The Beauty and the Sorrow

The Beauty and the Sorrow

*An Intimate History
of the First World War*

PETER ENGLUND

TRANSLATED BY PETER GRAVES

ALFRED A. KNOPF　　NEW YORK　　2011

THIS IS A BORZOI BOOK
PUBLISHED BY ALFRED A. KNOPF

Originally published in slightly different form in Sweden as *Stridens Skönhet Och Sorg*
by Atlantis, Stockholm, in 2009. Copyright © 2009 by Peter Englund.
Copyright © 2009 by Bokförlaget Atlantis AB. This translation, with a revised foreword
and additional new text by the author, was originally published in
Great Britain by Profile Books Ltd., London, in 2011.

Library of Congress Cataloging-in-Publication Data

Englund, Peter, 1957–
[Stridens skönhet och sorg. English]
The beauty and the sorrow : an intimate history of the First World War /
by Peter Englund. —1st. American ed.
p. cm.
"Originally published in Sweden as Stridens Skönhet Och Sorg by Atlantis,
Stockholm, in 2009" [i.e. 2008].—T.p. verso.
Includes index.
ISBN 978-0-307-59386-3 (alk. paper)
1. World War, 1914–1918—Personal narratives. I. Title.
DA640.A2E5413 2011
940.3092'2—dc23
2011020828

Manufactured in the United States of America
First American Edition

This book is dedicated to the memory of

CORPORAL JARED W. KUBASAK

whom I met in the fall of 2005 while embedded with
the 3rd Armored Cavalry Regiment in Iraq,
and who was killed there in action
on December 12 the same year

All the suffering and torment wrought at places of execution, in torture chambers, madhouses, operating theatres, under the arches of bridges in late autumn—all these are stubbornly imperishable, all these persist, are inaccessible but cling on, envious of everything that is, stuck in their own terrible reality. People would like to be allowed to forget much of it, their sleep gliding softly over these furrows in the brain, but dreams come and push sleep aside and fill in the picture again. And so they wake up breathless, let the light of a candle dissolve the darkness as they drink the comforting half-light as if it was sugared water. But, alas, the edge on which this security is balancing is a narrow one. Given the slightest little turn and their gaze slips away from the familiar and the friendly, and the contours that had so recently been comforting take the sharp outlines of an abyss of horror.

RAINER MARIA RILKE, *Malte Laurids Brigge*, 1910

The summer was more wonderful than ever and promised to become even more so, and we all looked out on the world without any cares. That last day in Baden I remember walking over the vine-clad hills with a friend and an old vine-grower saying to us: "We haven't had a summer like this for a long time. If this weather continues this year's wine is going to be beyond compare. People will always remember the summer of 1914!"

STEFAN ZWEIG, *The World of Yesterday*, 1942

Contents

To the Reader   xi

Dramatis Personae   xv

1914   1

1915   73

1916   201

1917   315

1918   421

THE END   497

Envoi   507

Sources and Literature   509

List of Illustrations   515

Index   519

To the Reader

The famous American war correspondent Stanley Washburn was invited in 1915 to contribute to *The Times History of the War*. He refused, even though he had been asked by none other than the mighty Lord North-cliffe: "I told him quite frankly that I did not want to write anything during the war which was published under the name of 'history,' saying that, in my opinion, no one who lived in a campaign could possibly be sufficiently well informed, nor have the proper perspective, to write anything of that nature."

I have had reason to think of Washburn's words on a number of occasions. I am an academic historian by profession but I have also tried my hand as a war correspondent in the Balkans, in Afghanistan and, most recently, in Iraq. As a historian, I have often longed to be present where and when events happen, but once I had arrived in, say, Kabul, I discovered the same thing as many other people in the same situations: to be right in the middle of events is no guarantee of being able to understand them. You are stuck in a confusing, chaotic and noisy reality and the chances are that the editorial office on the other side of the planet often has a better idea of what is going on than you do—just as a historian, paradoxically enough, often has a better understanding of an event than those who were actually involved in it. You become aware that distance is frequently the ingredient that makes understanding possible. But distance exacts a price: perhaps inevitably, much of the direct experience is lost.

This is a book about the First World War. It is not, however, a book about what it *was*—that is, about its causes, course, conclusion and consequences—but a book about what it was *like*. In this volume the reader

will meet not so much factors as people, not so much events and processes as feelings, impressions, experiences and moods.

It is not my intention to compete with the many excellent histories of
the Great War that have appeared over the years. I hope, rather, to complement them by giving a picture of the multiplicity of war constructed
from the authentic wartime experiences of twenty individuals—male
and female, civilian and military, old and young—of more than a dozen
nationalities and often far from home. For even though those of us alive
today perceive the war through the optic of its conclusion and, not least,
what came after, and therefore quite rightly regard it as the tragedy it
was, it took a while for the majority of those who lived through it to see
it that way. Some of them never did.

The reader will follow these twenty individuals, all of them now
more or less forgotten, and all of them low in the hierarchies. And while
the First World War has become synonymous in public consciousness
with the mud and sludge of the Western Front—not without good reason—many of these people play their part in the other theatres of war:
on the Eastern Front, in the Alps, the Balkans, East Africa and Mesopotamia. The great majority of them are young, not much more than
twenty years of age. Three of the twenty will perish, two will become
prisoners of war, two will become celebrated heroes and two will end up
as physical wrecks. Many of them welcome the war when it breaks out
but learn to detest it; a few of them detest it right from the first day; one
of them loves it from beginning to end. One of them will lose his mind,
another will never hear a shot fired. And so on. Everything here is based
on what they have left behind.

My cast of characters has been chosen with a view to providing an
all-round picture of the First World War, both as an event and as an
experience. Many different actors could, of course, have played a part,
for vast quantities of letters, journals and memoirs are preserved from
the war years. The book is structured as it stands quite simply because
I wanted to depict the war as an individual experience, to go beyond
the usual historical and sociological categories, and also beyond the
usual narrative forms in which, at best, people such as these appear as
no more than tiny specks of light, flickering by in the grand historical
sweep.

Although most of the twenty will be involved in dramatic and dreadful events, my focus remains primarily on the everyday aspects of the war. For this is, in a sense, a work of anti-history, an attempt to deconstruct this utterly epoch-making event into its smallest, most basic component—the individual, and his or her experiences.

Berlin-Uppsala, early November 2010

Peter Englund

Dramatis Personae

The main characters in order of appearance, their wartime occupations and their ages when the war began.

LAURA DE TURCZYNOWICZ *American wife of a Polish aristocrat, thirty-five*

ELFRIEDE KUHR *German schoolgirl, twelve*

SARAH MACNAUGHTAN *Scottish aid worker, forty-nine*

RICHARD STUMPF *German High Seas Fleet seaman, twenty-two*

PÁL KELEMEN *Hungarian cavalryman in the Austro-Hungarian army, twenty*

ANDREI LOBANOV-ROSTOVSKY *Russian army engineer, twenty-two*

FLORENCE FARMBOROUGH *English nurse in the Russian army, twenty-seven*

KRESTEN ANDRESEN *Danish soldier in the German army, twenty-three*

MICHEL CORDAY *French civil servant, forty-five*

ALFRED POLLARD *British army infantryman, twenty-one*

WILLIAM HENRY DAWKINS *Australian army engineer, twenty-one*

RENÉ ARNAUD *French army infantryman, twenty-one*

RAFAEL DE NOGALES *Venezuelan cavalryman in the Ottoman army, thirty-five*

HARVEY CUSHING *American army field surgeon, forty-five*

ANGUS BUCHANAN *British army infantryman, twenty-eight*

WILLY COPPENS *Belgian air force fighter pilot, twenty-two*

OLIVE KING *Australian driver in the Serbian army, twenty-nine*

VINCENZO D'AQUILA *Italian-American infantryman in the Italian army,*
twenty-one

EDWARD MOUSLEY *New Zealand artilleryman in the British army,*
twenty-eight

PAOLO MONELLI—*trooper in an Alpine regiment of the Italian army,*
twenty-three

1914

Go to war not for the sake of goods and gold, not for your homeland or for honour, nor to seek the death of your enemies, but to
strengthen your character, to strengthen it in power and will, in
habits, custom and earnestness. That is why I want to go to war.

KRESTEN ANDRESEN

Chronology 1914

28 JUNE   Murder of the Austro-Hungarian Archduke Franz
Ferdinand and his wife in Sarajevo.

23 JULY   Austria-Hungary delivers an ultimatum to Serbia.

28 JULY   Austria-Hungary declares war on Serbia.

29 JULY   Russia mobilises against Austria-Hungary in support of
Serbia.

31 JULY   Germany demands that Russia cease mobilisation but
Russia continues.

1 AUGUST   Germany mobilises, as does Russia's ally, France.

2 AUGUST   German troops enter France and Luxembourg;
Russians enter East Prussia.

3 AUGUST   Germany demands passage for German troops through
Belgium. The demand is refused.

4 AUGUST   Germany invades Belgium. Great Britain declares war
on Germany.

6 AUGUST   French troops enter the German colony of Togoland.

7 AUGUST   Russia invades German East Prussia.

13 AUGUST   Austria-Hungary invades Serbia. The campaign is
ultimately unsuccessful.

14 AUGUST   French troops enter German Lothringen (Lorraine) but
are pushed back.

18 AUGUST   Russia invades the Austro-Hungarian province of
Galicia.

20 AUGUST   Brussels falls. German armies sweep south towards
Paris.

24 AUGUST	The Allied invasion of the German colony of the Cameroons begins.
26 AUGUST	The Battle of Tannenberg begins. The Russian invasion of East Prussia is pushed back.
1 SEPTEMBER	The Battle of Lemberg begins. It turns into a major defeat for Austria-Hungary.
6 SEPTEMBER	Start of the Franco-British counter-offensive on the Marne. The German march on Paris is checked.
7 SEPTEMBER	The second Austro-Hungarian invasion of Serbia begins.
11 SEPTEMBER	Start of the so-called Race to the Sea in the west.
23 SEPTEMBER	Japan declares war on Germany.
12 OCTOBER	The first of a series of battles in Flanders begins.
29 OCTOBER	The Ottoman Empire enters the war on the German side.
3 NOVEMBER	Russia invades the Ottoman province of Armenia.
7 NOVEMBER	The German colony of Tsingtao in China is conquered by Japanese and British troops.
8 NOVEMBER	The third Austro-Hungarian invasion of Serbia begins.
18 NOVEMBER	The start of an Ottoman offensive in the Caucasus.
21 NOVEMBER	British troops occupy Basra in Mesopotamia.
7 DECEMBER	The second battle for Warsaw begins.

Laura de Turczynowicz is woken early
one morning in Augustów

What is the worst thing she can imagine? That her husband is ill, injured or even dead? That he has been unfaithful?

It has been a perfect summer. Not only has the weather been perfect—hot, sunny, wonderful sunsets—but they have also moved into a newly built summer villa, tucked away by the lakes in the beautiful Augustów Forest. The children have played for days on end. She and her husband have often rowed out on the lake during the short, white nights of June to greet the rising sun. "All was peace and beauty . . . a quiet life full of simple pleasure."

It has to be said that the simplicity of her life is relative. The large villa is superbly furnished. She is surrounded the whole time by servants and domestics, who live in a special annexe. (Each of the five-year-old boys has a nanny and the six-year-old girl has her own governess. The children are taken round in a special pony-trap.) They move in the society of the best noble families in the region. They have spent the winter on the French Riviera. (The journey home was fast and simple: European borders are easy to cross and there is still no need for passports.) They have a number of residences: as well as the summer villa and the big house in Suwalki, they have an apartment in Warsaw. Laura de Turczynowicz, *née* Blackwell, has a sheltered, comfortable existence. She screams at the sight of a mouse. She is frightened of thunder. She is modest and rather shy. She scarcely knows how to cook.

In a photograph taken a summer or so earlier we can see a happy, proud and contented woman, dark blonde, wearing a wide skirt, a white blouse and a large summer hat. We see someone used to a privileged and tranquil life, and a life that gets steadily better. She is by no means alone in that. Though there have been rumours of unrest and distant misdeeds, she has chosen to ignore them. And she is not alone in that, either.

So it really has been a perfect summer and it is still far from over. This evening they are supposed to be holding a lavish dinner party. But where is her husband? He has been working in Suwalki for several days and should have been back yesterday, in time for the party. They held back dinner for him but he did not arrive. This is not like him at all and she is growing more and more concerned. Where can he be? She waits, watches. Still no sign. She has not been this worried for a long time. What can have happened? She does not fall asleep until it is almost morning.

Laura is woken by a violent banging on the window.

It is four o'clock in the morning.

She leaps up to quieten the noise as quickly as possible, before it wakes the children. She can see a figure down below the window. Her first, confused thought is that it is one of the servants on the way to the market and in need of something—money or instructions, perhaps. To her amazement she is greeted by the pale and earnest face of Jan, her husband's manservant. He passes her a card. The handwriting is her husband's.

She reads: "War is declared. Come immediately with the children. Let the servants pack up what you wish to bring and come on later in the day."

TUESDAY, 4 AUGUST 1914
Elfriede Kuhr watches the 149th Infantry regiment leaving Schneidemühl

A summer evening. Warm air. Faint music in the distance. Elfriede and her brother are indoors, at home at Alte Bahnhofstrasse 17, but they can hear the sound. It slowly grows louder and they realise what is happening. They rush out into the street and away towards the yellow fortress-like railway station. The square in front of the station is swarming with people and the electric lighting is on—Elfriede thinks that the drab white light makes the leaves on the chestnut trees look as if they are made of paper.

She climbs up on the iron railings that separate the station building from the crowded square. The music is coming nearer. She sees a goods train standing waiting at Platform 3. She sees that the engine is steamed up. She sees that the wagon doors are open and through them she catches a glimpse of reservists, still in civilian clothes, going off to be mobilised. The men lean out and wave and laugh. Meanwhile the sounds of the music are growing louder and louder, ringing out clearly through the air of the summer evening. Her brother shouts: "They're coming! Here comes the 149th!"

This is what everyone has been waiting for: the 149th Infantry Regiment, the town's own unit. They are on their way to the Western Front. "The Western Front"—a very new term indeed, and Elfriede has never heard of such a thing until today. The war is about the Russians, isn't it? Everyone knows that. The German army is mobilising in response to the Russian mobilisation and everyone knows that the Russians are going to attack soon.* It is the threat from the east that is occupying the minds of people living here in Pomerania, and Schneidemühl is no exception to that. The Russian border lies less than a hundred miles away and the main railway line from Berlin to Königsberg runs through the town, which will presumably make it a self-evident target for the powerful enemy in the east.

The same thing is true, more or less, of the people of Schneidemühl as of the politicians and generals who, fumbling, groping and stumbling, have led Europe into war: information exists but it is almost always incomplete or out of date, and for lack of facts has been padded out with guesses, suppositions, hopes, fears, idées fixes, conspiracy theories, dreams, nightmares and rumours. Just as in tens of thousands of other towns and villages all over the continent, the picture of the world in Schneidemühl these days has been formed out of hazy and deceptive material of that kind—rumour, in particular. Elfriede Kuhr is twelve years old, a restless and intelligent girl with sandy-coloured hair and green eyes. She has heard people say that French planes have bombed

---

* Which was quite true: before the end of the month there were two Russian armies on German territory.

Nuremberg, that a railway bridge near Eichenried has been attacked, that Russian troops are moving towards Johannisburg, that Russian agents tried to murder the Crown Prince in Berlin, that a Russian spy attempted to blow up the aeroplane factory on the edge of town, that a Russian agent tried to infect the communal water supply with cholera and that a French agent has tried to blow up the bridges over the River Küddow.

None of this is true, but that emerges only later. Just now people seem prepared to believe anything, the more unbelievable the better.

For the people of Schneidemühl, as for the majority of Germans, this is ultimately seen as a defensive war, a war that has been forced on them and which they have no choice but to see through to its conclusion. They and their counterparts in similar towns and villages in Serbia, Austria-Hungary, Russia, France, Belgium and Great Britain are filled with both fear and hope and, not least, with a warm and powerful feeling of self-righteousness because they are now facing a momentous struggle against the forces of darkness. A wave of emotions surges over Schneidemühl, Germany and Europe, sweeping everything and everyone before it. But what we perceive as darkness is to them light.

Elfriede hears her brother shouting and then she sees it for herself. Here they come, row upon row of soldiers in grey uniforms, short boots of pale, untanned leather, huge knapsacks and pickelhaubes with grey cloth covers. A military band is marching in front and as they approach the great crowd of people at the station they strike up the tune that everyone knows so well. The soldiers sing it and, when they come to the chorus, the spectators immediately join in. The song roars out like thunder in the August night:

> *Lieb' Vaterland, magst ruhig sein*
> *Lieb' Vaterland, magst ruhig sein*
> *Fest steht und treu die Wacht, die Wacht am Rhein!*
> *Fest steht und treu die Wacht, die Wacht am Rhein!*[*]

The air reverberates to the sound of drums, the tramp of boots, the singing and the cheering. Elfriede notes in her diary:

---

[*] "Dear fatherland, put your mind at rest, / Fast stands, and true, the Watch, the Watch on the Rhine!" "Die Wacht am Rhein" had the status of a kind of unofficial German national anthem from the middle of the nineteenth century.

Then the 149th marched up shoulder to shoulder and streamed onto the platform like a grey tidal wave. All the soldiers had long garlands of flowers around their necks or pinned on their breasts. Asters, stocks and roses stuck out of the rifle barrels as if they were intending to shoot flowers at the enemy. The soldiers' faces were serious. I had expected them to be laughing and exultant.

Elfriede does, however, see one laughing soldier—a lieutenant whom she recognises. His name is Schön and she watches him bidding farewell to his relations and then pushing his way through the crowd. She sees the bystanders patting him on the back, embracing him and kissing him. She wants to shout to him, "Hello, Lieutenant Schön," but she doesn't dare.

The music plays, a sea of hats and handkerchiefs waves above the crowd, the train with the civilian-clad reservists whistles and pulls away, and everyone in the crowd cheers, shouts and waves. The 149th will soon be leaving too. Elfriede jumps down from the railings. She is swallowed up by the throng and feels as if she is being smothered. She sees an old woman, eyes red with weeping, who is screaming in heartrending tones: "Little Paul! Where is my little Paul? Let me at least see my son!" Elfriede, standing there crushed in this jostling and jolting mass of backs and arms and bellies and legs, does not know who Paul is. Shaken, or possibly simply thankful to have something to focus on in this overwhelming confusion of images and sounds and emotions, Elfriede says a quick prayer: "Please God, protect this Paul and bring him back to the woman! Please God, please, please, please!"

She watches the soldiers march past and a little boy alongside her sticks his hand pleadingly through the cold bars of the iron railings: "Soldier, soldier, goodbye!" One of the grey-uniformed men reaches out and shakes the hand: "Farewell, little brother!" Everyone laughs, the band plays "Deutschland, Deutschland, über alles" and some of the crowd sing along with it. A long train, decorated with flowers, puffs into Platform 1. At a call on the bugle the soldiers immediately begin to climb aboard to the sounds of oaths, jokes and commands. A soldier hurrying to catch up with the rest passes Elfriede as she stands there behind the railings. She plucks up courage and stretches out her hand to him, shyly mumbling, "Good luck!" He looks at her, smiles and takes her hand as he passes: "Until we meet again, little girl!"

Elfriede's eyes follow him and watch him climb into one of the goods wagons. She sees him turn round and look at her. Then the train jerks into motion, slowly at first and then faster.

The cheering rose to a roar, the soldiers' faces crowded in the open doors, flowers flew through the air and all at once many of the people in the square began to weep.
    "Until we meet again! We'll be home with you soon!"
    "Don't be afraid! We'll soon be back!"
    "We'll be back to celebrate Christmas with Mum!"
    "Yes, yes, yes—come back in one piece!"

And from the moving train comes the sound of a powerful song. She can catch only part of the refrain: ". . . in der Heimat, in der Heimat, da gibt's ein Wiedersehen!"* Then the wagons disappear into the night and are gone. Into the darkness and warm air of summer.

Elfriede is deeply moved. She walks home, choking back tears. As she walks she holds the hand the soldier touched out in front of her as if it contains something very valuable and very fragile. As she climbs the badly lit steps to the porch of Alte Bahnhofstrasse 17 she kisses her hand, quickly.

Sarah Macnaughtan returns to London today, 4 August, after a long and enjoyable stay in the country. The summer this year has been unusually hot and sunny and there has been nothing to disturb the profound peace that she and her friends have enjoyed. (The news of the double murder in the Balkans, which reached them at haymaking time, was quickly forgotten, or repressed, or simply filed away as yet another of those regrettable but distant events that unfortunately occur from time to time.) She writes:

Hardly anyone believed in the possibility of war until they came back from their August Bank Holiday visits and found soldiers saying good-bye to their families at the stations. And even then there was an air of unreality about everything, which rendered realisation difficult. We saw women waving handkerchiefs to the men who went away, and holding up their babies to railway car-

---

* ". . . at home, at home—that's where we'll meet again."

riage windows to be kissed [. . .] We were breathless, not with fear, but with astonishment.

THURSDAY, 20 AUGUST 1914
Richard Stumpf is copying a poem aboard SMS Helgoland

Richard Stumpf is deeply upset. Yet another declaration of war, yet another country allying itself with Germany's enemies. This time, Japan. The rulers in Tokyo are among the first of a growing band of war opportunists who, in this uncertain and fluid situation, have seized the chance to grab something for themselves, usually territory. Japan has delivered an ultimatum to the Foreign Ministry in Berlin demanding the withdrawal of all German warships from Asia and the handing over to Japan of the German colony of Tsingtao.*

Stumpf's anger overflows and out pours the racist invective: "Only these yellow, slant-eyed Asiatics would think of making such a shameless demand." He is, however, convinced that the German troops in Asia will give these "thieving yellow apes" a thorough thrashing.

Richard Stumpf is a twenty-two-year-old seaman in the German High Seas Fleet. His background is working class—he worked as an iron plateworker for two years before enlisting—but he is also a practising Catholic, member of a Christian trades union and an avowed nationalist. Like so many others he is overjoyed when war breaks out, not least because it means that Germany can finally settle accounts with the perfidious English: he thinks that the "real reason" Britain has taken sides in the conflict is "envy of our economic progress." "May God punish

* Tsingtao, transcribed as Quingdao nowadays, lies on a peninsula on the coast of the province of Shangdong and was ceded to Germany at the end of the nineteenth century in compensation for the murder of a number of German missionaries. (The German influence is still evident in that by far the best beer in China is brewed here.) Japan's unlimited imperialist ambitions on the Asian mainland had already led to wars with both Russia and China and this demand marked a further step in Japanese expansionist plans—under the pretence of fulfilling the duties inherent in the 1902 alliance with Great Britain. Japanese forces had been in a state of readiness to attack Tsingtao since the middle of August—that is one week before Japan delivered the ultimatum referred to above.

England" is a standard greeting by some members of the forces on enter-ing a room; the obligatory answer is, "He will punish them."

Stumpf is intelligent, chauvinistic, inquisitive and prejudiced. He is musical and reads a great deal. His photograph shows us a dark, serious young man with an oval face, eyes close together and a small but deter-mined mouth. On this particular day Stumpf is at sea, at the mouth of the River Elbe, on board the great battleship SMS[*] *Helgoland*, the vessel he has served on ever since enlisting.[†] That is where he was on the day war broke out.

Richard remembers that the atmosphere was subdued when their ship came into harbour because no exciting news had reached them while they had been at sea—people could be heard complaining about "all this fuss over nothing." But no one had been allowed ashore and instead they had spent their time loading ammunition and unloading "inessentials." At half past five in the evening the signal "All men on deck" had been given and they had all formed up. Then one of the ship's officers, holding a sheet of paper in his hand, had grimly announced that both the army and the navy were to mobilise that night: "You know what that means—war." The ship's band had struck up a patriotic tune and everyone had sung along with it "enthusiastically." "Our joy and excite-ment was boundless and lasted well into the night."

In the midst of all the cheering it is already possible to detect a nota-bly asymmetrical aspect. Colossal energies have been released and seem

---

* Seine Majestäts Schiff—His Majesty's Ship.

† Launched in Kiel in 1909, the *Helgoland* was an incarnation of the pre-war naval race in that she was built as a direct response to the British HMS *Dreadnought*, the largest and most powerful battleship in the world at the time. HMS *Dreadnought*, with her steam turbines, armour and heavy armament, was epoch-making: overnight she made all earlier armoured ships out of date and made the naval strategists of the world forget all budgetary restraints. SMS *Helgoland*'s armament was of a class with *Dreadnought*'s and her armour was, in fact, slightly heavier. (This was because German battleships were not intended to have the same range of operation as British ships and consequently some of the weight saved in terms of coal-carrying capacity could be used for extra protection.) With her twelve 30.5cm guns she was the most modern ship in the German High Seas Fleet and she and her sister vessels *Ostfriesland*, *Thüringen* and *Oldenburg*, raised expectations very high—among the public, the admirals, her own crew and with Kaiser Wilhelm. Everyone knew that the expensive (and foolish) High Seas Fleet project was one of the Kaiser's favourites and the implementation of it in the years before the war is what set Germany on a collision course with Great Britain.

to be dragging everyone with them. Stumpf, for instance, notes with some satisfaction that many radical authors who have made a name for themselves as sharp and persistent critics of the Wilhelmine age have now produced works of extreme and inflated patriotism. What has been swept away in this flood tide of high emotion is the question *why* they are at war. Like Stumpf, many people think that they know what it is "really" about, believe they have discovered the "true cause," but this "really" and "true cause" have already disappeared behind the fact that they are at war. The war already shows signs of becoming an end in itself and few people are still talking about Sarajevo.

Stumpf himself thinks that some of the propaganda against the growing band of Germany's opponents goes too far. Such as a vulgar postcard he has just seen in a shop: it depicts a German soldier putting an enemy soldier over his knee in order to smack his bottom, and he is saying to his waiting comrades, "Don't push! You'll all get your turn." And then there is the very popular jingle made up by street boys and scribbled in chalk on railway carriages carrying mobilised soldiers: "Jeder Schuss ein Russ, Jeder Stoss ein Franzos, Jeder Tritt ein Britt."* But other things move him deeply, like the poem by the popular writer Otto Ernst, published in the nationalistic paper *Der Tag*, which comments on the fact that Germany is now at war with seven countries. Stumpf is so taken by the poem that he copies it word for word in his diary. Two of the verses are as follows:

> *O mein Deutschland, wie musst du stark sein,*
> *Wie gesund bis ins innerste Mark sein,*
> *Dass sich's keiner allein getraut*
> *Und nach Sechsen um Hilfe schaut.*
>
> *Deutschland, wie musst du vom Herzen echt sein,*
> *O wie strahlend hell muss dein Recht sein,*
> *Dass der mächtigste Heuchler dich hasst*
> *Dass der Brite von Wut erblasst.*[†]

* "Every shot a Russian, every bayonet stab a Frenchman, every kick a Briton." A further line was also added to the jingle: "Jeder Klaps ein Japs," that is, "Every slap a Jap." Numerous silly rhymes of this kind were composed.

† "O my Germany, how strong you must be, / how healthy right to the core, / since no one dared alone / but sought the help of six others. // Germany, how upright your heart must

And the conclusion:

> *Morde den Teufel und hol dir vom Himmel*
> *Sieben Kränze des Menschentums,*
> *Sieben Sonnen unsterblichen Ruhms.*[*]

The inflammatory rhetoric and excessively strident tone of the propaganda do not really signify a great deal. Quite the opposite. While there are undoubtedly conflicting interests involved, none of the problems is so insoluble as to make war necessary, and they are certainly not sufficiently acute as to make war unavoidable. This war became unavoidable at the point only when people considered it unavoidable. When causes are vague and goals uncertain, however, it becomes necessary to fall back on the bloated and honeyed words of propaganda.

Richard Stumpf laps them up and staggers around, intoxicated by the words, while SMS *Helgoland*, bulky and enormous in her grey warpaint, sways on the water and bides her time. The enemy has not even been seen yet and one can sense some impatience on board.

TUESDAY, 25 AUGUST 1914
Pál Kelemen reaches the front at Halicz

In the beginning he had difficulty shaking off the feeling that this was just another exercise. It had all started in Budapest. Pál remembers how people looked as he loaded his luggage into a cab and how, dressed in his hussar's uniform of red trousers, blue tunic, pale-blue embroidered *attila* and high leather boots, he had to force his way through the dense crowds at the east station and elbow his way up onto the train to find standing room in the corridor. He remembers the weeping women, one of whom would have collapsed if a stranger had not caught her. Among the last things he saw as the train slowly moved off was an older man running after it, trying to get a last glimpse of his son.

---

be, / O how brilliantly pure your rightness, / for you to make the most powerful hypocrite hate you / and the Briton to go pale with rage."
[*] "Kill the devil and grasp from the heights of heaven / the seven victory wreaths of mankind, / seven suns of immortal honour."

After a hot but not too uncomfortable journey he had reported to his hussar regiment in Szeben—as usual. The man who received him there had not even looked at him, merely told him where he should go. Later the same afternoon, in bright August sunshine, he had gone to the mobilisation centre in Erfalu and then been billeted with a farmer—as usual.

After that there had been a series of routine activities: drawing his kit, including horse and saddle, payment of wages and a long—unbearably long—run-through of practical issues in a room that was so hot that people fainted as the stream of words just went on and on.

Then the picture began to change.

First there was a night march to the train that was waiting for them. Then a slow journey during which they were greeted at every station by crowds of enthusiastic people, "music, torches, wine, deputations, flags, cheering—Hurrah for the Army! Hurrah! Hurrah!" Then unloading and their first march. But there was still no real hint of war, no distant growl of guns and the like; it *could* still have been an exercise. Warm, blue skies, the smell of horse dung, sweat and hay.

Pál Kelemen is twenty years old, born in Budapest, where he went to the Latin School and played the violin under the conductor Fritz Reiner, who was later to become famous. In many ways Kelemen is a typical product of urban central Europe in the early twentieth century: well travelled, well read, aristocratic, ironic, refined, distant, with a weakness for women. He has studied at the universities of Budapest, Munich and Paris, and has even managed to fit in a short period at Oxford. When they rode into Stanislau, the main town in Austrian Galicia—he as a young, elegant lieutenant in the hussars (is there anything more elegant than a Hungarian lieutenant of hussars?)—women rather than war were foremost in his mind. He thinks that you can tell from looking at the women that this is a provincial town: "White-skinned, very pale they are and their eyes have brilliant fire." (This, he thinks he can tell, is in contrast to city women, whose gaze is more weary, more veiled.)

It is only when the division reaches Halicz that the illusion that this might merely be a manoeuvre is finally smashed.

On the way there they meet fleeing peasants and Jews. The mood in the town is apprehensive and confused and the Russians are said to be not far away. Kelemen notes in his journal:

We sleep in tents. At half-past twelve at night: Alarm! The Russian is before the town. I think everyone is a little frightened. I fling on my clothes and run out to join my platoon. On the road the infantry is standing in ranks. Cannon growls. Rifles are rattling some five hundred yards ahead. Motor cars dash down the middle of the highway. The lights of their carbide lamps stream in long rows toward Halicz on the road from Stanislau.

Between the posted guards I climbed over the hedge gate and across the ditches of the embankment. My platoon awaited me, saddled up, and we stood ready for further orders.

When morning dawned, the population was pouring out of the city in long files. On carts, on foot, on horseback. Everyone making shift to save himself. All of them carrying away what they can. And exhaustion, dust, sweat, panic on every face, terrible dejection, pain, and suffering. Their eyes are frightened, their movements craven: ghastly terror oppresses them. As if the dust cloud they stirred up had fastened itself to them and could not float away.

I lie sleepless at the side of the road and watch the infernal kaleidoscope. There are even military wagons muddled into it, and on the fields retreating military, routed infantry, lost cavalry. Not a man of them still has his full equipment. The exhausted throng pours through the valley. They are running back to Stanislau.

What Kelemen is witnessing as he lies at the roadside is the result of one of the first bloody and confused clashes with the invading Russians. Like everyone else involved, he has only a very hazy picture of what has actually happened and it will be years before anyone pulls together all the various impressions into a narrative called the Battle of Lemberg. But it does not require a fully worked-out account from the general staff for anyone to understand that this has turned out to be a defeat for the Austro-Hungarian army on a scale that is as colossal as it is unexpected.

FRIDAY, 28 AUGUST 1914
Laura de Turczynowicz meets a German prisoner of war in
Suwalki

Laura has never understood this war, let alone welcomed it. She is one of the many people for whom what has happened is like a natural catastrophe, a dark and ultimately incomprehensible tragedy that has suddenly swept down on them from nowhere.

But she has also noticed how the initial terror has quickly changed into a strange euphoria, which has affected even her. The ancient quarrels between Poles and Russians seem to have vanished completely. It says a great deal about the current mood that when a rumour went round one evening at the beginning of August suggesting that the war was perhaps not going to happen, it was the cause of some disappointment. (Great Britain was apparently hesitating about going to war, and *that* was setting off alarm bells among the rulers in St. Petersburg.)

Today is Laura de Turczynowicz's thirty-sixth birthday and until now her life has had all the elements of a fin de siècle dream. Born in Canada, she grew up in New York and was a gifted opera singer who had performed at the Metropolitan and elsewhere. She moved to Europe to "study and sing . . . and play," achieved success at Bayreuth and Munich—her German is good—and found a husband in the shape of a charming Polish aristocrat with an upturned moustache, a professorial title and a considerable fortune. His name is Stanislaw de Turczynowicz, Count of Gozdawa, and they married in Krakow in Austria-Hungary, where she also gave birth to their three children. By birth, then, the little ones are subjects of the Austro-Hungarian emperor, her husband is a subject of the tsar, and she is a subject of the British king. Few people thought of such categories before August; there are many people who can hardly think of anything else now.

The war has become rather more noticeable.

A week after its outbreak they were wakened in the grey light of dawn by a muffled roar, like the sound of a waterfall. It was the sound of thousand upon thousand of Russian infantrymen on the march, part of the II Corps of Rennenkampf's army on their way to invade neighbouring East Prussia. In spite of the early hour the whole of the little town turned out to welcome the weary troops with food, drink and other gifts. Many of the upper-class Russian families that Laura and her husband mix with have left and gone home. The first wounded men from the front have been seen. Suwalki has been bombed—a solitary German aircraft flew over a few days ago and dropped a couple of small bombs at random, while the excited men of the town shot at it unsuccessfully with their hunting rifles. The loot plundered from German homes can sometimes be seen on the wagons returning from the front.

In spite of all this, the war has remained something of an abstraction, something happening far away. At least for Laura. The family is back in Suwalki, in the big manor house near the high road, and she herself is still living the pleasant life of a landed lady, surrounded by beautiful family treasures, well-filled larders and a staff of obedient servants. She has been helping to organise a small private hospital and her husband has not yet been called up.

A nurse from a mobile field hospital comes to call on her today. They have just arrived from the front, their stores exhausted and their staff weary. Their normal capacity is 150 beds, which is more than enough for three doctors and four nurses to cope with, but the recent hard fighting in East Prussia has meant that they are overwhelmed by the numbers of wounded men—the nurse estimates there to be 700. Can Laura help? Yes, of course she can.

Laura goes to the barracks where the field hospital is located. As she enters she can hear the anxious murmur of hundreds of voices. She walks round, goes into room after room packed with wounded men, men who have not received any treatment. Everything has run out, from bandages to disinfectant.

Since she can speak German she is asked to take a look at a group of wounded German prisoners of war who have all been gathered in one corner. One of them is rocking violently backwards and forwards the whole time, simultaneously praying and asking for water. Laura talks to him and he asks her to write to his wife:

> He told me that he had been a bookkeeper, that he was twenty-six years old, and had a wife and children, a little house of his own, had never harmed anyone in his life, took no interest in anything outside his work and family, until with three hours' notice he was ordered to join his regiment, and leave it all. "The great lords

have quarrelled, and we must pay for it with our blood, our wives and children."

Laura returns later with large quantities of medical supplies she has brought from their own small private hospital. The joy shown by the nurses at the military hospital when they receive these gifts seems to her almost "pitiful."

Laura walks around the military hospital. She sees something she does not recognise at first. It is an "object" in a bed and all that can be seen where the head should be is "a ball of cotton and bandages with three black holes, just as if a child had drawn mouth and nose and eyes." A voice suddenly emerges from this "thing," a voice that, far from being unearthly, speaks in educated Polish. That alone comes as a shock. It is as if Laura in her naivety has not been expecting anything like this to afflict people of her own sort. The voice pleads with whoever it is not to go away but to give him some water, water. Laura goes up to the bed. Then she gets her next shock. Swarms of flies rise from the bundle on the bed. The man's hands have been completely burnt away and a heavy stench of pus and gangrene comes from the bandages.

Laura recoils, sickened and horrified. She comes close to fainting. She has to get away from it.

Later she plucks up courage and returns to the thing on the bed. She helps to erect an insect net around his bed and assists a nurse who is changing his bandages. The man tells her he was wounded by a shell that exploded close to him and that he lay out on the battlefield for four days. He asks if his eyes are gone. The answer is "Yes, quite gone." He then asks if he is going to live or die. The answer is "Die." He asks for water.

Laura learns later that the German prisoner she had talked to, the twenty-six-year-old bookkeeper, was due to be transported onwards but died on the way to the railway station.

WEDNESDAY, 2 SEPTEMBER 1914
Andrei Lobanov-Rostovsky sees the sun go dark in Mokotov

Now it is their turn to be sent in. The reports are contradictory. Something seems to have gone seriously wrong with the Russian invasion up in East Prussia: Rennenkampf's army seems to be in retreat and Samsonov's in flight. That surely cannot be true? The Russian invaders seem to be having more success down in Galicia, and Lemberg is likely to fall any day now. Although there is a much greater need of reinforcements against the Germans in the north rather than against the Austrians in Galicia, Lobanov-Rostovsky's rifle brigade is destined for the southern front where it is to join in the hammering of the already yielding Austro-Hungarian divisions on the Polish frontier.[*]

At the moment they are being held in reserve in Warsaw, camped on a large field in Mokotov. Andrei Lobanov-Rostovsky is a sapper in the Russian army and a lieutenant in the Guards—the latter being a rank more dependent on birth than on aptitude. He is actually a sensitive and bookish twenty-two-year-old who reads ceaselessly, preferably French novels but also history. Lobanov-Rostovsky is well educated (he has just read law in Petrograd but has also studied in Nice and Paris), a little anxious by disposition and physically not particularly robust. His father is a diplomat.

The outbreak of war has been a remarkable experience. He has spent every spare moment rushing round the city along with all the other excited people who crowd round the newspaper offices to read the placards and telegrams. The excitement reached its height when news came that Belgrade was under fire: spontaneous demonstrations in support of the war took place on the same streets that witnessed spontaneous marches by strikers just a few days earlier. He watched as the crowds held up trams in order to take out any officers in them and hoist them up on their shoulders to the sound of cheering. He remembers in particular how, to the amusement of the onlookers, a drunken worker embraced and kissed a passing officer. August has been a month of dust and unusual heat and although, as a lieutenant, he has been on horseback throughout the long marches, he has come close to collapsing with sunstroke.

He has not yet seen action. The worst thing he has witnessed was when they were quartered in a small Polish town some time ago and a serious fire broke out: the newly mobilised soldiers, whipped up by excitement and fear of spies, killed eight Jews who, they claimed, were

---

[*] The various fronts on which the Russian army fought were, in practical terms, independent zones with their own reserves, own trains, own supplies and own goals, making a sudden transfer of resources practically impossible, at least as long as Russian generals jealously and petulantly stood guard over the territories they had staked out for themselves.

trying to prevent the fire being put out.* The atmosphere in general has been nervous.

At two o'clock the whole brigade forms up in front of the host of small tents in the field. It is time for Mass. Something strange occurs halfway through the service—the bright hazy sun begins to grow dark. A partial eclipse is taking place. Most of the soldiers find this a bit uncanny and the phenomenon makes "a tremendous impression" on the more superstitious among them.

Immediately after the service they break camp and all the units in the brigade begin to board waiting trains. As usual the whole business takes longer than reckoned and it is already night by the time it is the turn of Lobanov-Rostovsky's unit. And things do not go much faster once they are under way. The train trundles south through the darkness with an extraordinary lack of urgency. Slowness is the default speed of trains in 1914: these wagonloads of soldiers sometimes move no faster than a man on a bicycle.† The fact is that the lines are jammed with trains, trains which during this period of the war are all headed in the same direction with the same purpose: Forward! To the front!‡

* The muddled and unproven reasoning was that the fire had been started to signal to the Germans that there were Russian troops present.

† The reason is logistic. All armies move according to minutely worked-out and unbelievably complicated timetables in which one of the preconditions for the endlessly complex calculation of hundreds of thousands of departures and meetings is that the speed is constant in principle and low out of necessity. Some people claim it was often possible to pick flowers at the side of the track during the journey, though that may be an exaggeration. We can, however, be pretty sure that some people tried.

‡ As part of a major programme of military modernisation Russia had by this stage started upgrading its railway network, and it was the extension of railways in Russian Poland that really put the wind up the German general staff. The faster an army could be brought together and brought into action, the bigger its chances of victory—that was axiomatic. The German Schlieffen Plan—which was not a plan in the accepted sense but rather a simple memo based on the situation that existed after Russia's overwhelming defeat by Japan in 1905—was based on the premise that the French could be knocked out before Russia would be ready for action. The railways were an important factor in this: as late as 1910 the Russian army would not have been able to use more than 250 trains for the mobilisation of its forces. (As a comparison it is worth mentioning that regional traffic in the Cologne area alone at this time was served by 700 trains.) But the Russian modernisation programme meant that far more trains were available and, moreover, they were able to unload closer to the German border. Without it, Lobanov-Rostovsky's journey would have been even slower.

A DAY IN SEPTEMBER 1914
Florence Farmborough in Moscow sees death for the first time

"I wanted to see him; I wanted to see Death," is how she tells it herself. She had never seen a dead person before and, indeed, until very recently she had not even seen someone sick in bed, which is perhaps a little strange since she was, after all, twenty-seven years old. The explanation, of course, is that up until August 1914 she had led a fairly sheltered life. Florence Farmborough was born and brought up in rural Buckinghamshire, but she has lived in Russia since 1908. She has been working as governess to the daughters of a well-known Russian heart surgeon in Moscow.

The international crisis that developed during the hot and beautiful late summer of 1914 largely passed her by since she spent it with her employers at the family dacha outside Moscow. Once back in the capital she had been gripped by the same "youthful enthusiasm" as so many others. Her old and her new homelands were united in a struggle against the common enemy Germany and this energetic and enterprising young woman immediately began considering how she could contribute to the war effort. The answer came more or less immediately—by becoming a nurse. Her employer, the well-known heart surgeon, succeeded in convincing those in charge of one of the private military hospitals then being set up in Moscow to take on Florence and his two daughters as volunteers. "We are elated beyond words. We, too, in our small way are to help the country's cause."

They have been wonderful days. After a while the wounded began to arrive, two or three at a time. Much of the work was unpleasant in the beginning and she sometimes recoiled when faced with an unusually nasty and gaping wound. With time, however, she got used to it, and then the atmosphere was so good. There was a new sense of solidarity and unity, not least among the soldiers:

> There is always a remarkable camaraderie among them: White Russian mingles in a most friendly fashion with Ukrainian; Caucasians with soldiers from the Urals; Tatars with Cossacks. They are mostly patient, long-suffering men, grateful for what care

and attention they receive; seldom, if ever, does a grumble pass their lips.

Quite a few of the wounded are impatient to get back to the front as soon as possible. Optimism is high, among both the soldiers and the hospital staff. The wounds will soon heal, the soldiers will soon be back in service, the war will soon be won. The hospital usually receives only milder cases, which might explain why, after working for three weeks, she is yet to see a dead body.

As she arrives at the hospital one morning she passes one of the night nurses. Florence thinks that she looks "tired and tense" and the woman says in passing that "Vasiliy died early this morning." Vasiliy is one of the men Florence has helped nurse. He was a soldier but really only an officer's groom and, ironically enough, his wound was not a "real" war wound. Vasiliy had been kicked in the head by an agitated and frightened horse and when the surgeon operated on him a further irony emerged: he was suffering from an incurable brain tumour. He has lain silent in his bed for the last three weeks, a pale, frail little man whose difficulty in eating has caused him to grow thinner and thinner, though he constantly wants water to drink. And now he has died, without any drama, just as quiet and alone as he lived.

Florence decides to look at the body. She slips into the room that serves as a mortuary and carefully closes the door behind her. Silence. There lies Vasiliy, or what was Vasiliy, on a bier. He was:

> So small and thin and wizened that he looked more like a child than a grown man. His set face was grey-white, never had I seen that strange colour on a face before, and his cheeks had sunken into two hollows.

There are sugar lumps on his eyelids to hold them closed. She is troubled, not so much by the lifeless body as by the stillness and silence. "Death is so terribly still, so silent, so remote," she thinks. She says a short prayer for the dead man and then quickly leaves the room.

FRIDAY, 11 SEPTEMBER 1914
Laura de Turczynowicz flees from Suwalki

Dawn. The streets that run between the low, square houses in Suwalki are deserted. Could it be a false alarm? Well, almost all of them are clinging to the wild hope—dangerously close to self-delusion—that says "not here" or "it will pass us by" or "we probably won't be affected." And it is possible that the endless rumours are just a kind of wishful thinking that has taken on the form of true stories. So, in recent weeks, people have been quite capable of suggesting that Königsberg has been captured, that the Russian army is approaching Berlin, and any number of other things.

As usual, however, no one really knows what is happening at the front.

Long columns of horse-drawn wagons come and go. Reinforcements march through the town. Now and again an aeroplane flies over the town, dropping bombs or propaganda. Sometimes lines of grey-clad German prisoners of war tramp past. The volume of traffic has increased noticeably in the last few days, however, and yesterday came the first signs that things were not going as well as they should. Firstly, there was the arrival of hordes of peasants from the small places near the border with East Prussia: "men, women, children, dogs, cows, pigs, horses, and carts all mixed up in one grand mélange." Secondly, a new and unpleasant sound could be heard—the sound of gunfire in the distance. Someone suggested it was just Cossacks hunting down a disloyal officer. Well, one can always hope.

The night has been quiet, however, and the refugees from the villages have moved on.

From the windows at the back of the big house there is a good view of the flat plain that surrounds the town and of the main highway leading to East Prussia. At six in the morning Laura sees a great throng of wagons approaching. They are filled with wounded men, and the wounded tell them that the front has been shattered and the Russian army is on the retreat. What should they do? Leave Suwalki or stay there?

It is eleven o'clock. Laura is hesitant and confused, feeling alone and deserted. Her husband, Stanislaw, is in Warsaw on official business. She consults a number of senior officials. She tries to telegraph out, only to learn that the line is cut. Reluctantly she decides that they should leave the town before evening.

Lunchtime. She sits down to eat with the children and looks round the dining room:

> How pretty it looked, the curious old room with steps leading down to its great windows, the soft colours of the rugs, the table with its fine napery and pretty silver and glass.

Then everything happens very quickly. First of all they hear the crack of rifle fire, loud and clear, "as if in the very room." Next comes the rolling thunder of artillery fire, followed a moment later by the clatter of smashed china. The servant about to serve their soup has dropped the tray and the tureen in terror. For a moment they are all silent, then the little girl begins to cry.

Chaos. Laura issues orders to right and to left—they must all be out of the house within fifteen minutes. The governess takes charge of the children. Laura herself packs the valuables—gold coins, rouble notes, her jewellery box. The sounds of battle outside are growing. Everyone is rushing about more or less aimlessly, grabbing, tearing, screaming. Laura finds herself running around waving a bunch of coloured silk stockings as if they were a flag.

They load everything into two farm carts. There is chaos on the streets. She sees military transport wagons. She sees Russian soldiers, weapons at the ready. She sees people screaming, jostling, arguing. She sees an old woman balancing a small bed on her head and dragging a samovar behind her so that it bounces on the cobbles. "One solid mass of disorder—primeval man and woman put to flight by inexorable force— all conventions dropped as if they never existed."

So they set off, out into "that vortex of humanity—people running— laden like horses—getting tired of the weight—dropping it—but going on." Laura and the children and most of the servants ride in the first wagon, most of the luggage in the second. She casts a glance back at the house. A priest she knows urges them to get moving and blesses them with the sign of the cross.

They head for the railway station. Halfway there Laura sees a man—an old acquaintance of the family—climb up onto the second wagon and start beating the driver. Then the man turns the wagon round and makes off with it and all their luggage. The children's dog, Dash, a white spets, is standing on top of the load barking. Wagon and dog disappear into the stream of panic-stricken people.

It is a beautiful autumn day.

SUNDAY, 20 SEPTEMBER 1914
Sarah Macnaughtan is travelling to Antwerp

So much has changed already. The traffic, for a start. Ever since the outbreak of war the streets have been strangely empty, in the way she usually associates with Sundays. And then there is language. Military terms like "rashions," "revellies,"* "fall in" and "mobilisation" have crept into everyday language. (There are many people who pronounce the phrase "at the front" as if it was a single word, "atthefront.") Or the business of fashion: suddenly women are to be seen dressed in military or half-military or quarter-military dress, imaginative imitations of uniforms, perhaps a big, ill-fitting greatcoat, "thrown open, with a large belt at the back." Or if not that, at least some sort of badge or armband to show that One Is Doing One's Duty, or One Is Behind You, or One Is Doing Something—even if it is only knitting socks for soldiers.†

Sarah Macnaughtan is one of these women, but for her a symbolic or half-hearted contribution is not enough. She really wants to be involved, including being THERE. So Macnaughtan has done what other women of her class and in her position have done and found herself a place in one of the innumerable private medical units that have sprung up since the start of August—in Macnaughtan's case it is Mrs. St. Clair Stobart's ambulance unit. They have been practising in one of the London parks, on small boys with neatly simulated injuries, which they have then bandaged up equally neatly. Macnaughtan is happy and relieved to be getting out of London, to be taking the step from words to actions.

* The spellings are Macnaughtan's.
† "At music halls and revues, girls, dressed as admirals and colonels, saluted with alarming sharpness all the time." A year or so later she writes: "Women were, I think, exceptionally military those days."

Which is not the easiest thing to do, since the British army has so far rigidly refused to allow women anywhere near the front.* In spite of the fact that a host of women, like Sarah Macnaughtan, have enthusiastically volunteered, the very army they are trying to support has received them with reluctance or indifference.† Recent months have been characterised by these women's increasing sense of frustration with all the confusion and bureaucracy, real or imaginary, and with all the people whose resistance shows that they simply do not appreciate the gravity of the situation.

For she is a serious woman. In terms of her age, Sarah Broom Macnaughtan is actually rather too old for this war—she will be fifty in just a month's time—and she does not really have the physical attributes that are needed: she is small, thin and frail, with a head that seems altogether too big for her doll-like body. But she is in every sense a product of the Victorian age and there are few concepts that weigh heavier with her, that have a finer ring to them, than Duty. And Principles. Earnestness is integral to her lifestyle, her countenance and her attitudes. She is intelligent, religious, humourless, loyal, gruff, demanding, generous, moral and fearless. She lives alone, unmarried and childless, a woman who is economically and emotionally independent.‡ She has travelled a great deal, frequently in trying conditions, and she writes books. Hardly surprisingly, she is a committed suffragette, and nor is it surprising that she is prepared to throw herself wholeheartedly into this war, even though her initial reaction to its outbreak is one of surprise verging on shock. But now it is a matter of Duty. And Principles.

She is in such an agitated state when she arrives at the station to catch the train that is to take them to the coast that she has forgotten her passport. Fortunately the train is delayed and she has time to send her maid home in a taxi to fetch it. She is ashamed of her little mistake

* There was an embryonic women's volunteer organisation, the semi-official VADs (Voluntary Aid Detachments), which had a place in army planning but no place in its budget and was entirely financed by private funds. The British army was still very doubtful about it.

† Sharon Ouditt has analysed the thinking underlying this attitude: "To have conscripted women would have been to accord them equivalent status in the emergency and to have broken the stereotypical presentation of women as war's 'other' on which so much of the 'home fires' mythology depended."

‡ Her father, a Scottish JP with shipping interests, left her very well provided for.

and manages to hide it from the others, "for they are all rather serious." Their destination is Antwerp, where they intend to set up a field hospital.

The train takes them to Tilbury, where there are further delays. Their ship does not set sail until the grey of dawn is visible, and the seas are running rough out in the English Channel. Everyone is seasick. "I think I was the worst and alarmed everybody within hearing distance. One more voyage I hope—home—then dry land for me." She spends the whole crossing being sick.

SATURDAY, 26 SEPTEMBER 1914
Richard Stumpf helps prepare SMS Helgoland *for action*

Reveille is blown as early as four o'clock this autumn morning. The ship and its crew wake to a morning of frantic activity. The main task is to unload 300 tons of coal as quickly as possible. As usual, the officers do not tell the men anything but rumour says that the British fleet has put to sea and someone says it is on its way to the Baltic. Someone says it has already reached the Great Belt. Stumpf sees that the first and third squadrons have also come into the harbour. "Something big is happening."

Stumpf concludes that the coal is being unloaded to lighten the ship to allow them to pass through the Kiel Canal as quickly as possible. He writes in his diary:

> The whole crew worked hard all morning. At lunchtime, when we had unloaded 120 tons of coal, the squadron flagship signalled: "Cease the preparations." Yet another dreadful disappointment. The bloody English! We do, however, seem to be very well informed about the movements of their fleet.

After this he adds, "Nothing worth mentioning happened during the following days and weeks."

MONDAY, 28 SEPTEMBER 1914
Kresten Andresen learns to dress bullet wounds in Flensburg

It will soon be time. It might be just one day, perhaps two, or possibly three, but it will not be long before they too are on the way. This is more than just the usual barrack-room gossip, though, of course, the air is full of rumours, of guesses that are elevated to probabilities, hopes that change to facts, fears that are disguised as assertions. The nature of war is uncertainty, the unknowable is its medium.

But there are also clear signs, clear evidence. All leave has been stopped, and they have to stay in the barracks. And today there has been less drill and instruction in minor dietary matters and instead they have been instructed in the real necessities of life—how to dress bullet wounds, rules regarding iron rations, how to behave during rail transportation and what will happen if they desert (the death sentence). The four cornerstones of a conscript's life in summary: battle, rations, transportation and compulsion.

Kresten Andresen is troubled, worried and afraid. The thought of the front does not awaken any desire in him at all. He belongs to one of those national minorities which suddenly and through no fault of their own are finding themselves dragged into a great war in which they have no real interest. Faced with the dark energies released by war they can only look on, dumbfounded and questioning; they stand apart from the nationalistic rhetoric that has created the war and the wild hopes the war has created. These are times when many people are preparing to kill or be killed for countries with which they feel only a superficial connection: Alsatians and Poles, Ruthenians and Kashubians, Slovenes and Finns, South Tyroleans and Siebenbürger, Balts and Bosnians, Czechs and Irish.* Andresen belongs to one such group: he comes from southern

---

* It is worth noting that certain national minorities welcomed the war since a demonstration of loyalty and service was perceived as a way of winning increased respect. This was the strategy chosen by many Jews, particularly those who were well assimilated, in countries such as Germany and Russia; they met with greater success in the former than in the latter simply because German anti-Semitism was so much weaker than Russian (or French). German newspapers contain accounts of German Jews who left Palestine at the outbreak of war and made their way home, often with some difficulty, in order to become volunteers.

Jutland, ancient Danish territory that has now been inside the borders of the German Empire for more than half a century, and so he is a German citizen even though his language is Danish.*

In all of the countries with large national minorities there is an acute awareness of the problems minorities can create in wartime. Dealing with them is primarily seen as a matter for the police, which is the case in the Danish-speaking areas of Germany. The order for mobilisation had hardly been nailed up on the wall before hundreds of Danes considered to be leaders or potential leaders were arrested. One of those arrested—at night, in a closed car—was Andresen's own father.† The mood in the first weeks of the war was like that: jubilation mixed with hysteria, expectancy mixed with terror, fear becoming aggression. And then, of course, there were rumours, rumours and more rumours.

The outbreak of war had also been a notable experience for Kresten. He had just put the finishing touches to a manuscript: "A Book about Spring and Youth." It was a sort of long prose poem about folk-life, nature and young love (or rather, a longing for young love). The manuscript in itself was a kind of act of love, with its pale blue cover, its elegantly coloured vignettes and illuminated capitals—all of which he had done himself. The lines with which he ended his work were these: "A bell falls silent, and then another, and another. The bells are falling silent more and more, their sounds becoming fainter and fainter, dying away until they are completely silent. Death, where are thy spoils? Hell, where is thy victory?" At the very moment he was writing these last words his father entered the room and told him that mobilisation had started. So, at the bottom of the very last clean page of the manuscript, Kresten added a few lines: "O God, have mercy on those of us going, and who knows when we shall return!"

It is now Andresen's seventh week in German uniform. When he

---

* The Duchies of Schleswig, Holstein and Lauenburg became part of Prussia after the Dano-German War of 1864. They had a significant German-speaking population even at that time.

† Like so much of the early hysteria about potential spies and traitors, this faded with time, especially once it became clear that Danish-speaking recruits like Andresen served under the German flag without any problems arising. The majority of those arrested, including his father, were released. An entertaining and perspicacious account—drawn from her own experience—of the excitement and spy hysteria in Germany in August 1914 may be found in Klara Johanson's essay "Prisoner of War."

arrived at the overcrowded barracks in Flensburg he heard that they would do four weeks' training and then be sent to France. That same night he heard a battalion march off in battle kit singing "Die Wacht am Rhein." That was followed by seemingly endless days of drill out in the blazing sun—the weather really was stunning. Andresen has settled better than he dared hope. Although there are only a few Danish speakers in his company he does not feel excluded. And even though there are bullying NCOs, the officers usually keep them on a short leash. What he finds most difficult to take is that even during their free time no one talks about anything but "war and more war," and even he has now started getting used to the idea that that is what is in front of him, even though he would profoundly like to escape it. He shoots rather well—his first scores were two tens and a seven.

By this point several contingents have already set off, singing as they march to an uncertain fate. The reason Andresen is still at the barracks is partly because of something as banal as a shortage of equipment and partly because they are taking the volunteers first. And since he would prefer to avoid the whole business, he has never joined the ranks of the volunteers. When the company forms up today at the end of training, the question is put to them: a new contingent is to be sent to the front and who is going to volunteer?

They all put up their hands—all but three. Andresen is one of the three. He is asked why but is then left alone. Later, together with another Dane, he visits a friend and, "with solemn devotion," they eat a chicken Andresen's mother has sent him. In the evening he writes in his diary:

> We are so benumbed that we march off to war without tears and without terror and yet we all know we are on our way into the jaws of Hell. But clad in a stiff uniform, a heart does not beat as it wants to. We aren't ourselves, we're hardly human any longer, at most we are well-functioning automatons who do everything without any great reflection. O, Lord God, if only we could become human again.

The beautiful Indian summer that has lasted since the outbreak of war has given way to autumn winds. A strong, cold, north-westerly sweeps over Flensburg, making the leaves rustle and the chestnuts fall from the trees in showers.

· · ·

Today Sarah Macnaughtan is in Antwerp, which has been under siege by the Germans for the last two days. The sound of artillery fire is no longer merely a distant one, and Zeppelins have flown over and dropped bombs. The field hospital at which Sarah is working is situated in the city's main concert hall and has rapidly filled with wounded Belgian soldiers. She writes in her diary:

> A hundred beds all filled with men in pain give one plenty to think about, and it is during sleep that their attitudes of suffering strike one most. Some of them bury their heads in their pillows as shot partridges seek to bury theirs amongst autumn leaves. Others lie very stiff and straight, and all look very thin and haggard. I was struck by the contrast between the pillared concert-hall where they lie, with its platform of white paint and decorations, and the tragedy of suffering which now fills it.
>
> At 2 a.m. more soldiers were brought in from the battlefield, all caked with dirt, and we began to work again. These last blinked oddly at the concert hall and nurses and doctors, but I think they do not question anything much. They only want to go to sleep.

SUNDAY, 4 OCTOBER 1914
Andrei Lobanov-Rostovsky takes part in the Battle of Opatov

The artillery opens fire again in the grey light of dawn. Its rolling and quaking roar wakes Andrei Lobanov-Rostovsky, who is still drowsy as he has had only a few hours' sleep. He staggers up. From the high ground on which they have camped for the night he can see lines of white clouds flowering from the shell-bursts in the distance. He watches them spread out over the low hills to the south and west. He can see the flashing, swaying masses of smoke rolling and flowing inexorably on like a lava flow. He sees the dance of fire approaching the town and meeting it. Panic-stricken civilians are rushing around in the streets down there. Finally, Opatov is almost completely swallowed up by the smoke of exploding shells and burning houses until just one church tower can be seen sticking out above the rolling clouds.

The artillery fire intensifies. Massive waves of sound assault them from both sides: shells explode, rifles crack and machine guns rattle. They cannot see much and they themselves are untouched, but to judge from the noise there is a battle raging "in a semicircle around us." The company stays put up on the hill, as they have been ordered to do: "You are to stay where you are and wait for instructions." New orders arrive at eleven o'clock. They are to withdraw a short distance.

Half an hour later Lobanov-Rostovsky looks back. He sees an enormous plume of smoke in the October sky—Opatov is being consumed by fire. And not only Opatov: all the villages on both sides of their position have begun to burn. It is becoming more and more difficult for them to move along the road since it is filled with panic-stricken men, women and children rushing in aimless waves backwards and forwards as the noise of battle grows around them. Somewhere around there Lobanov-Rostovsky's company comes to a halt.

What has happened? Well, the Russian army's pursuit of the Austrians south of Krakow has been called off. The reasons are the autumn mud, problems of support (which is nearly always the cause when excellent and rapid advances suddenly grind to a halt), along with the unexpected appearance of German troops.[*]

At around twelve o'clock Lobanov-Rostovsky's company is surrounded by a "complete circle of fire." There is still no one who knows what is actually happening. To judge by the noise there is even fighting going on behind them, on the road to Sandomierz. They have not yet come under fire themselves but the shell-bursts are gradually creeping

* Using the railways, Messrs. Hindenburg, Ludendorff and Co. had managed once again to pull off a strategic move of the kind the Russian high command could only dream of: the Germans rapidly transferred forces from a sector that had been made secure (East Prussia) to a sector under threat (southern Poland). It did not, however, amount to another Tannenberg. Both sides had been marching hither and thither in a fairly aimless manner, either without locating the enemy or passing each other unnoticed. The two sides quite simply bumped into each other outside Opatov, with the Germans playing the part of eager attackers and the Russians adopting a tenacious but retreating role. The battle had no real significance either for the campaign or for the war, and both sides later claimed victory.

closer and closer. A mounted machine-gun unit passes them. After a short conference with an unknown staff officer, Lobanov-Rostovsky receives orders to take over command of the company's twenty one-horse wagons, which are loaded with explosives and other equipment, and to follow the machine-gun unit back and thus break out of the encirclement. He is given twenty soldiers to help him—the rest of the company stays where it is.

So he sets off. He is mounted, he has twenty men on twenty one-horse wagons and, rather unexpectedly, there is a cow, which was actually supposed to be slaughtered for dinner but has been given a reprieve by the unexpected turn of events. Lobanov-Rostovsky is very worried because the mounted machine-gun unit is moving so fast that it soon leaves them behind. His later account stated: "I had no maps and not the vaguest idea either of the country around me or of the spot where I actually was." At a bridge where three roads meet they become stuck in a huge traffic jam of refugees, cattle, horses and horse-drawn ambulances filled with the wounded. The bridge has been blocked by a cart-load of refugees which has ended up with two wheels hanging out over the water. While the soldiers struggle to lift it back up, shrapnel shells again begin to explode above their heads:*

> The confusion among the peasants was indescribable. Women and children were yelling with fright, men were trying to hold back their panic-stricken horses, one hysterical woman clung to my horse and cried "Mr. Officer, which is the safe way out?" to which, naturally, I could only point out the general direction. A man pushing three cows that would not go got them onto a side road just as shells began falling on it. He turned to another one to

---

* At the start of the war the shrapnel shell was by far the most common field-artillery projectile in all the armies. It is a typical example of a weapon that is brilliant on paper. Each shell contained several hundred hard lead bullets, which were ejected from the body of the shell by a small charge of black powder in its base and which thus made the whole thing function rather like a gigantic shotgun cartridge. The effect depended on a special timing fuse causing the shell to explode in the air immediately in front of the target—an operation that was not that simple. If it detonated immediately overhead, it meant that the bullets would just fly past the target. Furthermore, the target needed to be above ground, which was why this kind of projectile lost most of its value once the combatants had disappeared down into trenches. It was the black powder that created the characteristic, slightly downward pointing smoke cloud when a shrapnel shell detonated.

find it being shelled in its turn and finally, losing his head, rushed back towards his burning village.

Once across the bridge at last Lobanov-Rostovsky finds the road so full of fleeing civilians and their carts that he leads his little group out across the fields. The mounted machine-gunners disappear in the distance and once again he has no idea where he is. He tries to orient himself with the help of the noise of the battle. Now and then shells fall around them and now and then there are bursts from distant machine guns. He is guessing his way forward.

As they are on their way down to yet another bridge some shells explode just above the little column. The terrified man in the lead begins to drive his horse and wagon flat out down the dangerous slope leading to the bridge. To prevent panic spreading, Lobanov-Rostovsky gallops after him, catches up and does something he has never done or even dreamt of doing before—he beats the terrified soldier with his riding whip. Order is restored and they succeed in crossing the watercourse and continuing on along the bottom of a steep ravine.

Chaos rules in the ravine. Some artillerymen are struggling to rescue three guns that have become bogged down. Increasing numbers of wounded men are pouring down the slopes, down to safety. Lobanov-Rostovsky asks what is happening and which unit they belong to but the bleeding men are far too disoriented and confused to be able to give sensible answers. An officer with a rescued regimental flag lying across his saddle gallops past at top speed—a glimpse of some of the atavisms of 1914: not only fighting under a flying banner but also the almost sacred matter of honour, of not letting the flag fall into the hands of the enemy. The officer with the flag is greeted with shouts of encouragement: "Take care!" Shells are exploding on both sides of the ravine. The air is full of dust and it smells of fire and cordite.

After proceeding along the ravine for a while, compass in hand and followed not only by his own section but by three or four hundred wounded men, Lobanov-Rostovsky is shocked to realise that they are trapped. The course they are following will eventually lead them up out of the ravine and onto the main highway towards Sandomierz—which is a problem, since there is a German artillery battery nearby and it opens fire on the Russians as soon as they emerge from the ravine. Lobanov-Rostovsky and the others have to hurry back down. Further off, to the right of the main road, they catch sight of more German batteries. Lobanov-Rostovsky is crestfallen and at a loss.

Then something happens which, though surprising, is not that unusual.

The German guns closest to them are mistaken for Russian guns and their own countrymen on the other side of the main road begin to bombard them. The German batteries proceed to fight a ferocious artillery duel between themselves during which Lobanov-Rostovsky and the Russians with him are able to slip past. The German gun crews soon discover their mistake but by then the Russians are already up on the highway to Sandomierz and in relative safety. Retreating units join them from all the small side roads and they become part of "one long black ribbon of carts overflowing with wounded, remains of artillery batteries, and various bits and pieces of different arms." Now it is time for the next atavism: a cavalry regiment is riding towards the highway in perfect battle order—a beautiful painting from the time of the Napoleonic Wars. Germans? No, Russian hussars. The cavalry officers ride up. Their calm smiles are in glaring contrast to the confusion and terror prevailing among the retreating men. It turns out that the cavalry belongs to a completely different corps and consequently has no idea what has happened or is happening.

As Lobanov-Rostovsky and his little column approach Sandomierz towards dusk it seems that the worst is over. A newly arrived and rested infantry division is in the process of digging in on either side of the main highway. When the column tries to wend its way into the town, Lobanov-Rostovsky finds that the streets are too narrow and the crowds too big, so he orders his twenty wagons to wait at the side of the road. He notes that the cow is still with them and that she seems to have coped with the hardships remarkably well. The sky is overcast.

He recognises one particular unit among the ragged stream of men flowing past him. It is the infantry regiment he came across last night, when they were lying resting in the open on the streets of Opatov, a motionless, sleeping collection of heads and legs and arms and bodies, pale in the bright moonlight. Yesterday they had been 4,000 strong, now there are 300 left, along with six officers. The regiment has been virtually wiped out, but not beaten: they are still carrying their flags and they are in good order.

At dusk it starts to rain. Only now does it occur to Lobanov-Rostovsky that he has not eaten anything all day. With all the excitement and apprehension he has not felt hungry. Around eleven o'clock the rest of his company arrives, badly knocked about but holding up for all that, and as luck would have it the kitchen wagons are with them. At last they can all eat. The sound of the guns in the distance eases up and finally they fall silent. What will later be called the Battle of Opatov is over.

The rain continues to pour down. The time is around midnight.

Lobanov-Rostovsky and some of the others creep in under the stationary wagons for shelter while they sleep. This works well at first but soon the trickling rainwater finds its way in under the wagons.

He and the rest of the company spend the remainder of the night sitting by the roadside, silent and awake, waiting for dawn and daylight with almost animal-like patience.

TUESDAY, 6 OCTOBER 1914
Sarah Macnaughtan witnesses the fall of Antwerp

A blue sky. The leaves are turning. Pleasant autumn weather. The sound of artillery is coming closer and they can feel the ground shaking now, as well as hearing the noise of the explosions. She goes to the door occasionally and asks someone in the never-ending stream of fleeing soldiers and civilians how the battle is going. The answer never varies: "Very badly." Motor cars drive past slowly, hooting their way through the slow-moving throng of people, animals and wagons. Rumour has it that the city will soon be subjected to direct bombardment. Macnaughtan and her colleagues have carried food and water down to the cellars in case they are forced to take the wounded to shelter there.

Many of Sarah's duties are of a mundane order: making beds, washing floors, cutting bread, pouring beer, portioning out the food. Other duties are anything but: tending the wounded and comforting the dying. Sarah Macnaughtan does not really know what to feel, or to think:

With each batch of the wounded, disabled creatures who are carried in, one feels inclined to repeat in wonder, "Can one man be responsible for all this? Is it for one man's lunatic vanity that men are putting lumps of lead into each other's hearts and lungs, and boys are lying with their heads blown off, or with their insides beside them on the ground?" Yet there is a splendid freedom about being in the midst of death—a certain glory in it, which one can't explain.

British soldiers, men from the Marines, have begun to arrive too, both among the wounded and among those retreating. They give the same answer when asked how the battle is going: "Very badly." One of the field hospital women returns with some wounded British soldiers— she had driven her own car right up to the battle line and found the men in a trench. She says: "No one knew why they were in the trenches or where they were to fire—they just lay there and were shot and left."

No one seems to know anything.

At five in the afternoon they start serving dinner, which is earlier than usual. The darkness of autumn is beginning to make itself felt and the high-ceilinged concert hall quickly becomes dark. Soon she can hear the clatter of pans being dropped and chairs being knocked over as people stumble round in the darkness. There are wounded men lying everywhere, even on the floor. The atmosphere is tense. "Any sudden noise is rather trying at present because of the booming of the guns." At about seven o'clock they hear a new noise—a kind of double crack. Someone says it is the sound of the British long-range guns.

It would be wrong to say that Macnaughtan has begun to have doubts, but things are not really as she expected. She herself is not really as she expected. She writes:

> When I go into the little chapel to pray it is all too tender, the divine Mother and the Child and the holy atmosphere. I begin to feel rather sorry for myself, I don't know why; then I go and move beds and feel better; but I have found that just to behave like a well-bred woman is what keeps me up best. I had thought that the Flag or Religion would have been stronger incentives to me.

Later in the evening she tries to go out to get some air but a nurse stops her and asks whether she could look after one of the wounded men. Of course she can, and so she sits and watches a twenty-one-year-old man die. She thinks he gives a suspicion of a smile. More wounded men arrive but they are turned away at the door. There is no more room. The constant thunder of the cannon continues all night without a break.

SATURDAY, 10 OCTOBER 1914[*]
*Elfriede Kuhr listens to war stories at a coffee party in
Schneidemühl*

Autumn colours. An October sky. A chill in the air. The teacher has
brought along a news telegram and reads it out to the class: Antwerp
fell two days ago and the last fort has now capitulated, which means that
the long drawn-out siege is over and the German thrust down along the
coast towards Flanders can continue. Elfriede can hardly hear the last
words of the report because all the children are shouting with joy.

This loud roar whenever another German triumph is announced
has become a ritual in her school. Elfriede believes that many of them
scream simply because they are hoping that victory will be celebrated
with a holiday. Or that the headmaster, a tall, strict gentleman with
pince-nez and a pointed white beard, will be so affected by their youthful patriotism that he will at least let them off the last lessons. (When
the outbreak of war was announced to the school the headmaster was
so moved that he wept and found it difficult to speak at times. He is the
man behind the ban on using foreign words in school and sinners have
to pay a five-pfennig fine: the word is "Mutter" not "Mama," "Auf Wiedersehen" not "Adieu," "Kladde" not "Diarium," "fesselnd" not "interes-
sant" and so on.) Elfriede, too, joins in the shouting about the fall of Fort
Breendonck, not so much because she thinks that they will be excused
from classes but just because she thinks it is fun: "I think it's wonderful to be allowed to shout and scream for all we're worth in a place we
normally have to keep quiet all the time." In the classroom they have a
map on which all the victories of the German army are recorded by pinning up small black, white and red flags. The mood in the school and in
Germany as a whole is aggressive, arrogant, chauvinistic and exultant.

After school Elfriede goes to a small coffee party. Her parents are separated and she has no contact with her father. Her mother is a professional
woman running a small music school in Berlin, which is why Elfriede
and her brother live with their maternal grandmother in Schneidemühl.

---

[*] Kuhr gives the date as being 11 October, but that seems unlikely to be right, partly
because the capitulation referred to happened on 10 October and partly because even
German children did not go to school on Sundays.

As usual, the war is the topic of conversation. Someone has seen yet another transport full of Russian prisoners at the station. They used to attract attention "with their long, brown coats and ragged trousers" but hardly anyone bothers about them anymore. As the German armies continue to advance, the newspapers churn out new figures for the numbers of prisoners taken, a sort of stock market of war in which today's quotations show Suwalki standing at 27,000 and west of Ivangorod standing at 5,800. (Not to mention other tangible symbols of victory: the newspapers this month have reported that 1,630 railway trucks were needed to transport the booty taken after the great victory at Tannenberg.) But what are they to do with all the prisoners? Fräulein Ella Gumprecht, a middle-aged, unmarried schoolmarm with firm views, plump cheeks and carefully waved hair, knows the answer: "Why not shoot the lot of them?" The others think that is a dreadful idea.[*]

The adults swap war stories. Fräulein Gumprecht tells of a man who was tossed into a burning house by Cossacks but who managed to escape on a bicycle by dressing in women's clothes. The children respond by passing on a story their mother has sent them from Berlin:

A German lance corporal in the reserves, a professor of Romance Languages at Göttingen in civilian life, has the job of escorting French prisoners from Maubeuge to Germany. The guns are thundering in the distance. Suddenly the lieutenant in command notices that his lance corporal has become involved in a violent quarrel with one of the Frenchmen. The Frenchman is gesticulating excitedly with his hands and the lance corporal's eyes are flashing angrily behind his glasses. Fearing violence, the lieutenant rides over to them and, with an oath, separates them. Then the agitated lance corporal explains the issue: the French pris-

---

* The treatment of prisoners of war on the Eastern Front at this time—as Alon Rachamimov has shown—was far better than in the Second World War, during which both sides were guilty of numerous violations as well as clearly systematic maltreatment. Conditions were relatively humane during the First World War and over 90 per cent of prisoners of war returned home alive after the war. (Because of food shortage and, above all, typhus, German and Austro-Hungarian prisoners in Russian camps suffered most.)

oner of war, who is wearing tattered boots held together with string, used to be a professor at the Sorbonne. The two gentlemen are quarrelling because they cannot agree about the use of the subjunctive in older Provençal poetry.

They all laugh, including Fräulein Gumprecht, who laughs so much that she gets a piece of nut chocolate stuck in her throat. Grandmother, however, turns to Elfriede and her brother: "Children, don't you think it's such a shame that two professors end up having to shoot at each other? The soldiers should throw down their rifles and say 'We don't want to be part of this any longer.' Then they should just go home." This upsets Fräulein Gumprecht and she shrills: "What about our Kaiser, then? And the honour of Germany? And the good name of our German soldiers?" Grandmother raises her voice and answers: "Every mother ought to go to the Kaiser and say 'Peace now!'"

Elfriede is astounded. She knows her grandmother heard the news of mobilisation with sorrow. This is actually the third war in Grandmother's lifetime: first there was the war with the Danes in 1864, then the war with the French in 1870. And even though Grandmother, just like everyone else, is firmly convinced that Germany will be victorious yet again and that the victory will again be a quick one, she still cannot see that there is anything good in what has happened. But to talk like this! Elfriede has never heard anything like it.

TUESDAY, 13 OCTOBER 1914
Pál Kelemen spends the night in a mountain pass near Łużna

Forwards, then backwards, then forwards again. First of all the frenetic advances in Galicia in the opening months of the war to counter the invading Russians, with all the bloody fighting that resulted from that (the "battle for Lemberg," or possibly the "Battle of Lemberg"); then the retreat—a confused race from river to river until they were suddenly in the Carpathians and on the Hungarian border. Dreadful! After that a pause, silence, nothing. Then orders to advance again, out of the mountain passes of the Carpathians, down to the plains to the north-east and on to Przemyśl, which is under siege. The losses have been enormous.*

Winter is coming unusually early. It started with a heavy snowfall, which quickly made all the roads impassable, and also made it impossible for Austro-Hungarian units to move forward—or back, for that matter. Pál Kelemen's division is trapped in one of these snowed-up passes in the mountains. The biting, wind-driven snow is forming deep drifts around the horses. Freezing soldiers are crouching around small, weak fires or stamping their feet and beating their arms. "Nobody talks."

Pál Kelemen writes in his journal:

There is only one house left intact in the mountain pass, the modest hut of the border innkeeper.† They have installed the field telegraph station in the first room; in the second, the staff officers of the Cavalry Corps are quartered; I arrived here at eleven at night and sent a dispatch to the Command, reporting that it was impossible to proceed at present. So I lie down in a corner on a pallet, covered with my blanket.

Howling, the wind pierces the tiles of the rickety roof and clatters the windowpanes. It is pitch dark outside. Here inside there is only one wavering candle flame. The telegraph works incessantly, forwarding orders in preparation for tomorrow's attack. Scores of those who fell behind in the advance lie in the hall and in the garret—the weak, the sick, and the slightly wounded who start to the rear tomorrow.

I lie half asleep, exhausted, some other officers around me on small heaps of straw. The shivering men around the lodge have made a fire out of the planks of the adjacent stable, and the flames leaping into the dark attract still more stray soldiers.

A sergeant enters and asks permission for one of his comrades to come in here; he is scarcely conscious and would certainly perish of the cold outside. They lay him on a bundle of hay on the ground near the door, hunched up, his eyeballs half

---

* It is still not known exactly how many men were lost but it is likely to be somewhere around 400,000—and this was in less than a month. The historian Norman Stone has written: "The pattern of the war was now set: in the west a stalemate, and in the east a more or less constant Austro-Hungarian crisis."

† The border between Galicia and Hungary.

turned out, his neck drawn in between his shoulders. In several places his coat was pierced by bullets and the edge of it singed by the fire of some night encampment. His hands are stiff with cold, his gaunt, tormented face covered with a dishevelled beard.

Sleep overcomes me. The *titi-tata* code signals of the telegraph become a buzzing in the distance.

At daybreak I am wakened by the noise of the men preparing to march on, and with dull dizzy head I look around the miserable night quarters. Through the low window flowered with frost the day is breaking sallow grey, filling every nook and corner of the room with sober light. Only the soldier who was brought in last night is lying still, on his face, turned toward the wall.

The door of the inner room opens and one of the aides-de-camp, Prince Schönau-Gratzfeld, steps in, smoothly shaven, in pyjamas, blowing clouds of smoke from a long-stemmed Turkish chibouk into the foul bitter air.

He perceives the soldier lying motionless in the corner, goes up to him, but recoils with fastidious horror. Indignantly he commands the instant removal of the corpse, obviously dead from cholera, and, with appalled expression, returns to the inner room. After him two privates drag in a portable rubber bathtub adorned with an escutcheon and filled with warm water.

SATURDAY, 24 OCTOBER 1914
Laura de Turczynowicz returns to Suwalki

The journey has been as slow as it has been uncomfortable. At least on the final stage from Olita Laura has not had to travel in a cattle truck, though the train has still been unheated. And for the last twenty-four hours it has just been crawling along, stopping time after time out on the track for no apparent reason. Sections of the track have been repaired, but only just passably, and on those sections the carriages have swayed and rocked "like a ship in high sea."

At half past five in the morning they finally pull into the station at Suwalki.

She sets off on foot in the raw, cold autumn darkness, accompanied by an acquaintance from the town, a doctor's wife. The road is churned up and difficult to follow. It slowly gets light. She sees Russian soldiers on the march, some of them drunk. She sees damaged buildings and flattened fences.

The children and the household staff are still in Vitebsk, where they have taken temporary accommodation. Stanislaw has been called up by the Russian army and gone off to serve as head of the sanitation engineers in the newly taken city of Lemberg. But before he disappeared he managed to travel to Suwalki, which had just been recaptured, and bring back two trunks of clothes and the news that the house was still standing. He had not wanted to say anything about the damage, merely saying it would be best for her to go and see for herself.

Which is why she is here now. She would really like to bring the children back as soon as possible, now that the Germans have been pushed back towards East Prussia.

When they reach the doctor's house Laura goes in to get her breath back and to gather her strength. She is more than a little afraid of what she is going to find—as a woman who grew up in New York she has no experience of this kind of situation. She is offered coffee and at about half past seven she sets off again.

At last she reaches her house, which is waiting there for her in the morning light.

She goes in. She can hardly believe her eyes.

Everything has been torn, smashed, ripped out, spilled, hurled around, knocked over and fouled. Every drawer has been pulled out, every wardrobe emptied. She wades around in the confused wreckage of the things that had once made up her home. The smell is indescribably awful. Laura goes from window to window, opening them, breathing deeply and holding her breath before going on to the next window and opening it. The library has been completely vandalised. The contents of all the shelves have been emptied and the floor is invisible beneath a layer of torn books and papers, scattered documents and engravings.

The remains of the dropped soup tureen are still lying on the floor in the dining room, along with a thick, crunching carpet of broken glass, dirty china, filthy cloths—all of it trampled by rough boots. The German soldiers and officers who lived here until a couple of weeks ago simply hurled the dishes and glasses on the floor after using them, then used new ones and done the same with them.

Laura goes into one of the pantries. Glass jars are lined up in neat rows. They used to contain jam, marmalade, honey and bottled vegetables. All the jars have been emptied of their original contents and filled with human excrement instead.

She gives orders for Jacob, the workman, and his wife and daughter to start clearing up. Meanwhile, she is going to draw up a list of everything missing and take it to the police.

SUNDAY, 25 OCTOBER 1914[*]
Michel Corday takes the train back to Bordeaux

There are times when he moves among people as though he were on a different planet, surrounded by absurd incomprehensibilities. Is this really his world? In one sense, no. Michel Corday is a forty-five-year-old civil servant at the Ministry of Commerce and Post but he is also a socialist, a *litterateur* and a friend of peace. He writes literary criticism and political articles for the newspapers and has even published a number of novels, some of which have been reasonably successful. (He was in the army at one time and several of his works—*Intérieurs d'officiers* [1894] and *Coeurs de soldats* [1897], for instance—reflect that background, whereas others deal with the sufferings of society or of the heart.)

Michel Corday was originally a nom de plume,[†] and this retiring man with a moustache is in some ways a fairly typical turn-of-the-century intellectual with a double life: he cannot live by his pen alone and thus also needs his job at the ministry. The distance between his two lives is not, however, really that great: he has changed his name so that even his

* The date is an estimate. The dating in Corday's 1914–18 journal is rather erratic: the entries are chronological but it is not always possible to see when one date changes to another. His visit to his family in Saint-Amand Longpré took place sometime between 22 and 26 October and, since he had his professional duties to perform during the week, it seems reasonable to assume that he travelled during the weekend of 24–25 October.
† He assumed the name Corday because his family was loosely related to Charlotte Corday, the woman who murdered the revolutionary leader Marat in 1793—a deed immortalised in Jacques-Louis David's painting *The Death of Marat*. The fact that a staunch republican like Michel Corday chose to take the name of a Girondist like Charlotte Corday is interesting and suggests a degree of vanity or, at any rate, a desire to add a touch of notoriety to his background.

civil-service self is now called Corday. Everyone knows he is a writer and he is a close friend of Anatole France.

During the first days of September, when it really looked as if it was impossible to stop the Germans, the government had left Paris and the staff of the ministries had gone with them. They had left the city by car in a state of panic—"the refugees at the station had been trampling one another as if they were in a burning theatre"—and found a safe haven in Bordeaux. Corday's ministry was accommodated in an institution for the deaf and dumb in Rue Saint-Sernin. Now, however, since the Germans have been held on the Marne for over a month, more and more people are saying it is time for the government and the ministries to move back. Corday's own family was evacuated to Saint-Amand Longpré and this evening he is returning to Bordeaux after visiting them.

To Corday the outbreak of war was a disgrace and a defeat and he has still not reconciled himself to it. He had been ill at a seaside resort and consequently all the news reached him through newspapers and telephone calls. The picture had been slow to take shape. He had tried for a while to distract himself by reading but it did not work.

> Every thought and event caused by the outbreak of war came as a bitter and mortal blow struck against the great conviction that was in my heart: the concept of permanent progress, of movement towards ever greater happiness. I had never believed that something like this could happen. It meant that my faith simply crumbled. The outbreak of war marked my awakening from a dream I had nourished ever since I started thinking.

The children on the beach were playing war games: the girls were being nurses and the boys wounded soldiers. From his window he watched an artillery troop marching away singing and it made him burst into tears.

Out of the jubilation and chaos of those hot August days a new and alien world really has emerged.

It is partly a matter of externals: all these women who have stopped using cosmetics for "patriotic reasons"; all these uniforms everywhere—uniforms have become high fashion; all these growing queues at Mass and at confession; all the floods of refugees, laden with bundles; all the blacked-out streets; all the roadblocks manned by overzealous, domineering militiamen; all these troop transports carrying healthy men to the front and bringing the wounded back from it.

But also of internals: the permanent barrage of patriotic verbal formulae, as highly strung as they are obligatory; the new and uncompromising attitude—"kindness, humanity—all that has been swept away"; the hysterical tone that is manifested both in propaganda and in people's conversations about the war (one woman told him that we should not weep for those who are marching off to the front—it is the men who cannot take part in the struggle who are to be pitied); the confusing mixture of generosity and selfishness; the sudden inability to perceive nuances of any kind—"One dare not say anything bad about the war. The war has become a God." But Corday is doing his duty as a good civil servant.

On the way to Saint-Amand the train had been stormed by women pressing fruit, milk, coffee, sandwiches, chocolate and cigarettes on everyone in uniform. In one town he had seen boys wearing police helmets and acting as stretcher-bearers. It is impossible now to find a waiting room at any of the stations: all of them have been turned into temporary hospitals for the wounded or stores for military equipment. On his return journey, somewhere between Saint-Pierre and Tours, he eavesdrops on a conversation between two families: "Both of them talked of the men they had lost in terrifying tones of resignation, as if they were simply talking about the victims of a natural catastrophe."

In Angoulême a man on a stretcher is carried on board and placed in a neighbouring compartment. The man has been wounded in the back by a shell splinter and is now lame. He has a nurse travelling with him to tend his wound. There is also a blonde woman whom Corday takes to be either the injured man's wife or his mistress. He hears the woman say to the nurse, "He refuses to believe that I still love him." When the nurse goes to wash her hands after examining the wound, the blonde woman and the injured man begin to kiss passionately. When the nurse returns she pretends not to notice and just looks out into the night.

A small non-commissioned officer is sitting in the same compartment as Corday. He has just returned from the front. The two men chat. At four o'clock in the morning the train stops at a station and the soldier gets off. A girl throws herself at the little man and clings tightly to him. "Just to think that so much love, the love of all the mothers, sisters, wives and girl-friends, has so far proved powerless against all this hatred," he thinks.

The kiosks at the stations they pass display rows of cheerfully colourful illustrated papers, all of them with a publication date in the first days of August. No more have been printed since then. It is as if a new era has begun.

Laura de Turczynowicz and an acquaintance spend today in the Augustów Forest near Suwalki, searching for deserted or orphaned children. (They have already found several, including a four-year-old carrying a baby of six months, who were so desperately hungry they had been eating earth.) She meets a man who tells her that their summer villa has been destroyed by the Germans, but he has found Dash, the children's white dog, alive. She writes:

> Every hut was burnt down; gruesome work it was. Many times we saw dead men. I wondered why we struggled so to save our lives when so many had gone down. Going through the forest at dusk, we heard a child's cry, but could not locate the sound. In our search a wounded horse plunging through the underbrush came upon us. He passed so near I could have touched him. Frightened, I clung to a tree for dear life.

WEDNESDAY, 4 NOVEMBER 1914
Pál Kelemen is wounded north of Turka

It is a beautiful night—starry, cold and with a bright moon. Pál Kelemen's horse is reluctant to leave its warm stable and venture out in the chill, biting wind. The army is once again in retreat: forwards and back, forwards and back again. Since a new line of defence is being established, their orders are to see that the retreating units do not get stuck and come to a halt. By about two o'clock in the morning the new line should be ready and, hopefully, occupied by the fresh infantry that are already on their way up to the pass. The task Kelemen and his hussars have been given is close to impossible since it is difficult to gain any kind of overall picture of the situation in the darkness. The road is already in chaos. They ride slowly up against the flow, through a sluggish, grey stream of men, horses, wagons, guns, ammunition carts and pack-mules.

In the moonlight he sees what look like long, black streaks in the white snow: they are the freshly dug trenches. He can hear the sound of rifle fire—the Russians have begun to push forward there. He notes that the stream of retreating men has thinned out but that there are still scattered groups of fleeing troops. Kelemen and his men point them in the right direction. The road is icy and slippery as glass. They have to dismount and lead their horses. Kelemen writes in his journal:

> Meantime the Russian artillery has commenced firing along the whole length of the front sector. I get into the saddle again and push ahead that way. The moon is setting, and in the stiffening cold the sky is becoming overcast. Smoke balls of the grenades and shrapnel drift heavy beneath the clouds.
>
> Some abandoned army wagons stand on the road without men or horses. We have just passed them when I feel a sharp blow near the left knee and at the same time my horse grows restive. I imagine I have struck my leg against something in the dark. I touch the place and instinctively bring my gloved hand to my face. It is warm and moist, and now I feel a sharp throbbing pain.
>
> I say to Mogor beside me that I think I have been hit. He rides up close and discovers a small wound on the rump of my horse also. But horse and rider are still able to keep up. Here one could not possibly dismount. There is no dressing station anywhere in the neighborhood. And to try to get to the infantry first-aid on the front is far more dangerous, since they are now under barrage fire, than to ride on as far as we can.
>
> In numberless simple yet kindly ways, Mogor valiantly tries to divert my attention from the wound. He soothes me by assuring me that we will surely meet some marching troop soon where a doctor will be on hand.
>
> It grows steadily brighter. In the east, the sun comes up with gaudy rays. The sky is radiant, the snow-wrapped mountains sharply distinct from the dark green pine forest. My leg seems to be growing, lengthening. My face burns and I grip the bridle with rigid hand. My horse, fine intelligent animal, picks her way among the snowy clods of the road with feet still sure.
>
> At last we reach the southern slope of the pass. Here, protected from the wind, the road is not so hard, and by the time

the full splendor of the sun flows over the valley before us, the outlying houses of a village are in sight.

In the market place we meet Vas, who, agitated, asks the cause of our delay and grows panicky on hearing the story from Mogor. The village school has been hastily transformed into a first-aid station overnight, and, with Vas on one side and Mogor on the other, I ride to the schoolyard gate.

The scene is beginning to blur before my eyes. I cannot dismount any more; my left leg is numb. Two aid men lift me out of the saddle while Mogor leads the horse from under me. They set me down cautiously. As my left foot touches the ground the accumulated blood squashes in my boot. I cannot stand. With the thoughtlessness of the very young, Vas holds his pocket mirror before me, and I see a strange, yellow old face instead of my own.

FRIDAY, 6 NOVEMBER 1914
Sarah Macnaughtan looks for company in Veurne

They get up at seven o'clock and join the queue for the washbasin in the bathroom. It is a small house and it is in a state of increasing dirt and disorder. When they took it over, all eighteen of them, they found some toys left behind on a mat, a saucepan on the stove, and only three beds— unmade since the owners had fled in haste. (There is also Jane, a happy dog with a red coat that one of them found when out on a job.) Most of them sleep on the floor in the unheated rooms and it is very overcrowded. All this is less of a torment than Sarah Macnaughtan expected. She is a very private person, used to living alone and quietly, and up to now she has found it trying to eat and sleep and work in a group: "I find the communal spirit is not in me." Recently, however, she has surprised herself by starting to look for company, even literally following people around, staying close to them in a way that definitely feels a little embarrassing, but she cannot stop herself doing it. Then it is her turn to use the bathroom. She has to pump for a long time to get any water. She washes. The water is very cold and she notices that the drain seems to be blocked.

Later they all gather in a large room in the butcher's shop next door and have breakfast before walking to the deserted seminary in which the new field hospital is located. Since the fall of Antwerp Macnaughtan has been accompanying the retreat south-westwards along the coast. Her original unit—Mrs. St. Clair Stobart's Ambulance Unit—has returned to England, but she has hung on stubbornly and joined a different group of volunteers, Dr. Hector Munro's Flying Ambulance Corps. She celebrated her fiftieth birthday a week ago.

Antwerp came as a shock to her. Partly because of the defeat itself, partly because of the appalling things she saw—they seemed to be endless and she was not really prepared for them—and partly because of the fact that many, many, oh so many men (and many of them British) did not behave at all in the way she had expected. People lied, bolted, hid away, showed themselves to be cowardly, and some even deserted. The fact that the British press managed to portray the retreat of the British Naval Brigade from the city as some sort of inverted triumph has upset and annoyed her: "I find the conceit of it most trying. Belgium is in the hands of the enemy, and we flee before him singing our own praises loudly as we do."

She has begun to toy with the idea of not just writing about her experiences but also going out on some kind of lecture tour at home. Her main audiences would be the workers in the munitions industry and her aim would be to make them recognise the seriousness of the situation. She has heard numerous scandalous stories of slackness and carelessness and self-interest and greed. This war can actually be lost.

At eight o'clock the first brown-painted ambulances rumble away but most of the people hang around for a while longer in "a courtyard filled with motors and brancardiers [male helpers] and men in uniform, and women in knickerbockers and puttees, all lighting cigarettes and talking about repairs and gears and a box of bandages." It is ten o'clock before the last of the ten vehicles leaves to gather the latest harvest of wounded men. As usual, the noise of the artillery hangs in the background. The day before yesterday the Germans abandoned some of their positions on the Yser, beaten not so much by the Belgian army (which has its headquarters in the town here) as by flooding. Unusually heavy gunfire was heard from the south-east and the town of Ypres yesterday.

The work she has to do is still of a fairly everyday sort: cleaning, serving food, distributing clothes. Macnaughtan hopes to be allowed to go out with the ambulances but she almost certainly recognises that she is physically far too weak for that job.

The weather is fine. In the afternoon she decides to go back to the house. She is intending to work on her diary and to rest a little. But it does not happen. She cannot be at peace. She feels anxious and nervous. She pulls herself together and writes, but something is not right with her. "I feel as if all the time I was living in some blood-curdling ghost story or a horrid dream. Every day I try to overcome the feeling, but I can't succeed." Yesterday it was one of the wounded men shouting at her that he wanted her to kill him. Today the cheerful French lad with the lovely teeth (the one who makes their coffee at lunchtime) was put against a tree and shot as a punishment for threatening a French officer with a revolver during the night—the boy was apparently drunk at the time. Finally her anxiety gets too much for her and she rises, puts her diary under her arm and walks back to the seminary. She needs company: "I find that unless I am with somebody the ghosts get the better of me."

By dinnertime the brown-painted ambulances are beginning to return, one by one, at irregular intervals. Weary and dirty, the drivers and stretcher-bearers get out of their vehicles. Greetings are exchanged, and questions asked. "Did you get many?"

Dusk is falling. It is dark by six o'clock.

SUNDAY, 8 NOVEMBER 1914*
Alfred Pollard digs a trench outside La Bassée

They are not really needed here and sending them forward to dig is mainly a way of keeping them occupied until they receive new marching orders.† No one tells them to take care.

There is, after all, so much that is new and unfamiliar. The front line in the west has now become genuinely static and it is only up in Flanders that real fighting is still going on: the First Battle of Ypres. Instead, both sides are mostly occupied digging themselves in, which is not always as simple as it sounds. Since no one foresaw this strange war of position there was very little training for it and there was even less experience.

---

* The date may have been a day earlier or a day later.
† The officer commanding this section had been expecting an artillery unit as reinforcement, but as the result of a simple error Pollard's infantry battalion had been sent instead.

Later on Pollard remarks that "the trenches in 1914 were terrible": drainage and refuse collection do not function and there are no shelters or bunkers, only small sections of roof that at best keep out the rain but hardly do more than that. The whole landscape of a war of position is new—not least this deceptive emptiness. Where, in fact, is the enemy? There is no sign of him here. And where is the war itself in all this silence?

So they just trudged off to this position about half a mile from the front line, checked that there was no sign of the enemy and that they were not likely to be under threat, and they started to dig. On the first day the Germans let them get on with their picking and shovelling, without any cover (there was none, in any case), within sight, and in bright sunshine. On the second day, however, the Germans obviously thought that enough was enough.

This is Pollard's third month in the army. At five o'clock in the afternoon of 8 August he left the insurance company in St. James Street where he worked as a clerk, never to return. It was an easy decision for him. A day or so earlier he had been standing in a great crowd of people outside one of London's big army barracks and he had watched a unit of the Guards march past on their way to war. Everyone was cheering and shouting, him too, though there was a lump in his throat as the soldiers marched past in perfect step, their arms swinging rhythmically. He was not weeping with pride as many of the others were, nor was it that he was moved by the sudden gravity of the moment, a recognition that the country had been thrown into war without any real warning—and a big war, at that, not one of those distant colonial adventures but a colossal war that threatens to turn the world upside down. Not only threatens to do so but promises to do so, which is why some of the people were cheering: the war stood for a promise of great and radical change. But that is not what moved Pollard so deeply that he started weeping. His tears were tears of envy. He wanted so much to be one of them. "How could I be left behind?"

To many people the war really came as a grand promise of change, and it appealed to Pollard in a number of ways, not the least of which was that he was thoroughly fed up with his job and had even been thinking about emigrating. But now the war had come instead. He was twenty-one years old.

He and all the others had queued for almost three hours. When the gates of the recruiting centre finally opened, he and another man—an acquaintance from the tennis club—pushed and elbowed their way through and then sprinted for all they were worth to the main building in order to be first. After all, what if the number of places was limited? And what if it was all over before they even got to the front? (His brother enlisted as a volunteer in the same unit at first, but then deserted in order to join a different unit under an assumed name simply because this second unit was expected to be one of the first sent into battle.)

Pollard loved the drill, found the long marches "rather fun" and could hardly control his excitement when he was given his rifle: "I was armed. It was a weapon designed to kill. I wanted to kill." He often sat playing with his bayonet in secret, testing the edge: "The desire to get to the front had become an obsession." They marched through London to the sounds of a military band. Weapons training consisted of firing fifteen shots. The order for departure came so suddenly that he did not have time to let his parents know. As the train to Southampton passed through a station, he threw a short message addressed to his mother out through the window. It reached her.

After all this waiting Pollard is at the front at last. Digging. For the second day in succession. The air is filled with the smell of earth and rotting leaves. Suddenly there is a noise "like an express train travelling at an incredible speed," followed by a ringing, metallic detonation. In front of them, not far above the ground, he sees the billowing, swelling cloud from a shell-burst. Pollard leans on his spade and stares "fascinated":

> I was really under fire. My pulses raced with excitement. A second shell followed the first. Then a third. There was a commotion a little way along the line. Men were running. Someone rushed by calling for the doctor. A direct hit. We had suffered our first casualty.

FRIDAY, 13 NOVEMBER 1914
William Henry Dawkins writes to his mother from HMAT Orvieto

Heat and a sea wind. Life on board the troopship is strange. He has probably never lived so comfortably before. Even though William Henry Dawkins is no more than a newly commissioned lieutenant he is nevertheless an officer and has therefore been given a first-class cabin of his own on board a ship that until just a month ago was one of the Orient Line's best and most modern vessels. So there is a shower and a hot bath and he is not far from the beautiful dining room in which they serve three excellent meals a day: "Our meals are better than could be had in the best Melbourne hotel." There is a ship's orchestra to play for these uniformed passengers.

The only thing to disturb the idyll is the stink of the horses down in the hold. That and the temperature, which rises as HMAT* *Orvieto* and the other ships in the great convoy steam their way northwards across the Indian Ocean beneath a fiery sky. Many of the other ranks sleep on deck at night, hoping it will be cool. Since leaving Australia Dawkins has celebrated his twenty-second birthday. A photograph taken immediately before embarkation shows a young man with a gentle smile, oval face, narrow nose and open, inquisitive gaze. He has just started wearing a moustache and his uniform tie is tied in a four-in-hand knot.

But even though he and the other officers are literally living in luxury their existence is far from idle. They usually rise at quarter to six in the morning and the days are spent in physical training, instructing the soldiers, holding sporting competitions and running courses in subjects such as boxing and French. (The idea is that he and the 20,000 Australians and 8,000 New Zealanders in the convoy will be sent to the Western Front.) *Le prochain train pour Paris part à quelle heure?*

At the start of the voyage the war was very far away.† At first the vessel sailed with its full peacetime illumination, which in the case of a beautiful liner like the *Orvieto* meant that the ship was lit up at night with thousands of brightly coloured lamps. But now the ship has a strict blackout: they are even forbidden to smoke on deck after sunset. They are afraid of the German cruisers, which are known to be freebooting in the Indian Ocean: their ghostlike and unforeseeable raids across the breadth of the ocean have already sunk almost twenty Allied merchantmen. The convoy's departure from Australia was, in fact, delayed because a squadron of German cruisers was known to be in the region.‡

---

* His Majesty's Australian Transport.

† The first shots in the war between Germany and Great Britain were actually fired in Australia when a German merchant ship attempted to slip out of Sydney harbour on 4 August but was halted by warning gunfire.

‡ This was Maximilian von Spee's Pacific Squadron, which was soon to make a name for

Now they are heading north-west, surrounded by an escort of Allied warships. When Dawkins looks out over the starboard rail he can see the Japanese cruiser *Ibuki*, whose wide funnels, for some reason, emit much denser smoke than the British and Australian vessels. The thirty-eight ships in the convoy make an impressive sight and today Dawkins is sitting in his cabin writing to his mother:

> It is wonderful the power of Britain at sea. This huge convoy just proceeds uninterruptedly on its own course in its own time. Then again a lone ship like the *Osterley* runs its usual mail course to Australia and back. Again cruisers flying our flag appear at odd moments from odd places. All these things point to a complete mastery of the sea. Today we heard of the fall of Tsing-tao and there was a pretty exchange of compliments between ourselves and the Jap battleship.

William Henry Dawkins had intended to be a teacher. His family had neither money nor any tradition of education (when he was born his mother was a seamstress and his father a workman), but his parents recognised that he was a bright child and, with the help of a scholarship, he was able to continue his education at a boarding-school in Melbourne. At the age of just sixteen he began to serve as pupil teacher* at a school no more than twenty-five miles from his home. He would probably have been happy in the teaching profession, which he was actually very keen on, if he had not happened to see in the paper that an officer-cadet school was to be opened in Duntroon. He applied, took the examinations and, to his own surprise, was accepted.

The building of the cadet school was still unfinished when he and the rest of the first cohort of aspirant officers moved in. The place itself had been a bit of a disappointment: the location was dry, cold and isolated

---

itself and spread panic and destruction as it steamed east. At this point the squadron is off Chile on the west coast of South America, where on 1 November it inflicted a surprise defeat on a British flotilla at Coronel. Heavy British reinforcements were on the way to the South Atlantic to avenge Coronel and to stop von Spee and his squadron at any price.

* The education of new teachers in Australia relied on a kind of apprenticeship system whereby newly qualified candidates ("Junior Teachers") worked in the class under the guidance of an experienced teacher.

and they lived in prefabricated, single-storey barracks with asbestos cladding. But the education was good and Dawkins, who was ambitious, achieved the highest grades in both theoretical and practical subjects. He is, however, rather small, only about five foot six inches and slightly built, and that—together with his intellectual abilities—pushed him in the direction of a specialisation in which the mind is more important than brute strength. The majority of the thirty-seven men in the passing-out class of 1914 went on into the infantry or the cavalry, whereas he and one other high-performing cadet ended up in the engineers. That particular branch of the forces probably suited his temperament best; even though Dawkins is pleased to be part of the Australian Expeditionary Force and just as happy as all the others to cheer British successes, it is clear that he is not afflicted by war fever in its most intense form. The character that emerges from his letters is that of an ambitious, quiet, slightly prim young man—an elementary school teacher in uniform. He is a keen churchgoer and the eldest of six brothers and sisters, the two youngest of whom—the twin girls Zelma and Vida—he is particularly fond of and pays a lot of attention.

The outbreak of war did not come as a complete surprise to him, since rumours had preceded it. Few people, however, had taken the rumours too seriously: if anything was going to happen it would literally happen on the other side of the world, where it would affect foreign places of which few people had ever heard and even fewer could pronounce. When the news finally reached them and they understood that their country too had been dragged into it in some incomprehensible way, Dawkins and his fellow cadets had existed in limbo for the first few confusing days. What was going to happen to them? They still had four months' education and training left to do. Then they heard they were to take their examinations early so they could join the expeditionary force that was being put together. They had happily packed their possessions and given away or sold everything surplus to requirements, and a grand and emotional dinner had been given in their honour. Now they are on their way.

Even though Europe still lies far ahead, Dawkins has already seen something of war. Or almost, anyway. When they were passing the Cocos Islands four days earlier the convoy took the eastern route instead of the more usual western route because they were afraid of encountering the most notorious and feared of the German freebooters, the light cruiser SMS *Emden*.* Their caution proved justified: the *Emden* was, indeed, lying in wait. A telegram informed the convoy of this fact and the largest of the convoy's escorts was dispatched to deal with it: a message—"Attacking the enemy"—reached the *Orvieto* at 10:25 and "the boom of the gun was heard by some on board our ship." The *Emden*, which was severely outclassed, was shot to pieces before being beached.

The rumour is now going round the *Orvieto* that the wounded and prisoners from the twenty-five-minute naval engagement are to be brought on board. Dawkins is really looking forward to this. The convoy is now approaching Ceylon, where he hopes to be able to post the letter to his mother:

> I hope you are in the best of health. I am splendid and in perfect health. I do hope Aunty Mary is improving. Give my kindest regards to all who may enquire of me. I will close now—looking forward to getting your letter at Colombo. Best love to all, From Willie xxxxxxxxxxxxxx to the girls.

THURSDAY, 19 NOVEMBER 1914
Kresten Andresen goes through his kit before travelling to the front in France

One by one Andresen's friends have gone. Since he has carefully refrained from stepping forward as a volunteer he has managed to remain in the barracks for some time—a furtive, uncertain existence waiting for the inevitable. But the disappearance of the others—most recently his namesake Thöge Andresen—has had an effect on him. Thöge, unlike Kresten, volunteered for front-line service. His reason? Thöge wanted "to undergo his baptism into manhood in war." Kresten Andresen can certainly understand how Thöge and others like him feel. He writes in his journal:

---

* By this point the *Emden* had sunk seventeen merchant vessels and was already surrounded by an aura of romance, partly because of the cunning of her commander, Captain von Müller, but also because of his humanity. He always picked up the crews of vessels he sunk, treated them well and ensured that they were quickly put ashore. This chivalrous behaviour corresponded well to the expectations most people still had of the war.

Go to war not for the sake of goods and gold, not for your homeland or for honour, nor to seek the death of your enemies, but to
strengthen your character, to strengthen it in power and will, in
habits, custom and earnestness. That is why I want to go to war.
But I refuse to learn that lesson voluntarily since I believe that the
aim can also be achieved in another way.

Andresen knows that it cannot be much longer, but he is nevertheless grateful for the extra time he has won.

They were vaccinated against typhus and cholera yesterday. Today
they are being injected against diphtheria. He is going through his kit,
which is now all complete:

Grey uniform with red piping and bronze buttons
Dark cloak, army issue
Pickelhaube with green cover, R86
Grey uniform cap
Own boots, bought in Vejle
Laced boots, yellow, army issue
Rucksack, calfskin
Yellow Belgian belt
Ditto ammunition pouch
Ditto leather items and straps
Tent and tent pegs*
Mess-tin, aluminium
Mug, ditto
Flask, ditto
Spade
Grey gloves
Bread bag
Two tins of coffee
Tin for rifle grease
Iron rations, consisting of two bags of biscuits, a can of meat
      and a packet of peas

* The part of the tent a soldier carried with him was humourously christened by the
troops as "the hero's coffin" since it was often used as a shroud for the fallen at field
burials.

Two first-aid bandages
Rifle, Model 97
Pull-through
Two woollen jerseys
Two shirts
Two pairs of underpants, one blue
Thick, navy-blue jersey
Grey scarf
Muff
Two belts
Pair of knee-warmers
Pair of gloves
Identity tag, ANDRESEN, KRESTEN K.E.R.R. 86.
Four pairs of socks, one of them in open work (love gift)
Hood
White armband for use in night-fighting
Bag of salt with a silk ribbon
Half a kilo of ham
Half a kilo of butter
Tin of fruit spread*
New Testament
Flight of the Stag†
Field Postcards, 30
Writing paper
"Something for the Troops": Anise oil‡
Plasters
Sewing kit
Map
Three notebooks
A Danish Flag (Lacking at the moment)§

---

* A kind of marmalade made from a mixture of apples and oranges.
† A popular novel by the Danish author Christian Winther (1796–1876).
‡ An antiseptic.
§ Later he actually did carry a small Danish flag with him into the field, which—together with Winther's novel—he considered to be the embodiment of "the most precious of everything that is Danish." So Andresen was by no means immune to nationalistic sentiments; it is just that his were not German sentiments.

Bayonet
150 rounds live
Half a kilo of bacon
One Speckwurst sausage
One loaf of bread (army issue)

All in all his pack weighs about thirty kilos, which (as Andresen writes in his journal) "can be said to be quite enough." The newspapers are writing about some units composed of young students who went into the attack at Langemarck singing "Deutschland, Deutschland, über alles." Winter is approaching.

SATURDAY, 28 NOVEMBER 1914
Michel Corday lunches with two ministers in Bordeaux

There are six of them in the party and they talk about this and that. Given the huge gravitational pull of the topic, however, the conversation always comes back to the war. There is the fact, for instance, that although there is a word for a woman who has lost her husband ("widow") there is no word for a woman who has lost her child. Or that it is almost certainly possible for German Zeppelins to reach and bomb Paris. Or that they have begun putting up special lampshades on the street-lights in London and that the person who invented them is the famous choreographer Loie Fuller. Or there is the business of these peculiar chain-letters containing prayers that have started circulating: the recipient is urged to copy the prayers and send them on to nine other people or "misfortune will strike you and those you love."

No, the war is a difficult topic to avoid, particularly when two of the men round the table are in the government.

One of them is Aristide Briand, Minister of Justice and an old political animal if ever there was one, an adroit pragmatist (some would say opportunist), vaguely pinkish in outlook and outspokenly anti-clerical. The eloquent Briand is becoming an increasingly important figure in politics and many other ministers are envious of him because he has visited the front. This month he has come up with a particular idea: since the war in the west seems to have bogged down, why not send a Franco-British army elsewhere, the Balkans, for instance. The other politician is Marcel Sembat, Minister of Public Works, a lawyer, journalist and one of the leading figures in the French socialist party. Both men are now part of the coalition government set up after the outbreak of war. Not many people are surprised that Briand joined the government: he is known as a careerist, accustomed to power and its conditions and possibilities. Very many more people, however, particularly among the radicals, were surprised by Sembat's acceptance of office: there are many in that camp who see it as an act of treachery on a par with the German Social Democrats voting in favour of war credits.[*]

During the course of the conversation it becomes clear that not even the ministers have any firm grasp on how many soldiers there actually are in the army. This is partly because the higher echelons of the military, who frequently and openly show their scorn for the civilian powers, are notoriously secretive, and partly because registers and rolls are still in disarray after the great mobilisation of the late summer and the colossal losses of the autumn, which culminated at the Battle of the Marne. (How many died is a secret and will remain so until after the end of the war.) None of the civilian ministers dares raise a voice against the generals—the latter still have the status of infallible Gods of Thunder in all the warring nations. They have, however, managed to come to a rough estimate of the losses by using the figures for the total number of food rations served in the army every day. On the basis of this information the government is estimating how many bottles of champagne it will need to distribute to the troops on Christmas Eve.

After lunch Corday is rather distressed by how much his old idol Sembat enjoys his new role as minister, how much he *loves* the title. Corday notes in his journal:

> Exceptional circumstances have enabled him to enjoy a position
> of power that he previously rejected as a matter of principle; but

---

* Particularly since Sembat had worked closely with Jean Jaurès, the socialist leader who tried to prevent the outbreak of war by calling a general strike but who was murdered on 31 July 1914 by a young French nationalist. And as if that was not enough, Sembat was also known to be the author of a widespread and widely discussed pacifist manifesto.

it is sad to see these men now, to see them riding around in their cars, see them climbing into their special trains, see how gladly and openly they bask in their power.

FRIDAY, 11 DECEMBER 1914
Kresten Andresen witnesses the looting of Cuy

When they left Flensburg the town was wrapped in a blanket of wet, new snow. The ritual was the usual one. Women from the Red Cross showered him and the other soldiers with chocolate, cakes, nuts and cigars, as well as putting flowers in the muzzles of their rifles. He had accepted the gifts but said a determined "no" to flowers in his gun: "I'm not ready for my funeral yet." The train journey took ninety-six hours. He did not sleep for many of them, partly from nervousness, partly from curiosity. Most of the time he had just sat there at the carriage window (they had been lucky enough not to travel in cattle trucks as many others did) and greedily taken in everything he saw: the battlefields around Liège where virtually every house seemed burnt or demolished after the severe fighting in August (the very first major battle in the west); the dramatic landscape and many tunnels of the valley of the Meuse; the beautiful winter-green plains of northwest Belgium; the line of the horizon made jagged by muzzle flashes and the light of shell-bursts; villages and towns quite untouched by the war and resting in deep, deep peace; villages and towns badly scarred by the war and filled with its ghosts. They detrained finally in Noyon in northwest France and marched south in the moonlight along a road on which artillery pieces and carriages and motor cars rattled past them, while the sound of distant explosions grew ever sharper.

The regiment has now taken up position along a railway embankment immediately outside the small town of Lassigny in Picardy. To his relief Andresen realises that, apart from some unpleasant but on the whole ineffective artillery bombardment,[*] this is a quiet section. Their

---

[*] Andresen is observing the same thing as many other people: that shrapnel shells, by far the most common type of artillery ammunition, have a negligible effect on troops who are well dug in.

duties are not too taxing: four days in the muddy trenches followed by four rest days. It is all about watching and waiting, with the occasional night on duty at a listening post between the lines. The French are dug in about 300 yards away. The two sides are separated by some simple barbed-wire entanglements* and a flat field on which there are still drooping sheaves of rotting rye—the harvest for 1914. Otherwise there is not much to see. But there is plenty to hear: the *tsji* and *tsju* of rifle bullets, the *dadera-dadera* of machine guns and the *pum-tsiu-u-i-u-u-pum* of shells.† The food is excellent. They get two hot meals a day.

Some of it is better than he had feared, some worse than he had expected. Christmas is approaching and Andresen is homesick, which is

---

* Barbed wire of the kind we now know was invented in the United States for agricultural purposes. It made animal husbandry possible on a completely new scale. The first mention of it in a military context—as a barrier against attack—is during the Franco-Prussian War of 1870–71. It is known that American forces used barbed wire to protect their camps during the Spanish-American War of 1898. Even though barbed wire is referred to in British army ordinances as early as 1888, the opposing forces in 1914 went into battle without wire: the expectations were that the war was going to be both highly mobile and soon over. When the first trenches were dug in the early autumn of 1914, improvised barbed-wire barriers (at best) were constructed from wire collected from nearby villages. (It is clear that the phenomenon was still rather unusual since the term "barbed wire" does not occur immediately: some accounts, for example, refer to "barbed fence-wire" and at the early stage they used whatever wire they could get hold of, including wire without barbs.) Such defences, moreover, were often thin, frequently consisting of a single line of posts linked by three or four strands of wire. Soon, however, they began to produce barbed wire specially designed for military use: the barbed wire used in agriculture up until that point normally had seven paired barbs per metre whereas the new military wire had fourteen or more paired barbs a metre. The barriers also became wider and denser: a French ordinance of 1915 refers to a minimum barrier of two rows with the posts roughly three metres apart, whereas a British ordinance of 1917 prescribed that a barbed-wire barrier should be at least nine metres deep. And there were soon many variants in use, some of them moveable, such as "Spanish Riders," "Cubes," "Hedgehogs," "Gooseberries" and "Knife Rests." The British ordinance mentioned above also refers to a number of different types of fixed barbed-wire barriers such as apron, double apron, fence and apron, trip and loose wire, concertina (also called Brun wire), trip and crossed diagonals, rapid double fence, low wire, French rapid wire, high and low wire combination (this last named alone came in six different variants). There were also experiments with obstacles consisting of electric fencing but these were not found to be practical. The Frenchman Olivier Razac has written that barbed wire, although never a metaphor for the First World War, may be said to have played an important role in artists' attempts "to give form to the monstrous sublimity of the destructive forces unleashed by modern war."

† The onomatopoeia is Andresen's own.

made all the worse by the acute shortage of letters from home. The little town in which they are quartered between their spells in the forward line is under almost constant shellfire, with the result that it has slowly been emptied of its population. The word went round today that the last of the French had deserted their homes. The civilians had scarcely left their houses before German soldiers began looting them.

The rule is that you take what you want from empty, deserted buildings. Both the camps behind the line and the shelters in the trenches are cheaply and gaudily furnished with loot from French homes—everything from woodstoves and soft beds to household equipment and beautiful sofas and chairs.* (The bunkers are often decorated with ironic mottos. One popular one is: "We Germans are afraid of nothing but God and our own artillery.") Now that it is clear that the last houses are being deserted things proceed in the usual order—officers can take what they want first, then it is the men's turn.

Andresen goes along with ten or so others, all under the command of a sergeant major. Lassigny is a more and more depressing sight: where there had once been tall white houses with shutters on their windows, nothing remains but spiky, rain-blackened heaps of rubble, bricks and splintered wood. The projectiles from shrapnel shells and shell fragments lie scattered all over the streets. The little town is slowly being ground down into the earth. The church has been shot to pieces and is just an empty shell. Inside it the old bell is balanced on a couple of collapsed beams and will soon drop and hit the ground with a final, cracked peal. A large crucifix, blown apart by a shell, hangs on the facade of the church. Andresen is deeply moved:

> How brutal and ruthless war is! The finest values are trampled underfoot—Christianity, morality, home and hearth. And yet, in

* This careful furnishing of the trenches—it would soon be possible to find bunkers with electric ceiling lights, carpeted floors and panelled walls—is a consequence of the fact that the German army in the west was already beginning to set its sights on long-term defence. For purely ideological reasons the French army did not wish to create the impression that it intended to remain in its trenches and thus its trenches remained relatively improvised throughout the whole war. Hardly surprisingly, the Austro-Hungarian army in the east was quick to make conditions comfortable for itself. There are even said to have been bunkers with glass in the windows, though there seems to be a touch of the oxymoron about that.

our time, there is so much talk about Civilisation. One is inclined
to lose faith in civilisation and [other] values when they are not
shown more respect than this.

They approach the recently deserted houses. The sergeant major,
who is a teacher in civilian life, leads the way. He rummages eagerly
through cupboards and crannies, but there is not much to take. Most of
it has already been looted. The chaos is indescribable. Andresen stands
back a little, his hands in his pockets, feeling more and more sickened
but saying nothing.

In a door that leads to a recently stripped shop they are met by a well-
dressed but hatless woman, wearing a coat with a fur collar. She turns to
the soldiers and asks where her husband is. Andresen says that he does
not know. He meets her eyes and her gaze is dark: he finds it hard to tell
whether her expression is one of despair or of scorn, but he feels ashamed,
so ashamed that he just wishes that he "could run far away" and hide.

TUESDAY, 15 DECEMBER 1914
Elfriede Kuhr helps to feed the troops at the station in
Schneidemühl

Frost haze, white snow, biting cold. Many of the smaller children are
so cold that they no longer want to play soldiers. Elfriede, however, the
oldest of them, argues in favour of the pretend exercise. It is all about
learning to endure: "After all, the troops at the front are suffering much
worse cold than we are." Little Fritz Wegner is, however, really frozen.
She is forced to wipe his running nose time after time, which she does
not really think is appropriate to her dignity as the unit's officer.

Later she goes to the railway station. Her grandmother works there
almost every day as a Red Cross volunteer. Elfriede's usual job is to help
feed the soldiers who stop there. The transport trains continue to run
night and day: carriages full of healthy, singing men going east to the
battles that are still raging there and carriages full of silent, bleeding men
coming back. On this particular day several hospital trains will be arriving so there will undoubtedly be plenty to do.

Elfriede helps out when, in spite of being forbidden to do so, they feed 300 civilian workers who come in on a train from East Prussia, where they have been constructing trenches and other fortifications. She watches the hungry men eat, silent and afraid of being caught: soup, bread and coffee. They quickly devour 700 sandwiches before slinking back into the waiting train. She helps to make new sandwiches in a hurry. The sliced sausage is all gone so they spread drippings on the bread instead, and the pea soup has to be watered down, but when the train with the wounded arrives they do not hear any complaints.

Towards evening she is sent to buy more sausage. She has to go to two butchers before getting everything she needs. On the way back she meets Gretel, one of her friends:

> For protection against the cold she is so wrapped in clothes that only her nose and blue eyes are peeking out. I hung a whole string of onion sausages around her neck and said, "Give me a hand so you don't get called a lazy-bones."

The two of them help at the railway station, lugging big churns of coffee back and forth. Just before ten o'clock they get their reward—a sausage sandwich and pea soup—then they go home, completely exhausted but very contented. Outside it has started to snow heavily. "It was beautiful to see the way the snowflakes whirled past in the light of the gas-lamps."

SATURDAY, 19 DECEMBER 1914
Sarah Macnaughtan is serving soup in Veurne

Rain. Rain again. Rain and darkness. The days have begun to run together, one following another, each the same as the last. The work does not change, the sights remain the same. The news from the front no longer offers any variety: a bit of territory lost here, a symbolic bit of ground won there. It is as if the war has stalled, is not getting anywhere, is trapped in itself, while still mechanically continuing to demand its daily tribute of lives and bodies. And the waste flushes past Sarah every day as she stands there in her soup kitchen at the station.*

The only thing that is new is a baffling ailment which is afflicting soldiers who have spent a long time in waterlogged trenches: their feet become cold, swollen, numb and blueish—sometimes affecting them so badly that amputation is the only solution. For those who have not reached that stage, dry footwear helps and Macnaughtan has sacks of socks to hand out to those in need of them. (All the socks are home-knitted and have been collected in Great Britain; some of them are darned, some knitted from different sorts of wool, and some of them contain little gifts of chocolate and cigarettes.) Some of the soldiers come in barefoot even though the end of December is approaching. She can see that what she is doing is appreciated but she is still prey to doubt: "I can make none of them really better. I feed them, and they pass on."

Macnaughtan is still living in the damp attic of the little house. The owners have returned and the woman of the house spent a week cleaning up after the earlier lodgers. Sarah eats a modest breakfast in the kitchen with the family at half past eight and goes to the station around ten o'clock.

The first transports with wounded men usually start coming in about half past ten. Sarah's soup kitchen is no more than a space in an archway, curtained off with the help of some nailed-up sacking. She has all her equipment and pots and pans in there, in a space about eight feet by eight. The object she is most familiar with is a small coffee grinder with a picture of a blue windmill on it. The grinder is often on the go all day and she has "conceived an earnest hatred" of it. She sometimes loads coffee, hot soup and bread onto a little red cart and takes it out to feed the troops on waiting trains.

She eats lunch at the field hospital and then goes back to the house for a short rest. She is not really feeling too well. Life back at the little house is characterised by monotony. The family sits around a stove in one of the rooms and the father occasionally plays the pianola while

---

* The soup kitchen was Macnaughtan's own. She started it on her own initiative and with her own money in order to alleviate the hunger and thirst of the less severely wounded soldiers who, because their injuries were less acute, often ended up waiting a long time for onward transport. She had three Belgian women as helpers.

the girls cut out scraps from old papers. Macnaughtan is amazed that none of them read. She feels lonely. The streets are wet and muddy and a harsh, cold wind blows in from the sea.

Macnaughtan has noticed that care of the wounded has begun to improve more and more and there is much less to complain about than before. At the same time, however, people are becoming more quarrelsome than they were. She writes in her diary:

> No one is affable here, except those who have just come out from home, and it is quite common to hear a request made and refused, or granted with, "Please do not ask again." Newcomers are looked upon as aliens, and there is queer sort of jealousy about all the work. Oddly enough, few persons seem to show at their best at a time when the best should be apparent. No doubt, it is a form of nerves, which is quite pardonable. Nurses and surgeons do not suffer from it. They are accustomed to work and to seeing suffering, but amateur workers are a bit headlong at times. I think the expectation of excitement (which is often frustrated) has a good deal to do with it. Those who "come out for thrills" often have a long waiting time, and energies unexpended in one direction often show themselves unexpectedly and a little unpleasantly in another.

The evening is long and dark and she is feeling unwell with a severe headache. She thinks that the drumming of the rain on the windowpanes is a melancholy sound.

TUESDAY, 22 DECEMBER 1914
Michel Corday witnesses the opening session of the Chamber of Deputies in Paris

The government and the ministries have returned to the capital and the Chamber of Deputies is reopening. As a senior civil servant in one of the ministries he is able to follow all the proceedings from a balcony. Organising the session has not been entirely without problems: one of the questions that has been debated—with great animation—right up to government level is whether deputies should be permitted to appear in uniform or whether they must all dress in civilian clothes. All those in a position to do so would like to turn up in military uniform. They have finally decided to make the frock-coat obligatory.*

Corday is frightened by the speeches and the effect they have on the listeners: "Alas, how words cast a spell on these people!" He finds that the more a soapbox orator insists on his resolve to hold out "to the bitter end," the more exaggerated his voice and gestures become.

Afterwards, out in the corridor, he meets a man who is now the adjutant to a high-ranking general but whom Corday knows from civilian life as director of the Opéra Comique. He tells Corday that 1,500 or so theatregoers have to be turned away every evening, such is the public demand. And the boxes are mainly occupied by women in mourning: "They have come to weep. Only music can subdue and ease their sorrow."

The man tells him a story from his months as a staff officer. There was a woman who refused to be separated from her husband, a captain, and who followed him on his journey to the front. In Compiègne they were supposed to go their separate ways since it was time for him to go to the front line, but his wife still refused. And she stood her ground stubbornly. The ban on civilians visiting the war zone is, of course, also applicable to women whose husbands are there, indeed, it is particularly applicable to them. Their presence is considered a distraction. (The only exceptions are prostitutes, who are issued with special passes to practise their profession—it is said that some particularly desperate women take advantage of this to stay in contact with their husbands.) Those in command said that there was nothing they could do in a case like this other than to declare the captain's service at the front at an end and to send him back to the mobilisation centre. What did the man do when faced with this threat? He murdered his wife.

---

* Respect for hierarchy was what decided the issue: how would it look if a lieutenant were to rise to his feet and put pointed questions to his absolute superior, the War Minister?

SATURDAY, 26 DECEMBER 1914
William Henry Dawkins is sitting by the pyramids, writing to his mother

From anticipation to disgust to disappointment and back to anticipation. The feelings among the Australian troops in the great convoy on its way to Europe—or to what they thought was going to be Europe, anyway—followed that trajectory. Over a month at sea dampened much of their initial enthusiasm, and homesickness was growing apace among these young soldiers, many of whom had never been away from their families for so long. (The postal service was—for reasons that are understandable—both irregular and unreliable.) The gloom on board increased more and more, the water had begun to run out in the ever more intense heat, and when it was announced that they were not even to be allowed ashore in Aden the dissatisfaction became general. Nor did the disappointment diminish when they were told a few days later that the journey to Europe was being cut short and the whole force would instead go ashore in Egypt. Many of them, like Dawkins, had set their hearts on celebrating Christmas in England.

The main reason for the change of plan was the entry of the Ottoman Empire into the war. The Allies were already fearful that this new opponent would attack the strategically important Suez Canal. By landing the Australian and New Zealand troops in Egypt a significant reserve force was in place and ready for use if the worst should happen. The government in London was also planning to take advantage of the war to turn the nominally Ottoman Egypt into a British protectorate[*] and the presence of these 28,000 troops would be useful if this should lead to uproar, turmoil and protests by the Egyptians.[†]

William Henry Dawkins also found the news that they were to disembark in Egypt rather disappointing but he soon got over it and saw the advantages of the turn of events. Their big, tented encampment lies quite literally at the foot of the pyramids; it is well organised, has plenty

---

[*] Egypt had been under de facto British control since 1882. At this stage the powers in Britain were even beginning to plan the dissolution and dismembering of the Ottoman Empire, which would imply an almost unparalleled Allied expansion in the Middle East: Russia, for instance, was offered Constantinople.

[†] There were, however, no such problems.

of food and its own water supplies, shops, cinema and theatre. The climate is surprisingly pleasant for the time of year and Dawkins thinks it reminds him of spring in South Australia but with less rain and wind. There is, moreover, a local train into the frenetic city of Cairo, which is only ten miles away. The train is usually packed with soldiers searching for recreation and there are frequently passengers even on the roofs of the carriages. In the evenings the streets of the great city are full of Australian, New Zealand, British and Indian soldiers.

Dawkins shares a large tent with four other junior officers. They have covered the sand with colourful rugs and there are beds, chairs and a table with a cloth. Each of them has his own wardrobe and bookshelf, and there is a bathtub right outside. During the hot evenings the tent is lit by a candle and a hissing acetylene lamp. At this point Dawkins is sitting in his tent and once again writing to his mother:

> Yesterday was Christmas Day and our thoughts were in Australia. Some of my section had the most gorgeous dinner—about six courses. They said that they only had to shut their eyes and they could imagine they were home again. Here we have many bands and at daybreak yesterday we had our carols played. Mother— whoever dreamt of having Christmas under the pyramids—very strange, when one comes to think of it!

No one knows what is in store for them next. The time is filled with education and training, training and education. At present Dawkins and his engineers are practising digging trenches and excavating tunnels to lay mines—not particularly easy in the unstable desert sand. He often rides round on his horse which, although it lost some of its mane and coat during the long voyage, is otherwise in good shape. Dawkins ends his letter:

> Well, Mother, I must close now and I hope you had a very happy Christmas and got my cable. I remain your loving son, Willie xxxxxxxxxxxx for the girls.

1915

But the truth is, that personal experience in this thing called war is at best an awakening of memory from a dream of seas and foggy islands bewildering and confusing. A few personal incidents loom a little clearer, deriving what clarity they have from the warmth of personal contact. Then incidents fraught even with the greatest danger become commonplace, until the days seem to move on without other interest than the everlasting proximity of death. Even that idea, prominent enough at first, gets allocated to the back of one's mind as a permanent and therefore negligible quantity.

EDWARD MOUSLEY

Chronology 1915

1 JANUARY	Start of the Third Battle of Warsaw. It ends in a marginal Russian victory.
JANUARY	Protracted Russian-Austrian battles in Galicia and the Carpathians, which continue until April.
4 JANUARY	The Ottoman Caucasus offensive is broken off after a disaster at Sarıkamış.
14 JANUARY	British troops invade German South West Africa.
3 FEBRUARY	Ottoman troops attack the Suez Canal. The attack fails.
8 MARCH	British offensive at Neuve Chapelle continues for a week with insignificant gains.
22 MARCH	The Galician town of Przemyśl capitulates to its Russian besiegers.
25 APRIL	British forces land on the Gallipoli peninsula with the aim of opening the Bosphorus.
APRIL	Large-scale massacres of Armenians begin in the Ottoman Empire.
28 APRIL	A major and successful German-Austrian offensive is launched in the east.
7 MAY	The American passenger liner *Lusitania* is torpedoed by a German U-boat.
23 MAY	Italy declares war on Austria-Hungary and invades the Tyrol and Dalmatia.
23 JUNE	First Italian offensive on the Isonzo begins. Minor gains.
9 JULY	German South West Africa capitulates.

15 JULY   A large-scale Russian retreat begins in the east.

18 JULY   Second Italian offensive on the Isonzo begins.
               Insignificant gains.

5 AUGUST   Warsaw occupied by German troops.

19 SEPTEMBER   A German-Austrian invasion of Serbia begins.

25 SEPTEMBER   A major Franco-British offensive opens in the west.
               Minor gains.

26 SEPTEMBER   A British corps starts to advance up the Tigris.

3 OCTOBER   A Franco-British army lands at Salonica to come to the
               aid of the Serbs.

9 OCTOBER   Belgrade falls. The Serbian collapse begins.

11 OCTOBER   Bulgaria declares war on Serbia and invades
               immediately thereafter.

18 OCTOBER   Third Italian offensive on the Isonzo begins. No gains.

10 NOVEMBER   Fourth Italian offensive on the Isonzo begins. Small
               gains.

22 NOVEMBER   Battle of Ctesiphon. The British advance on Baghdad is
               broken off.

5 DECEMBER   The British corps that failed to reach Baghdad is
               besieged in Kut al-Amara.

10 DECEMBER   The evacuation of Allied forces from Gallipoli begins.

Richard Stumpf is scrubbing the deck of SMS Helgoland *off Heligoland*

A cold, leaden sea. Excited anticipation has subsided into a yawn. Not once have they gone into battle, not once have they seen the enemy. During the naval Battle of Heligoland Bight at the end of August they *heard* the thunder of the guns in the distance but never got the chance to join in. Stumpf describes that as "a black day" for him and the rest of the crew. The closest they have come to combat was when they *heard* the sound of British airships on Christmas Day. Since SMS *Helgoland* was shrouded in fog they were never actually attacked but, further away, one of the airships dropped bombs on a cruiser and a cargo ship and succeeded in starting a fire on one of them. Stumpf's ship had, however, opened fire at the sound—admittedly, blindly, which made it seem all the more impressive.

It is not that SMS *Helgoland* and the other vessels of the German High Seas Fleet have been keeping out of the way. German naval strategy rests on carefully choosing its encounters with the numerically superior British navy. It is the U-boats that are expected to perform the more everyday function of cutting off supplies to the British Isles and gradually weakening the enemy.* But there have been no big, impressive naval battles, the admirals on both sides being acutely aware that it would be possible for

---

* There had been a promising start in September when the German U-boat *U9* had sunk three British cruisers in the space of just over an hour—old cruisers, admittedly, but still . . .

them to lose this war in an afternoon. In Germany, however, the lack of success at sea had to be padded out with other stories. At the start of the war there were various German light naval squadrons scattered here and there across the oceans of the world, often attached to one or the other of the German colonies. These evasive freebooters very quickly started a sensational game of cat and mouse with the British fleet as it patrolled the seas.* But the High Seas Fleet has so far restricted itself to patrolling its own waters in order to protect the homeland from enemy landings, and just occasionally it has harassed the English North Sea coast with pin-prick attacks.†

Every other day since Christmas SMS *Helgoland* has been out on patrol, a wearisome job that usually means the crew gets little sleep. It is also extremely monotonous. Stumpf notes in his journal: "There is nothing happening worth mentioning. If I were to list my activities every day, they would always be the same things."

This particular day is also filled with routine tasks.

First of all Stumpf and the other sailors scrub the decks, then they polish all the brass fittings until they gleam. Finally, there comes a pedantic check of their uniforms. This last enrages Stumpf. He writes in his journal:

> In spite of the fact that because of the general shortage of wool we have been unable to exchange worn-out pieces of kit in the ship's stores for ages, the divisional officer inspects every wrinkle and every stain on our uniforms.‡ He dismisses every attempt at explanation with a standard answer: "Poor excuse!" Lord above, this sort of behaviour makes me so sick of the navy. Most of them aren't bothered any longer. We're glad that not all officers are like this.

Stumpf keeps his mouth shut during the "odious inspection" but silently wishes that an enemy plane might appear and "drop a bomb on

---

* As has already been mentioned (footnote ‡ on pages 55–56), the German Pacific Squadron had an unexpected victory at Coronel on 1 November 1914, though it was annihilated later at the Battle of the Falkland Islands on 8 December.

† In the middle of December 1914 German cruisers bombarded Scarborough, Hartlepool and Whitby. Casualties, mostly civilian, amounted to 137 dead and 592 injured.

‡ In this context a division is a distinct unit of a warship's gunnery crew.

the fellow's head." He comforts himself with the fact that they have the afternoon off.

Then an order arrives: SMS *Helgoland* should make her way back to Wilhelmshaven and go into dry dock. "Bloody Hell!" he writes, "another Sunday ruined." The war continues to fail to live up to Stumpf's expectations. The afternoon is wasted with problems in the locks. As dusk falls they give up trying to go any further and tie up for the night.

Sarah Macnaughtan has left her soup kitchen in Belgium and returned to London via Calais. Once there, she has a nervous breakdown. On this day she writes in her diary:

> It was difficult, I found, to accommodate myself to small things, and one was amazed to find people still driving serenely in closed broughams. It was like going back to live on earth again after being in rather a horrible other world. I went to my own house and enjoyed the very smell of the place. My little library and an hour or two spent there made my happiest time. Different people asked me to [attend] things, but I wasn't up to going out, and the weather was amazingly bad.

FRIDAY, 22 JANUARY 1915
Elfriede Kuhr is visited by a baker's apprentice in Schneidemühl

It is late. The doorbell rings and Elfriede opens the door. Outside in the frosty winter darkness stands the baker's apprentice, wearing clogs on his feet and dressed in his white working clothes, which are covered with flour. He holds out a covered basket, which contains freshly baked rolls, still warm from the oven. They usually have fresh bread delivered every morning, so why now? It's nighttime, isn't it? The baker's boy laughs: "No, not any longer, Miss." He tells her that because of new state restrictions on the use of flour they are no longer allowed to bake at night. Which he is not in the least sad about—now he can sleep at night like a normal human being. He rushes off, shouting back to her: "It's because of the war!"

Her grandmother thinks this is all for the good—Germans eat too much bread anyway. The newspapers are publishing strict warnings against using grain as animal fodder: "Any individual using corn as animal fodder is committing a sin against the Fatherland and may be punished." The nutritional pattern of the German people was about to undergo radical transformation: instead of consuming calories via the circuitous route of eating meat, more of them were to be taken in their original, vegetable state. (Eating corn provides four times as many calories as when that corn has to be converted to meat first.) Vegetables, not meat, were to dominate the German dinner table from now on. Three-quarters of the population in this district work on the land, which does not, however, mean that they all live under the same conditions. Small farmers and farm workers have already begun to feel the worsening conditions, whereas the big farmers are doing very well indeed. Elfriede has heard of big farmers who are still feeding corn to their horses and cows in spite of all the bans—you can tell from the plump bodies and bright, shiny coats their animals have.

No, the big farmers and estate owners certainly have not felt the war yet:

> For breakfast every morning they eat that wonderful wheaten bread, sometimes with raisins and almonds in it, and on top of that eggs, sausage, cheese, smoked ham, smoked goose, various kinds of preserves and I don't know what. They can all drink fresh milk whenever they want, they can all have coffee or tea. They even put whole spoonfuls of fruit jelly in their tea.

On this occasion, however, Elfriede's agitation and envy of the way of life of big farmers contains a touch of bad conscience. She too, in a certain sense, is sinning against the Fatherland: she has a very soft spot for horses and sometimes when she meets one she secretly gives the animal the bread or apple she is supposed to be eating herself. But you do not see as many horses as before the war: all those not directly needed for agriculture have been taken over by the army.

WEDNESDAY, 3 FEBRUARY 1915
Michel Corday meets a hero in Paris

Yet another lunch. The most illustrious member of the company is
undoubtedly Pierre Loti,* famous author, adventurer, traveller, and
member of the Academy; the oddest is a Lieutenant Simon, in civilian life a teacher of French in England and a translator. Translator?
Well, Simon has translated *one* book from English to French: it has
not exactly achieved any great popularity but, then, it does deal with a
German (Goethe). In spite of his weak literary credentials the lieutenant has, however, earned his place in this company. He is a veteran of
the Battle of the Marne, where he lost an eye and was wounded in one
arm. Outside the window lies a bitterly cold Paris.

A special aura hangs over the Battle of the Marne. Part of the reason
is self-evident: this is the point at which the apparently unstoppable German armies were stopped, Paris was saved and the defeat that threatened
was averted. (Besides which, the triumph of the Marne also served to veil
a truly great disappointment—the failure of the notably costly French
offensive into German Lothringen in the opening phase of the war.) But
there is another reason. The battlefield is quite simply accessible. War
zones are usually hermetically sealed areas to which civilians do not have
access and where special permission is needed just to make a telephone
call. (Even high-ranking politicians are faced with problems when they
want to visit the front, which they are very keen to do since it looks good
and gives them the opportunity to dress in peculiar, individual creations
in the style of uniforms. On one occasion when Briand visited the front
someone took him for the group's chauffeur.) The places where the Battle of the Marne was fought are, however, open to anyone and are situated within easy reach of Paris. They have consequently become popular
destinations for excursions. People go there and pick over the debris of
battle that still clutters the battlefield. They collect pickelhaubes, caps,
buttons, cartridge cases, shell splinters and shrapnel and take them
home as souvenirs. And for those who cannot make the little day-trip for
themselves, or cannot be bothered to, there is authentic memorabilia for
sale at certain markets—by the basket, freshly picked.

* If Loti is mentioned these days it is usually because he was much admired by Proust.

Lieutenant Simon begins to describe his experiences during the battle and to say how he came to be wounded. To his dismay Corday notices that the rest of the people round the table become preoccupied with other things and almost cease listening—the market in heroes and dramatic war stories is already inflationary. He is reminded of an officer who had both his legs amputated and who said, "Yes, at the moment I'm a hero but in a year's time I'll be just another cripple."

It is still impossible to say you desire peace. Anyone who hears a remark of that kind invariably responds with cries of shame: "Disgraceful!" The restaurants are once again full of people.[*]

SATURDAY, 6 FEBRUARY 1915
William Henry Dawkins is sitting by the Pyramids, writing to his mother

"My dear Mother," he begins, "unfortunately we have received no mails this week owing to the lack of mailboats." The post to the Australian troops in Egypt *is* erratic. Three weeks ago he and the others received the letters they had been waiting for since November—176 sacks of them arrived. Before that, nothing; then, too much—some people hardly had time to answer everything; now, again nothing.

Dawkins, however, has received news about how things are at home. He knows they are all well, that his mum has taken the twin girls to the dentist, that the flowers he tried to send to a girl he knows unfortunately did not arrive, that prices have gone up in Australia. As for himself, he is keeping pretty well. But he has begun to be bored by the situation and by Egypt: the interminable exercises are continuing and they have been hit by the first sandstorm of the year. They still do not know what is to happen next, whether they are to stay here in Egypt or to go on to Europe.

* It is perhaps worth a mention that on this day three of the men involved in the assassination in Sarajevo at the end of June 1914 were hanged. Gavrilo Princip, the man who actually murdered the Archduke and his wife, escaped the death penalty because he was under the age of twenty at the time of the deed. Princip was placed under lock and key in the Theresienstadt fortress, condemned to twenty years' imprisonment. He was to remain there until he died of tuberculosis on 28 April 1918, still fanatical and still untroubled by remorse for what he had caused.

The war has slowly crept closer but is still not within sight or hearing. Just a week ago British spotter planes discovered Ottoman units moving through the Sinai desert towards the Suez Canal, and the long-awaited attack took place three days ago. Two battalions of Australian infantry were sent to Ismailia—the place most threatened—as reinforcements and the attack was soon beaten back.* Dawkins and many of his companions are slightly envious of those who marched off to the canal and we can sense a touch of jealous disparagement in his comments to his mother:

> There has been a little scrapping down on the canal but you will no doubt get all the news at home and a good bit more too. Thursday was a notable day for us, our first instalments for the defence of the canal left, consisting of the 7th and 8th battalions. William Hamilton† is in the 7th, and also Major McNicholl my old C.O. They were envied very much but I doubt if they are having a very enjoyable time down there as it is fairly monotonous waiting for Turks who apparently are not very good fighting material.

He himself has spent most of his time building, ripping down and transporting pontoon bridges.‡ Today, however, has been a day off and he and a fellow officer have ridden to the ruins of the ancient city of Memphis. What impresses him most are the two gigantic statues of Rameses II. He writes in his letter: "They were splendidly carved and must have taken many years to complete." But now it is evening and he is sitting in his tent:

> You will have got over the heat of the summer by the time you receive this letter. Things will be getting a little cheaper in

---

* The Ottoman attack in the east was not the only threat to the British presence in Egypt. Towards the end of 1915 a Wahhabite-inspired grouping in Libya, who were fighting in the name of Islam against both French and Italian colonial expansion in North Africa, began a series of attacks across Egypt's western border. These attacks were supported by Ottoman units, and it took considerable effort on the part of the British forces to put a stop to them. (While on the topic of problems in North Africa, we should note that the troubles in Morocco that had started when it became a French protectorate in 1912 were still continuing.)

† An old acquaintance from the cadet college in Duntroon.

‡ The single word "Pontooning" often appears in his short diary during this period.

the flour and wheat line after the harvest I should hope. I am feeling fairly tired so will close with Love to all. From Will xxxxxxxxxxxxxxxxxxxxxxx to the girls.

FRIDAY, 12 FEBRUARY 1915
Florence Farmborough goes through her travelling wardrobe in Moscow

Now it is all behind her: six months at the private military hospital in Moscow; six months of diligent study to achieve her nursing qualification—she had no trouble with the practical side, it was the theory, in complicated Russian, that caused problems; the exam and the graduation ceremony in an Orthodox church, where the priest had trouble pronouncing her name—"Floronz"; and, finally, her efforts to be accepted for service with the newly formed Mobile Field Hospital No. 10 had been successful after the intervention—once again—of her former employer, the famous heart surgeon.

Farmborough writes in her journal:

Preparations for my departure are well under way. I am breathlessly impatient to be off, but there is much to be done and the Unit itself is not yet fully organised. My nurse's dresses, aprons and veils have been made already, and I have bought a flannel-lined, black leather jacket. An accessory to the jacket is a thick sheepskin waistcoat, for winter wear, whose Russian name, "dushegreychka," means "soul-warmer." I hear that our Unit will be stationed for a time on the Russo-Austrian Front in the Carpathian Mountains and that we will have to ride horseback, as direct communication can be established there only by riding: so high boots and black leather breeches have been added to my wardrobe.

Today Suwalki is once again taken by German forces. This time, however, Laura de Turczynowicz and her family cannot flee since one of her twin boys has fallen ill with typhus and cannot be moved. She is missing her husband, Stanislaw, more than ever. It is cold and they have deep snow. She writes:

> Suddenly hearing an uproar, I saw some of the bad elements of the town looting, searching for food, knocking each other down, screaming—a horrid sight! The Jews, who were always so meek, had now more self-assertion, strutting about, stretching up until they looked inches taller. It was hard work to tear myself away from the balcony. I, too, seemed unable to control myself, running from the balcony to the child and from the child to the balcony.
>
> At eleven the streets again grew quiet, the time was near, and I saw the first pikel-haube [*sic*] come around the corner, rifle cocked—looking for snipers! The first one was soon followed by his comrades. Then an officer, who rounded the corner, coming to a stop directly before our windows.

SUNDAY, 28 FEBRUARY 1915
René Arnaud is given an insight into the logic of historiography on the Somme

A cold spring morning. The sun has still not risen but Ensign René Arnaud is already awake. He makes his usual tour of the trench in the half-light, goes from sentry to sentry—each is on duty for two hours—checks them and at the same time checks that the enemy is not getting up to anything. They all know that this is the best time of day for surprise attacks. Not that they are especially common here on the Somme.

In fact, this is a quiet sector. The risks are small. A German shell may perhaps whoosh overhead from time to time, but not heavy stuff—just the occasional 77mm with its characteristic *shooooo . . . boom*. Then there are snipers, of course, lying in wait for anyone who is careless, and there is the danger of using the connecting trench, which runs up over a hillock and is open at one point to fire from a lurking German machine gun. That is where his predecessor was killed, hit in the head by a bullet from that machine gun. That was also the very first time Arnaud had seen a man go down. When the body was carried past on a stretcher, its head and shoulders covered with a piece of tarpaulin and its red uniform trousers hidden by blue overalls, Arnaud had not found it particularly upsetting in spite of his own lack of experience. "I was so full of life that it was impossible for me to see myself in his place, lying on a stretcher with that air of indifference that the dead always radiate."

At the outbreak of war Arnaud was one of those who were jubilant. He had just reached his twenty-first birthday but looked scarcely a day older than sixteen. His only fear was that the war might finish before he reached the front: "How humiliating it would be not to get to experience the greatest adventure of my generation!"

This last hour as darkness slowly turns to light can be nerve-racking for the inexperienced:

> When I halted at the edge of the trench and spied out over no-man's-land it would sometimes happen that I thought the posts holding our thin network of barbed wire were the silhouettes of a German patrol crouching there on their knees ready to rush forward. I would stare at the posts, see them move, hear their coats brushing against the ground and the sheaths of their bayonets clinking . . . And then I would turn to the soldier on sentry duty and his presence of mind would calm me. As long as he didn't see anything, there was nothing there—just my own anxious hallucinations.

Then comes the moment when the horizon grows pale, the first birds start to sing and the contours of the terrain begin to emerge indistinctly in the milky-grey morning light.

He hears a shot. Then another, then two, then more. In less than a minute rifle fire is rattling all along the trench. Arnaud rushes back to wake the sleeping men. At the doorway of the bunker he is met by soldiers already on their way out, weapons in their hands and trying to put on their rucksacks at the same time. He sees a red signal rocket rise above the enemy lines. He knows what it is—a signal to the German artillery.* The consequences are immediate: a storm of shells bursts in

* Red, green and white can be said to be the iconographic colours of night during the First World War. All the armies used rockets in these colours and they were used in combination to create different messages. Red usually meant "Enemy attack!" whereas green signified that one's own artillery was firing too short and needed to advance its firing range.

front of, over and behind the French trench. The edge of the trench shows up against the flowing fire of explosions. The air is filled with "whirring, whining and explosions." The smell of explosive gases is choking.

> My heart was beating, I must have turned pale and I was shaking with fear. I lit a cigarette as I instinctively assumed it would help calm my nerves. I noticed the men crouched there in the bottom of the narrow trench with their rucksacks over their heads waiting for the barrage to finish.

It occurs to Arnaud that the Germans may already be on their way through no-man's-land. He clambers quickly over the backs of the lying soldiers to where there is a bend in the trench from which he knows it is possible to view the enemy lines. The air is filled with crashing, howling and whizzing. Once he gets there he quickly becomes utterly focused on watching the Germans: "My concentration on what needed to be done freed me from fear." He stares intently at the slope that separates the French and German positions. Nothing.

Slowly the barrage eases and dies away.

The dust settles. Silence returns. Reports begin to come in. Two men have been killed in the section alongside them, five in the company to their right.

Gradually Arnaud manages to construct a picture of what had happened. Two bored sentries had taken it into their heads to shoot at a flight of migrating birds; as far as anyone could judge they were curlews on their way up to their nesting grounds in Scandinavia. The shots had misled other sentries who, afraid there was some invisible danger, started shooting too. It took only a moment for this panic firing to run along the whole trench. The sudden shooting obviously led someone in the German trenches to fear an attack and whoever it was then brought their artillery into play.

They were able to read the official epilogue to this incident in a French army communiqué the next day. It read as follows: "At Bécourt, near Albert, a German attack was totally crushed by our fire." Arnaud's own comment was: "That's how history is written."

. . .

On that same day, William Henry Dawkins writes to his mother:

> I received your letter dated 26th Jan during the week and it may
> be the last I receive in Egypt as we are moving shortly. To where
> no one knows. The 3rd Bde, 3rd FD Amb, 1st Fd Coy and 4th
> ASC marched out during the day for Alexandria and we will be
> following during the next fortnight. I tip the Dardanelles as our
> destination but it may be anywhere in France, Turkey, Syria or
> Montenegro. Anyway it is a move and at last we will be getting
> to work.

WEDNESDAY, 3 MARCH 1915
Andrei Lobanov-Rostovsky and the great snowstorm at Lomza

Winter is coming to an end, as is the German February offensive. Both
of these are phenomena which, in spite of the laws of meteorology
and the plans of strategists, cannot be absolutely predicted. So when
Lobanov-Rostovsky's regiment is set the task of launching an attack—
the last one or, perhaps, the last but one—in order to straighten out
some little bend in the front line or to eliminate some threatening
position or to carry out something or the other that will only really
show up on the abstract 1:84,000 scale of the staff maps—well, it seems
almost inevitable that there will be a severe snowstorm.

It has been a dreadful winter in many ways here in north-west
Poland. Hindenburg's most recent offensive has not had any great effect[*]
and the Russian front in this area has moved a little here and a little
there, but it has held. Andrei Lobanov-Rostovsky belongs to a Guards
division, one of those elite units that are frequently used as firefighters
and moved backwards and forwards to wherever the danger is greatest.
He has, however, been spared the worst of the fighting. First of all he was
ill in Warsaw, after which he spent days getting in and out of railway

---

[*] The Germans undoubtedly had a number of local successes: they pulled off a
complete encirclement at Augustów, where a whole Russian corps (Bulgakov's XXth) was
annihilated, and the German press was quick to beat the Tannenberg drum. Russian
losses had been high, at times horrific, but German losses were also significant and, as
mentioned, accompanied by few gains.

carriages or simply travelling on trains in one direction or another while the generals tried to decide where his division was most needed. "These oscillations in our itinerary showed that the situation was changing from minute to minute." They finally detrained in Lomza and the division marched off to a line drawn on a map, north-west of the station. "And when the enemy approached, [this] became the front."

The winter and the winter battles are supposed to be over. Now it is just a case of some fighting "of local interest." The snowstorm is not allowed to hold up the Russian attack, which starts according to plan. Yet again Lobanov-Rostovsky is just an observer: he is, after all, a sapper and not really in demand in situations such as this. What he finds particularly frightening is to see how war, or perhaps more accurately, the generals, refuse to bow to the forces of nature: "The noise of the artillery preparation and the flares of the cannon, through the howling wind and the swirling snow, appeared more sinister than ever." The losses are unusually high, even by the standards of this war, because the majority of the wounded freeze to death wherever they happen to fall. And those wounded men who do survive the wind and the snow and the temperatures below freezing often suffer from severe frostbite. The hospitals are full of amputees.

Andrei Lobanov-Rostovsky is not feeling particularly well. Above all, it is the uneventful waiting that is getting to him. He finds passivity and the lack of activity very depressing. The only thing that breaks the monotony is when a German plane flies over, usually at dusk or late at night, and drops a few bombs.

FRIDAY, 5 MARCH 1915
Sarah Macnaughtan is serving soup in De Panne

She is back, but not in Veurne, which is now too dangerous, too close to the front. One of the nurses in her old field hospital was killed by shell-fire and the house she lived in had all its windows blown out when a shell hit the house next door. So she is now in De Panne, a small seaside resort on the Channel coast, which is empty for the winter. There are a number of high-class hotels along the sandy shore and some of them have been turned into military hospitals. The front is within hearing.

What else could she do but come back? For a woman with her sense of duty and her principles there was no other choice. Her trip back to London at the beginning of January was never intended to be more than a short break and once she had recovered from her breakdown and rested for a while she returned via Calais. She is not, however, in good health and had spent more than a week confined to bed in an empty flat in Dunkirk. She still has her doubts, but she keeps them to herself. And her patriotism has certainly not been dented—indeed, her experiences have only served to reinforce it: "God knows, we are full of faults, but the superiority of the British race to any other that I know is a matter of deep conviction with me."

Her doubts are more about war as a phenomenon and as a tool.* She hates it not just for what it is doing to others but for what it is doing to her: "I think something inside me has stood still or died during this war." And even though she is proud of what she and other women are doing, she is not entirely comfortable with what the war is doing to her sex. An example of what she means are the ugly, coarse, mannish clothes that so many women are wearing as if they were something quite natural. No, Macnaughtan longs for nice clothes, for good manners, for "beautiful things, music, flowers, fine thoughts."

Macnaughtan is also finding it more and more difficult to work. As the front becomes ever more static and all hopes of a rapid victory disappear, the flexible and amateurish lack of rules and regulations has begun to be replaced by regulations, structures, systems. One Tuesday at the start of February a Belgian officer turned up at the railway station where she had her soup kitchen and threw them out of the small space they were using. (In formal terms, the soup kitchen is now under the Belgian army, the soup being cooked by other people and subject to official inspection.) And when she was in Dunkirk new regulations meant she was not even permitted to cross a particular bridge.

She feels that she is both unnoticed and unappreciated, and although it is quite out of character for her, she is actually feeling rather sorry for herself. When she fell ill immediately after arriving in De Panne no one took any notice: "Not a soul came near me, and I wished I could be a

---

* Even though she is convinced of the truth of the German atrocities, and equally convinced that Kaiser Wilhelm was a mad beast who must be stopped, she actually likes all the German prisoners she has met so far.

Belgian refugee, when I might have had a little attention from somebody."

Macnaughtan is working her usual afternoon shift today—just like
any other kitchen skivvy. It lasts from twelve to five and she serves dinner and washes up afterwards. She is bored. It is all in glaring contrast to
her life before the war; she never gets to see interesting places now, nor
meet interesting people. But she does not want to give up. She notes in
her diary:

> To give up work seems to me a little like divorcing a husband.
> There is a feeling of failure about it, and the sense that one is
> giving up what one has undertaken to do. So, however dull or
> tiresome a husband or work may be, one mustn't give them up.

Afterwards she goes for a short walk on the sandy beach. She is
annoyed. Her leather-covered Thermos has disappeared. Stolen, of
course. Everything gets stolen. The front is quiet.

SUNDAY, 7 MARCH 1915
Kresten Andresen sketches a donkey in Cuy

In his sermons the padre congratulates them on living in a momentous
period. Then they sing "A Mighty Fortress Is Our God," missing out the
second verse, however, since it could be interpreted as expressing doubt
about armed might.* The past few months have been strange. Battles
have been both few and distant. During the whole of his time at the front
Andresen has fired only three shots, and he is pretty certain that all three
lodged somewhere in the defensive barriers in front of their position.
Sometimes, when it has been really calm, he has felt that strange sense
of unreality that sooner or later affects all the participants and which
makes it difficult to imagine that there is actually a war going on.

Perhaps it is this calm and silence which has lately tempted him to
feel—and it is mainly a feeling—that in some incomprehensible way this
whole business is moving towards its close. In any case, he does a lot of

---

* "Did we in our own strength confide, our striving would be losing," and so on.

fantasising about peace. Andresen has also been having striking dreams: last night, for instance, he dreamt he was on the streets of London wearing his best confirmation suit, after which he was suddenly transported to his childhood home, where he was laying the dinner table.

Birdsong and a sky that forms a warm blue canopy over a landscape in which the dry yellows and browns are beginning to be touched with bright green. Spring has reached Picardy. The crocuses are in flower, violets and arum lilies are in bud in the woods, and Andresen has found both Christmas roses and snowdrops among the fresh ruins. This is usually the time for the spring sowing, but not here and not now. Andresen can just hear the sound of a steam-driven threshing-machine thumping away on some backstreet of the village. The grain the machine is spitting out will bring no benefit to the French farmers, however: they are even forbidden to plough their own land, a ban made even more bitter by the fact that it was not announced until they had already done much of the sowing—which will be no use to them now.

Andresen feels truly sorry for that part of the French civilian population that is still hanging on in the villages immediately behind the lines. Their food is . . .

> . . . extremely monotonous. The mayor gives them a few round loaves of bread, the size of an ordinary wheelbarrow wheel, half wheat, half rye. They usually eat it dry, sometimes with a little piece of meat or a couple of fried potatoes. Apart from that they live on milk, and some beans and beets.

Since he comes from a rural background himself, Andresen finds it easy to understand the French farmers' worries; he also finds it hard to tolerate the thoughtless waste that is an everyday part of war. At the beginning of their time here they made their beds every night with new, unthreshed wheat from the fields. And over in Lassigny, which has been shot to pieces, some of the streets are covered with a thick layer of unthreshed oats, laid down to muffle the noise of wagon wheels.

Perhaps, too, it is the countryman in Andresen that has made him fond of Paptiste, a little donkey kept on one of the farms in Cuy. His affection is not reciprocated: the beast emits little grunts whenever someone approaches and shows signs of wanting to kick them. Andresen, however, finds this donkey irresistibly comic in its stupidity and natural indolence. This particular Sunday he takes the opportunity to sketch a little portrait of the donkey as it stands there in the farmyard enjoying the warm spring sun. He is intending to send the drawing home when it is finished.

The donkey is not his only local acquaintance. He has also got to know two Frenchwomen in Cuy, one fair-haired, the other dark. They are refugees from a nearby village in no-man's-land. Their acquaintance-ship has probably been made easier by the fact that he is Danish rather than German. The dark-haired woman has an eleven-year-old daughter called Sous and she has christened Andresen "Kresten le Danois." The dark woman has had no word of her husband since the end of August. "She is very unhappy."

> The other day they asked me when peace was going to come but I don't know any more than they do. I comforted them as well as I could—they were weeping over all the misery. Otherwise you rarely see them cry, though they have every reason to.

Andresen has helped the dark woman to write to the Red Cross information bureau in Geneva to try to get news of her missing husband. He has also given Sous a doll, christened Lotte, which the girl happily pushes round in an empty cigar box. He has decided to try to make her a doll's pram.

FRIDAY, 12 MARCH 1915
Rafael de Nogales arrives at the garrison in Erzurum

What makes the greatest impression on him during the long and dif-ficult march over snow-clad mountains is the fact that there are no trees to be seen. Nor birds. He had thought that there would at least have been ravens or vultures or other carrion eaters since towards the end of the journey he had seen the remains left after the great catastrophe at Sarıkamış—the bodies of thousands of frozen horses and camels. "It really must be a wretched country when even the birds of prey shun it."

But he shows no signs of regret. This is what he wants.

When the war broke out last August there were many people who travelled a long and tortuous road to Europe in order to take part in it. Rafael de Nogales's road may, perhaps, not have been the longest but it was without doubt among the most tortuous. If anyone deserves the title "international adventurer," he does. Born into an old family of conquistadors and freebooters in Venezuela (his grandfather took part in the fight for independence), he grew up and was educated in Germany, but was driven by a lust for adventure of the more unusual kind.

Rafael Inchauspe de Nogales Méndez is quite untouched either by the nationalistic fervour or by the semi-utopian energies that moved so many millions. Nor, by this stage, does he have anything to prove to himself or to others. Fearless, impatient and carefree, he has lived a life of ceaseless action for years. He fought in the Spanish-American War of 1898, took part—on the wrong side—in the Venezuelan revolution of 1902 and was consequently driven into exile, was a volunteer in the Russo-Japanese War in 1904 (where he was wounded), panned for gold in Alaska (and considers himself one of the founders of the city of Fairbanks), and worked as a cowboy in Arizona. Rafael de Nogales is now thirty-six years old, energetic, charming, tough, educated, short and dark, with an oval face, sticking-out ears and eyes close together. In appearance, de Nogales might be described as a Latin Hercule Poirot—well dressed, dapper, and with a small and very well-trimmed moustache.

As soon as the news of the war reached him he took a mailboat to Europe, determined to take part. The vessel's name was *Cayenne*. His route was circuitous and when he finally reached Calais his arrival was filled with drama. The streets were deluged with refugees, mostly women and children carrying the "pathetic pieces" of what possessions they had managed to take with them. Time after time troops of soldiers or rattling artillery batteries went past, forcing people to hug the walls. Coming from the opposite direction they were met by cars loaded with wounded men in a variety of uniforms: "A battle seemed to be going on. God knows where." He remembered two sounds in particular: the first was the threatening buzz of the aeroplanes that sometimes circled overhead—"steely, eagle-like"; the second was the ceaseless clatter caused by thousands of people in clogs passing along the cobbled streets. All the hotels were overcrowded and de Nogales was forced to spend the first night sleeping in an armchair.

His upbringing tended to make him favour the Central Powers but the news that German troops had marched into one of their smaller neighbours made him "sacrifice my personal sympathies and offer my services to heroic little Belgium." That proved easier said than done. Heroic little Belgium politely turned him down, at which he turned to the French authorities, but they refused to allow him into the regular army and then, feeling hurt and embittered, he was advised to try . . . Montenegro. That resulted in him being arrested there, up a mountain, as a spy. The Serbian and Russian authorities likewise rejected his offer, in the politest possible terms, but nevertheless . . . The Russian diplomat he met in Bulgaria suggested he might possibly try Japan: "Perhaps they will . . ." By this stage de Nogales's irritation and disappointment were so great that he came close to passing out in the beautifully furnished hall of the Russian embassy in Sofia.

Rafael de Nogales simply did not know where to turn. Returning home was not an alternative, but nor could he stay "and do nothing, which would have been the end of me, if not from starvation then from boredom." An accidental meeting with the Turkish ambassador in Sofia decided things: de Nogales made up his mind to enlist on the opposite side instead. At the beginning of January he signed up for the Turkish army and three weeks later left Constantinople to travel to the Caucasus front.*

Now the white mountains are behind them and they are riding past the small forts that form the fortress's outer defences. The sky is grey, covering "this god-forsaken landscape like a leaden vault." Here and there they can see freshly dug trenches—or perhaps they are mass graves? He sees frozen corpses. He sees dogs tearing at them. (Later they discover that a typhus epidemic is raging.) The party enters Erzurum. The town is not an inspiring sight and its narrow streets are full of snow. But Erzurum is buzzing with activity in spite of the cold, both in its bazaar, where the merchants are sitting cross-legged in rows, wearing furs and smoking their "eternal hubble-bubbles," and in the garrison where units of soldiers, groups of bearers and caravans laden with materiel are coming and going. This is the headquarters of the Third Army or, at any rate, what is left of it.

In the afternoon de Nogales reports to the commander of the fortress, a colonel.

The war has ground to a halt because of the cold and the deep snow.

---

* The name Constantinople (Konstantinye) was also used by the Turks at this time to describe modern-day Istanbul.

Nor is anyone going to risk another winter campaign so soon after the enormously costly failure back at the turn of the year when 150,000 men marched out and 18,000 returned. Even the Russians, more than satisfied by their great and unexpected victory, are simply watching and waiting in their virtually impregnable mountain positions right opposite Köprüköy.

Now and then the distant thunder of Russian artillery can be heard. The hollow rumble rolls through the enclosing mountainsides and the explosions sometimes set off avalanches on Mount Ararat: "Enormous white masses of ice slide down and fall from ridge to ridge, from cliff to cliff, until they smash with a formidable crash on the silent banks of the River Aras."

THURSDAY, 18 MARCH 1915
Pál Kelemen looks round an empty schoolroom in the Carpathians

The wound he received that night in the pass did not prove serious. He is now back at the front after a stay in a Budapest hospital and a period of convalescence, during which he was in charge of remounts* in the Hungarian border town Margita, where he managed to start but never really consummate an affair with one of the carefully guarded middle-class girls, a strikingly tall and slim young woman.

The thrusts backwards and forwards in the various passes in the Carpathian Mountains have continued with wearisome predictability and an equally wearisome absence of any real result. Both sides have won some territory here and there in recent months, at the same time as losing enormous numbers of men, above all as a consequence of cold, disease and a shortage of provisions.† Kelemen himself has smelled the stench which pervades these areas as old corpses thaw out at the same time as new corpses are added. Few people are talking any longer of a quick conclusion.

* Remounts were horses brought in to replace those injured or killed.
† The Austro-Hungarian army had lost about 800,000 men in terms of the dead, wounded or, above all, sick or frostbitten, since the turn of the year. These figures were not known, however, until 1918. All the countries kept the figures of their losses secret and to ask for them was considered little short of treason.

Kelemen's unit is now serving behind the front, mainly as a kind of police reinforcement to protect and help the long, winding supply columns which are ever-present along the slushy roads. It is an easy job. And safe. Nor does he have any great desire to return to the forward lines. He and his hussars often billet themselves in empty schools in Hungarian villages. That is where he is today, as he writes in his journal:

> In ruined schoolrooms turned into filthy stalls by the straw dragged in, the desks are like a terrified herd, dispersed, driven one upon the other, scattered about, and the inkstands are like buttons torn off of some holiday garment, lying as rubbish in the corners and on the window sills.
>
> On the wall, the text and the music of the National Anthem, the map of Europe. The blackboard is lying backside up on the teacher's desk. Flung about in the bookcase are copybooks, textbooks, slate pencils, chalk. All mere trifles, yet pleasing, at least to me after having breathed abominations for hours. When I read in these elementary school books the plain words: earth, water, air, Hungary, adjective, noun, God—somehow I find again that balance without which I have been tossed about so long, like a contraband ship, her rudder lost, on unknown seas.

SATURDAY, 3 APRIL 1915
Harvey Cushing makes a list of interesting cases at a military
hospital in Paris

Grey, black and red. Those were the colours he had before his eyes the whole time as he and the others travelled by bus two days ago from the Gare d'Orléans, across the river, past the Place de la Concorde and on to the hospital out in Neuilly. Full of curiosity, indeed, hungry with curiosity, he had stared out at the streets of the city. Grey was for all the military vehicles, painted in the same uniform shade—staff cars, ambulances, armoured vehicles; black was for all those wearing mourning— "everyone not in uniform seems to be garbed in black"; red was for the soldiers' trousers and for the crosses on the hospitals and ambulances. His name is Harvey Cushing, an American doctor from Boston, and he has come to France to study war surgery. In a few days' time he will be forty-six.

Today Cushing is at the Lycée Pasteur in Paris—or the Ambulance Américaine as it is now called.* It is a private military hospital founded at the outbreak of war by enterprising American residents in France and financed by collections. Those who work there are mainly from the United States—they are volunteers from the medical faculties at various universities and they serve here for periods of three months. Some of them come for purely idealistic reasons. Others, like Cushing, are motivated mainly by professional interest since there is an opportunity here to treat injuries of a kind that hardly ever occur in a neutral country like the United States, screened off from international politics. And since Harvey Cushing is a brain surgeon, a particularly accomplished one indeed, he hopes to see and learn a great deal in wartime France.† He has not yet reached any firm conclusions as far as the war is concerned. As a reasonable, educated man he regards many of the extravagant and elaborate horror stories about what the Germans are doing and have done with a degree of ironic scepticism. He thinks he can see through the empty pathos. Harvey Cushing is small, fair and thin. His gaze is scrutinising, with narrowed eyes, and his mouth small and tight: he gives the impression of a man used to getting his own way.

Yesterday, Good Friday, was his first proper working day at the hospital and he has already begun to form a picture of what the work involves. He has met the injured, often patient, quiet men with broken, twisted bodies and infected wounds that are taking a long time to heal. Bullets and shrapnel are not the only things that are taken out of their wounds: there are also what are known in the trade as secondary projectiles—pieces of clothing, stones, splinters of wood, cartridge cases, bits of equipment and even fragments of other men's body parts. He has already had time to see some of the worst problems. Firstly, many of the soldiers' feet are sore, blue, frozen and almost unusable, which seems to be a result of standing in cold, muddy water day in and day out.‡ Secondly, there are

* "Ambulance" was the term used in France for a military hospital at that date.
† Cushing, educated at Yale and Harvard, had already by this time made a significant reputation for himself among his peers. Something of a prodigy, he became Professor of Surgery at Johns Hopkins University at the age of thirty-two and was a world-leading researcher in the area of various brain centres and their functions.
‡ The term "trench foot" has not yet been coined.

the malingerers and those who exaggerate their problems, whether from shame or vanity. Thirdly, "souvenir surgery"—the dangerous business of operating to remove projectiles which could, in fact, have been left in the body, operating partly because the wounded man himself would like to have that particular bullet or piece of shrapnel as a trophy that he can proudly show off. Cushing shakes his head.

Today is Easter Saturday. The cold but clear spring weather of recent days has turned into steady rain.

Cushing spends the morning walking through the half-full wards and listing the cases that are of most interest from a neurological point of view. Since there are few men there with serious head injuries he also includes various kinds of nerve damage. The patients come almost exclusively from the south-eastern sectors of the front, so the majority of them are French, with a few black, colonial troops (he has been told that the Germans do not take black prisoners, but he doubts the truth of this) and a small number of Englishmen (who are usually soon taken to hospitals up on the Channel coast or transported home). Eventually his list is complete. It reads as follows:

> Eleven upper-limb injuries varying from wounds of the brachial plexus to minor ones of the hand; five of them musculospinal paralyses with compound fractures of the humerus.
>
> Two painful nerve injuries of the leg; operated on by Tauer with a suture.
>
> Three facial paralyses. One of them had "un morceau d'obus" as big as the palm of a hand driven into his cheek which he proudly exhibited—i.e., the "morceau."*
>
> A cervical sympathetic paralysis in a man shot through the open mouth.
>
> Two fractures of the spine, one dying, the other recovering. A beam supporting the "tranchées d'obri" had fallen on him when a shell landing near by blew up the section where he was stationed.
>
> Only one serious head injury; this in the case of Jean Ponysigne, wounded five days ago in the Vosges and brought in here to the Ambulance in some mysterious fashion.

* A shell splinter or, to be more precise, a piece of shell.

One of the orderlies tells Cushing during lunch that a few days earlier he saw a legless veteran from the war of 1870–71 stand to attention, swaying on his crutches, to salute a man forty-five years younger than him, a victim of the current conflict who had also lost his legs. During the afternoon Cushing visits the section for dental surgery and is very impressed by the new, ingenious and efficient methods being developed. "It is remarkable what they are able to do in aligning the jaws and teeth of an unfortunate with a large part of his face shot away."

FRIDAY, 9 APRIL 1915
Angus Buchanan waits for a train at Waterloo Station

Another day of rain. As dusk falls over London the city seems unusually grey and damp. He has been waiting on Platform 7 since six o'clock this evening and there is still no sign of their train. There are many of them standing there. The platform is full of people, not only men in khaki uniforms but also crowds of civilians—relations and friends who have come to Waterloo to wave them off. The weather may be miserable but the mood among those standing in groups, waiting and chatting, is free and easy. If any of them are impatient about the delay, they are not showing it.

The men gathered on the platform make up the main body of a battalion of volunteers, the 25th Royal Fusiliers, and they are just setting off on their long journey to East Africa. They already know that it is not easy for European units to work in that part of Africa but the majority of the uniformed men here already have experience of hot climates and difficult terrain. "This old Legion of Frontiersmen" comes from places as varied as Hong Kong, China and Ceylon, Malacca, India and New Zealand, Australia, South Africa and Egypt; the battalion includes both former polar explorers and former cowboys. When the war broke out Buchanan himself had been in the far north of the Canadian wilderness, fully occupied collecting Arctic flora and fauna, and it was the end of October before he heard what had happened. He immediately set off south, reached the first larger settlement around Christmas but moved on at once, all in order to enlist.

Buchanan's company is led by the experienced big-game hunter Frederick Courteney Selous, well-known for two very popular books about Africa.* Selous is the embodiment of the classic Victorian explorer: fearless, optimistic, ruthless, innocent, tough and inquisitive. He has a short white beard and is sixty-four years old but moves with the ease of a thirty-year-old. (The battalion has a generous upper age limit of forty-eight, but a good number of the men are older and have clearly lied about their age—there was still that much enthusiasm around.)†

From the start the battalion has been surrounded by an aura of being an elite troop of chosen adventurers. Among those waiting on the plat-form are actually a number of men who have deserted from other units in order to join the 25th Royal Fusiliers. And it speaks for itself that this is the only unit in the whole British expeditionary corps which has not been put through any military training at all: the men are considered to be so experienced that it is unnecessary—indeed, it would be an insult to these *gentleman adventurers*. It is hardly strange, then, that there is "a spirit of romance" in the air this evening.

Most of the men do not know one another and many of these sin-gular individualists are quite unaccustomed to seeing their own indi-viduality—usually so marked—cloaked in uniform. They are very keen to become acquainted. Angus Buchanan is twenty-eight years old, a naturalist, botanist and zoologist with a particular interest in birds. He intends to collect specimens of East African flora and fauna when he has time to spare.

The hours pass. The hum of voices and laughter continues to rise from the many clusters of people. By eleven o'clock, however, family and friends begin to tire of waiting and disappear sadly in groups of two or three. After one o'clock only the uniformed men are left on the platform. The train rolls in and they climb aboard. Immediately before it departs the police appear and start searching the carriages for deserters, but they

---

* *A Hunter's Wandering in Africa* and *Travel and Adventure in South-East Africa*. Selous had become particularly well-known because, like many other explorers and adventurers, he made lecture tours describing his experiences. He has a place in history as being, along with the famous Cecil Rhodes, the first to point to the Rhodesian high plateau as a suitable place for the British to settle and practise large-scale agriculture. Later, ironically enough, he himself discovered the great difficulties involved in this, difficulties that anyone who has read Doris Lessing's African novels and short stories will be familiar with but which Selous, with his fervour for colonisation, gravely underestimated.

† The commander of the battalion, Colonel Patrick Driscoll, was also the man who had initiated its formation. During the Boer War he had led a celebrated force of irregulars—Driscoll's Scouts—and the idea is that the battalion should be a unit of a similar kind.

have all been forewarned and quickly climb out of the other side of the train, where they remain hidden until the police have left.

At two o'clock the train rolls out of Waterloo Station. The destination is Plymouth, where a steamer, HMTS* *Neuralia*, is waiting. It will take them all the way to East Africa.

ONE DAY ABOUT THE MIDDLE OF APRIL 1915
Laura de Turczynowicz sees a soldier eating an orange in Suwalki

The incident with the orange affected her very badly, which is perhaps surprising, given that she has already witnessed so much. But what she has been through in recent months probably explains her reaction—everyone has a breaking point. Her frenetic activity, always rushing from one thing to another, does not only stem from a genuine desire to help, it is a conscious method of keeping her own demons in check: "Every moment was occupied or I should have gone mad!"

Two whole months have passed since the Germans marched into Suwalki for the second time and Laura and her children have been stranded on the wrong side of the front line ever since.

The worst thing was the typhus. They had been unable to flee the advancing enemy because one of the five-year-old twins had fallen ill with it, and soon afterwards his brother had caught the same disease. She came close to losing them both:

> I was a machine—night after night with my patients—how pitiful they looked—little grey shadows of my darling boys. They never stopped talking—only their voices grew weaker—each night meant a battle with death.

During one of these long days and nights of anxious watching and waiting Laura happened to catch sight of "a wild, white, strange-looking woman" and it took her a moment to realise that it was herself she was seeing, reflected in a mirror on the wall. When at last, after three weeks of struggle and against all expectations, the boys recovered, her

---

* His Majesty's Troop Ship.

six-year-old daughter went down with it and all the worry and wearying anxiety began again.

But now the snow has started to disappear. Spring is here.

The shortage of food is a constant scourge. The stores she laid in at the outbreak of war are now almost gone, most of them stolen by German soldiers or confiscated by their officers. All that remains is quite a lot of flour, some jam, macaroons (large and tough), tea and a few well-guarded potatoes, and that is about it. (The Germans have failed to discover one of her hiding places—inside a sofa.) Fortunately she still has a little money, but neither she nor the servants can always find produce to buy with it. Sometimes she is lucky enough to procure some black bread, and sometimes not. Sometimes there is milk, sometimes not. Wood, only occasionally, and the house is often freezing. Potatoes and eggs go for astronomical prices.

The day she bought five live chickens was a day of joy. They are now shut in what used to be the library, sitting perched up on the filthy bookshelves or scratching round the floor and covering the books with their droppings. But she no longer cares. The books have lost any significance for her—it is as if they belong to a different world, a world that came to an end in August last year.

For Laura, these problems are inextricably linked with two other evils: the war in general and the German occupation in particular. The family exists in a constant state of emergency, in which their private life is just as restricted as their mobility. German soldiers can force their way in at any time, claiming some errand and behaving threateningly or authoritatively or both. And since the house is so large and imposing, it acts as a magnet for German officers, keen to find a billet there or just to use it for parties. There is an improvised typhus hospital in one wing but the rest of the building is mainly used by the German command.* Laura and her children and servants are squeezed into a couple of overcrowded rooms and strictly forbidden to enter the parts of the house where the Germans have their telephone exchange and telegraph. A tangle of telephone cables now runs from the house and there is a tall aerial sticking up from the roof.

* The famous German field marshal, Paul von Hindenburg, stayed there when passing through. Laura found him to be a chivalrous but self-centred glutton. The fact that he is the commander-in-chief on this front—and therefore ultimately responsible for all the misery—makes him repulsive in her eyes.

The town has changed. Street cleaning has broken down completely and there is rubbish and filth everywhere. The streets are littered with abandoned furniture and other objects. The front is still so close that they can hear the roar of the big guns all the time. The roads are jammed with the constant comings and goings of German supply wagons and automobiles, and German infantry sometimes march through, almost always singing. She has come to detest that sound.

Laura cannot help hating the Germans. They are her enemies and they have occupied her home and transformed her life into one of perpetual darkness and anxiety. Not all Germans are the same, however, and some of them have been sympathetic and even helpful. But many of them behave in an arrogant, superior, self-confident and sometimes brutal manner. She has seen Russian prisoners of war being mistreated on numerous occasions. German propaganda, which talks about liberation from the Russian yoke, has had little impact, except possibly among the Jews of the region, for whom the occupation appears to offer relief from the arbitrary nature and ingrained anti-Semitism of the old regime.* The strangely mixed behaviour—now helpful, now brutal—she has encountered from the German occupiers is to some degree a mirror image of official policy. In view of the current chaos, which was caused by the war but which the Germans in their arrogance are inclined to interpret as an inherent characteristic of eastern Europe and its motley and confusing mixture of peoples and languages, the high command in the east has introduced an ambitious and wide-ranging programme. It is intended partly to exercise complete control over the conquered areas and their resources and partly to save the inhabitants from themselves by instilling German discipline, German order and German culture into them.

The cannon are growling in the distance and Laura and the others live in constant hope that the Russian army will break through and liberate them. (They can usually tell whose artillery is firing since Russian batteries fire their guns to a particular rhythm: one—two—three—four—pause, one—two—three—four—pause.) She often fantasises that her husband, Stanislaw, is somewhere over there in the Russian lines, quite close, perhaps only five or six miles away, and that as soon

---

* Accusations of Jewish collaboration with the Germans fanned the flames of the old, ingrained Russian-Polish anti-Semitism. Even Laura has become suspicious of many of the Jews in the town.

as the German front is broken she will see him standing there in front of her again. But mostly she is filled with a sense of complete isolation, trapped with her children in an absurd and comfortless limbo. New York is very, very far away. The children have Dash, their little white dog, to play with.

It is possibly the absurdity of the whole situation that makes her react to the orange. She sees an ordinary soldier on the street carrying a juicy looking orange, and he raises the fruit to his mouth and bites it. She stares, aghast. She would have given almost anything for that orange, to have been able to take it home to her children. She knows that is not going to happen. What really upsets her most, however, is the soldier's manner—he eats it in such a slovenly way. The man chews his way through that beautiful, round, exotic, shining orange "as though it was something you ate every day here in Suwalki."

When the wind blows from the west Laura can smell a pungency in the air. It is the smell of the carelessly buried dead of the past winter. Rumour says that there are tens of thousands of them.*

THURSDAY, 15 APRIL 1915
Willy Coppens sees a Zeppelin outside De Panne

The enormous oval body of the airship moves majestically and almost silently across the evening sky. It is a dreadful but impressive sight indeed, bordering on the sublime. The fact that this is an enemy vessel is fairly irrelevant in the context. Just watching it reinforces Willy Coppens's old desire to be a pilot—a desire which, strangely enough, the Belgian grenadier first felt in almost exactly the same place where he is now standing and watching the German Zeppelin steer out across the English Channel over De Panne.

He was five years old at the time and there among the sand dunes he had watched his first kite hovering in the breeze. Afterwards he thought the paper kite "possessed some kind of occult power which in an irresistible and inexplicable way drew me up towards the infinity of

---

* A winter game among some of the bolder children in Suwalki was to go round the fields outside the town probing the snow with sticks to find the corpses of the slain.

the heavens." As the thin line tautened in the wind it emitted a singing sound that made him tremble with excitement—and fear.

Willy Coppens is a soldier in the Belgian army, or what is left of it after last August's German invasion—the invasion of the territory of a neutral state, which is what gave Great Britain its official excuse to enter the war.* And he now finds himself in the strip of trench-scarred Belgian ground, stretching from Nieuwpoort on the Channel coast down to Ypres and Messines on the French border, that has remained unoccupied by the Germans. His parents and brothers and sisters are in Brussels on the other side of the front. When the order for mobilisation came last August he was called up into the 3rd Company of the 3rd Battalion of the 2nd Regiment of Grenadiers, and his service number was 49800. Then they just hung around the mobilisation area and he found this waiting so "awful" by the end that "when the declaration of war finally came, it came as a clear relief."

The fact that his country was attacked and his home city occupied is something that obviously gives him energy and motivates him. The atrocities the Germans were guilty of during those weeks in August (the massacres at Dinant, Andenne and Tamines,† the sacking of Louvain and so on), which Allied propaganda has returned to time after time, depicting, dramatising and embellishing them to the extent that the original atrocities have begun to disappear beneath a highly coloured blanket of clichés, are things that he never even refers to. Perhaps Coppens is one of those people who have come to believe that it was all nothing but propaganda. Perhaps new and more tangible and personal sufferings have already replaced these second-hand horror stories. Or perhaps the adventure of it all has gained the upper hand. He is, after all, only twenty-two years old.

---

* As Niall Ferguson has shown, there was considerable hesitation among British politicians about whether Britain should enter the war at all. Why line up on the same side as autocratic Russia against a Germany that in many areas, not least social legislation, art and science, was seen as a model? To begin with, a majority of the government was quite clearly against entry. Some of them were prepared to accept a limited German breach of Belgian neutrality, others were ready—should it prove necessary—to allow British forces to breach that neutrality. They kept very quiet about that later.

† In Dinant 612 people were murdered, in Andenne 211 and in Tamines 384; women and children were among the victims. The perpetrators were in all cases German regular army troops, whipped up to hysteria by alleged local guerrilla actions.

But he certainly feels bitterness towards the Germans and has an intense hatred of them: afterwards, when thinking of that Zeppelin outside De Panne, he said that he "always regretted never having been given the job of bombing the enemy in his own country." But that is not what he is thinking at this moment, during this April evening, as he watches the Zeppelin disappear out over the sea. The men on board are less objects of his hatred than of his envy, and as he watches it receding into the waning light he thinks "how wonderful it must feel for those on board."

Coppens has actually applied for a transfer from the infantry to the air force. That was in January. He has still not received an answer.

The Zeppelin has already disappeared into the darkness by the time two Belgian planes come buzzing along in search of the great vessel. Coppens notes that they are "biplanes from a prehistoric era, quite unusable in war." He suspects they have been sent up purely as a matter of morale, a theatrical exercise—they have to do something, after all. Nor has any pilot yet managed to shoot down a Zeppelin.[*] They are still surrounded by an aura of technological invulnerability and brutality. Which is the reason the Germans use airships in spite of their vulnerability to anti-aircraft fire and their sensitivity to wind and weather. They frighten people. They are the first terror weapon.[†]

The Zeppelin that Coppens sees disappearing out over the Channel is one of a group of three to attack the south-east of England on this particular night. Zeppelin L 7 makes a sweep along the coast in the Norwich area but finds nothing worth attacking. Zeppelin L 5, under the command of Captain-Lieutenant Böcker, forms the spearhead of the

[*] The first Zeppelin to be brought down by an enemy plane was LZ 37 on the night of 6–7 June. It is incorrect to say it was shot down: the British pilot responsible for the exploit, R. A. J. Warneford, was actually on his way to attack the huge Zeppelin hangars at Berchem when he happened to meet LZ 37. Warneford flew above the great vessel and bombed it, causing it to crash. Warneford was awarded the Victoria Cross for his action. Ten days later he lost his life in a very ordinary air accident.
[†] What, of course, is most terrifying is that this is a completely new way of waging war. Firstly, to a very great extent it is the civilian population that suffers, and secondly, the threat comes from the air. The agitation in Britain was great and there were even demands that captured Zeppelin pilots should be executed.

attack and drops bombs over Henham Hall, Southwold and Lowestoft but without hitting anything.

The only one of the three to cause any damage that night is L 6 under the command of Senior Lieutenant Baron von Buttlar. His airship reaches the coast north-east of London but since there is still a strict ban on attacking the British capital von Buttlar drops five explosive bombs and thirty incendiaries over Maldon and Heybridge. Then he turns back out over the sea.

He leaves behind him one damaged house and one wounded girl.

FRIDAY, 16 APRIL 1915
William Henry Dawkins writes to his mother from the harbour on Lemnos

Finally on their way, and now they are no longer in any doubt about their destination—the Dardanelles. Rumours of the operation have been in the air ever since February. That is when news reached them that Allied warships, apparently to no great effect, had attacked the Ottoman artillery batteries blocking the straits, an attack that had been repeated a month ago with the same notable lack of success.* As early as the end of March a large section of Dawson's brigade had disappeared across the Mediterranean by ship to the island of Lemnos in the northern part of

---

* The purpose of this badly planned and reckless operation was to use warships to blast a way first through the Dardanelles and then through the Bosphorus, primarily to enable the shipping of war materiel to the hard-pressed Russians. The intention was also to relieve them in the Caucasus, although the dangerous earlier Ottoman offensive had already ground to a halt in the cold, snow and chaos by this stage. It was also hoped that the Ottoman Empire could be knocked out of the war. There was constant debate between what were called the "westerners" and the "easterners," in which the former (usually the military) wanted to prioritise efforts to break through on the Western Front, whereas the latter (usually politicians) wanted instead to operate against the weak flanks of the Central Powers, above all in the Balkan area and in the southern Mediterranean. The Dardanelles operation was to a large extent the idea of the young, manipulative and controversial First Lord of the Admiralty, Winston Churchill. As early as 1907 the British navy had looked at the matter and come to the conclusion that it was impossible for a purely naval attack to succeed—but such mundane facts did not appeal to Churchill's adventurous nature.

the Aegean Sea. He himself stayed behind for a while in the big camp outside Cairo. He was very well aware, however, that something big was going on. He wrote in an earlier letter home: "Rumour has it that we are to form part of a huge army—French, Russian, Balkanese and British with the role first of subjugating Turkey and then marching on to Austria."[*]

It is about time something happened. The months of inactivity, if exercises can be called inactivity, have had a corrosive effect on fighting spirit and above all on discipline. The Australians have shown a growing lack of respect for British officers, and soldiers of all nationalities have been behaving in an increasingly undisciplined way in Cairo. This culminated on Good Friday, two weeks ago, when riots broke out in the city's red light district. Some people consider Cairo to be one of the world's most sinful cities, full of brothels and gambling dens where those intent on pleasure can enjoy everything from narcotics to naked dancers. And in accordance with the old law of supply and demand all this has mushroomed thanks to the sudden influx of tens of thousands of young soldiers with a fair amount of money in their pockets. The problems are partly a result of the erosion of discipline and partly caused by growing friction between the troops and the local population.[†]

So on Good Friday hundreds of soldiers, primarily Australians and New Zealanders, started running amok on a street in the red light district. In a fit of unbridled disorder they smashed up bars and brothels, hurled the fittings out into the street and set fire to them. The noisy, violent mob grew as more and more soldiers joined them. The military police tried to intervene and were bombarded with bottles, so they opened fire, wounding four soldiers. British troops were summoned and went in with bayonets but were disarmed and had to watch their rifles being burnt. An attempt to use cavalry to subdue the rioters also failed. Little by little, however, the rioting died out of its own accord. Dawkins

[*] This is a somewhat forced but not completely inaccurate summary of what was planned. Troops were necessary since bitter experience had shown that it would not be possible for Allied warships alone to secure the Dardanelles. The first task of land forces would be to knock out the coastal artillery batteries that were causing major problems for the Allied naval forces, particularly by their ability to direct accurate fire on the minesweepers that went ahead of the fleet.

[†] In his letters Dawkins expresses his growing animosity towards Egyptians, referring to them as, among other things, "contemptible."

had been there, helping out by manning a road block across one of the streets. During the days that followed a camp canteen and a camp cinema were burnt down by angry, violent troops.

Just over a week ago Dawkins's unit was relieved to be leaving Egypt. The harbour in Alexandria had been full of troopships. Two days later they made land on Lemnos. The island is too small to house all of them so many of the soldiers have quite simply had to remain aboard the vessels that brought them here. Today William Henry Dawkins, aboard the troopship *Mashobara* in Lemnos harbour, is writing to his mother:

> There are quaint old windmills here which are used for the grain. They are big stone buildings with large windmill sails. The place is very clean, so are the people, thank goodness, quite a contrast. Everything is covered with green grass and the fields are very pretty with their red poppies and daisies studded all round. We were all ashore yesterday—took the company for a little exercise and touring—best expresses the outing. The people here are like other places, all out to make as much as possible out of the soldiers. There are no large shops here so we strolled about, one with a round of cheese under his arm, another with a string of figs, another with a pocketful of nuts, another with a bag of biscuits and everyone trying to get rid of their stuff onto the others. We had a jolly time.

Dawkins knows that they will soon be moving on and he knows the task that awaits him and his company when the time comes: they are to be responsible for the brigade's water supply. The *Mashobara* is carrying masses of pumps and pipes and drills and tools and digging equipment. In the meantime, one of the ships is being converted for special operations—they are, for instance, cutting large landing doors in the bows of the vessel. They have received the maps of the place where they are to be sent in. It is called Gallipoli and is a long, narrow peninsula that guards the entrance to the Sea of Marmara. He does not write anything about this in his letter, however, which he ends:

> As I can't think of any more news I'll have to close. Sending you best love to all. Your loving son Willie xxxxxxxxxxxxxxxxx to the girls.

1. Elfriede Kuhr—German
schoolgirl, twelve

2. Sarah Macnaughtan—Scottish
aid worker, forty-nine

3. Richard Stumpf—German High
Seas Fleet seaman, twenty-two

4. Pál Kelemen—Hungarian
cavalryman in the Austro-
Hungarian army, twenty

5. Andrei Lobanov-Rostovsky—
Russian army engineer,
twenty-two

6. Florence Farmborough—
English nurse in the Russian
army, twenty-seven

7. Kresten Andresen (left)—Danish soldier in the German army, twenty-three

8. Michel Corday—French civil servant, forty-five

9. Alfred Pollard—British army infantryman, twenty-one

10. William Henry Dawkins—Australian army engineer, twenty-one

11. René Arnaud—French army infantryman, twenty-one

12. Rafael de Nogales—Venezuelan
cavalryman in the Ottoman army,
thirty-five

13. Harvey Cushing—American
army field surgeon, forty-five

14. Angus Buchanan—British army
infantryman, twenty-seven

15. Olive King—Australian driver
in the Serbian army, twenty-eight

16. Willy Coppens—Belgian air
force fighter pilot, twenty-two

17. Vincenzo D'Aquila—Italian-American infantryman in the Italian army, twenty-one

18. Edward Mousley—New Zealand artilleryman in the British army, twenty-eight

19. Paolo Monelli—trooper in an Alpine regiment of the Italian army, twenty-three

20. Laura de Turczynowicz—American wife of a Polish aristocrat, thirty-five

1. *SMS* Helgoland, *Richard Stumpf's ship:* "Reveille is blown as early as four o'clock this autumn morning. The ship and its crew wake to a morning of frantic activity."

2. *A column of Belgian infantrymen on the beach at De Panne, 17 October 1916:* "[Coppens] now finds himself in the strip of trench-scarred Belgian ground, stretching from Nieuwpoort on the Channel coast down to Ypres and Messines on the French border."

3. *Sanctuary Wood, October 1914:* "The Germans have detonated a large mine under the British lines in a wood the British call Sanctuary Wood at Zillebeke outside Ypres, and then they occupied the enormous, corpse-filled crater it made."

4. *View of Kiel, with the naval base in the background, 1914:* "It is evening when they arrive in Kiel. [Stumpf] notes that they have begun to ease up a little on the blackout that used to be so strictly enforced."

5. *A street in Lens:* "The projectiles come whistling down here and there. An unusually big one hits a house a small distance in front of [Andresen] and he sees how the greater part of the roof is lifted thirty feet or more up in the air."

6. *Fort Douaumont at Verdun under heavy bombardment, 1 April 1916:* "[Arnaud] sinks down with his head between his knees. 'I was on the battlefield at Verdun but was hardly conscious of the fact.'"

7. *British water carriers at Zonnebeke, August 1917:* "On the road up towards Zonnebeke Canadian troops, caked in mud, jostle with lorries, cannon and mules laden with ammunition."

8. *Beach scene in Boulogne-sur-Mer, May 1918:* "In the afternoon Cushing is back at the large seaside villa where he is living. The warm spring air streams in through the open window. He looks out over the English Channel."

9. *A blown-up bridge at Villers-Cotterêts, September 1914:* "When [Arnaud] arrives at his destination today he hears that his regiment is still there, at Villers-Cotterêts. He hitches a lift in a butcher's van for the last section."

10. *Péronne, end of March 1918:* "[Pollard] is now on the train to Péronne, where he hopes to be met by someone from the battalion. He is so cold that he is shaking and he is still being plagued by unpleasant fever dreams."

11. *Sailors gathering ready to demonstrate in Wilhelmshaven, beginning of November 1918:* "[Stumpf] dresses in parade uniform in honour of the day. Then he and the rest of the crew go off to demonstrate. The attitude of the officers suggests that the sailors might well end up being victorious."

1. *The war reaches Africa, 1914:* "Roughly 10,000 armed men are looking for each other in an area the size of western Europe but where communications are almost non-existent. The most difficult task is not to defeat the enemy, it is to find him. Any sort of movement demands an army of bearers."

2. *German native troops in combat somewhere in East Africa:* "Those in command of the small groups are Germans, clad in all the usual accoutrements of the colonists—light-coloured uniforms, cork tropical helmets and commanding appearance—but the soldiers are all professional native soldiers, *askaris*, who have been given the same training, weapons and trust as white soldiers."

3. *The Pangani River in German East Africa:* "The German forces they are chasing through bush, jungle and swamp, across rivers, mountains and savannahs, are apparently untroubled by the climate and disease, which is hardly surprising given that their troops are native and consequently used to the former and stoical about the latter."

4. *British native troops of the King's African Rifles on parade in Lindi, September 1916:* "Battalions of black troops from Nigeria, Ghana, Kenya and the West Indies were left to hold the fort in the pouring rain."

5. *The wreck of SMS* Königsberg *in the Rufiji delta, summer 1915:* "[Buchanan] can also see puffs of smoke from the enemy artillery—105mm pieces that the Germans, with their usual talent for improvisation, have salvaged from the light cruiser SMS *Königsberg* after it was knocked out by the British."

6. *A black machine-gun crew under German command somewhere in East Africa:* "After retreating from the valley at Mohambika the Germans dug in firmly on the Tandamunti ridge. The two sides have been taking it in turns to attack and counter-attack ever since the middle of June."

SUNDAY, 25 APRIL 1915
Rafael de Nogales witnesses the destruction of the two most sacred buildings in Van

Dawn. He wakes from his sleep lying in a dream of down and Nile-green silk. The room around him is furnished in keeping with the luxurious bed: on the ceiling there is an Arabian lamp with different coloured crystals set in bronze; on the floor, hand-knotted rugs and a stand containing ornamental weapons of Damascene steel. There are also precious figurines in Sèvres porcelain. This used to be a woman's room, as he can tell from the kajal pencils and carmosine red lipstick scattered on a small table.

Some distance away the Turkish artillery begins to come to life. Battery after battery opens fire. They add their sharp cracks to the thickening curtain of noise until everything sounds just as it usually does: explosions, crashes, thumps, booms, roars, shots and pained shouts.

Later he rides off. This morning he is to inspect the eastern sector.

Rafael de Nogales is on the outskirts of the ancient Armenian city of Van in one of the north-eastern provinces of the Ottoman Empire, close to Persia and with the Russian border due north and less than a hundred miles away. There is an uprising in the city and de Nogales belongs to the force sent to crush it.

The situation is complicated. Armenian rebels occupy the old, walled part of the city and the suburb of Aikesdan. The Turkish governor's forces hold the citadel on the cliff above the city, as well as the rest of the surrounding district. Somewhere to the north there is a Russian army corps, currently held up in the difficult mountain pass at Kotur Tepe but, in theory at least, still a day's march away. The mood on both sides is swinging between hope and despair, between terror and confidence. The Christian Armenians have no choice—they know they must hold out until the Russian corps arrives—and their Muslim opponents know that the battle must be won before the Russians appear over the horizon because the arrival of the Russians will mean that besieged and besiegers swap places.

This is what accounts for some of the extraordinary brutality of the fighting. Neither side takes prisoners. During the whole time he is in Van, de Nogales sees only three living Armenians up close: a waiter, an interpreter and a man who was found down a well, where he had been for the last nine days, having for some reason fled from his own people. The last is interrogated, fed until he recovers a little and then shot "without further ceremony." The atrocities are also a result of the fact that the majority of those involved are irregular soldiers, enthusiasts, volunteers, civilians suddenly presented with the weaponry and unrestricted opportunity to repay old injustices—real or imagined—and to forestall future ones—real or imagined. Among the forces de Nogales has under his command are Kurdish warriors, local gendarmes, Turkish reserve officers, Circassian irregulars and out-and-out bandits.[*]

The war is providing pretexts, creating rumours, cutting off the spread of news, simplifying thought processes and normalising violence. There are five battalions of Armenian volunteers fighting on the Russian side and attempts are being made to foment a general uprising against Ottoman rule. Small, armed groups of Armenian activists are carrying out sabotage and minor attacks. And time after time since the end of 1914 unarmed Armenians have been massacred in blind reprisals for the deeds perpetrated by the activists, as a warning to other Armenians, and as revenge for the fiasco at the front.[†] Or just because they *can* be

---

[*] Massacres of Christians had occurred before and the conflict between the Armenians and the Ottoman central authorities was an old one, but one that had become worse during recent decades. The Great War led to a sudden, unforeseen and particularly nasty deterioration. Many Turks were obsessed by a kind of anxiety about survival. In October 1914, when those in power in Constantinople took the decision to join the Central Powers, the Ottoman Empire had just lost yet another war (the First Balkan War, 1912–13, in which the Empire was defeated by the combined forces of Serbia, Greece, Bulgaria and Romania) and suffered yet again the loss of territories mainly inhabited by Christians. Other parts of the Empire, such as Egypt and the Lebanon, were de facto in the hands of the western great powers. It was uncertain whether this erosion was going to continue. A new ingredient—and a pretty deadly one—had just been added to this ancient witch's brew: modern nationalism. Even before October 1914 this led the rulers in Constantinople to consider ideas of major ethnic relocations aimed at the creation of an ethnically uniform state or, at least, at freeing important provinces from their non-Muslim "tumours." Simultaneously, among the increasingly hard-pressed minorities— particularly among activist Armenians—nationalism aroused separatist fantasies and the hope of a state of their own.

[†] Actually multiple fiascos, since it was not only the over-precipitate invasion of the Caucasus that had come to a bitter end. The Ottoman incursion into independent Persia had also ended in defeat by this stage. The Russian corps which had now reached Kotur Tepe was coming—victorious—from those operations.

massacred. By unleashing the latest massacres, the stubbornly stupid cynicism of the local Turkish commander has sparked off precisely the kind of major uprising the measures were in some vague way supposed to prevent.

Rafael de Nogales has already heard the rumours, listened to the misgivings and seen the evidence (refugees, burnt churches, groups of mutilated Armenian bodies at the side of the road). In a small town on the way to Van he saw a mob hunting down and killing all the Armenian men in the place—except seven he himself saved by drawing his pistol.* It has left him with a bad taste in his mouth. The situation here in Van, however, is different and more straightforward. He is an officer in the Ottoman army and his job is to put down an armed uprising. And to do so quickly before the sluice gate at Kotur Tepe bursts open. De Nogales, moreover, does not like Armenians: he admires their loyalty to the Christian religion but finds them in general to be sly, avaricious and ungrateful. (His enthusiasm for Jews and Arabs is similarly limited. On the other hand, he finds it easy to like the Turk as "the gentleman of the Orient." And he respects the Kurds, although he considers them unreliable: he calls them "a young and vigorous nation.")

The task of taking control of Van is problematic. The Armenians are defending themselves with the wild, desperate courage that comes from knowing that defeat and death are synonymous. At the same time, many of the volunteers in de Nogales's units are undisciplined, inexperienced, headstrong and, to an extent, utterly undeployable in any real fighting. As if that is not enough, the old quarter of Van is an absolute labyrinth of bazaars, narrow alleyways and mud-walled houses, as difficult to reconnoitre as it is to penetrate. So the subjection of the city has mainly been left to the Ottoman artillery. Most of the cannon really belong in a museum—ancient muzzle-loaders that fire round-shot,† though de Nogales has discovered that these crude missiles actually have more effect on the houses than modern shells, which are so powerful they whizz straight through one mud wall and out through the next.

In this way they are blasting their way through Van's maze of streets

---

* He handed over these seven men to a high-ranking local official who promised to protect them. Later, de Nogales discovered that the official had the prisoners strangled the very same night.

† They would later use several mortars more than 500 years old—with considerable effect, though also at considerable risk to the artillerymen.

and alleys, quarter by quarter, house by house, "with scorched hair and powder-blackened faces, half-deaf from the rattle of machine-guns and the sound of rifles fired off at close quarters." When a house has been reduced to ruins and its defenders to corpses, they set light to the rubble to prevent the Armenians' returning under the cover of darkness. Pillars of smoke from the fires rise above the city day and night.

During his ride along the eastern sector de Nogales discovers a field gun which has just been buried in the rubble of a collapsing building. He leaps from his horse, pistol in hand and in the utmost danger, and manages to get the piece salvaged. A corporal alongside him is hit in the face by a bullet.

An hour later he is up on the breastwork of the citadel. Through his field glasses he follows an attack on one of the fortified Armenian villages immediately outside the city. Standing with him is the governor of the province, Djevded Bey, a gentleman in his forties who likes talking about literature, dresses in the latest Paris fashions and, in the evening, likes to eat his grand supper wearing a white necktie and a fresh flower in his buttonhole. In other words, to judge by appearances, a civilised gentleman. Given his close contacts with the rulers in Constantinople and his utter ruthlessness, he is, however, one of the most important architects of this tragedy. In fact he represents a new species in the bestiary of the young century: the articulate and ideologically convinced mass murderer in well-cut clothes who performs his butchery while sitting behind a desk.

De Nogales stands alongside the governor and watches the storming of the village. He witnesses 300 mounted Kurds cutting off the Armenian escape routes. He sees the Kurds slaughtering the survivors with knives. Suddenly bullets slice through the air close to de Nogales and the governor. The shots are being fired by some Armenians who have climbed to the top of the great cathedral of St. Paul in the old city. Both sides have so far shown respect for this ancient place of worship but now the governor orders it to be blown to pieces. Which duly happens, though it does take two hours of bombardment with round-shot before the high old dome collapses in a cloud of dust. By this stage a number of Armenian snipers have worked their way up to the minaret on the great mosque. The governor is not quite so quick this time to give the order to open fire. De Nogales, however, does not hesitate and just says, "War is war."

"In this way," de Nogales tells us, "the two greatest temples in the city of Van were destroyed in the course of a single day. For almost nine centuries they had been among the most famous of historical monuments."

This is also the day William Henry Dawkins steps ashore at Gallipoli.

He wakes as early as half past three in the morning and takes a hot bath. The ship, with all its lights doused, is heading north-east. They drop anchor when the sun breaks the horizon. They are surrounded by the shadows of other vessels and in front of them lies the long shape of the Gallipoli peninsula—a vague, watercolour silhouette. Breakfast follows, after which they prepare to disembark. Meanwhile the guns on the warships begin to thunder. Dawkins and his men transfer first to a destroyer which takes them closer to the shore. From the destroyer they move over to wooden landing-craft towed by motor-boats.

Waves. A dawn sky. Loud explosions. He sees his first wounded men. He sees the bullets from exploding shrapnel shells showering down, perforating the surface of the water and sending up hundreds of small fountains. He sees the shore getting closer. He jumps out of the boat and notes that the water reaches up to his thighs. He hears the sound of rifle fire beyond the steep slopes on the shore. The shore is stony.

At eight o'clock all of his men are standing drawn up at the water's edge. Bayonets fixed. Dawkins notes in his journal:

On the beach we wait about an hour. The General[*] and staff pass. The former appears quite bright which is a good omen. No one really knows what has happened. The rest of our company land. Myself and [a] patrol then work south along the beach searching for water. Find a small pool near a Turkish hut where the belongings of the inhabitants were strewn in all directions. Pass on over a ridge into a deep gully but infantry in rear of us yell and we have to return. Send a party to dig a well near the hut—another to sink a Tube well in the same valley—another to improve a

[*] William Bridges, the commanding officer of the 1st Australian Division, whom Dawkins knew reasonably well since he had also been in command of the Royal Military College at Duntroon.

small supply on the beach. In the gully near hut over shot bullets are landing in swarms. Infantry on hill in front keep yelling out frantically that we are under fire. Of course we are.

And so it continues. Dawkins and his men rush back and forth between the swathes of bullets from the shrapnel shells, digging, drilling, laying pipes. Two of his men are wounded, one in the elbow, one in the shoulder. The detonator from a shrapnel shell hits his boot but does not inflict a wound. Later he hears the din of heavy firing—"a splendid sound"—from the high ground immediately behind the shore: a Turkish counter-attack.* A thin but unbroken stream of wounded men is trickling back from the high ground the whole time. He sees a confused colonel, clearly affected by some sort of shell shock, ordering fire onto hills held by their own troops. Dawkins helps unload ammunition from a transport barge.

He falls asleep, "dead tired," at around nine in the evening but is woken after only an hour and a half by a major who tells him the situation is critical. For the rest of the night Dawkins helps to bring up reinforcements and ammunition to the hard-pressed and scattered infantry in the front line. The firing goes on all night. Dawkins lies down again at sometime around half past three in the morning.

SATURDAY, 1 MAY 1915
Florence Farmborough hears the breaking of the front at Gorlice

As for millions of others, bidding farewell at the railway station was actually the most sublime experience of all: for most of them it was the only sublime experience. The crowds on the platform at the Alexander Station

---

* The Ottoman infantry defending Gallipoli during these days was brave, outnumbered, had defective equipment and was simply being used as cannon fodder. This fact is well summarised in a famous utterance by the then commander of the 19th Ottoman Division, Lieutenant Colonel Mustafa Kemal, later famous as Kemal Atatürk. In a critical situation at Ariburnu on this very day, when he sent in a regiment whose ammunition was almost exhausted to stop a dangerous breakthrough by the Anzacs (Australian and New Zealand Army Corps), he shouted to his soldiers, "I am not giving you an order to attack, I am ordering you to die." That unit, the 57th Regiment, was indeed annihilated. Q.E.D.

in Moscow had been enormous. They had sung the Russian national anthem, shouted blessings and encouragement, exchanged embraces and good wishes and distributed flowers and chocolates. Then the train had puffed off to the accompaniment of thunderous cheers, passing waving hands and faces full of hope and uncertainty. She herself had been possessed by "a wild exhilaration [that] swept like fire through my veins; we were off, off to the Front! My very gladness left me speechless."

She and her unit are stationed in Gorlice, a small, poor country town in the Galician part of Austria-Hungary, occupied for over six months now by Russian troops. Gorlice lies very close to the front. The Austrian artillery fires on the town daily in a rather absent-minded way, as if doing it as a matter of principle rather than according to any plan. They do not seem greatly concerned that the majority of the casualties of their fire are, like them, subjects of the Emperor in Vienna. The tower of the big church is split down the middle. Many of the houses are already ruins. The town had 12,000 inhabitants before the war, now there are only a couple of thousand who have not fled and they spend their days crouched in their cellars. Up until now Farmborough and the other staff of the field hospital have devoted most of their time to alleviating the distress of the civilian population, primarily by distributing food. The shortages are severe. The landscape is a pleasant spring green.

Mobile Field Hospital No. 10 consists of three parts. There are two "flying detachments" which can easily be sent to wherever they are most needed: each of them consists of an officer, a non-commissioned officer, two doctors, a medical assistant, four male nurses, four female, thirty ambulancemen, two dozen two-wheeled, horse-drawn ambulances with a red cross painted on their tarpaulins, and the same number of drivers and grooms. Then there is the base unit, where there are more places for the wounded, where the stores are kept and where there are also more transport facilities, notably two motor cars. Florence is attached to one of the flying detachments. They have organised an improvised hospital in a deserted house, scrubbing it clean, painting it and setting up both an operating theatre and a pharmacy.

Gorlice, as already mentioned, lies on the front line at the foot of the Carpathians and shells plump down among the houses every day. This section has, nevertheless, been quiet for a long time and the Russian military have been lulled into some degree of apathy. Anyone who goes up to the forward line becomes aware of it. There are no fortifications of the stout, well-built kind that are the rule on the static Western Front to be seen here.* Instead, the trenches are shallow, rather carelessly scraped-out features, resembling ditches more than anything else, protected by a few thin strands of barbed wire. Admittedly it was difficult to dig down to any depth here during the winter, but the digging has not gone any faster now that the frost is out of the ground: this is a result partly of laziness, partly of a shortage of spades.

The Russian artillery rarely responds to the Austrian bombardment. It is said that this is because of a lack of ammunition but there are actually plenty of shells stockpiled farther back. The bureaucrats in uniform who control these things are happy to keep them there, waiting for bigger things. The Russian army is planning a new offensive farther to the south, in the direction of the famous passes over the Carpathians (the "Gateway to Hungary"!), which still stink from the corpses left scattered everywhere after the hard but fruitless battles of the winter. The resources will be put to better use there. The question is whether that is really true: for some days now a sense of anxiousness has been spreading among the Russian units at Gorlice and a rumour has been going round that the Austrians opposite them have been reinforced with German infantry and heavy artillery.

On this particular Saturday Florence and the others at the hospital are woken before dawn by heavy artillery fire.

She tumbles out of bed. Fortunately she has been sleeping fully dressed. Everyone—everyone except possibly Radko Dimitriev, commander of the Russian Third Army—has been suspecting that something was about to happen. Explosions of varying strength and intensity become more frequent as the Russian artillery around them joins in. The bullets from exploding shrapnel shells clatter down on the streets and roofs.

Through the rattling windows Florence can see the lights playing against the still-dark sky. She can see the great lightning flashes from the muzzles of the guns and the subdued flashes from the explosions.

---

* The trench system in the east was rarely as well-developed and labyrinthine as in the west. This was mainly because the front, as has been noted, was more mobile. The distance between the enemy lines, perhaps a couple of hundred yards in the west and frequently much less than that, was often a mile or more in the east.

She sees the beams of searchlights and the bright, multicoloured light from flares mixed with a muted glow as fires begin to rage. They crouch indoors. The walls and floors are shaking.

Then the wounded start coming in:

At first we could cope; then we were overwhelmed by their numbers. They came in their hundreds, from all directions; some able to walk, others crawling, dragging themselves along the ground.

In such a desperate situation the only thing the hospital staff can do is to be brutally selective. Those who can stand up on their own get no help—they are just sent on their way after being told to try to get to one of the base units. There are so many unable to walk that they are laid out in rows out in the open air, where they are first given painkillers and then have their wounds tended. "The groans and cries of the wounded were pitiful to hear." Florence and the others do what they can to help in spite of feeling that it is all in vain since this flood of ragged and torn bodies seems to be endless.

This goes on for hour after hour. Now and then there is a longer silence.

Daylight begins to dim and twilight falls.

Among the shouting and the screaming, shadowy figures move round illuminated by glaring, distant lights.

At around six o'clock the following morning Florence and her colleagues hear a new and terrifying sound: a sudden, vibrating roar like a waterfall, which is the noise of over 900 artillery pieces of every calibre imaginable all opening fire simultaneously—that is one for every fifty yards of the front. Seconds later comes the drawn-out, rough echo of the impact. The crash of metallic explosions in every key becomes a dense wall of sound, the din intensifies, whirls and spirals like some sort of natural force.

There is something new and unpleasantly systematic about this artillery fire and the way it is crashing down on the Russian front line. The German technical term is *Glocke*, a bell; the English, a creeping barrage. The fire waltz swings backwards and forwards and side to side along the Russian lines and connecting trenches. This is something quite different from the casual, incidental bombardment by the Austrian artillery, something even more than yesterday's thunderously powerful barrage. This is artillery fire as a science, calculated to the second and to the ton to produce maximum effect. This is something new.

They hear the word "retreat"—with disbelief at first.

Then the spectacle of long, uneven lines of mud-covered soldiers with weary faces passing them. Finally, the order for immediate withdrawal, leaving the equipment and the wounded. They are to leave the wounded? Yes, leave the wounded. "*Skoro! Skoro!*[*] . . . The Germans are outside the town!"

Florence takes her coat and her rucksack and rushes out of the building. The wounded are screaming, praying, swearing and begging the nurses "not to forsake them, for the love of God." Someone grabs hold of the hem of Florence's skirt. She twists the hand loose and disappears down the uneven road along with the others. It is a hot and sunny spring day but the light is nevertheless muted. The oil tanks outside the town have started burning and the air is filled with oily black smoke.[†]

WEDNESDAY, 12 MAY 1915
William Henry Dawkins dies at Gallipoli

We might perhaps wonder which was uppermost in his mind, his exertions on the shore or his toothache. In all likelihood it was the former. Dawkins was a conscientious and purposeful man. His visit to the doctor does show, however, that the toothache must have been there in the background all the time, a distraction, a filter,[‡] and his experience of those days must have been a strange mixture of the grand-scale epic and

* Quickly!
† There are almost as many war cemeteries in this area as there are in Flanders and they can still be seen today by anyone driving along route 977 from Tarnów to Gorlice. In contrast to the situation in Flanders, many of these cemeteries are in a melancholy state of decay, which may sometimes be romantic but is often depressing. Most of them contain the bodies of soldiers from several different armies.
‡ Dawkins had visited the dentist several times while they were still in Egypt but all of the problems had clearly not been dealt with. As late as 10 May he was seeking medical help—on the shore—for his pain.

the limited and private—as always—with a sort of empty zone between the two: he probably quickly lost his grasp of ordinary things, such as which day of the week it was.

Ever since they had landed a full two weeks earlier the weather had been fine, though the nights had been cold. Two days before, however, it had started to drizzle. And it was still drizzling. The great numbers of people and animals moving back and forth between the shore and the trenches up on the steep hills have trampled the paths into sticky mud and it is difficult to move on the wet, slippery clay in the ravines. William Henry Dawkins and his corporal sleep in a covered cleft in the slopes by the shore. The only piece of furniture is an old armchair that floated ashore a few days ago and Dawkins sometimes sits in it when giving out his orders. When he wakes this morning it is raining hard.

Everyone can see that this grand operation has ground to a halt.

There are actually only two points at which the Allies have succeeded in creating real bridgeheads: one of them is right down at the southern point of the peninsula and the other is here at Gaba Tepe, on the western side of Gallipoli.* Dawkins and the others, however, landed at the wrong place, well over half a mile north of the intended spot. In one sense that was fortunate since the Ottoman defence was unusually weak at that point, the terrain being so rugged that the defenders judged it highly unlikely the Allies would even try to land there.† The result was that the attackers could wade ashore without serious losses but, once there, it was only with the greatest of difficulty they could move through the confusing labyrinth of steep bush-covered ravines and sharp ridges that plunge steeply to the shore. By the time the hastily dispatched Turkish infantry had reached the place, the Australian and New Zealand companies had—at best—managed to advance a mile and a half inland. And that is more or less where it came to a stop, as an ironic reflection of the static Western Front. Just as in France and in Belgium, attack and counter-attack came in quick succession until both sides, relentless but exhausted, realised that their opponent was not going to be budged. At which point they settled down to the usual plodding drudgery of trench warfare.

* Now best known as Anzac Cove.
† There was no longer any question of surprise: the repeated naval attacks on Gallipoli during the months beforehand meant that the Ottoman generals—under their German commander-in-chief, Otto Liman von Sanders—had their eye on the place and sent all the reinforcements they could scrape together.

Part of this drudgery is care, maintenance and the provision of food and water. Those in charge had actually given some thought to these things: they knew that access to water was going to be a problem, especially as the hottest season of the year was approaching. So when they landed they had with them barges loaded with water from Lemnos, water enough to satisfy the most immediate needs until the engineers managed to sink wells. Dawkins and his crew had worked quickly, building several wells and setting up access points to the vital liquid for both animals and men.

Not that it was ever a case of abundance. There was, for instance, insufficient fresh water for the men to wash in and so they had to look after their personal hygiene by bathing in the sea. They were, however, advised to avoid cleaning their teeth in sea water because of all the animal corpses floating around as well as the filth from the ships lying anchored offshore. One of the problems was that a great deal of fresh water was lost because the thin and fragile pipes bringing the water from the pumps at the wells were punctured so often, either by artillery fire or quite simply by careless soldiers letting carts and guns trundle over them. Dawkins and his men have consequently been busy for some time burying the pipes deeper.

It is an ordinary morning, though grey and rainy. Dawkins organises his troops in the usual order and allots the various groups their tasks for the day. One of them is to continue sinking the pipes into the ground. Little glory in it, and hardly a motif for a lurid print in some illustrated magazine, but necessary all the same. Several of the worst troublemakers in the company have happened to end up in his platoon. But a combination of the seriousness of the hour and Dawkins's qualities as a leader—particularly his genuine care for his men—have helped calm down the worst of the unruliness and a marked sense of solidarity has developed between these apparently incorrigible moaners and skivers and their mild young captain.

It is still early when they set to work.

The rain is falling.

An unusually dangerous section awaits one of the groups this morning and it is easy to see where it is: there are thirty or more dead mules, killed by Turkish shells, lying along a stretch not much longer than a hundred yards. The ditch is already dug, however—it was dug at night. Now it is just a matter of laying the pipe and joining it up.

Everything is still calm and quiet. No sound from the Turkish artillery. The only unpleasant part is the dead animals, with their bellies swelling and stiff legs sticking out. The ditch goes past the cadavers, alongside them, under them and even through them in some cases. The seven soldiers become covered in blood. Dawkins is with them. The time is a quarter to ten.

Dawkins moves a little further down the ditch to inspect it. Then they hear the whine of a shell.

It is the very first one of the morning. The whine becomes a howl. The howl is followed by a hard, sharp report. The projectile explodes just above the heads of the seven crouching soldiers and their water-pipe, but it is a shrapnel shell and they are untouched: its payload of round bullets showers down into the ground fifteen yards further on. One of the soldiers, a man by the name of Morey, turns round. He is just in time to see William Henry Dawkins fall to the ground in that peculiar way characteristic of the severely wounded—the fall is not controlled by the body's usual reflexes but by the simple laws of gravity.*

They rush to him. Dawkins has been hit in the head, throat and chest. They lift him up from the wet ground and carry him to a shelter. Another shell explodes behind them with a short, powerful crash. They lay him down. Blood and rainwater run together. He says nothing. He dies before their eyes.

Sarah Macnaughtan makes the following entry in her diary on this day:

> The other day I heard some ladies having a rather forced discussion on moral questions, loud and frank. Shades of my modest

---

* Had it been an ordinary high-explosive shell Dawkins would have escaped but his men would have been injured or killed. Shrapnel shells spread their bullets in a long cone directly ahead whereas high-explosive shells send out their fragments at almost ninety degrees. It is consequently possible to escape injury from a high-explosive shell even if it detonates just a few yards away as long as one is along the line of the shell's trajectory. There is also the fact that metallurgy was still relatively undeveloped and high-explosive shells sometimes broke into just a few large fragments, which explains why people could sometimes survive even if they were very close to the detonation. One theory held that it was precisely experiences of this kind which were, purely physiologically, the cause of shell shock: the vacuum created by the detonation was thought to cause damage to the brain.

ancestresses! In this war time, and in a room filled with men and smoke and drink, are women in knickerbockers discussing such things? I know I have got to "let out tucks," but surely not quite so far!

Beautiful women and fast women should be chained up. Let men meet their God with their conscience clear. Most of them will be killed before the war is over. Surely the least we can do is not to offer them temptation. Death and destruction, and horror and wonderful heroism, seem so near and so transcendent, and then, quite close at hand, one finds evil doings.

A DAY IN THE SECOND WEEK OF MAY 1915
Laura de Turczynowicz sees a prisoner of war find a piece of bread in Suwalki

Laura hears a German nurse shouting at someone to stop at once. The yelling continues and Laura goes to see what it is all about. A Russian prisoner of war is grubbing around in a stinking heap of hospital rubbish and, refusing to let the German nurse's protests put him off, he just carries on searching.

Parts of Laura's grand house have been turned into a temporary hospital for all the civilian typhus cases in the town. She often works there herself. The building is afforded some protection by the notices warning about typhus, just as she herself is given some protection by the Russian Red Cross nurse's uniform she wears. (Going out alone on these streets full of men in uniform can be an unpleasant experience for a woman, all the more so as drunkenness is becoming increasingly common.) Shielded by her uniform, she has started feeding some of the starving Russian prisoners kept in the town as labour. Among their other jobs they have dug up the corpses of fourteen soldiers buried in her garden after the fighting of last autumn.

There are few things that upset her more than the treatment of the Russian prisoners of war. They are undernourished, filthy, ragged, verminous, frequently ill, badly housed and badly treated. Worse, perhaps, than the filth and the wounds and the rags is the fact that they are, almost without exception, worn-out and broken men, who have lost all hope and who, in their silent and submissive suffering, have begun to lose some of their humanity. They are being turned into, well, animals, or things even.* Laura is profoundly shocked by this and helps them whenever she can.

The German nurse is still shouting and the Russian prisoner is still digging. Then he finds something. Laura sees what it is—a filthy crust of bread, which the prisoner holds up triumphantly to his fellows before starting to eat it. The German nurse is upset. How can he eat something like that? Doesn't he realise the piece of bread will make him ill, possibly fatally ill? The man carries on chewing.

Laura is upset too and she turns to the German nurse. Can she not give the man something proper to eat? The nurse hesitates and is not sure whether she dare. One of the uniformed German hospital assistants hears the discussion and intervenes—she goes away and returns with a big bowl of thick, steaming soup in which pieces of real meat are floating about. The Russian prisoner gulps down the food.

Three hours later he is dead.

His stomach clearly could not handle the sudden abundance.

FRIDAY, 14 MAY 1915
Olive King is scrubbing floors in Troyes

It is a cold and windy day. For a change, it has to be said, since the weather has been pleasantly warm recently. They have even been able to sleep in the open air in a nearby pine wood, lying on the as yet unused stretchers. It is not, however, the warmth that has made sleeping outdoors attractive but the fact that the small manor house, the Château de Chanteloup, that has been requisitioned for their use has no furniture and is pretty filthy. In addition to which, most of their equipment has gone astray. With no tents and without a functioning kitchen they cannot take any wounded men. But the manor is pleasantly situated: it may be right by the road but

---

* There was a peculiar dialectic relationship between dirt and subordination in the east. Cleanliness was one of the virtues the German occupiers never tired of preaching and was something that they felt to be proof of their own superiority. As Vejas Gabriel Liulevicius has shown, there were circumstances in which the subordinates could play on this, and on the German fear of infection, in order to evade punishments and control.

it has a fine orchard and kitchen garden and there is an attractive wood close by.

Olive King is up early as usual. By a quarter past eight she is sitting behind the wheel of her ambulance, ready to set off to find benches and tables to furnish the place. She is accompanied by one of her superiors, Mrs. Harley, head of transport. Olive May King is a twenty-nine-year-old Australian, born in Sydney, the daughter of a successful business-man. (She is her father's girl in many ways, especially since her mother died when Olive was only fifteen.)

Her upbringing and education have been conventional, finishing off in Dresden where classes in music and painting porcelain were part of the syllabus, but her life since has been anything but conventional. There is a tension within her between, on one hand, an upright and naive longing for a husband and children, and on the other, an energetic and restless nature. She travelled a great deal in the years before the war, in Asia, America and Europe—though always accompanied by a chaper-one. She was the third woman to climb the 17,887-foot volcano Popoca-tépetl, south-east of Mexico City—and the first to risk descending into its smoking crater. But there is something missing. She prays to God in a poem written in 1913: "Send me a sorrow [. . .] To wake my soul from its engulfing sleep." She is yet another of these people for whom the gospel of the war is change.

It is thus hardly surprising that, motivated both by her adventurous spirit and by her intense patriotism, King found a way of becoming a participant rather than an observer very soon after the war broke out. She took the only course open to women in 1914, the medical service. It is, perhaps, telling that King did not train as a nurse but enrolled instead in the much more unconventional role of driver, at the wheel of a large Alda ambulance she had bought personally with her father's money. The ability to drive a motor vehicle is still a very exclusive skill, particularly for a woman.

The organisation King is now working for is the Scottish Women's Hospital, one of many private medical units started in the enthusiasm of the autumn of 1914, but this one is rather unusual in that it was founded by radical suffragettes and is staffed exclusively by women.*

---

* It was probably straightforward practicality rather than gender-political principle that drew Olive to this unit: the first medical unit she joined had been stopped almost

King is driving her own ambulance this morning—its number is 9862 but she always calls it Ella, which is short for The Elephant. And it is big, virtually a small bus, with space for as many as sixteen seated passengers. The specially built load area at the back is heavy and King is rarely able to push Ella up to speeds higher than twenty-eight miles an hour.

They return at about half past ten. Helped by Mrs. Wilkinson, another of the drivers, King unloads the benches and tables they have acquired and stands them out in the garden, then King and Mrs. Wilkinson change their clothes and begin scrubbing out the outhouse where the drivers are to be quartered. The two of them wield scrubbing brushes and sponges, use several changes of water and keep on scrubbing vigorously until the floor is completely clean. They have also thought about re-papering the room but that will have to wait.

Dinner consists of asparagus, which tastes good, is cheap, and is in season. As usual they have an audience as they eat. The dining-room window looks out onto the road and inquisitive passers-by look in to catch a glimpse of these strange women, who have not only volunteered to come and help with the war effort but who are also managing without men. Then she and a number of the others go to their rooms to write letters because the post goes early tomorrow. King tells her sister:

> I don't believe it will be many months now before the war is over. The failure, thank God, of that damnable gas will be a great blow to Germany, I believe. Isn't it magnificent that the new respirators are such a success? Thank God for it. I wish He would make all their brutal gas-shells explode among themselves and kill 500,000 Bosches [sic]. It would be a gorgeous revenge for our poor slaughtered soldiers and I wish He would send fires or floods to blow up or wreck all the German ammunition factories.

King writes this in her freshly scrubbed room, half-lying on a rickety stretcher that is presently serving as her bed. The room is empty

---

immediately after it landed unannounced in Belgium, and Olive and two other women drivers had been arrested under suspicion of being spies. Mrs. Harley, however, one of the leaders of the Scottish Women's Hospital and the woman accompanying Olive on the hunt for furniture, was the sister of Sir John French, commander-in-chief of the British Expeditionary Force: this, self-evidently, would have made it easier for the unit to gain permission to operate.

otherwise, apart from a chair and a wind-up gramophone. There is an open fireplace with a marble mantelpiece, which is where they throw their cigarette ends, matchsticks and other rubbish. The walls are covered with a wallpaper she is very fond of—it shows brown parrots sitting in rose bushes and eating nuts. She is cold and she is sleepy. When is her real war going to start?

WEDNESDAY, 26 MAY 1915
Pál Kelemen buys four loaves of white bread in Glebovka

The Russians are really in retreat now. That has become clear to him during the last few days while riding through one badly damaged place after another and seeing everything the retreating enemy is leaving behind— from scrap and rubbish along the roads, to dead and dying soldiers, as well as newly erected road signs with incomprehensible names in the Cyrillic alphabet. (A year ago this road led to Lemberg, now it leads to Lvov, and soon it will be Lemberg again.*)

Kelemen has nothing against being on the march again and certainly nothing against the Russian invasion forces being driven out. The news of the great breakthrough at Gorlice, however, was greeted with much less jubilation by the troops than might have been expected. "Everyone here has become indifferent," he writes in his journal, "worn down by the everlasting tension."

They have been in the small town of Glebovka since yesterday. When he and the other hussars rode in there were two things that gave him a shock: the first was a house with its windows intact, behind which he caught a glimpse of white lace curtains; the second was a young Polish woman—he always has his eye open for young women—moving among a crowd of soldiers and Russian prisoners. She was wearing white gloves. It will be a long time before he forgets those white gloves and lace curtains, forgets that immaculate whiteness in a world of filth and mud.

Today he has heard that there is white bread for sale and since he is sick of the standard-issue bread, which is either doughy or dried out, he has gone to buy some. He buys four large loaves and notes in his journal:

* After the war the road would lead to Lwów; today it leads to Lviv.

I cut into one. It was not yet cold. Its thick strong smell filled my nostrils. Slowly, almost with awe, I took the first bite and tried to savor the taste clearly, thinking that this is the same white loaf I was used to once, before the war.

I ate and I concentrated. But my palate would not recognise anything at all, and I ate the white loaf as if it had been some new food, the fame and the taste of which I had never known before.

Afterwards I realised that the bread was just the same as at home. It was I who had changed; the war had given such a foreign flavor to the good old white bread I used to take for granted.

THURSDAY, 27 MAY 1915
Sarah Macnaughtan's time in De Panne is coming to an end

Enough is enough. She is going back to England in a week's time. Probably for good. Macnaughtan is one of those people who were swept along in the first rejoicing wave of enthusiasm and who then, as reverses and disappointments mounted, has seen her energies draining away. She is tired. Tired in body and tired in soul. Tired of suffering. Tired of danger. Tired of the constant bickering. Tired of pettiness and incomprehensible rules. Tired.

She has carried on working in the soup kitchen at the station, dutifully but without any joy. She does the same things every day: ladles out soup, coffee, bread and jam, and shares out the sugar. At least the cold, dark, lonely winter is over but the return of the sun has its disadvantages because it can get very hot standing out there on the platform at the station, and the smells are much worse. Some helpful people have sent her a motor car, but it has already broken down.

It is still a Fight Against Evil, of course. That is not something she has any doubt about. (That feeling has, in fact, only grown stronger in the course of the spring since she heard of the sinking of the passenger liner and since she saw the victims of German poison gas for the first time.) And she still feels strongly that the war is about Duty and Principles and The Honour of the Name of Britain. But for how long can it actually continue?

Surely the expense of the thing will one day put a stop to war. We are spending two million sterling per day, the French certainly as much, the Germans probably more, and Austria and Russia much more, in order to keep men most uncomfortably in unroofed graves, and to send high explosives into the air, most of which don't hit anything.

Macnaughtan is struggling to solve the equation in her head. At the start of the month a volunteer soldier told her in confidence that he was longing to be wounded "so that he might go home honourably." When she considers her own role, she has come to the conclusion that she could be far more useful on the home front, as a propagandist. She is working on a little book about her experiences. (Somewhat adapted, admittedly, with a candid but mildly humorous tone and with the text carefully purged of all doubts and disagreeable elements. A publisher has already been found for the project.) She is also thinking of realising her plan to travel round giving talks to workers at a number of munitions factories.*

She is struggling to find a solution to the conundrum of whether a sacrifice can be magnificent even if it is meaningless—indeed, whether the very fact that it is meaningless can make it even more magnificent. She has heard a story about some artillerymen who were sent back to fetch a gun and their NCO is supposed to have said: "We shall be killed, but it doesn't matter." Their captain responded "heavily": "No, it doesn't matter." The story has affected her deeply. She writes in her diary:

> "It doesn't matter"—nothing matters. I rather dread going back to London, because there things may begin to seem important and one will be in bondage again. Here our men are going to their death laughing because it doesn't matter. There is a proud humility about my countrymen which few people have yet realised. It is the outcome of nursery days and public schools. No one is allowed to think much of himself in either place, so when he dies, "It doesn't matter." God help the boys! If they only knew how much it mattered to us! Life is over for them. We don't even know for certain that they will live again. But their spirit, as I know it,

---

* Macnaughtan had heard of the scandalous shortage of shells and the problems it caused during the battles around Festubert (and elsewhere) which had ended a few days earlier.

can never die. I am not sure about the survival of personality. I care, but I do not know. But I do know that by these simple, glorious, uncomplaining deaths, some higher, purer, more splendid place is reached, some release is found from the heavy weight of foolish, sticky, burdensome, contemptible things. These heroes do "rise," and we "rise" with them.

Spring has been late in coming but now it has arrived at last in its full force, "a marvel of green," but the lilacs and the warm sea breeze only make her even more homesick. One week to go.

SUNDAY, 6 JUNE 1915
Kresten Andresen is evacuated from the hospital in Noyon

Perhaps it is luck, just a quirk of fate, that will save him. One dark night at the beginning of May Andresen fell into a narrow sap trench and fractured his right leg immediately above the ankle. Since then he has spent most of the time in hospital, lying in a large ward that used to be a theatre and being cared for by kindly French nuns. He is bored because he has little to read and he is fed up with the poor food—the sick are not considered to need as much as soldiers at the front*—but he is nevertheless quite content. At least six weeks, the doctor has told him. With a little luck he can stay out of the front line until July even, and perhaps, perhaps, perhaps, the war will be over by then.

While lying in bed Andresen has, as usual, done a lot of fantasising about the war and what might happen soon, and about peace and what might happen then. Italy declared war on the Central Powers in May; the British attacked up in Flanders and the French attacked with great tenacity at Arras; exceptionally severe fighting has surged across the crater-covered Loretto Heights; and the rumour going round is that the United States and several Balkan countries will soon join Germany's

---

* Men serving at the front received certain items—soap, for instance—free whereas those in hospital had to pay for them. Since their pay was low and the prices in the few and poorly stocked shops were sky-high, this soon became a problem. Consequently Andresen's letters home during this month, as well as expressing his joy at being out of the firing line, contained many requests for material support.

opponents. Andresen is amazed at how self-confidently many Germans have reacted to the growing threats: they say that it will probably lengthen the war but that Germany will nevertheless be victorious in the end. For his own part he hopes that the great political developments—real or imaginary—will lead to peace. He knows what he intends to do in that case. Before August 1914 he worked as a teacher in Vinding for a full six months and he wants to return to that after the war, to continue working in popular education and with young people. And he dreams of building himself a small house, a house no bigger than "Aunt Dorothea's hen-house but very romantic both inside and outside."

In recent days, however, the situation has become severe around Roye, which lies only some six miles from the section of the front held by his regiment. They have been able to hear the sound of artillery fire day and night and it is said that the French infantry has broken through the line. He has been spared that battle, thank God. And that is not the only thing: since the hospital beds are soon going to be needed for the hordes of freshly wounded men, all the convalescents are to be evacuated—to Germany, according to the word that is going round.

He knows nothing of this at first, since he spends a large part of Sunday lying on the fresh green grass under a pear tree, the warm air filled with the softly rolling murmur of the distant guns. As evening approaches he goes and listens to a church concert and it is only when he has limped back to the hospital that he hears what is going on. Andresen immediately packs his things. To Germany! His weapons and the bulk of his military equipment go in one pile, his private possessions in another. Their names are called out, they are provided with travel documents, and each of them has a small cardboard label—name, unit, injury and so on—attached to his chest. Their marching orders come at eleven o'clock.

They climb into motor cars, five men to a car, and roar off into the summer night. Along the road they pass a number of high-ranking officers who are standing at the roadside studying a horizon which is sparkling with muzzle-flashes and shell-bursts, searchlights and the signal rockets that are slowly spinning down. But this is no longer of any concern to him.

We're all off to Germany and I really don't know how to express my joy. Away from the battle and away from the shells. Soon we shan't be able to hear the guns any more. And we are travelling through fertile countryside and past smiling villages. My travelling mood is one of joy, of Sunday peace and ringing bells. Home, home and onwards.

The intention is that they should change in Chauny and the rest of the journey will be by train. They gather in a large park and a doctor carries out a new examination of those waiting. When he reaches Andresen he studies his papers and then tears the cardboard label from his chest. That is the end of the journey for him. As far as the doctor is concerned Andresen is sufficiently recovered to return to the front in just a couple more days.

Andresen walks away, utterly crestfallen; everything is suddenly just "black and black."

When he eventually returns to the park he sees the others all lined up. Several of them shout to him. His name has been called out—he is going to Germany after all! Andresen has hardly joined the ranks before it is discovered that he lacks the cardboard label on his chest. He is once again ordered to leave the group: "Farewell leave! Farewell home! I'm going back to the war again!"

FRIDAY, 11 JUNE 1915
Florence Farmborough hears of the breakthrough on the San

This is their third week in Molodych. That first panic-driven retreat after the breakthrough at Gorlice has now been forgotten—well, almost forgotten. The Third Army has lost an unbelievable 200,000 men—140,000 of them as prisoners of war—since those days at the beginning of May, but now it has occupied a new and apparently strong position along the broad River San. Reinforcements have arrived, at last. And orders have come down from the highest level: here, right here, the Germans and Austrians will finally be stopped. No more retreats!* Battles have raged

---

* There was nothing new about this categorical command that there must be no retreat: the high command issued it time after time after the breakthrough of 2 May. It was, however, completely counter-productive in that it forced the hard-pressed Third Army to defend a number of indefensible positions, which simply served to increase its already substantial losses.

along the river and both sides have made minor attacks.* One evening Florence saw large numbers of grey-uniformed German prisoners for the first time; they came walking along a road in the moonlight, wearing their typical pickelhaubes and guarded by mounted Cossacks. Rumour has it that the enemy has suffered major losses. There is new hope.

There is virtually no fighting going on where Florence is and that certainly reinforces the feeling that the crisis is probably over. There has been plenty of time for other things, such as washing down by the river and celebrating Italy's entry into the war or her own name-day. She has done a lot of walking in the silent, green woods, picking the abundant flowers of early summer. Apart from the usual cases of typhus and cholera things have been so quiet that several of the nurses have become impatient and started talking of applying to other units where they might be of more use. Their superintendent has tried to calm them down, hinting that the unit will soon be moved anyway, possibly to the Eighth Army down at Lemberg and perhaps even to the Caucasus. (Good news of the kind everyone longs for is coming in from the Caucasus front: Russian units have begun moving south and across the Ottoman border, encouraged by talk of unrest and rebellion behind the Turkish lines.)

It is now three o'clock in the afternoon. Florence Farmborough is sitting outside her tent, resting after the day's work. Everything is calm, as usual. She sees four orderlies carrying off some bodies in order to bury them in the improvised cemetery in the adjoining field. She hears the clapping noise made by a pair of storks that have built a nest on the thatched roof of a farm. A man from the other rapid-response unit comes up to her and hands her a letter addressed to their doctor. She asks him in passing how things are at his unit. The man tells her "with suppressed excitement" that bullets from shrapnel shells fell close to them that morning and the unit is preparing to move. The Germans have broken through on the San river!

She is shaken by the news but is not really convinced that it is true. She can, however, hear the noise of heavy artillery fire in the distance but, towards dinnertime, when she asks around among the others they are as sceptical as she is. After dinner she returns to her tent, which smells of

---

* The enemy did succeed in crossing the San at several points around the middle of May, doing so with the same self-confident, brutally crushing power as at Gorlice, but at this point it seems that these intrusions have been checked and held back.

the heat. There she meets Anna, another of the nurses, and Anna wearily confirms the news. The rumours of a breakthrough on the San are true:

> It is said they are pouring over in masses and nothing can stop them. We have the men, but we haven't the means. Whole regiments are said to be without a cartridge, and only a certain number of batteries can continue shelling.

Anna adds: "The result will be that our armies will be butchered, and it is but a day's march into Russia." She conjures up a picture of a Russia invaded and laid waste and the mental image is too much for her. She throws herself down on the bed, covers her face with her arms and weeps noisily. Florence makes a clumsy effort to stem her tears: "'Annushka,' I said, 'stop; this is not worthy of your nature.'" Anna removes her arms from her face and gives Florence a dark look: "'Nature!' she flashed, 'what is this talk of nature?'" Then the words pour out of her. "'Is it God's nature to allow this wholesale destruction? Not only does one lose one's nature among all this carnage, but one's soul dies too!'" And she carries on weeping. Florence says nothing: "I did not attempt to comfort her; I could find no comfort to give."

Then the final confirmation arrives in the form of an order to prepare to move. They start packing, a task that is interrupted when a large group of wounded men suddenly arrives:

> When we saw them we knew that the worst had happened; they were dazed and their faces were lined with an anxiety which dominated the keenness of their pain and there was that something in their eyes that checked all questioning.

Darkness falls. The thunder of distant guns fades and falls silent. A battery of artillery pieces swings into a nearby field and unlimbers. Florence and the others take down their tents in the soft night mist. Then they hear noises from the road. When Florence goes closer she sees that it is full of mounted men—Cossacks. She sees a farm boy run past and disappear towards the woods, his head bent low. She hears screaming and tumult: the Cossacks are going through the farms systematically one by one and gathering all the animals they can take with them—pigs, cows

and chickens. They are also gathering all the men and tying them up.[*]
Florence sees some Cossacks wrestling a young man to the ground while
a woman screams shrilly.

Then the Cossacks go off along the road taking their two- and four-
legged booty with them. The screams of the women continue without
break. Later, when Florence and the rest of her unit move off in the
darkness on their overloaded horse-drawn carts, the wailing can still be
heard.

It is a beautiful, clear, starry night.

TUESDAY, 15 JUNE 1915
Alfred Pollard is waiting for dawn at Hooge

It is a hot day, with no wind. They are in full battle kit and have eight
miles to march before they reach the launching point for the attack.
Things are easy at the start as they trudge along the always busy road
from Poperinghe to Ypres. They are hemmed in by other units on foot,
both large and small, and by "limbers drawn by horses, limbers drawn by
mules; endless ammunition columns; siege guns and howitzers; strings
of lorries; motor cycle dispatch riders." They realise they are going to be
taking part in a big and important attack since they can also see cavalry,
battle-ready and waiting for that much-discussed hole to be punched

---

[*] Florence Farmborough is uncertain as to whether the Cossacks are simply carrying out
orders or whether this is a largely private bout of pillaging. Most of the evidence suggests the
former. As the Russian army once again began retreating it fell back on its old speciality—
what is usually called a scorched-earth policy. It made a systematic attempt to take as much
as possible of the resources of the country—cattle, in particular—with it, at the same
time as destroying whatever it had to leave behind, regardless of whether this condemned
the civilian population to great hardship or, indeed, outright famine. At this point the
Russians were occupying territory that belonged to Austria-Hungary, which explains
why they also removed the men of military age; this had also been done earlier, during
the invasion of German East Prussia in 1914, but not with the same degree of methodical
planning. (On that occasion the retreating Russians had forcibly taken rather more than
10,000 German men, women and children.) This organised pillage and burning continued
with undiminished force even after they had crossed the border back into Russia, resulting
in extreme suffering even for their own civilian population. This, of course, did nothing to
make the war any more popular among the latter.

through the German lines at last so that they can pour through—sabres drawn, picturesque pennants waving and suitably dramatic poses—and make the war mobile again.

This is Alfred Pollard's first attack. He is full of fervour, almost happy in fact. Months of frustration and disappointment are finally over. Up to this point the war has not turned out as he expected. He has been ill with jaundice, suspected of being a malingerer (him! malingerer!), been an officer's batman and worked as a cook. The woman he has fallen in love with hardly ever writes. The war he had fantasised about has not yet materialised—far less the heroism he'd dreamt of. But now, at last.

The mood of the men in his unit undergoes a marked change the closer they get to the front. He knows the phenomenon:

> Leaving the line, when every step means a further distance from bullets and shells, there is an atmosphere of gaiety; songs are heard, jokes are exchanged, laughter is frequent. Going up, on the other hand, is a very different business. There is an air of seriousness, remarks are answered in monosyllables; men are mostly silent, occupied with their own thoughts. Some laugh and chatter from a sense of bravado, or to prevent their imaginations from becoming too active; others to bolster up the shrinking spirits of their weaker comrades. Only a few are natural.

Immediately before the notorious stretch called Hell Fire Corner the mass of men marching in step along the road is directed away and out across the sun-warmed fields. They are still not under fire but a solitary shell comes whistling down from the blue sky, explodes and knocks the battalion's mounted adjutant from the saddle. So it has started. The ranks go very quiet. "We were going into something of which we had no experience. No man felt sure he would live through the coming ordeal."

Finally, they come to a halt in a field where they are to wait until dusk. During the wait the field kitchen is driven up and the soldiers are given hot tea. Immediately afterwards the horse-drawn kitchen wagons withdraw to the safety of the camp. As he watches them disappear Pollard wonders how many of his companions would really like to be going out of danger along with the cooks. Then he turns the question round and thinks that perhaps some of those leaving are envious of those who are staying.

When the sun goes down they continue their march. Spread out in a single line, they disappear into the half-darkness, following and stumbling along a railway track. The trenches waiting for them at the launching point for the attack are new, narrow and shallow. They have to wait there "herded into ours literally like sardines," in full kit, sitting in uncomfortable positions. They smoke and chat. There are simple, rough ladders ready and waiting—they have only three rungs. Although nothing is going to happen before dawn and sleep is the only truly reliable blessing left to the soldiers of this war, Pollard finds it impossible to doze off: ·

Not only was I too uncomfortable but I was far too excited. In a few hours I was to go over the top for the first time. I felt no trace of fear or even nervousness; only an anxiety to get started. The hours seemed interminable. Would the dawn never come?

An hour before the attack Pollard is sent up to the forward line to act as runner for the first wave. He is pleased. He does not think of the fact that it increases his chances of being killed or wounded. It is not a case of ignorance on his part. (In March, at the same time as the battle later known as Neuve Chapelle was ending in failure and dreadful losses for the British, he watched at close quarters and in a state of impotent despair as an attacking unit was mown down virtually to the last man by the crossfire from German Maxim machine guns.) It is rather a case of Pollard's naively childlike streak once again revealing itself: he feels that death can only strike others, not him. They have, moreover, been promised massive artillery support on this occasion—unlike in March when the contribution of the British artillery was little more than symbolic. And his role also means that he will increase his chances of doing what he has been longing to do for so long—use his weapons: "With luck I might bayonet a Hun."

The artillery firestorm begins: "Bang! Bang! Bang! Bang! Bang! Swisch! Swisch! Swisch! Swisch! Crump! Crump! Crump! Crump! Crump!"* It is soon so fierce that shouting is insufficient to make him-

* The description is Pollard's own. Anyone who has heard artillery fire will know that this is not merely a silly approximation of the different sounds: the slightly drawn-out "Bang" represents the firing, the "Swisch" is the shell passing overhead, and the shorter, more compact "Crump" is the shell detonating not too far away.

self heard, he has to scream right in the ear of the man he is talking to. When soil begins to fall on his head now and again Pollard realises that the Germans are returning their fire. The soldiers around fiddle with their equipment. Their captain turns round in all the noise, smiles and mouths the words, "Only a minute to go." They all stand up. The short ladders are put in place. The soldiers, their rifles with fixed bayonets on their backs, take up position by them, one foot ready on the lowest rung. The captain drops his hand as a signal and climbs up. Pollard is right behind him.

The attack is successful. The losses are appalling.

FRIDAY, 18 JUNE 1915
Rafael de Nogales witnesses the massacre in Sairt

They arrive rather too late, and he is very glad that they do. At a distance it is a pastoral idyll that opens out before their eyes. Herds of cows and buffalo are grazing quietly in the green fields and some dromedaries are resting by a spring under a turquoise sky. The town of Sairt is a peaceful sight: a labyrinth of oblong white houses with six slim minarets rising above them "like alabaster needles."

They ride closer.

That is when Rafael de Nogales's eyes fall on the hill.

That morning, with no beating about the bush (with a degree of satisfaction, in fact), a couple of the Turkish officers in his party said that now that all the preparations in Bitlis were complete they were just waiting for the order from above for the killing to start in Sairt. So they would have to hurry if he wanted to see it.

But they did not get there in time.

The hill lies right by the main road. It is covered with . . . something. Soon he can see what that something is. The slope . . .

> . . . was crowned with thousands of half-naked and still bleeding bodies, lying in heaps, tangled, as if in a last embrace in death. Fathers, brothers, sons and grandsons lay as they fell from the bullets or the murderers' yatagans. Heartbeats were still pumping the life-blood out of some slashed throats. Flocks of vultures sat

on top of the heap, picking the eyes out of the dead and dying, whose rigid gaze still seemed to mirror terror and inexpressible pain, while carrion dogs sank their sharp teeth into entrails still pulsing with life.

The field of bodies stretches right down to the road and in order to advance they eventually have to let their horses jump over these "mountains of corpses." Shocked and stunned, de Nogales rides into Sairt where the police and the Muslim part of the population are busy plundering the houses of the Christians. He meets some of the people in authority in the district, among them the head of the town's gendarmes, who had personally led the massacre. De Nogales receives confirmation once again that the murder of all Christian males over twelve years old is not, as in the past, a more or less spontaneous pogrom but is actually a thoroughly planned operation conceived at the centre.

He is given quarters for the night in one of the plundered buildings. De Nogales realises now that the attack is no longer aimed only at Armenians but at other Christian groups as well. This house, in fact, belonged to a Syrian family. It has been stripped of its contents apart from a couple of broken chairs. There is no trace of its former owners with the exception of an English dictionary and a tiny little picture of the Virgin Mary hidden away in a corner. Bloodstains are visible on the floor and walls.

Later, as he sits with a group of very polite and pleasant officers outside the garrison mess, the ghastly scenes continue. He is horrified but does nothing to prevent them. With the help of a forced smile he mimics understanding. A mob goes by, dragging the corpses of some children and an old man, their skulls bouncing slackly on the round cobbles of the street. The people standing around spit or swear at the corpses. De Nogales also sees a group of gendarmes leading an old man of venerable appearance:

His black robe and purple cap clearly showed him to be a Nestorian bishop.* Drops of blood were trickling down his forehead and flowing down his cheeks like the scarlet tears of martyrdom. As he passed us his eyes gave me a long look as if he could see that I too was a Christian, but then he passed on and away to that dreadful hill.

* De Nogales uses the term "Nestorian" for "Syrian."

At sunset Rafael de Nogales rides out of Sairt accompanied by his Albanian batman, the tall and well-built Tasim, and seven mounted gendarmes. De Nogales fears for his life. There is a rumour that those above want to see him liquidated, and doubts have been expressed as to his loyalty. The ride takes them south through trackless country. He wants to get to Aleppo. There he is going to apply for a discharge from the Ottoman army.

TUESDAY, 22 JUNE 1915
Laura de Turczynowicz hears the fall of Lemberg being celebrated in Suwalki

A summer evening. Laura is in the house bathing the children. A church bell rings. Then another bell begins to toll, followed immediately by two more, three more, many more. It sounds as if all the churches in Suwalki are ringing their bells and the warm air is filled with their harmonious, vibrating tones. But why?

As usual, they know little or nothing about what is happening on the battlefields. The war for them is less an event to be followed than a condition to be endured. Which should not be taken to imply that the battles are meaningless: Laura and all those round her have been hoping and praying for a Russian breakthrough, for the return of the Russian army, for liberation. Recently, however, they have heard the distant roar of battle growing louder, then weaker and finally fading away. There are rumours of German victories. So what has happened?

She is still hanging on to that wild hope. The bells are ringing and Laura's immediate thought is that the Russians have finally broken through and the Germans are ringing the bells to warn their troops in and around Suwalki that they are being encircled. A woman friend rushes in, out of breath, excited and expectant. What is happening?

Once she has got the children to bed Laura and her friend try to find out. They go out onto the balcony and look out over the streets. They can see German troops cheering and singing in the evening sunlight. Their disappointment is immediate: "We came down so rapidly from our high hopes, with hearts sick and sore from hope deferred, that I hardly cared what it was." But what was it?

One of the German hospital assistants sees her on the balcony and shouts joyfully: "Lemberg has fallen!"

The Austro-Hungarian city, which has been in the hands of the Russian army since September last year, has been recaptured. It is a great victory for the Central Powers, almost enough—but only almost—to erase the memory of last year's great defeat for the Austro-Hungarians in Galicia. It is also a personal disaster for Laura de Turczynowicz: Lemberg is where her husband, Stanislaw, is stationed* and she has not heard from him for a long time.

Anxiety and uncertainty overwhelm her. Is Stanislaw still alive? Has he been taken prisoner? Did he manage to get away? "The bells kept up their din—they seemed to beat one into the ground."

WEDNESDAY, 14 JULY 1915
Michel Corday celebrates Bastille Day in Paris

It is an overcast summer day with the sun occasionally breaking through the blanket of cloud. Michel Corday notes in his journal:

> Silent crowds of people. Wounded men, some of them with limbs amputated, soldiers on leave in greatcoats faded by the sun. As many people collecting money as there are spectators, and they are asking for contributions to a variety of benevolent causes. The regiments march past with their bands; remember that all these men are on their way to the slaughter.

At the Place de l'Étoile he sees the Foreign Minister Théophile Delcassé arrive in an open motor car. Delcassé is probably the man who has worked hardest to bring Italy into the war and he is clearly hoping to be cheered. The great crowd remains silent, however.† Corday interprets

---

* Laura had visited Stanislaw there in December, before the Germans had retaken Suwalki, and she would have moved to be with him, taking the family with her, but for the fact that there were regulations against taking children into the Russian-occupied zones.

† The expectations raised by the Italian entry into the war had not been fulfilled. This was partly because the over-optimistic advance of the Italian army was stopped almost

the silence as an unconscious protest against the war but at the same time he suspects that there would have been wild jubilation if there had been a victory to boast of. (One of the attendants at the ministry discovered a while ago that the small flags marking the front lines on the department's war map had cobwebs on them.) "The Marseillaise" rings through the air and woe betide anyone who does not remove his hat. There is the buzz of aeroplanes in the sky overhead.

President Raymond Poincaré speaks. Once again he produces an aggressive, highly emotive and cliché-laden speech about fighting "to the bitter end." Poincaré is notorious for his ham-fisted rhetoric. An article by him was published in May that some people assumed, in view of all its banality, to be a parody: it proved to be authentic. The president points to the ultimate aim of the war, which is "to banish the nightmare of German megalomania." Corday believes "There are premonitory signs here of the ill-omened results that could result from a one-sided peace. In that case he is condemning our country to a struggle so drawn out that it could almost be fatal."

For once, it is almost possible to be conscious of the war even in Paris. Almost.

THURSDAY, 29 JULY 1915
Elfriede Kuhr listens to nocturnal singing in Schneidemühl

It is dark. The air is warm. A late summer night. She does not know why she wakes up. Perhaps it is the bright moonlight. Because of the heat she is sleeping on a chaise longue out on the veranda. Everything is silent, utterly silent. The only sound to be heard is the reassuring tick of the grandfather clock in the living room. Quite suddenly Elfriede hears singing, faint but melodious and coming from the railway station next to the house. She pricks up her ears, does not recognise the tune and listens for the words. She hears more and more voices joining in and the singing

---

immediately in the rugged mountains that line the borders of Italy—the existence of the mountains seemed to come as a surprise to some of the more boneheaded of the Italian generals. And partly it was because the Italian attack led to an upsurge of commitment on the part of the Slav population of Austria-Hungary, for whom this attack—unlike the war against Russia and Serbia—provided a cause they were actually willing to die for.

grows stronger: "Es ist bestimmt in Gottes Rat, dass man vom Liebsten, das man hat, muss scheiden."*

The song rises ever stronger, ever more sonorous and clear into the bright, starry night sky, while she sinks, deeper and deeper and deeper. We are always reluctant to leave childhood and we do so step by step; at this moment Elfriede has been affected by one of those insights from which a child never really recovers and which an adult always laments. She curls up on her chaise longue and she weeps:

Why were the soldiers singing like this in the middle of the night? And why this particular song? It wasn't a soldier's song. Were the people singing it actually soldiers? Perhaps it was a transport train reaching our town and carrying army coffins with fallen men? Perhaps their mothers and fathers and widows and orphans and girlfriends were on the train? Did they weep as I wept?

Then she hears something from her grandmother's bedroom—the sound of someone blowing their nose. Elfriede gets up, tiptoes carefully in to her grandmother and says beseechingly, "Can I creep into bed with you for a while?" At first her grandmother is reluctant, but then she lifts the covers and says, "Come on, then." She cuddles up with her grandmother, presses her head to her grandmother's breast and sobs. Her grandmother's forehead is pressed against Elfriede's hair, and Elfriede can feel that she is crying too.

Neither of them explains why, they make no excuses and they ask no questions.

SATURDAY, 7 AUGUST 1915
Andrei Lobanov-Rostovsky is resting to the north-east of Warsaw

His company left the city yesterday, without losing any men, even though they had to travel along streets close to the river that were directly open to fire from German machine guns. They saw that the Germans were avoiding firing on civilians so Lobanov-Rostovsky hired civilian

---

* "It is determined in God's plan that one must part from those one loves most."

horse-drawn cabs to disguise his own wagons. Today it is calm and they are taking advantage of it . . .

> . . . to rest and take stock of our position and war materials. We were told by the Staff that the enemy had crossed the Vistula in several places but so far was not molesting our forces except for small cavalry patrols which had appeared near by. On the other hand, strategically speaking, we seemed to be at the bottom of a sack as the two corps on our flanks had retreated more quickly than we had.

SUNDAY, 8 AUGUST 1915
Vincenzo D'Aquila is laughed at in Piacenza

The smell of coal smoke. A baking sun. Dust. No one is there to meet them when the train stops at the station. The whole town seems empty of people, most of whom seem to have hidden indoors to avoid the worst of the heat. They have to find their own way through narrow, stifling alleyways to get to the army barracks to enlist.

He is more than a little disappointed not to be greeted with some gratitude at least, even if not with enthusiasm. D'Aquila and the rest of them have braved the Atlantic and the roving German U-boats in order to risk their lives "for the greatness of the Italian fatherland." Early one bright summer morning he crept out of the house in New York, hid in the hall until his father had passed and then set off for the harbour, where the vessel that would take him to Europe was lying. Not just him: he was one of about 500 Italian-Americans who were intending to enlist in the Italian army. He remembers that all sorts of people were crowded together on board: "the fools and the wise, the strong and the weak. Every walk of life was represented: doctors and quacks, lawyers and shysters, workers and drones, adventurers and vagabonds." He had also noticed, with some surprise, that many of them, in their eagerness, had come armed with weapons such as stilettos, small automatic pistols and sawn-off shotguns. He had walked impatiently round the foredeck waiting for the foghorn to announce that it was time to cast off, time for the adventure to begin. Vincenzo D'Aquila has thick, dark, curly hair, an open face, with a straight nose and a weak mouth. The impression he gives is of someone rather uncertain and slightly shy.

He was already feeling the first pangs of disappointment when they stepped ashore into the Mediterranean sun in Naples. He had been expecting an enthusiastic welcome, been hoping for "frantic cheering, flag waving, band playing, scattering of flowers by pretty Neapolitan maidens." Instead they were herded unceremoniously into a roasting-hot customs hall where they had to wait half a day before a lawyer in a Panama hat and light-coloured suit climbed up on a suitcase and gave a speech. That was all. Apart from that, no one seemed to care.

Things did not improve when it was discovered that some of his papers had got lost in the bureaucratic muddle and the army officials initially refused to enlist him. He was not the only one getting cold feet: quite a few of those who had been on the ship had second thoughts by this stage and had either taken French leave or packed themselves off home to New York again. D'Aquila has not reached that stage: he is still curious "to see what a real war looks like." (Although deep in his heart he is hoping that it will be over before he actually reaches the front, in which case he will be able to sail back to the United States without having to do anything to justify his status as hero.)

After weeks of waiting and just when D'Aquila is on the point of giving up, he is informed that they have found the missing documentation. After a hasty medical examination he is enlisted in the infantry and put on a train for Piacenza, where he is to do his basic military training. When the train stops at a small station along the way he sees a simple coffin containing the body of a dead soldier being lifted down on to the platform. The other volunteers are drinking wine and singing obscene songs.

The barracks of the 25th Regiment in Piacenza are virtually empty. Eventually they come across some men in uniform just sitting around. He and the other volunteers—with, one imagines, some pride—tell them why they have come. The uniformed men burst into mocking laughter. They find it incomprehensible—no, simply stupid—no, crazy—to leave a peaceful life on the other side of the globe voluntarily in order to take part in "the madness in which the old world was then engaged." The new arrivals are greeted with a shower of abusive names: "fools," "donkeys," "boneheads." The uniformed men themselves are intending to do anything they can to avoid the trenches. The volunteers are far from welcome as far as they are concerned: by coming here they will merely lengthen this unjust war—and all the suffering.

D'Aquila is now more than a little disillusioned. These repeated disappointments have stirred a hint of doubt in his passionate and easily moved temperament. "Our full-blown bubble of self-glorification was finally beginning to burst." He and his friend Frank, a naive and cheerful young man he met on the boat on the way over, go out into the town again. D'Aquila visits a barber to get a shave. They return to the barracks in the evening and are received by a non-commissioned officer. It is too late for regrets now. He spends that night in a large barrack room, sleeping on a mattress stuffed with straw.

WEDNESDAY, 11 AUGUST 1915[*]
Andrei Lobanov-Rostovsky oversleeps in the neighbourhood of Tchapli[†]

The corporal was actually supposed to wake them all at one o'clock. When Lobanov-Rostovsky and the men in his company bedded down at the farm, the idea was that they would just rest for a couple of hours in the dark and then set off on the march again. They are well aware that the rearguard is due to continue its retreat at two o'clock and after that time there will be nothing between them and the pursuing Germans.

Just a couple of hours' rest, then.

They are, in fact, beyond exhaustion. Earlier, Lobanov-Rostovsky was suffering from a lack of anything to do, now his problem is the opposite one. The company of sappers is fully occupied during the great retreat: if they are not blowing up bridges, setting fire to houses or tearing up railway lines, they have to assist various units in the building of trenches and everything that involves—not just digging or blasting their way down into the earth but also clearing fields-of-fire and erecting assault barriers. Unfortunately, they do not have any barbed wire, no more than they have planks and nails or even ammunition, but they

[*] Or possibly Thursday, 12 August.
[†] There are several Tchaplis (now usually transliterated Chapli) in modern Ukraine; this one is in L'vivs'ka oblast.

still erect posts which, at a distance, might fool the Germans into believing that the position is stronger than it really is. They have spent the last forty-eight hours building trenches for an infantry regiment—dreadful work and much of it done in the rain. They finished the position just in time to receive orders to abandon it.

The retreat goes on.

Lobanov-Rostovsky has a sensitive nature and he is not only tired, he is also depressed. He admitted this openly to his immediate superior, Gabrialovich, a day or so ago, confessing, "My nerves are beginning to go to pieces." Gabrialovich was indifferent, suggesting that his lieutenant was not depressed, just tired. Then he started talking about something else. Lobanov-Rostovsky is also quite concerned about his books—he has some French novels and a number of bulky history books. Anton, Lobanov-Rostovsky's loyal batman, sees no point in carting this lot around, especially as he is the one who does much of the carting. Lobanov-Rostovsky has to keep a careful eye on Anton to make sure he does not let the books disappear. The batman is particularly careless with the great three-volume work on Napoleon and Tsar Alexander by the French historian Albert Vandal: he often packs this in a way that puts the volumes at risk of sliding out while they are on the march.

So, just a couple of hours of rest, then. After that they will continue to retreat.

Lobanov-Rostovsky is the first to wake. He realises at once that something is wrong since it is broad daylight outside. He looks at his watch. Six o'clock. They have overslept by five hours.

He wakes Gabrialovich, not without some difficulty, who orders him to rouse the men, who are sleeping by the carts in the farmyard, and to bring them into the barn in complete silence. Then he is to take a cautious look to see whether the Germans have already occupied the town.

They have not.

They start moving immediately.

Their concern now is that, as well as being threatened by the German cavalry they know to be somewhere *behind* them, they are running the risk of being fired on by the Russian units retreating *in front of* them. No-man's-land in every sense. What is more, they know from their own experience that all the bridges are being blown or burnt, so will there be any way for them to cross the river?

In order to limit one of these dangers they reverse the usual order of march and put the wagons with the explosives, equipment—and books—in the lead and let the troops march along at the back. This seems to be effective since they reach the river without being attacked by their own side, and nor do they see any Germans. By great good fortune, on reaching the sparkling green river they find that one bridge is still standing: "Soldiers of an unknown regiment were preparing to destroy it and looked at us in wide-eyed amazement."

They reach the railway that runs to Bialystok at around eleven o'clock—that is also in the process of being demolished. A large armoured train is steaming back section by section while soldiers tear up the track behind it. Lobanov-Rostovsky's unit follows the train. First they blow up a bridge, then they come to a railway station which, as a matter of course, they set fire to.

The flames are already licking up the wooden walls of the building when Lobanov-Rostovsky notices a cat wandering around up on the roof, terrified and screaming helplessly. He goes and finds a ladder and climbs up to save the cat:

> The animal was scratching with his claws in such terror that it was unsafe to attempt to climb down with him so I hurled him from the two-storey building. He made two somersaults in mid-air, landed on four paws, and, with his tail erect, disappeared into the bushes.

MONDAY, 23 AUGUST 1915
Angus Buchanan guards the railway at Maktau

It is early morning. Standing guard is a cold business with the strong monsoon coming in from the south-west. At around half past five dawn begins to break and a wet mist rises and blankets the flat bush below them. The forms of the landscape become faint, vague, are blotted out. Visibility becomes virtually nil. Everything is silent except for the sounds of guineafowl, hornbills and other birds greeting the rising sun with their calls and chattering.

Buchanan and the rest of this temporary picket are guarding the Uganda railway, which passes through Maktau on its way up from

Mombasa on the coast to Kisumu on Lake Victoria. It has been a calm night. For once, one might say. Over the last week there have been almost daily engagements with German patrols from over the border who have been trying to sabotage the railway traffic. Yesterday they succeeded in blowing up a section of track, causing a train to be derailed.

That is what the war looks like in East Africa, at least for the moment: no major battles at all but patrols, skirmishes, tentative scouting, more or less successful ambushes—pinpricks across the borders. The distances are immense.* Roughly 10,000 armed men are looking for each other in an area the size of western Europe but where communications are almost non-existent. The most difficult task is not to defeat the enemy, it is to find him. Any sort of movement demands an army of bearers.

Both the climate and nature present a bewildering variety that is difficult to cope with. There is everything from damp, tropical jungle and snow-capped mountain massifs to dry savannah; what is routinely referred to simply as "bush" might consist of open plains resembling parkland or dense and almost impenetrable forests. What is more, the combatants are frequently moving across frontiers that in many ways are abstractions, arrogantly drawn on the map with a ruler and aniline pencil at some distant negotiating table in Europe without any noticeable regard for the people, languages and cultures of the places in question, nor even for the boundaries defined by nature herself.

Yet, however limited it may be, the fighting here has resulted in the colonialist logic that once created these peculiar frontiers, being replaced by a logic created by the war itself. Gone are the days of the autumn of 1914 when local governors attempted to prevent any military action. There is no longer any point in referring to old agreements or arguing that a war among whites will inevitably undermine their dominion over Africa's blacks.† The Belgians and the French have already marched into

* The scale of distances in Africa may be seen from the fact that when Buchanan's unit left Plymouth by ship it took them five days to reach Africa, but they sailed a further twenty days along the African coast before they reached their destination, Mombasa in British East Africa.

† The small civil war that broke out among the Boers in South Africa in August 1914 shows the kind of thing the colonisers were afraid of: it was between those supporting the South African government, which sided with the British (even though the Boer War was only twelve years in the past), and a militant minority seeking revenge against Britain by

Cameroon and Togo, and the rapid success of the latter invasion in particular has been the deciding factor in the decision that German East Africa must also be conquered. And just as the British fleet ignored right from the start the colonial administrators' edict that there should be no war in Africa, a military leader on the German side—Paul von Lettow-Vorbeck, who would soon achieve legendary status—disregarded the obstinate pacifism of his own civilian authorities, armed a steamship and sent it out to wage war on Lake Tanganyika, while also making aggressive raids into Rhodesia and British East Africa.

Which is why Angus Buchanan and the troops with him have just spent a cold and sleepless night on a hill near Maktau. German patrols are somewhere out there in the misty bush, though on this particular night they have kept their distance. Well, there are Germans and Germans: those in command of the small groups are Germans, clad in all the usual accoutrements of the colonists—light-coloured uniforms, cork tropical helmets and commanding appearance—but the soldiers are all professional native soldiers, *askaris*, who have been given the same training, weapons and trust as white soldiers. British decision-makers consider this to be utter madness: they want to avoid arming the Africans and hope instead to wage the war by bringing in units from South Africa and India, and by using white volunteers and troops shipped over from Europe.

Buchanan has seen little of the fighting so far, apart from one spectacular raid he and his fellow soldiers took part in last June. They attacked the small German harbour at Bukoba on the far shore of Lake Victoria. It took them a day and a half to cross the lake by boat, two days—part of the time in thunderstorms and torrential rain—to chase out the German defenders, and a couple of hours to loot the town. From a military point of view the action was meaningless, but it did serve to boost morale and looked good in the newspapers. Like quite a few of the events in this war, its primary purpose was to generate newsprint.

At nine o'clock in the morning Buchanan and his fellows are relieved. Taking their weapons and equipment, they walk back to camp through the shadows created by the fluttering leaves.

---

forming an alliance with Germany. This internal conflict ended in February 1915 with the defeat and surrender of the last pro-German rebels.

Life in the camp is the same from day to day. Reveille is at 5:30, parade and sick parade at 6:30, after which they work on the defences and fortifications until breakfast at 8:00. The meal almost always consists of tea, bread and cheese. Then another parade at 9:00, followed by more work on the defences and fortifications. As Buchanan's own account tells us:

> They laboured on in the heat, swearing and joking (I think a soldier will joke, aye, even in H—) and perspiring, and with faces and clothes smothered in the fine red lava sand, which was raised by the labouring picks and shovels, or which incessantly wafted downwards in gusts off the bare compound of the encampment.

The digging goes on until lunch, when they are given exactly the same food as in the morning except that the cheese is replaced by jam. The sun is now at its zenith in the blazing African sky and the heat makes physical work impossible so everything comes to a halt. Some of the men try to sleep "under stifling hot canvas," others wash clothes, bathe naked or play cards in the shade. There are always great swarms of flies everywhere. At 16:30 there is another parade, followed by an hour and a half's digging. Dinner is served after 18:00 and

> consisted always of badly cooked stew, an unchanging dish which became deadly monotonous, and which, in time, many men could not touch, their palate revolted so strongly against the unseasoned, uninviting mixture.

The diet is sometimes varied with the contents of parcels from home, sometimes with the meat of an animal they have managed to shoot. And sometimes merchants from Goa turn up, but their wares are exceptionally expensive, at least in comparison to normal British prices: a pound of tea, which at home would fetch a price of 1s 10d, sells here for 2s 6½d; a bottle of Worcester sauce, which goes for 9d at home, costs 2s here. The incidence of ill-health has increased enormously in recent months and Buchanan believes that at least half the cases are a result of the lack of adequate nutrition.

There is more digging after dinner and it does not stop until the light has faded into a twilight that saps all the colour from the world. The sun goes down quickly at this latitude. The remainder of the day consists of moonlight, the whine of mosquitoes and the smells of burning rubbish and red lava sand.

MONDAY, 30 AUGUST 1915
Sarah Macnaughtan gives a lecture in Cardiff

Her lecture tour began at the start of June and she has already spoken in many places: Erith, London, Sheffield, Barrow-in-Furness, Newcastle, Parkhead, Whiteinch, Rosebank, Dumbarton, Greenock; Beardmore's and Denny's shipyards. The venues have almost always been full and the audiences have sometimes numbered upwards of 3,000. Bands have played and the atmosphere has been tense—she has seen and heard grown men weep. The experience has been a powerful one for her, too: "The cheers of horny-handed workmen when they are really roused just get me by the throat till I can't speak for a minute or two." She recognises how important it all is: "Somehow I knew that I must speak, that I must arouse slackers, and tell rotters what is going on."

After the meetings she has a feeling of unreality. She lies in bed in the dark and all she can see is "a sea of faces, and eyes all turned my way." She refuses to accept payment for her lectures. She feels tired but satisfied.

Her energy is by no means at an end. One of the women she worked with earlier in Belgium has asked her whether she will come to the Russian front with a volunteer ambulance unit. After some private but well-concealed doubts Macnaughtan has said yes. Duty again: how could she have done otherwise? There is important work to be done in Russia: "The Russian wounded are suffering terribly, and getting no doctors, nurses, or field ambulances." Her maid has tried to advise her against going: "I feel sure you will never return alive, ma'am."

Macnaughtan is currently in South Wales to give a series of fourteen lectures to audiences made up predominantly of coal miners. Her tour of this district is supported by the Bute family, major mine-owners, who have her to stay with them in Cardiff Castle for the duration of the tour. There she walks in the garden, meets the organising committee and writes a little. At midday she stands on the back of a lorry and addresses several hundred dock workers.

The big meeting of the day is later that evening and is held in Cardiff's grand City Hall. The event has been advertised as "Stories and Pictures of the War" and it is packed. A military band plays and Macnaughtan is introduced by the Lord Mayor, who takes the opportunity to tell them she has just been awarded the Belgian honour "Chevalier de l'Ordre de Léopold." All eyes turn to the little woman on the stage.

And Sarah speaks.

About the war: that it is the result of a German plan, a plan that has been many years in the preparation, and it has to be seen as a test of character for all of them. About Great Britain: that the nation is afflicted by selfishness and greed, and that strikes and quarrels and the class struggle are crippling the country. About duty and principles: that this is a time when they must all gather round the flag; that they must ask whether all those present are really doing what they can. About the British army: that it may be small but it is the finest army in the history of the world (she is interrupted by applause at this point). Macnaughtan is a good speaker: energetic and clear and with a good rapport with her audience.

A local journalist reports the rest of the speech:

> Miss Macnaughtan then related a number of interesting incidents, one of which was, that when a party of wounded Englishmen came to a station where she was tending the Belgian wounded, every wounded Belgian gave up their bed to accommodate an English soldier. The idea of a German occupation of English soil, she said, was the idea of a catastrophe that was unspeakable. People read things in the papers and thought they were exaggerated, but she had seen them, and she would show photographs of ruined Belgium which would convince them of what the Germans were now doing in the name of God. However unprepared we were for war, the wounded had been well cared for, and she thought there never was a war in which the care of the wounded had been so well managed or so efficient. (Applause.) They had to be thankful that there had been no terrible epidemic, and she could not speak too highly of the work of the nurses and doctors in the performance of their duties. This was the time for every man to do his duty, and strain every nerve and muscle to bring the war to an end and get the boys home again. (Applause.)

The speaker who follows her asks the audience whether they are prepared "to fight for right till right had won." They all rise to their feet, raise their hands in the air and roar a resounding "Aye" in unison. Then Macnaughtan shows her lantern slides of villages and towns destroyed by the Germans. The meeting comes to an end.

ONE DAY AT THE END OF AUGUST 1915
Laura de Turczynowicz is filled with despair in Suwalki

The summer is coming to an end. Lemberg has fallen. Zamość has fallen. Przasnysz has fallen. Windau has fallen. Pułtusk has fallen. Ivangorod has fallen. Warsaw has fallen. Kovno has fallen. Novo-Georgievsk has fallen. Brest-Litovsk has fallen. For Laura and the people in Suwalki the seemingly endless series of German victories on the Eastern Front are not just distant abstractions on a map, they also have direct consequences. The armies are moving north-east and the town no longer has any "military significance." The columns of horse-drawn wagons and singing infantrymen are becoming a less frequent sight and units that have been stationed in the town for some time are now moving on. Things are getting quieter. It is weeks since anyone heard the sound of cannon.

The children are ill again. Dysentery this time, with bloody diarrhoea. Once again she is trapped in a nightmare cycle of vigil and endless worry. A German army doctor who has helped her before helps her again and gives the children cholera serum. The outcome is uncertain. And the shortage of food has become acute.

Laura does not know how much longer she can go on. (She is not alone in this. More and more people in the town are committing suicide, acts of pure despair caused by a lack of food or an equally dreadful lack of hope. One acquaintance hanged herself in a wardrobe.) She has applied several times to the German authorities for permission to leave Poland—she is an American, after all. But permission has been refused every time. She writes:

Something broke down in me those days. I had come to the point where I knew if we were not released it meant giving up my children; and now I wished to give them up rather than see them suffer. I had clung to them so desperately, calling on them not to leave me. They had been left to me, but now I was willing to leave the decision to the Higher Power, not forcing things my way. Looking Death in the eyes, one loses the fear of Him.

One of the twins is in a particularly bad way. She spoon-feeds him with red wine, one drop at a time.

THURSDAY, 9 SEPTEMBER 1915
Michel Corday takes the train to Paris

An autumn morning, and an autumn feel to the air. Michel Corday is on the train to Paris. As usual he finds it hard not to eavesdrop on the conversations of his fellow passengers. Some of them are leafing through the morning papers they have just bought. One of them asks: "Anything new?" The answer is brief: "A Russian victory." Corday is amazed. Are they unaware of the fact that the Russians have been retreating ever since the German-Austrian breakthrough at Gorlice and Tarnów in the middle of May? Those laconic remarks are the only references to the war on the whole trip from Fontainebleau to Paris.

He recalls another railway journey, when he saw a woman at a station skimming through the official war communiqué in a newspaper and then exclaiming in a very satisfied voice: "We have advanced 400 metres!" Then she immediately proceeded to talk about other things. Corday comments: "That's enough for them. Enough to satisfy them completely."

Once he reaches his office he talks on the telephone to Tristan Bernard, a close friend and successful vaudeville writer. Bernard shares Corday's scepticism about the war and is always quick to make caustic comments about what is going on. Talking of the developments on the Eastern Front he has said that the Russians "always retreat in good order whereas the Germans advance successfully in disorder." (With reference to the attacks on Tout-Vent and Moulin-sous-Touvent, two places very distant from each other, he claims that one of the attacks was a mistake caused by someone at headquarters quite simply muddling up the names: the attack that was never intended to happen was the one that succeeded.)

These two men know—as do many others—that the Allies are pre-paring to mount a major offensive up in Artois and in Champagne. Most people are pinning enormous hopes on this. Since the two of them know their conversation might well be listened in to, they have developed a pri-vate code so that they can discuss the planned action. They pretend that they are writing a play together and questions about dates are camou-flaged as questions about page numbers. Thus, when Bernard enquires whether the manuscript has been expanded or cut, what he really wants to know is whether the date for the offensive has been brought forward or moved back. (At one point there was a rumour that the operation had been cancelled and the question then asked was, "Is it true the man-uscript has been thrown in the fire?") Bernard now asks Corday how many pages the manuscript adds up to. Corday answers, "Fifteen."

Later Corday reads a circular the Ministry of Education is sending out to all schools before the approaching autumn term. The circular exhorts teachers in all subjects to remind their pupils about the war in the most explicit way possible: "heroic examples and the noble lessons that can be drawn from them" should be given special emphasis.

On this same day Florence Farmborough, who is exhausted, writes in her journal:

> At 7 a.m. I tumbled out of bed, I was on duty from 7:30 onwards, and walked downstairs with a heavy head and legs which felt they would crumble under me at every step. Ekaterina, whom I relieved, looked white and drawn from sleeplessness; she was puffing away at a cigarette outside the dressing-room door. "Slava Bogu!" [Thank God!] she said brusquely. "Now I can go and get some sleep," and she threw the end of her cigarette away. There had been no wounded to occupy her hands; I could well believe that the hours had hung heavily.

Today Laura de Turczynowicz is making a short trip in a cab to visit the area where the family's summer villa had been. Her mind is easier: her application to be allowed to leave Poland and return to the United States has at last been approved by the German authorities. She writes:

We drove a little way from Suwalki. I wondered why we didn't come to the woods of Augustów—but then understood. The woods were all gone—graves, myriads of graves instead. I begged the man to turn around; it was too much to bear. The town, in its desolation was not much better—roofless houses, and windowless—and doorless; no animals, no people, and no children! They were gone—wiped out! There I made also a pilgrimage to say good-bye to the old house, our palace! Most of it I had not seen in months, and now I am sorry I looked upon it in its desecration.

FRIDAY, 10 SEPTEMBER 1915
Elfriede Kuhr visits the military cemetery outside Schneidemühl

There is a war cemetery immediately outside the town and it has grown significantly in the last six months. The road there passes through a dark pine wood and then through a beautiful ornamental gateway. Elfriede and a schoolfriend have decided to visit the cemetery today. Elfriede is carrying a bouquet of roses in her hand.

They see an empty, freshly dug grave. Alongside it six spades lie waiting. Elfriede drops her bouquet into the grave and says to her friend, "When a soldier is buried here he will rest on my flowers." At that moment a small funeral procession enters through the carved gateway: a group of soldiers with rifles comes first, followed by an army chaplain and then a small cart with a plain black coffin. Bringing up the rear is a small funeral party carrying a large burial wreath. The little procession stops at the open grave and the soldiers form up.

> The coffin was lifted from the cart and carried to the grave. The command "Attention! Present arms!" rang out. The soldiers stood as if rooted to the ground. The coffin was slowly lowered into the earth. The soldiers removed their helmets and the chaplain said a prayer. Then another command: "Load! Ready! Fire!" The soldiers fired three volleys over the coffin. Six men then stepped forward, took up the spades and shovelled earth on to the coffin lid. It made a dull, hollow sound.

Elfriede stands there trying to imagine how the man in the coffin is slowly disappearing beneath the earth that is being thrown in. "Now his face is covered . . . now his chest, now his stomach."

Afterwards they ask the cemetery superintendent who was being buried. "An airman—non-commissioned rank," he answers. "Almost certainly an accident. But you never know. Sometimes they drink too much."

SUNDAY, 12 SEPTEMBER 1915
Laura de Turczynowicz travels from Suwalki to Berlin

It is a cold morning, grey and misty. As the cart carrying Laura and the children moves off she takes a last look back. Her glance does not settle on the house but on the piano, the piano that German soldiers carried outside during an alcohol-fuelled party sometime at the beginning of the summer and which has remained out there in the open air ever since. The instrument, once so elegant but now ruined by the rain and the sun, stands crookedly, leaning to one side, with one leg broken.

Laura feels surprisingly little as they leave the grand house behind them. In the same way as the house has been emptied of its contents bit by bit, she has been emptied of emotions. What had once been her home is now just a place of suffering.

Right up to the last minute she is afraid something is going to happen, that someone will suddenly appear and stop them. The station is full of German soldiers who will be travelling on the same train. The children and Laura and their white dog, Dash, climb down and Laura is introduced to the captain who is to be her escort on the journey. Laura is tired since she neither could nor dared sleep the night before, but the captain and his men are even more tired. They have been on the move for six weeks almost without a break and the German officer is so far gone in exhaustion that he can hardly make himself understood.

Laura takes charge of their luggage and makes sure that all three pieces are on board. Then it is time to say a few hasty words of farewell to the cook. Laura gives her a little money and tells her where she has hidden a bottle of ether to be used to put Dash down if there is insufficient food to keep him. It is impossible to take the little dog with them and he has begun to sense it and is becoming agitated.

Then the train departs.

Laura sees the cook disappearing from sight. She sees a friend of the family waving goodbye with her hat. She sees the flat, devastated autumn landscape open out round them. She sees ruins. She sees prisoners of war working. She feels relief but she also feels worried because they are on their way into the country of the enemy. East Prussia. Germany.

Marggrabowa. They get out to change trains and to have their papers inspected. The station is full of people, many of them well-dressed ladies and young women waiting for a transport train of wounded soldiers due to arrive soon. Laura and the children can find no bench to sit on so they sit on the floor in a corner and wait. Time passes. The children are tired and whining. People standing around look at them inquisitively. The children become more and more restless, moan and make a fuss. Laura is at the end of her tether and snaps at them to be quiet and, forgetting herself, does it in English.

The reaction from those around is immediate. *"Engländerin!"* a couple of the women shriek. Laura tries to explain—*"Nein, Amerikanerin!"*—but no one listens. She is surrounded by a circle of threatening figures, most of them women, who hurl abuse and throw things at her. Laura presses into the corner, hiding the terrified children under her skirts. After what seems like "a century" the officer escorting her pushes through the crowd and leads them away. They get into the waiting train and Laura sits rubbing gobbets of spit from her clothes.

Insterburg. It is evening by now and they change trains again. The children are "miserable, a little hungry and thirsty." In spite of having first-class tickets they soon lose their compartment. The train rolls on all night through the dark, foreign countryside.

Berlin. It is six o'clock in the morning.

Three days later Laura de Turczynowicz and her three children cross the border into Holland. At Bentheim they and their luggage—what is left of it—are subjected to a thorough search. Under the supervision of a German official, a woman, they are stripped naked and their clothes are examined so closely that even the linings of their jackets and their shoes are slit open. Laura's hair is parted with a toothcomb to ensure that there are no hidden messages written on her scalp. Apart from the clothes they are standing in she is permitted to keep only the children's birth certificates, three photographs and a prayer book. That is all. Then they are allowed to continue. As the train enters Holland she begins to shake uncontrollably.

SATURDAY, 25 SEPTEMBER 1915
René Arnaud sees the start of the great offensive in Champagne

A south-westerly wind. Grey, low clouds. Rain. An ordinary autumn day. But here in south-eastern Champagne and also further to the north, up in Artois, it is anything but ordinary, for the big day—*le jour*—has at last arrived. In Champagne, two French armies—Pétain's Second and de Langle de Cary's Fourth—are about to attack on a front ten miles wide with the aim of driving the Germans up along the Meuse towards Belgium. That is one axis of the offensive. Simultaneously, in Artois, the British and the French are to attack round Loos and the Vimy Ridge. That is the other axis.

It is true that exactly the same thing was tried as recently as last spring, and in almost exactly the same places. And it is true that the successes were small and the losses considerable,[*] but things are different this time: the preparations have been much more thorough and the numbers of attacking soldiers and supporting guns are much greater— about 2,500 artillery pieces have been installed in Champagne. No one seems to wonder whether all these weapons are perhaps being used in the wrong way: the only solution they can imagine is to use more weapons,

---

[*] Up in Artois the French lost more than 100,000 men and the British about 26,000: the gains were marginal—no more than a mile or so. The first British attack, at Neuve Chapelle on 9 May, was a total failure, which was quickly blamed on the worthless preliminary bombardment by the artillery—a barrage of no more than forty minutes with almost exclusively light guns, severely handicapped by a shortage of high-explosive shells. This marked the start of the "Shell Scandal" in Great Britain, which led both to demands for the resignation of the Asquith government and to a radical reorganisation of munitions production and, indeed, of the whole war economy. It was this crisis that really caused the British public for the first time to recognise what it was going to take to win the war.

more guns, more shells. The solution to the equation equals mass and weight.* And the aim of this double offensive has been set very high: it is not just a case of winning some ground; the aim is nothing less than "to drive the Germans out of France," to quote Order of the Day No. 8565 issued by Joseph Joffre, commander-in-chief of the French army, to the troops who are now waiting to attack. The intention is that the order will be read out to the men. And this operation is to be no more than a beginning—breaking through the German lines here in Champagne and up in Artois will signal the start of a general offensive.

It marks a return to the illusions of 1914, more particularly to the dream of a rapid victory.† Expectations are pitched at the same very high level as the aims and the preparations: if Joffre can pull off what he is promising, the war could be over by Christmas!

René Arnaud is one of the men looking forward to the offensive. He has been impressed by the preparations in terms of their scale, their thoroughness, their mass and their weight: the enormous troop movements, the digging of new connecting trenches, the huge stockpiles of shells, the assemblage of both heavy and light artillery, the number of cavalry ready and waiting and, of course, "the constant buzz of brown and yellow aeroplanes above our heads, targeted unsuccessfully by enemy shells from which white puffs of smoke would suddenly burst into flower in the sky like Japanese paper flowers cast onto water, to be followed immediately by the sound of muffled explosions." Based on the evidence he can see before him and on Joffre's promise, Arnaud, too, is convinced that this is the turning point. He writes in a letter home:

---

* However thorough their preparations, there was one factor the Allies could do nothing about, which was that the Germans held the ridges and higher ground along almost the whole of the front. This is because the Western Front became fixed wherever the Germans decided to break off their retreat (or their advance) and they had, of course, chosen to halt where the terrain was most advantageous to them. This gave the Germans the advantage of better visibility and, in places where the water table was high—particularly in Flanders—allowed them to dig in much more thoroughly and to a much greater depth than the Allies, who were stuck with the lower-lying ground. These factors were a major cause of concern to the Allies in virtually all their offensives.
† This illusion should be seen as a consequence of earlier experiences rather than of a complete lack of imagination. The most recent European war had been the Franco-Prussian War of 1870–71, and that had certainly been decided quickly. Which shows how deceptive historical parallels can be.

Our commanders have promised us success to such an extent
that they must be completely convinced of it. And if we were to
fail, what a miscalculation that would be, what a crisis of morale
and fighting spirit that would imply for all the troops engaged!

The preparations include the distribution of a completely new piece of
equipment—the steel helmet. They are quite light, painted blue (to match
the new, pale blue-grey uniform), decorated with a small ridge across the
top and a flaming grenade badge on the front. The French army is the
first to introduce this novelty. As with quite a few other "new" pieces of
equipment (steel shields for the trenches, spiked clubs for assault troops,
sharpened infantry spades and all the different kinds of hand grenade)
they remind one of earlier centuries and reveal how, paradoxically, the
hypermodern can be a return to the past. Helmets are a necessity in the
trenches: it has become obvious that head wounds account for a dispro-
portionately large percentage of battlefield injuries and that they are far
more likely to be fatal.[*] Although the helmets are unlikely to provide protection against a rifle bullet, they will stop a bullet from a shrapnel shell
without difficulty. Arnaud and his men, however, find it difficult to take
these contraptions seriously—they seem so . . . unmilitary: "We shrieked
with laughter when we tried them on, as if they were carnival hats."

Arnaud's regiment, in a state of readiness for the start, is positioned
in a wood out on the right flank. In front of them they can see a shallow river and beyond the river lies another wood, Bois de Ville, where
the Germans are said to be, but they have seen and heard very little of
the enemy. (The battlefield is, as usual, empty. Not a man in sight.) That
wood is their first objective, once the main attack has secured the German
forward lines, that is; then the idea is that the German defences on both
sides of the breakthrough should be rolled up. When the German lines
have "crumbled," Arnaud's regiment is "to pursue the retreating enemy
with the assistance of the cavalry" and so on. Soon. Mass and weight.

---

* Early statistics indicated that just over 13 per cent of all battlefield injuries were head
wounds and no less than 57 per cent of these were fatal. Head wounds were much more
common than in earlier wars: the troops were now spending much of their time in
trenches where, for obvious reasons, the head was the most exposed part of the body.
The custom of cutting the hair short was introduced during the First World War, not (as
is often assumed) as a way of dealing with lice but because it made the treatment of head
wounds faster and simpler.

They have been witnesses to the firestorm for four days now and it has undeniably been spectacular:

The shells from our 155mm guns have been falling regularly on the edges of Bois de Ville with terrifying explosions. From the protection of the raised ground behind us a battery of 75mm guns has been firing its four pieces one after the other, making the air vibrate as if from the ringing of four bells. The shells whined as they passed over our heads and then, after a short silence, came the four sharp barks as they struck home. Under this torrent of fire we thought that everything in the enemy lines must inevitably be pounded to dust.

The clocks are ticking away. The attack is set for 9:15. Arnaud peers through the misty grey rain at the point he knows the first attack will take place.

Then it starts. Arnaud sees very little. Just "black shapes advancing slowly in broken lines." The dots work their way towards the German forward trenches, which are veiled in smoke. Then the attackers are swallowed up by the clouds and are no longer visible.

Soon there are rumours of a great victory and that the cavalry has broken through. There is great excitement. But why has Arnaud's regiment not been ordered to attack? They remain in the wood and wait. What has happened?

Three days later, on Tuesday, 28 September, all attacks are called off. The offensive has been held by the German second line and by the rapid arrival of German reserves. (It has been proved yet again that soldiers on trains move faster than soldiers on foot.) The French have taken roughly two miles of ground at a cost of 145,000 men dead, wounded, missing or captured. Arnaud's regiment never needs to attack Bois de Ville.

THURSDAY, 30 SEPTEMBER 1915
Alfred Pollard is wounded outside Zillebeke

How is he supposed to feel? Pollard is depressed and hungover and ashamed, having just received a terrible dressing-down from the colonel because, in his haste, he forgot to put on his puttees. But he is also excited about the mission he has been given. He has always longed for a chance to shine—and now is his opportunity.

Not that he takes things easy. His platoon commander has had an eye on this big, aggressive and utterly fearless twenty-two-year-old who takes every opportunity to be involved in the fighting, who never fails to volunteer for dangerous tasks and who sometimes sets off into no-man's-land of his own accord. On one of these trips Pollard found in a crater a Burberry coat with only a few shrapnel holes in it and, alongside the coat, a detached head standing upright, with no sign of a body. He found the sight "so droll and yet so pathetic." He now wears the coat in bad weather. He sometimes fantasises about the head. Was he a friend or foe? Was he a brave man, killed "whilst he was dashing forward in a charge full of the lust of battle" or was he just someone "cowering down in sickening fear"?

Pollard has just been promoted to sergeant and second in command of the battalion's bombing platoon,* which he trained himself and then, with his usual zeal, drilled time after time in the art of throwing grenades.

His moment has come. The great British attack at Loos began five days ago, well prepared and with large numbers of men, but yet again their efforts have failed to produce any significant results beyond colossal British losses. (Two of the divisions involved have lost half their strength, dead and wounded, in just a couple of days.) And as usual, the fighting has spread to other sections of the front. The Germans have detonated a large mine under the British lines in a wood the British call Sanctuary Wood† at Zillebeke outside Ypres, and then they occupied the enormous,

---

* Most British battalions had a bombing platoon, its members specialists in the use of explosives. During the First World War this meant primarily Mills grenades and gun cotton.

† It was given its name during the fighting of October 1914 when fleeing British soldiers gathered there and a local commander gave them permission to stay there temporarily rather than return to the fighting. By this stage, however, the wood was anything but a

corpse-filled crater it made. Pollard's bombing platoon has been ordered to retake the crater.

The platoon has been divided into two sections, one of them under Pollard's command, the other led by the platoon officer, Hammond. The plan is that the two groups should work their way forward through the trenches and then move round the crater from opposite sides until they meet. Their main weapons are hand grenades, which they are carrying in sacks. The private soldiers are also carrying clubs for hand-to-hand combat. Pollard feels no fear of what is to come, in fact he is grateful to have been given the task. He views the whole thing as a bit of a competition and he is determined that his part of the platoon will get further round the crater than Hammond's.

Pollard's mind is not, however, entirely dominated by his eagerness for action. For some considerable time he has been corresponding with a woman whose family he knows, a woman who has been sending him gifts and friendly, encouraging letters. He is head over heels in love, has christened her "My Lady," "the most divine and wonderful creature who has ever existed," and—bearing in mind that severed head—he hopes that her name will be the last words to pass his lips if he should meet the same fate. (Her name, incidentally, is Mary.) A few weeks ago he wrote a letter in which he proposed to her.

Yesterday he received her reply. In her letter Mary expressed something close to dismay at his proposal, telling him that if she were ever to consider marriage he would probably be the last man she would choose. Shocked and depressed by the response, Pollard went off to a pub in a nearby village and got drunk on champagne. He was still drunk when he was woken up with the news of his mission.

A short bombardment begins at three o'clock and immediately afterwards the group of men sets off through the trenches in all the noise. There are tall, leafy trees all around them. They have gone little more than fifty yards when they are stopped by a tall barricade of sandbags. They all start throwing hand grenades over it: *Bang! Bang! Bang! Zunk! Zunk! Zunk!* Three minutes later the response arrives in the form of German stick grenades that come sailing down. More bangs and zunks. This continues

---

sanctuary, but the name had stuck. It is perhaps worth mentioning that there is now a curious little café there, where, for a small fee, the fenced and preserved remnants of some trenches as well as a quite improbable collection of rusty bric-a-brac from the 1914–18 war may be viewed.

for a while until Pollard loses patience. According to the method he was taught at the grenade-training school, Pollard, as the leader, should be in position number five in the group, but he now goes to the front instead.

After three soldiers have each thrown five grenades in quick succession, Pollard and six men climb up out of the trench in order to circumvent the barricade. The Germans have obviously been expecting this because the men are immediately caught in cross-fire. Four of the six fall. Pollard, however, survives and jumps down into the trench, where he is met by the explosion of a German grenade. The shock wave hurls him back against the barricade and he can see small red spots all over his uniform where splinters have entered his body. He gets up.

His group tears down the barricade and rushes on through the twists and turns of the trench. They are throwing grenades in front of them the whole time. The Germans they are pursuing are falling back but others at the side climb up in the trees and open fire on Pollard's group from a range of no more than forty yards. One by one Pollard's men drop. He turns to give one of his soldiers an order but at the same moment the man receives a bullet in the throat. Pollard then enters a strange, dream-like state:

> It was just as though my spirit were detached from my body. My physical body became a machine doing the bidding, coolly and accurately, which my spirit dictated. Something outside myself seemed to tell me what to do, so that I was never quite at a loss. At the same time I felt quite certain I should pull through.

They reach a second barricade of sandbags and pass it in the same way as the first. As Pollard turns to one of his remaining men to hand him a sack of hand grenades, the man simply crumples. At the same moment he feels his right arm drop and the sack slip from his grasp. A bullet has gone right through the man in front of him, turned through 180 degrees and continued on into Pollard's shoulder, blunt end first. There it lodges. Through a haze he sees a red patch spreading on the sleeve of his tunic. His knees give way. Someone gives him a mixture of water and rum to drink. He gets up unsteadily and urges his men on.

Among the last things he remembers is thinking that he must not faint: "Only girls faint."

Then he faints.

SUNDAY, 3 OCTOBER 1915
Vincenzo D'Aquila spends the night firing his rifle

The order is at once both clear and incomprehensible. This very morning Vincenzo and the others have been sent to the trenches as replacement troops for the 7th Company of the 2nd Battalion of the 25th Regiment. They are soaked after having spent the night in the open. The trench itself is right in the forward line, looking towards the cone-shape of Monte Santa Lucia on the Isonzo. D'Aquila ends up in a sideshoot of one of the sap trenches. There is a deep and steep-sided valley separating the Italian lines from the Austrian, and the latter also have the advantage of being at a higher level. D'Aquila's company commander is a warrant officer by the name of Volpe.

The beginners are given instructions. Once the sun sets they must all start firing. All of them. And they should keep on firing all night. The aim is partly to disturb the enemy and partly to guard against possible surprise attacks in the darkness.

The last broken rays of the setting sun fade away on the horizon and the scene shifts from grey to black. The shooting starts. Along the whole section of the front held by the battalion rifle muzzles flash rapidly. D'Aquila is amazed by this aimless firing out into the darkness and by the enormous waste of ammunition: time after time he has heard how ill prepared Italy was for this war, how there is a shortage of everything from money and food to guns and ammunition and so on. He is also amazed that he, against all probability, is now in a position to take the life of another human being. Like very many of the other volunteers his thoughts have mainly focused on his *own* death, not on the fact that he is expected to kill other people.

D'Aquila looks at the sky. It is bright and starry. No, he neither will nor can kill anyone. But what will happen if he refuses to obey orders? D'Aquila comes to a decision. He wanted this, and he came here of his own free will. He will not refuse to attack when the time comes; when they tell him to leave the trench and storm those apparently impregnable Austrian positions up there on the small mountain, he will do so. He will take his chances. But he will not kill. No. Not now, and not ever. And perhaps some higher power will see his decision, recognise it with approval and, in the name of symmetry, spare D'Aquila himself from all harm. D'Aquila raises his loaded rifle, aims it up into the darkened sky and pulls the trigger. In the course of the night he fires hundreds of rounds in this ineffectual and meaningless way.

Not until dawn is approaching does the firing begin to slacken off. As the wisps of morning mist rise, silence falls over the mezzotint autumn colours of the valley.

Pál Kelemen is on the Serbian border that morning and he notes in his journal:

> We are in camp on the vast endless plain. Military and horses all around. Lead gray clouds hang low on the horizon. The Danube marshes start here; the rich Hungarian plain melts into the immense stretch of reed. German infantry is marching southward with resounding steps. Under the wind the sedge bows weakly, as if everything must tremble at the roar of the heavy guns over on the Danube.

WEDNESDAY, 6 OCTOBER 1915
Florence Farmborough leaves Minsk suffering from toothache

There is a new bite in the air. Gradually the nights are getting longer and colder. One of Florence's molars has been giving vague but definite twinges of discomfort that today has developed into a distinct and painful throbbing. She is sitting in her wagon, silent and dogged, her face covered by the veil she wears as protection against the sun and the dust on the march.

They left Minsk three days ago, its streets filled with people in uniform and its shop windows full of expensive goods. The city came as a revelation to her, not least because it sparkled with colours like pinks and whites, colours she and her companions have almost forgotten after months of existing with the many shades of brown of the earth, of the road and of uniforms. With simultaneous feelings of embarrassment and pride she and the other nurses have been able to compare themselves—badly fitting and discoloured clothes, rough, red and scabby hands, weary and sunburnt faces—with the well-dressed and immaculately made-up society ladies of Minsk. And then they moved on, in slightly strange high spirits, to the familiar sounds of the dull echo of artillery fire and the indistinct buzzing of aeroplanes, passing through fields still green and woods turning yellow and red and rust-brown.

The great Russian retreat is practically at an end. Both sides are beginning to dig in for the winter. Florence's unit is now marching at a noticeably slower pace. On an ordinary day the long, swaying column of horse-drawn wagons covers eighteen miles at most. But they are pleased to no longer be fleeing; they are even beginning to hope for a new turn of events.

Traces of the retreat are still visible in the surrounding fields and ditches. There are scores of dead animals of all kinds, animals that people had taken with them to prevent them falling into the hands of the enemy but which, fairly predictably, died as a result of the long daily marches. She sees dead cows, dead pigs and dead sheep. They awaken a memory:

> I remembered seeing a horse fall during the early months of the Retreat; I think it was in the dreadful sand of Molodychi. The men cut it hastily out of the gun-carriage harness and left it lying by the roadside, without so much as a word of regret. As we passed, I remember how its sides heaved and its eyes looked at us like the eyes of a human being being forsaken, and left to suffer and die in solitude.

They come to a halt. The long column stops. They have reached a place where the road cuts across a peat moss covered with spruce trees and some of the wagons in the other flying unit have stuck fast. Slowly, one at a time, the wagons are dragged free, and then they scatter spruce branches over the ground to make passage a little more secure.

They jerk into motion again and Florence sinks back into her isolated world where little or nothing exists apart from that aching tooth. Only once does she lift her veil and that is when they drive into an area where the stench is unusually strong. She hears agitated and questioning voices. It turns out they are passing a heap of some twenty cadavers, many of them horses, that have been lying there infecting the air for weeks.

No one knows exactly what is to happen next. The latest order says that they should attach themselves to the 62nd Division, which is located somewhere in the district.

Laura de Turczynowicz and the children are now on a transatlantic liner taking them from Rotterdam to New York. The quiet and security of Holland have been exchanged for all the noise and sense of isolation an ocean voyage involves. There are a number of American Red Cross nurses on board but Laura avoids them, having discovered that they are all pro-German. A doctor on board has examined the children and found them to be "surprisingly well" and only in need of "quiet for the nerves and proper food for the body." But in spite of leaving Europe and the war behind her, Laura is still gripped by anxiety—it is as though anxiety has become a bad habit. In Holland she took the opportunity to send a telegram to Petrograd, to be forwarded to her husband, Stanislaw. In it she tells him that they are all alive and now on their way to the United States. But is Stanislaw himself still alive? It is a long time since she received any word of him. And does anyone know where Laura is going? Does she know herself? "The nearer we got to America the more alone I felt."

THURSDAY, 28 OCTOBER 1915
Vincenzo D'Aquila witnesses the unsuccessful storming of Monte Santa Lucia

It is like having a seat in the front row, and not just in a metaphorical sense. The position D'Aquila finds himself in really was designed for observation, a place from which the course of attacks could be monitored through field glasses. The weather is clear for once, so watching the columns storming up the mountainsides should not present a problem.

Orderlies, batmen and the rest of them have got the observation post ready. The damage done to the carefully applied camouflage of branches by the wind during the night has been fixed; tables and chairs have been laid out and the field telephones have been tested. Everything is overlaid by a fuzzy blanket of sound, in which the noise of one explosion scarcely has time to fade before another replaces it. On the other side of the valley the final stage of Italian drum fire is pounding the Two Sisters—Monte Santa Lucia and Monte Santa Maria—and their forested slopes are wreathed in the white smoke from explosions. Binoculars and sherry are laid out.

Somewhere down there the 7th Company is waiting in a trench to start the attack. D'Aquila is not with them: with the unexpected help of his company commander he has managed to find a posting in which there is no risk of having to kill nor of being killed. He has become an assistant on the headquarters staff because, thanks to his American background, he has a novel and unusual skill—he can type. The shock that hit him that first night in the trench has not receded and D'Aquila has instead entered a state that resembles a confused religious crisis. It manifests itself in two ways: on one hand, it takes the form of brooding on what a Christian can permit himself to do in this situation; on the other, there is his hope that faith can somehow save him and, in his ever more agitated mind, this hope has gradually become his comfort. He has twice taken part in night patrols out into no-man's-land and on both occasions, in spite of considerable dangers, has returned unharmed. Has he been chosen? And he sees his unexpected posting to the brigade staff as yet another intervention by a higher power.

What he experiences during his time on the staff, however, does not make him any the less anxious and guilt ridden. Rather the opposite.

The staff officers emerge from their protected bunker. They have breakfasted on chocolate and toast and rounded it off with wine. Now they go down into the well-protected observation post. All the underlings immediately make room for them and greet them with smart salutes. The senior officers accept the salutes in a rather distracted manner and take their seats. The orderlies push in their chairs and hand them binoculars.

The performance can begin.

The bombardment ceases. The last shells whistle through the cool air and fall on the Two Sisters. The bursts of white smoke disperse in the air.

Silence falls.

It remains silent for a long time.

Then it becomes possible to see movement in the forward Italian trenches. Spread-out chains of men in grey-green uniforms are beginning to move towards the steep mountainsides. One of these clusters of men, scrambling, climbing, crawling and jumping, is D'Aquila's company, the 7th. It all happens slowly. At this distance their posture and their way of moving is reminiscent of people looking for something. Then comes the hollow rattle of Austrian machine guns—Schwarzlose machine guns. One by one they open fire from invisible nests somewhere up there on the wooded peaks. In spite of days of bombardment the Italian artillery has failed to silence them. There are two weapons that now dominate the battlefields: the artillery and the machine gun. Ordinary foot soldiers have increasingly become their servants (and their victims), whose task is to occupy terrain that has been swept clean by the hail of shells and to protect the machine guns while they perform their function. As they are doing here. The machine guns rap and the lines of men are thinned out, slow down, fall to the ground, turn back.

This jerky, disjointed procedure is repeated time after time down there in the valley. A company will rise from its trenches, work its way a little up the mountainside, lie down to avoid the lash of machine-gun fire and finally flee back, decimated. After a while another attempt will be made, which will also fail, since there are fewer men than before; they, too, will turn back, their ranks even thinner, only to be ordered out yet again. And so it continues.

D'Aquila is horrified, not just by the realisation that some of those dark, motionless stains on the distant hillside are his comrades but also by the indifference of the senior officers and the complete absence of any tactical finesse. All the warring parties have recognised by this stage that the firepower of the armies has become so overwhelming that attackers will inevitably suffer heavy losses. Yet many generals still subscribe to the pre-war illusion that it is possible to compensate for firepower with pure and simple willpower—the will to struggle on forward through the hail of bullets, irrespective of losses. But whose will, that is the issue? Towards the end of the day D'Aquila hears a conversation on the field telephone. The captain of a company of Alpini telephones and begs that his men be spared from making further attacks. His elite Alpine troops have stormed the mountainside fifteen times and fifteen times they have been beaten back. Of 250 men, barely twenty-five are left. The commander rejects the request and tells the man holding the receiver to remind the captain of the oath he swore to Italy and to the Crown.

The Alpini company attacks one last time. That attack also fails. The captain is not one of the survivors: the rumour is that he took his own life.

On 30 October D'Aquila is given an order to type out on his machine: it announces that all attacks are to be suspended for the present. Thus ends what has since been called the Third Battle of the Isonzo. Not a single one of its objectives has been achieved.[*]

A few days later the Italian army celebrates All Saints' Day with particular reverence. D'Aquila eventually discovers that one of those killed in the unsuccessful attack was his good friend Frank.

Sarah Macnaughtan is on her way to the Russian front. She and her party have arrived in Petrograd on the 28th after a long journey through Norway, Sweden and Finland. They move into a hotel. Then there is the first of a series of meetings. (No one knows exactly where their unit is to be sent in.) She notes in her diary:

> There is a story I try to tell, but something gets into my throat, and I tell it in jerks when I can. It is the story of the men who played football across the open between the enemy's line of trenches and our own when it was raked by fire. When I had finished, a friend of mine, evidently waiting for the end of a pointless story, said, "What did they do that for?" (Oh, ye gods, have pity on men and women who suffer from fatty degeneration of the soul!)

SUNDAY, 31 OCTOBER 1915
Pál Kelemen witnesses the hanging of a Serbian guerrilla fighter

The invasion of Serbia by the Central Powers is going completely to plan. Public opinion at home thinks that it is about time too: in 1914 the Austro-Hungarian army had gone on the offensive against their

---

* The Italian army suffered 68,000 casualties, 11,000 of them fatal. These figures were, of course, not made public until after the war.

1. *The mobilising Russian army gathers horses in St. Petersburg, 31 July 1914:* "The war is about the Russians, isn't it? Everyone knows that. The German army is mobilising in response to the Russian mobilisation and everyone knows that the Russians are going to attack soon."

2. *Russian prisoners-of-war on the Uszoker Pass in the Carpathians, spring 1915:* "The thrusts backwards and forwards in the various passes in the Carpathian Mountains have continued with wearisome predictability and an equally wearisome absence of any real result."

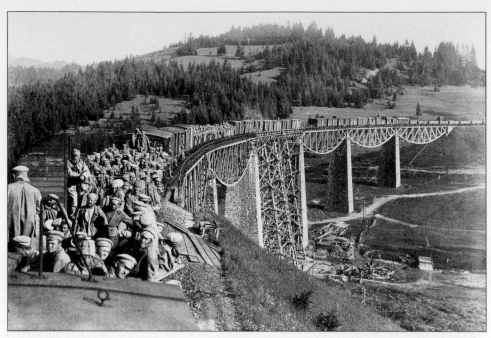

3. *The transport of Russian prisoners captured during the battles of May and June 1915:* "Finally, the order for immediate withdrawal, leaving the equipment and the wounded. They are to leave the wounded? Yes, leave the wounded. '*Skoro! Skoro!* . . . The Germans are outside the town!'"

4. *Austrian cavalry crossing the Vistula at Praga in Warsaw, 5 or 6 August 1915:* "We were told by the Staff that the enemy had crossed the Vistula in several places but so far was not molesting our forces except for small cavalry patrols which had appeared nearby."

5. *German troops in Minsk, 1915:* "The city came as a revelation to her, not least because it sparkled with colours like pinks and whites, colours she and her companions have almost forgotten after months of existing with the many shades of brown of the earth, of the road and of uniforms."

6. *View of Elfriede Kuhr's Schneidemühl, 1917:* "Once again Elfriede goes to the railway station. She is going to visit Dora Haensch, her best friend, whose parents run a small restaurant in the station building."

7. *Red Square, Moscow, October 1917:* "It is less than two months since she was last in Moscow but the city has changed enormously. The darkened streets are patrolled by all-powerful and trigger-happy soldiers wearing red armbands."

8. *A trainload of homeward-bound Austro-Hungarian troops has stopped in Budapest, November 1918:* "Gradually the housing outside the sooty carriages begins to get denser as they enter the suburbs of Budapest. At about twelve at night the train stops very briefly at a small station in Rákos."

1. *An Austro-Hungarian supply column near Santa Lucia, October 1917:* "The trench itself is right in the forward line, looking towards the cone-shape of Monte Santa Lucia on the Isonzo. . . . There is a deep and steep-sided valley separating the Italian lines from the Austrian."

2. *Italian Alpini in their element, 1915:* "Thanks to his mountaineering experience, [Monelli] succeeded in being selected for the Alpini, the elite mountain infantry. He joined up in June, in Belluno."

3. *Austro-Hungarian mountain troops working their way forward in the Alps, 1915:* "A chill blast, my heart becomes agitated. The first shot of the war: a warning that means that the machinery has been set in motion and is inexorably dragging you with it. Now you're in, and you'll never get out."

4. *Cima Undici, 1916:* "The Alpini battalion Paolo Monelli belongs to has been on Monte Cima for some days and they have occasionally come under artillery fire. But what is happening?"

5. *Monte Cauriol, 1916:* "By this point they have been on many dreadful mountains, but this one promises to be the worst of the lot. They stormed and took Monte Cauriol about a month ago—a feat in itself."

6. *An Austro-Hungarian military hospital on Monte Ortigara, 1915:* "For about a fortnight they have watched battalion after battalion dispatched towards the top of Monte Ortigara and each time they have also watched the result: first to come are the stretcher-bearers with the wounded and the mules with the dead, then—after a few hours or a few days—what remains of the battalion trudges past."

7. *Italian prisoners-of-war and some of the victorious German troops in Udine, October 1917:* "Neither newspapers nor communiqués are reaching them and they exist up here in the clouds of unknowing, fed on nothing but rumours, which are—as usual—confusing, contradictory and full of fantasy. Such as that the Germans have taken Udine. Such as that 200,000 Italians surrendered as prisoners."

1. *Supplies, the wounded, and swimmers at Anzac Cove, 1915:* "Dawkins and the others, however, landed at the wrong place, well over half a mile north of the intended spot. In one sense that was fortunate since the Ottoman defence was unusually weak at that point, the terrain being so rugged that the defenders judged it highly unlikely the Allies would even try to land there."

2. *V Beach on the southern tip of the Gallipoli Peninsula, 1915:* "There are actually only two points at which the Allies have succeeded in creating real bridgeheads: one of them is right down at the southern point of the peninsula and the other is here at Gaba Tepe, on the western side of Gallipoli."

3. *An Austro-Hungarian supply column in Serbia, October–November 1915:* "The invasion of Serbia by the Central Powers is going completely to plan. Public opinion at home thinks that it is about time too: in 1914 the Austro-Hungarian army had gone on the offensive against their Serbian neighbour on three occasions and three times it had been driven back."

4. *Captured Serbian troops on their way to surrender their weapons in Montenegro, February 1916:* "The defeated Serbian forces are now retreating to avoid the threat of encirclement and huge numbers of civilians are accompanying them on their uncertain flight south."

5. *A German aeroplane takes off for combat, watched by members of the local population in Macedonia, 1915:* "What real fighting there is is going on up in Macedonia, nicknamed Muckedonia by the British troops because of the mud and dirt there."

6. *A British army camp outside Salonica, April 1916:* "Sarrail's Army of the Orient is still in Salonica, in lofty defiance both of Greek neutrality and of the fact that there seems to be little or no point to the whole business any longer."

7. *Salonica immediately after the Great Fire, August 1917:* "The years of Western occupation with its accompanying flood of troops from virtually all corners of the world has served only to reinforce the glaring contrasts and the cosmopolitan spirit of the city."

1. *Fortifications at Erzurum, 1916:* "Now and then the distant thunder of Russian artillery can be heard. The hollow rumble rolls through the enclosing mountainsides and the explosions sometimes set off avalanches on Mount Ararat."

2. *View over Kut:* "The British corps has halted its southward retreat at the small town of Kut al-Amara and here they are going to wait to be reinforced or, to be more accurate, to be relieved since they are now surrounded by four Ottoman divisions."

3. *Heavily laden British riverboats on the Tigris, 1916:* "Both sides keep small flotillas of heavily armed boats on the Tigris, mainly to protect their own supply chain since the river . . . is a living artery for both armies."

4. *Jerusalem has capitulated and welcomes the victors, 1 December 1917:* "Gaza fell in November . . . followed by Jerusalem in December—the former a great blow militarily, the latter a political and prestige catastrophe."

5. *The ruins of Gaza after the fall of the city, November 1917:* "The silence of death ruled everywhere. In the middle of the streets, piled up among soot-blackened rafters and smashed carriages, lay hundreds of bodies, the burnt and shattered remains of people and animals."

6. *Under fire on the Palestine front:* "It is hardly a month since the First Battle of Gaza, a confused affair with heavy losses. Both sides initially thought they had lost the battle, but it finally ended in an Ottoman victory since the British, partly because of a shortage of water, withdrew from the ground they had gained."

7. *View of Bursa:* "It was in Bursa that the top British generals were being held prisoner and for a while Mousley was able to share their privileges in such matters as good and plentiful food, relatively recent newspapers and considerable freedom of movement."

Serbian neighbour on three occasions and three times it had been driven back. Not this time. On 6 October the combined German and Austro-Hungarian armies attacked, on 8 October they took Belgrade (for the third time since the previous August, incidentally), and on 11 October the Bulgarian army also invaded. The defeated Serbian forces are now retreating to avoid the threat of encirclement and huge numbers of civilians are accompanying them on their uncertain flight south.[*]

Pál Kelemen and his hussars are among the pursuers. They are advancing rapidly in the late-October rain and there have been periods when he has not been out of the saddle for days at a time. They have ridden past burning, looted buildings, along roads overcrowded with refugees—mostly women of all ages and children. And all the time they have been riding towards the sound of distant gunfire.

This Sunday the squadron is standing by the ruins of a Serbian inn. Hundreds of wounded men are lying on the muddy ground surrounding the building. There is still fighting going on against the rearguard of the retreating enemy—not here, but two mountain ridges further on, which is why there is some consternation when a soldier is brought in with a leg wound during the afternoon. He has been fired on from a cottage. An hour and a half later another soldier arrives, having been shot at from the same place; this one has a stomach wound.

A patrol is sent to investigate and it returns after a short while, bringing with it a badly dressed individual of medium height. His hands are tied together. The patrol is followed by people who are clearly relations and neighbours of the prisoner—some women and children and several older men. Pál Kelemen notes in his journal:

> They tried the man with the aid of an interpreter and heard the principal witnesses. It seems that, in spite of repeated warnings from his fellow villagers, he was firing viciously on our soldiers. As he surveys the crowd gathered there, he looks half savage, dropped from another world.
>
> The sentence is soon passed; the guerrilla must hang.[†]

---

[*] As a result of these movements alone, 15 per cent of the Serbian population died before the end of the war. No other nation suffered to the same extent as the Serbians in the years 1914 to 1918.

[†] Both the German and the Austro-Hungarian armies developed a hard-line culture for dealing with guerrillas, partisans, *komidatschi*, *francs-tireurs* or whatever they may have

The cook of the station, a Viennese pork butcher, undertakes the role of hangman with pleasure. He fetches a long rope and gets hold of an empty box to serve as trap. The *komidatschi* is told to say his last prayers and answers that he does not need them. The women cry, the children whimper and stare, petrified, while the soldiers stand around the tree wearily matter-of-fact but with excitement in their eyes.

The *komidatschi* is brought up by two soldiers. He shows no particular emotion but looks around with a truculent stare as if he were insane. They put the sling around his neck and pull the platform from under his feet. The rope was not hung high enough, and, with a supplementary powerful tug, the butcher adjusts it. The man's face is slowly distorted. Long jerking convulsions shake his body, dying. The tongue twists out of his mouth as he swings with stiffening limbs.

The spectators disperse in the twilight, the soldiers leaving first, then the civilians. Later Kelemen sees two soldiers coming along the road. They notice the body swinging in the autumn wind, go up to it and laugh. One of them gives the corpse a hard thump with the butt of his rifle, then they both salute and go on their way.

---

been called—that is, armed men, who shoot from ambush and fight without uniforms. Both colonial and historical experience played a part in forming the rather indeterminate mental image of such irregular fighters. They were viewed as a particularly uncivilised phenomenon since a civilised war should be fought only by uniformed men, without the involvement of civilians, and should the latter join in, they must be punished in the most severe way possible—with the death penalty. Taken in conjunction with seriously exaggerated rumours of atrocities committed *against* their troops, this hard line, which was theoretically laid down in the name of civilisation, led both armies to be guilty of the worst mass murders of civilians Europe had witnessed for more than a century. Things were at their worst during the opening phase of the war in 1914 when over a thousand civilians in Belgium—men, women and children—were killed by German troops as reprisals for imagined guerrilla actions. And Austro-Hungarian troops (particularly Hungarians) repeatedly ran amok in Serbia, killing everything and everyone they encountered. The hysteria of August 1914 had calmed down by this point but both armies continued to take an extremely severe stance against anyone who fought without being clothed in the external accoutrements of a regular soldier: guerrilla fighters should, quite simply, be hanged.

SUNDAY, 7 NOVEMBER 1915
Richard Stumpf sees two acts of Lohengrin *in Kiel*

It is a pleasantly warm and sunny November day. SMS *Helgoland* is
entering the Kiel Canal and rumours immediately begin to spread
through the crew. Hard land battles have been raging around Riga and
perhaps they are on their way up into the Baltic to offer support. Or
perhaps the English are on their way in through the Great Belt. Or perhaps neutral Denmark is being dragged into the war. Or perhaps it is
all . . . yet another torpedo firing exercise. Stumpf settles for the latter
"so that I won't be disappointed yet again."

The atmosphere on board is dreadful. Stumpf and the rest of them
are sick of the inactivity, sick of the worsening quality of the food, sick
of the harsh discipline and sick of being bullied by the officers. The ship
has a special punishment unit and every day twenty to thirty men can
be seen running round and round the ship carrying their rifles and full
battle kit. It takes very little to be punished: a dirty handbasin, a forgotten sock, a visit to the lavatory when on duty, an objectionable comment.
Stumpf writes in his journal:

> The fighting spirit of the crew has sunk so low that we would
> be delighted to get a torpedo in the belly. It's what we would all
> like to see happen to our despicable officers. If anyone had been
> heard wishing any such thing a year and a half ago he would have
> received a good thrashing. There is an evil spirit loose among us
> and it is only our good upbringing that stops us imitating what
> happened in the Russian Baltic fleet.* We all recognise that we
> have more to lose than our chains.

As they pass up through the canal Stumpf sees how the woods and
hills shine in many different shades of yellow, red and brown. There will
soon be snow.

It is evening when they arrive in Kiel. He notes that they have begun

---

* Stumpf's reference is to the mutiny on the Russian battleship *Potemkin* in 1905. His
memory, however, fails him on this: the *Potemkin* belonged to the Russian Black Sea fleet
not to the Baltic fleet.

to ease up a little on the blackout that used to be so strictly enforced. Is there something lurking behind that? Or is it just a sign that the serious and dedicated mood of the first year is slowly beginning to wear thin? The crew is allowed ashore. (Because, as he suspected, what they have to look forward to is not a battle but a couple more days of torpedo exercises.) Richard Stumpf rushes to one of the theatres in the city and manages to catch the last two acts of Wagner's *Lohengrin*. Afterwards he comments in his diary:

> It's a pity I can't get to more occasions like this. They make you feel like a human being rather than just a worthless beast of burden.

TUESDAY, 9 NOVEMBER 1915
Sarah Macnaughtan watches soldiers drilling in Petrograd

Snow and cold. Sarah Macnaughtan is confined to her comfortable room in the Hotel Astoria nursing a lingering cold and studying Russian. Trying to, anyway. She is finding it difficult to concentrate. Her eyes are drawn time after time to the window and out over the open square in front of the hotel, where a troop of soldiers is drilling.

Macnaughtan and her companions have been in Petrograd for just two weeks and the time seems to have been wasted. Nothing has happened. They have no idea where their six ambulances are—the vehicles were sent by ship through Archangel—and nor do they know where they are to be sent to serve. If anywhere. In complete contradiction to earlier assurances, the Russian Red Cross is unwilling to accept them. And Russian bureaucracy has proved to be even more impenetrable than British. They are lost in a maze of meetings, audiences and formal dinners. All to no effect. She writes in her diary:

> We want to be one in the great sacrifice war involves, and we offer and present ourselves, our souls and our bodies in great causes, only to find that there is some strange unexplained quality of resistance meeting us everywhere.

They are perhaps going to be sent to Dvinsk, where there has been heavy fighting ever since September—and perhaps not. The rumours emerging from the front are as confused as they are contradictory.

The soldiers on the square are drilling in the snow and Macnaughtan notes their inadequate clothing. Their coats are made of a cotton material, not of wool. This is just one example of the shortages that have hit Russia and her army. On the other hand, it is possible to get hold of just about anything if you have money. The well-heated hotel restaurant is full to overflowing every evening with well-dressed people gorging themselves on copious quantities of food and alcohol to the accompaniment of an orchestra. (She has a strong suspicion that some of the women are prostitutes.) She feels uncomfortable—sickened, even—when she is sitting in the restaurant.

And while this is going on, soldiers are starving, freezing, being wounded, maimed and dying at the distant front and there is suffering to be seen at close quarters, too. Just the other day Macnaughtan was helping to distribute food at a barracks full of people who had fled before the German advance in Poland. It is not just the smell and the disorder and the poverty that fills her with disgust, the people do so as well. The Polish refugees seem to her "as being very like animals, but not so interesting." These are the lucky ones—many more are said to be still out on the roads, sleeping in the snow.

And here we are in the Astoria Hotel, and there is one pane of glass between us and the weather; one pane of glass between us and the peasants of Poland; one pane of glass dividing us from poverty, and keeping us in the horrid atmosphere of this place, with its evil women and its squeaky band! How I hate money!

These contrasts existed earlier, of course, but the war has made them more acute, more glaring and, morally speaking, more offensive. Which restaurants are the best is a popular topic of conversation.

It is probably all this hanging about and enforced inactivity that account for her lack of strength. The energy that flowed into her during her lecture tour of Great Britain has begun to leak away. She can feel her thought processes slowing down. When Macnaughtan arrived in Petrograd she had the idea that she would use the waiting time to write another book, but she simply does not have the strength. She sniffs and leafs through her Russian textbook. The soldiers down on the square carry on drilling backwards and forwards. They lie down, stand up, lie down, stand up.

FRIDAY, 12 NOVEMBER 1915
Olive King and the light in Gevgeli

She had never really wanted to leave France. In a letter to her stepmother in the middle of October she allows something approaching dejection to show through for once:

> I sometimes feel I'm never going home, as if this rotten war were going on for ever. Every few weeks it seems to increase rather than slacken off, more countries getting dragged in, everything getting worse & worse. As for us, we don't know at all where we are going . . .

Then the women in the Scottish Women's Hospital heard that they were to be sent by ship to the Balkans, where a Franco-British corps under General Maurice Sarrail—sent in great haste and with almost no equipment—had landed in October at Salonica in neutral Greece in the hope of helping the Serbs by opening a second front.* King did not want

* Towards the end of September news had come that Bulgaria was mobilising, a clear sign that the country—after much vacillation and even more duplicitous scheming—had finally decided to join the Central Powers. This put the wind up the Greeks who, in turn, placed their small army on a war footing and invited the Allies in, which is why Sarrail's corps were sent to Salonica. The next day it emerged that the Bulgarians had fallen on their old enemy, Serbia, and invaded the southern parts of the country at the same time as Germans and Austrians were marching into the north. Sarrail's corps received a chilly, even threatening, reception because Eleftherios Venizelos, the Greek prime minister who had invited the Allies in, was driven from office by the German-friendly King Constantine I, with the result that Greece changed its political stance and once again became neutral. (The landing at Salonica was, therefore, according to A. J. P. Taylor, an act that in its way was as ruthless as the German invasion of Belgium.) Next came the short-lived victorious fanfares announcing that Sarrail's corps was pushing north along

to go at first. Ella, her big ambulance, was altogether too heavy and her engine too weak for the dreadful road conditions there.

The sea voyage that took King and the other members of the Scottish Women's Hospital to Greece lasted three weeks. A hospital ship on the way to the same destination was sunk by a German U-boat. In Salonica they were met by utter confusion—military, political and practical. Orders were followed by counter-orders in the "oceans of black mud" that constituted the streets of the city. Finally, in November, they were sent by train to Gevgelí, on the border between Greece and Serbia, to set up a field hospital.

Their tents came with them, but no tent pegs, and the ones they hastily improvised will not hold in the rocky ground. People have to go round night and day hammering in the loose tent pegs and tightening the slack guys. It is one of her main tasks. Another is to assist with the collection of the patients' clothes for washing and disinfection. She is not particularly bothered by lice and the weather is not so cold that they cannot wash their hair and bodies in the river.

They have electric light in the dining room, driven by the generator used for the X-ray machine, but it is switched off at half past seven in the evening and after that there is little to do but go to bed since they are not permitted naked flames in their tents because of the fire risk. Darkness falls early and it is already pitch black by five o'clock. On the other hand, it gets light well before six in the morning. She watches the sun rise every day, enjoying the sight as the surrounding hills take on the texture of wine-coloured velvet and the mountain peaks glow pink in the morning light.

Slightly to her surprise, Olive King realises she is happy. In today's letter to her father she writes: "This is just the loveliest place, the mountains are glorious, & the air so fresh and invigorating. We work all day like giants, & eat like wolves."

---

the Salonica–Belgrade railway—short-lived because they were immediately followed by the not very surprising news that the Serbs had finally crumbled under the overwhelming forces against them and that the scattered remains of their army were now somewhere up in the snow-covered Albanian mountains and hurrying south.

SUNDAY, 14 NOVEMBER 1915
Pál Kelemen visits the officers' brothel in Užice

The campaign has ended in victory. Serbia has been occupied. Sarajevo has been avenged. The victors can now begin to collect their reward and this evening Kelemen and some of his colleagues are visiting a brothel reserved for officers. It is in Užice, a small town on the Đetinja river. Kelemen notes in his journal:

Dim hall, carpets, and hangings on the wall. A wreck of a civilian sits strumming the piano. Four tables in the four corners. Four girls in the room. Two of them are lolling over an artillery lieutenant. At another table a group of Army Service officers are having black coffee. Beneath the lamp a first lieutenant of the Honvéd-Hussars sits reading the newspaper, days old.

This is the scene as we enter. We sit down at the only table left free and would like to have red wine, but on tasting it we all prefer coffee. In the corner Mohay, my cadet, tinkers with the gramophone without any luck. A spring must be broken.

One of the girls goes out, comes in again. Skipping over a chair, she sits at last in our cadet's lap. The other one, a black-haired girl in a red dress, lies stretched on a bench and stares at me.

Time passes. The evil-looking pianist is still playing. Something very familiar—the music that was played to me in a girl's room at home when I came to say farewell. Ages ago, far from here.

I get up and leave. They are wrong to think the wine has sickened me.

SATURDAY, 27 NOVEMBER 1915
Kresten Andresen attends a birthday celebration in Lens

Cold rain, and windy. Trees bare and swept clean. Grey, grey, everything is grey—the weather, their uniforms, the ever more watered-down coffee. But he has a free day. He does not have to be back at his post until tonight so Andresen grabs the opportunity to visit some friends from back home who are now serving in the 2nd Company. He has not spoken Danish to anyone for ages and he has been feeling lonely.

Night and day; in the trenches life indeed often changes character in accordance with the light. This is something he has become aware of during this most recent posting. He digs and digs, mainly at night and mainly at the foot of the notorious Loretto Hill that the French finally took during their May offensive. The front, however, is quiet at the moment. The French and the Germans move about quite openly during daylight hours, within sight of one another. And neither side shoots. (It is said that some really courageous fellows even visit the enemy trenches.)

This is an example of the kind of tacit pact that has developed here and there during the war: live and let live; don't disturb us and we won't disturb you.* But that is only during the day. The nights are almost always more uneasy, noisier, nastier. Darkness breeds uncertainty and uncertainty breeds fear. It is, as Andresen writes in his journal, like the story "of the man who changed form—during the day he was a human being, at night a wild animal." It is usually at night that people are killed.

They are quartered in Lens at present, a medium-sized mining town, and that suits him since there is more to see and more to do than out in the country. Andresen is walking up Rue de la Bataille when it happens.

Shells.

The projectiles come whistling down here and there. An unusually big one hits a house a small distance in front of him and he sees how the greater part of the roof is lifted thirty feet or more up in the air. He sees a big piece of shell land in the gutter. He sees the water splashing. He is paralysed at first but then he says to himself: "You have to run." And he runs, through the hot, dense layer of air created by the pressure waves, through the sound of more explosions coming at him from both sides, until he reaches shelter.

When he dares go out again dusk is already falling. Things are quiet by now and there are people out walking on the pavements. In many places householders and shopkeepers are sweeping up the shards of glass

---

* The generals on both sides detested this sort of behaviour. And it is worth noting that certain types of unit—Guards units, for instance—were immune to it, as were certain nationalities (such as Hungarians and Serbs) when they were facing one another.

from broken windows. At one spot he sees a soldier standing guard by a heap of straw: a direct hit from a shell killed two soldiers and a horse at this point, quite literally blowing them to pieces. The straw has probably been spread to conceal the grotesquely jumbled remains. Andresen can see, however, that the wall alongside is spattered with blood. He shudders and hurries on and very nearly stumbles over something . . . wormlike, lying on the pavement.

Andresen finally reaches the 2nd Company. Lenger, one of the Danes there, is celebrating his birthday and serving coffee and home-baked cakes. Andresen can at last speak Danish again, but unfortunately he soon has to set off back to his unit.

At nine o'clock they march out to do the night's work. He thinks at first that they are going to Angres, a village they have worked at in recent nights, but they march beyond that. The night is cold and cloudless, with a bright, shining moon. They finally halt at an altogether different place, not far from the Vimy Ridge. There they are set to dig an absolutely new trench. Now and then flares go up to the left of them and in the silvery light of the rockets the ridge shines as if covered with snow.

SUNDAY, 28 NOVEMBER 1915
Edward Mousley meets the retreating British corps in Azizi

There is nothing very remarkable about Azizi—just a bend in the river and a few mud houses. Edward Mousley has been sailing up the Tigris by riverboat from palmy Basra down on the coast to Qurna, Qala Salih, Amara and Kut al-Amara. He has heard the name Azizi mentioned several times and some people say it is where the British corps in Mesopotamia is located at present—Force D, as it is officially designated. Others say that the corps is at the gates of Baghdad and that the daring operation to take the great city is about to be crowned with success.

Edward Mousley is a twenty-nine-year-old lieutenant in the British field artillery. He was born in New Zealand, read law at Cambridge and was stationed in India until very recently. Since the operations in Mesopotamia are primarily being run by the colonial government of India it is only natural that reinforcements are also brought in from India. (The majority of the troops in the British corps are actually native Indians.)

Reinforcements are what Mousley and the others in the riverboat are—replacements for the men killed, wounded, missing or sick. Photographs of him show a self-confident man, with close-set eyes, a small, well-trimmed moustache and intense gaze, wearing a signet ring. There is a touch of ironic nonchalance in his posture. He has not served in the field before and has never been under fire.

Mousley was not one of those who grabbed the first opportunity to get into battle. He was summoned by a telegram that reached him when he was out on exercises. He then immediately began to get ready "to exchange training for reality." His colonel treated him to some good advice, his fellow officers to a steady stream of drinks. He was not in perfect health since he was still suffering the after-effects of a bout of malaria, but he did not allow his ill health to delay him. He put a number of surplus items—his motorcycle, for instance—into store to await peacetime and his return, but to his great joy he was allowed to take his most precious possession with him—his beautiful horse, Don Juan. Then, along with a number of other uniformed men, he embarked in a small mailboat and it carried them across the ocean.

Force D's march north is neither really necessary nor properly thought out. The whole business rests to some extent on the magic of a name ("Baghdad has fallen"—what a fine headline that would make in London, at the same time as being one in the eye for Constantinople, Berlin and Vienna), and to some extent on an all-pervasive and over-ambitious arrogance. British operations in the Persian Gulf began immediately after the outbreak of war, even before the Ottoman Empire had sided with the Central Powers: their original purpose was the very limited one of securing the oilfields down on the coast.* As so often happens in situations like this, however, the appetite had increased with the eating.

An initial effortless success on the coast encouraged the British to advance further. When that was also successful and, moreover, when the Ottoman army showed every sign of wanting to take to its heels whenever it was given a serious prod, the British took a few more leaps up along the Tigris until General Nixon, the commander-in-chief in that

---

* The great importance of oil at that stage was not, however, to power aeroplanes and cars, since these were relatively few in number, but as fuel for the British fleet. The British Admiralty had discovered that oil had a number of advantages over coal, not the least of which was that it was much easier to load.

theatre, who had remained back in shady Basra, looked at his map and said with a satisfied grunt that they might as well have a go at taking Baghdad, too—it was no more than 250 miles away after all, *right*?

Wrong. The 250 miles on the map have, so to speak, stretched in the doing and the corps has found itself advancing through swarms of flies, scorching heat and flooded watercourses. And meanwhile the supply line down to Basra has been getting longer.

Mousley has already seen signs that the capture of Baghdad is not perhaps going according to plan. Two days ago they passed a heavily armed sloop carrying a unit of the general staff: it was covered with shot-proof defences improvised out of bales of something or the other. In other words, traffic along the river is anything but safe. Now the steamboat carrying Mousley heads inshore and he realises at once that something really serious has happened. He sees a nervous urgency in the way people are moving around. He sees that the horses are weary and ungroomed and that wagons and harness gear are coated with dust. And he sees whole battalions, still wearing their tropical cork helmets, lying sleeping on the bare ground in "roughly organised rows."

He walks around among the exhausted men and animals and sees a small flag flapping above a mud hut, indicating that the commander of the corps artillery has his post there. The officer tells Mousley what has happened. Five days ago a major battle was fought at Ctesiphon, only fifteen miles south of Baghdad. The Ottoman army had dug in there and the British corps had succeeded in storming the first line of defence but then got stuck. Both sides suffered very serious losses and, since both sides had heard rumours that their opponent was about to receive significant reinforcements, the battle concluded in an original though not wholly unusual way with both sides withdrawing in confusion from the hot, dusty and corpse-covered battlefield.

The British force, however, no longer has the necessary strength to continue to Baghdad and is, in fact, overwhelmed by the numbers of wounded. The corps has four field hospitals with a capacity for 400 patients but after the battle they are having to care for 3,500 men. In the battery in which Mousley is to serve, the 76th, all but one of the officers have been wounded. And, unlike the British corps, the Ottoman army actually has received reinforcements, with the result that they have now turned round and are pursuing the retreating British.

That evening Mousley joins in the building of the ground defences that form a half-moon around Azizi. He thinks that it is all going surprisingly quickly and easily and, like a good many others at the start, he has difficulty in shaking off the feeling that he is taking part in a peacetime exercise. But he has only to look at the worn and battered state of the wagons, at the reduced numbers of horses pulling the guns and carts, and at the guarded expressions on the faces of the soldiers, to know that this is not the case.

As many as possible of the wounded are loaded onto barges and riverboats, and all superfluous equipment is also being shipped out. Mousley is one of those who lightens his baggage of unnecessary items such as his riding gear, bits and pieces of uniform and his camp equipment. He does, however, keep his horse, Don Juan.

When darkness falls, Mousley lies down to sleep alongside his gun battery, which is ready for action. The Ottoman army is somewhere out there in the darkness, and now and again the crack of shots can be heard. He hears jackals yelping—they have been shadowing the British corps all the way back from Ctesiphon, waiting for more corpses, whether human or animal. "Their ghost-like song" becomes fainter and more distant as weariness overwhelms him. Finally, he falls asleep.

THURSDAY, 9 DECEMBER 1915
Olive King takes the last train from Gevgelí

The order they receive provides final confirmation of the complete collapse of the Serbs. For Olive King it also marks the end of a period of upheaval, but also a strangely happy time.

The work in Gevgelí has been hard. The field hospital has 300 beds, but it was soon treating almost 700 patients. The winter has arrived in earnest, and in the last months they have been hit by several severe snowstorms, with tents being blown down or blown away. It is so cold that it is difficult to sleep at night. King has discovered that digging is the best way to keep warm. Her working day lasts anywhere from sixteen to twenty hours, her main task being to look after the paraffin lamps that now light the tents: light them, clean them, trim the wicks, fill them—all of which she has found deadly dull. She has begun to learn Serbian. Lice are spreading. She reports happily to her sister:

We never get any papers here, & have no news of any sort. This is a grand country & a grand life for making you fit. I haven't felt so splendidly well since I was in Arizona.

The not altogether surprising news has now reached them, however, that the field hospital is to be pulled back. Since there is no longer a Serbia to support there is no point in trying to push forward to Belgrade. The Army of the Orient, as Sarrail's corps is now known, is about to withdraw briskly towards neutral Greece—with Bulgarian troops on its heels. Yet another eccentric and grandiose Allied plan to use a circuitous route to break the deadlock of the war has collapsed and ended in disappointment.* King and the twenty-nine other women in the field hospital have less than twenty-four hours to evacuate their patients, pack the equipment and break camp.

The only way to get out of Gevgelí is by train. The roads are in an appalling condition or controlled by the Bulgarians. Thirteen French ambulances have set off down them and have disappeared—ambushed, or so it is said. So the net is closing around them.

It is midnight and Olive King watches the rest of the field hospital disappear on a train. She and two other drivers, along with the field hospital's three ambulances, for which there was no room, are the only ones remaining. Olive finds the idea of leaving Ella behind simply inconceivable.

One southbound train after another arrives, fully loaded with people and materiel. There is space for three women but absolutely not for three ambulances, one of them unusually cumbersome. They wait and hope. They watch the sun rise and hear the echoes of shooting rolling down from the snow-covered mountains. "It is a strange fact that the thought of personal danger never once entered our heads. Our only concern was for our precious cars," she later recalls.

The last train arrives.

Bulgarian troops are not much more than half a mile away.

And, yes! They see three empty flatbed trucks and without waiting for permission they drive their ambulances up onto them. The

* The day after this the evacuation of the Allied forces from Gallipoli began and the Ottoman Empire achieved its greatest military success of the modern age.

train rolls out of the station. Gevgelí is burning. Just before the town disappears from view King sees the station building explode as a shell hits it.

MONDAY, 13 DECEMBER 1915
Edward Mousley directs artillery fire at Kut al-Amara

He gets up earlier because, as from today, he has a new role—he is to act as the forward observing officer. The task is both arduous and dangerous since it means he has to work his way as far forward as possible through a primitive system of sandy trenches, and there are places where he and his signaller will have to creep along what are really no more than ditches. He is no longer wearing his sun helmet since it is far too visible. He is instead wearing a woollen cap, hardly the most comfortable headgear in this heat.

The British corps has halted its southward retreat at the small town of Kut al-Amara and here they are going to wait to be reinforced or, to be more accurate, to be relieved since they are now surrounded by four Ottoman divisions. The corps commander, General Sir Charles Townshend, has allowed his force to be encircled, partly because his troops are too exhausted to continue the retreat and partly because this gives the enemy something else to do rather than to advance on down to the coastal areas and the oilfields. The mood among those under siege is, however, good and all of them are convinced that it is just a matter of time before they are relieved. Mousley is unconcerned, even though he—like many others—is deeply critical of the hazardous attempt to take Baghdad with much too small a force and deficient preparations. But things are going to turn out all right.

In the course of the day he crawls on all fours for at least a couple of miles. There are times he is crawling through a dense, foul stench where the bodies of the fallen have just been thrown over the sides of the trenches and ditches and are now lying black, swollen and rotting out in the baking sun. There are times when he is no more than thirty yards from the enemy trenches. He directs the shells with considerable skill and great satisfaction and they pass no more than twelve or fifteen feet above his head, sometimes landing within twenty yards of him. He thinks that forward observation of this kind is *great fun*.

There are Ottoman snipers on the lookout everywhere and they are extremely accurate. When the telephone cable is not long enough Mousley uses flags to signal back to his battery, even when the enemy is shooting. He is under fire for the whole day.

Later he notes in his diary:

But the truth is, that personal experience in this thing called war is at best an awakening of memory from a dream of seas and foggy islands bewildering and confusing. A few personal incidents loom a little clearer, deriving what clarity they have from the warmth of personal contact. Then incidents fraught even with the greatest danger become commonplace, until the days seem to move on without other interest than the everlasting proximity of death. Even that idea, prominent enough at first, gets allocated to the back of one's mind as a permanent and therefore negligible quantity. I firmly believe one gets tired of an emotion. A man can't go on dreading death or extracting terrific interest from the vicinity of death for over long. The mind palls before it, and it gets shoved aside. I have seen a man shot beside me, and gone on with my sentence of orders without a break. Am I callous? No, only less astonished.

WEDNESDAY, 15 DECEMBER 1915
Willy Coppens puts up at a hotel in Étampes

The room is small or, rather, peculiarly long and narrow, but the view is good. When Coppens goes over to the window he can see the square and the railway station and beyond that, behind a screen of leafless trees, the ruins of the Tour de Ginette. This room at the Hôtel Terminus also has another advantage: the famous French flyer Maurice Chevillard[*] stayed here—always something to boast about. It was in any case the

* Well-known before the war for his daring, indeed dangerous, stunt flying.

only available room at the Hôtel Terminus and the Hôtel Terminus is the only hotel in Étampes with a bathroom, shared in proper order by all the guests.

Coppens has come to Étampes, south of Paris, with great expectations. At his own expense he has completed two months of basic flying lessons at a private flying school in Hendon, near London. After being instructed by choleric gentlemen in machines so small, frail and low-powered that they may only be used when it is absolutely calm (all flying ceased when the leaves on the trees began to stir), he made his first solo flight ten days ago. (This was after thirty lessons and a total of three hours fifty-six minutes in the air.) Immediately afterwards he took his official flying test, which consisted of steering the plane in a series of flat figures of eight and then landing, with his engine turned off, exactly in front of the instructor. All went as it should, and with Royal Aero Club Pilot Certificate No. 2140 in his pocket Coppens is now in Étampes to start the military part of his training.

There is, however, some contrast between "the wild delight" he felt on gaining his certificate and the reception he received when he got off the train in Étampes earlier today. Or lack of one, for there was no one to meet him.

The square in the little provincial town is as desolate and joyless as the December evening. From his window he sees nothing but "uninteresting houses occupied by uninteresting citizens." The cafés are empty. However, during these past months the town has reluctantly started to come to life since, as in many other places, the war, chance and—not least—the fact that a railway line passes through it, have given it a new significance, in this case as a pilot training centre. There are several military aerodromes outside Étampes and the air is continuously filled with the drone of aircraft, except on Sundays when all the exercises are suspended and silence reigns. A chance meeting with a friend from before the war (they had studied mechanical engineering and gone motorcycling together) is what led Coppens to the Hôtel Terminus and his arrival has not been without its bad omens: he saw a funeral procession in the distance and it seems that the dead man was a French pilot who had lost his life in a flying accident.

He takes his dinner that evening in a small hotel next door, which, unlike the Hôtel Terminus, has its own dining room. There he meets his old motorcycling friend and several other Belgians who are also here to be trained as military pilots. They are served by a rather haughty but verbose young woman called Odette.

Meanwhile,* in Tel Armeni on the border of Mesopotamia, Rafael de Nogales once again comes across evidence of the massacre of Christians. He is busy admiring the particularly beautiful and romantic scenery when he becomes aware of the smell of putrefaction among some ancient ruins on the edge of the town:

> I began to search for where the smell was coming from and backed away in horror from some wells or cisterns filled with Christian corpses in an advanced state of putrefaction. A little way away I came across yet another subterranean tank which, to judge by the smell, must also have been full of corpses. As if this wasn't enough there were unburied bodies on every side, or bodies barely covered with heaps of stones from which a bloody strand of hair or an arm or a leg stuck out here and there and had been gnawed by hyenas.

WEDNESDAY, 22 DECEMBER 1915
Edward Mousley on the sound of bullets

It is evening. He is lying awake in the bunker, well-wrapped in his Burberry sleeping bag. The only thing that breaks the darkness in the windowless space is a solitary stearin candle in a niche in the earthen wall; it casts a shadow that cuts across the floor and the ceiling. Edward Mousley looks towards the door, which is framed with sandbags. He can see an ammunition cart. He can see rifles. He can see a battery telescope. He can see a field telephone. He can see a wall scarred by shrapnel. He can see rows of palm leaves, clipped off and hanging down. The air is cool and there is no wind.

They are in a state of readiness this evening in Kut al-Amara. They

---

* Probably on the same day, though possibly 16 December.

are anticipating yet another Ottoman night attack and Mousley's battery of eighteen-pound field guns, which has been dug in among a grove of date palms, will be expected to fire a defensive curtain. Out in the darkness the chattering of a machine gun can sometimes be heard, and now and then the sharp crack of a bullet hitting the wall behind his head. It is less than a month since he was attached to the corps in Mesopotamia and the physical sensations of warfare are still of much interest to him. The sound of bullets, for example. He writes in his diary:

> One hears a sudden crack just ahead like the sharp snapping of a stick, and in the early days of one's initiation a duck is inevitable. I don't say one ducks, but one finds one has ducked. For a time every one ducks. It is no use telling people that if the bullet had been straight one would have been hit before hearing it strike the palm. Some people go on ducking for ages.

The night remains calm. At one stage the Ottoman machine-gun fire increases considerably and Mousley creeps out of his warm sleeping bag to check. But nothing happens apart from a few more horses being killed, an Indian groom wounded—and more leaves being clipped off the palm trees.

The same day Florence Farmborough, who has just returned from leave, writes in her diary:

> So eager were we to commence work again that on the following day we squabbled as to which of us should be on duty, but as Anna was celebrating her name-day, the verdict was given in my favour. A new surgery had been equipped in my absence; it was a clean, whitewashed, homely little room; I looked round it with pride. As night fell, I found myself strangely wide awake. I sat reading in the candlelight, ears alert to the slightest sound outside—although wounded, I knew, were unlikely to come, for the Front was peaceful.

FRIDAY, 24 DECEMBER 1915
Vincenzo D'Aquila is in hospital in Udine

First of all he hears the sound of small bells and then he sees a small group of people coming along the corridor. A priest in a surplice is walking in front and he is flanked by two nuns carrying candles. D'Aquila tries to decide which of his brothers in misfortune they will be visiting this time.

They enter the ward. Someone is to be given extreme unction.

Vincenzo D'Aquila is in the military hospital in Udine where, like so many others, he is suffering from typhus. He was brought here by ambulance a few days ago along the skiddy winter roads. He was lying on a stretcher high up in the vehicle and his head almost hit the roof every time the ambulance drove over a pothole. When they eventually arrived D'Aquila was in such a bad state that the orderlies thought he was dead and carried him into the unheated mortuary, which was where he was later found lying on a stretcher on the floor.

His illness has worsened. His high temperature has overheated his brain and in his delirium he has been shouting for Kaiser Wilhelm in order to hold him personally responsible for the war. When the nurses placed something on his head he thought it was a golden crown: it was an ice-bag. He has heard voices, supernaturally beautiful voices, and he has heard music.

These bells, however, are very real. The priest and the two nuns walk through the ward. D'Aquila follows them with his eyes, feeling sorry for the poor soul for whom the bell is about to toll. Imagine dying on Christmas Eve, at "the moment which all the world is supposed to commemorate with the greatest of good cheer and happiness."

The small group passes bed after bed, their bells tinkling. It is as if time becomes extended, stretched, slowed down in D'Aquila's fevered mind. Time does not count. It's as though the whole of eternity can be contained in a single moment. The three figures come closer and he does not take his eyes off them.

They come to a halt at his bed. The nuns go down on their knees.

He is the one who is to die.

D'Aquila does not want to, does not intend to and will not. The priest mumbles his prayers and anoints D'Aquila's brow with oil, but to D'Aquila's mind he has become an executioner whose actions are intended to take his life. D'Aquila, however, is so weak that he cannot utter a word. His eyes meet the priest's. One of the nuns blows out the candles and he is left alone.

D'Aquila tells us what happens next:

Everything about me was in pitch darkness which helped, I suppose, to produce an extraordinary feeling of suspension. It was for all the world like standing still in the air, neither moving to the right nor to the left, forward nor backward, neither rising up nor sinking down. The ether itself stood still. It was a state of immobility carried to absolute zero [...] Abruptly, after an oppressive dose of suspended animation in this impenetrable medium [...] a wall of light like a silvery screen appeared against the jet black background. A kaleidoscopic as well as multi-coloured projection of my entire life cycle, from my very birth and babyhood up to that moment when I received the Sacraments of the dying, was then slowly unrolled to my gaze, evidently for my absorption and edification.

Everything changes and he goes from fighting against death to welcoming it with joy.

The visions continue. He becomes a woman giving birth. He flies through the universe, past planets, stars and galaxies, but then his whirling path through the cosmos bends and he returns to earth, to northern Italy, to Udine, to the hospital on Via Dante, where he passes through a narrow little window into the hospital ward and to that thing at the outermost limit of existence—his own waiting body.

CHRISTMASTIDE, 1915
Paolo Monelli receives his baptism of fire on Monte Panarotta

The time has come. The time for his baptism of fire. They start marching at midnight. A long chain of soldiers and loaded mules stretches out across the snow. Paolo Monelli is thinking of two things as they march forward: one of them is home, the other is how happy he feels that he

will be able to tell them all in the future about what he is about to experience. It is cold; the sky is cloudless; the stars are pale; moonlight is playing over the glistening white snow. The only sounds to be heard are the
squeak of their nailed boots in the ice, the rattle of empty cooking pots,
the occasional oath and short, muttered conversations. After six hours
they reach a deserted, looted Austrian village. They rest there during the
day, waiting for darkness when they are to make a surprise attack on an
Austrian position on Monte Panarotta.

Paolo Monelli was born in Fiorano Modenese in northern Italy. His
original intention was to be a soldier but he started studying law at university in Bologna instead, which is where two of his passions coincided:
his interest in mountaineering and winter sports and his writing. During his time at university he wrote a string of texts on these topics, which
were published in the local daily, *Il Resto del Carlino*. It goes without
saying that he and his student friends enlisted as volunteers when Italy
declared war on Austria-Hungary in May of this year. This is more than
just a gesture on Monelli's part since, as the only son of the family, he has
the legal right to be excused from military service. He has consciously
avoided taking advantage of this and instead, thanks to his mountaineering experience, succeeded in being selected for the Alpini, the elite
mountain infantry. He joined up in June, in Belluno.

At the very last moment, however, Monelli was smitten with regret.
On the morning he was to leave he was woken early by a knock on his
window and he suddenly felt a vague and fleeting pang of fear. He remembers the feeling as having a touch of the hangover about it in that he had
gone to sleep in a state of intoxicated and carefree euphoria and woken
up with a feeling of dark and thoughtful regret. (The girl he spent the
evening with wept, but he did not take that too seriously.) Dark images
of the sufferings, both great and small, that lay ahead ran through his
mind. Joining up had seemed the obvious thing for him to do, but he
was not really sure *why*.

> Is it that I'm bored with my empty peacetime life, am I attracted
> to the risky game up there among the peaks, is it that I can't bear
> the idea of not being involved in what others will be talking about
> later—or is it simply an honest and humble love of my country
> that is persuading me to give my eager assent to a life of war?

And he remembers that it was cold on the morning he set off.

His regrets, however, are soon replaced by excitement. He describes a "voluptuous feeling of emptiness—the pride of healthy youth—the excitement of expectation." Up to this point he has hardly seen the war, let alone experienced it. (The first time he heard rifle fire in the distance he associated the reports with the clicking sound of billiard balls hitting one another.) Photographs of him reveal a rather slender man with sloping shoulders, thick dark hair, deep-set inquisitive eyes, sensual lips and a dimple in his chin. He looks younger than his twenty-four years, and in the pocket of his uniform jacket he carries a copy of Dante's *Divine Comedy.*

Monelli spends the day in a white cottage, where he lies down to rest on a low divan in a rococo-style bedroom. He has difficulty in getting any peace, perhaps because he is disturbed by the tramping feet of all the soldiers running up and down the wooden staircase, perhaps because his mind is too full of what is to come. Later they start to go through the plan for that night's attack. It is not going to be easy. They do not really know how to reach their target and, as they sit poring over the map, they cannot even locate their own position.

At nine in the evening they form up and march off. The night is bright, starry and cold. They enter dense woodland. Their nervousness increases. To their own ears, the sound of their boots crunching through the snow-crust is so thunderously loud that it will give them away. Monelli notices that he is hungry. Then comes the echo of a single shot: *Ta-pum. Alarm.*

> A chill blast, my heart becomes agitated. The first shot of the war: a warning that means that the machinery has been set in motion and is inexorably dragging you with it. Now you're in, and you'll never get out. Perhaps you didn't believe that before—right up to yesterday you were playing with life but simultaneously felt sure you could pull back out of your involvement at any point. You talked casually of heroic deeds and sacrifices—things you knew nothing about. Now it's your turn.

Monelli watches one of his comrades, whose face no longer wears its usual closed, inscrutable expression but is instead glowing with inner excitement. His comrade sees a couple of Austrians running away between the trunks of the trees below them and looses off two shots. "At that point," Monelli tells us, "something fell away and I no longer felt any anxiety. I am as controlled and clear-thinking as if I was exercising on the drill-ground."

Then—nothing.

Patrols are sent out to scout around.

Monelli and the rest of them keep watch, half-asleep. Dawn breaks. A cheerful lieutenant appears, his face red with exertion, and gives an order before disappearing off to the right. Rifle fire crackles in the distance. Monelli hears the groaning of a wounded man.

Then—nothing.

The sun rises. They start to eat breakfast.

Then the sound of machine guns. The noise of battle grows, spreads, comes closer. A few men with light wounds pass them. Somewhere up in front there is a battle going on.

They stop eating. Some of the men swear. The platoon forms a line and sets off across the snow. Monelli wonders, "Is this death, this chaos of screams and whistles, these branches being clipped off the trees, this drawn-out wheezing of shells up above?"

Then—nothing.

Stillness. Silence.

The mood is high during their return march. Admittedly they did not even locate the position they had orders to take, but the soldiers are happy to have come through unscathed and Monelli himself is pleased, indeed almost jubilant, to have undergone his baptism of fire. They pass back behind their own lines through a gap opened up in the barbed wire. There, however, the divisional commander is standing waiting, cold, stiff and glowering. When Monelli's battalion commander, a major, appears among the ranks of his marching men, the divisional commander stops him and gives him a dressing-down. They should have located the position. They should have taken the position. Their losses have been suspiciously small. And so on. After which the divisional commander remains standing at the side of the path and glares acidly at the soldiers as they file past. When it is all over the general takes his place in the back seat of a waiting motor car and disappears.

Towards evening they are back at the deserted village. Monelli goes into the cold white cottage and once again spreads out his sleeping bag on the low divan in the room with rococo decorations. Through a hole in the roof he can see the stars twinkling.

SUNDAY, 26 DECEMBER 1915
Angus Buchanan goes out on night patrol near the Taita Hills

They are surrounded by deep darkness. Above them are the stars but no moon as yet. Buchanan and his companions are wearing moccasins since it is virtually impossible to move silently through the bush while wearing heavy army boots. Their mission is the usual one: to prevent German patrols carrying out more acts of sabotage on the Uganda railway. It is about half past nine in the evening and the small group of men is moving quickly along a road which will lead them to a point about five miles away, where they intend to lie in ambush. They are moving in single file with long gaps between the men. Now and then they stop to listen.

Angus Buchanan has just been promoted to lieutenant. His career in the 25th Royal Fusiliers has been a quick one—last April he was a private. It is not without some sorrow that he has left life in the ranks, which he describes as "a gay, care-free, rough-and-tumble experience."

After marching in silence for a while they hear a sudden, loud crash. They come to a halt.

The noise is coming from the left-hand side of the road.

They can hear the crashing of branches being snapped and the rustling of the undergrowth. Enemy patrols do not move round in such a careless fashion. And right enough, they catch sight of a rhinoceros. They all stop immediately. In the darkness it is impossible to see whether the magnificent animal is showing any signs of aggression towards them. There are a few tense moments. Rhinoceroses are common in this region and are particularly dangerous—much more dangerous than lions. Buchanan has learned that the latter will attack only if they have been wounded. During the current year thirty British soldiers have been killed by wild animals in East Africa.

The rhinoceros lumbers off through the undergrowth. The danger is over.

The four men creep on in the dark.

They find the still-glowing embers of a campfire under a large mango tree. The enemy is somewhere out there in the darkness.

The moon rises and they can see the elongated, weightless shapes of their own shadows gliding along the dusty white road. Just a little way off there is the shimmer of a river.

At midnight they reach a place where they have a good view of the railway. They hide in the bush and wait. And wait. And wait.

Night passed quietly, stirred only by African sounds. Among the high trees on the river-bank, beyond the railway, monkeys yelled occasionally and snapped off dry branches as they swung from limb to limb. A solitary owl hoo-hooed away out in the distant darkness . . . Sometimes, too, an animal of prey would betray its presence and its prowling: the deep blood-curdling howl of the hyena and the dog-like bark of the jackal at times awoke the silence, for one or two brief moments, ere, phantom-like, they were swallowed in the dark, fathomless pit of night, and lost on their onward trail.

When the sun rises yet another uneventful night has passed. They light a small fire and make tea before walking back in the morning sun.

The soldiers are in the process of clearing large areas around the camp and huge stacks of provisions of all kinds are visible. Rumour has it that they are expecting significant reinforcements: "Daily our spirits rose at the prospect of the coming advance into the enemy's country."

1916

This is the war. It is not the risk of dying, not the red firework display of a bursting shell that blinds us as it comes whizzing down . . . , but the feeling of being a puppet in the hands of an unknown puppeteer—and that feeling sometimes chills the heart as if death itself had taken hold of it.

PAOLO MONELLI

Chronology 1916

10 JANUARY	Start of a Russian offensive in Armenia. Some gains.
JANUARY	Russian troops enter Persia.
21 FEBRUARY	Start of the German offensive at Verdun. Major gains. The battles continue until November.
4 MARCH	Great Britain and France divide the German colony of Cameroon between them.
6 MARCH	The Battle of Verdun spreads to include the western side of the Meuse.
9 MARCH	Germany declares war on Portugal. (The two countries have fought earlier in Africa.)
17 MARCH	The fifth Italian offensive on the Isonzo is broken off. Insignificant gains.
20 APRIL	The start of the Easter Rising in Ireland.
29 APRIL	The British corps besieged in Kut al-Amara capitulates.
14 MAY	Austro-Hungarian offensive around the Asiago plateau in the Alps. Some gains.
31 MAY	The Battle of Jutland—the great sea battle in the Skagerrak.
1 JUNE	Ottoman offensive in Armenia. Intensive fighting against Russian forces the whole summer.
4 JUNE	The Russian Brusilov offensive begins in the east. Major gains.
1 JULY	The great British-French offensive on the Somme begins and continues until November.

6 AUGUST   The sixth Italian offensive on the Isonzo begins. Some gains.

9 AUGUST   The town of Görz (Gorizia) on the Isonzo is captured by Italian troops.

14 AUGUST   A peace initiative by the Pope comes to nothing.

28 AUGUST   Romania declares war on Austria-Hungary. A German declaration of war follows.

29 AUGUST   Romanian offensive into Transylvania begins. Minor gains.

14 SEPTEMBER The seventh Italian offensive on the Isonzo begins. No gains.

4 OCTOBER   German and Austro-Hungarian counter-offensive begins in Transylvania.

10 OCTOBER   The eighth Italian offensive on the Isonzo begins. No gains.

1 NOVEMBER   The ninth Italian offensive on the Isonzo begins. Insignificant gains.

27 NOVEMBER Significant Russian successes in Persia.

5 DECEMBER   Bucharest occupied by German and Austro-Hungarian forces.

12 DECEMBER German peace initiative is rejected by the Allies.

Edward Mousley sees the sun rise over Kut al-Amara

It is called The Stack. It is a pile of sacks of flour some fourteen feet high and topped with an observation post. The view from the top is excellent. It is possible to see the horizon in almost every direction and to follow most of what the besieging Ottoman force is getting up to north of the town. The Stack stands in the middle of what they call The Fort, a large, walled enclosure at the north-eastern end of the British lines of defence around Kut al-Amara.

Edward Mousley has been in the Fort since yesterday, when he was sent there to replace a forward observer who had been wounded. The way there is long and dangerous: he had to navigate almost two miles of trenches to reach the position and enemy snipers are everywhere, shooting at anything that moves. Because of the Fort's isolated situation, the food served is unusually bad even by Kut standards. They have started slaughtering their draught animals and mounts (though Mousley's beloved Don Juan has been spared so far) and the soldiers closer to the town often dine on horsemeat. That is less common out here because of the distance.

Mousley has been awake since half an hour before dawn. He and the other forward observer in the Fort take breakfast in turns and on this particular early morning they have the same old stuff to eat: rice and tinned meat, washed down with tea—butter and sugar have already run out. Mousley likes watching the dawn and seeing the shadows of the night lift from the flat plain of the desert. The sky this morning is stunningly beautiful as it grows light, with shades of dark green, lilac and violet playing across an archipelago of fast-moving clouds driven by a south wind. Since this is New Year's Day he would like to think he is observing an omen and that the fate of the army, like that of the racing clouds, is to sweep rapidly on to Baghdad. Everyone in Kut al-Amara is calmly waiting for the relief force which, according to the optimists, is just a few days away, though the pessimists prefer to measure the time in weeks. They have been laying bets on it. Sometimes they play football, though the heat is deadening.

There is another reason he likes the dawn: it is the easiest time to register gunfire because later in the day mirages begin to form. It is also easier for the simple reason that enemy fire is not so heavy at that time. The enemy has worked out that British artillery fire is directed from the Stack, which means that as soon as the British guns open fire enemy projectiles begin to rattle against the walls. (He describes the sound of a salvo hitting the walls as *r-r-r-rip.*) They have to reinforce the double layer of sacks at regular intervals since the stream of bullets eventually gnaws through the outer layer and shots begin to penetrate into the protected area.

Later in the day Mousley notices through his binoculars that Ottoman soldiers are starting to set up an artillery position. He warns one of his batteries, gives them the coordinates, and soon the guns open up. The enemy soldiers, however, prove to be not so easily frightened. With his binoculars he can see them leaping for cover when a shell comes whistling over but immediately returning to the task of digging and picking even before the cloud from the shell-burst has dispersed. Fearless fellows. So Mousley changes the barrage pattern. His battery begins to fire its guns one by one so that there are fewer shells but they land more frequently. That seems to have an effect and after a while he sees stretcher-bearers and medical orderlies with carts arriving at the Turkish position.

The Fort is one of the cornerstones of the defence of Kut al-Amara and like the Stack it is almost continuously under fire. (When Mousley walks along the wall there are bullets smacking in through the low loopholes and he has to rush past one after the other.) So the infantrymen holding the Fort spend most of their time underground and the whole place is a maze of connecting trenches and bunkers, along with deep pits used for the storage of provisions and ammunition.

In the afternoon Mousley visits one of the Fort's outer defences. The

Ottoman infantry tried to storm it on Christmas Eve and after the British machine guns were knocked out and the Ottomans had broken into the bastion ferocious hand-to-hand fighting ensued. The attackers were eventually put to flight, by which time the bastion was full of dead bodies. The same soldiers who drove off the attack a week ago are still in the position and are pleased at their achievement. They show Mousley the large numbers of Ottoman dead still lying around—the bodies are in an advanced state of decay and the stench is horrendous in places. In spite of the smell and the danger from enemy snipers some of the men have risked venturing onto the carpet of bodies to look for souvenirs. One Indian soldier shows Mousley his trophies: three Ottoman tropical helmets and an officer's sword.

Dinner is really enjoyable—a small portion of potatoes, a fillet of horsemeat, dates and bread. The meal is rounded off nicely, too, since an officer offers him a Burmese cheroot and around seven o'clock Mousley retires to his bunker to smoke it reverently.*

The bunker he shares with another forward observing officer, a captain, is big for two people—about sixteen feet by ten—but unfortunately its ceiling is so low that it is impossible to stand upright. Mousley lies in bed, smoking and staring up at a ceiling constructed of a layer of beams with a diameter of six to eight inches, on top of which there is a three-foot layer of sand. He notes that the weight of the covering is making the beams bend. While looking at the sagging ceiling he tries to remember an axiom from Aristotle—something like, "just as some planks are stronger than others, so all will break if sufficient weight be applied."

On that day Paolo Monelli writes in his diary:

> Isn't this what you wanted? To be sitting by a fire, part of the war, one evening after a successful reconnaissance, waiting for more

---

* Cheroots were popular at the time, particularly among white men in tropical countries, since smoking them was thought to provide some degree of protection against a number of tropical diseases. (A Burmese cheroot usually contained rather light tobacco.) It might perhaps be worth mentioning that the cigarette made something of a breakthrough during the years of the First World War. Both the previously dominant cigar and the cigarette, as well as the intermediate cheroot, had an obvious advantage over the pipe in that they allowed the user to have both hands free.

serious missions. Thoughtlessly happy songs, the feeling that this is the best time of your life. And all your most morbid misgivings have been dispelled.

SUNDAY, 2 JANUARY 1916
Vincenzo D'Aquila emerges from his delirium in Udine

No one thought he was going to survive but an injection of something—opium, perhaps?—in some unfathomable way reversed his spinning descent down into the abyss. The first thing he can remember is one of the nurses shouting in amazement: *"Tu sei renato!"* You have been reborn! But for what?

It is only slowly that D'Aquila remembers fully what has happened.

From the calendar in the ward he can see that today's date is 2 January 1916. He is confused and lies with his head on the white pillow trying to understand. The war is still going on, that much he realises. But what actually happened when he was rescued from the expectation of death in the trenches? Was it his intelligence or his cunning that he had to thank for his salvation? No, it was his faith. He cannot let go of what the nurse said about him being reborn and a grandiose idea takes hold of him—if his own faith saved him from the war, could it not do the same for all the other soldiers?

A nurse comes up to his bed and gives him some thin slices of sponge cake and a glass of warm milk. After eating, he lies back and falls into a deep and tranquil sleep.

MONDAY, 10 JANUARY 1916
Pál Kelemen visits the scene of the assassination in Sarajevo

The last few months have involved little more than patrols and the other duties of an occupying force. The mountainous landscape is blanketed in snow but it is not particularly cold. The remnants of the shattered Serbian army have disappeared over the Albanian mountains in the south and Allied vessels are said to have shipped them out to exile in Corfu.

The major battles in Serbia are over and what remains to be done is to finish off the guerrilla war. Some parts of the country have been completely emptied of their male population. Time after time Kelemen has seen columns of men of all ages passing by:

> Shrivelled old men, crippled by hard labor, shuffle helplessly along, resigned to their fate like doomed animals. At the back are driven the cripples, the halfwits, and the children.

He is familiar with the snail tracks left behind by these pitiful processions—emaciated corpses lying in the ditch every mile or so, or the heavy, sour smell given off by their unwashed bodies, which hangs in the air even after they have passed round the next bend in the road.

For those who have no scruples there are numerous opportunities for exploitation. The Serbian towns have plenty of women prepared to offer their bodies in exchange for provisions, perhaps for a little chocolate or even just for salt. He has been unable to bring himself to participate in the shabby, unrestrained sex which now goes on almost openly in the occupied towns. Perhaps he is too respectable. Or is he quite simply too vain? For what would be proved by something won so cheaply?

His unit has been stationed in Bosnia since the end of December and Kelemen is in Sarajevo today. He notes in his journal:

> It is close to midnight. I have left the company and start home along the river bank. The snowfall has ceased; everything lies wrapped in white. In the Turkish quarter of Sarajevo on the other shore, snow lies thick on the domes of the mosques, and when the gusty wind blows off the mountain peaks, part of the white cover glides down with a reverberating crash, breaking the calm of the sleeping country.
>
> The streets are deserted. A turbanned night watchman shuffles away before me in his straw slippers. I reach the bank of the river Miljacka and stand on the corner just where the fatal shots were fired at the Crown Prince of the Monarchy. There is a marble slab on the wall of the house. June 28th, 1914.
>
> From the center of the city, the fine musical tinkle of sleigh bells approaches. And now the sleigh too can be seen, turning toward the river bank, the light narrow vehicle drawn by small steaming horses.

In the uncertain sheen of the street lamp I glimpse the outline of a slight woman wrapped in furs and the silhouette of the man beside her. With rapid hoof-beats the whole vision flies away. The sleigh with the two lovers in it has already passed the third corner. The sweet tinkle grows faint, and I stand alone on the cold river bank below the marble slab at the source of world tragedy.

SUNDAY, 16 JANUARY 1916
Florence Farmborough follows the course of a raid in the Chertoviche region

The cold and the heavy snowfalls are their most important allies. Both German and Russian armies remain stationary in rapidly dug trenches and overcrowded bunkers. Florence and the rest of the hospital unit have little to do. Most of their patients are suffering from injuries caused by the cold, or possibly from wounds resulting from a sniper's bullet, since those specialists in preying on their fellow men are never so active as in situations like the present one.[*]

Florence is rather pleased with life just now. She has just had ten days' leave in Moscow and really loved being there: "The light, the colour, the warmth, which I had so wished for—all were there." She went to the opera, saw the ballet, even danced. And the quiet evenings at home with her host family, with soft cushions, singing and playing the grand piano, that too had been undiluted pleasure, though after a while she had been troubled by a vague sense of restlessness. Something was missing:

> Gradually it was borne to me that to be happy while the world was unhappy, to laugh while the world was in pain, was incongruous; in fact, impossible. I realised that my happiness lay with my duty, and, as a Red Cross nurse, I had no need to be told where that was.

---

[*] Sniping was often encouraged, or even demanded, by those in command as a way of sustaining tension on the front, where calm conditions could lead to a spontaneous outbreak of peaceful restraint or—worse—out-and-out fraternisation between friend and foe.

In the end she had found herself counting the days until she could put on her uniform again and return to the front.

It is not only Florence who is in a good mood. Morale has recovered a little since the long retreat of the autumn and winter. The deadlock of recent months has allowed the shattered divisions to fill their ranks with new blood, their supply trains with new provisions and their arsenals with new materiel. The army of tsarist Russia now has fully two million men at the front and almost every one of them has his own rifle, which is considered to be an unusually good situation.[*] The shortage of shells that was being talked about for the whole of last year—though it was to some extent exaggerated—has been dealt with: they now have about 1,000 projectiles for every field gun, which is thought to be ample. And all the men have been fully rested.

As a result of all this, optimism in the Russian army is growing again. The fact that they have lost about four million men in the course of little more than a year and a half has been more or less repressed[†] and they hope—indeed, many of them believe—that the new year will at last bring the turning point they have been looking for and discussing. And there is a lot of talk of future Russian offensives.[‡]

There is a new spirit of aggression among the soldiers. Florence has known for a while that some sort of operation is being prepared along their sector of the front. Yesterday, at a dinner, she found out what it is to be: there is to be a reconnaissance in force by two battalions, which will target an important section of the German line of defence. The aim is to test enemy strength and to bring back some prisoners at the same time. Many of the men in the attack will be raw recruits, keen young men who have volunteered to be in the advance guard. Their job will be to stealthily cut passages through the German barbed wire—a dangerous task which, in their inexperience, they imagine is going to be little more than an exciting escapade. (They have been specially equipped

* Just a few weeks earlier over 400,000 men had no weapons of their own.
† Although at this stage, no one had any accurate idea of overall losses, not least because the Russian army was notoriously bad at keeping reliable statistics about its casualties. This defect was inherited by the Red Army.
‡ Those in the know were aware that the Allied powers—Great Britain, France, Italy and Russia—had decided to introduce synchronised attacks and advances in 1916. The idea was to make it more difficult for the Central Powers to use the transport advantages of their geographical position to move reserves easily to areas under threat.

with snow camouflage in the form of white overalls.) Florence and a section of her unit are to remain in a state of readiness immediately behind the front line in order to treat the men who are wounded.

By morning they are ready to move forward and set up a first-aid station but the hours pass while they wait impatiently. They do not get their marching orders until almost half past ten in the evening. They had been intending to use tents but to their joy they are given permission to set up their equipment in a cabin in a small wood just over a mile behind the trenches. The weather is dreadful—a strong, cold wind and sleety rain.

The doctors are nervous. Who can predict how the Germans will respond to a raid like this? The front is still calm and quiet. Not a shot is to be heard. They sit and wait. And wait. Midnight passes. After a while the divisional commander turns up and they offer him tea. The waiting continues. At two o'clock the commander receives a telephone report. Good news and bad news: the first attempt to cut through the German wire had to be abandoned but another attempt is being made.

More waiting, more silence, then another telephone call. Everything is going according to plan. The reconnaissance units are working their way through the barriers. The people in the little cabin breathe out and exchange smiles of relief.

More waiting, more silence. Three o'clock comes, then four.

Then it happens.

The silence is broken by the combined growling roar of artillery pieces, machine guns and rifles. This must surely signal that the Russian attack has begun. The noise grinds on. Another telephone report. The reconnaissance group has been discovered at their task and now find themselves under heavy fire from the German artillery. The breakthrough has failed.

The wounded begin to come in, some carried on stretchers, others helped by their fellows, some limping in under their own steam. The scene is dominated by two colours—white and red. The blood stands out in sharp contrast on the soldiers' new snow suits. She sees one holding a grenade in his hand, so shocked that he refuses to let go of it. She sees another man, hit in the stomach—his intestines are hanging out and he is already dead. She sees a third man, shot in the lungs and his breath is bubbling as he fights for air. She sees a fourth being given the last rites but he is already so far gone that he can hardly manage to swallow the wafer. White and red.

When it is all over Florence goes out into the fresh air. Everything is once again silent and calm, though the sound of scattered shots can be heard from a neighbouring sector. The reconnaissance force has failed, seventy-five men have been killed and about two hundred wounded. The commander of the regiment is missing and rumoured to be lying badly wounded somewhere out there in the wire and winter darkness.

TUESDAY, 18 JANUARY 1916
Michel Corday takes the Métro to the Gare de l'Est

Cold air. Winter sky. This morning Michel Corday is accompanying an old friend to the railway station. The friend is an officer in the engineers and is returning to his unit. The two men take the Métro to the Gare de l'Est. In the underground they hear an infantryman on his way back to the front at the end of his leave talking to an acquaintance: "I'd give my left arm to avoid going back." This is not just a figure of speech because Corday then hears the infantryman say he has been trying to get himself wounded as a way of being taken out of the front line: he did so by putting his hand through one of the loopholes in the trench under enemy fire and holding it there for an hour—without success.

Other topics of conversation on this day: the war has cost, on average, 3,000 human lives and 350 million francs *each* day. There is talk of reducing these costs in order to be able to fight for longer. The expression "war paid by instalments" is to be heard. There is also considerable agitation that Montenegro—France and Serbia's Balkan ally—capitulated yesterday. Not that Montenegro had much choice: the mountainous little country was occupied by the same German-Austrian troops who pushed the Serbian army out of its own country. Someone also tells a story about the capture of a badly wounded German officer at the front: as he dies he whispers, "It's true, isn't it, that Goethe . . . is the world's greatest poet?" This is seen as a typical expression of German self-conceit.

It is ten o'clock in the morning when Corday and his friend arrive at the Gare de l'Est. There are uniformed men everywhere, sitting in their hundreds on luggage trolleys or on the stone balustrades. They are waiting for their trains or for the clock to strike eleven: it is strictly forbidden to serve anything to drink to men in uniform before that time.* Corday has heard of a minister who wanted to buy a pot of tea for two women and the fiancé of one of the women, only to be politely refused because the fiancé was in uniform and the time was wrong. Then the minister tried to order tea just for the women and was again refused on the grounds that there was a risk that the soldier might drink some of the tea served to the women. The waiter did, however, point obligingly to the entrance and suggest a solution: the fiancé could do what an officer with another party was doing—leaving the tea room so that the people in his group could have something to drink.

The platform, too, is swarming with soldiers returning from leave. There are emotional farewells by the carriages, women lifting up their little ones so that the men hanging out of the windows can give them a last kiss. Corday observes the scenes in his usual voyeurish way. His eyes fall on a soldier whose face is completely contorted, transformed into a mask of sorrow. The man's suffering is so obvious, so palpably clear, that Corday has to turn away. He leaves the platform without looking back.

WEDNESDAY, 26 JANUARY 1916
Vincenzo D'Aquila is transferred to the San Osvaldo mental hospital

It is early and one of the orderlies brings in D'Aquila's old uniform and tells him to change. He is then taken to an office where a doctor in a captain's uniform is waiting. His name is Bianchi. D'Aquila salutes him smartly. The doctor receives him kindly and, feeling rather uncomfortable with the whole situation, hesitates. D'Aquila sees a pile of papers lying ready on the desk and manages to pick out fragments of what is written there. It is an order for him to be transferred for "observation and custody" to the San Osvaldo mental hospital. "Symptoms: cerebral typhus of a maniacal type—dangerous to himself and to others."

D'Aquila has gone mad—or that is what the doctors think his behaviour demonstrates. In D'Aquila's clouded and confused mind the whole experience of falling ill, followed by an apparently miraculous recovery,

* The prohibition applied to both alcoholic and non-alcoholic beverages. I have been unable to ascertain the reasoning behind it.

has driven to an extreme his belief that he is somehow being "chosen." His mind is filled with the wild idea that he has been brought back from the dead for a specific purpose by a higher power. And his mission? To stop the war. He imagines he can see the workings of the supernatural in the hospital wards. He believes he is performing faith healing.

And there is certainly no lack of people to heal. Immediately after his reawakening he was moved to a convent just outside Udine, where the military are sending soldiers with different kinds of mental problems. The number of cases is growing day by day. The doctors do not, in truth, know what to do with all these men with their strange cramps, grotesquely obsessional behaviour and inexplicable paralyses, men whose bodies are uninjured but whose minds seem to have succumbed. In a bed to the right of D'Aquila there is a young man who sits up every tenth minute, day and night, and carefully examines his pillow for lice. In the same ward there is a fellow who repeatedly thinks he is back at the front and rolls out of bed roaring, *"Avanti Savoia!"* He wriggles backwards and forwards on the cold floor, ducking to avoid imaginary bullets until he faints, at which point the orderlies pick him up. Then he remains unconscious until the next attack (both clinical and imaginary) sets him off again.

For lack of anything better, they call it "shell shock."

D'Aquila has seen it all and been appalled by it. It has merely served to reinforce his firm conviction that he both must and actually *can* put a stop to this utter madness—the war. He had a prophetic dream one night: right outside the hospital he saw two groups of fighting men clash with each other and he went outside and stood between them:

With upraised hand I motioned to the soldiers to stop shooting. Next I felt a sharp pain on my right side where an enemy bullet had hit me. But I did not reel. Instead I calmly extracted the bullet with my fingers and held it aloft to show the combatants my invulnerability. Instantly the firing ceased, the men threw their weapons to the earth and started to embrace one another, crying, "The war is over!"

D'Aquila believes himself to be a prophet and argues, not without some finesse, with both doctors and priests. They call him mad, but it is the world that has gone mad, isn't it? It may perhaps sound like some gobbledegook philosophy when he says he will stop the war (him, just a solitary, unknown corporal) but surely someone must make a start, mustn't they? So he has been wandering around in his dressing gown, preaching and debating. He suspects there are conspiracies. He thinks he has discovered secret messages from a higher power hidden in his underwear.

Captain Bianchi is strangely embarrassed, fiddles with his spectacles and blames orders from higher up. Once again D'Aquila starts arguing his case: it is the world that is mad, not him. He analyses, prophesies, orates: "Are we not told by Christ to love our enemies?" And so on. The captain listens patiently, shakes his hand, wishes him good luck and escorts him out into the yard, where an ambulance is waiting, its engine idling. As D'Aquila climbs aboard the engine splutters and cuts out. See, another sign from the heavens!

Eventually the driver and a mechanic get the vehicle started. They drive through Udine towards San Osvaldo at ferocious speed. The morning is cold and clear.

A DAY IN FEBRUARY, 1916
Pál Kelemen watches transport convoys on a mountain road in Montenegro

So Montenegro—one of the enemies of the Central Powers, although perhaps not the most important of them—has been knocked out. Pál Kelemen and his hussars took part in the operations, once again without seeing any fighting to speak of. They are now back to their familiar old routine—road patrols and guard duty. He notes in his journal:

> General Headquarters is being moved. As the railway bridge is not yet repaired, the provisioning service between the two stations is carried on by motor truck. But in spite of the very inadequate facilities for transporting the general food supply, all the vehicles have been requisitioned to help move Headquarters.
>
> Columns of trucks wind over the mountains, packed with cases of champagne, wire-spring beds, floor lamps, special kitchen equipment, and various crates of delicacies. The troops

receive a third of their normal rations. The infantry at the front has had only a morsel of bread for four days, but the staff officers' mess serves the usual four-course dinners.

SATURDAY, 5 FEBRUARY 1916
Olive King is looking forward to a day off in Salonica

She is sharing a tent with three other women. They make their own breakfast in the morning on a portable British military stove fuelled with meta tablets: it is small and pretty ineffective but does manage to boil water for coffee and just about heat a tin of sausages. Not much is happening in Salonica. As usual. The front is quiet, so quiet that the troops in the front line have even started digging vegetable plots in which they intend to grow peas. The only warlike activities on offer are the bombing raids made by the occasional German Zeppelin. The first more serious raid was made at the end of December and there was a second one four days ago. The effect of these attacks has been negligible.

Just as on all the other static front lines, the war in the air has been given a degree of attention out of proportion to its real importance. It has to stand in for all those things people had hoped for from the war but which are now so difficult to find: colour, excitement and drama, a scenario in which the courage and skill of the individual has some significance. A shot-down German plane was paraded through the whole of Salonica with a great hullabaloo the other day. (The fact that it was forced down just behind the French lines was mostly a matter of luck: there was only one bullet hole in the whole aircraft, but the shot had gone through the petrol tank.) King was there to watch. Allied cavalry clattered along in the lead, followed by several motor cars full of proud Allied pilots; then came the aeroplane, in pieces, carried on three lorries; after that were more Allied motor cars, with another column of mounted troops bringing up the rear. King gives an account of the events in a letter addressed to her sister:

That was the limited procession, to impress the Dagos, & they certainly stared open-mouthed, but the amusing part was the mass of lorries, ambulances, cars, trams, bullock wagons, packhorses & etc. which had been held up by the procession, & came straggling along after it.

In the darkness outside it is raining. King is lying in her tent writing to her sister and she keeps it short since she only has half a candle left. After that she goes to bed, which never takes very long. She simply takes her boots and skirt off and creeps half-dressed under the blanket and her overcoat. She and the other three in the tent have tomorrow off and she is looking forward to it. She is thinking of starting with a long lie-in, and for breakfast they will share the three eggs she bought earlier this evening.

SUNDAY, 13 FEBRUARY 1916
Rafael de Nogales and the wild duck on the Tigris

There is a chill in the air. The morning's rain has turned into a heavy snowfall by eleven o'clock and the flat desert landscape around them is transformed into an exotic white. Rafael de Nogales is on a steamship going south down the mud-coloured Tigris, towards the front. He is once again in search of battle and danger. He left his post on the staff in Baghdad yesterday in order to serve with a brigade of cavalry involved in the fierce battles around Kut al-Amara.

Apart from the cold, it is a pleasant, almost idyllic journey:

> The only things to break the monotony of the landscape were the *djirts* and waterwheels turning slowly on both river-banks, the contours of which were broken at regular intervals by dusty groves of palm trees and small, yellow-coloured villages. Here and there flocks of wild duck flew with beating wings across the leaden sky, perhaps frightened into taking off when the crew of a dhow further upstream hoisted their triangular sail to the accompaniment of one of those long, mournful songs that resemble a wail of lament rather than music and which are as long drawn-out and melancholy as the horizon of the desert.

De Nogales had actually attempted to get a discharge from the Ottoman army when he arrived in Aleppo, exhausted and sick after his long and dangerous ride from Sairt. Nothing he saw during the journey made him change his mind. Quite the reverse. Time after time he stumbled across traces of the massacre of Christians and he saw long columns of deported Armenians, above all women and children, being reduced to "filthy, ragged skeletons" as they were marched to death under the watchful eyes of Ottoman soldiers.

A telegram from the war ministry in Constantinople, however, informed him that his request had been rejected but offered him treatment in the headquarters hospital. De Nogales did not dare accept the offer: as a witness to the massacres he was in fear of his life. After being in close contact with the German military delegation in Aleppo, however, he felt sufficiently safe—after a month's convalescence—to report for a new posting.*

First of all he landed up in an administrative job in a small, distant place in the province of Adana, where he carried on an unequal, but to some extent successful, struggle against the disorder, corruption and appalling incompetence that characterised the Ottoman army's transport system. In December, however, an unexpected telegram summoned him to a new posting, this time on the staff of Baron Colmar von der Goltz, the German field marshal who was in command of the Ottoman Sixth Army in Mesopotamia.†

Still feeling some disquiet but eager for new excitement and glad to escape this internal exile along the caravan routes in Adana, de Nogales set off south towards the Mesopotamian front. The halting of the British push towards Baghdad was judged to be a great success and an even greater success was on the cards if the British corps surrounded in Kut al-Amara could be made to surrender. There is now fierce fighting going on around the small town, and also further downstream, where British units are attempting to force their way through to relieve the siege.

After travelling for a few hours they meet another boat on the river. The two vessels stop alongside each other and he sees a small man in the uniform of an Ottoman colonel come across on a gangplank. The man, who has a pointed beard and a "proud but unassuming" manner, is Nureddin Bey, the Turk who was not only in command when the British

---

* He also realised—or feared—that he would be stopped if he tried to go west or to Constantinople.

† Dubbed Goltz Pasha by the Turks.

advance was checked at Ctesiphon but was also largely responsible for the successful encirclement of Townshend's corps. Nureddin is now on his way to Constantinople, "stripped and humiliated," removed from his post as governor of Baghdad. Halil Bey, the new governor, may not be able to boast of any great military talent but he has first-class political contacts and now, with the scent of a great victory in the air, he is eager to usurp the role of official victor.*

Halil's nephew was Enver Pasha, one of the leading Young Turks and an aggressive nationalist who was the driving force in taking the Ottoman Empire into the war on the side of the Central Powers. In practical terms Enver was now the ruler of the empire as a sort of military dictator, and it was he who had dismissed Nureddin from Baghdad and replaced him with his uncle.

Because of its scale this war produces heroes at a phenomenal rate and the newspapers are full of them. Once used, they are cast aside just as rapidly. Death or oblivion awaits most of them. Also in Baghdad is another architect of the victory at Ctesiphon†—Field Marshal von der Goltz. In spite of his high rank the seventy-two-year-old German is virtually isolated, and he is ill, spending most of his days alone in a small, dirty tent.

As evening approaches, de Nogales sees rows of thin spirals of smoke "rising into a pepper and salt sky of grey and gold." The front is not far away and they have reached the point at which river transport will become land transport. Here he can see the spinning cogs of the enormous machine that keeps the war going—most armies need something like fifteen men working behind the lines to supply one fighting soldier.

Weaponry has undergone great change over the past fifty years,

---

* One of Halil's first actions as new commander was to order a regrouping of the Turkish forces that were aiming to prevent the British relief force reaching the men besieged in Kut. The regrouping was notably ill conceived and left one flank of the Turkish line exposed, a weakness the British recognised and immediately mounted an attack to exploit. The result was the Battle of Hanna on 13 January, which would probably have been won by the British had it not been for faulty reconnaissance. Halil's manoeuvre eventually proved successful: the honour for the victory at Kut al-Amara fell to him and to immortalise the fact he added Kut to his name. He survived until 1957 as the "Hero of Kut," a celebrated, if not necessarily deserving, Turkish military hero.
† And at Kut, although he never lived to see it. He died two months later, a fortnight before the siege there was broken, officially carried off by typhus, although there were a number of rumours, never substantiated, that he was poisoned by Turkish officers.

becoming ever more deadly, but the means of transport have hardly changed at all. This is one of the main reasons that the war so often stalls and becomes static. Once the trains have reached their termini the further progress of the armies relies on exactly what it relied on in Caesar's or Napoleon's day—the muscles in a man's legs or in a horse's back. But these ever more complex organisations demand more and more equipment, and the weapons, with their increasingly rapid rate of fire, demand more and more ammunition.*

The majority of campaigns, particularly those fought beyond the well-developed railway network of western Europe, are decided more by logistics than by tactics. However brave an army's soldiers may be and however advanced their weapons, it will inevitably find itself at a disadvantage if the transport system that is supposed to support it is weak or underdeveloped. The conflict has increasingly become an economic competition, a war between factories. And logistics is the Ottoman army's weak link.

During his service de Nogales has witnessed any amount of Ottoman ineptitude and corruption but on the Mesopotamian front they have mobilised everything they can. What de Nogales sees as his boat draws closer is, in its way, impressive. There is no mistaking the Turks' determination or their energy. At the same time, however, there is something timeless about the scene:

> With every moment that passed I could see more and more clearly the line of steamers, dhows, nankeens, terradas, cufas and rafts moored along the left bank of the Tigris, all busily loading or unloading military supplies and provisions, which were standing in tall, pyramid-shaped stacks along the steep banks of the river. Thousands of buffaloes, camels and other beasts of burden, tended by Arab herdsmen in picturesque dress, were graz-

* A German army corps needed only 457 wagons for its transport in 1871 whereas in 1914 it needed no fewer than 1,168—an increase of over 250 per cent. All these extra wagons had to be pulled by horses, and the extra horses needed fodder, which also needed to be transported. Weight for weight, a horse eats ten times as much as a man, which in turn demands more wagons and more horses to pull them, and so on. A contemporary head-count suggests that there was one horse for every three men. About eight million horses died in the war, which means that the horse population suffered proportionately greater losses than the human one.

ing peacefully over a vast expanse covered with white tents that spread as far as one could see in the hazy distance. Cavalry patrols and infantry platoons were marching backwards and forwards to the sound of military music through an enormous uniformed throng, from which rose a ceaseless mumble of voices like the roar of a distant sea. Now and then the hubbub was pierced by the shrill braying of the animals, the hoarse notes of sirens, the singing of imams calling men to prayer and the yells of Persian, Arab and Jewish merchants who, gesticulating grandly, offered our soldiers tobacco, olives and plates of greasy fare.

De Nogales spends the night aboard the *Firefly*, a sooty, bullet-riddled British gunboat that fell into Ottoman hands during the fighting at Umm two months ago. Both sides keep small flotillas of heavily armed boats on the Tigris, mainly to protect their own supply chain since the river, which is unusually difficult to navigate this year because of drought, is a living artery for both armies.

The faint roar of distant explosions can sometimes be heard and on the distant horizon oily smoke rises densely above some groves of palm trees. Somewhere over there is Kut al-Amara and its beleaguered defenders.

One of the men over there in the encircled town is Edward Mousley. At the moment he is suffering from dysentery and waking up this morning was more than usually unpleasant: apart from the inevitable diarrhoea he has severe pains in the small of his back and in his head, and he has a high temperature. The doctors' orders are simple: "Improve your diet." Mousley comments: "They might as well have recommended an ocean cruise." Food supplies are slowly but surely shrinking in Kut al-Amara. Some of the men who want to stay on their feet at any price keep themselves going on opium pills and various other home remedies, such as a mixture of castor-oil and Chlorodyne, a well-known analgesic patent medicine with a minty taste: its active ingredients are opium, cannabis and chloroform.*

* Chlorodyne, primarily intended for the treatment of cholera, was invented by a British army doctor in India and was much copied by competitors. It was very popular at the

The situation at Kut al-Amara is unchanged—they are all waiting for new efforts to relieve them. Some of them are growing impatient whereas others are simply waiting, bordering on apathetic, having
stopped believing in a quick rescue. They talk jokingly of feeling "siegy"
or "dugoutish." And the screw has just been tightened one more turn:
they were bombed by an enemy plane today. Mousley despairs: "The circle is closed. We are being shot at from all directions, including above."
The most upsetting news of the day is that people at home in Britain
do not know anything about what is happening in Mesopotamia; they
think the corps has just gone into some sort of winter hibernation.

Mousley notes in his journal:

I finished [reading] a novel today. It has at least made me long for
England again. We are all full of longings; and the chief blessing
of civilisation is that it supplies the wherewithal to quieten them.
Lord! For a glass of fresh milk and a jelly. Temperature 103° and
shivering. I am going to have an attempt at sleeping. Everything
is quiet. The sentry's steps beside my roof make the earth shake.
It is the seventieth day of the siege.

MONDAY, 14 FEBRUARY 1916
Kresten Andresen is in Billy-Montigny and thinking of peace

Winter turning to spring. Puddles covered with ice. The landscape is
light brown. There have been some quiet months, which has pleased him.
Andresen has had a few tours of duty in the front line but as a digger, not
as a fighter. During the day they sat in a cellar listening to the shell-
fire, and at night they marched up to the forward line and dug and dug.
Their positions are in a state of constant development, both in depth and
extent, and the sight of mile after mile of deep trenches and ever thicker

---

time, though the concoction was highly addictive and could even lead to death if taken
in immoderate doses. It was eventually discontinued in its original composition—to the
great sorrow of its many enthusiasts. Chlorodyne offers a good example of how the late
nineteenth and early twentieth centuries were one of the most liberal periods in history
where drug abuse was concerned; those involved would not, of course, have thought of
it in that way.

belts of barbed wire has become depressing rather than impressive. He has told himself and the others that a solution by military means is no longer possible—the more time passes, the more impenetrable the lines become. He has also heard that this is one of the sectors where the German and the French soldiers have come to a kind of silent understanding to leave each other in peace as far as possible. Now and then, however, severe fighting breaks out and then dies away just as quickly, following a logic he finds impossible to discern.

Apart from the nights of digging Kresten Andresen has been having a relatively comfortable life. He has been spared anything really unpleasant and any great danger, but he is still unsettled and longing for home. He has withdrawn from his German comrades to a great extent, finding them over-partial to drink, and even from everyday life, which he finds monotonous and melancholy. They sometimes play practical jokes on each other, like putting pepper in each other's "pig snouts"—soldiers' slang for gas masks. Whenever he can he seeks out other Danes to talk to and spend his time with. He has been reading Molière and become friendly with one of the draught horses. When news reached them that Montenegro had capitulated to the Austro-Hungarians, it was enough to set off endless speculation that this was just the first step, that others would soon follow suit and a general peace would break out by Easter or not long after. And so on. Andresen writes in his diary:

> The offensive that was going on here has now come to a complete halt and everything is perfectly calm. It's a long time since I heard the big guns. And I believe the war will be over before August. But that doesn't mean that we'll get home immediately. There is bound to be a terrible mess in all the old world. I believe that life will stop for a while before blooming with renewed vigour.

SATURDAY, 19 FEBRUARY 1916
Sarah Macnaughtan is on her way from Kasvin to Hamadan

At eight o'clock they get into the motor car and set off. The low houses of Kasvin soon disappear behind them and the plain opens out. Snow everywhere. The wind is piercingly cold. She thinks: "I always had an idea that Persia was in the tropics. Where I got this notion I can't say." Northern Persia—that is where Macnaughtan and her party have ended up.

The road that brought them here has been crooked and unpredictable. At the beginning of December the Russian authorities—in the shape of a grand duchess—finally informed them that they would be serving in the Caucasus and so they travelled there by train via Moscow. The further south they get (Vladikavkaz, Tblisi, Batumi and back to Tblisi), the vaguer the idea of the "Front" becomes. Where is the "Front" actually?[*] And what are they actually supposed to be doing? Only one of the ambulances they shipped out from Britain has got through and it turns out to be in need of repairs. (The car they are driving is one she bought in Tblisi with her own money.) And are motor vehicles any use at all on the awful mountain roads down in the Caucasus? The only thing they know is that a Russian infantry division has advanced quite a long way into Persia and the fighting is said to be continuing.

The fact that the war has spilled over into neutral Persia and that her unit will be working to support an army of invasion is not something that Macnaughtan has given any great thought to. Events are following a logic of escalation of their own,[†] separate from and beyond the high-flown ideals she was doing so much to propagate during last summer's lecture tour. When one is submerged, as Macnaughtan is, in an ever-changing torrent of events, it is difficult to say what is what, what has anything to do with the High Ideal or the Struggle for Victory, or what is simply an expression of crass national self-interest or equally crass imperial expansionism. Does she really want to ask herself those questions anyway? Russia, when all is said and done, is an ally of Britain.

But her nagging doubts have been stirred into life again.

The motor car drives on along the frozen road, hemmed in by high

---

[*] She puts the word in quotation marks in her diary.

[†] It is not particularly surprising that Persia was drawn into the war. Even before 1914 this weak and unstable state had been a playground for Russian and British imperialists, who had in practice divided the country into spheres of interest. The outbreak of war made the whole situation even worse. After just a few months British troops occupied an important centre for oil production on the Persian coast and the Germans countered with a vigorous propaganda campaign and an intensification of espionage activities. When the Persian gendarmerie, trained and led by Swedish officers, placed itself under German control in November 1915, Russian troops immediately invaded the country.

banks of snow. There is a sharp wind. They stop at a small tea-house, eat some sandwiches and drink a glass of port: "I think a glass of this just prevented me from being frozen solid." Then they drive on, slowly leaving the plain behind them and travelling up into the mountains. She is freezing.

The experiences of these past months in Russia have, however, served to reinforce her conviction that the British are superior to all other peoples and cultures. And, half-jokingly, she has begun to wonder whether they are on the wrong side in this war. At least in the east:

> I often despair over [Russia], and if the Russians were not our Allies I should feel inclined to say that nothing would do them so much good as a year or two of German conquest. No one, after the first six months, has been enthusiastic over the war, and the soldiers want to get home.

There is very little in Russia that she can find anything good to say about: the climate is harsh, the towns are filthy, the people unmannerly, the officials corrupt, the morals low, the social gatherings poor, the food monotonous and their homes ugly. One of the few bright moments occurred on Christmas Day, when she was invited to dine with Grand Duke Nicholas in Tblisi: she was utterly delighted, partly by Nicholas himself—"an adorably handsome man, quite extraordinarily and obviously a Grand Duke"*—and partly because he proposed a toast to her! But then everything returned to the grey reality of waiting, inactivity and contradictory information. Macnaughtan is not in the best of health.

At three o'clock in the afternoon they reach the top of the snow-covered pass, where they meet some Russian officers and eat lunch together. Then they get into the car and begin the slow journey down. She sees birds. She sees wolves. She sees hares. She sees a jackal. She sees abandoned vehicles. She sees a regiment of Cossacks. She sees transport

---

* Until September 1915, when he was dismissed as a result of various court intrigues, Grand Duke Nicolai Nicolaevich—an unusually tall man—was the head of Stavka, the supreme command of the Russian army. Following his dismissal, the position was taken over by Tsar Nicholas II, a military dilettante. The Grand Duke was then transferred to the Caucasus front, where, thanks to the good planning of his subordinates, which he was happy to go along with, and to his own ability to summon reinforcements, the Russians were now fighting a successful campaign against the Turks.

wagons. She sees horse-drawn guns. There really is a war going on some-where in the distance and that thought serves to liven her up. Not much is happening at the front at this stage but General Baratov's division will soon be resuming its slow advance on Teheran and then she and her companions will be needed to tend the wounded.[*] That is the intention, anyway.

It is beginning to get dark. Hares caught in the car's headlights remain sitting in the road as if bewitched. Once the sun has gone it sud-denly becomes even colder. She sees the surrounding hills disappear in an icy mist.

They reach Hamadan at ten o'clock—"a clay-built, flat Persian town." The car gets stuck on the awful road into the town and Mac-naughtan continues on foot while some of the party remain with the car. Two Russian officers escort her to the hospital where she is to work. She notes that one of them is drunk. She becomes even more annoyed when they arrive, only to be met by "an unpleasant Jew doctor" and two young nurses and to find that no preparations have been made for her arrival. (To make things worse, the officers have started flirting with the nurses.)

After a great deal of confusion and a long wait in the cold she gives up. It is now about midnight and she goes to a house occupied by an American missionary couple. They are helpful, give her a cup of tea and a bed for the night in an unheated room, where she goes to sleep rolled up in her "faithful plaid."

THURSDAY, 2 MARCH 1916
*Pál Kelemen observes a woman at the railway station in
Bosna Brod*

The fevers and the weariness he has been suffering from recently have at last been diagnosed—malaria. Not the worst kind, but he still needs

---

[*] A number of people have been trying to gain Macnaughtan's support for the Armenian refugees who are currently pouring into this part of the Caucasus. There is much talk of last year's massacres and, having spoken personally to a number of eyewitnesses and survivors, she is in no doubt about the scale and brutality of the events. But she has a distaste for the Armenians—"an odious set of people"—and prefers to work with the Russian army at the front.

nursing. He is, of course, very pleased that the bed waiting for him is in a Hungarian hospital. Kelemen said farewell to his men and to his brother officers in the light, mild spring rain, and it was an emotional farewell—his sergeant actually wept. Then he left the camp on that marshy field outside Cattaro and sailed on a military transport ship to Fiume.*

They sailed along the Dalmatian coast with the ship's lanterns doused, through the ice-cold Bora wind and past the most dangerous part of the Adriatic Sea: the sea is a cul-de-sac, secured by an enormous Italian mine-barrage down by Otranto. He could not understand the ill-concealed excitement of the crew: he "couldn't comprehend that somebody's eyes could still gleam at the sense of danger, or that such living, defiant energy still exists." While all the rest of them were out on the freezing deck nervously keeping a lookout for Italian mines, Kelemen sat alone in the ship's mess getting drunk on red Vöslauer Goldeck wine.

Today he is in Bosna Brod, sitting waiting for a train. It is a railway junction and swarming with soldiers.† Lorries tear back and forth along the streets, and at the station he can see engines and carriages of every variety and age. There are great stacks of tinned food and ammunition everywhere. The loading and unloading is being done by elderly, bearded militia in dirty uniforms. The station restaurant is packed with military men and government officials of all kinds, but sitting at one table is a young woman and all Kelemen's attention is focused on her:

> She has on a plain worn dress with some kind of a fur about her neck. I keep looking at the frail, weary figure, the traveling cushion, the shawl and handbag, the boxes on the chairs, and the coat on the peg.
> For one moment she turns an apathetic face towards me,

---

* Cattaro was the Italian name—it is now called Kotor and is in Montenegro. Fiume was the Italian name of what is now Rijeka in Croatia. It is worth mentioning that Fiume, formally speaking, was Hungarian territory, not Austrian, and had been a semi-autonomous *corpus separatum* since the eighteenth century. Bosna Brod is now Bosanski Brod in Bosnia-Herzegovina.

† The crowds at the station are partly a result of one of the peculiarities and weaknesses at the heart of the Austro-Hungarian dual monarchy. Different parts of the empire had their own railway systems, in terms of both rolling stock and tariffs. Both goods and passengers had to be transferred when moving from one railway system to another. In the case of Bosna Brod, the village made its living out of the fact that the gauge of the track in Bosnia was different from the gauge in Austria.

but then, with total indifference, is occupied again with her own affairs. There is a field postcard before her on the table;[*] a pencil has lain in her hand for a long time but she has not written a single word. Perhaps because I am watching her, perhaps because she is roused from her musing by the clatter of a fresh company departing for the front, she makes up her mind at last, and with long strokes writes down the address. Then her head droops to her hand and she sits motionless again with fixed gaze.

The train with the field company is just pulling out. Whooping, shouting, and singing echoes into the restaurant. She raises her head a bit but does not look outside. Watching from behind the broad pages of an opened newspaper, I see tears well into her eyes. For a while she will not take her handkerchief; then she touches her cheeks with it. She picks up the pencil and writes a few words more.

The conductor comes in from the platform, clangs a bell, and in stentorian voice shouts the arrival of the homebound train. The girl pays, and, with the fuss and helplessness of a woman traveling alone, puts on her coat and gathers up her many little things. Suddenly she catches sight of the unfinished postcard on the table, takes it and tears it up, her gloved hands trembling, and throws it on the tablecloth. The busboy carries her suitcase out after her.

SATURDAY, 4 MARCH 1916
Richard Stumpf sees SMS Möwe *returning in triumph to Wilhelmshaven*

A clear spring night. The whole German High Seas Fleet is lying just off the mouth of the Elbe, rocking gently on the watered-glass surface of the sea. Perhaps something is going to happen at last! Everything has been made fast for battle and even the officers' luxuriously furnished cabins

---

* Members of the armed forces could write home postage-free using field postcards, and their correspondents could reply without payment as long as they used the special stamps or postcards attached to them. Light parcels could also be sent free of charge.

have been emptied of everything unnecessary. The officers are wearing their pistols in order "to be able to enforce their orders with arms"—this is a novelty and ultimately has to do with the growing sense of frustration among the crew.

The ships weigh anchor in the middle of the night. Richard Stumpf hears the familiar sounds, above all the tremors emanating from the three steam engines. They are transmitted through the metal of the hull like a vibrating pulse. He does not, however, know in which direction they are headed. Instead of their usual northerly course leading out into the empty North Sea, the great mass of grey-painted vessels, silent and blacked-out, steers north-west past the East Frisian Islands and then on along the coast. Strange.

The morning turns out clear, warm and sunny. Stumpf is acting as lookout on the ship's bridge and for once he is genuinely pleased—with the weather, with the mission and with life (well, almost). The reason is not just that the weather is good and the fleet is at last going to *do* something but that this morning a copy of a telegram was posted on the notice board outside the radio cabin: addressed to SMS *Möwe* and from the commander of the High Seas Fleet, the message consisted of just two words: "Welcome home!"

They all know about SMS *Möwe*. *Möwe* represents everything Stumpf and millions of other Germans thought the war at sea would be like: bold manoeuvres on the oceans of the world, in which the elements would be defied and an apparently superior opponent outwitted time after time and with very definite results.

SMS *Möwe* began life as *Pungo*, a very ordinary freighter used to ship bananas from the German colony of Cameroon during peacetime. The war had been going on for only a few days when French forces, soon to be followed by the British, invaded the German colony.* There, as elsewhere, the invaders' hopes of rapid success quickly ran into the sand. Following a clumsy and protracted campaign that lasted throughout 1915, the German outposts did eventually fall one by one.† And since it was obvious

---

* The main pretext was the need to knock out the radio station at Douala, which had a powerful short-wave transmitter that could be used to coordinate the small German naval units that were scattered across the ocean at this point. Ultimately, of course, it was all about improving their own colonial position.

† Just two months earlier the remaining German population had moved into the Spanish

that the German banana trade with Cameroon was ruined at least for the duration of the war, the *Pungo* was converted to the *Möwe* in the autumn of 1915 in order to serve as a merchant raider. The German fleet has perhaps a dozen such vessels. On the outside they look like ordinary freighters from neutral countries (mainly Scandinavian countries) but they are heavily equipped with both mines and concealed guns. Their prime target is Allied merchant shipping and they have caused fear and confusion out of all proportion to their numbers. It is also more than a touch embarrassing for all concerned that these insignificant vessels have succeeded in sinking more ships than the combined might of the great, costly and muscular High Seas Fleet.

The fact that all these battleships have largely been languishing in port has led to a good deal of derision from many people in civil life: the whole of this great and expensive fleet, which in pre-war days consumed one-third of the military budget, is seen as passive and even, some whisper, unusable. The last commander-in-chief of the navy, finally dismissed because of his cautiousness, used to be the target of pointed remarks, particularly from women, whenever he went out on the street. The following lines have been seen scribbled on walls or heard sung by boys on the street in Wilhelmshaven:

> *Lieb' Vaterland magts ruhig sein*
> *Die Flotte schläft im Hafen ein.* *

Given this situation, then, ships like SMS *Möwe* have had to make up for the manifest deficit in naval exploits. She sailed away in December— under a Swedish flag—and has had a daring voyage by any account. She mined the waters close to the great British naval base at Scapa Flow, thereby sinking the elderly battleship HMS *King Edward VII*. She then sailed on round Ireland to reach the French coast, before passing Spain and the Canary Islands and finally crossing the Atlantic to the coast of Brazil. She has been laying mines and holding up Allied merchant vessels

---

enclave of Rio Muni, where they were interned. And on this very day, 4 March 1916, Cameroon was officially divided up between the French and British after Mora, the last German outpost, surrendered, having been guaranteed favourable terms.
* "Dear Fatherland, be quite calm / The fleet is asleep in harbour." The lines are a play on the refrain of "Die Wacht am Rhein."

all the way: she has taken fifteen ships in three months, thirteen of which were sunk and two taken to harbour as booty.*

Just as they are about to sit down for lunch they hear shouts from the port side. Stumpf and his companions rush to where the cheering is coming from. When they emerge into the March sunshine they see the little SMS *Möwe* puffing along between the lines of great grey battleships, and the flags of the fifteen ships she has taken or sunk are fluttering from her mast. The first officer calls for a cheer and they all join in, "wildly, with all the strength of our lungs." The crew down on the low deck of the *Möwe* are all lined up and respond with their own happy hurrahs. Stumpf notes with amazement that "there were a number of negroes wearing blue shirts and red caps standing on her deck, and unbelievably enough, they were cheering too."

Then there is a remarkable balletic scene—the whole squadron performs a perfectly coordinated turn by way of greeting:

> It was an indescribably splendid sight. Just a short distance away the island of Heligoland gleamed in the golden rays of the sun, the sea was dark-green and it looked as if fifty prehistoric monsters were dancing a triumphal dance around the returning *Möwe*. I really lamented my lack of a camera on this occasion.

A triumph, for once. Later the whole of the first squadron sails into Wilhelmshaven yet again and takes on coal until eight in the evening. They are supposed to go out again immediately—rumour says that this time it is for real.

A few days later Richard Stumpf notes in his journal:

> Yet again there was no battle! As I write this we are back in the mouth of the Jade river, safe, sound and in one piece, without having fired a single shot. I have just given up all hope! Our fighting spirit has sunk to new depths.

* There can be no doubt as to how risky *Möwe*'s activities were: only four days earlier, on 29 February 1916, another of these merchant raiders—SMS *Greif*—was sunk in the North Sea. The British had their own equivalent, the so-called Q-Ships, small vessels with carefully concealed armament, which were designed to ambush German U-boats.

WEDNESDAY, 8 MARCH 1916
Florence Farmborough comments on the life of the civilian
population in Chortkov

They are back in enemy territory. Chortkov, where they have been for
a month now, lies in the Austrian part of Galicia. The town was badly
damaged last year when Russian units, expecting to be driven out, set
fire to many of the buildings. Jews form a large part of the population.
Florence writes in her diary:

The position of the Hebrews living in Chortkov is most pitiful.
They are being treated with vindictive animosity. As Austrian
subjects they enjoyed almost complete liberty, experiencing none
of the cruel oppression poured out on to the Russian Jew. But
under the new Government their rights and freedom have disappeared and it is obvious they resent the change keenly.

When it snows—and it has snowed a great deal this winter—one
Jew per household is compelled to go out and clear the streets under the
supervision of Russian soldiers wielding knouts, and they do not hesitate
to administer a whipping with them. There is a ruin opposite the house
where Florence and several of the other nurses are quartered. One of the
town's rabbis used to live there. Next door to it is a synagogue which has
been vandalised.

This morning Florence receives a visit from a Jewish seamstress who
has made her a grey cotton dress. The woman is upset. When Florence
asks why, she tells her that three Cossacks pounded on the door the evening before and demanded house room. (All soldiers have that right and
the majority quarter themselves on Jewish families, sometimes twenty or
thirty men to a house. The overcrowding is indescribable.) She told the
Cossacks quite truthfully that all her rooms were already overcrowded
with soldiers, but they forced their way in all the same and began to
carry out a sort of improvised search. They soon found what they were
looking for—a revolver they had obviously planted there themselves.
The seamstress and her husband protested, upset and, indeed, terrified
since possession of a weapon was strictly forbidden and punishable with
death. It was all a trick, of course, and the Cossacks offered to forget the

whole business as long as they were paid ten roubles. The seamstress and her husband had no choice:

> So the ten roubles were scraped together and handed over to the Cossacks who, as they left, commented in loud, scandalised voices on the treachery of the heathen Jewish race. Such tales of injustice are commonplace in this part of the world; it would seem the very name "Jew" is, to Russian soldiers, a word of scorn.

Otherwise the last months have been quiet. Apart from the costly and ineffective attacks made far to the north, on Lake Narocz outside Vilnius, no one has seen any signs of the Russian offensives everyone was talking about so expectantly. Something close to a sense of disappointment has begun to spread and even Florence feels frustrated by all the waiting.

The front is so quiet at the moment that there have been very few wounded to take care of, so Florence and the other nurses have been try-ing to help the civilian population instead. There have been many cases of typhus and smallpox and the outbreaks have been made worse partly by the extreme overcrowding, which has facilitated the rapid spread of infection, and partly by the shortage of food. The shops in the town are well stocked with luxuries like corsets, high-heeled shoes, silk ribbons and chamois-leather gloves but it is difficult to get hold of simple basics like butter, eggs and yeast—and what little there is of them sells at ridic-ulous prices.

A severe typhus epidemic raged here last year and the smallest and youngest were hit hardest. Between ten and twenty children a day were dying at one point. Florence has seen a good deal by this time but she writes in her diary:

> Sometimes it seems to me that not one of those dreadful wounds which I saw and treated during last year's retreat touched me so deeply as the sight of these suffering children, with their small wan faces and limp little bodies.

One of the people she nurses is a four-year-old called Vasilj who comes from a poverty-stricken peasant family from outside the town. His father, who was conscripted into the Austro-Hungarian army at the start of the war, has disappeared and his mother makes her living by doing washing for Russian soldiers. The boy caught smallpox last year and because of the illness and malnutrition he has stopped growing. When Florence picks him up his arms and legs feel like thin twigs.

Another of those seeking her help today is a young Ukrainian woman. She says she is eighteen but she looks younger. She came yesterday, surly and scared, to get help with her skin problems and they started by cutting off her filthy, matted hair. Then they gave her green soap to wash with. "Her body, full of sores, told its own sorry story of prostitution." The girl survives by selling her body to soldiers. She has come back today with a slightly easier mind now that she understands that the nurses really want to help her.

Florence is standing by the door as the girl is leaving. She sees her turn round. She sees her bow her head to the doctor and mumble a thank-you. As the girl passes her, Florence has "a momentary glimpse of tears below her tightly compressed eyelids. She, too, was a victim of War."

Edward Mousley is woken by the sound of shelling. His first thought is that it is their own artillery in Kut al-Amara; then he thinks it must be the Ottoman artillery bombarding the British relief force which, according to the latest reports, is less than twenty miles away on the north bank of the Tigris. He climbs up onto the roof to investigate and sees flashes in the distance; they are coming from the guns of the relief force, which is pounding the Turkish lines at Dujaila on the *south* bank of the river. That is only about eight miles away. The relief force has clearly crossed the river covertly and, after marching under cover of darkness, is making an attempt to break through to them.

The excitement among the besieged troops is enormous. As daylight grows stronger they can see Ottoman units making hastily for the threatened position. Mousley knows there are plans for the besieged to support the relief force by making a sortie, either to the north or to the south depending on which side of the river the relief force arrives, but he does not hear an order to put the plan into operation. Around nine o'clock he can see rows of heads moving along the Ottoman trenches and all of them are heading south-east.

The sounds of battle grow more intense and Ottoman units continue to pour in the direction of Dujaila.

Then everything goes very quiet and there are no more flashes to be seen on the horizon.

Mousley assumes that the silence means the British infantry has reached its target and that fighting is going on with cold steel at close quarters.

The silence continues. The besieged men are becoming increasingly nervous. What has happened? Why are they not making a sortie?

The hours pass and nothing happens. The big guns round Dujaila remain silent.

Evening comes.

Everything is quiet.

Meanwhile, Sarah Macnaughtan is still in Hamadan in northern Persia. She is ill and alone. She writes in her diary:

> I lie in bed all day up here amongst these horrible snows. The engineer comes in sometimes and makes me a cup of Benger's Food. For the rest, I lean up on my elbow when I can, and cook some little thing—Bovril or hot milk—on my Etna stove. Then I am too tired to eat it, and the sickness begins all over again. Oh, if I could leave this place! If only someone would send back my car, which has been taken away, or if I could hear where Mrs. Wynne and Mr. Bevan* are! But no, the door of this odious place is locked, and the key is thrown away. I have lost count of time. I just wait from day to day, hoping someone will come and take me away, though I am now getting so weak I don't suppose I can travel. One wonders whether there can be a Providence in all this disappointment. I think not. I just made a great mistake coming out here, and I have suffered for it. Ye gods, what a winter it has been—disillusioning, dull, hideously and achingly disappointing!

THURSDAY, 9 MARCH 1916
William Henry Dawkins's father receives his dead son's belongings

Today Arthur Dawkins has signed receipt of a parcel shipped by Thomas Cook & Son from the Australian military authorities in Egypt. The parcel contains William Henry Dawkins's personal effects. They are:

---

* Her two companions.

1 Electric Pocket Lamp
1 Bible
1 Leather Sovereign Purse
1 Pocket Book
1 Diary
1 Pr Scissors
Belt
3 Jack Knives

In Kut al-Amara, at three o'clock on the same afternoon, Edward Mousley writes in his journal:

> The relieving force did not get through. We have heard this unofficially. We all have the feeling it is "the big effort," and not a side show. We are disappointed, but having had little else than disappointments we are accustomed to them.

SATURDAY, 11 MARCH 1916
Angus Buchanan and the mist on Kilimanjaro

They make a road as they march along—not by building it but simply because of their weight. This column consists of 4,000–5,000 soldiers, thousands of mules and horses, numerous cannon, ammunition wagons and various kinds of supply wagons, and even a number of motor vehicles that are skidding around at the back of the queue. Their progress is not rapid.

At the start of the march, when they were still moving across the flat sandy plain, Buchanan looked back through the swirling dust and saw in the distance the tracks they were leaving behind them: they resembled "the fine line of a sinuous thread across the blank space of an incomplete map." Their advance guard has had the occasional short brush with the enemy, who seems to be pulling back. They have discovered and set fire to a German encampment that had been hastily deserted.

Now they are going to conquer German East Africa.

On paper it undoubtedly looks like a big and impressive operation.

The Germans, just as in Europe, are going to be attacked simultaneously from a number of different directions: a British force will attack
from Northern Rhodesia, the Belgians will invade north of Lake Tanganyika and the Portuguese are expected to threaten the south (a state
of war between Germany and Portugal has existed for the last two days).
The main operation, however, is to take place in the north-east corner
of German East Africa, in the areas around Kilimanjaro. The idea is to
trap and destroy the main enemy forces in a classic encirclement operation. The column Buchanan and the rest of the 25th Fusiliers are accompanying is supposed to sweep down from the north and act as the anvil
to hold the retiring German forces so that the hammer—the main
force advancing from the west*—can pound them to pieces. The destination for both columns is Moshi. (This small town is the final station
on the long railway the Germans have built from Tanga on the coast.)
It is the logic of a great European war but grafted onto the geography of
Africa.

"Sweep down"? Well, what was meant to be a rapid advance on the
enemy rear has degenerated into a slow, jerky thrash through unknown
terrain. Since the column got into the bush, its speed has diminished
significantly. What is more, they have just arrived in tsetse-fly country,
and the horses and mules imported for the operation are particularly
susceptible to the diseases spread by the insects. The animals are dying
at a horrifying speed and in equally horrifying numbers.† (Whose idea
was it to use these horses and mules here? Clearly not someone with any
experience of this part of Africa.) All day they have been passing dead
and dying draught and riding animals lying beside the track they are
trampling out. It takes no more than twenty-four hours from the death

---

* This consists mainly of troops from South Africa, which after some hesitation decided
to side with the British Empire. (As usual, it is the thought of future territorial gains
which persuaded yet another nation to choose sides in the conflict. The war in Africa, just
as in the Middle East, is little more than a continuation of the imperialist competition for
territory that the great European powers indulged in during the middle of the nineteenth
century.) Many of the soldiers now marching side by side with the British are old Boer
fighters who a decade earlier had been bitter foes of the British. The commander-in-chief
of the whole operation is also an old Boer commander, the legendary Jan Smuts. War
creates many strange alliances.
† In the course of the operation the main column lost 5,000 of its 7,000 mules.

of one of these creatures for the corpse to "become a swarming mass of blowfly larvae—horrible to behold." (The same thing is true for fallen soldiers, of course.) The stench is overpowering.

Another bit of bad news is that the rainy season is just round the corner. Last night the heavens opened and it poured down. At present they have neither tents nor blankets (they are packed somewhere in the distant baggage train), so Buchanan and his fellow soldiers managed only three hours' sleep—out in the open, directly on the ground, freezing and soaked. Endurance is far harder than bravery.

They have been marching south all day, the whitewashed peak of Kilimanjaro over on their left, and towards dusk they finally break out of the bush into open country. It is more or less at that point that the column swings east and heads for the great mountain. At last they catch sight of their destination, Moshi, away in the far distance. The name means "smoke" in Swahili, referring to the wreaths of cloud that permanently crown the dome of the 19,340-foot mountain. As the sun sets they hear the sound of gunfire. The march comes to a halt: the advance guard has bumped into some enemy scouts. It does not, however, turn into a serious engagement because, true to their usual pattern, their opponents simply disappear without trace. After waiting for a short while, the winding column lurches into motion again.

They set up camp by the Sanja river at nine o'clock. In the far distance, in the darkness between their own bivouac and Moshi, they can see fires. In the last seven days they have marched less than forty-five miles. During the night they hear occasional shots fired by nervous sentries. Otherwise everything is calm.

The anvil has slowly begun to reach its allotted position—but where is the hammer?

The following day it becomes obvious that the German forces have already slipped out of the trap and disappeared to the south, surprisingly quickly, in good order and without any major losses. Moshi has been taken. The German part of the population has fled, leaving only Africans, Greeks and the ubiquitous merchants from Goa. In other respects the operation is a failure.

It rains almost all day on Monday, on Tuesday likewise.

WEDNESDAY, 15 MARCH 1916
A letter is written to Vincenzo D'Aquila's mother

D'Aquila's family in the United States know that he is in hospital, but little more than that. His mother sends one telegram after another to the Italian military and to the hospital enquiring about her son: she wonders how he is and whether he can perhaps be allowed to come home to the United States to be looked after there. She finally receives the following answer from the director of San Osvaldo:

Udine, 15 March 1916

Dear Madam:

I am sorry to be unable to comply with your request since the military authorities have already arranged for his transfer to the Asylum in Siena, which removal was effected on March tenth.

His physical condition was quite satisfactory; on the other hand, however, his delirious, grandiose and absurd ideas persist. I fear we are faced with a mental affliction of long duration.

(Signed)

THE DIRECTOR

SATURDAY, 18 MARCH 1916
Paolo Monelli is bombed in Roncegno

All of a sudden—just look at that, shit from the air, two bombs explode only five metres away from you, and you still don't know whether you are injured or not. (After an eternity of deafness you hear—as if from an infinite distance—the voice of the companion lying hugging the ground alongside you: "Monelli, are you wounded?" "I'm just going to feel to see.") And then you think that this sense of grace is deceptive. In a blind rage the field doctor hurls kitchen plates at the airborne intruder.

TUESDAY, 28 MARCH 1916
Kresten Andresen encounters spring and discontent in Billy-Montigny

Spring but still not spring. Bushes and beech trees are showing little mouse-ears of green, the apple trees are in bud and anemones and other flowers have opened in the woods. But it is still cold and the wind is bitter.

Andresen is having some bad days: "I'm sick and tired of the whole business and finding it difficult to keep my spirits up." This is in spite of—or perhaps because of—the fact that he has recently been home for ten days' leave, the first leave he has had since the war began. He had only just returned when he was admitted to hospital yet again, this time with a severe throat infection and fever. He has still not taken part in any really fierce fighting: in a letter to a relative he almost seems to be apologising for this, apologising that he does not have any particularly dramatic experiences to pass on. (He has, however, sent souvenirs home; mainly shell fragments.) For him it is not so much a matter of the awful reality of war as its awful tedium. His service consists largely of working behind the lines or digging at night.

This is his twentieth month in uniform and he has started to lose any hopes he had for an early end to the war. He remembers, not without some bitterness, how almost exactly a year ago he believed the war would soon be over. Those frustrated hopes are undoubtedly part of the reason for his depression.

He is not alone in feeling frustrated about the way this war just grinds on and on at an ever higher cost. Inflation and food shortages are afflicting all of the warring countries and, apart from Russia, it is Germany and Austria that are suffering most. It is not just that the Allied naval blockade is proving to be deadly effective.* Food production has

---

* The British blockade had the paradoxical effect of forcing Germany to tighten its control of resources and to put the economy on a war footing that was much more efficient than Britain's for a considerable time.

also been hit by administrative carelessness, by lack of transport and by the fact that so many farmers and farm workers have been called up to serve under the flag. And those who have remained in agriculture often cannot resist the temptation to sell their products through the black market, where prices can be up to ten times higher. (It has, for instance, been estimated that roughly half of all the eggs and pork produced in Germany and Austria go straight into the black economy.) Add to that the rapidly rising prices of everyday items and the result is an equation impossible for most families to solve, particularly those in the towns. Every single graph has begun to point in the wrong direction: ill health, undernourishment, child mortality, discontent and criminality among the young are all on the increase.

Andresen has met other soldiers returning from leave and they have had some astonishing stories to relate:

One of them told us of something approaching a riot in Bremen where large crowds of women smashed shop-windows and stormed the shops. Mortensen from Skibelund met a man from Hamburg who left Hamburg four days before his leave was up because his wife no longer had any food to give him.

For some inexplicable reason a couple of the malcontents have taken to directing their outpourings of rage at Andresen—one of them, for instance, accused him of extreme patriotism. A soldier from Hamburg came up to him today and, with the Social-Democrat party paper *Vorwärts* in one hand, began to question him about the attitudes of the South Schleswig Reichstag representatives to the war. Andresen responded: "There are many people there who think for themselves." The men at the front, too, have begun to feel the impact of the food shortages: they rarely get butter to put on their coarse army bread—it has been replaced by an unappetising variety of jam that the soldiers lampoon with abusive ditties. (Military humour has also coined a string of alternative names for this jam, such as "Hindenburg Cream" or "Kaiser Wilhelm's Memorial Butter.")

The front is calm:

I've hardly heard the sound of gunfire in the week I've been back here. All the forces are gathering down at Verdun. There is talk here that a fort has fallen, but there are so many rumours flying around. What's the situation with Romania? Everything seems calm to me, but it is no doubt the calm before the storm.

MONDAY, 10 APRIL 1916
Edward Mousley sees the slaughter of the last horses in Kut al-Amara

They have been slaughtering the draught animals and the mules for some time but they have consciously been sparing the riding animals. That is no longer possible. Another attempt to relieve them has run into the sand and orders have now been given that the last horses will have to be slaughtered in order to feed the besieged garrison, which will soon be starving.

Mousley tears up some fresh grass and goes to where the horses are lined up. His own horse, Don Juan, obviously recognises his owner and welcomes him eagerly in the way he has taught the horse to do. Mousley feeds him the grass.

Then the slaughter begins.

A non-commissioned officer shoots the horses. There is the crack of a gunshot and one by one the big, heavy animals crumple to the ground. The blood flows. At first Mousley watches, noting that the horses follow the proceedings, trembling as they wait their turn. Like the other horses Don Juan stamps uneasily but otherwise remains quite still. When it is almost Don Juan's turn Mousley can watch no longer; he asks the man with the gun to take careful aim and to tell him when it is all over. Then he kisses the horse's cheek and walks away. He can see how the horse turns and watches him go.

Then there is another crack from the gun.

His dinner that evening is Don Juan's heart and kidneys. (These parts of the horse are always reserved for the owner—Mousley has also kept Don Juan's black tail.) Admittedly it feels strange, but he does not think there is anything wrong about it. He writes in his diary: "I am sure he would have preferred that I, rather than another, should do so."

. . .

Sarah Macnaughtan is now in Teheran. Ill and exhausted, she has decided to cut short her service in Persia and travel home. She has had so little to do that her time here can, in reality, hardly be called service. She writes in her diary:

> It is such an odd jump I have taken. At home I drifted on, never feeling older, hardly counting birthdays—always brisk, and getting through a heap of work—beginning my day early and ending it late. And now there is a great gulf dividing me from youth and old times, and it is filled with dead people whom I can't forget. In the matter of dying one doesn't interfere with Providence, but it seems to me that now would be rather an appropriate time to depart.

TUESDAY, 25 APRIL 1916
Elfriede Kuhr witnesses a disturbance at Schneidemühl railway station

Once again Elfriede goes to the railway station. She is going to visit Dora Haensch, her best friend, whose parents run a small restaurant in the station building. Two soldiers come in while Elfriede is there. One of them is a young man with elegant, regular features and the other is big, broad and very drunk. The drunken soldier shouts for beer but plump Herr Haensch refuses him. Then the drunk leans over the bar to pour himself a glass but Herr Haensch takes him by the shoulders and shoves him away. The drunk immediately pulls out his bayonet and lunges at Herr Haensch, who runs for the back door with an unexpected turn of speed, while Dora and her mother scream. Several guests get up and grab chairs, which they raise either as weapons or as shields. The drunk's companion, who has meanwhile sat down at a table with his legs stretched out in front of him, calmly says to his comrade, "Get out of here—and quick." Which the drunk duly does.

Herr Haensch returns immediately, accompanied by a warrant officer and two soldiers of the watch. The warrant officer goes up to the drunk's friend, who is still sitting at his table calmly leafing through a newspaper, and asks in a pleasant tone for the name of the man who has fled and the name of the regiment he belongs to. The soldier with the newspaper refuses to give the information, at which the warrant officer goes closer to him and says something that Elfriede does not catch. The young soldier stands up and yells, "You are a swine, sir. I didn't want this bloody war and I've been forced to play at being a soldier. Fine. Well, then! If you want to say something to me then be good enough to use a military form of address. You can pester me as much as you like but I will not disclose my friend's name!"

The heated discussion continues: the young soldier stubbornly refuses to answer the officer's questions and finally he is arrested himself. Elfriede watches him being led away between the two guards, who have gleaming bayonets fixed on their rifles. The arrested soldier's face is so pale that his lips look almost white. Everyone starts talking again as soon as the door closes behind the four men. The restaurant is filled with excited voices. Elfriede puts her hand on Dora's heart and feels that it is pounding hard, hard.

Elfriede tells Dora that she cannot decide who was right—the warrant officer or the man who refused to give his friend's name. Herr Haensch hears Elfriede's comments and yells at her, "Now just you listen to me, there is no doubt about it. The warrant officer was obviously right. The army has to have discipline, otherwise . . . otherwise there'd be chaos." The enraged Herr Haensch gives Elfriede a hefty slap on the backside and pushes her out of the restaurant.

Confused and upset, Elfriede makes her way home. She can see both sides of the argument—on one hand, the elegant young man who refused to inform on his friend and, on the other, the warrant officer who was just doing his duty:

> But most of all I was upset by myself. I can never really decide for myself what is right and what is wrong about this war. I rejoice at our victories but at the same time the thought of all those dead and wounded makes me beside myself. I heard yesterday that there is a military hospital hidden in the forest for the soldiers who have had their faces shot away. They apparently look so horrific that ordinary people can't even look at them.* Things like that make me despair.

* Such cases existed in all the warring countries, as did the policy of isolation—for the most part, voluntarily—in closed nursing homes. In France, 9,900 men with destroyed faces formed a special veterans' association after the war.

Today is Elfriede's fourteenth birthday and she has started wearing her hair in a different and more grown-up fashion.

In Kut al-Amara that night Edward Mousley watches as one last effort is made to bring in supplies for the besieged British garrison. An armour-plated riverboat, full of provisions and manned by a special crew of volunteers (all of them unmarried), has tried to work its way up the Tigris under cover of darkness in a desperate effort to creep past the Ottoman lines and reach the beleaguered troops. The boat, SS *Julnar*, is sighted, however, and fired on from all sides until she finally runs aground. Mousley writes in his journal:

> Here the Turkish guns confronted her at a few yards' range. Her officers were killed, Lieut. Crowley [*sic*] captured,[*] and she was taken within sight of our men waiting to unload her by the Fort, and of the sad little group of the garrison who beheld her from the roof-tops of Kut. She lies there now. It appears that the tragic but obvious end of so glorious an enterprise is a last hope. We have scarcely rations for tomorrow.

SUNDAY, 7 MAY 1916
Kresten Andresen and his dull life in Billy-Montigny

The green of early summer. The warmth of early summer. Birdsong. Just now it is the utter waste of time that is troubling him most: the fact that the days just pass, one the same as another, with nothing happening that has not happened before, with the same routines, the same words, and nothing being done. He is also terrified that he is becoming so forgetful. He searches in vain through his memory for so many of the things he had learned earlier—history, the history of literature. He has hardly put a book down before he has forgotten what is in it. As usual, he is ready to listen to any tiny rumour that peace will come soon, even though he has

---

* Lieutenant Commander Charles Henry Cowley, who was executed immediately afterwards by his captors. He was awarded a posthumous Victoria Cross.

been disappointed so often in the past. The front is absolutely quiet, and he is happy about that.

Andresen is writing a letter home today:

Dear Parents!

The same day I sent you my last letter from this place I fell over and sprained the top joint in the middle finger of my left hand, as Misse has perhaps told you. The transport I should have gone with has now left. But my finger should certainly be better within the week. It was actually straightened out quickly. I'm wandering round enjoying life and enjoying nature. My washerwoman has lent me a good French novel and when I get tired of reading I do some sketching. I'm intending to send you a couple of small drawings—I've already sent one to Aunt Dorothea. Not that they are really worth having—this life is so unbelievably stupefying that I'm absolutely no good at anything any longer. I don't know what to do about it. But I do believe the condition has something to do with the fact that we never get anything to eat but incessant oatmeal soup! And army bread and that never-ending jam.

MONDAY, 8 MAY 1916
Sarah Macnaughtan arrives back at her London home

A young man helps Macnaughtan in through the door of her house at 1, Norfolk Street. She is welcomed home by two of her sisters and by Mary King, her old maid. When Macnaughtan sees her maid, she says, "You were right, Mary. Russia has killed me."*

Only a few fragments remain of her memories of the journey from Persia to Great Britain: the missionary, who was her companion and helper on the journey north; the car journey of more than 300 miles over snow-capped mountains and up to the Caspian Sea; the boat that they missed by only one hour; the week she spent recovering at the British embassy in Petrograd; her walk—on sticks—across the ice at Helsingfors to reach another ship.

---

* See Monday, 30 August 1915, page 153.

Macnaughtan has stopped keeping a diary by this point. The last entry was about a month earlier:

> I should like to have "left the party"—quitted the feast of life—when all was gay and amusing. I should have been sorry to come away, but it would have been far better than being left till all the lights are out. I could have said truly to the Giver of the feast, "Thanks for an excellent time." But now so many of the guests have left, and the fires are going out, and I am tired.

They carry her upstairs to her bedroom. Her prematurely grey hair is thin. She, too, is very thin, very weak and very, very pale.

THURSDAY, 18 MAY 1916
Angus Buchanan leaves Mbuyuni and learns something about mules

The worst of the rains are over. After almost two months of waiting in the wet around Kilimanjaro it is time to march on in search of the elusive enemy. The capture of Moshi was a success but they failed yet again to defeat the enemy. Like many of his companions, Buchanan is reluctantly impressed by their German opponents, not least by their native troops, who have demonstrated their discipline, skill and great courage. So this is not going to be easy. The Germans are already behaving like the guerrilla army they are well on the way to becoming, whereas the British corps moves with all the weight and cautious, clumsy slowness of a regular army.

The main force marches out from Mbuyuni during the afternoon. Buchanan happens to be in command of the battalion baggage-train for the day, which consists of pack animals—mules—since they are once again setting off into rugged terrain. There is the scent of steaming, damp, sun-baked vegetation.

It turns out to be, in his own words, "a memorable march." Most of the animals are new and some of them have never carried pack-saddles before so they rear and play up. Time after time the mules break free or twist themselves out of the unaccustomed harnesses and Buchanan and several other soldiers spend the whole evening riding back and forth along the column chasing animals that are on the run. They stop every now and then to mend a harness or to re-saddle "the rearing, frightened, stubborn brutes." This continues all night.

When they eventually make camp Buchanan knows that four of his mules are missing, but, even then, they still have two more than they counted at the start of the march. In the darkness they simply caught all the animals they found running loose and some of them clearly belong to other battalions. They decide, as usual, to keep the animals they have found and not report it to anyone.

TUESDAY, 23 MAY 1916
Paolo Monelli takes part in the retreat down from the
Cima Undici

They were taken up to the front in lorries in great haste, the drivers telling them what they knew, which was not much, just rumours about continued retreats. An Austro-Hungarian offensive around the Asiago plateau has been going on since 15 May and the enemy has had great success, at least by comparison with the fruitless pushes by the Italian army over on the Isonzo. Unless the Italians succeed in stopping them they will reach the lowlands and will then be in a position to carry on to the coast, to Venice. It is only about twenty miles to Vicenza. The Alpini battalion Paolo Monelli belongs to has been on Monte Cima for some days and they have occasionally come under artillery fire. But what is happening? And why?

Monelli and the rest of them are not receiving any news but they are still trying to understand what is going on, trying to read the signs— and the signs they can find are anything but good. Their own artillery is becoming ever weaker and yesterday evening the last guns in their sector—a battery of light mountain cannon—disappeared. Worse still is the fact that the noise of battle, explosions and muzzle-flashes, slowly moved closer to them and then went *past* them. One of the companies in their battalion has already been recalled down into the valley, so when they wake this morning they find themselves all alone on the mountain top. Someone says that Cima Dodici has fallen. Cima Dodici? They all turn their heads—that mountain lies *to their rear*, surely? "We are caught like rats in a trap."

Then orders reach them: they are to stay there until darkness falls—they are the rearguard and any resistance they can put up will give others the chance to get away. "What is going to happen to us? What is going to happen to Italy?" They can see with their own eyes how Austro-Hungarian battalions are streaming down from the mountain next to them. They can only watch helplessly since the enemy is out of range and the Alpini do not have any heavy weapons. Monelli and his companions are left in peace; it is as if everyone has forgotten about them, including the enemy. The morning turns into day and there is nothing for them to do but to wait there, cut off and isolated, "and the torment of waiting is all the more bitter because of the feeling of catastrophe that has gripped us."

At lunchtime Monelli climbs up to the cave where the battalion staff officers are located. At its mouth he meets the battalion commander, a major, his eyes red from lack of sleep. The major stands there twisting his beard. He is drunk. "Come here," he says to Monelli and gives him some wine. "Have you made your confession? By tonight we'll be surrounded." The major has been ordered to stay in position. "And so we'll stay in position and then we'll be captured. And then we'll be blamed and mocked."

The wine works. (The major calls it "a friend that never deserts you.") Slightly intoxicated, Monelli begins to see the situation in a somewhat brighter light. It will be evening in a few hours. Perhaps they will manage to escape. And if the enemy attacks before then the company will do its best to win a little time, "and then perhaps the division will manage to get its office papers back to safety."

The miracle happens. No one attacks them.

When darkness falls they begin to work their way in small groups down the mountain and into the woods.

Cold rain is falling. A nearby village is burning and the shapes of the trees and rocks are distorted by its reflected glow. They cross the river half an hour before the bridge is due to be blown and they take a short break on the other side. They have a drink of the water, metal mugs jangling against the stones of the watercourse, and eat some dry biscuits. Before they continue up over the next ridge they take the time to bury the last man to die that day. His name is Giovanni Panato and he was struck by a fragment of a randomly fired shell while they were climbing. That is often the case: a random cause has a random effect. Panato shouted out when he was wounded but struggled on, only to collapse and die at last.

As they pack their things, their mugs clinking as they are shoved back into the rucksacks, the soldiers start asking questions. Why are they retreating? Why don't they stay and fight? Monelli has trouble coming up with answers:

> What do they know and what do I know about what is happening? Nothing. We fight, we march, we halt, we are just numbers among the mass that pours forward, that manoeuvres along this mountainous front in the ice of the mighty Dolomite Alps, with a dull grudge in our hearts, a painful feeling of not knowing, of not seeing.

At the same time, in some distant castle with thick carpets on the floor, there are the people Monelli calls "those mysterious gods who spin the threads of our fate," in other words, "an officer who writes, a clerk who copies, an adjutant who leaves the room, and a colonel who swears."

> This is the war. It is not the risk of dying, not the red firework display of a bursting shell that blinds us as it comes whizzing down (and rise to his feet, look around, quite confused by the great anguish*), but the feeling of being a puppet in the hands of an unknown puppeteer—and that feeling sometimes chills the heart as if death itself had taken hold of it. Chained to the trench until orders to be relieved arrive as suddenly as a cannon shot or a snowstorm, tied to ever-present danger, to a fate that is inscribed with the number of your platoon or the name of your trench, unable to take your shirt off when you want to, unable to write home when you want to, seeing the most modest needs of

---

* "Quando si leva che intorno si mira—tutto smarrito della grande angoscia," from Dante's *Inferno*, Canto XXIV. As has been mentioned (page 196), Monelli always carried his volume of Dante.

existence governed by rules over which you have no influence—
all this is war.[*]

They continue in the darkness, uphill again. Their steps are heavy in
the mixture of mud and snow. He sees yet another burning village and
can hear explosions and rifle fire behind them. The rearguard—or, more
accurately, the rearguard's rearguard—is under attack: it is poor old da
Pèrgine and his men.[†]

Their progress becomes even more leaden, staggering and vacant,
their steps dully mechanical. After a while no one even has the energy
to complain. Monelli and his companions have not slept properly for
several nights and their weariness is painful, numbing, almost narcotic
in its effect. Wrapped in the dull ache of exhaustion they let the world
around flow slowly past, stripped of all its significance. They no longer
pay any attention to explosions and burning houses, hardly think of the
fact they are being pursued and could be attacked at any moment. Rests
are no longer of much help either, since when they wake from a brief nap
(on the ground, in the snow) they feel even more numbed, even more
desperately grey and weary.

They walk on through the forest all night until a cold pale dawn
arrives.

The sun is already rising when they reach their own lines. Two sentries try to stop them, demanding passwords. The exhausted men hurl
a torrent of oaths at the sentries and stagger past them. Further on, they
come across men from other companies and other battalions, a confused
jumble of soldiers, carts and nervous mules, "the sharp sound of shod
hooves on stone." A light drizzle is falling.

Rest, at last, at last. Monelli crawls into a small tent. He falls asleep
with his hands tightly clenched, and in his dreams he continues to march
a march that has no end.

---

* Monelli continues (and personal experience permits the present author to vouch for
the truth of the statement): "The press correspondent who visits the trenches does not
know this [war]; the officer from the general staff who pops up to ensure that he gets a
medal by being with us does not know this [war]. Once they are hungry or tired or think
they have done their job, they take out their watch and say, 'It's late. I have to go now.' "
† Garbari da Pèrgine, the officer who volunteered to lead the rearguard. Monelli felt
confident that "our rear is safe for [da Pèrgine] is defending it: he asked for that dangerous
task because, he said, he knew the positions well."

That same day René Arnaud and his battalion are still waiting in the village of Belval-en-Argonne. They can just hear the sound of the guns away at Verdun. They are extremely nervous, suspecting that they will soon be thrown into the great battle. Being at the front when things are calm can undoubtedly be dangerous but is not particularly costly in terms of lives: there might be the occasional raid to be undertaken, but it is mostly the British who do things like that. But to be sent to the front in the context of a major offensive is a completely different matter. Then there will inevitably be losses, huge losses:

> We tramped around, swapped rumours and discussed things. I can still remember Truchet, the battalion doctor, standing there with his head bowed, legs apart and an anxious, restless expression on his face as, more nervous than ever before, he scratched his black beard with his left hand: "This is a disgrace! This slaughter should be stopped! They're allowing thousands of men to be massacred just to defend a heap of out-of-date old forts. It is horrible! Oh, what a fine bunch of generals we've got."

TUESDAY, 30 MAY 1916
René Arnaud reaches the front line on Hill 321 outside Verdun

> The worst mental suffering in wartime is when one's thoughts rush off and anticipate what one has not yet done or experienced, when the imagination is given ample opportunity to consider the dangers that await—and to multiply them a hundred times over. It is a well-known fact that the fear induced by thinking of a danger is more nerve-racking than meeting the danger itself, in the same way that desire is more intoxicating than the satisfaction of desire.

So writes René Arnaud. The great battle has been going on almost continuously since the end of February, when the German army launched its carefully prepared offensive. Arnaud and his men knew that sooner or later it would be their turn,* that they too would soon be travelling

---

* Of the 330 infantry regiments in the French army, 259 at some stage served at Verdun.

up along "La Route," the only road that can be used to supply this sector of the front and along which lorries pass at an average rate of one every fourteen seconds. To those who receive the order to march to Verdun it feels like a sacrificial progress.*

Arnaud has heard people talking about the statistics. An officer recently returned from Verdun said straight out, "The whole thing is very simple. You will be relieved when three-quarters of your men have been knocked out. That's the going rate."

Arnaud and the rest of his battalion have spent the day in the seventeenth-century citadel of Verdun, an enormous structure of staff rooms, stores, endless corridors, subterranean casemates and bomb-proof barrack rooms. A warm smell of cabbage, mouldy bread, disin-fectant, sweat and sour wine permeates the whole place. The sound of distant shell-bursts, like a ceaseless growl, penetrates through the small loopholes in the three-foot-thick stone walls. The Germans have three times as many artillery pieces per yard of the front here as they had dur-ing the great breakthrough at Gorlice—and it shows.

The heat is stifling. Arnaud has been lying on his straw mattress thinking about the statistics. Three-quarters. Which of his men will not be returning from out there? Which of the battalion's officers will get through the coming week without being wounded or killed? Statistically speaking, just three or four. Will he be one of them?

They receive their orders during the afternoon:

> Tonight the 6th Battalion is to relieve the battalion from the 301st Regiment that has been stationed on Hill 321. The battalion will leave the citadel at 19:15 hours to arrive at 21:00 hours at the point where the road to Bras meets the Pied du Gravier ravine. A gap of 50 metres is to be observed between each group.

Arnaud talks to his men, who are busy filling their packs with tinned food, dry biscuits, tools and ammunition. The atmosphere is a nervous one. He tries to calm them, not by making patriotic speeches—he knows

---

* The road was later christened La Voie Sacrée (Sacred Road) by Maurice Barrès, one of France's best-known nationalist politicians and wordsmiths, and it perhaps caught on, suggests the author Ian Ousby, because it seems "to evoke the thought of *Via Dolorosa*, 'the road of suffering,' and thus compares the suffering and sacrifice of the soldiers at Verdun with Christ's progress to crucifixion on Golgotha."

that never works in this kind of situation—but by invoking precedent: "We have always been a lucky company. We are going to return from Verdun."

They move out in single file in the dusk, group by group, out of the dark and safe interior of the citadel and through the empty and silent ruins of the town. Now and then a heavy shell lands close to the cathedral. The long chain of heavily laden men crosses the river by a pontoon bridge, its planks echoing under their feet. Arnaud looks at the dark water and wonders "how many of us will ever cross this bridge again."

While they are taking a rest a man "with a flabby, swollen face and crafty eyes" comes up to Arnaud, holds out some papers and appeals to him. The man is clearly making a last-minute attempt to be excused. He points out he is a tailor and has never been in the front line before because he has a hernia. The papers confirm this. Arnaud, who is already bitter that, given the prospect of being sent to Verdun, one of the professional officers in the battalion suddenly managed to wangle a transfer to the baggage-train, merely snarls at him.

Arnaud cannot help feeling sorry for the man as he watches him going away crestfallen, his head bowed and the papers still in his hand. And he thinks that he, too, might have tried the same thing were it not for the badges of rank on his arm.

Immediately after this they pass a unit on its way out of the fire, all of them with muddied clothes and feverish eyes; he cannot help envying the young lieutenant commanding them—"How I wished I was him!"

They begin clambering up the high sides of the ravine that leads to the battlefield.

The thunder of the artillery grows, all the individual sounds merging together. The sky to the right of them is glowing where shells are falling over Fort de Douaumont, captured by the Germans on the fourth day of the battle and now a centre point for the fighting. Indeed, it has become more than that and is now a landmark, a magnet, a myth (for both sides), a symbol which, in the way of symbols, has acquired a significance beyond its strategic importance and become the focus of keen competition between German and French propagandists, its capture a measure of success at a time when successes have become more and more abstract in nature whereas reverses are all too concrete. Since the battle began at the end of February roughly twenty million shells have landed on the battlefield.

The darkness grows deeper as they continue moving forward along an empty road. Suddenly there is a lightning flash above them, followed by a short, sharp report. Instinctively they all duck. The first enemy shell. Now and then they take a break. They can smell the stench of rotting flesh. Arnaud is afraid and becoming more and more impatient. Finally, they meet their guide:

> We set off at a fast pace, across a ravine, up some steep slopes, turned off to the right and then swung to the left. Shells were exploding on both sides of us. We jumped down into a connecting trench, climbed out of it again, leapt down again and at last scrambled up yet again. I was following in line behind the last group and was marching as though asleep.

They come to a halt immediately in front of a ridge that is being fired on by the German artillery. Their guide has disappeared into the night. Arnaud is under a lot of pressure: he has no idea where they are but he knows that they must be in position before sunrise. If they are not in a bunker by then they will be spotted by the German forward observers and machine gunners and that will be the end of them. So he goes to the front of the company and they quickly set off again, down into a little hollow peppered with shell holes, past a hill where 15cm shells are thumping down regularly in salvoes of four and into an empty connecting trench. They come across two officers half-asleep beside a lit candle in an improvised bunker: they have no idea where Hill 321 is.

Arnaud moves on, gambling that it is to their right:

> I could already sense that cold edge to the air that means that dawn is not far off. I hurried along, followed by swaying bayonets and water bottles. If only we can get there before it's light! In the distance the contours of the ridge were beginning to show up against a sky that was still dark. The bombardment became more intense, as it always does before dawn. "Get a move on! Get a move on!"

At last—bunkers, shadowy figures, Hill 321.[*] He finds the commander of the battalion. He is given a guide to accompany them for the

---

[*] Hill 321 is the point of an elevated section that starts from the ridge where the Ossuary is now located. The actual spot can be found by going about 400 metres north-west from the parking area, along what is called Le Chemin de l'Étoile. Those visiting should wear stout shoes and avoid blind alleys.

very last section, up a seemingly endless slope. Once up on the plateau they are met by a hail of shells but still move forward. Then they meet a captain, the officer in command of the company they are to relieve. The handover in the grey light of dawn is the simplest imaginable— the captain points out where the Germans are, where the line of their own trenches runs and rounds it off with a quick, "This is the front line. Good night."

What the maps show as a trench turns out to be little more than a ditch that is hardly a metre in depth. His soldiers lie down and soon go to sleep, leaning against one another. Arnaud himself is utterly exhausted, both by the physical exertions and by the enormous strain. He sinks down with his head between his knees. "I was on the battlefield at Verdun but was hardly conscious of the fact."

WEDNESDAY, 31 MAY 1916
Willy Coppens lists the accidents during the spring in Étampes

There is a special procedure to be followed whenever a fatal accident occurs. All flying comes to a halt, the flying machines are rolled into their hangars and all the trainees gather round to hold a wake over the mangled body—"a depressing business." The funeral takes place the following day, and the citizens of the town and all the classes in the school, as well as the other trainee pilots, all file past the grave. (Those killed in accidents are always buried in Étampes' own small cemetery.) Then the hangar doors are opened and flying lessons start again.

Willy Coppens has seen this procedure repeated many times during the spring. Accidents are, in fact, very common occurrences.[*] It is the noise, above all, that sticks in his memory. First of all the screams of the spectators, followed by "that dreadful sound of splintering wood." And finally, silence, that indescribable silence when the engine has stopped, the pieces of wreckage have settled and the body has hit the ground with a strange sort of dull crunch, that empty silence that lasts for a few seconds—and for eternity.

[*] And would continue to be. During the war more Belgian pilots died in crashes than in battle.

The first smash Coppens saw with his own eyes occurred on 1 February. He and a couple of others were lying wrapped in their fur-lined flying coats sunning themselves in the weak winter sun and waiting for their turn. The air was alive with the rising and falling buzz of flying machines circling the aerodrome when he suddenly heard one of the nicely ticking engines begin to race and someone shouted, "My God, he's going to kill himself!"

> At the very moment I raised my eyes I saw a Farman machine on its way down in an inexplicable and almost vertical dive, at a speed that was far too fast, which is why it broke apart in the air. The body of the aeroplane literally burst apart and the wings, stays and other parts flew in all directions. I could pick out the tail, the engine and the pilot. Everything fell straight down and crashed right in front of us in a field some 400 metres away.

Some of the onlookers rushed there immediately. Coppens was not one of them. He did not want to look. And the accidents had simply continued:

> On 8 February we buried the French pilot Chalhoup.
> On 6 March Le Boulanger performed a turn that was much too tight, lost speed and spun to the ground. He was severely injured when we dragged him from the wreckage.
> On 14 March we buried Clement, a French pilot.
> On 26 April Piret was doing a turn in a Blériot machine, lost speed and glided down sideways to the ground from a height of 90 metres. Once again he escaped with minor injuries.
> On 27 April Biéran de Catillon turned a Henri Farman[*] upside down in a truly terrifying way but escaped without serious injuries.
> On 16 May François Vergult crashed a Maurice Farman without any harm to himself.
> On 17 May Adrien Richard crashed another Maurice Farman on landing and they built us a new aeroplane from the wreckage of the two machines.

---

[*] Maurice Farman and Henri Farman were two very similar types of aeroplane, both having the engine and propeller behind the pilot.

On 20 May De Meulemeester, an excellent pilot, went into a spin after performing a pretty risky manoeuvre. Even though he fell from a greater height than Le Boulanger he was not injured as badly and was back on his feet after a day or two. On 27 May Evrard[*] ripped the undercarriage off a B.E. 2.

Today, 31 May, there is yet another smash. This time it is a pilot by the name of Kreyn, who lands his Maurice Farman so clumsily that there is a screeching crash. He is saved by something that is a recent introduction—a flying helmet. Not everyone wears one.[†] Some of them think it is just too ugly and too reminiscent of the padded caps that worried Flemish mothers put on their children when they are learning to walk.

Coppens cannot wait to take his test. He will then get golden wings on his uniform, the rank of sergeant and five extra Louis d'or in his pay every month.

Richard Stumpf writes in his journal on the same day:

At last, at last—finally it's happening, the great event that has been the object of our desires, thoughts and feelings for the last twenty-two months. This is what we have been hoping for, working for and training for with such passion for years.

What he is describing is the Battle of Jutland, the great naval battle in which 274 German and British warships clash off the Danish coast during the afternoon and evening. By nightfall fourteen British and eleven German warships have gone to the bottom and over 8,000 seamen have lost their lives. Stumpf's ship, SMS *Helgoland*, fired sixty-three shells during the battle and was hit only by one. The crew came through unharmed. There is another entry in his journal for that day:

---

[*] Lili Evrard was, however, killed in another accident that summer.
[†] There were even pilots who went without goggles: eyes get used to the wind after a while and the tears stop flowing. And the speed was not that great. In some aeroplanes with the propeller behind the pilot (such as the Farman just referred to), it was perfectly possible to take to the air wearing a uniform cap without it flying off in the wind.

I am convinced that it is actually impossible for a man to describe the thoughts and feelings that go through his mind during his baptism of fire. If I said I was afraid I would be telling a lie. No, it was an indescribable mixture of pleasure, fear, curiosity, apathy and . . . the joy of battle.

Quite soon, and with some justification, the confused battle is being described as a minor German victory. It had no impact on the war.

THURSDAY, 8 JUNE 1916
Angus Buchanan goes hunting for food on the Pangani river

He would actually rather not get up, he would like to stay here, lying wrapped in his warm blankets. Angus Buchanan can see the thin pin-pricks of light from the stars above him but he can sense the coming sunrise. "Just five minutes more."

"Come on!" A hushed voice stirs him and he sits up in the early morning light. Under a bush alongside him Gilham, the other lieuten-ant, is lacing his boots and the two men grin at one another, sharing their secret. In spite of the fact that hunting is forbidden, as is leaving the camp, the two of them are intending to do just that. They are sick of the endless stew made of unappetising tinned meat and, anyway, rations have been cut because supplies are running low. Both of them are hungry, and how are they supposed to manage without food?

Many of the soldiers are on the verge of malnutrition, as a result of which the number of cases of sickness in this heat is rising steeply. The sick then have to be sent back for nursing care and that takes up a sig-nificant part of their already limited transport resources. And the sick still need feeding: the men being sent back eat just as much food as those moving forward to join the fighting units, so the rations for the latter have to be cut even further. It is a vicious circle. Units that started as regiments have shrunk to 170–200 men, more the size of companies.[*]

---

[*] Although Buchanan might be thought guilty of exaggeration here, since a regiment commonly comprised 3,000–5,000 men, the claim of some historians that for every man lost in battle during this campaign a further thirty were killed or incapacitated by disease lends credence to his assertion.

The German forces they are chasing through bush, jungle and swamp, across rivers, mountains and savannahs, are apparently untroubled by the climate and disease, which is hardly surprising given that their troops are native and consequently used to the former and stoical about the latter. They are often familiar with the terrain, can move through it with impressive ease and know what can be foraged. And thanks to good treatment and good pay they have developed a high degree of loyalty to their German masters.

The British have been forced to reconsider their reluctance to arm Africans and use them in the fighting. Part of the point of the operation Buchanan has been involved in since the end of the rainy season has been to push the Germans out of Tabora, the region where they recruit their best *askaris*. Von Lettow-Vorbeck has also proved to be a master of improvisation: supplies are no longer reaching him from Germany so he has started manufacturing his own ammunition, taught his troops to make their own boots and acquired heavy artillery by salvaging the guns of the cruiser *Königsberg* after the British navy chased her into the Rufugi delta.

Buchanan and Gilham take their army rifles and creep out of the camp past rows of sleeping men. They take Buchanan's African servant Hamisi with them. At first they have to fight their way through dense, dry bush. The worst parts are the thickets of thorny shrubs and trees, and the worst of the lot are those the Africans call "*mgoonga*,"* which have thorns that are inordinately long, sharp and prolific. They avoid these small trees if at all possible and Buchanan says: "I will carry memories of Mgoonga as long as I live." Their hands, arms and legs are soon bloody.

After an hour the landscape begins to open up and they are now far from the camp for their shots not to give them away. Buchanan and Gilham load their rifles and creep forward silently. Hamisi falls back a little and follows them at a distance.

They have gone little more than half a mile when a kudu jumps out, but the graceful antelope bounds off and disappears into the bushes before they manage to get a shot at it. Buchanan swears. After a mile and a half they have come across nothing but animal tracks—those of impala and warthog—and have set up a couple of flocks of guineafowl.

* Swahili *mgunga*: *Acacia polyacantha* ssp. *polyacantha*—the falcon's claw acacia or white thorn tree.

It is time to turn back. The sun has begun its voyage across a clear blue sky and within an hour it is going to be almost unbearably hot. Their morning's hunt for these quick and elusive animals has been as fruitless as the division's hunt for the quick and elusive companies of German Schutztruppen.

Buchanan, Gilham and Hamisi take a different route back and it turns out to be a lucky choice. First of all they run into a gerenuk, which both men fire at and both miss. When they move on, the bush becomes denser again and Buchanan can no longer see Gilham, but he does hear a sudden shot followed by a triumphant shout: Gilham has spotted another gerenuk and brought it down. The two men yell with glee. Meat! Antelope meat, no less! Buchanan looks tenderly at the animal lying there dying at their feet. He has never seen the species until today:

> slender and delightfully delicate of build with a coat of close, short, glossy hair, dark chocolate brown, above the central sides, where a distinctive horizontal line clearly separated the dark upper part from those a shade or two lighter below.

The three men butcher the animal. Hamisi carries most of the bloody pieces and Buchanan and Gilham carry what he cannot manage. Scared of being discovered, they creep very cautiously back into camp.

They will be able to eat their fill today.

That same day René Arnaud and his men on Hill 321 at Verdun come under attack from the German infantry. The artillery fire eases off and then grey-clad figures appear in the cratered landscape in front of them:

> The sound of the shooting and the garlicky smell of the powder-smoke soon led to a kind of intoxication. "Shoot the swine! Shoot them!" Suddenly I saw a big man moving in front of me and to the right; I aimed and had that intuitive feeling that comes from a shot that is going to find its target; I pulled the trigger and as the recoil hit my shoulder the large body disappeared. I wondered later on whether it was my bullet or someone else's that hit him, or whether he had just thrown himself to the ground because of the fierce rifle fire. Anyway, he is the only German I think I have

"downed"* during three and a half years of war, and I'm not even sure in his case.

The attack is eventually beaten back with the help of hand grenades.

SATURDAY, 10 JUNE 1916
René Arnaud leaves Hill 321 on the front line at Verdun

By the time the news comes Arnaud has lost count of time. He does not know how long they have been up here on this broad ridge. (He will later calculate that it was ten days.) So much time has passed and so much has happened that Arnaud has given up hope of being relieved; indeed, given up hope of anything. It is as if he has been numbed by days and nights of bombardment and by the two attacks they pushed back. Danger hardly affects him, nor does the sight of yet another dead man:

> This indifference is perhaps the best condition for a man to be in in the midst of battle: to function instinctively, from habit, without either hope or fear. The long period of overwhelmingly powerful emotions has finally ended with emotion itself dying.

For a moment or two he cannot understand why the men sent to fetch their food rations should have returned empty-handed in the twilight. But they are quick to explain: "We're going back tonight." They all start jumping with joy. "We're going back tonight!"

There is still one thing to be done, however. Their captain, who has been drunk on cognac most of the time, turns up and tells them that they cannot leave the position until all the dead have been picked up and gathered in a half-finished trench immediately behind them. They cannot leave their own dead lying around when a new company takes over. The men grumble but Arnaud convinces them it must be done.

The unpleasant task is performed by the light of signal rockets and exploding shells. One body after another is lifted onto the piece of tarpaulin they are using as a stretcher and they trudge off with it to the

---

* The word Arnaud uses in ironic quotation marks is *descendu*.

improvised grave. Even though the dead are already "far gone and falling to pieces" they can recognise every one of them: Bérard (killed, like so many others, by the German machine gun over by Le Ravin des Dames— it could sweep their position from end to end); Bonheur (the runner who was so fond of wine); Mafieu (the cook who had been made a foot soldier as punishment for being drunk on duty); Sergeant Vidal (with his black beard and mournful eyes, killed by a bullet in the middle of his forehead when they were driving back a German assault the day before yesterday); Mallard (the man from the Vendée with his black hair and blue eyes— his foot was accidentally blown off by his own hand grenade and he bled to death); Jaud (Arnaud's old corporal, dark and suntanned, with the gentle eyes of a child and an awful beard); Ollivier (courageous, loyal little Ollivier with his straight fair hair); Sergeant Cartelier (tall, slim and recognisable anywhere by the special low boots he wore in spite of regulations); etc., etc., etc.*

The days have been hot and the stink of putrefaction comes in waves as the bodies are lifted and carried away. The men have to take regular breaks to breathe fresh air before returning to their task.

They do not finish until almost two o'clock in the morning and Arnaud feels "a bitter sense of satisfaction to have done what has to be done." He watches the unit that is coming to relieve them—heavily laden men who leave a smell of sweat hanging behind them. The lieutenant taking over the position is a whiner. All that is left of the barbed-wire barriers are some bent and twisted spirals, and the command post is just a hole between two piles of sandbags. Arnaud is furious about the complaints at first: "Have we really been through all this suffering just so that an idiot can come along and pretend that we haven't been doing our job?" But he calms down and thinks that the surly lieutenant will soon find out what it means to hold Hill 321 for ten days and ten nights.

The march back from the front line goes remarkably quickly. It is as if their weariness has been washed away. Nobody wants to take a long rest break, preferring to get as far as possible from the firing before the sun rises. The route back passes Fort de Froidterre and they stop in its

---

* Not all were killed by the enemy—both sides at Verdun lost men to their own misdirected shells. The mistakes were partly the result of human error—inaccurate aiming and the like—and partly because of mechanical failure caused by excessive use. The usual firing life of a field artillery piece was about 8,000 rounds.

shelter long enough to meet a troop coming from the other direction and going up into battle. It is a mirror image of themselves ten days earlier: "their coats are bright blue, their tanned leather equipment still yellow, their cooking pots still gleaming silver." Arnaud is wearing a coat covered in mud, binoculars round his neck, crumpled puttees, ten days' stubble and a damaged helmet—the crest was shot away during fighting at close quarters on 8 June. Most of his soldiers have neither rucksacks nor belts. Some of them no longer even have a rifle.

While Arnaud and his men are contemplating these impeccably kitted-out newcomers they see a shell land in their midst. Not one of Arnaud's men reacts; instead they continue on their way, following a muddy road. They can see dead men and dead horses along the roadside banks, and even a deserted ambulance. The men plod on as quickly as they can, in a "fearful and disordered way as if they were fleeing from a battle." Their eyes are fevered, their faces muddy. They do not look round except to cast repeated glances over their shoulders and swear at the observation balloon hanging over the German lines in the dawn light—it could call down artillery fire on them at any time. The estimate Arnaud heard on their way to Verdun has proved right, almost exactly: of the hundred men he led to the front only thirty are returning.

They reach the crossroads they passed ten days before. Arnaud sees Verdun shining red, white and silent in the morning sun and thinks: "War is beautiful—to the eyes of generals, journalists and scholars."

They cross the river and slowly put the dangers of the battlefield behind them. They take a break on the fringes of a wood and Arnaud sees a reservist sergeant reading a news sheet. Arnaud asks him what has been happening and the sergeant snorts, "Just the same old thing." He gives Arnaud the paper and Arnaud reads it before exclaiming: "It's us! It's us!" His men gather round him and he reads the press communiqué aloud:

8 June, 23:00 . . . On the right bank, after massive bombardment, the enemy made several assaults on our positions east and west of the Thiaumont farm. All the attacks were repulsed by our defensive fire and our machine guns.

9 June, 15:00 . . . On the right bank the Germans continued to mount fierce attacks along an almost two kilometre front east

and west of the Thiaumont farm. All of the assaults to the west failed and the enemy suffered severe losses . . .*

One of the men interjects that the communiqué has carefully re-frained from mentioning their own losses, but all of the rest are strangely gratified and repeat time after time—like a comforting mantra—"It's talking about us." And these brief notices about their battle perhaps offer one reason for it being fought at all; perhaps this event was intended to become text right from the start; perhaps the company suffered its ten days of martyrdom so that someone would be able to say that Hill 321 (not in itself of any great military importance) was held.

Indeed, from the French point of view, the defence of Verdun is mostly symbolic, so that the generals, the politicians, the journalists and the public can say to one another, "Oh yes, the town has been held, is being held and will be held." But has anyone properly considered what that little transitive verb *tenir*, "to hold," actually stands for? "To hold" means one thing to the top generals, another to the megaphones of the nationalistic press in Paris, yet another to the commanders in the field, and something entirely different to foot soldiers like Arnaud and his thirty surviving men. The cruel and tragic forms the battle has taken are, therefore, not just the sum of the collective forces of destruction among those doing the fighting, they are also the sum of the rhetorical and semantic confusion among those at whose behest the battle is being fought.

But they have now come through one of the very worst and most climactic points of the battle. Over the course of little more than a week, the Germans have mounted some of their most concentrated assaults since February along the whole of the front, achieving significant suc-cesses. Among several other places, the important French strong point, Fort de Vaux, has fallen after quite exceptionally severe fighting.†

Later, Arnaud hears the whistle of the narrow-gauge railway that

---

* It is worth noting that the material provided by these official communiqués, which was relied on and used constantly at the time (*The Battle of Verdun* by the pseudonymous Henry Dugard was, for instance, published as early as 1916), still holds historians in its clutches. For all its merits, the huge French work *Les 300 Jours de Verdun*, which appeared for the ninetieth anniversary of the battle in 2006, relies heavily on precisely such communiqués.

† The German assaults were renewed immediately after Arnaud's decimated battalion was pulled out of the battle. And Hill 321 did fall in the end.

winds its way between Verdun and Bar-le-Duc. He realises that he really has survived:

> I had climbed down from the scaffold of suffering and returned to the world of peace and life. I thought I was the same person I had been before spending ten days face to face with death. I was wrong. I had lost my youth.

Florence Farmborough writes in her diary that day:

> It was a hot, rather sultry day. In the morning Alexander Alexandrovich, one of our Transport Heads, offered to drive us to see the deserted Austrian trenches; we gladly consented. One excelled all others in luxury and cosiness: we decided it must have been the "blindage" of an artillery officer. It contained chairs, tables, pictures on the armoured walls and books; there was even an English grammar.

SUNDAY, 25 JUNE 1916
Edward Mousley steals a tropical helmet from a dead man in Nusaybin

The march continues. It is almost two months since the encircled British garrison in Kut al-Amara capitulated to the Ottoman army and just over 13,000 men were taken prisoner.* In spite of promises to the contrary, the prisoners were plundered and the officers were separated from the men. While the officers were put on riverboats for transport to Baghdad, the other ranks were forced to march the whole way in spite of the fact that many of them were already in a bad way and the hottest period of the year had just started—temperatures could reach 50° C in the shade.

Mousley was ill at the time of the capitulation and consequently had

---

* Only 3,000 of these men were white and British, the rest were Indian. Any civilians in Kut al-Amara thought to have collaborated with the British (by acting as interpreters, for instance) were hanged, in some cases after being tortured.

to wait for special boat transport to Baghdad. Ironically, the vessel they eventually boarded was the *Julnar*, the steamer used in the last desperate attempt to relieve them back at the end of April. As he was being carried on board he noted that there were bullet holes everywhere. During the interminably slow journey the boat stopped at intervals to unload the bodies of prisoners who had died.

In Baghdad Mousley recovered enough strength for the next stage. With Russian troops less than 125 miles north of the city, the Ottoman authorities were anxious to get the British prisoners away from the area as quickly as possible to prevent them being liberated if the Russians advanced. They were taken by train to Samarra and from there they had to march under guard, first up the Tigris to Mosul and then west out across the desert.

The column of captured officers is permitted to transport its baggage on mules and camels, and the weakest men are allowed to ride. The march has been terrible despite that and they are leaving a trail of sick and dying men, collapsed mules and discarded equipment along the way. Corpses, dried and shrivelled by the burning sun, mark out the trail of those who preceded them. Meanwhile, their progress is also being shadowed by armed Arabs, waiting to plunder and kill those who fall by the wayside. They have been tormented by sandstorms, heat, hunger and, worst of all, thirst. They have survived on figs, black bread, tea and, in particular, raisins—all bought at excessive prices in the places they have passed through. Like everyone else, Mousley has more or less lost all sense of time. "I knew two seasons only," he writes in his diary, "when we walked and when we did not." He is weak and feverish. He has lost almost two stone in weight, has severe stomach problems, and his eyes are painful.[*]

---

[*] Higher-ranking British officers, however, with General Townshend at their head, were being treated extraordinarily well. (Mousley writes sarcastically that Townshend travelled like a prince.) At about this time the Swedish explorer Sven Hedin was present at a remarkable dinner laid on by Halil Pasha. The guest of honour was none other than Townshend, whom Hedin had met during one of his pre-war journeys. Hedin tells us that the Englishman "was taking his fate with equanimity. The atmosphere was happy, even. It really was an occasion for forging fraternal links. Halil filled his glass, made a speech to his guest of honour, wishing him good fortune in the future. And the English general clinked glasses and thanked him for the hospitality he had received in Baghdad. Then the celebration was over and Townshend travelled home in Halil Pasha's motor car."

They have now reached the small town of Nusaybin, in which they are to spend a night or two before continuing the march to Ras al-'Ayn, where there is supposed to be railway transport waiting for them. They set up camp in the shade of an old Roman bridge. The sky above them is a cloudless and scorching vault and Mousley is weaker than ever. He has just recovered from a bad attack of heatstroke, having lost his topee in an unusually strong sandstorm yesterday, and the handkerchief he put on instead provided little protection.

He happens to hear that there is a collection point for sick prisoners somewhere in the town and that a British lieutenant has just died there. Mousley intends to go and try to get the dead man's topee—he is, after all, not going to need it anymore. He spends a long time working his way "through tiny streets and dark quarters and backyards" before eventually locating the place. Passing through a wall via a small gateway hidden by a hanging carpet, he enters an open courtyard.

Along the inner sides of the walls rows of emaciated men are lying under improvised sunshades of grass and leafy branches. Most of the skeletal figures are completely naked apart from a piece of cloth around their loins. Their faces are hollow and covered with week-old bristle. They are the British troops from Kut al-Amara and, apart from some black biscuits, they have virtually no food at all. They have to fetch their own water from a watercourse some 200 yards away and the long scrape marks in the dust and sand show where the prisoners have crawled there and back to get a drink.

Some are dead, many are dying.[*] He sees a man with his jaw fallen open and his face covered in flies; at first Mousley takes him for dead, but the man is alive and when he makes a weak movement great swarms of disturbed flies pour out of his open mouth. Mousley has seen this before, the mouths of dying men filling and emptying with hosts of flies in time with their feeble movements: he calls it "the beehive phenomenon."

Mousley searches for the dead lieutenant, finds his tropical helmet and takes it. Then he returns to his column and alerts the other officers to what he has seen. They go to the town commandant in order to

---

[*] During the Second World War the Japanese army used the following rule of thumb to decide how long a starving man had left: "Anyone who can stand up—30 days left to live. Anyone who can sit up—20 days. Anyone who has to urinate lying down—3 days. Anyone who can no longer speak—2 days. Anyone who can no longer blink—dead by dawn."

protest. All the soldiers still capable of moving now join the officers, who collect what money they can to leave with the men who are too feeble to march. The sixty pounds they collect is given to these unfortunates so that they can at least pay for some food and care.

Mousley returns to the Roman bridge, where he writes in his journal:

> At night, when the remorseless sun is gone, we wander up and down our tiny front between the sentries, smoking what Arab tobacco we can get and casting many an anxious glance towards the western horizon over which, far, far away lies Ras-al-Ain, the railway terminus. Between this and that there are many marches throughout long nights and days. Shall we reach it?

TUESDAY, 27 JUNE 1916
Florence Farmborough nurses the wounded in Buchach

As of today the Brusilov offensive is entering its fourth week and good news—indeed, surprisingly good news—is still coming in. The army to which Farmborough's unit is now attached (the Ninth) has achieved the best results of all, having driven its Austro-Hungarian opponents back in something resembling a frantic retreat or, more accurately perhaps, a retreat in utter panic.* Florence and her colleagues are very pleased—the high expectations they had for the new year and the much discussed great offensive have truly been fulfilled. The weather is hot.

Florence has now seen crowds of prisoners of war (something that was unusual earlier),† and she has seen and been reluctantly impressed by the enemy's well-constructed though now shell-shattered trenches. She has also seen the aspects of success that are less often mentioned: the

---

* A first attempt to stop the rolling advance of the Russian divisions was made at the Dniester river and, when that failed, at the Prut river. The Russians had broken through the Austro-Hungarian positions on the Prut ten days before and the Ninth Army was able to take Czernowitz and push forward into Austrian Bukovina.

† Since the start of the Brusilov offensive on 4 June the Russians had taken almost 200,000 prisoners of war and about 700 artillery pieces. The Austro-Hungarian defence in Galicia had effectively imploded and the Austro-Hungarian army never recovered from this catastrophic defeat.

freshly filled mass graves, beside which the survivors are sitting sorting through the heaps of boots, belts and other equipment that had belonged to their fallen comrades. And she has seen the victors staggering around after drinking themselves stupid on captured or looted alcohol.

Her medical unit is stationed in Buchach at present, a pretty little town straddling the Strypa river. The town has been badly scarred by the fighting and many of its inhabitants have left, but it is still vividly colourful thanks to the masses of acacias in flower. Florence's unit has taken over a house that used to belong to the Austrian superintendent of schools, who left Buchach along with the Austrian troops. The building has already been looted by the time Florence and her companions arrive and books, pictures, geological samples and dried flowers lie scattered all over the floors. Those Austrians who still remain in the town have been ordered out of their houses and will be sent east. Florence has witnessed a repetition of the scenes of last summer, except that it is now mainly German speakers who are fleeing, and she has seen thousands of them on the move, people of all ages driving their animals before them and with their possessions piled up on overloaded carts.

But good news is not the only news to reach them. Good news has a price and it is people like Florence who have to try to save what can be saved from the flood of crushed and broken fragments of humanity that continues to pour into the field hospital.

Yesterday evening she assisted when two men with stomach wounds were operated on. The prognosis for this kind of injury is extremely poor, mainly because it is difficult to avoid fatal infection when the gut contents have been spilled into the stomach cavity. She was impressed by the skill of the surgeon in cutting away the torn pieces of the gut and then patching together the parts that were still functioning. Men with stomach wounds make difficult patients, not only because they usually die but because, dehydrated from blood loss, they are always calling for water, which they cannot be allowed to have because of the danger of complications. Once the procedures were finished Florence remained in the improvised operating theatre because she had heard that more wounded men were expected. She fell asleep on a chair there and did not wake up until around midnight.

It is six o'clock in the morning before any more wounded men arrive and Florence is there to help tend them, the only break being for an early breakfast. One of the wounded is a young soldier, just a boy, who has been hit in his upper left arm. She takes the bullet from the wound, which proves unusually easy since most of its force had been spent and the rear part of it is sticking out. The boy cries and complains the whole time, even when the wound has been cleaned and bandaged: "*Sestritsa*, it hurts!"* Another of them has a very odd wound: he too had been struck by a bullet, which had then bounced off his shoulder blade, changed direction and passed through the right-hand side of his body, gone down through his groin and lodged in his right thigh. A third patient, another young man, is covered with dirt, dust and dried blood and she begins by washing his face:

> "Little Sister," my patient said, with an attempt at a smile. "Leave it dirty! I shall not go visiting any more." At first I thought he was joking and some light-hearted repartee was on the tip of my tongue; then I saw the ugly gash on his head and I understood what he meant.

Later on she sees one of the two patients with stomach wounds whose operation she had assisted at the evening before. He is going downhill. His craving for water is such that she has to get a male orderly to help hold him down on his straw mattress. His mind is beginning to wander and he shouts that he and his comrades are now down by the great river drinking, drinking, drinking.

FRIDAY, 30 JUNE 1916
Kresten Andresen is repairing connecting trenches on the Somme

A blue sky. Sun-warmed grass, smelling of summer. Yet more digging. Andresen has spent much more time with a pick and shovel in his hands than with a rifle and hand grenade—and he is not complaining about it. Sentry duty in the forward line is dangerous, unpleasant and exhausting; and never more so than now when the British are subjecting the German lines a dozen or so miles away to a virtually continuous barrage of drum

---

* "Little Sister," a term commonly used by Russians when addressing a nurse.

fire, presumably in preparation for a major assault. Now and again the fire waltz even sweeps across Andresen's connecting trenches and they continually need to be repaired. The white chalky soil is heavy to dig but, once dug, provides excellent bunkers.

The work follows a set pattern: eight hours digging with a fairly long pause for food in the middle, after that the men can do whatever they like. One of the connecting trenches he is working on runs through the flickering, fragmented sunlight of a wood still clothed in summer greenery, where the blasted trees lie on the ground like pickasticks; the trench then runs on along a stream and straight through an old water-mill. They sleep in deep subterranean bunkers, safe but crowded. The beds are so narrow they have to sleep on their sides and the wide gaps between the slats of the beds make it extremely difficult to sleep comfortably. The mattresses are stuffed with wood shavings that tend to stick together in lumps. And the air supply is more than a little suspect:

> When you've been lying there asleep for five or six hours you get a tight, spongy feeling across your chest, as if you had asthma, but it goes away fairly quickly once you get up into the fresh air and light.

Andresen is not really well. He cannot shake off his persistent cold, his stomach is playing up and he often suffers from headaches. They have watched many dogfights up in the clear blue summer sky. The British seem to have the upper hand in the air. "The famous airman Immelmann was recently shot down here.[*] I was in bed asleep in the bunker but those who were up above saw it."

As usual he is hungry to hear any talk of peace. At the moment there is a particularly persistent rumour going around that the war will end on 17 August. That will be a Thursday.

---

[*] Max Immelmann, Germany's second most successful air ace at the time with seventeen victories (to Oswald Boelcke's eighteen). He was the first airman to receive the Pour le Mérite, then Germany's highest military honour, which subsequently became known as the "Blue Max" among German pilots. It remains uncertain whether he was downed by British bullets or mechanical failure.

SUNDAY, 2 JULY 1916
Angus Buchanan buys some chickens in Kwadirema

It is Sunday and for once the Sabbath is being respected. They have been in camp for a couple of days—waiting, so the word goes, for supplies to be built up before they continue their march. They have been suffering food shortages recently and the men have once again been going hungry.

The day is a very quiet one and Buchanan is not even doing machine-gun drill with his men. The result is not entirely beneficial, however, as it is easy to feel homesick when there are no distractions on a close, windless Sunday like today. Buchanan would be happy just to hear how things are at home, but news is rare in the bush and letters even more so. For several weeks now they have been hoping that the post will reach them.

But the day is by no means completely wasted. Apart from having a chance to rest Buchanan is pleased that he manages to pull off a fine business deal. He met two natives a few days ago and they have been away to their village: now he can barter with them and, in exchange for some clothes, he gets flour and thirteen chickens. This unexpected addition to their calories is a great joy and there will be chicken for dinner. It also stirs the zoologist in him. (Not that the zoologist ever switches off completely. Whenever he has the time and the energy Buchanan collects plants, eggs and, above all, birds. He catalogues everything he finds with the care—bordering on love—of the scientist. His latest find, made on 14 May, was a pygmy kingfisher, a female of the species *Ispidina picta*, to which he gave the reference number 163.) One of the chickens he has bought has a peculiar white plume on her head and for some reason he cannot bring himself to kill her, deciding instead to keep her for a while. She might produce eggs—she might even turn into a pet.

FRIDAY, 7 JULY 1916
René Arnaud's battalion prepares for a return to the front at Verdun

The news comes as a shock in the heat of high summer: they are to be sent back to Verdun "in order to fill a gap." None of them believed they would have to return there, especially after suffering such heavy losses. As a result of the losses the two regiments in the brigade have been amalgamated and Arnaud and his fellow soldiers have had to unpick the number 337 from their collar flashes and stitch on the number 293—the 337th Regiment no longer exists, not since fighting at Verdun just a month ago.

Arnaud is doing his best to reassure the men in his company but does not feel he has succeeded. And he, too, is depressed. All of them are obviously thinking the same thing as him: "You can survive it once, but hardly twice." During the evening the commanding officer of the regiment gives them a briefing in one of the small subterranean rooms in the Verdun citadel. The unit is to retake a recently lost piece of ground between Thiaumont and Fleury, not far from the place they were defending at the beginning of June. The lieutenant colonel subjects his officers to the same kind of inspiring speech Arnaud has already used on his own men—with the same meagre result. Arnaud can see how tense the commander is, how hard he is clenching his jaws and how he no longer believes his own words. Arnaud does, however, feel a little calmer—initially his battalion is to be held in reserve.

When Arnaud goes out into the corridor he sees fifty or so men from his battalion standing in a queue outside another room, which is where Bayet, the acting battalion doctor, a rotund man with cropped hair and large glasses, is located. The men are reporting sick and thus hoping to avoid the purgatory that awaits them. Every conceivable ailment and condition is cited: hernias, rheumatism, badly healed wounds. The battalion doctor is sweating with the effort, surrounded as he is by a cluster of men "clinging to him like drowning men clinging to a life-buoy." Arnaud hears later that several of the battalion's senior officers have also reported sick: "In short, there was a general state of disintegration."

That evening Arnaud meets Doctor Bayet and makes an attempt of his own to be declared unfit. He feels he does it in a rather subtle way. Arnaud starts by complaining about one of the officers (one of the highly decorated ones) who has seen fit to report sick, and he suggests that he himself would *never* do such a thing, even though he actually has good reason to because of a heart problem. As if incidentally, he unbuttons his uniform jacket and asks the doctor to listen, hoping frantically that the doctor will hear something and send him to the rear clutching yet another medical exemption. The doctor listens and then says in a bored voice that perhaps there is a slight murmur. But that is all he says. Feeling ashamed of himself, Arnaud buttons up his jacket: "This demonstration of weakness stopped me condemning others from then on."

Once it is dark they march out of the citadel again. The lines of heavily laden men wind their way across the river and towards the dark heights with their glowing aurora of explosions. When they have climbed the first of the steep ridges Arnaud lies prostrate on the ground, his heart pounding wildly. "I was exhausted, morally more than physically. I thought I was going to pass out, perhaps even hoped that I was going to." After a long march through a narrow connecting trench they reach a simple bunker with a corrugated-iron roof. There he falls asleep.

The attack takes place at dawn two days later. It fails. The losses are considerable and one of the men to fall is the commanding officer. Arnaud's unit does not take part in the attack and he survives.

A DAY IN JULY 1916
Rafael de Nogales witnesses the execution of a deserter outside Jerusalem

Virtually every morning there are two or three new bodies dangling from telegraph poles and other improvised gallows around the Holy City. Most of them are Arabs who have been caught after deserting from the Ottoman army. They are the very opposite to Rafael de Nogales in that they did not choose war, war chose them. They represent the silent majority of those now in uniform (irrespective of the colour of the uniform): unlike de Nogales, who eagerly allowed himself to be swept up by the energy, danger and illusions of war, they are men who have been forced into it reluctantly, questioningly, unenthusiastically and—last but not least—mutely.

It is not that de Nogales looks down on them: there is a sense in which he actually understands the deserters. The Ottoman army has yet again been afflicted by supply problems, largely as a result of corruption, wastage and organised theft. And undernourishment has once again opened the way for disease, particularly typhus. Since the whole region is suffering from food shortages, typhus has taken on epidemic proportions, its impact being felt in particular by the many new Jewish immigrants to the city who, because of the war, have been deprived of all assistance from their former homelands. The simultaneous combination of hunger and homesickness has meant that the number of desertions from Arab units has gone through the roof.*

The typhus epidemic and the desperate supply situation in Palestine means that the so-called Pasha Expedition (a corps consisting partly of Turkish units and partly of German and Austro-Hungarian troops equipped with considerable quantities of artillery, lorries and other modern equipment) does not stop for its planned rest period in Palestine after its long trek through Asia Minor but continues on to Sinai in the intense heat. They have been sent to take part in a second attempt to cut the Suez Canal.† De Nogales was impressed by the sight of these columns of motor lorries and brand-new cannon rumbling past.

Non-stop hangings have been the Ottoman commander's answer to the desertions but their effect has been negligible. (De Nogales takes the view that such draconian measures are an attempt to cure a sickness for which the commander himself is at least partly responsible: he is thought to be involved in the corruption that has led to food shortages among the troops.) Which is why he has decided that the latest deserter will be given a very public execution by firing squad and die before the eyes of his comrades in the Jerusalem garrison.

The execution is to take place today.

The condemned man is yet another Arab, this time an imam.

A long procession winds its way out of the shady multitude of roofs and cupolas that is Jerusalem. At the front is a military band playing Chopin's Funeral March. It is followed by a group of high-ranking officers and civilians. Then comes the man who is to die, strikingly well dressed in a brilliant white turban and a kaftan of bright red cloth. Behind him marches the firing squad. And behind them there is a long tail, consisting of the Jerusalem garrison—or large parts of it, anyway—including Rafael de Nogales.

This long snake of people gathers round a small, low mound of earth

---

* Many Arabs were conscripted to uniformed but unarmed labour battalions, used, for instance, in the maintenance of roads and for digging trenches.
† For the first attempt see 6 February 1915 (page 82). The Pasha Expedition was equally unsuccessful.

on which a thick post has been driven into the ground. As the death sentence is being read out de Nogales carefully observes the man who is about to die. He seems "very little concerned by the fate that is awaiting him and is calmly smoking his cheroot with all the scorn for death that is characteristic of Muslims." After listening to the reading of the sentence the man sits down cross-legged on a mat opposite another imam, who is supposed to be his spiritual comforter, but the spiritual comfort gets out of control when the two of them indulge in an ever more animated theological debate that threatens to end in blows.

The condemned man is made to stand up and is tied to the post. A blindfold is put over his eyes. He continues smoking calmly throughout this procedure. When the command "Ready" is given and the squad raises its rifles into firing position and takes aim, the man quickly moves his cheroot up to his lips. The shots ring out, the two shades of red in the kaftan and the body meet and the man crumples, "his hand pinned to his mouth by a bullet."

THURSDAY, 20 JULY 1916
Olive King distributes clothes in Salonica

The day begins to cool down. There are nine sacks lined up in the clothing store and Olive King is waiting impatiently. The sacks contain the clothes, equipment and personal possessions of nine patients due to be shipped out of Salonica today and her task is to ensure that they are issued to the rightful owners. None of them has arrived yet and she hopes to have time to bathe in the warm sea before the camp gates are locked. Eventually she goes over to the ward where the nine patients are and asks them to hurry up. Now she can hand out the sacks, but one of the patients opens his and protests that these are not his belongings. Accompanied by the patient, Olive King starts a hopeless search for the right sack.

She will not be able to bathe this evening.

She finishes a letter to her father instead and confesses to something she has hitherto treated as "a deep and dark secret"—the fact that she no longer has long hair:

I cut my hair when we first came out here (that's why I've never sent you any snapshots since I've been here) & it's just been the greatest imaginable blessing, saves such a lot of time & always tidy & comfortable. It really looks quite nice, & has grown so thick, & it's lovely not having anything blowing in your eyes driving. As soon as it was done I couldn't imagine why I'd never done it before.

Sarrail's Army of the Orient is still in Salonica, in lofty defiance both of Greek neutrality and of the fact that there seems to be little or no point to the whole business any longer. The overcrowded city is now surrounded by a belt of fortifications almost as deep as those to be seen on the Western Front.* In other words, a standstill. What real fighting there is is going on up in Macedonia, nicknamed Muckedonia by the British troops because of the mud and dirt there. It is hotter than down on the coast and disease is rife up there, particularly malaria, but also dengue fever. Battlefield casualties are few.

Olive King is considering enlisting in the Serbian army, partly because she is tired of all the trivial jobs, all the waiting and all the well-organised inactivity in the fortified enclave of Salonica, and partly because she has discovered that the nurses in general and their new supervisor in particular detest women volunteers like her. King says that she has "had enough of women's discipline—or rather, lack of it" and would rather work for a real military organisation. There is also another factor in the equation, in the form of a charming Serbian liaison officer she has become acquainted with. Large parts of what remains of the Serbian army have been shipped from Corfu to Salonica.

The evenings can be pleasant, at least as long as the wind is not blowing too hard and filling the air with dust. She reads or she writes letters. She and some friends sometimes find tortoises and organise races with them. Sometimes they crawl through the wire and go to a small café just

---

* In answer to a question as to what the Army of the Orient was actually doing, the French ex-Prime Minister Georges Clemenceau is supposed to have snarled: "Digging! Let them be known in France and in Europe as 'the Salonica gardeners.'" It might also be mentioned that Sarrail expended more energy poking his nose into Greek politics than in fighting against the Central Powers on the other side of the border, and that Clemenceau returned to office in 1917.

behind the camp. It is often empty and there they drink lemon juice and soda and dance for hours to the rasping tones of a wind-up gramophone. There are only two records of dance music—"Dollar Princess" and "La Paloma"—and they play them time after time.

MONDAY, 24 JULY 1916
Sarah Macnaughtan dies at home in London

She regains hope after her return from Persia. For a while, anyway. Relations and friends visit, sometimes in such numbers that her maid feels compelled to impose a strict limit on how many minutes each can stay. The doctors are vague about what is wrong with her. It is possibly some sort of tropical disease and they have put her on a special milk diet, but she has trouble keeping it down. Just a month ago it seemed that she might recover: her weight increased, she began to organise her correspondence, she made short visits to her library downstairs and she talked of refurnishing the house. Plans were made to move out to the country so that she could enjoy the summer there.

Things have changed since then.

It is weeks now since she left her room, and yesterday she sank into a sort of coma. It is no longer possible to communicate with her.

Some headlines from today's *Daily Mirror:* "British Smash Through Defences Into Pozieres"; "Drivers' Protest—More Buses Stop Today"; "Big French Air Raid on Rhine Town"; "Is It to Be Another Year of War?"; "Last Week of Gorringtons Summer Sale"; "Red Cross Regatta on the Thames"; "Grand Duke Pushes on in Asia Minor."

During the day, she unexpectedly becomes rather restless. Perhaps it is simply a fear of death, or perhaps her body is summoning its last reserves of physical and mental strength before her final journey. One of her sisters is downstairs playing hymns on an organ and the sounds can reach up to Macnaughtan through her open bedroom door. No one knows if she can hear them. She dies later in the afternoon. The room is full of flowers.

·   ·   ·

Michel Corday makes the following entry in his diary on the same day:

> An old man in dirty-grey uniform, with a cap drooping over his
> ear, tawny top-boots, sword clanking against his spurs, a score of
> mysterious ribbons on his chest, so radiant with pride as to light
> up the whole boulevard. Next to him, there was a poor devil on
> two crutches, with his drill coat, his corduroy trousers, one leg
> amputated right up [to] the thigh. A pitiable contrast!

THURSDAY, 27 JULY 1916
Michel Corday has dinner at Maxim's

It is a beautiful, hot summer in Paris. The cafés are well patronised
and the tables that cover the pavements are full. On Sundays the local
trains out into the green countryside are packed with trippers. Groups of
young women dressed in white swish along the streets on their bicycles.
For those seeking the sea air, it is utterly impossible to find a vacant hotel
room at any of the many resorts along the Atlantic coast.

Michel Corday and an acquaintance are in Maxim's, close to the
Champs-Élysées, and he is once more struck by the contrast between
what he sees going on and what he knows to be going on. He thinks yet
again about how infinitely far away the war seems to be. The restaurant
is famous for its cuisine and for its fashionable art-nouveau décor, which
has made it something of a time capsule, a refuge from the present, a
reminder of happier days, a promise of a future. Yes, the war *is* a long
way away, but it is nevertheless present, although people prefer to keep
quiet about the way it manifests itself here—through alcohol and sex, or
perhaps more accurately, drunkenness and lust.

The restaurant is full of men in uniform, from different branches
of the armed forces and of many different nationalities. There are also
a few well-known faces, such as Georges Feydeau, the writer of farces,
and François Flameng, professor and war artist, whose watercolours are
to be seen in virtually every new number of the widely read magazine
L'Illustration. Flameng is one of those civilians who cannot resist the
gravitational pull of the military world and he has come up with his own

uniform-like style of clothing: this evening he is wearing a kepi, a khaki jacket with rows of medal ribbons on the chest, and puttees. There are also women present, many of them—the majority, perhaps—are high-class prostitutes.

The quantity of alcohol consumed at Maxim's this evening is enormous. There are some pilots who are having what is called a champagne dinner and eating nothing at all. The level of drunkenness in the place is high: incidents that before the war would have led to sharp reprimands or to people looking away in embarrassed silence are now tolerated or even give rise to appreciative laughter from the other diners. Corday sees some British officers who have imbibed so much that one of them can hardly stand: the man tries to put on his uniform cap but, to the obvious delight of those sitting around him, misses his own head. Two extremely drunk men are standing at separate tables and hurling crude insults at each other across the elegantly ornamented room. No one pays any attention to them.

The business of prostitution is being conducted with virtually no attempt at concealment. If a customer wants to buy the services of a woman he simply speaks to one of the restaurant managers. Corday hears one of them respond quickly to a potential client: "Ready and at your service this evening." After which he names the price, provides an address and directions and concludes with "the hygiene requirements."

Even in France, where legalised brothels have a long history, the war has led to a massive increase in the sex industry. This, of course, is due partly to increased demand—swarms of soldiers arrive in Paris on leave every day and whores have poured in from all over the country—but also because the authorities, encouraged by the military, frequently choose to turn a blind eye to the problem. Even so, arrests for illegal prostitution have risen by 40 per cent.

There has also been a significant increase in sexually transmitted diseases.* Many of the armies routinely issue condoms to soldiers going on leave. Not that it does much good.† Surprisingly, not everyone tries to

---

* One of Corday's fellow diners, Georges Feydeau, would die from syphilis before the war ended.

† In the Austro-Hungarian army soldiers who became infected with an STD were punished. Attempts were made to reduce the prevalence of such diseases by the old approach—control at source. (One of the first measures the Germans introduced after taking Warsaw in August 1915 required all women involved in "professional fornication"

avoid infection: infected prostitutes sometimes earn more than healthy ones since they attract soldiers who *want* to catch a venereal infection in order to evade service at the front. The most grotesque expression of this can be seen in the trade in gonococcal pus, which soldiers buy and smear into their genitals in the hope of ending up in hospital.[*] Those who are really desperate rub it into their eyes, which often results in lifelong blindness.

Even the prostitutes are doing their bit for the war. Some brothels used to take in homeless refugees and Corday believes that all the high-class whores in Maxim's this evening will have what is called "a godson." This means that, for patriotic reasons, they have "adopted" a soldier, which in turn means that when that soldier comes home on leave the prostitute in question will have sex with him free of charge.

The drunken uproar in the restaurant continues, to the accompaniment of popping corks, shouting, laughter, shrieks, yells and chinking glass. An officer in a particularly well-tailored uniform roars: "Down with civilians!"

On the same day Florence Farmborough writes in her journal about a wounded young officer whose death she has witnessed:

> The terrible odour of putrefaction that accompanies that form of gangrene was harassing us desperately, but we knew that it would not be for long. Before Death came to release him, he became calmer—he was back at home, among those whom he loved. Suddenly he seized my arm and cried, "I knew that you would come! Elena, little dove, I knew that you would come! Kiss me, Elena, kiss me!" I realised that in his delirium he had mistaken me for the girl he loved. I bent and kissed his damp, hot face, and he became more tranquil. Death claimed him while he was still in a state of tranquillity.

---

to register and undergo medical checks.) Even so, 22 per cent of the Canadian troops in France suffered from venereal disease of some kind during 1915 and 20 per cent of the Allied soldiers who visited the French capital in the summer of 1917 became infected.

[*] The same reasoning motivated a similarly disgusting trade in the coughed-up phlegm of tuberculosis sufferers.

SUNDAY, 6 AUGUST 1916
Elfriede Kuhr plays the piano at a party in Schneidemühl

It is a confusing time, dreadful and exciting, painful and alluring, ago-
nising and happy. The world is changing and she is changing with it,
both as a result of the things that are happening and also quite independently of them. Wheels are moving within wheels, sometimes in opposite directions, but still moving as one.

Once upon a time many people had rejoiced at the war as both a
promise and a possibility, a promise that all that was best in mankind
and culture might be realised, a possibility to tilt against the unease and
the disintegration that had been discernible all over pre-war Europe.[*]
But wars are and always have been paradoxical and deeply ironic phenomena that frequently change what people want to preserve, promote
what people want to prevent and demolish what people want to protect.

In complete contradiction to the fine hopes of 1914, there is a tendency for certain phenomena—traditionally lumped together under the
heading of "dangerous disintegration"—to mushroom out of control.
Many people are concerned about the ever-increasing freedom in rela-
tionships between the sexes and the growing levels of sexual immorality.
Some of this is blamed on the fact that so many women, like Elfriede's
mother and grandmother, have been permitted or even compelled to
take work previously done by men—men who are now in uniform. This
has, of course, been absolutely crucial to the war effort and consequently
should not really be called into question, but it is not difficult to find
people who maintain that this "masculinisation" of women will prove to
be fatal in the long run.[†] Some of this is blamed on the fact that the long
absence of men at the front causes a drastic increase in sexual demand,

---

* The British field marshal Lord Roberts, for instance, thought that a war was the only
antidote to "the great human rottenness that is rife in our industrial cities." Remember,
too, Thomas Mann's fine hopes in 1914 that the war would make German culture both
"freer and better." For more examples of the war as hope, promise and liberation, see
Känslornas krig by Jens Ljunggren.
† Interestingly enough, this might be compared with the fact that soldiers who had
a breakdown as a result of their experiences at the front were frequently considered
to be "hysterical," for which reason their behaviour could be interpreted as a form of
"feminisation."

which has in turn led to a huge rise in such behaviour as masturbation, homosexuality and extra-marital affairs, which were previously strictly forbidden or denounced.* (Germany, like France, has witnessed an increase in prostitution and sexual diseases.) Some of it is blamed on the fact that the ceaseless flood of men in uniform backwards and forwards across the country causes there to be a sudden excess of young, sexually active men in certain places at the very time there are fewer resident men capable of supervising the women left at home. A marked rise in extra-marital pregnancies and illegal abortions, for instance, has been reported from garrison towns. Schneidemühl is no exception to this: the town is home to an infantry regiment and to the well-known Albatros factory, which both manufactures military aircraft and brings in large numbers of young pilots for training.

(Biplanes, both those that have crashed and those that have had to make an emergency landing, are not an unusual sight in the area, even in the centre of the town. And Elfriede knows that fatal accidents are not unusual: every week she sees funeral processions making their way either to the war cemetery in the forest or to the railway station, where the coffins are put aboard trains.)

Up until now Elfriede has watched all this from a distance—curious, confused and watchful. A thirteen-year-old girl at her school has been expelled after being made pregnant by an ensign. And during a visit home from the music school she runs in Berlin, Elfriede's mother was amazed to see that "the levels of elegance here are not far behind what you can see on the Kurfürstendamm." Elfriede thinks she knows why:

It's because of all the officers from away who are in the 134th Reserve Battalion or in the 1st and 2nd Reserve Air Squadrons. Because of these men, our women and girls spend a lot of time doing themselves up.

---

* In June 1915 a German magazine published the story of a cinema proprietor who stood up in front of the audience during the interval and warned them that a man in uniform had just entered the establishment intending to catch his wife and her lover, whom he knew were in there somewhere. To avoid the scandal the cinema proprietor pointed out that there was a small, discreet emergency exit on the right-hand side: 320 couples immediately left the cinema in the semi-darkness.

The older girls can often be seen hanging round with soldiers, as indeed can some adult women, ultimately perhaps "out of sympathy" because the soldiers "are on their way to the front where they will be killed or wounded anyway." It is obvious that the proximity of death and the sheer volume of deaths have helped to break down what would otherwise be strict moral codes.* Elfriede has not yet let herself be tempted but she has noticed that soldiers have begun talking to her in a new way. She believes it is because she is now wearing a proper skirt and has her hair pinned up like a grown-up.

The big sister of one of her classmates often organises small parties for the young pilots. Coffee and cakes are on offer, couples chat and, indeed, even kiss a little while Elfriede plays the piano. So far the whole business has just been a titillating game for Elfriede. On these occasions she has pretended to be "Lieutenant von Yellenic" (the persona she often resorts to when playing war games), playing background music in the officers' mess for friends, "just like in a novel by Tolstoy."

As she arrives at today's party she meets a young, blond and blue-eyed pilot officer on the stairs:

He stopped, greeted me and wondered whether I was also "one of the people who had been invited."† I said no, I was just the one who played the piano. He pulled a face and answered: "I see. That's a pity." "Why is it a pity?" I asked. He just laughed and disappeared into the room.

TUESDAY, 8 AUGUST 1916
Kresten Andresen disappears on the Somme

No more sun, just mist and haze. The front line has not moved much since the middle of July but the battles continue to rage. The landscape is strangely colourless. All the colours, particularly the greens, are long gone. The storm of shells having kneaded everything to the same drab,

---

* To quote Frederic Manning: "In the shuddering revulsion from death one turns instinctively to love as an act which seems to affirm the completeness of being."
† The words used in her journal are "mit von der Partie."

grey-brown shade.* There are dense ranks of artillery pieces on both sides; in some places they are wheel to wheel and they are firing day and night. Today British foot soldiers are attacking the village of Guillemont— though it is a village in name only, since weeks of bombardment have reduced the place to tangled heaps of stones, beams and debris. Nor is it really a village on the maps used by the British high command: there it is marked as *an important position* that must be taken, not because it would break the German line but because it would provide room for manoeu- vre. (There are several reasons for the British attack, not least that King George V is presently visiting his troops in France and General Douglas Haig, the British commander-in-chief, would like to be able to welcome His Majesty with some small victory.)†

The British attack has been well prepared. They have dug new con- necting trenches from the closest point in the shell-shattered wood at Trônes so that the infantrymen can launch their attack as close as pos- sible to the German lines. An experienced and battle-hardened division, the 55th, has been chosen to carry out the attack and the preparatory bombardment has been both lengthy and merciless.

One of the German soldiers who will have to face the attack is Kresten Andresen.

His regiment has been sent in to reinforce one of the most exposed sectors on the Somme. To one side of Guillemont there is Longueval, then Delville Wood, then Martinpuich, Pozlères, Thiepval, Beaucourt and Beaumont Hamel—all places well known from the army commu- niqués of the past month and now shrouded in a dark aura of stinking corpses and shattered hopes. Two days ago he wrote to his parents:

I hope I have now done my bit here, for the present anyway. One can never know what will happen in the future. But even if we

* This drabness in terms of colour is another point at which the conflict failed to correspond to the pre-war expectations of various overly romantic aesthetes: the war actually turned out to be dreary in colour as well as in its everyday routines.
† The British decision to mount an offensive on the Somme had nothing to do with the strategic importance of the region (it had none); it was launched there quite simply because this was where the British and French front lines met and the offensive was intended to be an exercise in cooperation. The main German defensive line lay where the British Guillemont Road Cemetery is now located, that is immediately outside the rebuilt village.

are sent somewhere in the very depths of the sea, we could not go anywhere worse than this place.

The losses have been great, not least among his Danish friends. Most of them have fallen victim to the constant artillery barrage:

My good, dear friend Peter Østergaard—I can't understand why he should fall. How many sacrifices are being demanded of us. Rasmus Nissen is badly wounded in his legs. Jans Skau has lost both his legs and is wounded in the chest. Jens Christensen from Lundgaardsmark is wounded. Johannes Hansen from Lintrup is badly wounded. Jørgen Lenger from Smedeby—wounded. Asmus Jessen from Aarslev—wounded. There is no one left now: Iskov, Laursen, Nørregaard, Karl Hansen—they are all gone and I am almost the only one remaining.

The drum fire has been dreadful. Shells of every possible calibre have rained down on them, particularly those of the heaviest calibres, 18cm, 28cm, and 38cm. When a brute of the latter variety explodes, Andresen writes, it is like meeting "a monster from the sagas." Suddenly everything is silent and dark. Then, after a few seconds, the dust and smoke clear enough to see for a few metres before another shell comes screaming in. On one occasion they came under heavy fire in a connecting trench without any bunkers.* He and the others could do nothing but press themselves against the side of the trench, press their helmeted heads down on their knees and clutch their rucksacks in a pathetic attempt to protect their chests and bellies. In one of his most recent letters home he wrote: "At the beginning of the war, in spite of all the terrible things, there was a sense of something poetic. That has now gone."

Kresten Andresen now finds himself in the forward line. He has tried to come up with anything good that can be said about his situation and actually thinks he has found something. Chatting to a Dane in a different company a few days earlier he said, "we might easily be taken prisoner." Perhaps that is what he is hoping for when the enemy firestorm lifts and the British soldiers of the 55th Division climb out of their trenches a couple of hundred metres away.

* This was not at all unusual since connecting trenches, unlike the main trenches, were not designed for fighting but to facilitate movement.

The clumsiness of the attack on the place the British troops call "Gillymong" is reminiscent of many other British attacks on the Somme.

The British artillery is, of course, laying down a so-called creeping barrage, which in theory means that the foot soldiers are advancing behind a curtain of fire intended to keep the German defenders down in their bunkers right until the last minute. In practice and as usual, the artillerymen follow their own timetables, which means that the fire moves forward a certain number of metres at given intervals irrespective of whether the British infantrymen are keeping up or not.[*] Soon the barrage disappears into the distance leaving the lines of advancing infantry behind, and then these lines run straight into the German curtain of fire[†]—and even into each other: in all the smoke and confusion two British battalions end up fighting one another. The men who manage to push forward in spite of this soon come under cross-fire from German machine guns hidden in a sunken road immediately before the village.

A number of isolated groups do reach the German trenches on the edge of what was once Guillemont and chaotic close-quarters combat breaks out there.

Kresten Andresen is still alive around the middle of the day on 8 August.

During the afternoon German units carry out a counter-attack. They are very familiar with the terrain and have soon recaptured the lost stretches of trench and overcome the British attackers. (Ten officers and 374 soldiers are taken prisoner.) In one trench they find a wounded man from Andresen's company: when he was wounded he hid in a bunker because he had heard that the British bayoneted the wounded to death.

---

[*] The infantry carried with them an array of devices to help the artillery observers further back see the forward position of the advancing attackers. On this day, for instance, British infantrymen had small flashes of polished metal stitched on their backs—these were supposed to gleam in the sun and show where the men were. The problem was that the day was overcast and, in addition to that, the swirling clouds of smoke and dust caused by exploding shells meant that there was very little chance of actually seeing what was happening during the attack.

[†] German artillery fire was, generally speaking, more lethal than that of the British and French because the Germans did not attempt the rather futile task of blasting enemy fortifications out of existence but concentrated instead on bombarding the troops as they prepared to attack and then, once an attack was under way, laying down curtains of exploding shells in no-man's-land. In one section of his famous book *Le feu* Henri Barbusse has described what it is like to move through a wall of explosions of this kind.

He had, however, seen the British taking German prisoners back to their own lines with them.

When the 1st Company is mustered it is discovered that there are twenty-nine men who cannot be accounted for among either the living or the dead. Kresten Andresen is one of them.

There has been no word of him since.

His fate is unknown.*

SUNDAY, 13 AUGUST 1916
Florence Farmborough views a battlefield on the River Dniester

The countryside spread out before their eyes is breathtakingly beautiful. On both sides run long, winding hills, covered with trees; in front is an undulating plain, framed by the high, dramatic peaks of the Carpathians in the distance. But as the column approaches and then reaches yesterday's battlefield, the idyll is shattered. They pass the recently deserted sites of gun positions; they roll through villages so smashed by shells and dissected by a web of trenches that all that remain are piles of stone and wood; they drive past blackened crater fields full of deep, spiky hollows. The size of a crater depends on the calibre of the shell: an ordinary field artillery shell of 7cm or 8cm makes a crater less than a metre across; the real monsters of 42cm make a hole twelve times that size, or more.

They come to a halt on a small hill. Yesterday this was one of the best fortified positions in the Austro-Hungarian line of defences. Today it is

---

* The paths of one of the forgotten and one of the most famous participants in the war almost crossed at Guillemont. On 24 August Lieutenant Ernst Jünger and his 73rd Regiment of Fusiliers were sent into action there. Jünger has described it in his superb war memoir *In Stahlgewittern* (The Storm of Steel). By the time of Jünger's arrival the village had been completely obliterated: "only a whitish mark on the field of craters still showed the spot where the chalky stone of the houses had been ground to dust." There was an all-pervasive stench of putrefaction and millions of fat blowflies filled the air. Even Jünger, normally so cool, was shaken by what he saw. "The ploughed-up battlefield was a scene of horror. The dead lay there among the living defenders. When we dug bunkers we saw how the dead lay in layers one above the other. One company after another had been mown down as they made a stand shoulder to shoulder under the drum fire; then their corpses had been buried under the tons of earth hurled up by the projectiles and new men had taken the place of the fallen."

just a mess of crumpled barbed wire and partially collapsed trenches. The enemy dead are still lying on the ground. They died so recently that even in the summer heat they show no signs of putrefaction—indeed, they seem as if they might almost be alive. She sees three bodies pressed together and it is only the contortion of their limbs that convinces her that these people really are dead. At another spot she looks at an enemy soldier lying outstretched in a shattered trench: the man's face is completely unmarked, his skin still has the light of life. Just as so many others have done when faced with death in its less dramatic manifestations, Florence thinks: "He might have been resting."

They climb back into their cars and continue their journey. They soon begin to understand the scale of this battle, which led to yesterday's great breakthrough. From being a single battlefield it becomes multiple fields and they come to places where there has not yet been time to remove the Russian dead:

> The dead were still lying around, in strange, unnatural postures—remaining where they had fallen: crouching, doubled up, stretched out, prostrate, prone ... Austrians and Russians lying side by side. And there were lacerated crushed bodies lying on darkly stained patches of earth. There was one Austrian without a leg and with blackened, swollen face; another with a smashed face, terrible to look at; a Russian soldier with legs doubled under him, leaning against the barbed wire. And on more than one open wound flies were crawling and there were other moving, thread-like things. I was glad Anna and Ekaterina were with me; they, too, were silent; they, too, were sorely shaken. Those "heaps" were once human beings: men who were young, strong and vigorous; now they lay lifeless and inert; shapeless forms of what had been living flesh and bone. What a frail and fragile thing is human life!

These maimed and torn bodies are a reality in themselves but also a picture of what war does to man's conceptions and hopes, indeed, to the old world as a whole. As much as anything else, the war began as an attempt to preserve Europe exactly as it was, to uphold the status quo, but it is now changing the continent in a more sweeping way than anyone could have imagined in their worst nightmares. An ancient truth is making itself manifest yet again—the truth that sooner or later wars become uncontrollable and counter-productive because men and societies will tend to sacrifice everything in their blind drive to be victorious. That has rarely been more true than it is at present, when those in power, unintentionally and without any plan, have unleashed uniquely uncontrollable forces: extreme nationalism, social revolution, religious hatred. (Not to mention a grotesque level of debt that is undermining the economic health of all the states involved.) Farmborough, shaken by what she has seen, finds refuge in her faith: "Oh! One must believe and trust in God's mercy, otherwise these frightful sights would work havoc in one's brain; and one's heart would faint with the depths of its despair."

Later, when they stop and set up camp, they still find themselves surrounded by dead bodies but now, after the passage of more hours, the inevitable processes of putrefaction have begun to set in. They can smell the unpleasant sweetness in the air and hear the buzzing of the gorged flies. The men in the unit are unconcerned by the corpses—or pretend to be—other than as problems of hygiene. But Florence and the other nurses feel very ill at ease when it is time to eat. There is a corpse immediately behind her tent, half buried by the earth thrown up by an exploding shell, but his head is clearly visible. One of the nurses goes and places a piece of cloth over the dead man's face. A little later Florence regains her courage and takes out her camera to photograph the many dead Austrians. She has taken only two photographs when she is overwhelmed by a sense of shame: what right does she have to intrude on these lifeless beings? It was not that long ago that she went out of her way to see her first cadaver, not that long ago that she "wanted to see Death."

And so the day continues, with death ever present.

Later again, while waiting to be given things to do or orders to move on, she overcomes her feelings and goes off exploring. She walks past a village that has been completely razed by Russian artillery fire ("God help the inhabitants"), past a stinking and still uncovered mass grave and arrives at last at the logical end point of this whole business— a small and rather pretty war cemetery that is probably a few years old. She already knows that the Austro-Hungarian army takes its war cemeteries very seriously and that it also treats its fallen enemies with great respect. The small plot is carefully fenced and the way in passes through a beautifully carved gateway, over which is a wooden cross and an inscription in German: "Here rest the heroes fallen for their Fatherland." And "heroes" refers to the dead of all nationalities, since Russians and Germans lie buried here alongside Austro-Hungarian soldiers. A fallen

Jewish warrior has not been made to lie under a cross: his grave has been marked instead with the Star of David.

At suppertime they receive nothing but good reports. They already know that operations in the north are coming up against great difficulty but they have seen today with their own eyes that the great offensive in the south is continuing and, to their joy, they hear that as a result of this new breakthrough the Austro-Hungarian armies are retreating at such a speed that the Russians have lost contact with them. The enemy appears to be at the point of complete collapse. This breathes new life into their hopes. Germany will find it hard to continue without Austria-Hungary and the Italian army will have room to manoeuvre and be able to complete its invasion of the double-monarchy without any resistance.[*]

Florence also hears another little piece of news that makes her personally happy. One of the states that has been dragged into the war is Persia, which was invaded by British and Russian troops less than a year ago. Fighting has been going on since then. This evening Florence is told that one of the men who has done most to re-establish so-called order in Persia is a Briton, Brigadier General Sir Percy Sykes.[†] Being British, Florence cannot fail to be proud of this.

So in spite of everything the day ends with smiles. The sun goes down and the night wind wafts the ever stronger smell of thousands of putrefying heroes into the tents.

On that day Angus Buchanan and the column he is part of are at a watercourse. They have been racing south-west in pursuit of a rapidly retreating enemy force that is destroying all the bridges behind it. He writes:

---

[*] Four days earlier the Italian army—after enormous efforts and equally enormous losses—had finally taken the Austrian town of Görz on the Isonzo and changed its name to Gorizia, the name it still bears today.

[†] This Sykes should not be confused with the British politician (and ex-soldier) Sir Mark Sykes who, together with the French diplomat François Georges-Picot, had come to a top-secret agreement (the Sykes–Picot Accord) earlier in the year. Under the accord their respective governments agreed that after the war the Ottoman Empire should be divided up and a large part of its territory would be placed under the direct control of Russia, France and Great Britain. Among other decisions, Mesopotamia would go to Britain, Lebanon to France and Armenia to Russia. A War to End All Wars, indeed. The result of all this—as we all know to our cost—has been (to borrow the title of a book by David Fromkin) *A Peace to End All Peace*.

We have now descended into low, unhealthy marsh country, where the atmosphere is close and damp, and fly-ridden. For the remainder of the day and the next two days, swarms of us, like busy ants, laboured to and fro on the construction of the large timber-buttressed bridge being thrown across the high-banked river. At the end of the latter day fever laid hold of me, and left me with just enough energy doggedly to carry on.

TUESDAY, 29 AUGUST 1916
Andrei Lobanov-Rostovsky almost takes part in the Brusilov offensive

The incident that put his life at stake and gave him what was perhaps his worst experience during all his years at the front began as a silly joke. The news reached them some time on Monday that Romania, after a year of devious vacillation, had joined the Allies and declared war on the Central Powers. It seemed to be good news* and some of the men in the company Lobanov-Rostovsky had been sent to support could not resist the temptation to rub the Germans' noses in it: they put up a large sign, in German, informing their opponents in the trenches opposite of the Romanian decision.

At first the Germans do not seem to react at all. Everything is still quiet when Lobanov-Rostovsky returns to his post in the forward line at nightfall. It is actually quieter than usual. No rattling of machine guns

---

* It was not good news. Romania's entry into the war proved to be a burden for the Allies, particularly for Russia, which was eventually forced to send significant forces south in a costly and vain effort to help the new ally. The strength of the Romanian army was impressive—on paper—and it had undoubtedly won a degree of prestige in the two Balkan wars of 1912–13, but that turned out to be essentially unmerited. Its equipment was in short supply or antiquated; many of its soldiers were dressed in the handsome, colourful uniforms of the nineteenth century; its officer corps was weak, inexperienced and usually preoccupied with the wrong things. One of the first measures taken by the Romanian army after mobilisation was to issue an order stipulating that only officers above the rank of major had the right to wear eye-shadow in the field. The entry of Portugal into the war, which happened in March of this year, similarly failed to provide the Allies with any noticeable or measurable benefit.

and for once the night sky is not lit up by the cascades of green, red and white sparks from signal rockets.

In spite of the calm, or perhaps because of it, he feels nervous. He reaches for the field telephone, rings the command post and asks what the time is. The answer is "23:55."

Five minutes later it starts. German punctuality.

The prevailing calm has not actually been an illusion. He and the rest of the Guards division are stationed on the Stokhod river, where the front line stabilised after the Russian army's notably successful summer offensive—an offensive which has been named after the man who planned and led it, the intelligent and unorthodox Alexei Brusilov. The offensive started at the beginning of June and has been going on in stages throughout the whole summer. The results have been amazing. The Russian forces have not only taken territory on a scale unequalled since the autumn of 1914 (some units are now back in the Carpathians and posing a direct threat to Hungary) but they have also inflicted such losses on the Austro-Hungarian army that it is on the point of collapse.

What Brusilov and his southern army group have achieved should not really have been possible: without any great superiority in terms of numbers or firepower they have successfully carried out a rapid offensive against an enemy who was well entrenched.*

Two paradoxes explain why most offensives end in failure and why the fronts so often become static. The first is this: in order to succeed, offensives need both thorough preparation and the element of surprise. But one excludes the other. An attacker who makes all the preparations considered necessary will inevitably be discovered and the surprise element comes to nothing. If surprise is prioritised, however, it is necessary to forget about careful preparation. The second paradox is this: in order to succeed, offensives need both weight and mobility. Weight—above all in the form of thousands of artillery pieces, many of them heavy, some

---

* This operation, just like the British offensive on the Somme, ultimately came in response to a plea for help from hard-pressed allies: the French were under pressure at Verdun, the Italians at Asiago. When Brusilov agreed to the pleas of his superiors and offered to mount a general offensive, asking for no more than very modest reinforcements, some of his colleagues shook their heads in dismay. Madness, they thought: everyone knew (didn't they?) that mounting an offensive demands massive superiority in terms of numbers, control of the air, millions of shells and so on.

extremely heavy—is needed to blast a way through the enemy's defensive lines. Mobility is needed to be able to exploit the gap thus created before the defender has time to react and plug it with reserves or new, hastily excavated lines of defence.

But in this case, too, it is only possible to have the one at the expense of the other. If an army has as many cannon, howitzers, mortars and so on as are necessary to achieve a breakthrough, it will become so slow that it is unable to convert the breakthrough into anything more than a salient filled with corpses and shell craters. And then the enemy reserves are brought up and everything can start from the beginning again. If, however, an army is sufficiently mobile to exploit a breakthrough quickly, it is unlikely to have the weight to break through in the first place. These (rather than any particular imbecility on the part of generals) are the main reasons for this drawn-out war of position.*

Brusilov's model was brilliant in its simplicity. It relied primarily on surprise, but that was to be achieved without the massive assemblage of men and materiel; nor did he need that kind of preparation since—the second point—he was not aiming for huge superiority in just one small sector (as had recently been the case with Evert's earlier Russian offensive in March) but was attacking at a series of points along the whole of the southern front. This meant that the German and Austro-Hungarian generals did not know where to send their reserves and the result was that the attacking forces for once came out on top.†

---

* In reality, battles were less a competition between the trenches and machine guns of the defenders and the assault units and artillery of the attackers than a pitting of the defenders' reserve units (which could be moved quickly to threatened sectors by train) against the slow forward push of the attackers' advance units, whose artillery trailed behind and frequently encountered enormous problems in advancing across a landscape that it had only just (and usually very successfully) blown to pieces.

† It helped, of course, that Brusilov was attacking the Austro-Hungarian army, which by this stage was suffering from an "almost Spanish-Hapsburg combination of serenity and incompetence" (to quote Norman Stone). There is also the fact that the railway network was considerably less developed and troop density much lower than on the Western Front. (This also explains why the war in the east was, in general, much more mobile than in the west.) Many of the Central Powers' divisions had spent much of their time on trains, being shunted from one threatened point to another by irresolute commanders; Lobanov-Rostovsky himself had been in this situation during the previous year's February offensive. Moreover, many of the German and Austro-Hungarian units that arrived were exhausted and well below strength after having been pulled out of the witches' brew of Verdun or from the harsh plateau around Asiago.

The place on the Stokhod river where Lobanov-Rostovsky is currently located is precisely the point at which the Brusilov offensive ran out of steam and chugged to a halt because of massive German reinforcements and equally overwhelming Russian losses. There were also logistical problems in that the Russian attackers were moving ever further from their railway network whereas the defenders were being pushed ever closer to their own. There was a long series of attacks and counterattacks in the region but things have now been quiet around the Stokhod for some time. Neither side has the strength to do much: the summer of 1916 in the east, just as in the west, has seen more blood spilled than anyone could have imagined.

The last few months have been relatively peaceful for Lobanov-Rostovsky. We can perhaps see evidence of his not notably soldierly disposition in the fact that he has been transferred from the sappers to a posting that involves even less combat: he is in command of a column of bridge-builders, which consists of eighty men, sixty horses and a number of unwieldy pontoons, and they have marched in the rear of the army the whole time, along with the artillery. But even from that position he has noticed two things. Firstly, the ability of the Russian army has really improved, particularly in Brusilov's army group; thus, for example, Russian trenches are much better built now than they were in Poland just a year ago, and camouflage skills are outstanding. Secondly, many of the Russian units are in very good shape: he has seen them march past "singing and in good order." He has also observed that the units are at full strength, though the officers are boyishly young, the fresh products of the cadet schools. Most of the veterans of 1914 are gone—dead, missing, in hospital or invalided home.

Lobanov-Rostovsky has, for once, been sent up to the front, where he has been put in temporary command of a couple of searchlights, the usual officer in command having had a nervous breakdown after six weeks in the forward line. Along with their generators, these searchlights have been dug in as far forward as possible and the idea is that they will be switched on if the Germans try to make a surprise attack by night. The infantrymen under his command think this is a stupid idea and they tell him openly that they do not want him and his searchlights there. Searchlights attract fire. But orders are orders.

The searchlights, however, have not been put to use and Lobanov-Rostovsky, true to his character, has been able to spend most of his time with his books. In the slightly touching way of bookish people, who always try to read their way to an understanding of the great and incomprehensible events that are affecting them, he has been spending a good many hours studying various German military theorists and war historians such as Theodor von Bernhardi and Colmar von der Goltz, as well as Carl von Clausewitz, the dark master himself.

Well, now. That rather childish sign triumphantly announcing Romania's entry into the war on the side of the Allies—a direct result, by the way, of the great and unexpected successes of the Brusilov offensive—sparks off an equally petulant reaction on the part of the Germans. On the stroke of midnight a raging firestorm is unleashed on the trench where the sign was put up and the German artillery plays every instrument in its orchestra in unison with the unpleasant accuracy it alone is capable of: the shrieking falsetto of the light field guns, the bass of the howitzers and the baritone of the mortars.

Andrei Lobanov-Rostovsky finds himself right in the middle of this whirling storm of steel, dust and explosive gases. He and some of his men squeeze into an improvised bunker and, as if afflicted by cramp, he still has the field telephone jammed against his ear. There is a short break between explosions and he hears fragments of a conversation: "Ninth Company reporting. Fifteen dead so far. Otherwise all right." Then a fresh salvo crashes down, this time very close. Everything shakes. Dust. Noise. The telephone falls silent. Light filters in through a newly blown hole in the roof. To be caught under drum fire is a new experience for him.

> It is impossible to convey the sensation in words, but anyone who has been through such an experience knows what I mean. Perhaps the nearest description would be a continuous and violent earthquake together with thunder and lightning while some foolish giant amused himself by taking hundreds of flash-lights. I lay in my hole amidst the thundering and roaring, trying painfully to think and to do the right thing.

He endures the same experience that has already been suffered by millions of soldiers when they make their real debut in the trenches: the visible world shrinks and very little can be seen, but the senses of smell and hearing are drastically amplified. The noise, in particular, becomes overwhelming and deafening. Two thoughts shine through the dark confusion of his mind. "The one: If anything happens to me, what a pity I didn't have time to finish that book of Clausewitz! The other: I am being watched by my soldiers, so I must conceal my fear."

After a while in this cauldron of chaos Lobanov-Rostovsky loses all sense of time. At one point he feels—not hears, not sees—feels that *something* is coming, and before his senses manage to register any more than that, a salvo of 15cm shells lands in a circle around him. When he comes to, unhurt but covered in earth, one of the NCOs lying alongside him says that the searchlight has been hit and smashed to pieces. The shells continue to fall from the dark sky in an unbroken stream.

Suddenly everything is dark and still.

And then silence: "The change was so sudden that the transition was physically painful."

It is three o'clock on the dot. German punctuality.

Now that the attack is over Lobanov-Rostovsky starts to tremble violently. He shakes so much that his whole body is covered in sweat.

Nothing more happens that night.

SATURDAY, 16 SEPTEMBER 1916
Michel Corday is working late at the ministry in Paris

Early autumn, with high, clear skies. As usual, the newspapers are annoying him. The front page is dominated by bold headlines announcing new Allied victories and it is only on the third page that he encounters a negative item: there is a three-line reference to the continued retreat of the Romanian army.

No trace of anything else. Corday has just read a letter written by a colonel and telling of an appalling event that happened recently at Verdun—yes, that battle is *still* going on, though with rather less intensity. (French troops attacked Douaumont a week ago and took some trenches. Two days ago German units mounted a counter-attack. Also, on the Somme, after being dormant for a time the battle has hotted up again: yesterday they used a completely new war machine for the first time—some kind of motorised vehicle, armed with a cannon and machine gun, protected by armour plating and running on caterpillar tracks.)* The colonel's letter tells of a disused railway tunnel at Tavannes which the troops have been using for a long time as a bunker, cantonment and ammunition store. This blocked-off tunnel was always packed with people, either soldiers who have become separated from their units or men seeking shelter from the continuous shelling. On the night of 5 September one of the ammunition dumps exploded and between 500 and 700 soldiers died in the resulting fire. There has not been a single word about this in the papers. (Nor was the disaster reported to the leading politicians.)

Censorship is strict and its regulations wide, convoluted and inscrutable.† The newspapers often contain white spaces where articles have been removed at the last minute. In other cases it is a matter of semantic manipulation—sometimes bordering on the ridiculous. Writers who use the expression "after the peace" are urged to write "in the post-war period." A colleague he knows, who works in a neighbouring department, has just managed to convince the papers to stop using the words "horse competitions" and to use instead the phrase "equine selection tests." "We are saved!" Corday snorts.

But it is not really the censorship or language regulations that Corday finds most upsetting, it is the fact that journalists are so willing to allow themselves to be turned into megaphones for nationalistic politicians and blinkered military men. Corday writes in his journal:

* The name "tank" has its roots in an attempt to deceive. The project was, of course, top-secret and anyone who asked was told that these big vehicles were "water tanks" to transport water to the troops. The latter part of the description stuck.

† A few examples from this period. An article with the headline "We Are Not Beaten" is stopped, as is another article that reports that around 50,000 Frenchmen have been killed in the war so far. A suggestion that the Allies have most to win by prolonging the war is also banned; a report pointing to the deaths of a large number of small children during the war in Romania likewise. Any detailed discussion of German peace feelers is forbidden. Only the most extreme and nationalistic German newspapers are quoted, the aim being to suggest that these offer a picture of German opinion in general. The official British documentary film of the Battle of the Somme, which has just arrived in France, has scenes cut out—including the most famous in which a group of soldiers is seen storming out of a trench and one of them falls back dead. (It is perhaps worth mentioning that this scene was probably staged.)

The French press has never revealed the truth, not even whatever truth is attainable under censorship. Instead we have been
subjected to a heavy bombardment of fine-sounding prattle, of
limitless optimism, of a systematic vilification of the enemy, of a
determination to hide the horrors and sorrows of the war—and all
this has then been concealed behind a mask of moralising idealism!

Words are one of the war's most vital strategic resources.

In the afternoon Corday walks to his office in the ministry. Along
the boulevard he encounters numerous bemedalled, wounded officers
on leave: "They seem to have come here specially in order to receive their
reward in the form of admiring glances." He passes the queues outside
grocers' shops. A fairly important propaganda point so far has been that
the Germans are suffering shortages of all kinds of goods whereas everything is available in France, but shortages have now begun to be felt here.
Sugar is difficult to get hold of, butter is sold only in 100-gram rations
and there are no longer any oranges in the shops. The city scene does,
however, have one new element—the nouveaux riches, or NR, as they are
sometimes known. They are black marketeers, war profiteers and others who have made big money out of contracts with the military or as a
result of the shortages and the like. NR are a permanent feature of all the
restaurants, where they are often to be seen eating the most expensive
items and drinking the finest wines. Women's fashions are extravagant
and ostentatious and the jewellers have rarely done better business. The
war is talked about less than ever, at least among the lower classes.

Michel Corday is working late this evening. He and a colleague from
the Ministry of Education work long and hard on a report for the Committee on Inventions. It is almost two o'clock in the morning by the time
they finish.

A DAY IN LATE SEPTEMBER 1916
Pál Kelemen goes to a railway restaurant in Sátoraljaújhely

Having more or less recovered from malaria and feeling well rested after
his long convalescence (which has included both going to church and

indulging in drinking sessions), Kelemen has once again been given light duties. Today he is on his way back from the Carpathian front, where he was making a delivery with packhorses close to Uzok. A captain of infantry in Uzok has given him his first real leave for a year and a half— in discreet exchange for a pair of new and very smart riding boots. Kelemen's destination is Budapest, and he is in the best of humours.

He has to change trains in Sátoraljaújhely and while waiting there he spends his time in the railway restaurant. It is full of passengers, old and young, women and men, civilian and military, "in disorderly confusion around tables covered with discolored cloths." His eye falls on a young, highly decorated ensign with the face of a boy:

> Seated at the head of one table, he is calmly eating a wedge of yellow, cream layer cake that lies on its side on his plate. His eyes move constantly about the hall but the gaze is blank and tired and returns each time to the slice of cake he is consuming with obvious pleasure. He wears a shabby general issue field uniform with both the large and the small silver medals on his breast. Probably returning from furlough on his way back to the trenches.
>
> The lively picture of the restaurant is changing from moment to moment. But he sits there beside the wall, as if there were no confusion around him, concerned only with his own pent up thoughts—and the second piece of cake that is rapidly diminishing on his plate.
>
> He takes a draught of water and helps himself to a third wedge from the pedestaled glass stand where the richly iced cake is set out, invitingly cut into portions. He is no longer eating because it tastes good. He is trying to store up in himself for the coming hard times, delicacies typical of home.

SATURDAY, 23 SEPTEMBER 1916[*]
Paolo Monelli communes with a dead man on Monte Cauriol

By this point they have been on many dreadful mountains, but this one promises to be the worst of the lot. They stormed and took Monte

---

[*] Or possibly a day or so earlier.

Cauriol about a month ago—a feat in itself, since the mountain is high and the Austro-Hungarian position was a strong one. Since then things have gone as they often do: after all the effort and losses involved they had insufficient strength to continue. The enemy brought up fresh troops and began a counter-attack—for no other reason than that this essentially meaningless spot was beginning to feature in communiqués and newspaper reports and was thus transformed into a trophy to be won or to be defended.

Monelli's company have beaten back several counter-attacks. There are dead Austrians hanging on the barbed wire. But the Italian losses, too, have been very high. They are under almost continuous fire and artillery bombardment from the surrounding mountains. Monelli notes that practically no one is left from the original platoon. The stench of decomposing bodies hangs in the air day and night. There are twenty or more dead men rotting away in a crevice very close to them, one of whom is an Austrian medical officer. The body is lying in such a way that Monelli can follow the slow process of decay: yesterday the nose burst and some sort of green fluid began to seep out. Strangely, however, the corpse's eyes remain almost unchanged and Monelli thinks they are staring accusingly at him. He writes in his journal:

It wasn't me who killed you—and you were a doctor, so why did you go and take part in that nocturnal attack? You had a loving fiancée who wrote you letters, perhaps untruthful, but so comforting, and you kept them in your wallet. Rech took the wallet from you on the night they killed you. We've also seen her picture (a pretty girl—and someone made indecent comments) and photos of your castle and all the cherished possessions you had there. We piled everything in a little heap and sat around, ensconced in our bunker with a bottle of wine as reward for our toils and happy to have beaten off the attack. It wasn't long ago that you died. You are already nothing, nothing more than a grey lump crumpled against the cliff, destined to stink. And we are so alive, ensign, so inhumanly alive that I've tried in vain to find a touch of regret in the depths of our consciousness. What good has it done you to have looked at the world with such avidity, to have held her young body in your arms, to have gone to war as if it were a vocation? Perhaps you too were intoxicated by the great mission, by your place in the advance guard, by the fact that perhaps you were fated to sacrifice yourself? But dying for whom? The living who are in such a hurry, the living who have become used to war as the fierce rhythm of life, the living who do not believe that they themselves will need to die—they are no longer thinking of you. It is as though your death has not only ended your life but annulled it. You will still exist for a little while as a number on the sergeant's muster-roll, a pathetic subject for memorial speeches; but you, man, you do not exist and it's as if you never had existed. We call them dead men, but what's lying there is actually no more than carbon and hydrogen sulphide, covered in ragged shreds of uniform.

The stench of the corpses in the crevice has become more and more distressing and when darkness falls four soldiers are given the job of dragging away the bodies. They are given a glass of brandy each and gas masks against the smell.

TUESDAY, 26 SEPTEMBER 1916
Vincenzo D'Aquila is discharged from the mental hospital in Siena

It is exactly twelve o'clock. He is down in the inner courtyard with several other patients when the telephone call comes. One of the male nurses waves him over, tells him he is to report to the hospital superintendent's office and adds: "Say goodbye to your buddies, Corporal, you're leaving us." D'Aquila calls to his brothers in misfortune, they say their goodbyes and wish each other well, and he is suddenly afflicted by contradictory emotions, "sadness over leaving the boys—gladness to be in the free air again." After changing into his uniform and collecting his possessions he goes over to the administration building, finds the superintendent's office and knocks on the door.

It is in Siena that D'Aquila has begun to return to life. He still believes it is necessary to stop the war and that war is unjust and wrong, but he now recognises that it is going to be difficult to take on such a colossal task while shut behind bars in a mental hospital. He has worked in the hospital laundry, hung up sheets and folded endless numbers of pillowcases. He wants to be set free and declared of sound mind, and he will not actually admit he has been mad. The doctors have countered that by saying that if he has not been mad they are in no position to say now that he has recovered. In answer to a direct question, D'Aquila told them that he has no intention of ever going back to the front.

There are doctors who suspect D'Aquila of bluffing, of simulating mental illness, and there have been attempts to show him to be a malingerer. The business of sorting the malingerers from the genuinely afflicted is one of the main functions of the staff. Not that all the staff are equally zealous in this respect and D'Aquila has actually seen some of them helping patients to simulate their symptoms. They have warned them when the doctors are coming and they have smuggled food to those who are officially refusing to eat. D'Aquila himself is convinced that a high proportion of the mental patients he meets *are* malingerers and, without any sense of self-contradiction, he views them with a degree of scepticism that borders on scorn. At the same time, however, there are some people who suspect he is doing just that, especially since he has been heard to say things such as, "While the war is going on a mental hospital is better than a trench." When not folding pillowcases or walking in the yard he has joined in with the other inmates, reading newspapers and magazines, playing cards and dominoes, and—with an earnestness that exceeds their knowledge—having endless discussions about the war situation and what can be expected next.

In August D'Aquila led a short-lived hunger strike against the monotony of their food: rice soup, for instance, was a permanent item on the menu. The result was a threatening dressing-down from the superintendent and three days' solitary in a padded cell, and since then the superintendent has him marked down as a malingerer. Discharging the young man as having recovered is probably seen both as a way of getting rid of a troublemaker at the same time as punishing him: D'Aquila will now have to return to active service and if he refuses he will de facto be classed as a deserter.

The door opens and D'Aquila is received not by the superintendent but by one of the doctors, a little professor by the name of Grassi. The doctor shakes his hand and congratulates him on being discharged.

D'Aquila leaves Siena that day and travels to Rome. His journey takes him via Florence, where he has a few hours to wait for a connecting train. He walks out into the town but comes to an abrupt halt, amazed and angry, on the beautiful Piazza della Signoria. With a sudden and resounding crash his different worlds collide. There is no sign here of the questions and torments that have been occupying him for the last year and which quite literally drove him out of his mind. There is nothing here that even suggests that a war is going on. People are drinking coffee, eating ice cream and flirting. In one part of the piazza there is an orchestra playing Viennese waltzes.

SUNDAY, 15 OCTOBER 1916
Alfred Pollard finds traces of the summer's battles on the Somme

The darkness of autumn. Cold. Damp. A full moon. Tonight Alfred Pollard is out scouting in no-man's-land again. He is on the Somme. Face blackened with burnt cork and revolver in hand, he is creeping forward through an endless series of shell holes:

> I had not proceeded very far before I felt something yield and scrunch under me. It was the skeleton of a corpse, its bones picked clean by the army of rats which scavenged the battle-fields.* The rags of a tunic still covered its nakedness. I felt in the pockets to try to discover some means of identification, but they were empty. Someone had been before me. Further on I found another; then another and another. They were the bodies of those slain in the terrible fighting at the beginning of July. All were British.

Angus Buchanan writes in his diary on the same day:

> Seven German *askaris* gave themselves up overnight. They report food scarce, and also that numbers of natives are deserting and going off west through the bush, their purpose to try to find their way back to their homes. They also say, as we have heard before,

---

* Front-line soldiers of all nationalities felt a mixture of disgust and hatred for the trench rats because they lived on the corpses, and they lived well, growing unusually large. Two indicators of how long a body had been dead were putrefaction and rat damage. The two processes were in competition and it was often the rats that won.

that the German carriers are partially bound when in camp, so they cannot run away in the night, if they wanted to escape.

THE MIDDLE OF OCTOBER 1916
Florence Farmborough loses her hair

Florence has been suffering from paratyphoid fever. One night a few weeks ago when her fever was at its worst Florence thought she had three faces: one was her own, one belonged to one of her sisters and the third seemed to be that of a wounded soldier. Sweat poured from each of them and they had to be wiped all the time. She knew she would die if the wiping ceased. She tried to shout for a nurse but found that she no longer had a voice. She is now convalescing in the warm autumn sun in the Crimea. The hospital in which she is being cared for is actually a sanatorium for tuberculosis sufferers but she has been allowed to stay there anyway. Everything is still green outside and she has made an unexpectedly quick recovery. She writes in her journal:

> My hair was in bad condition and coming out in handfuls. So, one day, the barber came to my room and not only cut my hair, but shaved my head! I was assured I should never regret it, and that it would grow again stronger and thicker than it had ever been before. From that time, I wore my nurse's veil round my head and no one—save the few initiated—could ever guess that the veil covered a bald pate—devoid of even a single hair!

Michel Corday notes in his journal during this period:

> Albert J., currently on leave, mentions how much the soldiers hate Poincaré, a hatred based on the idea that he was the one who started the war. He points out that what makes the men take part in attacks is the fear of appearing cowardly to the others. He also says—with a laugh—that he is thinking of getting married since that will give him the right to four days' leave and a further three days when a child is born. Also, that he hopes to get the certificate

exempting him from military service once he has produced six
little ones.

THURSDAY, 19 OCTOBER 1916
Angus Buchanan is confined to bed in Kisaki

The bed on which he is lying is made of grass and even though he is
now feeling much better than he has felt for the last few days he is still
very weak. Dysentery. Everyone knows the symptoms: stomach pains,
a high temperature, painful and bloody bouts of diarrhoea. Buchanan
has managed to remain one of the healthy ones for a long time but in the
long run it was inevitable that he too would be afflicted.

The campaign with all its weary traipsing about has continued. In
what has increasingly taken on the character of a pure guerrilla war,
the enemy has been pushed away from the Pangani river towards the
interior of German East Africa and Buchanan and his companions have
been chasing them southwards through the bush. Sometimes they have
passed through inhabited regions, in which case supplies have temporarily improved as they have been able to barter goods with the local
population.* On one occasion Buchanan managed to exchange an old
shirt and waistcoat for two hens and half a dozen eggs.

They have had some successes, however. On the Lukigura river at
the end of June they succeeded for once in engaging the usually elusive
German units in a real battle. In spite of being in a pretty poor state the
25th Royal Fusiliers gave a good account of themselves again, firstly by
making a rapid flanking march and then by putting their enemy to flight
with a bold bayonet charge. The important town of Morogoto, located on
the central railway, was taken at the end of August, though only after significant losses and some exhausting and sometimes completely pointless
marches through very difficult terrain that ranged from the hilly to the
waterlogged and marshy. Dar es-Salaam, the biggest and most important
harbour in the colony, has been in British hands since the beginning of
September. As Buchanan's division marched south, the Germans continued to retreat, step by step, and with repeated skirmishing.

* Money was of no interest to the local population: they already had more than enough
of the worthless German emergency paper currency.

Everything came to a halt at the end of September after further costly and unsuccessful efforts to get to grips with an enemy who somehow always managed to slip away. By then the supply lines were too extended, the supplies too few and the men too exhausted. Buchanan's company is a pitiful sight. Most of the men are emaciated, many of them have no clothes above the waist and lack socks in their boots. News seldom reaches them and letters from home sometimes take six months to arrive. They have only a very vague picture of what is happening in the war.

Earlier this autumn Buchanan caught malaria but has since recovered; then came the dysentery. To keep him company he has the hen with the white comb that he decided to keep. The hen has become very tame and is now a pet. During the marches she travels in a bucket carried by an African servant and when they make camp she runs around free, scratching for food. In some strange way she always finds her way back to him through the forest of feet and hooves, and she lays him an egg every day. On one occasion he saw her kill and eat a small poisonous snake. At night she sleeps beside him.

Buchanan is lying on his bed of grass writing his journal. He is ill and depressed, not least by their lack of tangible success:

Feeling better today and cheerier, but I wish, since I've lost patience, that we could get along with "the Show," and then be quit of Africa for a time, for I have a passionate desire that we should be free to change, just for a little, the colour and the quality of a long familiar picture whose strange characteristics are now indelible. Sometimes, I'm afraid, I feel as if I was in prison, and long for the freedom of the life beyond these prison walls. Those are times when thoughts quickly fly in and out of the old scenes—dear old familiar scenes—and they are touched now with a deep and sure appreciation. Would that they could stay; would that, by the strength of their willingness, they could lift me in body over the vast space and set me in some fair peaceful land.

That same day Paolo Monelli is listening anxiously to the sound of the preparatory bombardment by the Italian artillery, which is hammering away at Monte Cauriol, where the fighting is still going on. He writes in his journal:

The sky is overcast, grey and low. Mist is rising from the valley and cutting off the two peaks, ours and the one we are to attack. If we are going to die, we shall die cut off from the world and with a sense that no one is really interested. Once one is resigned to the thought of sacrificing oneself, one would like to think that it might happen in front of an audience. To die in the sun, in full view, on the open stage that is the world—that is how one imagines dying for one's country: but the way it is here is more like a condemned man being strangled secretly.

SUNDAY, 29 OCTOBER 1916
Richard Stumpf finds life monotonous on board SMS Helgoland

He wonders which is worse—the permanent clouds of blue tobacco smoke that fill their quarters below decks or the ubiquitous coal dust "that seeps into our guts the whole time." Stumpf is as gloomy as the day itself. He recalls the expectations he had when he enlisted almost exactly four years earlier and he is plagued by the contrast with how things are now. The emotional surge that followed the great Battle of Jutland has faded away. They are back to the old, grey routines—grey as the battle-ships themselves: short, uneventful patrols along the coast interspersed with long periods in port. The High Seas Fleet, if anything, is behaving even more shyly and cautiously than before. His "iron prison," SMS *Helgoland*, is once again lying at her moorings, this time waiting for a broken cylinder in the port engine to be repaired.

The tobacco smoke drives Stumpf up on deck yet again: "These stinking bloody pipes! They make me feel ill and they ruin my appetite. I'm only too glad to hear that the price of tobacco in the canteen has gone up."* The smoke bothers him and the monotony bores him. And

---

* Ian Gately has shown that there were increasing restrictions in Europe on tobacco smoking before 1914, but that the war undermined this change of attitude. Vast quantities of tobacco were consumed in the war years and tobacco was part of a soldier's basic rations right from the start. British soldiers received two ounces of tobacco a week whereas the Germans were given two cigarettes or cigars a day. (The British navy received a ration double that of the army and if the same was true of the German navy it would explain why Stumpf suffered so much.) Tobacco in one form or another was a standard item in

he has few friends on board. The other sailors find him strange, both because of his intellectual interests and because he spends all his time writing. There are no outlets for Stumpf's energies here, nothing for him to get his teeth into mentally or physically; and at the moment he has nothing to read, though he has ordered some books from Berlin.

It looks like being another wasted day for Richard Stumpf. In the early afternoon, however, the whole crew is called up on deck to welcome the arrival home of a U-boat returning from patrol. Stumpf watches the crews on nearby ships begin to cheer and throw their caps in the air. There she comes—the slim hull of U-53. The whole of the U-boat crew is lined up on the deck: "They are wearing oilskins and their faces are beaming with joy."*

Stumpf is envious of these radiant submariners and wishes he could be one of them. At the same time he longs for the war to be over soon; as usual, his emotions are divided:

> Did we really have such a good life in peacetime? Even if it might seem as if we did, we weren't really satisfied. I remember that many of us hoped for war so that things would get better for us.

---

parcels sent by the aid organisations and by relations. The French soldiers' newspaper *La Baïonette*, for example, in addition to expressing constant nagging concerns about shortages, published paeans to tobacco at regular intervals. The popularity of smoking was probably due to a combination of factors. The mildly narcotic effect of the nicotine, along with the fact that it gave the men something to do in stressful situations, would undoubtedly have helped calm the nerves of many. At least as important for those in command of the armies, anyway, was the fact that tobacco suppresses appetite. A third factor was that the smoke helped to mask the stench of putrefaction: it was not unknown for units in trenches particularly affected by rotting corpses to be given extra rations of tobacco.

* U-53 had been all the way to the United States and even docked at Rhode Island harbour (the United States was still neutral at this stage). The purpose of the voyage had been to act as escort to the enormous ocean-going merchant U-boat *Bremen*, which had been sent to the United States to bring back strategic raw materials. After the *Bremen* mysteriously disappeared during her maiden Atlantic voyage, U-53 simply returned home, torpedoing five vessels on the way. The German navy had seven huge merchant U-boats of the *Bremen*'s class (U-151), designed to ensure the supply of vital goods. The recognition of the effectiveness of submarines during the war led Germany to construct a range of U-boats as well as the standard type: UB-boats were designed to attack in coastal waters and UC- and UE-boats were small vessels designed mainly for mine laying in coastal and ocean waters, respectively.

Whenever I remember how we used to worry about getting a job, about pay disputes and the length of the working day, it makes the thought of peace less attractive. But at the moment it seems like paradise, a time when we could buy all the bread, all the sausage, all the clothes we wanted. Not that that was much help to all the poor buggers with no money to buy anything! Perhaps the real crisis will come when we are all lucky enough to be at peace again.

SATURDAY, 16 DECEMBER 1916
Angus Buchanan sees reinforcements arrive in Kisaki

It is a period of recovery—for everyone. Angus Buchanan has recovered from his dysentery and his battalion, or what remains of it, has recovered from the hardships of the autumn. In a very short time both Angus and the battalion have regained surprising levels of energy. Buchanan himself has continued collecting birds, has been off on a lengthy reconnaissance mission beyond the Mgeta river and, in spite of a touch of malaria, bagged his first two elephants—a young bull followed immediately by a large cow elephant. Meanwhile the troops have been working hard preparing the route for their continued advance through enemy territory, felling numerous trees and building several bridges over the Mgeta. At Kirenwe they have also cut a wide road through the primeval forest.

Today their spirits were lifted even further by the arrival of a column of about 150 men, a welcome reinforcement for the weakened battalion. At their head is a man wearing a big soft hat and armed with a hunting rifle—it is Buchanan's old company commander, Frederick Courteney Selous. He is now sixty-five years old. Just a few months ago Selous had been so ill that he was sent home to Great Britain and no one expected to see him again. Now, however, he looks to be in extraordinarily good shape and Buchanan and his companions are happy and impressed. "How fine an example of loyalty he gave, in thus, at his great age, returning again to the front to fight his country's battles." Selous is doubly welcome since he can tell them how things are going at home and what is happening in the war in general.

Later, when the day begins to cool and the shadows lengthen, they discuss this and that. Selous talks about his large collection of butterflies, which he took back to Great Britain, and Buchanan tells him about the elephant hunt. Meanwhile the black bearers in Buchanan's machine-gun platoon build a grass hut for the man they call Bwana M'Kubwa, the big boss. In a few days they will all be moving south-east towards the Rufiji river, where the enemy is said to be entrenched. There is a new sense of expectancy in the air.

SATURDAY, 30 DECEMBER 1916
Alfred Pollard writes a letter to his mother

It has been a good year for Sergeant Alfred Pollard DCM. The successful fighting around the crater in Sanctuary Wood in September 1915, during which he was wounded, resulted in the Distinguished Conduct Medal, which he is very pleased with, though in his heart of hearts he is a touch disappointed since he had hoped for the Victoria Cross.

After a period in hospital in England and while waiting to be declared fit for active service, he spent his time going to the theatre and to music halls (all free for wounded soldiers), attending parties, practising his grenade-throwing technique in his mother's garden and writing an application for officer training, which was successful. He has been back in France since May and has been given responsibility for training the battalion in hand-grenade combat. He has also returned to his old habit of making nocturnal trips into no-man's-land.

The only thing to have upset Pollard was the news that his older brother had been killed at the end of the summer. At that point—out of concern for his mother, who only has one child left now—he considered applying for a less exposed posting. But he soon dismissed the idea and decided instead to avenge his sibling from that day on: "Rather would I do my utmost to kill as many [Germans] as possible." He celebrated Christmas at a French château behind the lines, where he was once again instructing soldiers in where, how and when to use hand grenades. He has been given a new nickname—Bombo.

Today he is writing to his mother:

Dearest Mater,

I hear you have not been very well. I hope you are all right again
now. The post is absolutely up the stick, probably owing to
Christmas. I have received the footer clothes and the uniform
and Perk's cake; all very acceptable. I am at present at the school
as I told you and intended to remain here, but really, mater,
internal inspiration tells me I must go back up the line when the
battalion go. I don't suppose that will be until nearly the end of
January so don't start worrying, but I feel it's up to me to go with
them. I have sent in my resignation but may be retained until the
end of the course. Anyhow, you might wash out addressing me to
the school and continue addressing me to the battalion. I am very
sorry, mater, but I know you will understand.

I have had some splendid riding lately. Yesterday afternoon I
rode into a town about seven miles away. Coming back we had a
three mile gallop without a check. Rather splendid! There were
two rows of trees by the side of the road with soft earth between
them.

Well cheerioh!

Two weeks later the battalion marches back to the front and Pollard
is with them. Is there some sort of death wish in this? Probably not. He
is carrying a new mascot in his pocket—a small china doll with a lilac
ribbon round its waist and an angelic expression painted on its face. It
is a gift from the sister of Mary, the woman who turned down his marriage proposal so firmly.* Pollard has christened the doll Billiken and he
always carries it with him from now on.

---

* See 30 September 1915, page 166.

1917

And the savage in you makes you adore it with its squalor and wastefulness and danger and strife and glorious noise. You feel that, after all, this is what men were intended for rather than to sit in easy chairs with a cigarette and whiskey, the evening paper or the best-seller, and to pretend that such a veneer means civilization and that there is no barbarian behind your starched and studded shirt front.

HARVEY CUSHING

Chronology 1917

31 JANUARY	Germany announces unrestricted U-boat warfare.
3 FEBRUARY	USA breaks off diplomatic relations with Germany.
21 FEBRUARY	German troops in France make a planned withdrawal to behind the so-called Hindenburg Line.
24 FEBRUARY	British forces recapture Kut al-Amara in Mesopotamia.
9 MARCH	Food riots in Petrograd worsen and turn into a revolution.
11 MARCH	British forces march into Baghdad.
26 MARCH	The First Battle of Gaza. The Ottoman defenders repel the British.
6 APRIL	USA declares war on Germany.
9 APRIL	British offensive at Arras. Some gains.
16 APRIL	Major French offensive at Le Chemin des Dames. Minor gains.
19 APRIL	The Second Battle of Gaza. Ottoman defenders once again repel the British.
29 APRIL	Mutinies in the French army. They become widespread and continue until the beginning of June.
12 MAY	The tenth Italian offensive on the Isonzo begins. Some gains.
1 JULY	Russian offensive in the east. It collapses completely towards the end of the month.
31 JULY	Major British offensive around Ypres in Flanders. It will continue until November.
3 AUGUST	Renewed Allied offensive in East Africa.

5 AUGUST   German-Austrian offensive in Romania.

19 AUGUST   The eleventh Italian offensive on the Isonzo begins. Some gains.

21 AUGUST   German offensive around Riga. Significant gains.

24 OCTOBER   Start of the joint Austro-Hungarian and German offensive at Caporetto. Major gains. A general Italian retreat.

31 OCTOBER   The Battle of Beersheba in Palestine leads to a British breakthrough.

6 NOVEMBER   Passchendaele captured by the Canadians. The offensive runs out of steam.

7 NOVEMBER   The Bolsheviks take power in Petrograd following a coup.

9 NOVEMBER   The Italian army establishes a new line of defence along the River Piave.

1 DECEMBER   The last German forces retire from East Africa into Mozambique.

2 DECEMBER   Peace negotiations begin between Germany and the new Russian Bolshevik regime.

9 DECEMBER   Allied troops march into Jerusalem.

THURSDAY, 4 JANUARY 1917
Angus Buchanan attends the burial of his company commander at Beho Beho

In the beginning it looks like yet another failed pincer movement. The 25th Royal Fusiliers—or, to be more accurate, the 200 men remaining of the original 1,200—have been on their feet since before dawn. They have the reputation of being the most reliable and fast moving of the British units and they have once again been sent on in advance to carry out an encirclement. Their target, and that of the main force, is the village of Beho Beho. While the other units approach the hamlet from the east, Buchanan and his companions are to move round stealthily and approach from the west, preventing the German unit known to be in the village from slipping away in its usual manner. Sunshine. A baking sky. The scent of hot foliage.

After two hours of cautious marching through the bush they reach the position in which they intend to wait for the retreating enemy. There is a small road in front of them, leading from the village. The sound of sustained gunfire hangs in the hot air: the main force has started its attack. The men of the 25th Royal Fusiliers spread out in a long, extended line, lie down in the cool cover of the shade provided by the trees and wait. The sounds of battle in the distance show no sign of easing off and after a while the men begin to feel some impatience. Is this yet another operation that has come to nothing?

That is the story of the operations in German East Africa. The British columns have moved in a series of clumsy leaps from valley to valley, slowly pushing the mobile, elusive companies of Schutztruppen south-wards. They will soon be at the Rufiji river.

On paper this looks like success and most of the German colony is now in Allied hands. But this has happened only at enormous cost in terms of suffering and resources. The war has also affected this part of Africa in a way no other conflict has done. Before it is all over the British alone will have recruited a million black bearers (virtually all the stores are carried on African backs for part of the journey), one in five of whom will not survive the war.

What the Allied commanders under the leadership of Smuts have failed to understand is that von Lettow-Vorbeck, their tough, intelligent and cynical opponent, does not give a damn about the colony. Right from the start, this master of guerrilla warfare has seen it as his task to draw in as many enemy troops as possible, because every man, every gun, every bullet shipped to East Africa means one man, one gun, one bullet fewer on the Western Front. And the German has succeeded in this beyond his wildest dreams: Smuts now has five times as many sol-diers as von Lettow-Vorbeck but has come nowhere near defeating the German.

A couple of excited scouts come running back in the heat. They have seen the enemy approaching along the road. Orders are given and the line of lying men rises and moves towards the road with their weapons at the ready. Buchanan is in command of two Vickers heavy machine guns and manages to get them set up in firing position. Further along the road they can see German *askaris*, who have just left the village. Buchanan tells the story:

> On these we immediately opened machine-gun and rifle fire, surprising them completely, and inflicting severe casualties. Not-withstanding this they retaliated, gamely enough for a little, but our firing wore them down, and soon those that remained were silent, and fleeing in the bush.

Much of the new military technology had problems functioning in the African terrain and the African climate. Motor vehicles often came to a standstill, artillery got bogged down and aeroplanes failed to find their targets in the dense vegetation. The machine gun, however, proved to be as murderously effective in Africa as it was in the other theatres of war. (Those with experience from earlier colonial wars already knew this.) During fighting in the bush or in the jungle there is a tendency for rifle fire to go too high. Heavy machine guns, however, can have the same effect as scythes as they send swathes of bullets backwards and forwards through the thick cover about three feet above the ground, dropping anything that is hiding there: and they are all the more effective in that they can easily be put into a fixed firing position by using ratchet wheels.

Buchanan and his men carry on past the fallen and the wounded, on towards Beho Beho. They take up position on a small open ridge just outside the village and a prolonged exchange of fire with the black troops in the village ensues. The sun is bakingly hot.

The hours that follow are difficult.

The low ridge on which they are lying is covered with gleaming white pebbles that reflect the sun's rays in a way that would be beautiful from a distance but which make the heat almost unbearable for men forced to lie down pressed to the ground. They all get painful blisters, even those with the advantage of the brown, leathery skin caused by years in the African sun. The enemy troops in the village, on the other hand, are in the shade and also have the advantage of being able to station themselves in the trees and snipe accurately at the men lying out on the roasting pebbles of the ridge.

The firing continues and losses begin to mount among the men of the 25th. One of those hit is Buchanan, who takes a bullet through his left arm. After a little while a shout runs along the line—Captain Selous, their company commander, is dead. He had moved forward fifteen yards or so in an attempt to pinpoint the position of some particularly troublesome snipers and scarcely had he raised his field glasses to his eyes before a bullet struck him in the side. He was turning round with the obvious intention of trying to return to his own line when another bullet hit him in the head and killed him. They react with horror to the news since they all "loved him in an uncommon manner, as their officer and as their grand old fearless man." No one is affected more than Ramazani, Selous's African servant, who had accompanied him as his gun-bearer on his many big-game safaris before the war. Out of his mind with sorrow and a desire for revenge, Ramazani hurls himself into the firefight with no regard for the well-aimed bullets coming from the concealed rifle-men in the village.

Towards four o'clock the enemy slips away and disappears into the bush yet again. Buchanan and the rest of the British troops are able to enter the empty village.

That evening they bury Frederick Courteney Selous and the other dead men in the shade of a baobab tree.[*]

TUESDAY, 16 JANUARY 1917
Michel Corday wonders how posterity will view the war

Something is happening. There is a change of mood, partly revealed by a declining interest in the war or, perhaps more accurately, by a greater tendency towards escapism: the romanticised tales of soldiers and hero-ism that filled most magazines during the first years of the war are dis-appearing and being replaced by whodunnits, crime fiction and other kinds of typically escapist literature. And it also shows in an openly stated antipathy to the war, even though articles and speeches by chau-vinists and nationalists, opportunists and bombasts still set the tone of what passes for public debate.

Faithful echoes of the latter kind of thinking can still be heard among "ordinary" people and it has long been taboo to advocate peace or, indeed, even speak of it. "Peace" has become a dirty word, giving off a vague odour of defeatism, pro-Germanism and a spineless propen-sity to compromise. The word alone is enough to make people object, swear, roll their eyes and so on, and it has even been censored. Victory—absolute, unconditional, total victory—has been the only acceptable idea. Just as in the other warring states, the sufferings and losses have not promoted a desire for compromise but have made attitudes more rigid, even more disinclined to accept anything short of "victory." Anything else would mean that all the sufferings and losses have been in vain, wouldn't it? And why compromise, anyway, when there is no chance of being defeated?

---

* Another eyewitness account says it is a tamarind tree.

But something is happening. Something has changed in the language being used, though so far it is only on the street, person to person.

It is no longer impossible to hear people talking about their desire for—yes—"peace." A couple of days ago Corday was standing in the cold waiting for a tram when he overheard a conversation between a woman and an army padre who had just come back from the Somme and Verdun. The padre said to her, "There are already more than enough mothers in mourning. Let's hope that the whole business will soon be over." More recently, on the same tram, he heard an upper-class woman, well wrapped up in her fur coat, say loudly to a soldier, "You wouldn't have had to put up with thirty months of this if it weren't for the thousands of scoundrels and idiots who voted for the war parties." Many of her fellow passengers grinned and squirmed in embarrassment, but a working-class woman sitting near Corday muttered: "She's absolutely right."

It is not only weariness and exhaustion that are beginning to make their voices heard. This change of mood is also a reaction to last month's peace initiatives, one from the German chancellor Theobold von Bethmann-Hollweg* and the other, a few days later, from the American president Woodrow Wilson. The rulers of the Allied countries immediately rejected the first out of hand, and they responded to the second with such a series of objections, demands and hazy claims that it is obvious to everyone that there is no immediate hope of peace.

But the Word itself has nevertheless resurfaced. "Peace."

The publication of a letter from the Kaiser to his chancellor is one element in the propaganda for the German peace proposal. Among much

---

* Bethmann-Hollweg's proposals, one of the wasted opportunities of the war, arose partly from his recognition that Germany's chances of achieving an unconditional victory had diminished even though, following the defeat of Romania and the failure of the British offensive on the Somme, Germany's position was apparently stronger than before. The proposals were also a rather desperate attempt to resist the favourite idea of the German hawks and militarists—their desire to wage an unrestricted U-boat war. The German chancellor, and many with him, correctly feared that this would drag the United States into the conflict. His proposals were, however, rather vague: he did not formulate any conditions or offer any promises—least of all a commitment to allow Belgium to emerge from the war unscathed. These were not the first German peace proposals. Feelers had been put out in the direction of Russia in 1915 but, since Paris and London had a lot more to offer (Constantinople, for instance) than Berlin, Petrograd responded with little more than silence.

else, Kaiser Wilhelm writes, "To put forward a peace proposal is to perform a moral act that is necessary to free the world—including neutral countries—from the burden that is now in the process of crushing it." *Every* French newspaper has attacked this letter, usually by questioning its authenticity, and they have also given the American proposal a chilly, even scornful, reception: "Pure imagination! Illusions! Delusions of grandeur!" Corday has actually heard a man snort and accuse the American president of being "more German than the Germans."

How can anyone hope to offer a fair picture of the possibility of peace when the press, the only real medium for the masses, is both strictly censored and in the hands of propagandists, warmongers and ideologues? Corday finds no great comfort in the thought that a succeeding generation will be able to make sense of the tangle of emotional storms, *idées fixes*, exaggerations, half-truths, illusions, linguistic games, lies and deceptions which this war has produced. He frequently tries to recall what it was that happened, *really happened*, when this great landslide began to move in the late summer two and a half years ago; he eagerly gathers the small splinters of fact that he can find here and there, scattered like the forgotten clues left at the scene of a crime that has long since gone cold. The question, however, is what information will it really be possible to obtain after it is all over.

He has known for a long time that the image of the war and of public opinion presented by the press is biased to the point of mendacity. He wrote in his journal in April 1915: "Fear of the censor and the need to flatter the basest instincts [of the public] lead [the press] to publish nothing but hate and abuse." The politicians and generals who were involved in whipping up public opinion in favour of the war in 1914 have become prisoners of their own hate-fuelled rhetoric. It has made the very idea of a compromise peace unthinkable, and it has even made certain tactically motivated withdrawals impossible because withdrawal would immediately be converted into symbolic defeat in the eyes of the press and the man on the street: this was what happened with Verdun.* But now, perhaps, something has at last begun to move.

---

* A vocal and influential body of opinion in Germany also rejected all compromise and considered it self-evident, for instance, that Belgium would in some way remain German. The same people also regarded German colonial expansion as a given.

So it goes without saying that the newspapers will be anything but reliable as a source for future historians. What about private letters? Corday has his doubts even there: "Letters from the front give a false feeling about the war. The writer knows that his letters might be opened. And his main aim will be to impress future readers." Photographs, then? Perhaps people will be able to turn to them to discover what things were really like, on the home front, for instance. Corday thinks not, and he writes in his journal:

> Either vanity or shame prevents certain aspects of life from being reflected in our illustrated magazines. So posterity will find that the photographic documentation of the war is full of very big gaps. For example: it will not show the almost total darkness that exists indoors because of the restrictions on lighting, or the gloomy, dim streets where the fruit merchants are illuminated by candles, or the dustbins that remain unemptied on the pavement until three in the afternoon because of a shortage of manpower, or the queues of anything up to three thousand people waiting outside the large grocery stores to get their sugar ration. Nor—to look at the other side of the coin—will it show the huge numbers filling the restaurants, tea rooms, theatres, variety shows and cinemas to bursting point.

A DAY IN JANUARY 1917
Paolo Monelli learns how to deter nosy visitors

Both the winter weather and the gunfire have eased and the winding mule tracks have begun to be well trampled. It is in conditions like these that visitors tend to show up, curious about these notorious mountain peaks and keen to be able to say "I was there."

They are not welcome.

If they are of lower status the soldiers simply bombard them with snowballs and pieces of ice from a distance and then, when they arrive confused, breathless and covered in snow, pretend to know nothing about it. More subtle methods are needed for those of higher rank. The men have laid a number of explosive charges a short distance away from their defensive position and the moment they receive a telephone warning that some bigwig down below has started to put on his snow kit they detonate some of these charges. This causes a cascade of snow and stones and, unfailingly, the Austro-Hungarian position on the mountain top opposite responds by firing off half a dozen shells. (*Zeem choom zeem shoom!*)

The battalion commander will then say dolefully that he does not know what is going on: "Everything's been so quiet up there until now." At which the high-ranking visitor down below "is immediately smitten by a nostalgic longing for the valley" and vanishes.

THURSDAY, 1 FEBRUARY 1917
Edward Mousley sees snow falling on Kastamonu

He survived the march and reached the railhead at Ras al-'Ayn. He and the rest of the men who finished the two-month desert march from Baghdad were then transported north-westwards in cattle trucks. And the places rolled past. The Euphrates. Osmaniye. The Anti-Taurus Mountains and the Mediterranean as a silver sliver in the distance. Gülek Boğazı. The Taurus Mountains. Pozantı. Afyonkarahisar. Eskişehir. Ankara. From Ankara they were on foot again, northwards and upwards, over mountains covered in conifers, growing colder all the time, all the way to Kastamonu, about forty-five miles from the Black Sea. There the prisoners were quartered in a couple of large houses on the edge of the town, in Christian districts that were half-empty after the attacks on the Armenians.

Conditions are good in Kastamonu, very good when compared with those they endured in the months following their capitulation. They are treated well, and Mousley and the others begin to suspect that the horrors of the march were not so much planned as a result of the usual Ottoman combination of harsh indifference and incompetence. There is also the fact that the men at Kastamonu have the advantage of being officers: the conditions for the non-commissioned ranks and ordinary soldiers are extremely harsh. Whereas Mousley and the officers have to combat boredom, nightmares and the aftermath of the march and illness, the other ranks who survived transportation have been put to hard labour in various places.*

In Kastamonu Mousley is allowed to visit the shops and the bath-house once a week, accompanied by a not excessively zealous guard. The prisoners are also allowed to attend church and to send and receive post, including parcels from home. They play chess, bridge and rugby and are sometimes allowed to go for long walks among the high hills that sur-round them. They are planning to start a small orchestra. Mousley has had a recurrence of his malaria and been forced to go to a Greek den-tist to get his teeth fixed—they were badly affected by the monotonous diet during the siege. He has even put on some weight. Most of them try to stick to certain routines, such as changing for dinner, even if it only involves taking off one ragged shirt and putting on another equally ragged one. The Ottomans enforce a strict ban on fraternising with the inhabitants of the town, though they may occasionally get drunk.

He has been very cold since the start of winter. There is a shortage of wood and what little he can get hold of tends to be damp. When he puts it in the small stove there is more smoke than fire. Boredom and monot-ony are the worst things, however, and Mousley spends much of his time smoking and sleeping in the room he shares with another officer. It is a long time since he wrote anything in his journal.

When he looks out of his window this morning the light is colder and paler. Snow. The whole world has changed. The jumble of reddish brown roofs he is used to seeing are white and the town has suddenly become picturesque, almost as pretty as a picture. The streets are empty and the only signs of life are the sing-song voices of the muezzins in the minarets. The sight of this sudden transformation, the result of snow— "this pure and godly element, silent and secretive"—does something for him, filling him with remarkable energy that displaces his apathy. It makes him start hoping again, makes him want to remember again.

He takes out his journal and makes the first entry since the begin-ning of October: "February 1st, 1917.—Four months have gone. As I write the earth is white with feet of snow." Later he and some other British officers go to a hill about a mile away, where they do some sledging "and

---

* Around 70 per cent of the other ranks taken prisoner after the capitulation at Kut al-Amara will die. That mortality rate is on the same level as that in the worst Nazi and Soviet labour camps.

pretend that we are schoolboys again." They have a snowball fight on the way home.

FRIDAY, 2 FEBRUARY 1917
Richard Stumpf regains hope in Wilhelmshaven

The barometer is continuing to rise and in the morning those who have come off watch are allowed to go on a march or, perhaps more accurately, to make a short excursion to Mariensiel. The ship's band marches in the lead, playing its instruments, the formalities are kept simple and they are all full of high spirits. The ice is gleaming and is still thick. Stumpf is impressed by its strength and beauty, but he thinks it will soon break up and disappear without trace. On the way home they march through Wilhelmshaven.

SMS *Helgoland* is once again being refitted, repaired and modified. This time it is the ship's 88mm rapid-fire cannon that are being removed. The Battle of Jutland revealed their range to be insufficient and the guns have been deemed ineffective—"a view," as Stumpf writes in his journal, that two years earlier would have caused anyone voicing it "to be shot as a traitor." These guns have not fired a single shot and those manning them (including Stumpf) have been wasting their time. He tries to comfort himself with the fact that the guns are more needed ashore.* Stumpf also believes that great things are brewing. He has regained his faith in the future: "The whole world is holding its breath as Germany gathers herself to deliver one final, devastating, knock-out blow."

Once back on the ship they have lunch and then the duty officer arrives with a piece of paper—"wonderful news." "Listen to this, men, a telegram from Berlin. 'As of today we shall be waging unrestricted U-boat war.'" The announcement makes all of them "extremely happy" and soon nothing else is being talked about on board. Most of them seem to be of the opinion that it is only a matter of time before Great Britain is forced to her knees. This is a "sentence of death for England."

---

* A historical curiosity: when used on land these rejected 88mm cannon proved excellent as anti-aircraft guns. Also, one of the most feared guns of the Second World War, the German 88mm cannon, was ultimately developed from them.

This is the German version—put into action—of the fight "to the bitter end" French politicians have proclaimed for so long.

Stumpf is one of the doubters, though he is willing to give the whole business four months, after which the situation should have become clearer. He does, however, see this as a way of responding to the British blockade, which is what caused this cold and miserable "turnip winter" in Germany. That is what they have to eat most of the time, turnips of various kinds prepared in various ways. (The basic ingredient does not change but the variety of recipes is endless: they eat turnip pudding and turnip balls, mashed turnip and turnip jam, turnip soup and turnip salad. Some people refer to turnips as Prussian pineapples.) The turnips are often cooked with a meagre addition of slightly rancid lard, the faint odour of which is masked by adding apples and onions to the pot. The shortage of fat has led to an increase in intestinal ailments and the monotonous diet has caused many people to suffer from oedema. On average, Germans, both military and civilian, have lost about 20 per cent of their body weight and the majority of the sailors on the ship are a good deal thinner than they were. Stumpf has lost only five kilos, but he receives food parcels from his parents in Bavaria.

Unrestricted U-boat warfare? Why not? Let the British have a taste of their own medicine: "I hope they suffer the same acute hunger as our people in Saxony or Westphalia."

WEDNESDAY, 7 FEBRUARY 1917
Alfred Pollard finds a trench full of corpses outside Grandcourt

For once he is hesitant about a mission. In the first place, he has only just come back from one—in fact, he is hardly back. Pollard has not even had time to climb down into the trench when he meets the colonel waiting there impatiently for him, and the Old Man says he will have to go out again. It is about one o'clock in the morning and his orders are to lead a patrol into the village of Grandcourt "at all costs." The colonel repeats that ominous phrase "at all costs" twice, so Pollard understands that it is important. The air force has reported that the Germans have pulled back and the colonel wants their regiment to be the first to move into the empty village. (As a matter of prestige.) Pollard's second concern is that he does not know how they can reach the village, given that the open River Ancre runs between their position and Grandcourt. He asks the colonel how they are supposed to cross the river and the colonel's answer is a brief one: "I must leave that to you, Pollard."

There is a full moon and the ground is covered with snow. Pollard and his four-man patrol work their way down a hill and reach a deserted trench. Deserted, yes; empty, no. It turns out to be full of the bodies of British soldiers from another division. When he sees the stiff bodies of his countrymen lying there powdered with snow, he recalls that someone told him about a platoon in a forward position that had been attacked in a German night raid—and finished off with bayonets. To the last man. He had heard the story but forgotten it. There are so many stories of units being wiped out and platoons disappearing.

As they move on and continue down to the river, Pollard remembers the first time he saw a trench full of dead men. It was during his very first attack, on that hot day at Hooge in June of 1915:

> I was a mere boy looking on life with hopeful optimism, and on war as an interesting adventure. When I saw the Hun corpses killed by our shell-fire I was full of pity for the men so suddenly cut off in their prime. Now I was a man with no hope of the War ending for years. I looked at a trench full of corpses without any sensation whatever. Neither pity nor fear that I might soon be one myself, nor anger against their killers. Nothing stirred me. I was just a machine carrying out my appointed work to the best of my ability.

In the white snow Pollard finds the tracks of the German unit that attacked the men in the trench. It proves to be a piece of luck because they lead him across a frozen bog and down to the river, where he finds a small and rickety bridge. He slips across it with his revolver drawn, going first as usual. Everything is quiet. He waves to the others to come over. Step by step they creep into the snowy village. Everything is quiet. The reports were correct—the Germans have left the village.

Although neither Pollard nor anyone else on the Allied side knows it yet, this is part of a series of planned German withdrawals aimed at straight-

ening out the front line. New, well-fortified positions are ready and waiting for them further back.

FRIDAY, 9 FEBRUARY 1917
Olive King is repairing her ambulance in Salonica

A raw February wind. The smell of snow in the air. Another winter in
Salonica, another winter in this overcrowded, over-fortified army camp
of a town with its seriously underemployed army. The streets are like a
fancy-dress parade of uniforms: the blue-grey of the French, the khaki
of the British, the brown of the Serbs, the brownish green of the Russians and the green-grey of the Italians. In addition to this polyglot
conglomeration there are colonial troops from India, Indo-China and
North Africa. A number of attempts were made last autumn to push
the Bulgarians back in the north, but the front has hardly moved. Now
everything is at a standstill again. The weather, as usual, is changeable:
hot and sunny at one moment, cold and windy the next. It has been
snowing for two days but the snow has failed to take the chill out of the
air. Lying under her ambulance, Olive King is freezing.

King had planned to spend the morning at one of the hot bath-
houses down by the harbour but her ambulance had other ideas. It is in
need of repairs, which is why she is lying on the floor in a freezing garage
working on it. Her fingers are blue with cold and she fumbles everything.
There is a strong wind blowing outside.

Olive King is now a part of the Serbian army—Olive and her two
vehicles. (In addition to old Ella she has also bought a faster, lighter Ford
ambulance, which is the one she is repairing at the moment.) And since
the Serbs lost almost all their vehicles during the great retreat, she has
more than enough to do. There is no more endless patrolling from lamp
to lamp for her, no more lugging around sacks of ragged clothes: instead,
she is dispatched on long, difficult trips on narrow, dangerous mountain roads, roads that would scarcely have been graced with the name in
western Europe—bridle paths, perhaps, or mud tracks. Just now, conditions are at their worst. If the temperature is above zero, everything
turns to sludge; if the temperature dips below zero, she can expect an ice
rink.

King has come much closer to the war and the war has come closer to her. Mrs. Harley, whom she has worked with ever since their days hunting for furniture in France and who—"at an age when most old ladies are content to sit at home knitting socks"—has endured hardships enough to break women half her age, was killed a month ago. She was struck by bullets from a shrapnel shell fired by enemy artillery—Bulgarian? Austrian?—while working with refugees up in Monastir. From her own journeys to the front up in the north King has not only brought back two Bulgarian rucksacks full of battlefield souvenirs—cartridge cases, shell splinters—she has also returned with memories of a battlefield decked with half-buried corpses. She has also, for the very first time, actually seen the "loathsome enemy" (in the form of Bulgarian prisoners of war).

And she has fallen in love, which is hardly strange—there is something in the atmosphere, in the situation, in being forced to live in uncertainty, that breaks down the everyday fears and conventions which would otherwise put barriers in the way. To judge from the evidence, this love means more to her than anything else at the moment. More than the war, which has become a mere backcloth, figures in a landscape, monotonous routine, sometimes absurd or bizarre, sometimes dangerous or downright nasty, and frequently simply irritating. Like now, when dreams of a hot bath are suddenly put paid to by a faulty footbrake.

The object of her love is a charming Serbian liaison officer, Captain Milan Jovičić, known as Jovi, a man of her own age and happy, bright and droll. The whole thing blossomed through dinners and simple parties—one can imagine the scratchy tones of "La Paloma" played time after time—but also under the stress of shared danger. When she was confined to bed with her first bout of malaria last September he visited her at least twice a day and often stayed for hours. Her love seems to be reciprocated. They have to be secretive about it, but there is still a good deal of gossip about them. Which she finds annoying.

This is not just an affair. She has had affairs before, but this is something far more.

King is aware that something has happened to her during these years and it frightens her. Or, perhaps, she is most frightened by how others will react to it. In a letter to her father, written after she had enlisted in the Serbian army, she wrote as follows:

Bless you, darling Daddy, I love you so much, you'll never have any idea how much. I often wonder if you'll find me very changed. I think I've got pretty selfish in the war, & I know I've got more horribly independent than ever.

She does not mention a single word about being in love. Jovi is just referred to as "a pal," which itself is radical enough compared with what would have been acceptable before the war. But not many people think any longer about supervision, chaperones and the proper forms of social intercourse between unmarried men and women. Not here, not now.

At lunchtime Olive King takes a break from her work in the chilly garage and walks through the snow back to the small flat she shares with two other woman drivers. As soon as she gets in she lights the little paraffin stove, which is the only heating in the room and has to be kept alight whenever they are in the house at this time of year. She is worried about the price of paraffin, which seems to be going up all the time— a can costs nineteen francs and lasts only a couple of days. "If America comes in, she ought to let us have it at reduced rates."

King decides to stay in her room for now. She has done her bit for the day and the other mechanic will have to finish the job. She starts thinking about those wonderful Tasmanian apples and wonders if they are still in season at home in Australia. She wonders whether her father might be able to send her a box.

A DAY IN FEBRUARY 1917
Florence Farmborough reflects on the winter in Trostyanitse

It has been a bad winter both in big ways and in small. In December she received news that her father had died at the age of eighty-four, and last month the famous heart surgeon, the father in her Russian host family, also died. And the front has once again come to a standstill. In the snow and low temperatures on this part of the Eastern Front all major military operations have stopped and Florence's hospital unit is receiving patients only in dribs and drabs. A couple of wounded one day, perhaps, a couple of sick the next, but they have nothing to do most of the time.

Food shortages have, as usual, worsened during the cold months and this year they have been worse than ever. There have been bread riots in both Moscow and Petrograd, war weariness has become more and more acute and the growing dissatisfaction is being aired with surprising openness. Rumours of disorder, sabotage and strikes abound. Before 1914 a string of economic experts had stated that any war would have to be short since a long war would bring economic catastrophe. They have now been proved right. Money—real money—in all the warring countries has run out and the war on both sides is being financed either with credits or by printing banknotes. So the food crisis in Russia is not just about the cold, not just about immediate shortages, it is also a result of spiralling inflation. Moreover, joy about all the many victories of last summer soon turned to disappointment and disaffection when it became clear that the sacrifices had not led to a final turning point or decisive solution.

Over and above the general loathing of the war, increasingly vocal criticism of the war leadership and even of the Tsar himself has bubbled to the surface. Rumours about what has happened or possibly is still happening at court are particularly common: the murder of the notorious monk Rasputin, which was committed a month and a half ago, seems to reinforce the image of a corruption that goes right to the top.* Much of this has passed Florence by, preoccupied as she has been by the deaths of two people close to her, but she does feel sorry for the Tsar, who can best be described as well-meaning but incompetent.

So yes, it is a bad winter. When the general sense of disquiet is added to their general lack of activity, it all leads to nervous tension, irritability and endless petty squabbles among the staff of the hospital unit. Florence, too, shares these feelings:

> We seem to be waiting for something to happen. Things cannot continue as they are. Many questions are asked, but none can answer them. "Will the war continue?" "Will a separate peace be arranged between Russia and Germany?" "What will our Allies do in such an emergency?" . . .

---

* In itself the murder changed nothing, but it does seem to have led to all the hatred and bitter criticism previously aimed at the Tsarina's bizarre favourite being directly targeted at the royal family.

It is a dull oppressive winter; the frost and ice do their best to numb our thoughts and hamper our movements.

SUNDAY, 25 FEBRUARY 1917
Elfriede Kuhr's grandmother faints outside the horse butcher's in Schneidemühl

There is a butcher who sells horsemeat on the street where Elfriede lives. He is a Jew and his name is Herr Johr. Elfriede is well aware that there are people who dislike Jews but she is not one of them. Once she even started a fight with a boy who had called one of her Jewish friends a swine. Many Jews and even Poles live in the area and as far as Elfriede is concerned they are all Germans, even if of different kinds.

Unfortunately, Elfriede's grandmother fainted today, outdoors, in the cold, outside Herr Johr's shop. Some passers-by carried her inside and slowly she came to, lying on the sofa in Herr Johr's living room. Her legs were so shaky, however, that Herr Johr felt it necessary to bring her home in his van. When they see their grandmother being carried to her bed and notice how pale and cold her face is, Elfriede and her brother are frightened. Fortunately, however, one of their neighbours is visiting and she makes their grandmother a cup of coffee. There is no longer any real coffee, of course, just ersatz made from roasted grain, but their neighbour does put real sugar in the cup rather than the artificial sweetener that is now usual. Elfriede's grandmother drinks it and after a while begins to feel more herself: "Now I feel warm again, children."

Why did she faint? Possibly, like many other people, she has been working too hard. Or possibly, like everyone else, she has been eating too little.

But Elfriede cannot help feeling anxious and when it is time to do her physics homework she moves into the bedroom so that she can keep an eye on her grandmother while she does it. School is not uppermost in her mind just now, anyway. A little under a week ago she and a friend had gone ice skating on a flooded meadow down by the river; there were masses of people there, all skating round and round to scratchy music from a wind-up gramophone. While she was there she bumped into the young lieutenant she had met for the first time on the stairs at the party given by her school friend's big sister. His name is Werner Waldecker. Quite by chance she had met him on the street shortly after the party and got into conversation with him—an exchange that had ended with him kissing her hand and expressing the hope that they would meet again. And they did, five days ago on the frozen meadow. Afterwards, by which time it was getting dark, he took her to the Konditorei Fliegner where, though there were no éclairs, they drank mulled wine and ate sugar pastries and she was very happy. Lieutenant Waldecker walked her home and tried to kiss her on the steps of the porch. She had slipped shyly from his embrace and disappeared into the house, though she later regretted doing so.

Not much is happening at the moment according to the war map they have hanging in the classroom. Nothing of any note has happened in Africa or Asia for several weeks. Yesterday, unfortunately, 289 men capitulated in Likuyu in German East Africa, and several Turkish trenches were taken by the British south-west of Kut al-Amara in Mesopotamia. That is all. Things are also quiet in Italy and the Balkans; nor is anything new happening on the Western Front, apart from the occasional raid. It is only the Eastern Front that is providing the newspapers with anything more than the occasional notice, and almost all the fighting there has been concentrated in one area—Romania—for months. That part of the map is now a patchwork of small black, white and red flags and there could well be a major victory there soon. The last was on 6 December when Bucharest fell and the children were given a day off school. Elfriede used that sudden holiday to go for a walk.

SUNDAY, 18 MARCH 1917
Andrei Lobanov-Rostovsky tries to get into the Hotel Astoria in Petrograd

"Just follow the general trend," the doctor had said. It is two o'clock in the morning and bitterly cold. Lobanov-Rostovsky leaves Anton, his batman, to deal with the luggage at the station and sets off directly for the hotel. Oddly, there are neither taxi-cabs nor horse-drawn cabs available outside the station and he has to go on foot. There is something strange going on, something that does not fit. He passes armed patrols on the dark streets and they "eye him suspiciously." He passes a burnt-down police station. On Morskaja, the fashionable shopping street, he notes clear evidence of the disturbances: the shop windows are smashed, the shops have been looted and there are bullet holes on the walls of the buildings.

Lobanov-Rostovsky was, of course, aware of the disturbances that had broken out on 8 March when women took to the streets to protest about bread shortages.* And he had already witnessed trouble at the railway station in Kiev, where a mob broke into the first-class dining room and, to the accompaniment of much roaring and yelling, tore down the portrait of the Tsar from the wall. Nicholas II abdicated three days ago. Lobanov-Rostovsky heard the news last Thursday as he was leaving hospital: an officer came up to him and passed on the sensational information—in French, to be discreet. In his journal Lobanov-Rostovsky greets the news with optimism: "A new Emperor, or a Regent more energetic and intelligent, and victory is assured."

This is possibly a hard-won hope. He has been ill with malaria since the turn of the year and was only discharged from hospital on 15 March, the day before the abdication. When he reported back to his battalion he was told he was being sent to the reserve battalion in Petrograd. The news filled him with despair since he had heard that troops there were being sent out onto the streets to shoot demonstrators and strikers. He met a doctor, who tried to calm him down and asked if he was thinking of taking his own life. Lobanov-Rostovsky then confessed to his doubts: "It's the imbecility of the government which is causing this revolution. It's not the people's fault, and yet I am sent to Petrograd to fire on the people." The doctor consoled him and gave him a piece of advice that stuck in his mind: "Just follow the general trend and everything will work out all right."

Lobanov-Rostovsky arrives at the Hotel Astoria, where his uncle and aunt are staying. The hotel shows the marks of the disturbances, of street fighting even, since the walls are pockmarked by bullets. The large win-

* Widespread discontent lay behind the protests but the reason they broke out when they did was at least partly due to the weather. A period of extreme cold eased around 8 March and it became much warmer, which meant that many more people were prepared to join in the demonstrations.

dows on the ground floor have been smashed and badly boarded up. The lobby is completely dark and the swing doors are locked. No one appears when he pounds on them. Strange. He goes round to a side door, knocks on it and is immediately surrounded by a group of armed and aggressive sailors. They aim their weapons at his chest and fire threatening questions at him: "Where's your pass?" they ask. He replies that he does not have one. "Why are you carrying a revolver?" A young naval lieutenant arrives and manages to convince the armed men to let Lobanov-Rostovsky go: "Comrades, let this man out. He has just arrived and didn't know there was a revolution."

Once out on the street again, Lobanov-Rostovsky hurries back to the railway station to drink tea and wait for the dawn.

He tries again at about eight o'clock. Factory whistles are sounding in the distance. Snow is falling from a grey morning sky. The temperature has risen and the streets are wet and slushy. Apart from the traces of fighting, everything looks almost normal. Crowds of people stream past on their way to work as usual. There is one thing, however, that is different: there are patches of red everywhere, both on the buildings and on the people. All the passers-by are wearing something red: a rosette or a paper flower or just a piece of cloth tucked into a buttonhole. Even the motor cars and elegant horse-drawn carriages are decorated with something red, as are the house fronts and the windows. The large pieces of cloth hanging on the facades of the houses appear almost black in the weak morning light.

Lobanov-Rostovsky gains entry to the hotel this time. The lobby offers a sorry sight: shards of glass and smashed furniture everywhere and the thick red carpets are covered with frozen puddles of water. People are streaming in and out. An excited group is clustered around a table in one corner—they are recruiting for some kind of association of radical officers. The heating has stopped working and it is the same temperature indoors as out on the street. He can find no trace of his relations. "Everything seemed to be disorganised, and nobody knew anything."

Although he couldn't have known it, some of the bloodiest clashes of the whole revolution had taken place in the luxury Hotel Astoria. That was where many of the higher-ranking officers and their families were staying and someone, or perhaps more than one, had fired out on passing demonstrators. The demonstrators had responded with machine-gun fire, after which armed men had stormed the lobby and heavy fighting had broken out amid the crystal chandeliers and mirrored walls. Many officers had been shot or bayoneted to death and the hotel's wine cellar had been looted. (It was quite usual during these days in Petrograd for acts of genuine indignation and protest to be mixed with vandalism and outright criminality.)*

Lobanov-Rostovsky ventures out again onto the slushy streets. As evening approaches he is not much wiser about the situation, but he has located his uncle and aunt. They had fled from the Astoria to the Admiralty during the disturbances—and found heavy fighting raging there too. As to the reserve battalion of the Guards Regiment he was supposed to be joining, he receives completely contradictory pieces of information:

> [The unit had] refused to join the revolution and had been completely exterminated; it had been among the first units to join the rebellion, and the soldiers had killed off all the officers; all the officers were safe, and so on.

Not without some anxiety he decides to take a taxi to the barracks the following morning and report for service. "Just follow the general trend and everything will work out all right."

SATURDAY, 24 MARCH 1917
Andrei Lobanov-Rostovsky is elected officer by the soldiers' committee

There are signs of disintegration everywhere. The soldiers are sloppily dressed, do not salute and show no respect. He has effectively been a prisoner in the barracks, waiting for the soldiers' committee to come to a decision. Are they going to approve him?

The decision came today. Yes, they have decided that he is to serve as their officer. That does not mean he has the same status as before: as the leader of the battalion explains to him, officers are like constitutional

---

* Orlando Figes has shown that the idea that the March revolution was peaceful is largely a myth. In reality more people were killed in these disturbances than during the more famous and momentous coup by the Bolsheviks in October of the same year.

monarchs, they have formal responsibility but no real power. Lobanov-Rostovsky feels relieved—if he had not received their approval he might well have been imprisoned instead. Or even worse. He writes:

> It appeared that the deciding voice was that of a sergeant who had served under my orders and told the committee about the time at Rejitsa in 1916 when, on my own responsibility and against the orders of the commander of the regiment, I had given my men permission to go on leave. Presently two members of the committee came to see me, informed me of their decision, and asked me very politely if I would do them the honour of remaining with the battalion. That same evening we learned that five officers of the Moscow Regiment who had been elected by their soldiers the day before had been murdered by them during the night.

MONDAY, 26 MARCH 1917
Rafael de Nogales takes part in the First Battle of Gaza

Rafael de Nogales has not slept a wink for a day and a half and he is exhausted. He has been deep behind the enemy lines leading a patrol with orders to find and blow up the pipeline for drinking water the British have built from the Suez Canal, up through Sinai and all the way to the front line outside the old coastal city of Gaza. Over the last thirty-six hours they have covered some ninety to a hundred miles of desert terrain and their mission has been a miserable failure: they failed even to find the pipeline. When he and his companions get back to camp the first thing he is intending to do is get some sleep.

Things are anything but calm, however. All available units are preparing for battle because there have been reports that a significant British force is crossing the big wadi* which lies in front of the line of defence at Gaza. The sight of all this activity is enough to give de Nogales renewed energy: "The overpowering tiredness I was feeling disappeared in an instant." He gets a fresh horse and rides off ready for new duties.

* A dried-up river bed.

First of all de Nogales is ordered to lead the baggage train and all its camels, packhorses and wagons back to a safe position. The only things left behind are the white tents, which they hope will disguise their regrouping. He then comes back to join the rest of the Turkish cavalry, which has been positioned to cover an important section of the large wadi. This is a point at which the British will certainly launch an attack since it marks the left flank of the Ottoman line of defence, which virtually hangs in the air just there. If the British break through at that point they will be within easy reach of the Ottoman rear and will also be a threat to the headquarters at Tel el-Sharia.

This major British attack is another sign that the tide of war is turning in the Middle East. Ever since the second Ottoman attempt to cut the Suez Canal failed last summer, the British have been mounting a counter-offensive and their efforts have been characterised by the kind of systematic approach that comes only from bitter experience. They have breached Palestine's final and in some ways most effective line of defence—the desert—by constructing a narrow-gauge railway, as well as that impressive freshwater pipeline that de Nogales could neither find nor blow up.

It is a cold and foggy night.

At dawn the sound of heavy artillery can be heard from the direction of Gaza. The noise gradually intensifies as the rattle and crack of machine guns and rifles join in. An attack has been launched.

A first report comes in: the British have thrown up bridges and crossed the wadi with unexpected speed. Tanks accompanied by infantry have begun to shoot their way into Gaza at the same time as cavalry have advanced around the town and are threatening to cut it off from the rear. A German officer to whom de Nogales speaks is pessimistic: the position of the city is pretty hopeless and it may have already fallen. As it grows lighter they can see the clouds of smoke in the distance, billowing up from the explosions and fires that encircle Gaza.

The Ottoman cavalry regiments continue to wait for the British assault but nothing happens. Instead they are ordered to mount and advance along the wadi towards Gaza. De Nogales is given the job of leading the ammunition carts to safety but he leaves that task in order to search for a unit that has gone astray. Having found the unit, he eagerly accompanies it into battle as it fights its way towards Gaza against the British forces encircling the town. De Nogales says that, despite his weariness, he is spurred on by the mixture of enthusiasm and nervous rapture that "is inevitably inspired in even the dullest heart by the howl of the first shells and the dry cracks of shrapnel-shells exploding overhead."

British warplanes fly overhead and drop bombs. Soon he is able to survey a "magnificent panorama" of the battlefield around Gaza which, in a swathe twenty miles wide, is wreathed in thick smoke from which red flames and shell-bursts continuously spit forth.

It is not until later that de Nogales remembers his original mission. He leaves the battle and he and his batman ride back to sort out the column of ammunition wagons. Their horses are tired and running with sweat. The two men find the convoy just in time to see it being accidentally bombarded "with an enviable rate of fire and precision" by one of the German artillery batteries which are in Palestine to help the Ottoman army. After suffering considerable losses, particularly among the draught animals, they are saved from further bombardment by a German pilot who notices what is happening and manages to signal to the battery to cease fire.

As the evening light fades de Nogales leads the column to the headquarters at Tel el-Sharia, where he meets Colonel Friedrich Kress von Kressenstein, the commander of the Gaza front. The German is nervous and sending telegrams right and left since he is convinced the battle is lost. The same thought has occurred to de Nogales, too, the whole situation being marked by confusion. Consequently he is more than a little surprised to hear—just as he is about to mount his horse and ride to the battlefield—that the British have for some inexplicable reason begun to withdraw.

The battle is over. Both sides have conceded defeat but the British were simply the first to retire.

In the evening de Nogales rides into a moonlit and devastated Gaza:

The silence of death ruled everywhere. In the middle of the streets, piled up among soot-blackened rafters and smashed carriages, lay hundreds of bodies, the burnt and shattered remains of people and animals. On the blackened walls of buildings that were still smoking and tottering on the point of collapse could be seen big purple patches that resembled red carnations, carnations of blood marking where the wounded and dying had rested their chests or heads before drawing their last breath. When the last streaks of the red and gold sunset had died away into the deep darkness of the sky, the wailing calls of the muezzins rose from the minarets to announce to the faithful followers of the prophet that the Angel of Death has spread his wings over a desert where thousands of Christian soldiers are now sleeping a glorious and eternal sleep under the starry sky of Palestine.

He rides back to the camp, where his horse almost collapses from exhaustion. De Nogales wraps himself in a blanket and lies down, his head resting on the horse's flank. He falls asleep almost at once.

A DAY IN APRIL 1917
Pál Kelemen practises with a machine gun outside Kolozsvár

The modern age has even caught up with the Austro-Hungarian army. The cavalry, the pride of that army, the jewel in its military crown, the men with the finest uniforms, is to be wound up. It no longer has any meaningful function and can hardly ever be sent into action. They have tried, and whole regiments have been mown down by a couple of machine guns. On the whole, the cavalry have done little more than herd prisoners of war, patrol behind the lines and put on splendidly colourful parades. Their horses, moreover, demand huge quantities of fodder which, like everything else nowadays, is in short supply.*

The fact that the Austro-Hungarian cavalry is considered to have by far the most beautiful uniforms on the continent is of no help to them. No longer mounted, they are having to say good-bye forever to their fur-edged blue tunics, embroidered red trousers, leather helmets with a comb, their plumes and their buckles, their braiding and gold buttons, their galloons and high boots of polished light-tan leather and from now on they will be wearing the same drab, practical, cheap and anonymous

---

* One contemporary estimate reveals that forty trains a month could supply a division of 16,000 infantrymen whereas it took four times as many trains to supply the same number of cavalry. A further disadvantage was that the long, broad columns of cavalry could easily block vital approach roads.

hechtgrau (pike grey) as the infantry. One more piece of the old Europe is disappearing. Kelemen's regiment, too, is being disbanded and the men retrained as foot soldiers, which he detests, probably not just because infantry service is more dangerous and more strenuous but because the aesthete and the snobbish side of him recoils from it. When he turned up for the machine-gun course that was to turn him into an infantry officer, the captain who greeted him—a man of more than middle age, unshaven and wearing a creased uniform jacket—immediately came down on the fact that Kelemen was still wearing the gold epaulettes typical of the cavalry. He said abruptly: "This has to come off." Kelemen is having his own little rebellion and is still wearing them.

The course is unbearably tedious, as are the other men on the course and the town they are staying in. Tedium is the order of the day. This afternoon they are in horse-drawn wagons and on their way out to an isolated firing range to practise with live ammunition. They pass through a village. The empty, flat Hungarian plain stretches out to the horizon. It has recently been raining and the sun is covered by thick clouds. They arrive and Kelemen notes in his journal:

> The spire of the village is far behind us. At our right is a thatched-roof shelter that serves now as the shooting range of the machine gun detachment. The target figures stand like bizarre scarecrows in the loamy soil, and in a freshly dug trench two machine guns are placed ready for practice.
>
> They begin to speak. The bullets whizz with frantic speed toward the target dummies. After the vast silence, the ceaseless rattling makes the ears ache. I walk about as far as possible from the machine gun stand and turn away toward the darkening firmament until westward sooty stripes announce the falling evening. Toward the south tinted clouds still float and the white walls of a remote farmhouse shine dimly in the sun's last rays. The immense field reverberates with the shrilling of bullets.
>
> I thought that only soldiers were witness to the practice of those grisly instruments of murder. But from the direction of one of the draw wells, with quick flapping wings, a swarm of wild duck flies up and eddies, irresolute in the air. One of the guns is turned on them. A line of birds drops to the earth.—Tomorrow, a good dinner.

FRIDAY, 20 APRIL 1917
Rafael de Nogales and the final phase of the Second Battle of Gaza

They are a good distance behind the lines and convinced that the worst is over. The battle had reached its peak the day before and de Nogales rode in two cavalry charges. The first time they were ordered to attack it felt like receiving "a sentence of execution"—the Ottoman cavalry were to charge British machine guns. By some miracle it had turned out all right, though he had been wounded in the thigh. His bodyguard, Tasim, stopped the flow of blood with a plug of chewing tobacco, "which stung a little but was very efficacious."

It is hardly a month since the First Battle of Gaza, a confused affair with heavy losses. Both sides initially thought they had lost the battle, but it finally ended in an Ottoman victory since the British, partly because of a shortage of water, withdrew from the ground they had gained. The Second Battle of Gaza is mainly a result of the over-optimistic (thoroughly inaccurate, in fact) reports sent to London by the British commander in the region afterwards. They stirred the government into hoping—yet again—that a great breakthrough was imminent: all that was needed was a few more men, a few more artillery pieces, another attack, and so on.

Strengthened by rapidly shipped-in reinforcements (including eight tanks and 4,000 gas shells) and by the promise of more if they managed to open the road to Jerusalem, the British launched a major assault yesterday. The whole thing degenerated into a sun-baked copy of the failures on the Western Front, with air attacks, massive but pointless artillery bombardment, broken-down tanks and infantry attacks that were smashed to pulp while running into a well-constructed system of trenches.

The cavalry division de Nogales belongs to has contributed to the success by harassing the British flank. He and the other officers are visited at dawn by a messenger from the commander in Gaza, Colonel von Kressenstein, who sends his congratulations and thanks them for their efforts. The Second Battle of Gaza is now practically over and the British have not broken through.

A quarter of an hour later, in the light of dawn, the whole division is on its way towards Abu Hureira, a marshy area further back, where there will be water for their horses and rest for themselves. As the air warms up, the great host of riders stirs up an enormous cloud of dust that hangs in the air behind them like a giant tail. De Nogales is worried—the British will undoubtedly be able to see the cloud and realise that a major force is on the march. The divisional commander, however, brushes aside his concern with a smile and when they arrive at the marshy zone they halt in serried columns, regiment by regiment.

They have hardly had time to dismount before it starts.

At first they just hear the buzz of engines. Immediately afterwards six or seven British biplanes appear. Bomb after bomb explodes among the tightly packed rectangles of men and horses, bombs that within half a minute have inflicted greater losses than they suffered the whole of the previous day:

> Almost two hundred horses lay on the ground in their death throes, or fled in all possible directions, maddened by pain and with blood spurting from their dangling guts. Any riders whose feet had been caught in the stirrups were dragged with them and any soldiers foolish enough to try to stop them were trampled under their hooves.

Rafael de Nogales is impressed by the pilots and thinks they have carried out a "particularly brilliant attack."

A nearby German anti-aircraft battery manages to hit two of the planes, one of which flies unsteadily away towards the horizon, the other nosedives straight down. De Nogales watches the plane and sees it hit the ground in a plume of smoke. He immediately remounts and, accompanied by a patrol of lancers, rides as fast as he can towards the distant column of smoke, which is about three miles away.

His thought is to save the pilot's life. Or at least his body.

He knows that the Arab irregulars currently fighting for the Ottoman army will kill, butcher and loot any wounded enemies they find. During the night he has repeatedly come across the naked and mutilated bodies of British soldiers. He also met a guide who was leading a horse laden down with rifles, bloody uniforms, boots, belts and so on, all of which he had looted from dead troops. The man had even held out a long, pale object, which in the light of a torch proved to be a man's arm hacked off above the elbow—hacked off for the sake of the fine tattoos that decorated it. Feeling slightly nauseous, de Nogales had bought the arm and made sure it was buried.

They reach the shot-down plane, but it is already too late.

The pilot is lying dead under the wreckage. His body is naked and his feet have been chopped off, probably because the looters didn't want to waste time unlacing his boots:

> The dead officer was blonde, his hair somewhere between tawny and red, and he was still very young. The only apparent wound on his body was in the chest, where a piece of shrapnel had entered and penetrated the lung. Because of the tremendous impact caused by a fall of more than a thousand metres his blue or hazel eyes had been pushed out of their sockets.

One of the dead pilot's colleagues is buzzing around above them, seeking revenge.

Something stirs in de Nogales. Perhaps it is because of the dead man's beauty, or perhaps (as de Nogales puts it himself) it is because he feels respect for an honourable and fearless enemy, an officer and a Christian like himself, but he cannot bring himself to leave the body there as prey for the desert dogs. Drawing his revolver he forces a man to load the body on his camel and take it back to Abu Hureira.

There de Nogales ensures that the pilot is given a proper burial. It is impossible to get hold of a coffin in a hurry so he wraps the dead man in his own cloak. He also takes off the little gold cross he has worn since he was a child and pins it like a medal on the dead man's chest.

WEDNESDAY, 25 APRIL 1917
Alfred Pollard writes a letter to his mother

What keeps him going is the same hope that leads the generals to persist with their plans and attacks: the belief that although his own side is suffering severely, his opponents are suffering even more. So it is just a question of time, of holding out a bit longer, just a bit longer. Then the enemy's front will collapse and the war will be decided, won, finished. (The use of the term "push" derives from the same mentality: all that is needed is a decisive "push" and the Germans will be forced to their knees.) The planned German withdrawal in France back to the Hindenburg Line is interpreted—not without some justification—as a sign of weakness.*

Pollard's unit is one of those that has followed on the heels of the Germans. On one occasion he led his company up on a hill and for the first time in almost three years he suddenly found himself looking out over a spring-green landscape that was almost completely untouched by war. He really believed at that moment that they were on the threshold of victory, that they had only to push a little bit more, a little bit more. He was genuinely frustrated when the news reached him that his unit was to be relieved—now, when the end was so close. "However, orders are orders and have to be obeyed." His company, down to only thirty-five men, marched back along muddy roads. The spring sun was warm enough for them to take off their tunics.

At the beginning of April when the British army launched yet another offensive, this time at Arras, Pollard was back at a base camp recovering from an injury of a banal kind: he had tripped in the dark and sprained his foot badly. He wanted to take part in the offensive at any price and quickly returned to the part of the front where his battalion was waiting to be sent into battle. And, once again, his task has been to lead patrols into no-man's-land.

Today he is writing to his mother about his latest exploits:

> I had a most exciting adventure in a Hun trench the other day. I cut through their wire and got into their trench thinking it was unoccupied, but soon discovered it was full of Huns and consequently had to beat a hasty retreat. I got out all right fortunately. I hear a rumour that the Brigadier has recommended me for a bar to my M.C. in consequence of this little business so if you keep your eyes glued on the paper you may shortly see my name in it. Don't think I've been taking any unnecessary risks because I have not. I've merely done what I've been asked to do.

---

* The Hindenburg Line was a heavily fortified and well-prepared defensive line between Arras and Reims. It was built to shorten the German front by thirty miles and thus free up some ten divisions. The Germans made a strategic withdrawal to behind the line in March 1917.

Well, dear old lady, although out of the line we are still away from civilisation. By the way I have received another box of new records but cannot play the wretched gramophone until those governor springs arrive so please hurry them up.

Best of spirits and having a good time. By the way, I have killed another Hun. Hurrah!

SUNDAY, 29 APRIL 1917
Alfred Pollard stops a German attack at Gavrelle

The fierce firestorm up on the forward line is not enough to disturb his sleep. He is woken instead by a messenger, who has brought him a very terse order: he is to organise cover for the flank *immediately*. Pollard leaps out of his bunker: "There was no time to enquire what had happened. It was obvious that something had gone wrong. I must act at once."

The strange thing is that when he gets out into the clear spring sunshine everything is absolutely quiet. There is neither the sound of exploding shells nor even any rifle fire. The apparent calm serves only to make him even more uneasy. Pollard feels his heart begin to pound. His instincts tell him they are in deadly danger. He starts scanning the trenches in the forward line. Everything seems to be in order on the right. He looks to the left. Suddenly he sees it: over there, about a mile away, there is a German counter-attack under way. No soldiers can be seen moving but he can hear the characteristic sound of hand grenades— *Bang! Zunk! Zunk! Zunk!*—and see the small grey clouds of smoke left by the explosions.

This continues for five minutes.

Then the utterly unexpected happens.

The positions that are under direct attack seem to be holding firm, but some of the British troops manning the trenches alongside have started to run—away from the enemy. The panic is spreading quickly and a dense crowd of men is fleeing across the field.

Then Pollard sees that the German counter-attack is rapidly rolling forward through the gap that has been left, through the connecting trenches, towards the second line and straight towards the position he is in. At a moment like this, with German storm troops only minutes away, a brave but more averagely constituted man would have considered it sufficient to organise a defence quickly and then await the inevitable clash. The German force is a strong one, at least a company, possibly a whole battalion.

But Pollard is not average.

At first the sense of shock almost makes his knees give way and he is forced to grab hold of the edge of the trench to avoid falling over.

> Then the curious feeling came to me which I have described before that I was no longer acting under my own volition. Something outside myself, greater than I, seemed to take charge of me. Acting under this mysterious influence I ran forward.

First of all, he manages to stop some of the panicking men and he positions them in shell holes with orders to shoot—it does not matter if they hit anything or even take aim. Then he draws his revolver. Gun in hand, with three men behind him, armed with no more than six hand grenades, he prepares to charge towards the Germans in the connecting trenches. And he does this giving hardly a thought to the fact that his enemy is possibly a hundred times more numerous.

He gives his small party some rapid instructions. Pollard will go in front and the three men are to follow him with hand grenades primed. Whenever they hear him fire his revolver they are to throw a grenade so that it lands about fifteen yards in front of him and beyond the next bend in the trench.

They set off.

They run forward.

For the first hundred yards they see no one. All is clear and they move on quickly. They meet a solitary British soldier, "the fourth member of my little army." They carry on along the empty connecting trench.

After just another hundred yards Pollard rounds a corner and sees a German soldier, bayonet fixed, coming towards him. Pollard fires. He sees the German drop his rifle and collapse, hands clutching his stomach. Two hand grenades fly over Pollard's head towards the next bend. Another German appears. Pollard fires again and this one falls in a heap, too. The hand grenades explode. He sees a German turning back but he also sees several other Germans pushing forward. He fires again. More hand grenades sail over his head and detonate: *Bang! Zunk!* The remaining Germans withdraw.

At this stage, with the German attack turned back against all odds, a brave but more averagely constituted man would have considered his work done, particularly since all the hand grenades were now finished.

But Pollard is far from average.

His blood is up, and he feels "a thrill only comparable to running through the opposition at Rugger to score a try." He rushes after the fleeing Germans in the connecting trench. He catches glimpses of figures in field grey, fires and misses. Finally, he comes to his senses and begins to organise the defence. His speciality is hand grenades and to his joy he finds heaps of them left behind by the Germans. Pollard prefers the German stick grenades to the British version, partly because they can be thrown further and partly because they have a more powerful explosive charge and make a considerably louder bang—purely psychologically, the noise is very important. They take with them as many as they can carry.

Within no more than ten minutes the Germans have pulled themselves together sufficiently to mount a counter-attack. The fighting takes the form of a duel with hand grenades. Grenades fly through the air in short arcs. Explosion follows explosion. Dust and grey smoke hang in the air. Pollard removes his helmet so that he can throw better and after a while he also rips off his gas-mask bag. *Bang! Bang! Bang! Bang!* When German grenades land between their legs they pick them up quickly and hurl them over the side of the trench. The Germans, shaken and taken by surprise, obviously have no idea that they are facing only four isolated men. But anyway, space is so tight down in the depths of a connecting trench that only two or three men at a time can take part in the fighting. If the Germans had thought to climb out and advance over the flat ground alongside the trench, Pollard's little troop would have been overcome in a matter of minutes.

The supply of captured grenades is shrinking fast. One of Pollard's men notices this and asks whether it is time to start pulling back. Pollard refuses: "I'm not going back one foot, Reggie."

Then everything goes quiet.

The Hun attack has ceased as suddenly as it had started. They count their hand grenades—they only have six left. He and a couple of his soldiers go back along the connecting trench to collect the grenades they had left behind. On the way they meet men from Pollard's company moving forward to assist them. Thus strengthened, they repel the next German counter-attack without too much difficulty.

Everything goes quiet again.

Pollard spends the rest of the afternoon organising the defence of the connecting trench.

Things remain calm.

As night approaches, they are relieved. Pollard is utterly exhausted by then. As they are marching back they pass through a belt of poison gas but he is simply too tired to put on his gas mask. By the time they get back to the cookhouse wagons he feels very sick, but a cup of hot tea eases the worst of his nausea.

TUESDAY, 1 MAY 1917
Willy Coppens spends four and a half minutes over Houthulst

He is guilty of over-estimating himself, of that there is no doubt. Even though his plane has still not had its forward-firing machine gun mounted, which means he is completely reliant on his observer's armament, Willy Coppens has decided that he is going to fly deep into enemy territory and find an opponent to shoot down. Coppens feels virtually "invulnerable" today. It has something to do with his confidence in his own ability—he is now a competent pilot even though his combat experience is limited—but it also has something to do with his confidence in his machine: a Sopwith 1½ Strutter, the fastest and most modern aircraft type Coppens has ever flown.*

* This aircraft was a proven workhorse, used by a number of different air forces in a variety of roles and in many theatres of war—everywhere from the Western and Eastern Fronts to the Balkans, Italy and Mesopotamia. Its strange name derived, according to Kenneth Munson, from "the short inner wing-struts, sloping outwards and rising diagonally on each side from the upper part of the fuselage." It was the first British aircraft that could shoot through its propeller, its makers utilising a synchronisation mechanism copied from a German aircraft which had veered off course in dense fog and landed on the wrong side of the front line. The 1½ Strutter had been a decisive factor in the Allies' gaining superiority in the air during the summer of 1916.

They cross the front line at Ypres and for once everything is quiet in the shell-shattered swathe of country around that shell-shattered town. A little to the south there is a British offensive going on at Arras, and right down on the Aisne there is a battle still raging around Le Chemin des Dames.*

Their flight path takes them north-east. At a height of just over 3,000 metres they pass over Langemarck and the old battlefield of 1914. As the plane flies in over the great forest of Houthulst Coppens finally sees what he is looking for. He catches sight of four German single-seaters; they are below him but have started to climb in his direction. As he tries to manoeuvre into a position to attack, he keeps a careful watch on them— so careful that he does not see four other enemy planes creeping up from the opposite direction.

A classic beginner's mistake.

Coppens remains oblivious until the first clattering salvo strikes home.

Probability is the enemy of fighter pilots in this war: there are simply too many things that might go wrong. The aircraft are easily combustible, the construction fragile, the engines weak, protection non-existent and the armament unreliable. They have no parachutes.† The fact that aircraft engines must be hand cranked and do not have a starter motor means that there is nothing to be done if they cut out in the air. (The usual altitude for air combat is between 3,000 and 6,000 metres. It is always cold at that altitude, which as well as giving constant discomfort to the pilots in their open cockpits can also easily lead to engine failure because of problems with the cooling and lubrication systems.) It is not only the sudden silence after a crash that Coppens finds distressing; the sudden silence when an engine cuts out in the air is almost as bad.

---

* Because of the losses suffered and the disappointment caused by the lack of success, this would soon lead to a wave of mutinies in the French army. For the moment, however, both battles were, so to speak, pausing for breath, in a way typical of battles of that kind. The attackers were replenishing their supplies of ammunition and materiel and replacing the exhausted and diminished units in the front line with fresh, rested forces. The defenders, of course, were doing the same, and thus the whole process of attrition would soon start again more or less from square one. Often, this pattern was repeated ad nauseam.

† Even when suitable parachutes became available most air forces forbade their use since they were considered likely to encourage pilots to ditch their aircraft unnecessarily. Nor were life jackets provided. Some pilots tried to make their own by pumping up old car-tyre inner tubes and wearing them round their waists.

Few if any combatants were faced with such appalling odds against survival as Allied pilots in the late spring of 1917. People talk with horror of "Bloody April." With the help of technically better machines, improved training and new tactics, the German air force has slowly achieved superiority in the air. This superiority is peaking just now, during the Arras offensive. During the past month the French pulled back many of their badly mauled squadrons in order to rebuild them, but the British chose to continue the battle in the vain hope that superior numbers would make up for technical and training deficiencies.*

The result has been a massacre. Great Britain has lost one third of all her fighter planes in the last month. On average, a British fighter pilot has only seventeen and a half flying hours before being killed.

Willy Coppens is now perilously close to becoming one of these statistics. The salvo from the German fighter rattles along his machine. A fragment of a bullet that struck a stay-wire hits the left side of his head with great force but without leaving a wound. The blow, however, knocks him to the right and the joystick—and consequently the plane—follows his involuntary movement. Which is a piece of pure luck, since it means that the rest of the salvo goes in at a slight angle, along the fuselage of the plane rather than broadside.

Coppens describes the experience as being "squirted all over with molten lead" and afterwards he willingly confesses "that being shot at is bad for the nervous system."

In all the panic, however, he remembers the advice he was recently given by a French pilot. If a larger, two-seater machine like his is attacked by a smaller single-seater there is only one thing to do: keep turning, turn back and forth. The simple point being to give the fighter as little chance as possible of hitting its target.

So that is what Coppens does; he turns, pendulums, twists, swings and sways, all the time losing height in irregular spirals. His aircraft hardly remains in level flight for a second at a time. Coppens himself scarcely sees the enemy, now and then catching a glimpse of one plane or another with a big black cross painted on it diving at his aircraft or climbing up into position for a new attack. He can hear them, though,

* In numerical terms, the situation looked good. At the start of the fighting the British had 385 fighter planes to the Germans' 114. But statistics are not everything.

and at regular intervals he can also hear his observer firing his machine gun at the enemy in short bursts.

Once Coppens has crossed back over his own lines the four German fighters break off the attack and fly away. It has taken four and a half minutes but it feels like "an eternity" to him. During the short battle he lost 1,200 metres of height.

After they land he and his observer inspect the damage. They count thirty-two bullet holes, twenty-nine of which are so close to the cockpit that Coppens can touch them without leaving his seat. One bullet went right between his knees and then passed very close to his right hand resting on the joystick. But apart from the fragment that he finds embedded in the leather of his helmet he has not been hit. He calls it "a miracle." Invulnerable?

In Kastamonu, where Edward Mousley is sitting writing his journal, it is spring and green.

> The band has made great strides. I'm now first violin and leader of the "Orchestra." We have five violins, two cellos and a double bass, besides the drums, two clarionettes [*sic*], flute and banjo, and the Human Crotchet* has made commendable progress in writing out our music from bits of anything we got through the post, piano solos, and many we have had to write from memory. We perform on Saturday evenings alternately at either house. Sometimes we sound almost like a seaside band at Home!!! I long for the old Queen's Hall concerts again.

Mousley also spends his time writing for *Smoke*, a hand-written newspaper which is secretly passed around among the British prisoners of war in Kastamonu. He is also sketching out a project about international law and the possibility of starting a supranational organisation after the war, "a possible Society of Nations or International Body." He longs to be home. He thinks about escaping.

---

* The nickname of one of the other prisoners. Presumably a reference to his appearance.

MONDAY, 21 MAY 1917
Harvey Cushing sees wreckage in the Atlantic

It is their tenth day at sea and for once the weather is good. The sun is shining and the sea is calm. The ship is called SS *Saxonia* and it is carrying Harvey Cushing and the rest of the staff of Base Hospital No. 5, one of the very first American units to be sent over to the war in Europe. It is just a month since the United States entered the war—to make the world "safe for democracy." The intervention has, economically speaking, made things safe for the British, anyway. They have been fighting this war on credit, credit that appeared to be running out at the end of last year, and some members of the British government had been talking sombrely of the risk of economic collapse. Now, at the eleventh hour, Britain has been propped up with American money and, not least, with cheap American raw materials.

The voyage so far has been undramatic but anxious. SS *Saxonia* has been sailing alone* and the ship has been zig-zagging constantly across the ocean, ever watchful for the periscope of a U-boat. All of them are wearing life jackets twenty-four hours a day and they practise taking to the lifeboats time after time. At evening time everything seems to be coloured various shades of blue-grey: the ship, the sea, the clouds.

Military formalities have begun to lay a heavy hand even on this essentially unmilitary unit. Armed guards can now be seen on different parts of the vessel, exercises are performed on deck, shoes are well polished, and when the officers do their daily gymnastic exercises they ensure that the other ranks cannot watch in case it undermines their respect for their superiors. Cushing has some difficulty getting used to it. He was more than a little surprised when he was given his spurs (purely a token of being an officer, since Base Hospital No. 5 has no horses) and a pistol (Model M 1911)—"a villainous-looking, greasy automatic," which he rarely carries and has no intention of using.

It is not that Cushing has any doubts about the war. He has been convinced for a long time that the United States would be drawn in sooner or later—indeed, must become involved. And he has been working both long and hard to prepare his professional colleagues back in Boston for

* The convoy system had not yet been fully introduced.

it. The month he spent in France as a sort of medical observer in the spring of 1915 helped to increase his hatred of the war as a phenomenon but lessened his fear of it as an event. He was rarely afraid on the occasions he visited the front. As he wrote in his journal that spring: "the further away from home you get and the closer you actually get to the scene of the war, the less you hear about it and the less terrifying it seems." As a neurologist he then became very interested in the phenomenon of "shell shock," and this purely professional motivation still remains. But other, much more powerful factors have been added to that.

At that time he had been a neutral observer and he had treated the endless stories of German aggression with scepticism. That cool and distant stance has been eroded. The decisive moment came on 8 May 1915. He was off Ireland on his way back to the United States when his ship sailed into the wreckage of RMS *Lusitania*, which had been sunk by a German U-boat the day before with the loss of 1,198 men, women and children, 124 of them American citizens. They had ploughed their way through wreckage for a whole hour and Cushing, in a state of shock, had seen deckchairs, oars and boxes drifting past and, worst of all, the bodies of a woman and a child alongside a collapsible life raft. A trawler was circling in the distance, picking up bodies—for a bounty of one pound each.

Those are the memories that come to the surface now, on this day in May 1917, when he sees wreckage. This time, no more than a plank, some pieces of rubbish and a life jacket. That afternoon they are joined by an escort vessel, a small and aged destroyer with the number 29 painted on its bows. The destroyer takes up station 500 yards behind them and they cheer and wave, considerably relieved. Cushing thinks that more people will risk sleeping below deck tonight.

They practise stretcher-bearing on the upper deck later that afternoon—their inexperience shows. The training is done with the help of an instruction manual. All of their new army suitcases are stacked in the bow and if everything goes according to plan they will dock in Falmouth at six o'clock tomorrow morning.

TUESDAY, 29 MAY 1917
Angus Buchanan is put ashore on a white sandy beach in Lindi

There are times when three months can pass quickly. That is how long Buchanan's unit has been down in Cape Town, that is how long their visit to "a beautiful, peaceful land"—pure heaven—has lasted. This period of rest was utterly essential and it is doubtful whether the 25th Royal Fusiliers could have continued without it. The mood of both officers and men during the latter part of their time in East Africa was one of depression and apathy.

There is, anyway, little that can be done during the wet season and battalions of black troops from Nigeria, Ghana, Kenya and the West Indies were left to hold the fort in the pouring rain.

The rested units are now on their way back to East Africa by boat, refreshed and ready, as the word has it, to finish the business off. Von Lettow-Vorbeck's forces may have been pushed back into the south-eastern corner of the colony, but they are still undefeated. The new South African Allied commander Major General Sir Louis "Japie" van Deventer, is intent on more direct combat and fewer of the ingenious but usually fruitless pincer movements. ("Hard hitting" is his chosen method.) All of those tortuous marches through bush and jungle were aimed at reducing combat losses while outmanoeuvring the enemy, but time after time they led to lines of communication being stretched to breaking point. The general feeling is that the lives saved on the battle-field by the tactics of Smuts—the previous commander—were lost several times over in the hospitals.* And many of those who, like Buchanan, were evacuated to South Africa to recover were in such a miserable and emaciated condition that it caused widespread concern. Most people had not seen white men in that condition before: blacks, yes; whites, never.

The convoy loaded with troops for the coming offensive is made up of five vessels. They have dropped anchor just over a mile from a beach of white sand, which is where the troops are to disembark. Just a short distance away is the town of Lindi, which is already in British hands. Buchanan writes:

* Of the 20,000 South African troops sent to East Africa, half were transported home suffering from serious illnesses.

We viewed the shore with mixed feelings; adventure still held an attraction to us, but the country had, in its latent possibilities, the power to appal the searchings of imagination, and it was with feelings more sober than otherwise that we contemplated the land before us. For there lay the bush-land, as it had always lain before us, an over-dark picture which no man could surely read.

A small steamer comes up alongside the cruiser and the men pick up their packs, their equipment and their rifles and climb down into it. The steamer transports them to a waiting longboat, which takes them the final, shallow stretch. Then they are carried, dry-shod, on the backs of the black oarsmen, up onto the white sand.

THURSDAY, 31 MAY 1917
Richard Stumpf sees twenty Iron Crosses awarded on SMS
Helgoland

When there are no new victories you have to make as much as you can of the old ones. The first anniversary of the Battle of Jutland is marked by great celebrations throughout the High Seas Fleet. The captain of SMS *Helgoland* gives a speech "with fiery eyes." The further he gets into his highly charged oration, the more polemical and shrill he becomes:

"Our enemies are working with a special purpose in mind, which is to break the bond between our Supreme Commander and his navy and his army. Once the House of Hohenzollern has been overthrown they will compel us to accept a parliamentary form of government similar to that in England and in France. Which means that, just like them, we shall be ruled by merchants, lawyers and journalists. In those countries, whenever they grow tired of a general or a military leader they simply dismiss him. But when this war is over we shall need an even stronger army and an even stronger navy. You must oppose all those who want to introduce parliamentary government into Germany, and you must never forget that the greatness of Germany stands and falls with her imperial dynasty, with her army and with her young navy.

Remember one thing: the social democrats in all the countries we are at war with desire to destroy us."

The finale is three cheers for "His Majesty, Our Supreme Commander in War," after which twenty Iron Crosses are awarded on a more or less random basis to men who took part in the battle.

Stumpf, as usual, feels divided, concerned and angry. The energy of the speaker and the power of the words take hold of him and he feels more than thinks that some of what has been said might possibly be true. But if his emotions pull him in one direction, his reason pulls him in another. He understands very well why the captain holds these views, and perhaps he would think the same way if he was an officer. But he is nothing but an ordinary seaman, a "propertyless proletarian," as he puts it himself, and, as such, it is impossible for him to support "any increase in the autocratic power of the Kaiser, the army and the navy." Indeed, "it is easy to talk about such a thing if you don't have to pay for it yourself." Stumpf has no fear of a parliamentary system and he thinks there are many good men among the leaders of Germany's enemies. Just now, he would "rather be an English slave than a German seaman."

The restlessness, irritation and disappointment that have built up in Stumpf during the years since the outbreak of war are only partly a result of the frustration he feels at the rigid discipline and the monumental tedium caused by the inactivity of the fleet. He is also filled with anger, an anger directed at Germany in its current form, particularly at what Stumpf regards as the fundamental principle that lies at the heart of the country—the class system. That, ultimately, is what has caused the ultra-patriot of 1914 to become the confused but angry radical of 1917.

The war has developed into something that few people foresaw and even fewer desired, and the class system is one of the things that has been unmasked: where decades of socialist and anarchist propaganda failed to lay bare the lies, hypocrisy and paradoxes of the old order, a couple of years of war have succeeded in doing so. And there are few places in which the absurdities of Europe have been so thoroughly exposed as in the German High Seas Fleet.

The officers and the crew live together, are both metaphorically and literally in the same boat, but their living conditions are actually grotesquely different. That is true of everything from their food and their living quarters (officers' cabins are furnished like upper-class homes, with oriental rugs, padded leather armchairs and original art) to their working conditions and leisure (ordinary seamen are rarely given leave whereas officers can sometimes be excused from duty for months on end and, when in port, often sleep in their own homes). The proximity which is inevitable aboard ship has revealed these hitherto hidden distinctions with unprecedented clarity. At the same time, the absence of activity, of battle and of victories—in short, of blood—has made it possible to question the differences.

Things are different in the army. Even though there are eye-catching differences in conditions there too, there are practical reasons why they are not so glaring, and they can even be excused to some extent by reference to the demands and sacrifices of army service. There is no more dangerous occupation in this war than that of a junior officer in the infantry.* In the navy, however, in the virtually immobile High Seas Fleet, the demands on officers are small and their sacrifices even smaller. So what justification can there be for their privileges other than that they come from a privileged class? And is there not a real possibility that all this high-flown talk of honour and duty and sacrifice will eventually lose its power and stand revealed as a pretext to keep the masses in their place?

Stumpf sees manifestations of the class system even in this anniversary celebration. The officers naturally keep their own company in their luxuriously appointed mess and enjoy a bacchanalia that goes on until four o'clock in the morning. The ordinary seamen are treated to nothing more than "a few barrels of watery beer" and their party is held up on the deck. What bothers Stumpf most, however, is not that the officers get so much and the crew so little—what really upsets him this evening is that so many of the ordinary seamen are still prepared to bow and scrape to their masters (who grin at them condescendingly) in order to be rewarded with some words of appreciation and some crumbs from their table:

> The officers' mess resembled a lunatic asylum. But what was even more scandalous was to see the seamen begging beer, cigarettes

---

* The chances of a first or second lieutenant surviving the war were considerably less than those of an ordinary soldier. Estimates suggest that junior officers proportionally suffered six times the losses of other categories of servicemen.

and schnapps off these drunkards. I could have screamed out loud at the way they humiliated themselves. Some of them lost all self-control and assured the officers that they were good sailors and good Prussians, and as a reward they got an extra glass of beer. It finally reached the stage where they were cheering individual officers and their generosity.

WEDNESDAY, 6 JUNE 1917
Paolo Monelli marches up to the front line at the Cima della Caldiera

Evening. They march. The long column of the battalion makes its way steadily upwards in the dusk. They all know where they are going. Those who were here during last year's battles point out the places they recognise and name the names of men who fell. "Via dolorosa." At first, looking down, down into the valley bathed in moonlight, gives Monelli a marked feeling of vertigo, but soon his growing tiredness means that he slowly loses interest in everything around him. Finally, there is only the tramping of feet, and weariness.

They march across the plateau under the cover of darkness, feeling the vague waves of cold coming up from the snow that is still left. He sees some big fires and he sees men sleeping: these are the units that will be in tomorrow's attack. He thinks, *Poor devils*. Then he thinks:

> Every man's lot seems more wretched than my own. Not to have been selected to take part in the first wave of the attack seems to me to be an immense piece of good fortune and I am amazed that these men can sleep so calmly, these men who once outside the trench tomorrow will let go of everything that protects their lives. I am afraid for them. (It's not so different from the times I have been seized by vertigo when standing on a boulder watching a man clinging to a sheer rock-face—and then the next day I have followed in his footsteps.)

They reach their goal at dawn and make camp. He sees cliffs, snow and the occasional pine tree.

MONDAY, 11 JUNE 1917
Angus Buchanan comes under attack at Ziwani

Where is the enemy? Where are our own people? These are the questions that always come up during night operations. At the stroke of twelve, under cover of darkness, Buchanan's 25th Royal Fusiliers, together with one of the growing number of black battalions, are put ashore at a spot up the Lukuledi river ten miles from Lindi and the coast. The idea is a good one: in this way they, in combination with a force that is advancing in the north, will outflank the strong German positions closer to the coast.

The problem is that a march that would be difficult enough in daylight will be something approaching a nightmare in the dark, and in the bush. For once, however, those in command have thought about this. The idea is that Buchanan's battalion will march through flat bush country along a narrow-gauge railway that they know runs from the river in the direction of Mkwaya. Which is what they do, with the result that his unit moves quite quickly. They all got wet and cold while disembarking on the muddy river bank and the march warms them up. But the questions remain: where is the enemy and where are the rest of our own people? They hope that the black battalion is advancing on a parallel course somewhere to the left of them.

Buchanan hears a solitary cock crowing, loud and clear. He realises that they are approaching a settlement and that dawn is close. He can see a weak glimmer of light on the horizon. He can hear the first muffled explosions of artillery in the distance. It is one of their own gunboats, which has been seen and engaged in an exchange of fire. Soon he can also hear the sound of the British aeroplanes that have been sent up to spot the enemy, who is keeping himself well concealed in the fragrant, dark-green bush.

They pass Mkwaya in the pale light of dawn and there the column turns west in the direction of Mozambique. Two hours later it is broad daylight. When they come up onto a ridge near Ziwani they get their first sighting of what they have been watching for since midnight—the enemy. On the other side of the valley, less than a mile away, large groups of German *askaris* are on the move. He can also see puffs of smoke from the enemy artillery—105mm pieces that the Germans, with their usual talent for improvisation, have salvaged from the light cruiser SMS *Königsberg* after it was knocked out by the British. When Buchanan and the others move down into the valley they discover that the enemy is already there and they immediately encounter strong German patrols. There are some confused exchanges of fire and the British withdraw to the top of the ridge. It soon becomes clear that the battalion on their left has also made contact with the enemy and the 25th Royal Fusiliers are ordered to dig in on the ridge for the time being.

This work takes the rest of the morning and goes on again after lunch.

At two o'clock, however, something happens.

From a distance of no more than thirty yards there is sudden, deafening and intense gunfire from *askaris* equipped with both rifles and machine guns. They have crept forward through the bush and tall grass completely unseen. Buchanan compares the noise to the clash of a violent thunderstorm.

When he comes to describe the events later he finds it difficult to give a clear picture once the fierce close-range fighting began:

> From then on one lost all reckoning of time, all reckoning of everything, except that there was something big on that kept every energy alive and working at fever speed.

One small piece of luck for the British is that the attackers make what is a very common mistake when fighting in dense vegetation: they instinctively aim too high, with the result that most of the bullets go over the defenders' heads. There is, however, one drawback: the swathes of bullets shoot down bees' nests that are hanging in the trees and the infuriated insects attack everything and everyone they can find. The stings of this species are particularly painful, and when the otherwise reticent Buchanan writes that the pain drives them "almost crazy" he is not exaggerating. This type of thing happened on several occasions during the campaign in East Africa and on one occasion Buchanan saw a man so badly stung that he quite literally went out of his mind.

The fighting is over by the evening. The attackers withdraw and the 25th Royal Fusiliers remain on the ridge. All the British troops are covered with yellow swellings, in some cases their faces are so swollen that they have difficulty in seeing. Tomorrow they will go back towards Lindi.

THURSDAY, 14 JUNE 1917
Michel Corday strolls along a Paris boulevard in the evening sun

A whole new theme—not a mere variation—has been added to the old one. Understandably enough, it is related to the American entry into the war. Michel Corday has been in the Chambre des Députés listening to René Viviani. Corday does not have a high opinion of Viviani. It is not just because the man is a weak politician surrounded by rumours of drug abuse, but mainly because of what he did, or rather did not do, in 1914. Viviani, a man of the left who was prime minister at the time of the outbreak of war, had done nothing to avert the catastrophe; indeed, he was one of those who pushed for the war credits that were a necessary precondition for fighting the war.

Viviani's days as a "Man with Power" are already more or less over, but there is still considerable use for his talents as a speaker, which are undoubtedly great. Viviani specialises in stylish and excited rhetorical flourishes and, as always in these situations, the manner in which something is said is at least as important as the words spoken. The speech he made was, indeed, "an oratorical triumph." He said more or less the same thing as everyone else is saying and on this occasion, as usual, he put the needle down on the same scratched old record that proclaims fighting "to the bitter end." But something new was added, something that made Corday catch his breath. The war has a new goal, a new meaning, a new excuse. Its real purpose is now said to be so that "our sons' sons will not need to lose their lives in such conflicts." So that's what it is all about! They are fighting a war to put an end to all wars. A new idea. Neat. A neat slogan.

It is almost seven o'clock in the evening as Corday strolls along one of the boulevards in warm, low sunshine. Street life is a motley scene and in many ways a reflection of the war:

> [There are] prostitutes with hats the size of parasols, knee-length skirts, bosoms bared, diaphanous stockings and made-up faces; young officers with unbuttoned collars and magnificent medal ribbons; Allied soldiers—muscular British, inoffensive Belgians, unfortunate Portuguese, Russians with their impressive marching boots, young men in tight battledress.

Corday also comes across a representative of a new phenomenon, the soldier beggar. Of late it has become usual to see them at restaurants or cafés. They are often wearing medals on their chests, fine medals like the Croix de Guerre, awarded for heroism in the field. They sell picture postcards or sing patriotic songs to collect a little money.

The begging soldier Corday meets on the pavement has an arm missing. He is also drunk. He is meandering through the stream of people, asking one, then another, for a few coppers or for a cigarette at least. And he repeats the same word all the time: "Peace . . . peace . . ."

Corday later talks to an acquaintance who tells him that the mutinies in the French army are not over and that over 400 mutineers have been shot so far.* His friend also tells him about one mutineer who, when threatened with this fate, said: "If they shoot me at least I'll know why I died."

WEDNESDAY, 20 JUNE 1917
Florence Farmborough returns to the front at Voloschyna

A summer sun. Heat. Thunder in the air. Up on the hill she can see tents covered with branches. She can see horses clustering under the few trees to enjoy the shade. She can see figures bathing in the muddy water of the river. Farmborough is happy to be back. Everything is quiet at the moment, but rumour says that the Russian army will launch a new attack in a few days and in that case they will have more than enough to do.

Farmborough has been away for only a few days to meet some British nurses in another unit, but it was long enough to make her sensitive to things that had earlier passed as everyday normality. Like the food. She hesitates when the standard soldier's gruel is served. The lumps of fat disgust her. And the fish soup is too salty. Despite her hunger she does

---

* This figure is grossly exaggerated. The courts martial set up after the mutinies sentenced around 23,000 men to punishment, slightly over 500 being sentenced to death. The aim, however, was to set an example and in the end fewer than fifty were actually shot—usually in front of their fellow soldiers. The stories that whole units were driven out into no-man's-land and then slaughtered by their own artillery are myths.

not eat anything apart from black bread, washed down with tea. She finds the conversation depressing and the mood is argumentative.

After dinner, I walked up to the top of our hill with Sofiya. In the far distance were the high mountain peaks, bathed in a soft, cobalt haze. The small villages of Saranchuki, Kotov and Ribniki were lying far below us in their respective valleys; we could see that the homesteads were ruined and deserted. The enemy's trenches were visible; they seemed perilously near the Russian lines—only 70 feet away, Sofiya said she had heard. There are scarlet patches of poppies in the fields around, marguerites too and a few corn-flowers. There is something so comforting, so home-like, about a field of poppies.

On the same day Elfriede Kuhr notes in her diary:

This war is a ghost in grey rags, a skull with maggots crawling out of it. New, hard battles have been raging in the west in recent months. We are fighting at Le Chemin des Dames, at Aisne and in Champagne. The whole region is a field of ruins, blood and mud everywhere. The English have brought in a new and terrible weapon, an armoured vehicle on rollers which can get across any kind of barrier. These armoured vehicles are called tanks.* No one is safe from them: they roll over every artillery battery, every trench, every position and flatten them—not to mention what they do to the soldiers. Anyone who tries to take shelter in a shell-hole no longer has a chance. Then we have that beastly poison gas. The English and the French (unlike the German soldiers) still don't have really safe gas masks with an oxygen supply. There is also a sort of poison gas that eats its way through clothes. What a way to die!

* See asterisked footnote at 16 September 1916, page 300.

MONDAY, 25 JUNE 1917
Paolo Monelli's battalion enters the inferno on Monte Ortigara

Now it is their turn. They have been waiting for this moment. For about a fortnight they have watched battalion after battalion dispatched towards the top of Monte Ortigara and each time they have also watched the result: first to come are the stretcher-bearers with the wounded and the mules with the dead, then—after a few hours or a few days—what remains of the battalion trudges past. That is how it works, such are the mechanics of it. Battalions are sent into the mill of artillery fire and remain there being ground mercilessly down until they have lost the majority of their men. Then they are replaced by new battalions, which stay until they have lost the majority of their men. Then they are replaced by new battalions, which stay until they have lost the majority of their men. And so on.

It is called a materiel battle. Now and again one side or the other will mount an attack, through valleys filled with craters still warm from shell-bursts, up towards some peak or over rocky ridges. But, for the most part, the infantry has no other task than to hang on grimly to a particular point, a point that seems to them to have been chosen more or less at random but which has some significance in the cartographic reality inhabited by the general staff or in the deluded world of victory communiqués. These "points" are often places that God or the surveyors saw fit to give an elevation to, which elevation has then ended up firmly established on the map as 2003 or 2101 or 2105—figures which in due course are transmogrified into "hills" to be conquered or defended.*

Things look bad this morning. The thunder of artillery fire is stronger than ever when Monelli wakes at dawn. He crawls out of his sleeping bag and goes out to see what is going on. After a while the battalion is ordered to form up. They set off, a long line of silent, heavily laden men moving uphill, always uphill along a narrow track that runs along the high, steep rock wall. The sun is rising higher in a blue sky and it looks like being a hot day.

---

* In the German army they refer to "blue points." Enemy trench lines are designated with blue figures on their maps.

The soldiers' faces express what Monelli describes as "a calm resignation in the face of the inevitable." As far as possible he avoids thinking, tries to lose himself in details and practicalities. And it works quite well. He notes to his joy that his voice sounds crisp and controlled when he is giving an order to one of his subordinates. He tests his feelings: does he have any premonitions? No, he does not, but a line of poetry by Giosuè Carducci, the Nobel prizewinner, has stuck in his head: *Venne il dì nostro, e vincere bisogna*—"Our day has come, and we must be victorious." Monelli feels he has been transformed into a tool, a good and strong tool governed by a power far outside his own body. He sees a column on its way out with its mules. He sees the clouds from bursting shrapnel shells, all black and orange.

Eventually they come to a cave, the mouth of which opens out towards the line of battle. Once they leave it they will come under direct fire. The mouth of the cave is narrow and crowded, full of telephonists and artillerymen who squeeze against the cold walls of the cave to allow Monelli and his companions through. They give him and the other Alpini long, searching looks that take Monelli by surprise and he immediately tries to put them out of his mind. But the thought has already sunk in: "Good God, so it's that bad."

The captain says just one word: *"Andiamo!"* Forward!

At which they take off at a run and rush one after another in quick succession out into the open air, rather like people jumping off the top board at a swimming baths. The Austrian machine guns begin to rattle. Monelli leaps forward and down. He sees a man hit in the head by a big shell splinter. He sees that the ground is full of small shell holes. He sees bodies, small piles of them at some points, and takes note that those places must be particularly dangerous, those are places to be careful. He takes shelter among some rocks and gathers his breath for the next stretch. "The whole of one's life passes in a moment of remorse, a premonition comes to the surface and is dismissed with terror." Then he sets off, hurls himself forward, some bullets whizz past—*zio, zio*—and he is past it. But he sees the captain lying back there.

They are warned about gas and he struggles to put on his gas mask. After five minutes he takes it off again—it is impossible to run with it on. They carry on down into the next dip in the ground. It is packed with dead bodies, both old corpses from the battles last year, which are now little more than skeletons dressed in rags, and fresh bodies, still warm and still bleeding—but all of them are united in the same timeless state. Monelli comes to another dangerous passage. There is an Austrian machine gun ready and waiting further on and it opens fire on anyone who dares try to cross—six or seven men have already been mown down. He sees a man hesitate—his friend has just been hit. The man is talking about going back but the way back is just as dangerous. He sees the man cross himself and then throw himself out across the rocky slope. The machine gun spits but the man escapes and runs, jumps and tumbles on down the slope. Monelli does likewise.

It is about twelve o'clock. The sun is shining. It is hot.

Now it is uphill again, up over a ridge. And there, finally, Monelli reaches his company's position. Position? It is no more than a long row of blackened rocks and great mounds of stones on a ledge, and they squeeze in behind them, motionless, silent, wide-eyed, utterly ineffectual under the heavy shelling, passive, but there. A young soldier sees Monelli and stands up to warn him, beckons him towards his own shelter, but is struck in the chest by a projectile and crumples.

Later Monelli and his battalion commander go looking for the brigade command post and eventually find it in a cave in the mountain. The sandbagged mouth of the cave is, as usual, jammed with people who have taken shelter from the constant artillery barrage. It is so overcrowded that the two of them climb over arms, legs and bodies and no one even reacts. The staff officers are located right at the back of the cave, where it is dark and absolutely silent. If Monelli and his commanding officer thought that the news that two battalions of reinforcements have arrived would be greeted with gratitude and perhaps even jubilation, they are disappointed. The staff officers have not heard of their arrival and greet them "without any enthusiasm." The mood in the dark cool cave is gloomy, more than gloomy in fact—it is marked by humiliation and resignation, a feeling of being abandoned to the inevitable. The brigadier, overcome with weariness, says, "As you can see, we are surrounded by the enemy and he can do what he wants with us."

In spite of that, they depart with an order to attack, improvised at random by the brigadier. Monelli thinks that someone at the highest level—the officer commanding the corps, perhaps—is in the process of a mental breakdown because the instructions they receive become increasingly contradictory and incoherent. When they do receive them, that is, since the constant artillery bombardment cuts the telephone cables about every five minutes. Then men have to be sent out into the noise and the smoke and the whirring shell splinters to find and fix the break. Being a signaller is the most dangerous occupation up on Monte Ortigara.

But it is not only the signallers who are victims of one of the many paradoxes of the war—in this case, the fact that the ability of the armies to cause destruction has increased much more than the generals' ability to control and direct their troops. Communications almost invariably break down during major battles, with the result that battles turn into a blind and confused melee of butting and jabbing amid the smoke of exploding shells.*

Darkness falls. The air is filled with three smells: the bitter odour of explosives, the sweet stench of putrefaction and the sour stink of human excrement. Everyone does his business wherever he happens to

---

* The technology for effective battlefield communication simply did not exist. The new wireless radio sets were too big, heavy and unreliable to be practical. Wired telephony worked well for permanent networks or when the shelling was not too heavy, but under concentrated fire cables were easily damaged. By this stage cables were being buried metres deep and, if possible, encased in pipework, but that kind of thoroughness was available only when the front was static and relatively calm. All the armies employed various methods of optical signalling (flares, heliographs, lamps, semaphore and flags), but those required good visibility—something that was in short supply when the fighting became heavy. A further possibility was to transport orders and reports physically. All sides experimented with dogs as runners but that method proved ineffective under heavy bombardment: dogs, like horses, tend to become crazed in heavy artillery fire. And all sides used carrier pigeons—the German army alone got through 300,000—which were sometimes the most reliable form of communication. According to one estimate, nine out of ten pigeons reached their destination. Carrier pigeons were even awarded military decorations and other honours, one of the best known being the last bird to be dispatched from the encircled Fort de Vaux at Verdun during the fighting in June 1916. It got through but died of its wounds and is now commemorated by a plaque at the fort. There is also the famous Cher Ami, a pigeon that, in spite of being wounded in the breast and having a leg shot off, managed to reach its destination with a message from a surrounded American unit during the fighting in the Argonne in October 1918: it was awarded the Croix de Guerre and its stuffed body is on show in the Smithsonian in Washington. If there was no alternative, human runners were used, usually dispatched in pairs in the hope that one at least would survive. This was obviously a mission fraught with great danger. (Adolf Hitler frequently acted as a runner during the First World War and was twice decorated for doing so. It provided him with the concrete if somewhat limited knowledge of military matters that he later used to trump various generals whose experience had been moulded more by the theoretical world of the operations room.)

be crouching or lying, simply taking down his trousers in full view of everyone else. Anything else would be stupid. Bitter, sweet, sour.

That night one of the companies attacks Hill 2003. They take it.

Three days later the Austrians take it back.

SATURDAY, 30 JUNE 1917
Paolo Monelli returns from Monte Ortigara

He has survived five days up there. There have been times when they have been under fire from every point of the compass at the same time. It has sometimes felt as if the whole mountain was being criss-crossed by powerful electrical currents: the earth itself has trembled, jumped, crackled, hissed. They have lived with dead men, lived off dead men, using their ammunition, eating their rations, drinking from their water bottles, stacking their bodies on the top edge of the barricade to stop the bullets, standing on them to avoid frostbitten feet. After two days they had already lost every second man, dead, wounded or shell shocked. It has occurred to Monelli that maybe one in ten will come through unharmed and he hopes and prays to be one of them. When the enemy artillery holds fire for a while, he seeks omens by randomly consulting lines in his pocket Dante.

And he has survived.

Monelli notes in his journal:

A sense of dumb amazement at being reborn, at sitting in the sun in the doorway of the tent and receiving new impressions. Life is something good to eat and we chew it in silence with healthy teeth. The dead are impatient comrades who set off in haste on unknown missions of their own. We, however, feel how the warm caress of life reaches us. Sipping gently at some pleasing family memory, and then the relief of once again being able to tell the poor old folk down there that the prodigal son is returning— something one did not have the courage to think about on the day we set off.

THURSDAY, 19 JULY 1917
René Arnaud sees Marie Delna receive a mixed reception in Noyon

Why shouldn't a performance be concluded in the traditional way with "La Marseillaise"? The commanding officer of the division is surprised and not a little upset. The theatre director, probably a touch embarrassed and nervous, explains that they "have learned from bitter experience that with morale as low as it is at present it is better to avoid singing the French national anthem in front of the troops."

It is three months since mutinies broke out in the French army and it is only now that the army can be considered fit for combat again. But only just. The tensions are still there under the surface.

The mutinies at the end of April are perhaps best described as an implosion of disillusion. The generals and the politicians blame socialist agitation, pacifist propaganda, the spread of revolutionary infection from Russia and so on. It has been a troubled spring in France in general. There is no doubt that there is the same war weariness as in Russia and, in some respects, it has manifested itself in the same ways: disobedience, strikes and demonstrations. These things are not, however, being driven by dreams of the future but by the nightmares of the present. And underlying everything is a colossal sense of disappointment.

The great French offensive in April began to the sound of the same fanfares of rhetorical exaggeration as the great offensive in Champagne in the autumn of 1915: the preparations were flawless, the Germans were at breaking point, a breakthrough was certain, the decisive point had been reached, victory was assured and so on. Sweeping promises that the war would be decided within forty-eight hours made even the most war-weary pull themselves together and make an effort. *Allons enfants de la Patrie / Le jour de gloire est arrivé!* But when the offensive ran into the sand with minimal success and maximal losses, something quite simply broke.*

---

* When things were at their worst, fifty-four divisions were involved and large parts of the Western Front were effectively undefended. (The fact that the German army somehow failed to discover and exploit this significant disruption has to be seen as the biggest intelligence blunder of the First World War—all the more so as the Germans were very skilful in exploiting and supporting the Bolsheviks in Russia as a means of undermining the Russian war effort.) Some of the French mutineers demanded an immediate peace, others threatened to march on Paris, while the majority were simply satisfied with refusing

Arnaud's own battalion was not affected by the mutinies—it comes from the Vendée, a region with traditions that are anything but revolutionary. They first became aware of the events one night when they were supposed to come out of the front line after ten days there, but they were informed that their relief was being postponed for twenty-four hours. The battalion that was meant to be taking their place had refused to enter the trenches until a number of carefully specified demands had been addressed.

It is probably because his troops held firm during the mutinies that their commanding officer insists that "La Marseillaise" shall be sung at the end. The theatre director submits—reluctantly. Today's theatre performance can also be seen as an expression of the solicitude the military command now feels compelled to demonstrate for its men as a result of the mutinies. The performance takes place alfresco so that as many men as possible can attend. Since it is high summer, being outdoors is no great problem.

Towards the end of the performance the star of the show takes to the improvised stage. The star is no less a figure than Marie Delna, perhaps the finest contralto in Europe, with a decade of successes behind her: the Paris Opéra, naturally, but also La Scala in Milan, Covent Garden in London and the Metropolitan in New York. A very big star, indeed. And big in girth too, these days, as Arnaud and the rest of the audience note: the fragile, sylph-like creature they are familiar with from posters and photographs has metamorphosed into an enormously fat woman. She sings as beautifully as before, however, standing on the stage in some sort of white chemise with a tricolour in her hand. *Aux armes, citoyens! Formez vos bataillons! / Marchons, marchons!* Thundering out such exhortations might well seem a touch provocative in the current situation when so many people are unwilling to do the first or the second, and especially the third.

When she has finished singing the final verses the applause from the majority of the soldiers is mixed with hissing. The commanding officer goes berserk with rage and gives orders for the men who hissed to be identified. Which proves to be a pointless exercise.

---

to carry out attacks and submitted lists of demands for simple, concrete improvements in food, medical care, leave and so forth. The resulting executions were consequently few in number whereas the improvements in material conditions for the troops were quite considerable.

SATURDAY, 21 JULY 1917
Alfred Pollard receives his Victoria Cross at Buckingham Palace

There are twenty-four Victoria Crosses being awarded, but there are only eighteen men waiting in the fenced-off area at Buckingham Palace: the other six are being awarded posthumously. Standing alongside are a number of people in civilian clothes—they are the close relations who will receive the medals on behalf of the men who have died. A military band is playing and there is a guard of honour formed up and bearing flags. A crowd of onlookers can be glimpsed behind the tall, gilded railings that surround the palace.

The celebrations began as soon as it was announced that Pollard had been awarded the Victoria Cross, but they were nothing compared to what was waiting for him when, along with another winner of the VC, he travelled home for a month's leave. Since then his life has been a round of parties, visits to the theatre, invitations to dinner, cheering and pats on the back. He has sometimes been embarrassed but has always been pleased. When the two of them try to pay for their own drinks there is always someone who pushes in front and insists on treating them. If they arrive at a posh restaurant they are immediately recognised, taken to the front of the queue and shown to the best available table. Pollard is famous. His picture is in the papers.

Pollard is also engaged. To Mary Ainsley, "My Lady," the woman who once so firmly turned him down. He suspected that one of her reasons was that he was then just an unknown ordinary soldier, but now, *now*! Now he is an officer and has been awarded the highest and most prestigious military honour the British Empire can bestow. The war has given him a new level of self-confidence and one evening he put his arms round her and poured out a torrent of "half incoherent phrases" about how much he loved her and wanted her. During a walk the following morning, Mary said that she still did not love him but that it would be wrong to disappoint him when he loved her so much—and love is something that can grow. The engagement ring is made of platinum, set with diamonds and a black pearl. They have spent the last few days at a hotel on the coast together with some friends, swimming, taking boat trips, walking, going to concerts, enjoying good dinners and having their first quarrel.

But now he is here, waiting outside Buckingham Palace along with seventeen other men. There is a special hook on each man's uniform to make it easy for His Majesty to attach the medal. Then the formalities start. Everyone comes to attention and the guard presents arms. The band breaks off the piece it is playing and strikes up "God Save the King" instead. The guard of honour lowers its flags. The King appears. The King! He is accompanied by a shoal of adjutants. The eighteen men stand rigidly at attention. The music dies away. "Stand at ease!"

They are called forward one by one, Pollard being the sixth in line. Just like the others he marches forward ten paces and comes to attention in front of the monarch. A colonel reads the official citation, which starts, "For the most conspicuous bravery and determination." When the last words of the citation have been read—"with an utter contempt of danger, this officer, who has already won the DCM and MC, infused courage into every man who saw him"—the King hangs the medal with its wine-red ribbon on the hook on his chest and utters some words of praise. He then shakes Pollard's hand, hard, so hard that a cut Pollard got during his seaside holiday opens up again. The newly decorated twenty-five-year-old takes a step back and salutes.

That is the high point of Pollard's war; indeed, the high point of his life.

Alfred Pollard, the insurance clerk from London, doomed to a life of insignificance and tedium, has now achieved everything he has ever dreamt of, become the man he always believed he was. And it is the war that made it possible.

After the ceremony there is a packed programme of festivities and tributes, and tomorrow he will return to the continent. There is a rumour going round that a big British offensive is being planned somewhere in Flanders. He is aware of a new and unusual emotion: for the very first time ever he is not burning with impatience to get back into battle.

That day Willy Coppens goes into combat in a single-seater aeroplane:

> Over Schoore I met a two-seater machine circling round at an altitude of 3,200 metres. I attacked it with determination but without the least effect. The passenger in the two-seater fired

back at me but also achieved nothing—my plane showed no trace of a hit. At 500 metres I let go of my prey, who disappeared, and I was left cursing my incompetence.

A DAY IN JULY 1917
Paolo Monelli witnesses the execution of two deserters

Dawn. The whole company is standing waiting in a small woodland glade. The firing squad is also there, as is the doctor. And the priest, who is trembling with fear at what is to happen. The first of the two prisoners arrives:

Look, there is the first of the condemned men. Weeping but without tears. A rattle from his tight throat. Not a word. His eyes no longer express anything. His face just shows the dull fear of an animal about to be slaughtered. When he is led up to a fir tree his legs will not hold him and he crumples. He has to be tied to the trunk with some telephone cable. The priest, pale as a corpse himself, embraces him. Meanwhile the platoon is formed up in two ranks. The front rank will do the shooting. The adjutant of the regiment has already explained to them: "I'll give the signal with my hand—then fire."

The two soldiers are men from his own unit. During the dreadful fighting up on Monte Ortigara they were sent down to the valley on fatigue duty. But after three days in the front line they had had enough and they did not come back. A military tribunal down in Enego condemned them to death for desertion. Discipline in the Italian army is harsh to the point of being draconian.* After being sentenced the men

* The Italian army executed just over 1,000 of its own men during the war, which is far more than the number executed in the British army (361), not to mention the German army (48). Over 15,000 Italian troops were condemned to life imprisonment for crimes against military discipline and many of them remained in prison long after the war was over, in some cases until 1945. The Italian commander-in-chief, Luigi Cadorna, insisted on "iron discipline."

were returned to their unit, which is responsible for carrying out the execution itself (in the presence of all the men, to act as a terrifying example), escorted by two military policemen who did not have the heart to tell them the fate that awaited them. Locked up in a small hut, the two men screamed, shouted, wept, pleaded and tried to negotiate: "We promise to go out on patrol every night, Lieutenant." No use. So they stopped screaming, shouting, pleading and trying to negotiate. The only sound to be heard from the locked hut was weeping. Both of them are experienced soldiers who have been in the army since the beginning of the war. All armies function on a mixture of external compulsion and consent (spontaneous or orchestrated); indeed, this whole war originated in a meeting of those two concepts. And the shakier the consent becomes, the harsher the compulsion applied. But only up to a certain point. When the only thing remaining is compulsion, there is nothing left and the whole edifice collapses.

The adjutant raises his hand and gives the silent signal.

Nothing happens.

The soldiers look at the adjutant, look at the blindfolded man tied to the tree. Among the soldiers in the firing squad there are comrades, brothers-in-arms, "perhaps even relations" of the condemned man.

Another sign is given.

Nothing happens.

The adjutant claps his hands nervously. It is as if some sound is necessary to convince the soldiers that it is time for them to shoot.

A salvo crashes out.

The condemned man falls forward but is held up by the wire with which he is bound and slides down the tree trunk a little instead. In this short movement he has changed from a man to a body, from subject to object, from being to thing, from he to it. The doctor steps forward and after a short token examination pronounces him dead. No one can be in any doubt of that. Monelli sees that half his head has been blown away.

Then the other man is led forward.

In contrast to his fellow deserter he is quite calm and has something resembling a smile on his lips. He speaks to the members of the firing squad in a strange, almost ecstatic tone of voice and says, "This is right and just. Just make sure that you aim properly—and don't do what I did!" Confusion breaks out in the firing squad. Some of them want to be excused on the grounds that they have already shot one man. Words are exchanged. The adjutant swears and threatens and manages to re-establish order in the squad.

Shots ring out. The man crumples. He too is dead.

The firing squad is dismissed and the men walk slowly away. Monelli can see how shaken they are, and he sees fear and pain on all their faces. Nothing else is talked about all day and their voices are quiet and unobtrusive, from shame or from shock:

> Questions, doubts arise in our reluctant minds, and we push them away fearfully because they sully our high principles too much—the very principles that we accept with our eyes shut as though they were matters of faith—and because we are afraid that without them it would be too difficult for us to do our duty as soldiers. Fatherland, necessity, discipline—a line in our instructional manual, words whose meaning we don't really know and which are just sounds to us. Death by firing squad—that makes the words clear and comprehensible to our sad minds. But those gentlemen down in Enego, no, they did not come here to witness the reality of the words of the sentence they pronounced.

THURSDAY, 2 AUGUST 1917
Angus Buchanan takes part in the storming of the Tandamuti ridge

Another night march, another attack. The bald ridge lies in front of them and rises from the dense surrounding vegetation like the back of some drowned prehistoric creature. On the crown of the hill there is a small stand of trees in which a fort is concealed. The fort is the target of the attack.

The main attack begins at nine o'clock. The constant rattle of machine-gun fire and the dull crack of grenade launchers sound through the bush. The first wave of men to go in is a black battalion, the 3/4 King's African Rifles. They take heavy losses and their attack stalls on the bare slope. The second wave is called up, Angus Buchanan's unit, the 25th Royal Fusiliers. They are beginning to respect the black troops and there is even a kind of comradeship developing with some of the more experienced African units—something that would have been quite unthinkable before the war. Buchanan is in command of the battalion's machine-gun platoon and he and his gun crews follow the chain of riflemen along the corpse-strewn slope of the ridge and up towards the summit. The gunfire is now a continuous roar.

As the German forces have been pushed back into an ever diminishing corner of the colony and started to base their resistance on a number of fortified positions, the fighting has become fiercer and more costly. Although the total number of troops involved is considerably fewer than during earlier campaigns, losses in combat are three times as great.

Both sides are feeling an increasing sense of desperation: the Germans because they are defending the last scrap of territory remaining to them on this continent, the British because those in command have received increasingly brusque statements that this campaign must be finished—and sooner rather than later. It is not just that war credits are running low, the tonnage of the merchant fleet is doing the same. Since sanctioning unrestricted U-boat warfare at the end of January the Germans have been sinking more ships than the Allies can manage to build.* In a situation in which every fourth vessel fails to get through and in which the supplying of the British Isles is threatened, convoys to East Africa are regarded as something of a luxury.

After retreating from the valley at Mohambika the Germans dug in firmly on the Tandamunti ridge. The two sides have been taking it in turns to attack and counter-attack ever since the middle of June. And now it is happening again.

The two companies of the 25th Royal Fusiliers move quickly on towards the clump of trees but are held up by a *boma*, a wide barricade of intertwined thorn bushes, at least as effective as barbed wire. They bounce off this and are pushed back towards the left. Meanwhile, however, Buchanan has managed to position his machine guns no more than fifty yards from the barrier. There is a sharp exchange of fire and within a short space of time four of Buchanan's "most able and invaluable

---

* During January 1917 German U-boats sank thirty-five vessels with a combined weight of 109,954 tons; by April those figures had risen to 155 vessels and 516,394 tons, though the losses declined following the introduction of the convoy system and a policy of more aggressive mine-laying. Air Force pilots also became more skilled at sinking U-boats. (The first submarine sunk at sea by aircraft was the French *Foucault*, dispatched by Austrian seaplanes in the Adriatic on 15 September 1916.)

gunners" have fallen. But Buchanan holds on and the chattering fire from his guns sweeps back and forth across the enemy position while grenades from the grenade launchers further back swish almost silently over their heads and explode with smoke and fire among the trees.*

Buchanan notices that the return fire from the fort is slowly growing weaker and he thinks he can hear German buglers blowing the retreat beyond the ridge. But with victory within his grasp he receives an order to pull back: the Germans have mounted a counter-attack further over and there is a risk of being cut off. When Buchanan and his men move away from the ridge they hear the sound of heavy gunfire in the distance. All their bearers have disappeared and their sacks, boxes and chests are lying scattered along the path. No sooner have they worked out that *askaris* must have swept right through their baggage train than they themselves come under fire from close range.

Later again they reach the field hospital and find it has been looted by German troops, but in a remarkably orderly manner:

[The Germans] had the audacity to order the native orderlies to supply the German whites with tea, while they removed all the quinine and such medicines of which they were in need. But the whites had treated the wounded with consideration, and, with revolvers drawn, had ordered their wildly excited blacks to stand clear of any possibility of interference.

While the war on all the other fronts is characterised by increasing brutalisation, the warring whites in East Africa frequently behave in a notably chivalrous manner towards each other. This camaraderie is not just a remnant of the pre-war idea that the colonies should be excluded from any conflict, but is also an expression of the feeling that they—as a drop of white in that continent's ocean of black—share a kind of collective colonial fate.† On the whole, white prisoners are treated very well, sometimes being given better food than the soldiers. On one occasion

---

* Many soldiers detested being under attack from grenade launchers and mortars since, unlike other artillery pieces, their projectiles made very little noise as they travelled through the air and therefore arrived without audible warning. (They were, however, rather slow, so it was often possible to see them coming.)

† Educated Africans were beginning to think that the war would lead to colonialism destroying itself.

during this campaign a German doctor crosses the British lines and asks for the return of a bag of medical equipment which was left behind; he is given the bag and allowed to return to his own side. And when von Lettow-Vorbeck is awarded the Pour le Mérite during the fighting, the British general opposing him sends a courteous letter of congratulation.

At around eleven o'clock in the evening Buchanan and the rest of the battalion—those who are still on their feet—reach the camp at Ziwani. They are utterly exhausted, having been on the move or in battle for twenty-two hours.

In a week's time they will attack the same ridge yet again.

That same day Harvey Cushing writes in his journal:

> 2:30 a.m. Pouring cats and dogs all day—also pouring cold and shivering wounded, covered with mud and blood. Some G.S.W.'s of the head,* when the mud is scraped off, prove to be trifles— others of unsuspected gravity. The pre-operation room is still crowded—one can't possibly keep up with them; and the unsystematic way things are run drives one frantic. The news, too, is very bad. The greatest battle in history is floundering up to its middle in a morass, and the guns have sunk even deeper than that.

WEDNESDAY, 8 AUGUST 1917
Florence Farmborough crosses the border into Romania

They start their march at seven o'clock in the morning. It has been raining and the roads are muddy but she finds the open, hilly scenery attractive, with its colours and contours softened by the gentle morning light. They cross the Prut on a bridge that is being worked on by Austrian prisoners of war and she sees that their tents are soaked through after the rain. Some of the prisoners are just sitting motionless, waiting for the morning sun to rise high enough to dry their sodden clothes.

* Gunshot wounds.

Once the wagons have clattered across the wooden roadway of the bridge and rolled down to the opposite bank they are in Romania. What is it that has raised their feelings of hope? Yesterday, when they were told that they would be going south into the neighbouring country, the staff of the hospital unit greeted the news with joy. Part of it is simply that they are getting away, not just from the advancing Germans but also from the scenes of collapse, demoralisation and retreat that have characterised the last week.

By this point the "freedom offensive,"* the new government's last effort to continue the war, has collapsed. Florence's unit belongs to the Eighth Army, which initially seemed to be successfully breaking through the enemy lines south of the Dniester but which ground to a halt after advancing less than twenty miles. The reasons: a shortage of supplies and lack of enthusiasm on the part of the soldiers. The latter have been holding meetings, asking questions, discussing conditions, choosing committees and demanding the right to elect their own officers. The number of desertions has increased enormously and now occurs quite openly. Whole divisions have refused to attack the enemy. Florence has noticed, to her amazement and disquiet, that a large proportion of the soldiers really do not want to fight any longer. Their displeasure has also found a new target to set alongside their own officers—the female nurses. Is it because they are volunteers or because they are women, or both? Whatever it is, they now find themselves the victims of sneering, swearing and sexual innuendo: for the very first time Florence has felt afraid of their own side's soldiers and has kept well away from them.

Over the frontier, with luck, they will be spared the sight of the continuing disintegration of the Russian army. And over the frontier Romanian and Russian units together have started their own little version of the freedom offensive and by all recent accounts they are having some success. So they greeted this march with joy, not because it was taking them away from the war but because it was taking them somewhere they could make a real contribution.

They halt out in an open field to eat an army concoction in which "fish and meat had been lumped together into thick *kasha* soup, and

---

* Now better known as the Kerensky offensive after Alexander Kerensky, the incumbent prime minister in Russia's Provisional Government, who had ordered it that July when minister of war.

there were strange greenish leaves which had certainly not been reared on a cabbage-plot." The sun is high in a blue sky and it is hot. Florence hears people arguing—politics, of course. She picks up some of the details: Kerensky will undoubtedly dismiss Brusilov—their hero—as being the man responsible for the failure of the offensive. Other angry voices join in and even Florence is upset. But she does not let herself get dragged into the discussion and goes off with her friends to cool down with a bathe in the river. Unfortunately they cannot find anywhere private enough—there are soldiers everywhere—so they return to the column up in the field and crawl into the shade under one of the big wagons. She manages to write some letters before the order is given to move on. By then it is about four o'clock in the afternoon.

Later on they come to a long, steep hill and have to wait their turn since the horses need help to haul the heavily laden wagons up it. She writes in her journal:

> A bevy of stalwart young soldiers assisted each horse and cart to reach the summit, and there was much shouting and unnecessary whipping of horses. They, poor frightened creatures, knew what was expected of them and did their best; but their deep, spasmodic breathing and foam-streaked, perspiring bodies told of the strenuous exertion which every movement demanded of them.

They carry on along poor roads, up and down through the hilly terrain, through villages with neat little wooden houses, their windows covered with curtains, past women and children in exotic, beautifully embroidered clothes. She hears an old woman let out a yell of terror at the sight of all these uniformed men and Florence thinks that the words remind her of Italian. So this is Romania. They stop in a small town and buy apples from the Jewish merchants—for roubles. There are no eggs to be had since the soldiers have already bought them. The summer heat is made more bearable when they enter a beautiful, shady pine wood.

As evening approaches they make camp on a hillside close to a village. The heat is such that they disdain their tents and set up camp beds in the open air. Their leader has managed to get hold of a newspaper only three days old and he reads it aloud to them by the campfire. Much of it is about the usual political chaos in the Russian capital and Florence is only mildly interested. There is, however, one story that grips her and some of the other nurses: it is the news that, because of the critical situation, infantry battalions consisting solely of women are being formed.

She already knows that woman soldiers exist in the Russian army and has actually met some of them among the wounded. She remembers one in particular, a twenty-year-old woman she nursed in Galicia who had a nasty wound on one temple where a bullet had grazed her. The woman wanted to get straight back into battle. The new all-woman battalions have been formed on the initiative of "Yasha Bachkarova,"* a Siberian woman from a simple background who initially fought alongside her husband and then stayed in the army after he was killed. She has been wounded and decorated several times and has been promoted to the rank of sergeant. The newspaper quotes her: "If the men refuse to fight for their country we will show them what the women can do." A battalion composed entirely of women has already seen action during the "freedom offensive," when they were sent in to hold a trench abandoned by deserters. Florence and the other nurses think this is fantastic news.

It is a warm evening and a big, shining moon is hanging in the starry sky.

SATURDAY, 18 AUGUST 1917
Olive King sees Salonica burn

By this afternoon it is clear that a major conflagration is raging in the city and Olive is keen to see it at closer quarters. So when there is a call for cars to help rescue the supplies at the Serbian Quartermaster General's depot she is obviously quick to grab the opportunity. It is not until she drives past Venizelos Street that she realises how serious the situation is. What started as an ordinary enough fire has now accelerated into something on an enormous scale. The whole of the Turkish quarter seems to be in flames:

* Maria "Yashka" Bachkarova, who was eventually executed in 1920 as an enemy of the people for her connections with the White Russian military. Her unit was known as the 1st Russian Women's Battalion of Death.

It's impossible to describe the scenes of pandemonium in the streets, the jammed mass of panic-stricken people getting their goods away in bullock carts, on their own backs, in little open fiacres, or in those long narrow falling-to-pieces little Greek carts that make driving here so difficult. There was a continuous roar of the flames, every moment came a great crash & millions of sparks as some buildings, [sic] a Vardar hot-wind gale was blowing & showers of sparks & burning fragments poured over us all the time. It was not yet dark, but everything was lit by the weird golden glow, like a wonderfully brilliant sunset.

Until today Salonica was a confusing, picturesque and, in parts, very beautiful city with the unmistakable stamp of centuries of Ottoman government. There were minarets, a strong city wall and an excellent bazaar. Anyone walking round the labyrinth of narrow streets and medieval lanes would feel quite convinced that he or she was, in a purely geographical sense, in Europe but would simultaneously recognise immediately that the place felt, smelled and sounded like the Orient. And, in fact, until less than five years ago the city was under Ottoman rule. Far from detracting from the place, its oriental character was an important part of its attraction, and the years of Western occupation with its accompanying flood of troops from virtually all corners of the world has served only to reinforce the glaring contrasts and the cosmopolitan spirit of the city. Here mosques, Byzantine cathedrals and Greek Orthodox basilicas stand shoulder to shoulder with trams and cinemas, variety theatres and bars, expensive shops, fine restaurants and first-class hotels. For some people, however, Salonica is not just a polyglot conglomerate (King and many of her friends speak a unique pidgin, in which the basis is English but with a significant admixture of French and Serbian) but much more a Babel of sin.

Well, if that really is its true character, the time for punishment seems to have arrived. The strong wind causes the fire to spread with unexpected speed.

King makes several trips into the growing sea of fire, rescuing necessities or people's private possessions. Whenever she stops she has to run round the outside of the little Ford ambulance putting out the sparks that are falling on it. And as she drives she has to sound her horn almost continuously to force a way through the dense crowds of people, some of them hysterical and panic-stricken, others so distressed that they have become virtually apathetic. She notices that the two most common things people salvage from their homes are large mirrors and bronze bedsteads. When the flames eventually reach the harbour and the sea she realises that a wall of fire three miles long is now separating her from the garage. She still drives on and, when she runs out of petrol, she continues on foot in order to find more fuel.

Military discipline largely breaks down in this flame-flickered confusion. As usual, chivalry and heroism are mixed with selfishness and cowardice. There is a wave of looting. A number of large casks of wine burst in the heat and their contents pour out across the street "like blood." Both soldiers and civilians hurl themselves to the ground and drink the sludge. The next time King passes the spot it stinks of wine and she sees blind-drunk, vomit-covered people lying all over the place. A stockpile of shells ignites with an enormous explosion. Sporadic gunfire can be heard.

When the sun rises after a long night the sky is so full of smoke that it never becomes properly light. King drives down to the harbour. The electric cables for the trams have partially melted and are hanging down across the street so she has to zig-zag between them. She sees soldiers and civilians raking through the smoking ruins in search of loot.

Olive King has been behind the wheel for over twenty hours. When she returns to her room, exhausted and hungry and in need of some sleep, she finds a homeless woman and nine children in the hall. Almost half the city has been burnt down and 80,000 people have lost their homes. It will take the best part of two weeks to put the fire out and the city will remain a sooty ruin for the rest of the war. The Salonica that existed before the fire will never be rebuilt.

SUNDAY, 26 AUGUST 1917
Harvey Cushing finally sees a three-dimensional map

The front is quiet but everyone knows the lull is only temporary. Most of the morning is spent changing the wounded men's bandages. Cushing thinks that many of those he operated on earlier seem to be recovering—or perhaps it is just that he is in a better frame of mind after managing to get two nights' sleep in succession.

There are no American units to speak of involved in the fighting yet so Cushing and his hospital unit have been moved north to the Flanders front. Another British offensive, the biggest of them all, has been going on there since the end of July. It already has a name: the Battle of Passchendaele, or the Third Battle of Ypres.

Four major attacks have been launched so far. It has rained almost the whole time and the battlefield has been churned into a sea of mud. Up to now the successes have been as small as the losses have been great, but it is difficult to know much about what is happening and few people have an overview since censorship is strict and the official communiqués uninformative. Cushing, however, has made some fairly accurate guesses about the course of the fighting from his observations of the stream of ragged, bleeding men being brought in by a seemingly endless convoy of mud-spattered ambulances. How many men have been wounded? Is their morale holding up? How long has it taken them to reach the bandaging station? Most of the wounded are so caked in mud that it takes an unusually long time to remove their clothes, clean away the dirt and find their wounds. Those who have already been given a tetanus injection have a "T" written on their foreheads with an indelible pencil. There is a steadily expanding cemetery next to the hospital, the graves being dug by Chinese labourers in blue tunics.

Severe head wounds are Cushing's speciality and he tries to get through eight procedures a day. He operates in a tent, wearing a thick rubber apron and army boots. One of his special techniques is to use—with immense care—a powerful magnet to extract shell splinters from the brains of wounded men. Few men arrive with common or garden bullet wounds, and bayonet injuries are a rarity. Almost all Cushing's patients are the victims of shellfire and almost all of them have multiple injuries. Cushing has become something of an expert on wounds: he has learned, for instance, that the most devastating injuries often lurk behind the smallest entry wounds.

There is a ring of observation balloons around the horizon. Sometimes bombs fall near the hospital. If they have any time at all to spare they play tennis on a court close by. Today, after lunch, Cushing and a colleague drive round the other hospital units in the neighbourhood to visit friends. The weather is nice and dry for a change. The sound of artillery fire hangs in the air. The road from Mont des Cats to Rémy runs along a high ridge with an excellent view and, to the north, they can pick out the front line at Ypres as a ribbon of muzzle-flashes.

A Canadian colonel allows Cushing to see something he has been curious about for some time—one of the big, three-dimensional maps of the battlefield, made of sand to a scale of 1:50 and used in the planning of attacks. Everything is carefully marked: every wood, every building, every height contour. Allied trenches are marked with blue ribbon, German trenches with red. Cushing reads the names written on small labels: Inverness Copse, Clapham Junction, Sanctuary Wood, Polygon Wood. Cushing is little wiser after reading them but to judge from the map the next attack will have Glencourse Wood as its objective—the wood projects as a red bulge into all the blue lines.

They are not the only ones studying the map, as a number of officers and NCOs are doing the same and trying to learn the terrain. These are the men who will be going over the top tomorrow.

Cushing and his colleague return just in time for dinner, after which his commanding officer disappears with Cushing's unread copy of yesterday's *Times*. When Cushing asks for it, the senior officer hides the paper behind his back and points Cushing in the direction of an army bulletin pinned up on the door of the mess. Cushing is annoyed, and he also finds the document with its codenames and map coordinates completely incomprehensible:

Morning	Report	aaa	YAWL	reports
S.O.S.	sent	up	about	5
a.m.	this	morning	on	left
of	CABLE	and	right	of
LUCKS	front	Enemy	attacked	on
front	J.14.A.5.8	to	right	at
5	a.m.	Posts	at	J.14.A.7.4
were	driven	in	Posts	at
J.14.A.8.8	are	still	maintained aaa	[. . .]

At about midnight Cushing lies in his tent listening to the storm of heavy artillery fire building up in the distance. Immediately after that rain starts drumming on the tent again.

. . .

The following day someone tells Cushing that 17,299 cases were discharged or sent on for further treatment elsewhere from the three field hospitals in this sector between 23 July and 3 August. (The dead, of course, are not included in this figure.) The Fifth Army has twelve other field hospitals like theirs.

TUESDAY, 4 SEPTEMBER 1917
Edward Mousley is travelling to Ankara by horse and cart

Breakfast is first class: sausage, cakes, tea and jam—Mousley has just received a parcel from home. The men guarding them eat bread, olives, melon and onions. Then they all set off from the little inn, which is infested with bedbugs. Mousley and the other prisoner of war—a British soldier with a badly inflamed broken arm—ride in the wagon at the start but once the road begins to climb up over the mountain they get out and walk alongside: the draught animals are simply too weak to pull them. The mountainside is covered with tall pines. A large group of mounted gendarmes is accompanying them, partly to prevent them escaping and partly to protect the party from attacks by bandits. They pass a waterfall.

Mousley has actually been thinking about escaping and last summer he was one of a group of prisoners who spent months preparing a daring escape from Kastamonu. Their intention was to follow a track through the mountains up to the Black Sea, where a small boat was supposed to be buried in the sand—with oars but no sail. Disguised as a Turk, Mousley even managed to make several practice runs to test out the best way of fooling the guards. He was almost caught on one of these occasions and after that he was kept under close watch. Part of the group did, however, escape but were (probably) recaptured after (possibly) being betrayed or (more probably) caught while making a clumsy attempt to pass as Germans.

But now Mousley is leaving his confinement in Kastamonu. He is still suffering from the after-effects of his time in Kut al-Amara. The real problem is severe bruising to his back, which was struck by a shell fragment that damaged some of the vertebrae—the pain frequently keeps him awake at night. But the reason for his journey to Ankara is to get specialist treatment for his eyes: all the dust and muck driven into them by the explosion is causing almost continuous inflammation which, so far, is more annoying than dangerous but could become serious. He received a letter from acquaintances in the foreign ministry in London and he managed to use it to frighten the Turkish commandant into believing that London was taking a special interest in his case, with the result that the Turkish officer arranged for his transfer to Ankara. Mousley himself is pressing to be treated in Constantinople, the thought in the back of his mind being that it will be easier to escape from there.

The journey up the mountain takes the greater part of the morning and they do not reach the pass until three o'clock. The peak is not far away, cloaked in mist. At the pass they take a longer break and eat lunch before starting down. Mousley thoroughly dislikes Ali, the officer in command of the transport. Ali is choleric, power mad, aggressive and cowardly, but they try to keep him in a good mood by constantly giving him cigarettes. Mousley has a much higher opinion of Mustafa, the ordinary soldier guarding them, and the two prisoners have developed a good relationship with him. They are actually quite impressed by the way this "patient soul of the Turkish peasant" does his duty faithfully and uncomplainingly in spite of suffering badly from malaria.

The temperature rises. Even though Mousley and his companion are now once more able to ride in the wagon it is not a very pleasant journey. It is hot and jolting, the horses are so weak that they sometimes fall over and have to be helped up, the harness is forever in need of repair and, at one point, they come close to driving off the steep road. Mousley's eyes are playing up more and more but he is in an unusually good mood in spite of that. He writes in his journal: "But these have been wonderful days of movement, a voyage of rediscovery of the world, a passing from sleep to dreamland, from death to life."

Along the way he recognises details from when they were being taken to Kastamonu as prisoners: a little cottage here, a mill there, that demolished Armenian house. They spend the night in another of those small inns. After having a smoke they go to sleep up on the roof, perhaps because the place is full of bugs or maybe just because it is too hot inside.

.　.　.

The same day Angus Buchanan sets off from Camp C23, yet another hot and unhealthy camp in the jungle:

> On 4th September the battalion left C.23 and advanced to the centre and left camps before Narunyu, to occupy the front line there; relieving the 8th South African Infantry, who were tottering with sickness and unfit for further service in active fields.
>
> Here utter physical exhaustion, and fever, which had gripped me for some time, began slowly to master endurance.

MONDAY, 10 SEPTEMBER 1917
Elfriede Kuhr cooks "peasant's omelette" in Schneidemühl

Everyone is talking about food at the moment—and about the need to stock up. No one wants to go through another winter like the last one, the "turnip winter." Fortunately they have a cellar full of potatoes at Alte Bahnhofstrasse 17 (they bought a whole load off Herr Kenzler), as well as turnips. They have almost no bread, however, nor cooking fat. Their diet is utterly drab and monotonous.[*]

Elfriede, however, has become a real expert at making "peasant's omelette," a dish both she and her brother are very fond of. First of all she rubs the iron pan with a piece of old bacon rind, adds salt and puts in sliced potatoes, frying them carefully so that they do not burn. Then she whisks an egg together with water, flour, salt and pepper and pours it in along with some onion or chives—if there are any. The knack is to have just enough water in the mixture to cover the potatoes but not so much that it drowns the taste of the egg.

Two days ago Elfriede and her friend Trude went for a long walk with Lieutenants Leverenz and Waldecker. It was still warm and summery and they walked all the way to Königsblick. Lieutenant Waldecker walked with her, listened to her, put his arms around her, laughed at her stories, looked at her in such a strange but loving way, kissed her fingertips, the end of her nose and her forehead. At one point Lieutenant

---

[*] The problem was not just that imports were being cut off by the British blockade; the previous year the government had banned the import of "exotic" foods such as mandarins, raisins, pineapples, ginger and vanilla.

Leverenz had wagged his finger at his colleague and said in an annoying way, "No, no—under-age!" And then Lieutenant Leverenz and Trude had kissed each other time after time but Lieutenant Waldecker had contented himself with holding Elfriede's hand and pressing her head to his shoulder. They did not return home until the evening and when they parted on the stairs at Alte Bahnhofstrasse he whispered in her ear that he loved her. He, Lieutenant Waldecker, in his fine pilot's uniform, his officer's cap at an angle, his leather gauntlets, his Iron Cross, his blue eyes and his blond hair. She was so happy and pleased, it made her go weak at the knees.

In spite of this, or perhaps because of this, she still plays her usual games of pretend with Gretel Wagner. Elfriede likes it most when she is being Lieutenant von Yellenic and Gretel is being Nurse Martha. There is a new twist to their games now: usually, Lieutenant von Yellenic is terribly in love either with some absent imaginary lady or with Nurse Martha. Unfortunately, however, the object of his/her love is already married to a major so there can be no question of anything more than platonic love at a distance.

This is taking up most of her time at the moment, though she still goes down to the station sometimes to help her grandmother in the Red Cross canteen as she used to, or just to watch the troop transports and hospital trains. But her visits are less and less frequent, and the black-white-red flags on the war map on the classroom wall no longer interest her. These days they seldom talk in school about what is happening on the different fronts—it comes up only when someone's friend or relation has been killed. And it is a long time since they had a day off to celebrate a victory. The war, as Elfriede writes in her journal, has been going on so long that it has almost "become a kind of normal condition. We can hardly remember what peace was like. We scarcely think of the war any more."

FRIDAY, 28 SEPTEMBER 1917
Michel Corday pays a visit to Anatole France in Tours

The train pulls into the station in Tours at lunchtime. Anatole France is standing on the platform, an elderly, corpulent gentleman with a short white beard and a red hat on his head. They travel by car with him out to La Béchellerie, the author's country estate, beautifully situated on a little hill a mile and a half outside the city.

The war has been a trial to the old man. Not that it has affected him directly. He has no relations at the front and he has been living here quietly on a tributary of the Loire ever since August 1914, when he—like many others—moved south to get away from the apparently unstoppable German armies. No, it is more that the war, right from the start, has turned out to be such a bitter and disillusioning defeat for everything he used to believe in.

The pain of it all has been especially difficult for this old man. He was accustomed to hearing the soothing and harmonious sound of choirs singing his praises, but then he was suddenly deluged with torrents of abuse and threats, simply because he stood by what he had said earlier and refused to be swept along by the war fever of 1914. Caught off guard, hurt and afraid, the old man had then (at the age of seventy-one) offered to volunteer, which had brought him nothing but ridicule. Anatole France is now more ignored than persecuted and although he still ventures to make occasional small, dispirited and modest suggestions, they are passed over in silence. Corday has the impression that Anatole France has completely lost faith in humanity, though the great writer cannot stop brooding over what is happening. He has told Corday that he sometimes imagines the war will continue forever and that thought almost drives him out of his mind.*

They are given lunch when they get to La Béchellerie. The solid stone seventeenth-century building is very beautiful and packed with the things Anatole France, a manic collector, has gathered over the years. One of the visitors to the house at this time likened it to "an antique shop," and there is a gilded torso of Venus standing in the middle of the drawing room. There are other guests at lunch, including a draper from the town, and he too is very pessimistic about the future:

The overwhelming majority of people in Tours want the war to continue because of the high wages it has brought to the work-

---

* He felt there was some justification for a reaction of that kind. In a letter to another acquaintance France wrote, "As if it wasn't enough that the war is causing such dreadful suffering; it is also making idiots of all those who haven't already gone mad."

ers and the increased profits made by tradesmen. The bourgeoi-
sie, whose only mental nourishment comes from the reactionary
newspapers, has been completely won over by the idea of a war
without end. In short, he declares, it is only the men at the front
who are pacifists.

They spend the afternoon in the library, which is situated in a small
building out in the garden. The conversation inevitably gravitates back
to the war, this scab that none of them can or will stop picking at. They
discuss the different peace initiatives of the last year—the German one,
the American one and, of course, the one proposed by the Pope just a
month ago.[*]
We can imagine the special atmosphere. A group of cultured people
in a room that is, one might say, buttressed by books—people like Corday and Anatole France, sensitive, refined, radical humanists, forced to
live like strangers to their own age, upset and confused by events they
cannot understand and forces they cannot influence. Is it really true that
all roads to peace are now closed? They grasp at thin, straggly straws
of comfort. Perhaps the translation of President Wilson's answer is
incorrect. Perhaps the German memorandum that accompanied their
response to the Pope is a forgery. Perhaps there is a hidden strategy for
negotiation. Perhaps, possibly, hopefully. Why, why, why?
Words and thoughts go back and forth across the warm, sheltered
room as the hours pass. Soon twilight begins to fall. A great moon rises
and colours the autumnal scene in silver and white.

---

[*] The first two of these proposals were by that time off the table: the American proposal
because the United States had entered the war and the German one because its originator,
Bethmann-Hollweg, had lost his battle against the hawks in Berlin and left office. In
July a majority in the German Reichstag had voted by 212 to 126 in favour of a resolution
demanding peace without either territorial gains or reparations: this ran completely
counter to the ambitions of the men who in reality now held power in Germany—the
military high command, with Hindenburg and Ludendorff in the lead. This meant that
the so-called civil truce of 1914 was broken and Bethmann-Hollweg's position as the man
trying to balance the scales became untenable.

SATURDAY, 13 OCTOBER 1917
Harvey Cushing lists the day's cases

The bad weather is continuing. It is raining most of the time and there is a strong, almost gale-force wind. Cushing has once again spent the day at the operating table. At 5:25 on Friday yet another attack was launched at Ypres—in spite of the awful weather, rising water levels, bottomless mud and poor visibility. From the survivors he is treating, Cushing has heard of wounded men drowning in shell holes.

He starts the morning by running through the cases waiting for him:

> Winter, E. 860594. *7th Borderers, 17th Div.—penetrating cerebellar. Sitting down. Helmet on. Blown into the air. Unconscious for a time, does not know how long. Later crept back to a trench—legs wobbly—dizzy etc.*
>
> Robinson, H. 14295. *1st S. African Inf., 9th Div.—penetrating rt temporal. Wounded yesterday c. 6 p.m. Knocked down but not unconscious. Helmet penetrated. Walked 20 yards— dizzy—vomited—numbness left arm, etc. No transport until this morning owing to mud.*
>
> Matthew, R. 202037. *8th Black Watch—penetrating right parietal; hernia cerebri. Thinks he was wounded three days ago, etc. A fine, big Jock.*
>
> Hartley, J. *26th M.G.C., 8th Div. Wounded at 11 last night, not unconscious. Walked to dressing station. Thinks they had reached their objective, etc.*
>
> Bogus, *3rd N.Z. Rifle Brigade, 1st Anzac. Frontal gutter wound. In line for two nights before show began—awful conditions. Had gone 1000 yards when wounded etc.*
>
> Beattie, *7th Seaforths, 9th Div. Stretcher-bearer, wounded while bringing out his third man—4 to a stretcher—300 yards from advanced line. Occipital penetrating (?)*
>
> Medgurck, *11th Royal Scots, 9th Div. Multiple wounds, including head etc.*
>
> Dobbie, *Household Batt'n, 4th Div. Wounded near Poelcapelle some time yesterday afternoon. Adm. here 7 p.m. In "resus" since. Severe. For X-ray, etc.*

Towards the end of the day Cushing feels reasonably satisfied. The operations have gone well and he has also successfully used the special magnet system to extract splinters from three of these men's brains.

Cushing realises that the attack has not gone particularly well and the wounded continue to pour in. But no one has seen any recent newspapers or official communiqués and it is impossible to know what has actually happened.

Two days later it is quiet again at Ypres. The weather is clearing up. There is a rumour that three British divisions have been so badly mauled that they are having to be pulled out of the fighting and reinforcements from the Second Army are on their way in. In the afternoon Cushing sees thousands upon thousands of birds gathering in swirling flocks close to a little copse near the field hospital. Someone tells him they are starlings.

WEDNESDAY, 24 OCTOBER 1917
Michel Corday comments on the street talk in Paris

A fourth winter of war is just round the corner and the mood in Paris is wearier than it was a year ago. In spite of the fact that shortages are less severe than before. Anyone with money can get hold of anything. Black marketeers are becoming more and more common, more affluent and more shameless in their behaviour. Many of the best restaurants have employed highly decorated veterans and war invalids as doormen and Corday wonders what they must think as they stand there holding the door for people who are no more than "voluminously embodied appetites rushing to their troughs." He notes in his journal:

One hears people in the street making their small plans. People often say, "After the war I shall ..." in the same calm tone of voice as they say, "After having a shower I shall ..." They classify this world-shattering event in the same category as natural catastrophes. They never suspect for a moment that they themselves would be able to stop it, that its parasitic life is dependent on their acquiescence.

SUNDAY, 28 OCTOBER 1917
Harvey Cushing sees the Canadian build-up at Zonnebeke

A light mist. Hazy sunshine. Thin clouds. A chill in the air. There is absolutely no part of him that affirms this war. Quite the opposite. The wrecks it creates pour in waves into his hospital and his daily business is to try to patch them back together. Experience has made him acutely conscious of the cost. Hardly a day passes without him washing blood and brain matter from his hands. And coming as he does from a sheltered upper-class life in Boston, he finds many aspects of his present life distinctly uncomfortable: the perpetual wet, the monotonous food, the cold that makes it difficult to sleep in the thin tent. He has brought his own collapsible bathtub with him.

And the costs—Cushing is horrified by the almost limitless waste of materials. There are bunkers in which the floor is insulated by layer upon layer of unopened tins of food. In one place they found 250 pairs of new waist-waders, intended for use in the most flooded trenches: they had simply been discarded by some unit after being used only once. The soldiers throw away everything that is heavy or not immediately necessary before they go into combat, in the certain knowledge that if they survive they will be able to report it as lost in battle and they will then be issued new equipment without further question. Discarded rifles can be seen everywhere, being used as signposts or props in the trenches or just rusting away. Five minutes' bombardment of a small piece of ground can consume ammunition costing £80,000.

He has seen and heard too much not to be critical of the British army's methods of waging war at Ypres. Take, for instance, the story he heard the day before yesterday from one of his patients, a non-commissioned officer from the 50th Division. The young man was lying trembling in his bed, pretending to smoke a cigarette. His battalion had gone astray in the rain and darkness and had tried to dig in. Since there was nothing but mud everywhere the best they could do was to throw up small heaps of sodden earth and lie down in the wet puddles behind them. After twice being ordered to advance in the darkness they were finally given the order to attack. They tried to follow the creeping barrage—tried, but it was moving too quickly. And suddenly they found themselves standing in front of a row of concrete German bunkers. "Well, there was practically nobody left."

Cushing cannot for his life understand why an attack cannot be called off if, for instance, the weather is quite atrocious. He put that question once to a senior British officer and was told that, unfortunately, it was quite simply impossible. Not at such short notice. There is much too much organisation involved, and the planning is too complicated for it to be possible. Too much, too complicated—in a sense, beyond human control. That is an image of the war as a whole.

This particular Sunday is fairly quiet and only the odd wounded man is brought in. But the battle is not over. New attacks are being prepared. One of Cushing's contacts in the Second Army has earlier promised to take him up to the front and today seems to be a good opportunity for such a visit. The two men sign in at one of the many control points, exchange their car for an ambulance and drive towards Ypres via Poperinghe. The closer they get to the town, the denser the traffic becomes. They zig-zag across the muddy road, between marching soldiers and motorcycle dispatch riders, convoys of lorries and horse-drawn artillery. They drive through a grey confusion of rubble and ruins. After passing the pockmarked Menin Gate they drive as far as Potijze, where they park their vehicle and continue on foot. For the sake of safety, since the forward line is only a mile or so away.

Cushing is astonished. Not just by all the rubbish lying everywhere in the sticky morass of mud—"dead horses, smashed tanks, crashed and crumpled aircraft, cordite buckets, shells, mortars, bombs, broken or discarded wagons, barbed wire"—but by the fact that the place corresponds in some way to his expectations. In fact, it looks just as it looks in the photographs.

On the road up towards Zonnebeke Canadian troops, caked in mud, jostle with lorries, cannon and mules laden with ammunition. At the side of the road there are troops waiting their turn to move on. The air is filled with the noise of innumerable artillery pieces: the noise rises and falls, rises and falls but never falls silent. Aircraft circle up in the hazy sunlight, surrounded by the brief watercolour puffs of smoke from anti-aircraft fire. He sees a German shell land hardly more than 200 yards away and watches the black earth spurt up "like a geyser." Then he sees another shell land, closer still. He is surprised by his own reaction:

And the savage in you makes you adore it with its squalor and wastefulness and danger and strife and glorious noise. You feel that, after all, this is what men were intended for rather than to sit in easy chairs with a cigarette and whiskey, the evening paper or the best-seller, and to pretend that such a veneer means civilization and that there is no barbarian behind your starched and studded shirt front.

In a moment of dizziness as he stands there on the edge of the abyss, this man—who knows only too well the sorrows and misery caused by war—suddenly and almost reluctantly thinks he can also perceive its greatness and its beauty or, anyway, the dark and devastating energies that shape the tragedy. But enough is enough. They return to Ypres. He watches the sun go down behind the ragged ruins of the medieval Cloth Hall and sees its last glowing rays caught by an observation balloon being winched down for the night.

Florence Farmborough notes in her journal for that day:

> In the early morning a man was led in who had been wounded by a German bullet. He soon came to know that he was the only soldier in that ward who had received a wound from an enemy. He strutted up and down feeling quite a hero among the many who had self-inflicted or accidental wounds.

TUESDAY, 30 OCTOBER 1917
Paolo Monelli is drinking brandy and waiting for news

Something big has been happening over on the Isonzo in the last week. With a single attack the enemy has succeeded in doing what the Italian army has failed to do with eleven offensives—that is, to achieve a breakthrough. And they are advancing. Monelli and the rest of the men on the northern front do not know exactly what has happened or what is happening. They are holding a good, strong position and until a few days ago were ready to sit out the winter in their newly constructed huts. They are at high altitude and there is already plenty of snow.

No, they know nothing. Neither newspapers nor communiqués are reaching them and they exist up here in the clouds of unknowing, fed on nothing but rumours, which are—as usual—confusing, contradictory and full of fantasy. Such as that the Germans have taken Udine. Such as that 200,000 Italians surrendered as prisoners. Or was it 300,000? The mood is gloomy. There is total silence in the officers' mess and Monelli is drinking brandy to take the edge off his feeling of hopelessness.

He writes in his journal:

Tragic news is reaching us from the front in the east. Our enemy is trampling the soil of our fatherland and our soldiers are throwing down their weapons. Here, nothing. Our waiting made worse by bureaucratic stupidities, by signatures and circulars, by the pedantry of nervous commanders and jokes from superiors we don't respect.

THURSDAY, 1 NOVEMBER 1917
Pál Kelemen sees an infantry battalion coming out of the front line on the Isonzo

A steady, silent rain is falling from a grey sky above a grey mountain. It is early evening and an Austro-Hungarian infantry battalion is pulling back after a period in the front line. Pál Kelemen is there and watches them stagger down the path from their positions up on the mountain plateau.

The Caporetto offensive* was actually only intended to give the hard-pressed Austro-Hungarian units on the Isonzo a small breathing space in the face of the threat of yet another major Italian push. But something—

* Caporetto is actually the name given to the place after the war, when the region became Italian; in 1917 it was still Austrian territory and the small town was called Karfreit. The name of the offensive is slightly misleading in that the real breakthrough took place north of Caporetto/Karfreit. This idyllic spot, now in Slovenia, is called Kobarid and has a small but excellent museum devoted to the battle.

mist, gas, surprise, the idiotic Italian dispositions, the experienced German units trained in new and mobile tactics*—produced a breakthrough far bigger and far deeper than anyone had dared hope. And then one thing led to another. Threatened with being outflanked, the whole of the Italian army on the Isonzo began a panic-stricken retreat towards the River Tagliamento. It was a huge triumph for the double monarchy.†

The battalion that Kelemen meets on its way down has not actually taken part in the attack but it shows the marks anyway. He notes in his journal:

> As they start forward or stand still, blocked by those ahead, or lie down at the roadside, it seems impossible that these are the fighting troops with which the statesmen and the generals are defending the Monarchy. That this tattered ravaged band with their shaggy beards, their crumpled, soaked, and dirty uniforms, their dilapidated footgear, and the exhaustion in their faces constitutes "our brave infantry."
>
> Now there is a halt. The whole battalion sinks down on the slope. Some of the soldiers take ration cans out of their knapsacks and with the long blades of their claspknives they lift out the food and shove it raw into their mouths. Their hands are black with dirt, horny, heavy moving. On their faces the wrinkles stretch and fold again as they chew. They sit on the wet stones and stare into the open tin cans without expression.
>
> Their uniforms are made of more inferior cloth than was

* The storm-troop tactics were used for the first time at the beginning of September when, without any great strain, they broke the Russian front at Riga and sent the whole of the Russian Twelfth Army careering wildly to the north. In France, later in the same month, German units trained in the new infiltration tactics beat back the British tank-supported breakthrough at Cambrai.

† The most famous description of the Italian collapse at Caporetto is Ernest Hemingway's *Farewell to Arms*. For all its literary merits, however, this is not a first-hand account. Hemingway did not arrive in Italy until the following year and was never present at the actual scene of the fighting. He wrote most of the book at home in Kansas City during the summer of 1928, after equipping himself with sundry maps and historical works. Another account, nothing like as well known although written by a man who was to become famous, is Erwin Rommel's *Infanterie greift an* (Infantry Attacks). The battles he took part in as a young lieutenant in an Alpine regiment are described in slightly Cubist language and in great detail, with the aid of plentiful cartographic material. He won the Pour le Mérite at Caporetto.

prescribed. The soles of their boots are paper, turned out for the profit of the army purveyors exempt from military duty.

At this hour at home, in houses untouched by war, dinner is being laid. Electric bulbs shine. White napkins, fine glasses, silver knives and forks glitter in the light. Men, clean and in civilian clothes, lead ladies to the table. Maybe even a band is playing in a corner. Drinks sparkle. With easy smiles they talk of trifles—in mixed company, conversation should be light and pleasant.

Do they think this evening of the shabby troops who, masters of a superhuman task, make it possible for so much to be the same at home? The same?—Even better for a good many.

SUNDAY, 11 NOVEMBER 1917
Florence Farmborough hears rumours of a coup

He is handsome, almost beautiful in fact, the twenty-year-old lieutenant who was brought in yesterday. Even as he was being carried in she noticed that he had "the regular classical features of the southern Russian; dark, curly hair; light grey eyes, heavily fringed with long dark lashes." She has also noticed that his body is well formed. His name is Sergei and his batman is with him. The latter has told them that the lieutenant is the eldest of a family of seven children, that he volunteered at the age of seventeen and was selected for officer training.

The young lieutenant is a difficult patient. He is agitated, in pain, frightened and demanding; against the doctors' express instructions, he wants to be lifted out of his bed; he shouts orders and yells at his poor batman, who obviously loves his lieutenant and makes awkward efforts to help him in every way possible. The prognosis is bad: the lieutenant has severe stomach wounds—his bladder is shredded and his intestines punctured in many places. But the surgeons have done what they can and all they can do now is hope for the best. The twenty-year-old lieutenant roars at his batman: "Away to the trenches, scoundrel! Away to the very foremost fighting line!"

Florence sees how the little man sidles away to the next ward to wait for his master's temper to pass. For some reason the lieutenant calls Florence Zina: he is probably becoming delirious.

They are still in a relatively isolated location on the Romanian front, but some rather sensational news reached them from Russia today. There was a coup in Petrograd three days ago, organised by the Bolsheviks, one of the revolutionary factions. Unrest has been spreading ever since. The picture is still confused and contradictory and a great deal is merely rumour, but it seems that the Bolsheviks are now in power in Petrograd while the Kerensky regime is still hanging on in Moscow. "Our worst fears have been realised: a civil war is in progress in Free Russia."

In the early afternoon someone makes the dreadful but not unexpected discovery that the lieutenant's belly is becoming discoloured. Gangrene. His death is now just a matter of hours away.

She sits at his side all night and lets the male orderlies take care of any wounded who are brought in. The lieutenant is rapidly sinking towards unconsciousness and death. He shouts for his mother several times, and the only thing Florence can do is to dull his pain with heavy doses of morphine.

He dies at half past five in the morning and his body is carried out into a small room. Florence sees him lying there—sees it lying there, rather—with eyes closed and hands crossed. His batman is sitting beside him, his face rigid and pale. The thunder of the artillery sounds very close but the batman seems unconcerned.

Afterwards Florence writes in her journal:

> I don't think I could stand any more. I had always hoped that my
> war experiences would, despite their misery and bitterness, act as
> a stimulus to my spiritual life, would heighten my compassion,
> would "strengthen my soul in all goodness." But now I wanted to
> find a quiet spot where the world was at peace.

On the same day Willy Coppens is at a party given by a British squadron in Uxem. He has been invited because he intervened in a dogfight between two British planes and seven Germans and his surprise action made the German pilots break off their attack. He writes:

> The dinner was very lively. The expressions of gratitude from
> the pilots I saved from the attentions of the German squadron
> increased at the same tempo as the generous quantities of drink

that were consumed. I became more and more convinced that I really was a hero, helped in this belief by the assurances of the others and a variety of alcoholic mixtures.

When he eventually returns to his own base on his motorcycle Coppens is very drunk and in the cold night air repeats aloud that he is a hero. During the night his friends nail up the door to his room so that he has to climb out of the window in the morning.

WEDNESDAY, 14 NOVEMBER 1917
Harvey Cushing takes the train from Paris to Boulogne-sur-Mer

Travelling by train is becoming more and more troublesome. To be sure of getting aboard it is necessary to be at the station at least an hour before the departure time and, once on board, the law of the jungle obtains, at least as far as getting a seat goes. Harvey Cushing has been on one of his many visits to Paris, where he is on various committees working to improve medical care in the forces and to spread knowledge of new methods of treatment. So that side of him is still alive—the practical and professional side, which was what drew him to France in the first place. But it is touch and go.

That, however, is not what is occupying Cushing's mind today as he sits on the rocking train that is taking him back to Boulogne-sur-Mer and the hospital where he has just started work. The time is just after ten in the morning.

The people sharing the compartment with Cushing present a picture of how big and complicated this war has become. There is a middle-aged French couple, she wrapped in a travelling rug and he immersed in the morning paper. There are several Russian soldiers, one of whom has colossal white mutton-chop whiskers. There are a number of Belgian soldiers, easily recognisable by the small tassels that dangle from their caps and which Cushing considers "silly." There is a Portuguese officer standing sulking out in the corridor (Cushing suspects that he has taken this man's seat). There is a pilot dressed in a dark blue uniform reading the risqué magazine *La Vie Parisienne*, notorious for its pictures of scantily dressed women (frequently torn out and used as pin-ups in the trenches and billets) and for the many contact advertisements from women seeking a (new) husband or, above all, from soldiers seeking a "godmother." People know or suspect that most of these advertisements are code for temporary sexual contacts and the American troops have received warnings from on high, exhorting them not to buy this French scandal sheet.*

Cushing has already started to put the prolonged and bloody battles around Ypres out of his mind. They finished just a week ago when Canadian troops finally took a heap of rubble, which was all that was left of the village that gave the battle its name—Passchendaele. It looks as if the British army command allowed the futile attacks to continue purely for reasons of prestige, refusing to call a halt to the whole thing until they could say that they had achieved their "aim."

Some aim. Cushing is feeling dark and pessimistic today. "One sometimes wonders what it's all about and what indeed we are all over here for," he writes in his journal, "and why we are actually here." Much of his gloomy mood is a reaction to the disturbing news from Russia and Italy. The Bolsheviks, with their slogan "Peace now!," have seized power in the east and the badly mauled Italian army has retreated from one river to the next. Will they really be able to hold their new line on the River Piave? (The reason Cushing's unit has had to take over the hospital in Boulogne-sur-Mer at such short notice is that the British unit that was running it has been ordered to move to Italy as quickly as possible.) Cushing himself feels that the Allies are in the worst state they have been in since the Battle of the Marne in 1914.

This mood of crisis leads, as always, to reproaches. Cushing glares at the Belgians and Russians in the compartment. The Belgians, he writes, no doubt wear those silly tassels "on the principle of dangling a wisp of straw before a reluctant mule." And the Russians just eat and do nothing: "The men won't fight of course and, worse, won't work." There is no solidarity among the Allies and reverses have come one after the other in rapid succession. Meanwhile, "the Hun is known to be planning to break the Western Front before spring." No, Cushing is not particularly optimistic and, like millions of others, feels that his fate is in the hands

---

* Given that the American forces also had a very strict ban on alcohol, warnings of this kind tended to reinforce the image of the Americans as moralising puritans.

of distant forces, forces that no one can control any longer. "Some kaleidoscopic turn may alter our destinies at any minute."

The pilot has put down *La Vie Parisienne* and started reading a novel
with the title *Ma P'tite Femme* instead. The train is swaying and clunk-
ing along.

THURSDAY, 15 NOVEMBER 1917
Paolo Monelli takes part in the defence of Monte Tondarecar

Wet snow and sludge. The army engineers have erected barbed wire
on the shoulder of the mountain and that is where the enemy *must* be
stopped. It is not the first time they have heard those words. Quite the
reverse. They have heard them time after time during the last month, but
the Italian retreat has continued in a series of leaps between mountain
tops and rivers: from the Isonzo to the Tagliamento, from the Tagliamento to the Piave. On the Asiago plateau in the north the line is still
more or less holding, but even there it is slowly moving back. If either
front gives way, the other will automatically be left in a difficult, indeed
impossible, situation.

The position they are to defend up on Monte Tondarecar is anything
but ideal. The field of fire is useless and the sector that Monelli's company has to defend is so long as to be ridiculous. On average he has eight
men for every hundred metres. Monelli himself is controlled and determined, even though he has been shaken by the retreats and the threat
of an Italian defeat—not just in a battle but in the war as a whole. He
really intends to fight here, however bad the position and the odds. The
latest entry he made in his journal is two days old. He wrote about how
sad it was that all those mountains had now been taken by the enemy.
"But," he concluded, "when they come face to face with our pain and our
hatred they will not get through."

The attack they have been waiting for begins.

Enemy storm troops rush forward. Shouts and screams. Monelli
glimpses a grey swarm moving rapidly. They are attacking in tight
groups, unusually tight for 1917. They consist of their own equivalents
in the enemy army—Austrian Alpenjäger. Shouts and screams and

gunshots. Weapons open fire, machine guns rattle, bullets whistle past. Monelli sees some of his own troops: De Fanti, Romanin, Tromboni, De Riva. They are unshaven and haggard and clearly just as determined to hold firm as he is. Their faces are remarkably calm. Shouts and screams and gunshots. The grey wave is slowing down, coming to a stop, being washed back. One of the other officers leaps up on the edge of the trench in triumphant ecstasy and screams abuse at the retreating enemy, who disappear back down into their own lines. They leave behind an uneven patchwork of motionless bodies. Shouts. Bodies hang heavily on the thin barbed-wire fence. That is how close they came.

This is repeated twice more. Then things settle down a little. A major in the artillery carefully looks over the edge and observes—with an expression that reveals his surprise—that the line actually did hold. He utters a few words of praise and disappears.

Monelli takes out his journal when the battle is over and, under today's date, writes just three words: "*Non é passato.*" He did not get through. That is all.*

MONDAY, 3 DECEMBER 1917
Elfriede Kuhr watches a coffin leave Schneidemühl

The day is bitterly cold but she stands there anyway. She waits for two endless hours, holding in her hand a rose she has bought with her savings. At about half past two the first rattle of drums can be heard. Then more noises: first the tramp of boots marching in perfect time, then wind instruments, then singing. She can see the procession now: the band in field grey at the front, then the padre, followed by the hearse and the mourners, and lastly a guard of honour of soldiers in steel helmets and carrying rifles.

The mourners? She ought to join them—after all, she is one of them.

Lieutenant Werner Waldecker is dead. He lost his life when his plane crashed two days ago. Elfriede heard the news when she got to school

---

* A vigilant reader might wonder how such an enigmatic entry can provide a picture of that day's fighting. Fortunately, in addition to other source material, the preface to the fourth edition of Monelli's book about his war experiences (written in April 1928) relates what happened in much greater detail.

yesterday. It is as if there is a "gaping black hole" in her head and all her movements are mechanical. The hole has now been filled with two questions. The first is, what does he look like now? Has his head been smashed, shattered to pieces? The second, how am I to keep my feelings hidden?

The hearse rolls towards her. She sees the coffin. It is brown and has a flat lid with a wreath lying on it. When the hearse draws level with her she takes a few steps forward and throws her rose up on the coffin. The rose slips off and falls onto the street.

The hearse moves on through the open gates of the goods section of the railway station and Elfriede follows it. The body will travel as registered freight. A reddish-brown goods wagon is waiting there on the track. The coffin is lifted from the hearse and there, among the stacked crates of goods, the padre recites something from a little black book. The men remove their helmets and recite the Lord's Prayer in unison. The men in the guard of honour raise their rifles and fire three rounds in quick succession. Silence follows. Elfriede can smell the cordite. The coffin and the wreath are lifted into the waiting wagon and two railwaymen in sooty working clothes close the doors with a bang.

She goes back out into the street and sees her rose lying there. She picks it up—the bloom is undamaged. She holds it under her nose and runs away, bent low. She can hear the military band playing behind her.

TUESDAY, 4 DECEMBER 1917
Andrei Lobanov-Rostovsky is alone on a mountain top on the
Pisoderi Pass

It starts off rather well. They leave the camp at the foot of the mountain at dawn and begin the long journey upwards. The road is narrow but well constructed, snaking up to the pass in sharp loops. The weather is good and the view is magnificent—wherever the eye looks it sees the high, dramatic peaks of the Albanian mountains. After a march of no more than six miles, however, the difficulties begin.

Andrei Lobanov-Rostovsky is in the Balkans, far from home and far from his own country. He is here as a volunteer in a unit sent to reinforce the Russian contingent in Salonica. His decision to volunteer has nothing to do with any thirst for adventure: rather the reverse, it is a carefully considered plan to get away from Russia, where a political revolution is turning into a social revolution. "Much blood is likely to be spilled and we can perhaps even expect terror."

He has tried, as always, to read his way towards understanding. He has been ploughing through historical literature for the last six months, books about revolutions (the French, of course, but also those of 1848) and about the struggle for power between Marius and Sulla in ancient Rome, for instance. He has sat pen in hand, taking notes and pondering, while Russia was beginning to fall to pieces around him. He thinks he has found an obvious parallel in the phases of the French Revolution. What would a sensible person have done in France at that time? He would have left the country in good time before the Terror and then returned after the fall of Robespierre. In that way he would have managed to leap over the destructive period and re-emerged when everything was getting back to normal again. That is what he hopes to do. That is why he volunteered to serve on this front. The uniform is his asylum.

Salonica, however, has come as an unpleasant surprise. It is partly the sight of the burnt-out city: "I had never seen desolation on such a vast scale as Salonica." Mile after mile of burnt houses. The civilians—Greeks, Turks, Jews, Albanians—living "wretchedly in tents or wooden shacks amidst the ruins of their burnt homes." And then there is the mood among the Allied units: it soon became clear to him that morale is at rock bottom and that they "all hated this front." Battles are infrequent but disease, above all malaria, is taking thousands of lives. In the better restaurants it is quite usual for bowls of quinine tablets to be put on the tables along with the salt and pepper pots. Off-duty soldiers frequently cause riots, and even in the officers' messes there are fights between men from the different armies. Lobanov-Rostovsky finds the latter particularly shocking, never having seen anything like it before. As a rule it is the same nationalities that gang together against others: the British, Russians and Serbs fight the French, the Italians and the Greeks. Somewhere up in the mountains a half-mad French colonel has proclaimed a little independent republic of his own, printed his own currency and issued his own stamps.[*]

Lobanov-Rostovsky's own plans are not working out as he predicted.

---

[*] The colonel was Henri Descoins; the republic the Autonomous Albanian Republic of Korçë, which reverted to Albania in 1920.

The tremors of revolution are being felt even down here in the Balkans. Unrest in his battalion has increased, especially since they received news that the Bolsheviks have seized power and started—yesterday, in fact— to negotiate an armistice with the Germans at Brest-Litovsk. The soldiers and the non-commissioned officers are grumbling, growling, contra- dicting and slow to follow orders, or they turn up late on parade. Sentries sleep at their posts. Officers are reluctant to issue ammunition to their men. And Lobanov-Rostovsky has actually been shot at, after which he was transferred and put in command of a signals company.

This is the company he is now leading over the mountains to join the Russian division stationed up at Lake Prespa, to which the only road crosses the Pisoderi Pass at 1,800 metres. The going is easy at the start but higher up snow is still lying and the narrow, winding road is cov- ered in ice. Lobanov-Rostovsky hears shouting behind him and when he turns round he sees that one of the horse-drawn wagons is sliding over the edge and falling. When they reach the wreckage one of the horses is already dead and he is forced to put the other one down. A little further on, the gradient is so steep that the exhausted horses can no longer get a grip and the soldiers have to push the wagon metre by metre up to the pass. The seventy mules that are carrying the telegraph equipment man- age rather better, but they are not properly trained for the job and two of them hurtle down into the abyss. The hours pass and the company is stretched out in a long, ragged line of men, wagons and animals, all dragging themselves uphill extremely slowly.

It starts to snow during the afternoon and they have still not crossed the pass. Lobanov-Rostovsky is patrolling on horseback backwards and forwards along the ever more extended column. Around six o'clock they reach the top, by which time dusk is falling. On a snowy field beside the road he sees a soldier trying to get a single mule to move on but in spite of his efforts the stubborn beast refuses to budge. Lobanov-Rostovsky says he will wait by the mule while the man goes to fetch help.

Lobanov-Rostovsky waits and waits. No one comes. What is going on? Have they decided to forget about him? Or are they simply unable to find him in the dark and snow? What to do? It has been a year of disap- pointment and reverses for him but now he has hit bottom:

I seldom felt so miserable during the entire war. A biting wind was blowing; fog was rolling in and covering the hills from view;

night was coming on rapidly, and there I was alone on the top of
a mountain, holding a mule.

Finally, he hears some voices in the darkness and he shouts. It is a
couple of latecomers with their wagon and horses. They help him with
the mule. It is two o'clock in the morning before the last wagon crosses
the pass.

WEDNESDAY, 5 DECEMBER 1917
Paolo Monelli is taken prisoner on Castelgomberto

As early as yesterday he began to suspect that the end was approaching. The end—in the singular, and with the definite article? This battle
might well have more than one outcome but the probability of its' having
a happy ending is shrinking by the hour. After an intense bombardment,
after being attacked with poison gas, after the threat of encirclement,
after failed counter-attacks, after confused close combat—after all that,
Monelli and his fellow soldiers have retreated and taken up position a
little lower down, in a wood on Castelgomberto. But once the sun rises
the Austrian storm troops are going to attack this position too.

This is the hour. The hour I have foreseen, however reluctantly,
ever since my first day in the war. It is as though some enormous
force has concentrated all the fighting and all the torment and
toil of the past into one single decisive, tragic moment.

It is cold, snowy and dark. Monelli and his men are freezing, as well
as hungry and thirsty. Yesterday's retreat was so hasty that there was no
time to eat the meal that had already been served, no time even to take
it with them. Their fear and their uncertainty are great. They do not
know where the enemy is. Monelli sends out a patrol to make contact
with their own troops—who are or might be or ought to be somewhere
to their left—but the patrol does not return. They get very little sleep.
They have a grenade launcher and they fire it blindly out into the darkness. They have ten boxes of grenades and would prefer to get rid of them

before the next attack comes. And anyway, why should the enemy enjoy the peaceful slumber they themselves are denied?

Dawn. As soon as there is enough light the Austrian machine guns begin to play on their position. And then the artillery. Smoke fills the earthworks, stinging their eyes and noses. The situation is becoming hopeless—the situation *is* hopeless. The company is shrinking, hungry and almost out of ammunition.

They surrender. Austrian soldiers surround them.

Monelli takes out his revolver, throws it away and watches it spin down a steep slope. He is filled with bitterness at that moment: thirty months of war and now this. He sees several of his old soldiers weeping. He hears one man exclaim, "But what will Mama say?"

FRIDAY, 7 DECEMBER 1917
Willy Coppens enjoys himself in De Panne

It is after lunch and they are already sitting in the cars ready to set off when a telephone message comes. A German aircraft is attacking some of the forward trenches. Can they send up a couple of fighter planes to drive him off? The German pilot has defied the awful flying weather that has kept the whole squadron grounded for two days and which has encouraged them to take a break from the tedium of hanging round the airfield by driving to De Panne for some entertainment.

Libeau* and his famous concert party are performing there in the hospital theatre. Libeau and his troop put on theatrical and musical productions behind the front and they often attract audiences of a thousand or more, most of them French or Belgian troops, many of them convalescents and all of them hungry for recreation and distraction. Two of the men climb out of the cars and hurry to change their clothes. The rest carry on to the theatre in De Panne, along the birch-lined road they now know so well. They do, however, see the first plane lift off into the grey skies. It is Verhoustraeten—Coppens recognises him by the special way he test-fires his machine guns. On this occasion it sounds almost like a greeting, and perhaps it is.

* Gustave Libeau (1877–1957), Belgian actor.

Later in the evening, during a pause in the entertainments, a brief telephone message reaches them: Verhoustraeten is dead, hit by a machine-gun bullet fired from the ground. His plane has crashed behind their own lines. There is a moment's silence among the young men in uniform but then the conversation continues "as if nothing has happened." Death is so normal, hovers so close to them that they simply cannot dwell upon it. Not if they want to continue doing what they are doing, anyway.[*]

But denial has its limits:

Later, after leaving the mess with a cheerful "Good night, gen-tlemen!," I walked past Verhoustraeten's room, which was next door to my own. It was now cloaked in darkness and there, in the doorway of his unlit room, I stopped, deeply moved because the whole drama of his disappearance suddenly became clear to me. Up to this point I hadn't understood the scale of the tragedy. I began to ask myself whether a sacrifice like this was really neces-sary, and I began to have my doubts.

THURSDAY, 20 DECEMBER 1917
Pál Kelemen is impressed by a battalion of Bosniaks in Paderno

The great offensive at Caporetto is over. Winter has come and the tough German divisions have gone off to practise their infiltration tactics on other victims,[†] while French and British reinforcements have arrived to support the reeling Italians. The front has firmed up along the River Piave.

---

* At the moment, at least, the situation is quite favourable. The slaughter of Allied airmen during the spring is a thing of the past and the war in the air is much more evenly balanced. Indeed, there are even signs that the Germans are under pressure. In this area, as in others, the weight of the Allied production apparatus has begun to make itself felt.
† Infiltration tactics meant that the attacking forces, instead of attacking on a long, unbroken front in the hope of overcoming the whole of the enemy line, functioned as small mobile units, which would try to exploit weak points in the enemy's defences and simply circumvent the strong ones. These small mobile units would then attempt to push as far as possible into the rearward areas, preferably reaching the enemy artillery, without which the tough strongpoints further forward would be lost.

Today Pál Kelemen meets a battalion of Muslim Bosniaks. Just like
the Muslim colonial troops in the service of the French, they have come
to be seen as elite units. And they are often sent into action where the
situation is unusually dangerous. Kelemen, urbane and refined as he is,
is rather baffled by these men, alien to him in many ways. He is frightened by their inexplicably warlike spirit. What can they hope to achieve
from this war? Bosnia was annexed by Austria-Hungary as recently as
1908. Kelemen thinks that at least some of the older Bosniaks there must
have "resisted the power whose reliable and diligent soldiers they have
become." But he still cannot avoid being impressed by them:

> Tall, lean, mighty fighting men, like the species of rare cedar now
> dying out. They stoop a little, as if embarrassed at having grown
> and developed so stalwart. When walking, they draw their heads
> down between their shoulders and their deep-set small eyes flash
> everywhere with piercing gaze. Seated, they cross their bowed
> legs beneath them, push the fez back to the crown of their heads,
> and smoke their long-stemmed wooden pipes with as much
> tranquillity as if they were at home in the fabled land of slim,
> lovely minarets. Almost all of them are in full manhood. Pointed
> beards frame the sunburned faces. They are resting now and eat-
> ing. The shabby tin cans of Army rations look strange between
> their crooked bony fingers.

On the same date Paolo Monelli reaches his destination, an old castle in
Salzburg, now converted into a prison camp. He has been marching for
almost two weeks in a column of weary, demoralised prisoners of war,
wearing ragged uniforms from which the medals and badges of rank
have been torn. Some of them have fought over food, and trouble has
broken out here and there, when some of the troops have exploited the
inevitable breakdown of organisation caused by being prisoners to rebel
against the strict discipline of the past and to attack their officers. Many
of them are happy that their war is now over—and they do not hesitate
to show it. Monelli has also noticed that, even though triumphant, their
enemy has his own significant problems: many of the Austro-Hungarian
soldiers standing at the roadside watching the column of prisoners have

looked undernourished and thin. (The enemy is clearly also suffering a desperate shortage of men since Monelli has noted several hunchbacks and even a dwarf among their number.) For Monelli and his companions life in the camp will begin today, but he has already recognised that his existence for the foreseeable future will pendulum ceaselessly between two states—boredom and hunger. He writes in his journal:

> We arrive at the castle in Salzburg on 20 December—a grim fortress with steep, thick walls on top of an inaccessible hill; no sun and we tremble with the cold in the empty rooms. In this northern winter, surrounded by fog and snow, the thought of traditional Christmas festivities is a torment. In this rhythm of misery, rendered even more bitter by hunger, there is no element of sweetness or delight to knock on the doors of a soul wrapped up in its own hatred.

MONDAY, 31 DECEMBER 1917
Alfred Pollard plays a joke on some Americans in Le Touquet

Perhaps it is his childish side showing through, perhaps it is his growing irritation with the Americans, probably it is a bit of both.

It is late in the evening as Pollard creeps cautiously into the long and narrow barrack room occupied by the American officers. He is accompanied by three friends. All the lights are out, but the light of the moon is filtering into the room through the windows. The only thing to be heard is the sound of men sleeping soundly, tucked up well in their sleeping bags and blankets.

Americans. Pollard, like most other people, knows that they are certainly needed. The French army has scarcely recovered from the colossal losses of recent years and from the mutinies in the spring; the British army is still drained of blood after the long, costly and failed offensive at Ypres; the Italian army is still reeling and weak after the sudden collapse at Caporetto in late autumn. And on the Eastern Front everything points to Russia being on her way out of the war. The Bolsheviks have come to power in Petrograd, voicing slogans about peace and concluding an armistice with the Germans—an armistice that is now two weeks old. All the German divisions formerly occupied in the east will now doubtless be moved west. So the Americans are certainly needed—their soldiers, their money, their industries.

If only they were not so, so . . . self-confident.

Pollard had expected the Americans to welcome advice, to be glad to share the dearly bought experience of the British army. But no. Many of the American officers he meets are either notably naive or unexpectedly arrogant and do not think they have anything to learn from their allies. They have, after all, been at war themselves for over a year. (Well, a war of sorts, if that is the right name for the skirmishes they have been having with Mexican bandits.*) The newcomers are clearly competent when it comes to exercises on the barrack square and their ordinary soldiers are keen, well built and well nourished. Even Pollard has to admit that. But the Americans think that the British methods of attack—which by this stage have become advanced, imaginative and increasingly successful but which demand close liaison between the various arms of the service, with creeping barrages accompanied by mobile and well-armed small units—are unnecessarily artificial and over-complicated.

When the British hear the Americans talk, they sometimes get the impression that the latter intend to turn the clock back to August 1914

---

* Since 1916 Mexico had been the scene of a civil war between the rebel Pancho Villa and President Carranza (a man with the interesting Christian name Venustiano). Allied propaganda in the United States worked hard to convince public opinion that Villa was some sort of German-controlled threat, and he went some way towards justifying their claims by accepting relatively small sums of money from German agents. Enraged by American support for President Carranza, Villa then attacked American citizens in northern Mexico and in March 1916 carried out a raid into New Mexico, where he attacked the small town of Columbus, killing some twenty Americans. The United States responded immediately by invading northern Mexico. (This was not the first time during this period that the American military had simply marched into various more or less sovereign countries. They fought against Spain in 1898, fought a colonial war in the Philippines between 1899 and 1902, went into Nicaragua in 1912, and sent the Marine Corps into Haiti in 1915 and into the Dominican Republic in 1916. This invasion of Mexico was the second within just a few years: they had mounted a military intervention in 1914 with the aim of toppling the sitting government.) For some time American forces chased the clouds of dust that the ever-evasive Villa and his men left behind them. Villa's raids across the border into the United States were still continuing at this point.

and advance in closed ranks with fixed bayonets. Pollard can only shake his head. The time will come when the Americans will learn their lesson but the price they pay will be in blood.

And there is another thing. The party animal in Pollard is irritated by the ban on alcohol in the American army and the hypocrisy it leads to. In private, virtually every American officer is quick to produce the bottle he keeps hidden in his kit. This evening, however—New Year's Eve, for Heaven's sake—all nineteen Americans on the course turned down the chance to celebrate and went to bed at ten o'clock. Pollard thinks that the placid Americans are more like bank clerks than real soldiers.

He is in Le Touquet at the moment, where he and officers of various nationalities are learning to handle the Lewis light machine gun. Pollard's summer has been a quiet one, his autumn likewise. He has had a number of postings behind the front, one after another. Among its other duties, his battalion has been guarding the Expeditionary Corps headquarters in Montreuil and in September it took part in suppressing the only minor revolt that this year of revolutions spawned among the British forces.* But Pollard's feelings are split. On the one hand, the lack of combat is getting to him, making him restless and bored. On the other hand, he has finally recognised the truth of what others have said in the past but he dismissed as rubbish—that "fellows who had a girl at home thinking of them were less keen on taking risks than the totally unattached." He can live with all these postings behind the lines. As long as he can be there at the end of the war, he will be satisfied.

The four Englishmen tiptoe up to the nearest bed, two men to a bed.

On the word of command, they lift their allotted bed and tip out the cocoon with its snoozing contents before rushing on to the next bed and doing the same . . . and then the next . . . and the next. Muffled screams

* The reference is to the mutiny in Étaples (known to British soldiers as "Eat-Apples") from 9 to 12 September. In Étaples, which was near the coast, there was a training camp where the discipline was unusually harsh. The whole thing started when a New Zealand soldier, who had been absent without leave, was arrested by the hated military police and accused of desertion. His fellow soldiers and other discontented troops gathered and demanded that he be freed; fighting broke out, shots were fired and one of the demonstrators was killed. More and more soldiers flocked to the spot and the military police were driven out of the camp without further ado. Disturbances and spontaneous demonstrations continued over the following days. On 12 September Pollard's battalion and two other reliable units were sent in, armed with clubs, and between them they succeeded in quashing the mutiny.

and loud protests echo round the walls. Some of the half-awake Americans start throwing wild punches but connect only with their fellow victims who, of course, hit back. A confused brawl begins in the darkness. Before anyone has managed to switch on a light, Pollard and his companions slip unseen and delighted out of the barrack room and into the night.

Nineteen-eighteen has arrived.

1918

This is going to be our evil inheritance, or our good inheritance, in any case our irrevocable inheritance—and we are going to be fettered by our memories for ever.

PAOLO MONELLI

Chronology 1918

18 FEBRUARY After an armistice, German forces begin to advance again in Russia.

3 MARCH Peace is made between the Central Powers and Russia at Brest-Litovsk.

9 MARCH Continued Allied offensive in Mesopotamia.

21 MARCH Start of a major German offensive in the west. Very significant gains.

29 MARCH French counter-attack in the west temporarily halts the German offensive.

4 APRIL Start of a renewed German offensive in north-west France. Significant gains.

9 APRIL Start of a German offensive in Flanders. Significant gains.

1 MAY The first American units go into battle on the Western Front.

7 MAY British forces take Kirkuk in Mesopotamia.

24 MAY British forces land in Murmansk.

29 MAY Start of the German offensive around Aisne. Major gains. The Germans soon reach the Marne.

15 JUNE Major Austro-Hungarian offensive on the Piave. Minor gains.

15 JULY Start of major German offensive on the Marne. Some gains. Three days later a powerful Allied counter-attack forces Germans to retreat.

8 AUGUST	Start of major Allied offensive at Amiens. Very significant gains.
3 SEPTEMBER	Start of the general German retreat to behind the Hindenburg Line.
15 SEPTEMBER	Allied offensive in Macedonia. Bulgarian army forced into a general retreat.
19 SEPTEMBER	Start of a major British offensive in Palestine. Major gains.
26 SEPTEMBER	Start of American offensive in Argonne. Significant gains.
28 SEPTEMBER	Start of major Allied offensive in Flanders. Significant gains.
30 SEPTEMBER	Bulgaria capitulates.
10 OCTOBER	After massive attacks, the whole of the Hindenburg Line is finally broken through.
24 OCTOBER	Allied offensive on the Piave. Very significant gains.
30 OCTOBER	The Ottoman army in Mesopotamia capitulates.
31 OCTOBER	Revolution in Vienna; the Austro-Hungarian dual monarchy is dissolved.
1 NOVEMBER	The Serbian army liberates Belgrade.
3 NOVEMBER	German mutiny begins in the High Seas Fleet in Kiel.
4 NOVEMBER	Armistice between the Allies and Austria-Hungary comes into effect.
9 NOVEMBER	German republic proclaimed following revolution in Berlin. Kaiser Wilhelm II announces his abdication.
11 NOVEMBER	Armistice. All military action ceases at eleven o'clock in the morning.

A DAY AT THE BEGINNING OF JANUARY 1918
Pál Kelemen watches the war in the air over Castellerio

A beautiful, clear and sunny winter's day. When the fronts are quiet, as here in northern Italy, the war in the air still continues. A big Italian Caproni bomber is droning along in the clear blue sky and the Austro-Hungarian anti-aircraft guns are aiming heavy fire at it. Puffy clouds of white smoke blossom like flowers in the sky, but always in vain.[*] The smoke from the explosions gradually thins and disperses in the wind. A solitary Austrian monoplane flies into view and begins chasing the slow, three-engined bomber. Pál Kelemen notes in his journal:

> Above us the big Caproni is seriously engaged with our little fighting monoplane. Our anti-air batteries send heavy charges against the sky without avail. The white smoke-clusters from the detonations spread and evaporate slowly on the sharply brilliant blue.
>
> Our flyer gets nearer all the time to the clumsily manoeuvring biplane, and the frequent cough of their machine guns can be distinctly heard on the earth. All of a sudden the Italian machine settles downward. Ours wheels above it for a brief moment, then flies off northward while at ever-increasing rate

[*] This is not unusual: in 1918 Austro-Hungarian anti-aircraft batteries on average achieved one hit for every 3,000 rounds fired, which was considered a quite respectable strike rate.

the Caproni speeds toward the ground, its motor stopped, the wings wavering, and plunges to earth.

By the time I get there the body of the Italian flying captain, killed by a machine-gun bullet, is laid out on the turf beside the plane. One wing of the gigantic bird of war, bent and broken, has pierced into the earth and oil is filtering out of the riddled motor.

The Italian officer is clad in a full leather suit, his faultless elegance disturbed only by the angle at which his cap is crushed over his clean-shaven face. A fine-worked silver wrist-watch ticks on unshaken and the whole body stretched out at ease seems to be only sleeping.

We search his pockets; his portfolio is handed to me. Besides letters, banknotes, slips of paper, there is a double-folded card in a hard black binding: "Season ticket to the circus, Verona."

Here on this barren shell-plowed field the circus is just a printed name on a piece of cardboard. The glittering lamps at the base of the box rows, the grubbed-up carpet of the sawdust, the snapping whip of the ringmaster, the bareback rider with her tulle skirt and flashing jewels, and all the other endless delights of youth have been left behind forever by one young life. The other slender rakish officers in the box will wait tonight in vain for this comrade. But the music of the circus band will still blare and the floury-faced clown will turn somersaults with paid good humour on a velvet cover on the sand. And the ladies will flirt from afar, just as if he were there, as he was perhaps even yesterday.

I should like to slide the card back under the bloodstained shirt so that, as in pagan times when everything that served the hero followed him into the tomb, this property of his also should disappear from the face of the earth and there should be at least one place left empty in his memory, in the circus in Verona.

Willy Coppens writes the following in his journal that day:

During a patrol over the southern part of our sector, in the direction of Ypres, I flew into a snowstorm and got completely lost. Our aircraft have poor compasses, located on the floor where they aren't much use. I don't recognise anything until I have the

Kemmelberg in front and then I get to Dunkirk, from where I have no difficulty in finding my way back to my unit.

MONDAY, 7 JANUARY 1918
Florence Farmborough arrives in Moscow

The train sways and clunks, sways and clunks its way through a white winter landscape illuminated by the weak morning sun. The settlements begin gradually to grow denser and at half past twelve they roll into the station in Moscow. The journey from Odessa has taken her a whole week, such is the confusion in Russia just now. The journey has not only been long, it has been extremely uncomfortable, and she has feared for her safety on a number of occasions.

The train has been full to overflowing with soldiers of all kinds in all kinds of moods: happy, aggressive, drunk, helpful, inconsiderate, euphoric, angry. During some stages of the journey there have even been people travelling on the roof, and sometimes people boarded the train by simply smashing the windows and wriggling through. They, like Florence, had left the front and the war behind them and wanted to get home as quickly as possible. The original idea had been that the whole of her disbanded hospital unit would travel together, but this soon proved impossible as they became separated in the crowds and confusion. She lost her precious seat when she went to help a pregnant woman who had been taken ill, so she has spent a large part of the journey standing with her aching head pressed against the cold window in the corridor. When she changed trains in Kiev and finally secured another seat, she did not dare move from it for two and a half days for fear of losing it—in spite of the fact that she had nothing to eat and very little to drink and was surrounded by the noise and smell of smoking, drinking and shouting soldiers. All of her luggage had been stolen by this point.

Florence is depressed and confused as she gets off the train in her worn, dirty uniform:

I had returned like a vagrant, bereft of all I had held dear. My Red Cross work was over; my wartime wanderings had ceased. There was an emptiness in heart and mind which was deeply distressing. Life seemed suddenly to have come to a full-stop. What the future held in store, it was impossible to predict; it all looked too dark and void.

It is less than two months since she was last in Moscow but the city has changed enormously. The darkened streets are patrolled by all-powerful and trigger-happy soldiers wearing red armbands. (Many of the people she knows intentionally dress in shabby clothes so as not to bring themselves to the attention of these patrols.) Gunfire can often be heard at night and her host family sleeps fully dressed so that they might leave the house quickly if necessary. Food shortages have grown much more severe and have reached famine proportions. The guaranteed daily ration consists of three and a half ounces of bread or two potatoes. It is now impossible to obtain even a simple basic like salt. There are still restaurants open but their prices are astronomical and the meat is usually horse flesh. The atmosphere is one of fear and uncertainty.

SUNDAY, 27 JANUARY 1918
Michel Corday contemplates the future

The bitter cold has begun to ease—just a couple of weeks ago the temperature was down to minus 18° C. The authorities have banned the sale of absinthe and forbidden the wearing of scarves by soldiers.* Cakes have been abolished (the tea rooms sell only pastries now), and the bread ration is soon to be reduced further—to ten ounces per person per day. There are rumours of imminent disorder in working-class districts, of imminent enemy bombing raids on Paris, and of an imminent German offensive on the Western Front. It is also said that an exclusively female circle of spies has been uncovered in the Parisian theatre world.

Corday writes in his journal:

The shipyard workers on the Clyde are intending to strike on 31 January "if peace negotiations have not begun before that date." This really does reveal a new challenge in the struggle between

---

* Corday does not explain the motives behind these measures.

the people and their rulers—the people are demanding to know why their rulers are forcing them to fight. It has taken four years for this legitimate desire to come to the surface. It has already achieved its aim in Russia. Now it is raising its voice in England. It is beginning to break out in Austria. We do not know how strong it is in Germany and France. But the war has entered a new phase: a conflict between the shepherds and their flocks.

TUESDAY, 29 JANUARY 1918
Richard Stumpf reads a call for a general strike

For the last two months SMS *Helgoland* has been in dry dock again. The major work being carried out means that the ship is filthy: "You can hardly touch anything without getting dirt on your hands." Stumpf has resigned himself to the situation. Discontent is simmering among ordinary people, but, although politics is the subject of much talk on board, sailors as a group are, in Stumpf's view, much too disunited, much too easily fooled, much too lazy and much too stupid to be able to do anything about the current state of affairs.

Stumpf has fallen back on his own resources instead and has found a new outlet for his energy: he plaits a kind of coarse, hempen shoe which he then sells to his fellow sailors. The business is going well and he has set up an improvised cobbler's shop in the ship's bakery, away from the prying eyes of the officers. The calendar says it is winter, the weather says it is spring.

On this particular morning, however, something happens that seems likely to go some way towards countering Stumpf's misanthropic pessimism. There is a rumour that socialist leaflets have been found on board and within a few minutes the whole crew knows what has happened. The sailors huddle in groups and the flyers are passed from hand to hand. He reads one of them himself and notes that it is unsigned and does not reveal where it was printed; he also notes that some of what it states is true but some of it is just "stupid platitudes and phrases." The main slogan is: "If Germany is not to be ruled by the sabre then you must prepare yourselves for a general strike."

The tremors that are just reaching the port of Wilhelmshaven have their epicentre in Vienna, hundreds of miles away. Around the middle of the month a wave of strikes broke out in the Austrian capital's armaments factories in protest at the reduction of the bread ration and the continuation of the war. The situation soon became so threatening that the Habsburg royal family fled the capital with an armed escort. The wave of strikes spread rapidly, including to Budapest and to the naval base at Cattaro, where the sailors arrested their officers and raised red flags. The unrest in Austria-Hungary is over for the moment but yesterday major strikes started among the munitions and metal workers in Berlin. The discontent in Germany is also about food shortages and the fact that the military men now in control are simply allowing the war to continue. The truth is that Germany is being ground down in a purely economic sense. The spark that set things alight was the news that the peace negotiations with Russia at Brest-Litovsk had broken down.* The strikers are demanding peace—a peace in which neither side will suffer annexations or reparations, a peace based on the right of peoples to self-determination.

The strike has spread right across Germany today and over a million people in Munich, Breslau, Cologne, Leipzig and Hamburg have withdrawn their labour.

Before lunch the crew is ordered to muster on deck, section by section. The officers address their men. On the one hand, they express their gratitude that the rabble-rousing leaflets were brought to the captain's attention so promptly and they exhort the sailors to do the same on any future occasion. On the other hand, the crew is given a strict warning against participating in strikes or other political activities.

Stumpf finds it difficult to know what is going to happen. He is well aware that there is widespread discontent: "If there was anyone capable

---

* Much of the responsibility for this may be attributed to the Russian Bolsheviks. Since 9 January the Russian delegation had been led by Leon Trotsky, who had been playing a carefully prepared (and transparent) waiting game. He expressed his negotiating strategy for dealing with the Central Powers with the kind of sophistry that was all too typical of him: "Neither war nor peace." It is hardly surprising that this slogan enraged his German military counterparts. It should also be said that a civil war was breaking out in newly independent Finland at this point: "White" and "Red" Finns began fighting against each other in a war that was also to some extent a sideshoot of the main war. This was partly because it was the main war that made independence possible and partly because German units gradually began to provide significant support for the Whites while Russians sided with the Reds.

of channelling this discontent, a major eruption would be virtually inevitable." There is plenty of grumbling among the sailors and the workers but the protests lack both focus and staying power. In his experience, the energy released simply becomes hot air after a short time. And when he looks at the dockyard workers on board the ship everything seems normal: they show no signs of wanting to lay down their tools, nor do they seem to be simply pretending to work.

But when Stumpf goes up close to one of the workers he hears him say, "Starting from tomorrow, we'll put a stop to all this hammering." By "hammering," Stumpf takes him to mean the war.

The following day there is an announcement that all shore leave has been suspended because of the unrest in Wilhelmshaven. At lunchtime almost all the shipyard workers lay down their tools and quickly leave the battleship. The sailors shout words of encouragement to them as they leave, advising them "never to come back." The sun is shining and the air is warm and spring-like.

On that day Harvey Cushing is in Wimereux, a small resort just north of Boulogne-sur-Mer. He is there to attend the funeral of his Canadian medical colleague John McCrae. McCrae's fame rests on a poem rather than on the fact that he was in charge of No. 3 Canadian General Hospital. The poem is called "In Flanders Fields" and there are few people who have not read its famous opening lines:[*]

> In Flanders fields the poppies blow
> Between the crosses, row on row,
> That mark our place; and in the sky
> The larks, still bravely singing, fly
> Scarce heard amid the guns below.

Since its publication in *Punch* in December 1915 it has become one of the Allied side's most often quoted and widely reproduced verses. And with its uncompromising message about the continuance of the struggle,

---

[*] The story—often quoted—that he wrote it in twenty minutes in May 1915 while sitting in the back of a little ambulance, overwrought after attending the burial of one of his friends, is sadly untrue. As is the story that he threw it away at first but a colleague rescued the crumpled piece of paper.

it was used in particular during the campaign to draw the United States into the war.

> *We are the Dead. Short days ago*
> *We lived, felt dawn, saw sunset glow,*
> *Loved and were loved, and now we lie*
> *In Flanders fields.*
>
> *Take up our quarrel with the foe:*
> *To you from failing hands we throw*
> *The torch; be yours to hold it high.*
> *If ye break faith with us who die*
> *We shall not sleep, though poppies grow*
> *In Flanders fields.*

McCrae died yesterday of something as banal as inflammation of the lungs. Cushing writes in his journal:

> We met at No. 14 General—a brilliant sunny afternoon—and walked the mile or so to the cemetery. A company of North Staffords and many R.A.M.C. orderlies and Canadian sisters headed the procession—then [McCrae's horse] "Bonfire," led by two grooms and carrying the regulation white ribbon with his master's boots reversed over the saddle—then the rest of us. Six sergeants bore the coffin from the gates, and as he was being lowered into the grave there was a distant sound of guns—as though called into voice by the occasion.

FRIDAY, 1 FEBRUARY 1918
Elfriede Kuhr's brother receives his call-up papers

It does not sound like a very pleasant experience. Elfriede's brother Willi is upset when he tells her how they all had to line up naked in a freezing barrack room. Willi has been exempted from military service so far for medical reasons: water on the knees and a weak heart "resulting from scarlet fever." But this has now been reconsidered. The German army, like all the other warring European armies, is suffering an acute man-power shortage. A doctor presses his stomach and listens to his lungs before announcing: "Sound as a bell!"

Willi spits and snorts: "The self-important fool! All he wants to do is to scrape together some more cannon fodder for Kaiser Wilhelm!" Elfriede and Willi's close friend Hans Androwski tease him and laugh: "What a magnificent sight you must have been—naked! A model of divine Olympian youth!" Then the tone of the conversation changes and they start discussing how Willi should handle the situation. Androwski, who is excused from service because of poor eyesight, says that what-ever happens he must avoid the infantry. The air force is best—behind a desk, of course, not at the controls of a plane. "Tell them that your hand-writing is fantastic!" Willi rejects everything they say and looks on the dark side: "Prussian military service. Now I'm right in the shit." Elfriede says that he had better not let their mother hear him say that—she still believes in the war and when Willi falls, Elfriede says ironically, she will see him as *a hero*.

Then they start talking about the war. Elfriede asks the same ques-tion as so many other people are asking: why, why have all these people died? "Millions dead for nothing, for nothing at all." Androwski does not agree. It has not been meaningless. By their deaths, all these fallen Russians have paved the way for the great revolution in their country. Elfriede becomes angry. "By their deaths? If that's the price I don't want any more revolutions." Willi does not say anything, just bites his nails.

FRIDAY, 8 FEBRUARY 1918
Olive King contemplates her lack of eyebrows

It is winter but it is unusually warm. Some Italian officers have appar-ently already been hardy enough to bathe. Olive King is no longer living in the little house on the edge of the burnt-out city of Salonica and has moved instead into a cabin improvised from an enormous wooden crate that once contained an aeroplane.

Bathing? Perhaps it is for lack of anything better to do. There is nothing new in Salonica. In spite of significant reinforcements join-ing the Army of the Orient, very little has happened. Critics of the

operation—and there are many of them these days—refer to the fortified city as Germany's biggest internment camp. There were attempts
to break through the Bulgarian lines to the north during 1917 but any
advances have been painfully small. (Sarrail himself, though, was
replaced as commander some months ago.) Part of the problem is that
disease is rampant. Nominally the Army of the Orient can reckon on
600,000 men, but once malaria, dengue fever and other afflictions have
done their bit there are only about 100,000 of them fully fit for service.
The hospitals are swamped.

Olive King, however, has not been suffering from any lack of activity.
Recently she has been making repeated trips to Corfu or, more accurately, to Santi Quaranta, the port right opposite the large island. The
American Red Cross has donated twenty-nine ambulances to the Serbian military medical service and she has been one of the people driving
the new vehicles to Salonica. The round trip takes eight to ten days and
by this point King knows the road well.*

The journey along these narrow, precipitous mountain roads is often
troublesome and sometimes dangerous. King has endured both snowstorms and breakdowns. She has noticed that she often bears the hardships better than the male drivers, "who hate the discomfort, the rain
& mud & cold." For her own part she says she lives "the gypsy life." Her
health is excellent apart from occasional toothache and the colds she
always treats with a mixture of boiling water, rum and masses of sugar.

It is quite clear that she is devoting herself to her work with the kind
of obsessive dedication shown by someone in need of distraction. To her
great disappointment her love affair with the Serbian captain Jovi has
come to an end. The last time they met was in October when, just after
she had been decorated with a Serbian medal for bravery shown during
the great fire, she met him on Corfu. (He was about to go to London on
an official mission.) They spent several days together and then said their
goodbyes at the boat back to the mainland. She cried a little—she would
actually have liked to sit down and howl. A period of loneliness and
depression followed, a depression that became severe when she received
a letter from Jovi telling her he had met someone else.

So now she is sitting in her wooden cabin writing to her father once

---

* The present-day road distance between Salonica and Santi Quaranta is 230 miles, but
King was not, of course, driving on modern roads.

again. He wants to have a photo of her and she promises to send one all in good time. It is not that there is any shortage of opportunities—there are a number of street photographers in the city and they have plenty of customers: "You nearly always see a Tommy standing up with a shame-faced defiant smile, surrounded by critical & jeering friends." But there are cosmetic reasons for delaying the photograph. When her stove would not light she poured in a sploosh of petrol and "whizz went my eyebrows and lashes and front hair, the second time this year." King does not want to have her photograph taken until they have grown back. She has already told her father in an earlier letter that she will probably never be able to return to an ordinary family life:

O, Daddy, I often wonder what you'll think of me when we meet after these five long years. I'm sure I must have got awfully rough & coarse, always being with the men, & I'm not a bit pretty or dainty or attractive.

On Monday she is off to Santi Quaranta again. Nothing, not a thing, is happening up at the front—as usual.

MONDAY, 18 FEBRUARY 1918
Willy Coppens flies over occupied Brussels

Coppens has done everything it is possible to do: tested the new engine, made sure the tanks are full to the brim, got hold of a small map, packed an automatic pistol and a box of storm matches (to set light to the aircraft if he is forced down behind enemy lines), and taken his best uniform cap with him (to wear if he is taken prisoner, since one cannot just be dressed anyhow in that situation). It is a beautiful, clear winter's morning with a blue, cloudless sky.

At 8:35 he takes off in his machine. His destination is Brussels. The city is over sixty miles away, deep inside German-occupied territory.

The purpose of the flight? There is no real purpose—as the Belgian generals have recognised, which is why they have imposed a ban on such long flights. Technically speaking, what he is planning to do is against orders and could lead to a court martial, but Coppens is prepared to take both that risk and the risk of flying so deep into enemy territory. To some extent it is just a matter of dash and élan, with the added attraction of doing something that is both dangerous and remarkable. During the night the very thought of this flight made him tremble with excitement. The flight is not just an enjoyable but empty gesture, however: the showing of the Belgian colours over a city that has been occupied for three and a half years is also a way of demonstrating defiance and a will to win—qualities that are needed at a time when weariness, uncertainty and doubt are more prevalent than ever.

Because how is it all going to end? There are probably not too many people who would bet on an Allied victory, and even the optimists coldly calculate on the war continuing into 1919. The French army has still not fully recovered from last year's mutinies, nor the British from the blood-bath at Passchendaele, nor the Italian from the catastrophe at Caporetto. Admittedly, the Americans are on the way, but there are still far too few of them. And Russia? Well, Russia has descended into revolutionary chaos and is to all intents and purposes out of it. There are, moreover, rumours of a massive redeployment of German troops from the increasingly quiet Eastern Front to the Western.

There is also something else drawing him to Brussels—his family. He corresponds with them by letter via Holland so he knows they are alive but he has not seen them since 1914. The simple fact is, he wants to see his home town again.

Just after nine o'clock Coppens passes over the front line at Diksmuide at an altitude of 5,400 metres. Beneath him he can see two French SPAD planes flying in the opposite direction. He is in luck. The French aircraft attract the attention of the German anti-aircraft batteries. He sees how they are surrounded by clouds of smoke from the detonating shells while he is allowed to continue untouched and apparently unseen. He is by no means an expert navigator so he is intending to stick to the usual procedure and fly by well-known and obvious landmarks, which is why his route does not make directly for Brussels. He steers a course up towards Bruges until he catches sight of the mass of red roofs in the distance, and from Bruges he follows the railway line that goes down to the capital via Ghent. Immediately south of Ghent, Coppens resists the temptation to launch an attack on a German two-seater that unexpectedly appears off to his right.

Now he suffers his first tremors of apprehension. When he looks behind him he can no longer pick out his own lines, and a little while later the River Yser and even Diksmuide are no longer visible. He is utterly alone. "Alone in a fragile craft" are the words that accompany him on his way. The feeling of isolation that comes over him is so strong that he ceases looking around him and fixes his gaze on the horizon ahead—even though this seriously increases the risk of becoming the victim of an unpleasant surprise.

When he is over Aalst, Coppens catches his first glimpse of Brussels. Leaning forward and screwing up his eyes, he can pick out the huge Palace of Justice, its colossal dome sticking up above the clustered roofs of the southern part of the city. Happy but confused, he begins to sing loudly, though the words are drowned by the drone of his engine.

Coppens passes over a train chugging along down there—the first sign of life.

At 9:52 he flies in over the city.

At the Gare du Midi he goes into a steep dive and sweeps low over the roof. At that height and at that speed his flight breaks down into a series of impressions of lightning. There, on the Avenue Louise, two trams are passing each other outside a couple of light-coloured buildings; there, at the market on Place Sainte-Croix, some stallholders are throwing vegetables into the air in joy; there are the trees in the Parc Solvay and the rippling mirror of the water reservoir; there, his parents' house, a tall white house with a red roof. Home! Coppens pulls his aircraft into a sharp turn to the right and inside one window of the house he sees the silhouettes of two women and instantly concludes that one of them *must* be his mother. At the rear of the house he sees the window of his own boyhood room. Through the gleaming glass he thinks he sees red curtains and something makes him think of the model aeroplane he hung on his ceiling perhaps eight years ago—it is probably still hanging there, somewhere in among the shadows.

After flying for thirteen minutes back and forth over Brussels, Coppens turns away from the city's tangle of roofs and lanes, palaces and avenues and makes for Ghent, and then from Ghent direct to Diksmuide and the front line. In the distance the North Sea is glistening in the sunlight. He knows now that he will almost certainly get back and he feels relieved, although the feeling is short-lived:

But when I thought of what I had just done and thought of my parents I was filled with despair yet again—despair that made me shrivel up inside. I have never again experienced such spiritual pain, almost impossible to bear.

At 10:45 Willy Coppens glides in and lands at the aerodrome at Les Moëres. He sees the narrow barrack blocks and the green tarpaulin hangars, but now his "feeling of despair has given way to one of triumph" and he laughs almost hysterically as he jumps out of the cockpit. He pats the hot engine cowling of his aircraft and walks away singing.

A DAY IN FEBRUARY 1918
Pál Kelemen witnesses an accident on the mountain road at Caldonazzo

He is still stationed on the northern Alpine front in Italy, with a view out over the flat Friulian plain. When the weather is really clear it is possible to catch a glimpse of the Mediterranean as a shining line far off in the distance. Rumour says there is to be a renewed Austro-Hungarian offensive, but where are the forces going to come from? The shortage of food and munitions is worse than ever and most units are far below their nominal strength. But warmth is beginning to return.

Provisions for the elevated sector in which Kelemen is located are brought in by lorry. Great skill is required to manoeuvre the heavy, clumsy vehicles along roads that wind and snake along the precipitous mountainsides. Pál Kelemen notes in his journal:

In the beautiful sunny weather a general comes out in his automobile to inspect one of the fortifications, beside him the indispensable aide—arrogant officer of the General Staff. Their car dashes recklessly ahead with continuous sounding of the klaxon, signalling from afar to the heavy provision truck to draw aside. It turns as far off the road as possible, but still there is not room enough for the big, varnished field-grey motor car to pass. The General Staff officer leans out, shouting angrily, "Pull over, there, you swine!" And the poor swine pulls over so far that he crashes with his truck, somersaulting into the abyss.

MONDAY, 11 MARCH 1918
Michel Corday attends a play at the Comédie-Française

It is the premiere of Anatole France's play *The Bride of Corinth* at the Comédie-Française in Paris. Michel Corday and his wife are, of course, present. The performance is interrupted in the middle of the second act: one of the actors steps forward to the footlights and announces that the air-raid alarm is sounding and German bombers are again on their way to Paris. Voices in the stalls shout: "Continue!"

The actors start performing again in spite of the fact that a fifth of the audience has disappeared. Corday is uneasy. He, too, would have liked to leave the theatre but is ashamed to do so in front of all his acquaintances on the balconies, so he and his wife stay. It turns into a strange experience. The sound of wailing sirens cuts through the high-flown speeches of the actors and at 21:25 the sounds of the first bombs are heard. They sound like slow, muffled drumming.

Paris has been bombed many times since the turn of the year, most recently three nights ago. The bombers—big, twin-engined Gotha aircraft[*] or, even bigger, huge, four-engined Zeppelin-Staakens—always made their raids after dark. The night sky was lit up by searchlights, exploding anti-aircraft shells and the silver streaks of signal rockets.

Paris is now a city with a total blackout. Once the sun has gone down people find their way around with small torches in their hands. (Criminals have been quick to exploit the situation and the number of street robberies has increased.) There are blue-painted glowlamps in the trams and in the Métro and Corday thinks that their light makes the heavily made-up faces of the street prostitutes take on the same colour as "rotting corpses." Important buildings and monuments have been shrouded in a protective covering of sandbags and the shop windows are covered

---

[*] Nicknamed "Wong-Wongs" by the British population because of the characteristic sound of the double, unsynchronised engines.

with aesthetically interesting patterns made by the strips of paper glued on to cut down the risk from shards of flying glass. After the raid of 30 January Corday saw pieces of curtain and wall-hangings and a woman's pink stocking flapping in the trees outside a bombed-out house in Avenue de la Grande-Armée. The windows were blown out in all the neighbouring houses and servants were going round sweeping up the shattered glass and putting in temporary fixtures made of newspaper.

Because of the dark and the great height the bombs are dropped from—usually over 4,000 metres—there is no point in the aircraft aiming at specific targets. The attacks are purely terror raids, even if on a limited scale. But they are having some effect and people have started to flee from Paris. The British and the French air forces are also carrying out raids, targeting the German cities in range—Stuttgart, Mainz, Metz, Mannheim, Karlsruhe, Freiburg and Frankfurt. Apart from Dover, however, London is the most bombed city in Europe.[*] At first it was fleets of Zeppelins but then, in the course of 1916, when these proved not to be up to the task, heavy bombers took over. But even there the number of casualties has not been really significant—the most in one raid being 162 during a daylight raid on 13 June 1917.[†] These bombing raids do, however, mean that yet another important taboo has been broken: the sole target of the attacks is the unarmed civilian population. Corday considers such behaviour barbaric.

In the interval between the second and third acts, Corday and his wife find their way down to the blacked-out foyer. It is empty apart from a statue of Voltaire hidden behind a pyramid of sandbags. The interval lasts for an unusually long time: the director of the theatre is involved in discussions as to whether the performance should continue. It is decided that the show must go on, even though the raid is by no means over. "Naturally," Corday comments sourly, for he is sure he is right in thinking that they all want to go home but are staying "for fear of being criticised by the others—who are all bursting to do the same. Pride means more than death!"

---

[*] Around 2,600 civilians were killed by Allied bombing raids against Germany; 1,736 civilians were killed or wounded by German bombing raids on Great Britain. In France, a combination of air raids and long-range artillery bombardment resulted in the deaths of over 3,300 civilians.

[†] London was only one of the targets on this occasion and the casualty count includes those who lost their lives in other places.

So they return to the auditorium for Act III. The raid is still going on outside when the curtain falls. The actors invite the audience to shelter in the cellars of the building. Corday and his wife follow the stream of people in evening dress down into the enormous vaults, where all of the marble busts that used to decorate the theatre are now lined up, cloaked in tarpaulins. Corday sees a uniformed man put his cap on Molière's head. The mood in the cellar is subdued and apathetic even though the actresses try to provide some distraction by reciting poetry.

At midnight someone shouts that the bombs have stopped falling. When they leave the theatre the streets are veiled in a dense fog. The little pricks of light from the pocket torches move around jerkily in the gloom.

TUESDAY, 12 MARCH 1918
Rafael de Nogales hears the thunder of artillery coming from the River Jordan

The headquarters is housed in a large Franciscan monastery. The mood is uneasy. Is the front east of the Jordan going to hold firm? The muffled rumble of British gunfire can be heard in the distance. The situation has become so critical that all officers and other personnel whose duties are not considered vital are ordered to take their weapons and report for battle. They are driven away in lorries in the direction of the artillery fire.

It is not perhaps the best time to pay a courtesy call, as Rafael de Nogales almost certainly knows when he enters the monastery to visit the commander. But how can he resist? The man he wants to pay his respects to is a man who is more than famous, having become something of a heroic icon. Otto Liman von Sanders, Prussian general, Ottoman field marshal. Grandson of a converted German Jew. Before the outbreak of war, inspector general of the Turkish army.* After the outbreak of war, the right man in the right place when the Allies landed at Gallipoli

---

* The significant growth of German influence in the Ottoman Empire in the years before the war made the Russians nervous and led them to consider their military alternatives. It was one of the factors in the background when Russia initiated its great programme of military modernisation, which in turn frightened the life out of the German general staff and led it to consider its own military alternatives. And so on.

and he, as commander of the Fifth Army, was involved in stopping what could have developed into a rapid catastrophe for the Central Powers but turned instead into an ultra-rapid catastrophe for the Entente. Someone who met the charismatic Liman von Sanders called him "a highly educated soldier with relentless energy, indefatigably active and stern with himself and with others." Unlike many of the other German soldiers sent to the Middle East to act as advisers and commanders, he has no great problem cooperating with the Ottoman generals.* A month ago Liman von Sanders had been dispatched here to Palestine to work his famous magic once again.

And it is needed. Gaza fell in November last year, followed by Jerusalem in December—the former a great blow militarily, the latter a political and prestige catastrophe. The front now runs from Jaffa in the west to the Jordan in the east. The British are presently continuing their efforts to hammer their way out of the bridgehead north of the Dead Sea.

The distant sounds of battle increase during the afternoon. Rafael de Nogales recognises that he, too, will probably have to leave for the threatened sector. Or as he puts it himself: "I began to get ready to contribute my grain of sand."

The phrase "grain of sand" is in itself not without interest. It is a sign that even de Nogales has at last been afflicted by the same feeling that has already led to the disillusion of millions—namely, that in his anonymity and interchangeability he has been reduced to a virtual nothing, a fleck, a drop, a mote, a particle, a thing infinitely tiny, swallowed by an enormous Something to which the individual is forced to give his all, but without his sacrifice affecting what happens in any perceptible or measurable way. That is why the decorated heroes and the famous generals are so important—they represent some hope that the opposite might still be true.

Since the Battle of Gaza de Nogales has spent his time far from the front, first in Jerusalem, where he received treatment for an ear complaint, and then in Constantinople, purely for recreation. There, one evening, while sitting at a magnificently spread dinner table, among happy people and magnolias in flower, it caught up with him, "that strange unease that *la vie en salon* often wakens in the hearts of those who wear

---

* Which did not, however, mean he had unlimited influence. He was ignored, for example, when he tried to put a stop to the genocide of the Armenians.

a sword and boots with gilded spurs. And without knowing why, my thoughts began to travel across the seas, to my distant homeland."

Just as de Nogales is about to set off for the front, some unexpected news comes in. The British have broken off the attack and withdrawn.

Magic. Or probably just the usual old reasons: misunderstanding, exhaustion, faulty intelligence.

SUNDAY, 17 MARCH 1918
Willy Coppens sees an insect turn into a human being

Nothing of any importance has occurred. The two patrols with three planes in each have joined forces to return to the aerodrome together. Then Coppens sees one of their pilots, De Meulemeester, suddenly throwing his plane into a steep dive. Coppens follows immediately.

Then he sees why—a slow German two-seater is below them.

De Meulemeester reaches it first, follows the rule book exactly and waits until the last minute before firing. The Belgian then shadows the German plane and continues firing salvo after salvo into his prey. Coppens follows. He sees a tail of blue steam pour out of the enemy aircraft and sees that the shots are still striking home. He sees the German plane suddenly keel over and break up. All that is left is a cloud of wreckage and debris.

Two objects emerge from this cloud of spinning and flying fragments. One of them is the fuselage, which plummets straight down, spewing black smoke. The other is the observer, still alive, falling head first towards the ground. The man is spinning slowly round in the air, slowly, his arms outstretched, like a man crucified. Coppens cannot prevent his gaze following the descent, even when the falling man shrinks to a dot, a minute dot. Time after time Coppens thinks that surely the man is going to hit the ground now, but the fall just goes on and on for what seems to be an eternity, until suddenly the dot stops.

Coppens is shaken:

The poor man! The poor man! This time, for the first time, I had seen the human being and could no longer hang on to my old feeling that it was some kind of gigantic insect I was dealing with.

When Coppens turns his aircraft round he passes the remains of the enemy plane, still drifting slowly down. A map that is floating round in the air attaches itself to one of his wing tips for a moment.

He needs "some kind of violent reaction" to shake himself free from the dreadful sight and the thoughts it has spawned. So he begins to put his plane through loop after loop, again and again. The others do the same.

THURSDAY, 21 MARCH 1918
Alfred Pollard hears talk of the German breakthrough on the Somme

The great German spring offensive began this morning. Even though they knew that the Germans had been moving masses of troops and materiel from the east, even though they had been expecting some sort of attack for a long time, it comes as a great surprise, not least because the attack is so successful. Most people had expected a repetition of the fate of Allied offensives, that is to say a slow, ultimately fruitless gnawing away at practically impenetrable defensive lines and taking heavy losses in the process. But, helped by a successful combination of stealth, an unexpected quantity of artillery and the infiltration tactics tested in Italy and the east, the German army has managed to achieve a great and unanticipated breakthrough.

Alfred Pollard writes:

The first we knew of the affair was an urgent order to pack up and be prepared to move at half an hour's notice. It was very interesting to see the effect of the order on the various fellows in the battalion. Those who had not been up to the line before were pleased; the others were divided into two classes. Some were down in the dumps, most were indifferent; a few like myself were frankly delighted. I was definitely filled with joy. After the terribly boring months through which I had just passed the prospect of some fighting was decidedly bracing.

SUNDAY, 24 MARCH 1918
Harvey Cushing finds it difficult to enjoy the spring in Boulogne-sur-Mer

Bombs have fallen during the night. Now it is a warm and sunny spring morning and Cushing is accompanying a general who wants to study the damage inflicted by the night raid. A bomb has hit the field hospital's stores and X-ray tubes; glass vessels and other laboratory equipment lie mixed with chemicals among the rubble that crunches beneath their feet as they walk around. The roof has been blown off but no one has been injured—not in the hospital, anyway. A little further away a number of houses have collapsed after being hit by another bomb and it is thought that there are still people under the wreckage.

They then move on to a nearby prisoner of war camp—No. 94 POW Camp—which the zealous general also wants to inspect. Cushing is interested and goes with him. When they arrive there the German prisoners are formed up outside the barbed wire in two groups of 500 or so. They are well treated, live in well-scrubbed barracks and are allowed to receive parcels from home. Some of the German NCOs have had new uniforms sent to them and they wear them on Sundays, decorations and all. They also stick rigidly to military etiquette in spite of imprisonment. The sound of heels being clicked can be heard throughout the visit. Cushing, however, is not particularly impressed by them. Even though the prisoners are obviously well nourished, he thinks they are short—even smaller than the British troops, who tend to be on the small side. He also thinks there are "few intelligent faces among them."

The British general, too, is punctilious about the formalities. He inspects both groups, passing from man to man. The general remarks on the fact that several of the Germans are wearing big, ill-fitting corduroy coats and he pounces on a prisoner who has mended his field-grey trousers with a *blue* patch. He then snoops everywhere in search of anything else he can criticise. On the rubbish tip he finds some potato peelings that could have been eaten and a bone that should have been boiled up for soup. When the inspection is over the prisoners march past the British general in columns four abreast, lifting their legs high in the classic Prussian goose-step.

In the afternoon Cushing is back at the large seaside villa where he is living. The warm spring air streams in through the open window. He looks out over the English Channel and sees three destroyers heading south. He sees some "absurdly camouflaged transports" moored closer to the shore, and he sees lines of fishing boats waiting for a wind. It is ebb tide and people are walking on the dry beach below the villa, enjoying the warm sunshine and looking for mussels.

Cushing is restless and ill at ease. The great German offensive is rolling on. It is mainly aimed at the British Fifth Army, which has still not recovered from the losses it suffered during the Third Battle of Ypres last autumn. The reports, as usual, are contradictory, censorship is tight and rumours plentiful—but the British do seem to be retreating. The hospital has received hardly any wounded men at all, which is a bad sign: the Germans are clearly advancing so quickly that the British are given no time to evacuate the casualties. Shells fired from some kind of giant gun have started to crash down on Paris. Cushing and the rest of them, however, have not received any new instructions and all they can do is "sit in the sun and stroll on the sands—and wait. This is the hardest thing to do."

He looks out of his window down onto the promenade and sees some officers sitting on a bench and playing with a child.

WEDNESDAY, 27 MARCH 1918
Edward Mousley turns thirty-two in Constantinople

Recent months have been full of variety. On Christmas Day, having been transferred to Constantinople, Mousley made an escape bid. It started well. By a mixture of bluff and good preparation he and his companions made their way along a well-reconnoitred escape route down to the Galata Bridge and sailed out into the Sea of Marmara in a boat acquired in advance by a helper. The boat contained a plentiful supply of eggs, to be used as food during their journey, but it lacked some vital pieces of equipment, bailing buckets in particular. The wind was strong, the sea running high and the current powerful. The mast broke and soon the whole escape attempt turned into a farce. Smeared from head to foot in smashed eggs, they headed for shore in a boat that was rapidly filling with water. They had no choice but to return surreptitiously to the house in which they were being held prisoner, where they managed to climb back in, sodden and covered in egg.

After that he had a nice surprise—a transfer to Bursa, a pleasant spa with famous sulphur baths. All this happened on the orders of Dr. König, his eye specialist, who had been the ship's doctor on the battlecruiser SMS *Goeben*, one of the two vessels involved in drawing the Ottoman Empire into the war in 1914.[*] It was in Bursa that the top British generals were being held prisoner and for a while Mousley was able to share their privileges in such matters as good and plentiful food, relatively recent newspapers and considerable freedom of movement. He played a lot of chess.[†]

Then the order came for him to be returned to Constantinople.

Mousley had hoped that this might mean he was going to be sent home as part of a prisoner exchange but yesterday he was taken instead to a notorious prison. He has just been informed that he is to be brought before a military court, charged with attempting to escape. He is locked in a small dark cell together with an Arab, a Turk and an Egyptian. When he looks through the bars he can see a long corridor, a lavatory and a burly guard walking up and down.

Today is Mousley's thirty-second birthday and he is very hungry and not feeling well. He asks for food but no one seems in the least concerned about him. He gets hold of a newspaper but that fails to cheer him up: the German offensive in France is rolling forward, seemingly unstoppable. He writes in his journal:

> My guards and gaol companions amused themselves by show-
> ing literally how Germany was now walking over the French and
> us. I, however, awaited the counter-offensive, if we were not too
> broken, and, in any case, the moment when the German advance

[*] The other was the light cruiser SMS *Breslau*. In August 1914 the pair were being chased by the British Mediterranean Fleet after bombarding Bône in French-controlled Algeria. They escaped through the Dardanelles and on reaching Constantinople were officially transferred to the Turkish navy (as were their German crews). The collaboration is widely regarded as instrumental in cementing the alliance between the Central Powers and the Ottoman Empire.

[†] Though not against General Townshend, who was spending his time as a prisoner of war comfortably housed in his own private villa on one of the Princes Islands off the shore of Constantinople.

must be outdistanced owing to the elaborate communications required for pushing on the great masses of men and materials of modern war. It was a most miserable birthday.

The only bright spot comes in the evening. Two of his cell mates start fighting and Mousley takes advantage of the confusion to slip away for a moment and leave a message with an RAF officer he knows to be in the adjoining cell.

SATURDAY, 6 APRIL 1918
Andrei Lobanov-Rostovsky draws his revolver in Laval

He is fairly certain he has never come this close to shooting someone during the whole war, and the irony is that he is threatening to kill one of his countrymen. Andrei Lobanov-Rostovsky's odyssey has continued, a journey not so much away from the security of home (even if that is the result) as away from the threat of the revolution.

It turned out that Salonica was no refuge from the troubles at home and that the tremors of the revolution were reaching even the Russian forces there, particularly after the Bolsheviks came to power. Why fight now? So Lobanov-Rostovsky continued his flight—to France, as company commander in a battalion of Russians willing to fight on, in Russian uniform though in the service of the French. (The overwhelming majority of the Russian soldiers in Salonica refused to join, forming revolutionary committees instead, waving red flags and singing the International. They had then been shipped off, closely guarded by Moroccan cavalry, to the penal servitude that awaited them in French North Africa.)

But the Russian Revolution is making itself felt even in France. Or, perhaps, just "the Revolution," because the mood is the same all over a Europe that is tottering grey, exhausted, disillusioned and drained of blood after almost four years of war, four long years in which all promises of quick victory and all hopes of inspiring renewal have been turned into their opposites. Lobanov-Rostovsky has not been long in the big camp at Laval where the Russian troops on the Western Front have been gathered, but he can already see signs "that the soul of the battalion [is] becoming contaminated."

Which is not really so strange. In the first place, Russia is no longer at war, the notably harsh conditions of the Brest-Litovsk Treaty between the victorious Germans and the hard-pressed Bolsheviks having been signed a month ago.* So, for the moment, Russians have no good reason to risk their lives. When the battalion arrived from Salonica the camp was already overflowing with demoralised and rebellious Russian troops, part of the Russian corps that had been stationed in France earlier. Meeting them has inevitably had an impact on the new arrivals. Moreover, Paris is not far away and the troops are easily affected by the agitation among the many radical emigrant groups in the city.

There have been many signs of unrest. During a parade a heavy bolt was thrown at the general in command of all the Russian troops in France. Whole platoons have suddenly gone on strike and, just as in Salonica, officers have received anonymous death threats.

Everything came to a head today because his battalion is to be sent up to the front for the first time. When Lobanov-Rostovsky arrives at the parade ground to inspect his company this morning, there is no one there. He is told that the soldiers have just held a meeting and decided to refuse to leave the camp. Lobanov-Rostovsky is worried and nervous to the point of cracking, but he realises that unless he does "something really drastic, everything [will] be lost." He does not know what to do, but he gives orders for his 200 men to be summoned from the barracks. It takes a long time but eventually they are all there.

He makes a short improvised speech to his company. He tells them that he actually does not give a damn for the political side of things but, purely formally, they are now part of the French army and have sworn to

---

* It was more of an expansionist decree than a treaty, under which Russia was forced to cede control of Ukraine, White Russia, Finland, the Baltic states, Poland and Crimea. Most of these were to become independent satellite states of Germany. The Caucasus was granted to the Ottoman Empire. Russia, moreover, had to hand over to the victors (or rather victor—the governments of Austria-Hungary and Bulgaria were frustrated and enraged that the fruits of victory were to go almost exclusively to Germany) enormous quantities of oil and grain, as well as a great deal of militarily important equipment such as locomotives, artillery pieces and munitions. The new Soviet Union of the Bolsheviks was set to lose 34 per cent of her population, 32 per cent of her agricultural land, 54 per cent of her industrial enterprises and 89 per cent of her coal mines. German forces had already marched into Georgia—with oil in mind—while German generals, intoxicated by this victory, are now talking wildly of transporting German U-boats to the Caspian Sea and perhaps even invading India.

fight until the war is over. And that it is his duty to ensure that the company goes to the front. Then he asks them if they are prepared to march. The answer is unanimous: "No!"

He has no idea what to do next so he waits a few minutes and asks the same question again. The answer yet again is a resounding no. His brain is working feverishly, and he is "watching the whole scene as though in a dream."

Lobanov-Rostovsky recognises forlornly that he has manoeuvred himself into an utterly untenable position and, more from despair than calculation, he draws his revolver, a gesture which he admits afterwards was "rather theatrical." Then he utters the following words: "This is the third and last time I am going to ask you. Those of you who definitely refuse, step out of the ranks. But I warn you that I will fire at the first man who does so."

There is complete silence.

Lobanov-Rostovsky calculates what the worst outcome might be. Is he really prepared to shoot anyone who steps forward? Yes, having uttered the threat he cannot do otherwise. There is, however, the risk that the soldiers will simply rush him and lynch him. Such things have happened before. In that case he will use the revolver on himself. "The seconds of silence which followed I remember as a kind of hallucination. Thoughts were whirling through my head. What to do next?"

The silence lengthens. Every moment of inaction, every second of hesitation on the part of the soldiers bring him closer to victory. The men realise this and the silence gradually softens; rebelliousness turns to docility. Someone shouts from the ranks, "We're not against you, personally, Captain." Still with his revolver in his hand, Lobanov-Rostovsky answers by appealing to duty and to principles. The silence continues. Then he asks those willing to serve to raise their hands—and the whole company declares itself prepared to go to the front. With a great sense of relief he gives his soldiers the rest of the day off: they will depart early tomorrow.

When Lobanov-Rostovsky leaves the parade ground he is staggering like a drunkard. The ground beneath his feet is spinning. He meets a fellow officer who stares at him in consternation: "What's the matter with you?" he enquires. "You're green and purple."

MONDAY, 15 APRIL 1918
Florence Farmborough arrives in Vladivostock

Early in the morning the train rolls slowly into Vladivostock. From the carriage window she can see the harbour, where there are four big warships moored, one of them flying the British flag. Florence Farmborough feels an enormous sense of relief at the sight of the Union Jack. It is as though all the tension, all the trouble and dark concerns are suddenly washed away just by the sight of that piece of cloth. She can hardly restrain herself:

> Oh! The joy! The relief! The comfort! The security! Who will ever know all that this glorious flag symbolised for us travel-stained, weary refugees? It was as though we had heard a dear, familiar voice bidding us "Welcome home!"

It is twenty-seven days since they left Moscow, twenty-seven days on a screeching, snorting goods train, together with strangers, most of them foreigners fleeing eastwards, in a dirty, uncomfortable wagon designed for prisoner transports. But even though the cold has been hard to bear and even though they have sometimes been short of both food and water—for a while they had so little water that no one was even allowed to wash their hands—she has been through worse. And their well-organised foreign papers, covered to overflowing with official stamps, have helped them get past suspicious Red Guardists and despotic railway officials.

The decision to leave was in a sense inevitable. She had no work and the situation in Russia and in Moscow was becoming untenable, with famine, lawlessness and imminent civil war. Even then it had not been an easy decision to reach, and before making it she was overwhelmed by a kind of depression. One of her friends came across her one day sitting and weeping, and she could not explain why, not even to herself, since there was no simple answer. She leafed through her journal entries and relived various unpleasant scenes with a shudder or with disgust, asking herself: "Was it *I*—really *I*—who saw that? Was it *I*—really *I*—who did that?" And she thought of all the dead bodies she had seen, right from the very first, little Vasiliy, the groom in Moscow who was not even a real victim of the war since he died of a brain tumour. She asked herself, "Will they be remembered? But who could remember all those many thousands and thousands?" When she said goodbye to her friends and host family in Moscow twenty-seven days ago she had felt clumsy and cold and words had been insufficient to express her emotions.

They leave the railway carriage and make their way into the town. She can see a polyglot mixture of nationalities and uniforms on the streets. There are Chinese and Mongolians, Tartars and Hindus, Russians (naturally), British, Romanians and Americans, French, Italians, Belgians and Japanese. (Two of the large warships down in the harbour are theirs.) The foreign intervention has started and what began as an effort to keep Russia in the war is on the way to becoming a stand against the Bolsheviks in Moscow. The markets and the shops are well stocked. It is even possible to buy butter. Once she gets to the consulate she meets a helpful official who passes over £20 sent by her brother in England. Sea transport out of Vladivostock can also be expected, though he is unable to say when.

She really enjoys being able to eat white bread and strawberry jam again.

That is the day Harvey Cushing writes in his journal:

> Unseasonably cold, with a high wind blowing from the north. An occasional plane struggles against it, but not many. This standing by with nothing to do but await orders is the very devil. It affects everyone alike, for we know that somewhere there is overwhelming work under which surgical teams are struggling.

THURSDAY, 18 APRIL 1918
Michel Corday overhears some card players in Paris

Yet another overcast day. The anxiety has eased a little, but only a little. The great German offensive has been going on for almost a month, but the push south towards Paris really does seem to have stopped and there has been a new series of attacks up in the north instead, in Flanders. At the same time, however, the Germans have started moving on the Oise and the Meuse.

The great topic of conversation in Paris is, of course, the giant cannon. Since 23 March the French capital has come under fire almost daily from some sort of special artillery piece, which can hurl its projectiles for eighty miles from a well-camouflaged position behind the German lines—a distance so sensational that the experts initially doubted its veracity.* The random bombardment (now here, now there, at a rate of two or so an hour), in combination with news of the rapid German advance initially caused something close to panic in the French capital.

Corday writes in his journal that the atmosphere reminded him for a while of the situation in August 1914. Every conversation began with the same anxious question: "Have you heard anything?" Stations were overflowing with people trying to find room on a train and the queues stretched right out into the streets. The banks were crowded with depositors seeking to withdraw their money for fear that it would all be lost if the Germans marched in. About a million people have left Paris by this time, seeking refuge in towns such as Orléans, the population of which has tripled at a stroke. Trade has diminished noticeably—firms dealing in luxury goods have been particularly hard hit and been forced to lay workers off.

Corday has noticed that most of those leaving the city do not want to appear cowardly and put forward a string of excuses to justify their flight. There is a joke doing the rounds: "No, *we* aren't leaving for the same reasons as all the rest. We are leaving because we are frightened." He feels he can sense a great deal of hypocrisy, not just in the furtive duplicity of motives for fleeing but also with regard to the type of people who are running away. According to Corday, many of those now leaving Paris have previously been vocal supporters of the war, exhorting others to "Fight to the bitter end!" Now that they are finally in real danger

* By using a very long barrel the "Paris Guns" fired shells up into the stratosphere, where the lower air resistance meant that the projectiles could travel further. The stresses created by firing the 21cm shells were so extreme that the calibre of the barrel widened slightly with every round fired, which meant that successive shells needed successively larger driving bands. Similarly, firing-chamber expansion meant that the explosive charge continually needed to be increased. Only sixty or seventy rounds could be fired before the barrel had to be rebored to 24cm. These guns were enormously expensive and time-consuming to manufacture, and, considering the outlay, achieved very little.

themselves they have immediately taken to their heels. (Corday also has the impression that it is the upper and middle classes who make up the bulk of the evacuees. They have the necessary resources to get out and the contacts that make it easier to do so.)

It is the very uncertainty of the situation that nourishes the fear. What is actually happening? Strict censorship—even of letters and post-cards—increases the sense of living in a no-man's-land between the fixed and the fluid, a twilight zone in which it is no longer possible to rely on what the press claims or the official communiqués state. In many ways these two media have merged anyway, and nowadays it is forbidden to claim in print anything that contradicts what is stated in a military announcement. Even what is said face to face may be punishable, and anyone claiming in conversation that the Germans are closer than the authorities maintain, or that enemy resources are probably greater than is officially admitted, may be charged with "alarmism." It is forbidden, for example, to discuss where the shells of the giant cannon landed or what damage they caused—to do so can lead to fourteen days in gaol.*

Prosecutions usually result from intelligence provided by informers. A regiment of civilian volunteers has been set up to eavesdrop on conversations on the street and call the police if they hear anything unacceptable. Telephone conversations, too, are listened in to. Today Corday notes some of the warnings recently issued in his ministry:

On such and such a day at such and such an hour someone from the office telephoned the prefect in Amiens and the latter answered that the situation was critical and that the British, as usual, were in flight. An utterly reprehensible conversation.

Or:

Extension such and such at your office rang a lady, number such and such, and asked what the situation was like. Inappropriate expressions were used during the conversation and this must not happen again.

---

* The punishment for this and similar offences was far harsher for those in uniform, whose crimes were subject to military jurisdiction.

Since the bombardment of Paris began Corday has noticed yet again how strong people's need for normality is—and how double-edged their talent can be when it comes to constructing everyday normality even in extreme conditions.

When the shells begin to fall, the police raise the alarm all over Paris by going round blowing their whistles and beating on small drums. This leads to more ridicule than disquiet (blowing a whistle and beating a drum simultaneously is more difficult than might be imagined) and street urchins, housewives and passing soldiers tend to laugh at them. Then the distant explosions come and Corday, who had never heard shells exploding before, describes the sound as "hollow, hard and echoing." He reports that when a shell landed one morning those nearby calmly continued beating their mats and that the sound of the mats being beaten drowned out the echo of the explosion. One of his friends did not even hear the explosion because the Algerians who have taken over the city's refuse collection were making so much noise emptying the rubbish bins.

Corday is horrified by the reactions: "Fifty metres away from the disaster people carry on buying and selling, making love and working, eating and drinking." A shell landed on the church in the Place Saint-Gervais during the Good Friday Mass. The church was full, since prayers were being offered for the many men who had fallen in the hard fighting of recent weeks. Seventy-five people were killed when the church roof collapsed.* On this occasion Corday was in the Métro and when he came up to street level at the Madeleine station a woman he did not know told him what had just happened. "Several young men sitting on a balustrade by the station entrance carried on swapping loud jokes."

Corday is sitting in a café today. There are four men at one table, playing cards and commenting on the bombardment of the last few days:

---

* Such a high casualty figure was rare. Accurate aiming from such a distance was impossible and the random landings of these giant projectiles usually resulted in far fewer victims than this. Indeed, many of them exploded harmlessly. Part of the explanation was that, in order to keep the weight of the shell down, the German constructors used a fairly small charge. Experienced soldiers hearing the explosions thought that it sounded like a much smaller 7.7cm shell. All in all, Paris came under bombardment forty-four times between 23 March and 9 August, during which 367 shells landed on the city and 250 people were killed.

I choose clubs . . . fourteen were killed . . . Trumps! . . . and forty wounded . . . Hearts! . . . women, too . . . Trumps! Trumps and one of spades!

SUNDAY, 19 MAY 1918
Willy Coppens shoots down his fifth observation balloon

The weather is beautiful. This morning Willy Coppens is flying towards Houthulst, where he knows there is a German observation balloon and he is planning to shoot it down. If he succeeds it will be his fifth kill, and five kills is the Belgian air force requirement for a pilot to be called a flying ace. There is a small flight of aircraft from his squadron keeping him company to protect him from German fighters. (An attack on a balloon is visible from a great distance; the sky will quickly fill with shell-bursts from anti-aircraft batteries and enemy aircraft will immediately rush to the scene to protect the balloon.)

They reach the front line at Diksmuide, where they see a flight of enemy aircraft heading south. Coppens and his escort turn towards them but the German aircraft seem to have no interest in a fight and just continue on their way. He sees the balloon. Puffs of smoke from the anti-aircraft batteries begin to blossom in the sky.

At 9:45 Coppens dives at the balloon and shoots it down in flames.

As soon as he lands he is immediately surrounded by the other pilots wanting to congratulate him. Not only the pilots: all the jubilation attracts some of the squadron's many dogs, among them the fox terrier called Biquet, the Alsatian called Malines and Topsy the cocker spaniel. Later that day Coppens and another of the pilots in his squadron are summoned to the headquarters in Houthem, where the commander of the Belgian air force officially congratulates him on having achieved the status of air ace. When Coppens returns he joins another patrol over the front lines at about half past six.

That evening his name is mentioned in the official Belgian press communiqué for the first time. Coppens is very proud and excited since he knows that the statement will not only be posted everywhere behind the front lines but will also be published in the foreign and the domestic press. He goes to De Panne and mingles with the people standing studying the latest communiqué and he tells of the "childish pleasure" he felt on hearing the soldiers reading it aloud and coming to his name—*his name!* "But that was in the beginning, before I got blasé and before I became well known."

The same day Richard Stumpf sees a warship being decorated for Whitsuntide. He notes in his journal:

> The little vessel *Germania*, which belongs to the munitions depot, anchored close to us. Her highest masthead was decorated with a large bundle of birch cuttings. Fresh green branches had also been tied along her rails and superstructure. I thought to myself that these people haven't lost their sense of beauty even after four years of war. Otherwise why would anyone risk his life by climbing right up to the masthead?

THURSDAY, 23 MAY 1918
Harvey Cushing buys sugar in London

The hospital is situated at 10 Carlton House Terrace, close to Pall Mall and with a view over St. James's Park. The fashionable address reveals that this is a private institution, solely devoted to the care of wounded officers and founded by a rich patron, in this case an upper-class Englishwoman, Lady Ridley.* Cushing has come to visit an acquaintance, the airman Micky Bell-Irving, who is being treated here.

Cushing is in London on official business. He is to meet a number of high-ranking people involved in the organisation of British military medical care in order to discuss close coordination of resources relating to the treatment of neurological disorders. He was certainly not sorry to leave Boulogne-sur-Mer. The second German spring offensive—up in Flanders—has fortunately ebbed away and there is an uneasy calm at the front. But German air attacks have continued undiminished. The night before Cushing left for England was bright, moonlit and cloudless and Boulogne-sur-Mer was heavily bombed.

* A cousin of the former First Lord of the Admiralty, Winston Churchill.

London is proving to be a confusing experience for Cushing.

In spite of the fact that the end of May is approaching, the city makes a grey and depressing impression. There are invalids everywhere. Most people seem to be longing for peace and there seems to be a general feeling that at least the war would have been over if the United States had not come in. And the mood has become much more open—the notorious British reticence has disappeared. Londoners have repeatedly come up to Cushing in the underground or on the street, obviously drawn by his American uniform, and politely offered him assistance or started explaining things that did not need explanation.

There are some food shortages in London, particularly of sugar and of butter, as Cushing has discovered. When he had breakfast in his hotel this morning he was served French bread with two small pats of some kind of unappetising, crumbling margarine, and there was no sugar for his coffee. At the same time, however, in a shop intended for American troops, he was able to buy two pounds of sugar for just a couple of pennies. His purchase was given to him discreetly wrapped in a box that had originally contained "Fatima's Cigarettes" and he gave it away immediately to an English acquaintance. Everything is available as long as you have enough money and the right contacts. Cushing does not think the general level of health has deteriorated, however, since people are eating less and walking more and "their minds are probably the clearer" for it.

Cushing enters the ward where his friend is being treated. Micky was injured not in combat but while he was practising aerobatics. He had looped the loop several times and executed a number of rolls when one of the wings suddenly broke and the plane spiralled down from about 5,000 feet. By some miracle, he survived, though seriously injured. One of his legs was so badly smashed that the surgeons had no alternative but to amputate it.

Micky is sitting up in bed clutching his stump with his hands. He is having appalling phantom pains in the amputated limb and is heavily drugged, but he greets his visitor with his usual friendliness and charm. So it takes a while for the American to realise that the drugged man in the bed has no idea who his visitor is. Cushing finds this distressing and writes in his journal later that Micky is "now a suffering wreck—death would have been less bad."

THURSDAY, 30 MAY 1918
René Arnaud makes his way back to his regiment at Villers-
Cotterêts

Arnaud's leave finished four days ago and he left Paris to rejoin his regiment and the company he now commands as a recently promoted captain. Rejoining them proves to be easier said than done as the regiment has been moved east, in the direction of the new German breakthrough. A couple of days ago the third phase of the German spring offensive opened, this time with massive attacks on the devastated old battlefields around Le Chemin des Dames. And, once again, the Germans have had considerable success: they have taken almost 50,000 prisoners and 800 artillery pieces and are moving with worrying speed towards the Marne, only sixty miles from Paris.

Arnaud has been following the same procedure for three days in succession. In the morning he leaves Paris by train for wherever the regiment was last located, only to find that it has moved on, so he is back in Paris by the afternoon, his mission unsuccessful. It is clear to him that the army high command does not really know what is going on and is trying by means of repeated chess-style moves to gather enough reserves for a counter-attack.[*]

When he arrives at his destination today he hears that his regiment is still there, at Villers-Cotterêts. He hitches a lift in a butcher's van for the last section. Arnaud does not fail to see the irony in this.

MONDAY, 3 JUNE 1918
René Arnaud leads an assault on Mosloy

He wakes with a jerk. There are trees around him and beside him is Robin, his lieutenant. "They are bombarding us." German 7.7cm shells

---

[*] Constant and confusing movements by train, backwards and forwards along the front line, were the lot of many German soldiers a few months later. By that stage it was their turn to be shunted back and forth in attempts to stem enemy pushes. It has been estimated that there were times when anything up to a third of the German army was sitting in slow-moving trains scattered across the French and Belgian countryside.

are landing around them. Short, loud cracks. He and the rest of the company hurriedly leave the copse in which they have spent the night and run for some buildings less than a hundred metres away. Fortunately for them many of the enemy projectiles turn out to be duds that fail to explode, a phenomenon that is becoming more and more common.

Down in a cellar they find the officer in command of the battalion holding this sector. Arnaud and his men have actually been sent to relieve a company in a different battalion, indeed, in a different division, but they got lost during the night and are not really sure what to do now. Once again, it is defensive combat that awaits them.

He thinks he can see signs in the French army of "a strange mixture of being on the way to losing control and on the way to regaining it." There are many indicators of crisis. Soldiers who have "lost contact with their regiments" are a common sight on the roads—he has heard the expression so often he is sick of it. An acute shortage of foot soldiers has meant that cavalry units have been hurriedly converted into infantry, something the ordinary soldiers view with malicious and ill-concealed joy since the men in the mounted units have been enjoying a comfortable life behind the lines up to now, waiting serenely for the promised but never realised French breakthrough.* The mood of shock and surprise that reigned a week ago has, nevertheless, begun to ease and the French army is gathering itself for a counter-attack. But panic is still lying just below the surface.

Arnaud explains the situation to the major down in the cellar, telling him they are lost and that he is therefore putting the company at his disposal. The major thanks him. The conversation is then interrupted by a fat sergeant major coming rushing down the steps:

"Major, the Germans are attacking with tanks."

"Bloody hell," the major exclaimed. "We'd better get out fast."

And with a quick movement, quite natural if hardly heroic, he grabbed his belt and his revolver, which were lying thrown on the table—but then he remembered me:

"Well, captain, since you're here, mount a counter-attack!"

"But . . . in which direction, mon commandant?"

---

* This joy was enhanced by the fact that the officer corps in the cavalry was a kind of special reserve for the unpopular French aristocracy.

"Counter-attack, straight ahead!"
"Yes, mon commandant."

Within a few minutes Arnaud's company is formed up in two lines with twenty metres between them. And off they go. He has been drilling his unit the whole winter. It has not been easy because many of the men are older, timid, inexperienced and untrained, men who have spent the greater part of the war in safe positions far behind the front line and who would have been permitted to remain there if it were not for the acute shortage of conscripts. Arnaud sees the lines advancing in excellent order and he feels pleased—it is almost as though they are on the training ground.

The company rushes forward, all of them take cover, wait, move on, throw themselves down again. At the third rush he sees that two men out to the left remain prostrate and do not accompany the rest—they are under fire. "Down, all men down!" They all stop. Arnaud scans the ground ahead. They are lying on the crest of a long slope and can see all the way down to the river. There are no enemy soldiers in sight. But yes, further away, under a tree, he sees the square shape of a German tank. It shows no sign of moving. Arnaud decides that enough is enough:

An inexperienced officer newly arrived at the front with his head full of prescribed theories would probably have assumed he should continue advancing, which would have led to the majority of his men being killed for nothing. But by 1918 we had enough experience of the realities of the battlefield to stop ourselves in time. The Americans, who had just left the front line close-by, at Château-Thierry, did not have this experience for obvious reasons and we all know the enormous losses they suffered during the few months they were active.

Arnaud hands over command to one of his warrant officers (Lieutenant Robin has been wounded in the arm) and goes back to make a report. He has carried out his orders.

As evening approaches they are relieved and sent to rejoin their regiment.

Arnaud hears later that there is a new duty waiting for him: he is to take command of the battalion since the major who had been in charge earlier has been wounded. The account of this, as given by the man bearing the message, is as follows: "That bloody heap of shit got a tiny bit of shrapnel in his hand and pushed off straightaway. The cunt—the wound wouldn't even have stopped my son going to school."

SUNDAY, 23 JUNE 1918
Olive King is awarded a medal in Salonica

It is a hot day and full of disappointments. Olive King knows that she is to be decorated again, this time with the Serbian Gold Medal for exemplary conduct, and that the ceremony is to take place at about ten o'clock. Making a reasonable estimate that she will be in time if she gets up at nine, she stayed up until 3 a.m. writing a report. (She is working hard on setting up a canteen for the underpaid and sometimes undernourished Serbian drivers she works with.) But she is woken up at six o'clock by someone pounding on her door and by a small face peeping in through her window and telling her she is expected at the garage. She takes a quick bath to wake herself up and sets off.

The ceremony does indeed take place at ten o'clock. A colonel makes a long speech in which he praises her contributions, after which he pins the round, gleaming gold medal on her chest. King notices a little box lying on the table alongside and thinks for a moment that yet another distinction is in the offing. But no—that is disappointment number one. At about half past eleven the next disappointment occurs. Artsa, one of the Serbian drivers, has promised to help her explain the sketches of the planned canteen to the Serbian engineering troops who are going to build it. But no—he fails to turn up as agreed. Having had no time for breakfast because of the morning rush, she is hungry and decides to have lunch. But no—the woman who services her cabin arrives unexpectedly to do the weekly cleaning and King has to stay there. Things improve somewhat in the afternoon and when the post arrives she is hoping for a letter from her father. But no . . .

Disappointments large and small. Apart from a few minor battles nothing has yet happened on the Salonica front. Breaking the deadlock is out of the question, especially now that 20,000 French and British troops have been shipped off to France to counter the renewed German offensive there. (Rumour has it that the Bulgarians, not the Allies, are planning an offensive down here—that is what some deserters from the enemy camp have said, anyway.)

Olive King is worn out, cross and irritable. She is longing to go home. She has been working here for thirty-three months without a break and without leave, but it is not just the monotony of Salonica and the trivial everyday setbacks that are wearing her down. Another love affair has come to nothing. Grief-stricken after the break with Jovi, she rebounded to another of the Serbs she works with, the said Artsa. Their romance became serious and he proposed to her, but her father forbade her to marry the young man. She obeyed him—apparently with no great resentment.

Something within her has come to an end. Thus, in an earlier letter, when she suddenly became ideological—contrary to her usual custom—and started preaching geopolitics and the aims of the war with a tremor in her voice, it is not too difficult to sense that the sermon is ultimately directed at herself. An attempt to plug the haemorrhage in her soul with words:

> Apparently there are still millions of people who have no notion of why Germany went to war. They have a vague notion that she wanted an outlet to the sea, & so walked over Belgium. She does want Belgium, & Holland too, but not in the same way that she wants Serbia, to join up with Turkey. The only way to save the British Empire is to support the Jugo-Slav dream of unity, to put a strong, friendly state where it will be a perpetual barrier to the "Eastern Push."

It is now evening and Olive King is sitting in her little wooden cabin with all the doors and windows open. It is hot and close. The cooling wind of the last two days has suddenly died down and she is "fed-up & weary of everything tonight." She drips eau de cologne on her feet and blows on it, feeling how the moisture evaporates with a short, cool caress.

SUNDAY, 30 JUNE 1918
Harvey Cushing discusses the future in Paris

Outside—a wonderfully warm and beautiful summer's day. Inside—
gloomy. It is the man in front of them who is spreading all this darkness.
His name is Édouard Estaunié and he is a fifty-six-year-old author who
won some success with his psychological, social-moralising novels just
before the war. (He belongs to the same generation as Marcel Proust and
is sometimes named in the same breath as Anatole France and Louis
Bertrand.)* The house is silent and empty. Estaunié has sent his family
away, away from the almost nightly raids by German bombers and away
from those long-range guns.

Cushing, too, has become thoroughly familiar with the bombing
raids. When he and a colleague were coming here a few days ago, their
journey on the Métro was disrupted by an air-raid warning. A little later
they were able to watch the attack from a balcony at the Hôtel Conti-
nental, which had a view out over the Tuileries: "Gothas—lights—
shrapnel—the explosion and flame of an occasional bomb—a small
fire—a pitch-black Paris." And they crossed the Place Vendôme, where
the pavements were covered in slivers of glass and the facades of the
building pockmarked by shrapnel. But it is not these attacks, which have
been going on for months, that have made Estaunié so depressed as he
sits at his desk. They may have contributed, but what really depresses
him is the overall state of the war.

The third German offensive since the end of March, north-east of
Paris this time, began little more than a month ago. The Germans demonstrated yet again that they can break through the Allied line wherever
they please and this time they surged forward faster than ever. Just two
weeks ago the Germans came to a halt and they are now no more than
forty or fifty miles from Paris. Everyone is expecting them to start moving forward again and the capital of France will be their next objective.

Cushing is taken to visit Estaunié by a colleague by the name of
Cummings. The three men talk about nothing but the war. Estaunié is

---

* In so far as Estaunié is remembered today, it is for his coining of the word *télé-
communication* in 1904. He was a qualified engineer and worked for the French post and
telegraph office.

horrified and depressed by the destruction of several big and beautiful French towns during recent months: "First Reims, then Amiens, now Soissons, soon Paris." Estaunié genuinely believes that Paris is about to fall, and he is convinced that the only thing left for them to do is to fight one final, heroic battle: "Better to go out against the enemy and lose 40,000 men than to lose them in a retreat like the last one." Cushing and Cummings try to argue against that—the army must be preserved at all costs, so that it can continue to fight. No, replies Estaunié, look at the Belgian army or the Serbian: they have been preserved but their countries no longer exist. France will also go down but she will go down fighting to the last man. *C'est effroyable.*

The two Americans keep trying to come up with a counter-argument and suggest that they themselves represent one such: the American army in France is steadily growing in strength. Cushing has heard that it now has fifty or more divisions, 750,000 men, in France and with the help of reinforcements on this scale it should surely be possible to halt the German assault. And then there is the lethal influenza that has just started spreading up in Flanders—rumour has it that it has already affected the enemy armies severely. But it is difficult to make any impression on the Frenchman's despair. Then Estaunié becomes philosophical: in the struggle between justice and barbarism throughout history, barbarism has always triumphed.

With pessimistic Gallic prophecies ringing in their ears Cushing and Cummings go sorrowfully out into the blazing summer sun. Finding themselves within walking distance of the Eiffel Tower, the Arc de Triomphe and other famous buildings, they spend the whole afternoon walking around Paris, eager to see as much as possible, eager to imprint it all on their memories. Both of them have a feeling that they might be looking at all this for the last time.

A SUMMER'S DAY, 1918
Paolo Monelli on life behind the wire in Hart

He has tried to escape twice, the first time only ten days after arriving at the castle in Salzburg. And twice he has been recaptured.

Some people have settled into captivity, determined to remain there until the end of the war. Monelli, however, is withering away in this grey and melancholy world of pettiness. He feels he is locked into an eternal, unchangeable, hateful present. Monelli is twenty-six years old and it is as if he is being robbed of his youth. Perhaps it is already lost. He daydreams a great deal, remembers a great deal, pines a great deal and conjures up pictures of his life in peacetime, images of simple everyday things that are now impossible, unthinkable even, like walking along a pavement wearing newly polished shoes, or drinking tea in a café with female acquaintances. He thinks about women a lot. There is a high level of sexual frustration among the prisoners. The food is bad and there is little of it, so hunger lurks dangerously close all the time.[*]

He is in Hart now, which is his third camp. They live in long barracks, stifling and fly-ridden in the hot summer sun. Over beyond the barbed-wire fence they can glimpse a rural idyll with the scent of new-mown hay, and somewhere beyond the blue-green mountains on the horizon lies Italy. Monelli finds boredom one of the hardest things to cope with:

> And today is like yesterday. Nothing changes. Today like yesterday like tomorrow. Reveille in the gloomy dormitories, evening inspection to make sure it is all dark and, bracketed between those two points, a meaningless existence in which people have stopped thinking of the future because they no longer dare to consider it, an existence that hangs there monotonously on the hooks of a few unchanging and frustrating memories.
>
> The stamping and tramping in the endless corridors of the linked barrack-block, where the only light comes from skylights in the roof and one is sometimes attacked by a nightmare that says that we are already dead and buried, that we are nothing but restless corpses that leave their graves for a short conversation with other dead men in the exercise yard. Hatred of the comrades whom the Austrians have forced you to become close friends with, the miasma of humanity, the dreadful stench of five hundred inmates, a hungry and egotistical herd, twenty-year-old bodies condemned to masturbation and inactivity. And it is not

---

[*] This was also true for the camp guards. There were food shortages all over Austria-Hungary by this point, largely because of chaotic conditions and a lack of transport.

that I think I am any better than them even though I can produce
the odd grain of wisdom now and then and even though a lively
conversation with friends about past battles can still enliven and
comfort me through the humiliations of the day.

Even I have learned to play chess; even I will sometimes press
myself against the diamond patterns of the barbed-wire fence as
an expression of my desire for passing women; even I will reluctantly hand over my kilo of rice to the communal pool as if it was
an obligatory contribution. And who knows, even I might stoop
to borrowing that pornographic book from a fellow-inmate.

TUESDAY, 16 JULY 1918
Edward Mousley writes a sonnet on a hill above Bursa

It is as if there are two people competing for space in his mind. Or perhaps
it is no more than the usual old conflict between reason and emotion.

One part of him senses that the war has reached a turning point.
It seems that the Germans will not get any further in France, and Germany's allies (the Austro-Hungarians, the Bulgarians and, not least, the
Ottomans) are showing every sign of war weariness. Mousley himself is
doing fairly well. He has convinced the Ottoman military court to find
him not guilty of attempted escape! He was helped by his own background as a law student specialising in international law and by his tactic
of mounting an aggressive counter-attack when in a tight corner. He is
now back among the captured senior officers in the spa town of Bursa
where, under close supervision, he is permitted to go fishing and watch
football.

One part of him is filled with despair as he sombrely watches the best
years of his life trickle away in captivity.

Today Mousley is once again on his way to take the waters and, as
usual, he is accompanied by an armed guard. It is a hot day and Mousley
feels unwell and tired. They walk up one of the hills that surround Bursa.
The view is magnificent, particularly of the high mountain, Kesis. After
a while Mousley realises that he is not going to reach the bath before it
closes and so he sits down by the roadside. There he writes a sonnet:

One day I sought a tree beside the road
Sad, dusty road, well known of captive feet—
My mind obedient but my heart with heat
Rebelled pulsating 'gainst the captor's goad.
So my tired eyes closed on the "foreign field"
That reached around me to the starlight's verge,
One brief respite from weary years to urge
Me to forget—and see some good concealed.
But skyward then scarred deep with ages long
I saw Olympus and his shoulders strong*
Rise o'er the patterned destinies of all the years
Marked with God's finger by the will of Heaven—
Tracks men shall tread, with only Time for leaven—
That we might see with eyes keen after tears.

"But," he admits when he ponders on this lyrical outburst later, "these moments were few." He then adds in the slightly pidgin language he has adopted during his years in captivity: "And the pressure of existence and shikar [hunt] for food and money, and general bandobast [organisation] of plots and plans and pots and pans engrossed much attention."

FRIDAY, 26 JULY 1918
Michel Corday looks at the women on a windy street in Paris

Corday is sitting on the train to Paris in the morning. Following his usual habit he is eavesdropping on the other passengers in the compartment. Someone says, "We are advancing everywhere!" A French lieutenant holds up that morning's paper in front of an American soldier, whom he does not know and who probably does not understand French, points to the bold headlines and says, "Excellent!"

A civilian gentleman is bubbling over with delight at the latest military successes. In the middle of the month the Germans began yet

---

* The Greek name for Kesis is Olympus. The sonnet was written at a time when there was still a large Greek minority living in this part of Turkey. The war that would end in their expulsion still lay some years in the future.

another offensive on the Marne but it has been stopped in its tracks by determined Allied counter-attacks. And now the enemy has ceased attacking and withdrawn back across that infamous river. The wild German bid to win the war with one knock-out blow has come to nothing. The failure is obvious to everyone, especially to all the armchair strategists in civilian suits. The result of the German gamble has been to make a number of dents in the Allied front line—dents that look impressive on the map but are vulnerable in practice. Corday hears an enthusiastic gentleman explaining the new and unexpected situation at the front to a somewhat doubtful captain:

> "I'm telling you, there are 800,000 men on their way there at the moment." The captain demurred uncertainly: "Are you sure of that?" The other man replied: "800,000, I promise you. Not a man less. And we're going to capture the whole bloody lot of them!" He leaned back and let his finger follow the operation on the map printed on the front page of the paper: "Look! There . . . and there . . . and there!" The captain was convinced. He said: "They really are thoroughly beaten! How they must hate it! Put yourself in their shoes . . ."

That same day Michel Corday hears about the death of a woman who ended up stranded behind the German lines in Lille at the beginning of the war. She succeeded in later rejoining her husband, who, when he heard her "praising the chivalrous behaviour of the German officers," murdered her with a cut-throat razor. Now he has been acquitted.

Later that day Corday and a friend are walking on a street in Paris. There is a strong wind. His friend is in an excellent mood, having received good news that morning from his son, who is an ensign in the army. And his friend's mood is further improved by seeing the wind pulling at the skirts of the women out walking. The war has changed everything, including women's fashions. Over the years, for reasons that are more practical than ideological, colours have become more muted, the material simpler, the designs more suited to work and an active life. And the changes have been thoroughgoing, affecting what is not seen as well as what is seen: the complicated and lavishly decorated undergarments that existed before the war have disappeared and been replaced by smaller items with less artifice, again designed for an active life. The almost obsessive curviness, inherited from the nineteenth century and requiring stiff corsets that restricted movement, has fallen out of fashion. Lines have become straighter and skirts have never been so short—and never have they been made of such thin and light material. The women on the street are having to struggle to preserve their modesty in the strong wind. There is a young woman walking in front of Corday and his friend. A sudden gust lifts her skirt to her waist and Corday's friend smiles contentedly.

SUNDAY, 28 JULY 1918
Elfriede Kuhr is working at the children's hospital in Schneidemühl

They do what they can. When the babies cannot get any milk they give them boiled rice or porridge or just tea. When there are not enough real nappies, as is frequently the case, they use a new sort made of paper. They are not very good—the paper sticks to the babies' skin and it hurts when the carers take them off.

Ersatz, everywhere ersatz. Substitute coffee, fake aluminium, imitation rubber, paper bandages, wooden buttons. The inventiveness may be impressive but the same cannot be said for the resulting products: cloth made from nettle fibres and cellulose; bread made from flour mixed with potatoes, beans, peas, buckwheat and horse chestnuts (which only becomes palatable a few days after being baked); cocoa made from roasted peas and rye with the addition of some chemical flavouring; meat made of pressed rice boiled in mutton fat (and finished off with a fake bone made of wood); tobacco made of dried roots and dried potato peel; shoes soled with wood. There are 837 registered meat substitutes permissible in the production of sausages, 511 registered coffee substitutes. Coins made of nickel have replaced coins made of iron, tin saucepans have replaced iron pans, copper roofs have been replaced by tin roofs and the world of 1914 has been replaced by that of 1918, in which everything is a little thinner, a little less solid, a little less substantial. Ersatz: pretend products for a pretend world.

Elfriede Kuhr is working in the children's hospital in Schneidemühl. It took her some time to get used to the work there, to suppress her feelings of nausea at the sight of blood or pus or bedsores or of heads covered in scurf. Almost all the children are suffering from malnutrition or have a disease that is in some way attributable to it. (Their inadequate diet a result partly of the successful British blockade of Germany and partly of the fact that the German agricultural and transport systems are being ground down by the almost superhuman war effort. Even when food is available there are no trains to transport it.) There is a sense in which these children are just as much war victims as the men killed at the front. Or the children who went down with the *Lusitania*. Child mortality in Germany has doubled in the last few years.[*]

Many of the little ones have been handed in by their mothers, young soldiers' wives who have reached the end of their tether:

> Oh, these babies! Just skin and bone. Little starving bodies. And how big their eyes are! When they cry it is no louder than a weak little whimper. There is a little boy who is bound to die soon. He has a face like a dried-up mummy. The doctor is giving him injections of cooking salt. When I bend over his bed the little one looks at me with those big eyes that remind me of the eyes of a wise old man, but he is only six months old. There is clearly a question in those eyes, a reproach really.

Whenever she can, she steals real nappies so that the little boy does not have to have those dreadful paper things.

Elfriede gets up at six o'clock in the morning, starts work an hour later and then works until six in the evening. Her brother Willi has been called up and is a private in the air force. At the moment he is still undergoing training. When she met him after he had joined up she thought he looked dreadful in his uniform and wearing a peculiar lacquered hat. Worst of all was seeing him standing at attention, rigid, absolutely still,

---

[*] Mortality among women also rose. It increased by 11.5 per cent in 1916 and by 30.4 per cent in 1917 compared with pre-war figures. Mortality among the elderly was 33 per cent higher in 1918 than in 1914. It has been estimated that 762,000 German civilians died from malnutrition and associated diseases during the war. The average weight of a nine-year-old in Vienna dropped from 30kg to 22.8kg; in the same city only 70,000 litres of milk were being consumed daily compared with 900,000 litres before the war. Numerous institutions for the mentally ill and for the elderly closed down simply because many of the inmates had died of hunger. On top of all this, the number of births fell by almost a half.

hands pressed against the seams of his trousers, his eyes fixed on some point in the far distance. It was just like when she had played at pretending to be Lieutenant von Yellenic, but this is for real and much better—and much, much worse. The last time Elfriede met Willi was on his birthday, a fortnight ago. On that occasion he said to her twice: "Everything's going to rack and ruin."[*]

TUESDAY, 6 AUGUST 1918
Pál Kelemen meets some American prisoners of war in Arlon

He is living comfortably in a two-storey building with his own bedroom, his own living room and his own entrance. It seems to be an apartment built to be rented out, but who would take their holiday in this part of Belgium? As a symbolic gesture of cooperation and gratitude[†] the Austro-Hungarian army has sent four divisions and a number of their famous 30.5cm mortars to the Western Front. Pál Kelemen belongs to one of these divisions. The train journey from Friulia took eight days, across the dreadful, empty battlefields on the Isonzo, up into Austria ("cities, cultures, women, but everywhere the thousandfold symptoms of the fatigue of war"), through Germany (where he saw the heavily bombed and panic-stricken city of Metz), past Luxembourg and across the Belgian border to the little town of Arlon. The place was under heavy artillery fire when the train rolled into the station. He was afraid.

Arlon has been occupied for four years and the German occupiers have done their best to impose a kind of normality on the town, but without success. Shops, hotels and restaurants are open as before but anyone can see that life is far from normal—even if you ignore the most obvious signs, such as the bombs dropped during air raids and the shells from long-range guns that continually plummet down, killing Germans and Belgians alike. In the first place, the town dies at exactly eight o'clock every evening, the curfew being upheld with Prussian precision and the

* The exact phrase he uses is: "Es kracht im Gebälk."
† After being saved by German intervention on numerous occasions since 1915 on the Eastern Front, in the Balkans and in Italy.

blackout being absolute. This is as different as it is possible to be from the carefree Austrian approach with its charm and its inefficiency: here strict discipline is the rule. In the second place, there are virtually no men here apart from the very old and the very young and the omnipresent Russian prisoners of war who make up the labour force. The men of Arlon either are away in the Belgian army or have been sent to Germany or elsewhere as forced labour. The Germans try to make full economic use of this and other occupied regions. There are women to be seen everywhere.

This ought to suit Kelemen, who has a great love of women, but he has quickly recognised that there is an unsurmountable barrier between him and the Belgians. The civilian population shows no respect for the occupiers and as far as possible even avoids looking at them. And if for any reason they are spoken to or faced with questions the locals simply pretend not to understand, and they do so with eyes and gestures full of scorn and defiance. In the hope of ingratiating himself a little with the woman who owns the house he is living in, Kelemen has tried to explain that he is a *Hungarian*, not a German, and that the Hungarians have frequently fought against the Germans throughout history. But the woman simply pretends not to understand. In Arlon itself he has already noticed "a charming young girl" and when he saw her standing in an open window a few days ago he immediately rode up and began conversing with her in French. He had hardly started his flirtation before an older woman appeared and drew the girl inside. It turned out she was the daughter of Arlon's chief of police—and he had been imprisoned by the Germans.

The fourth German offensive since March opened in the middle of last month, this time on the Marne, but it seems to have gone the way of all the others: initial major and rapid successes and significant Allied losses, which German propaganda blared out in bold headlines and in the triumphal tones of church bells, followed by a gradual slowing down of the advance as a result of supply problems and the tougher resistance put up by swiftly assembled Allied reserves. The involvement of American units is also becoming increasingly apparent. These new arrivals are fighting with a thoughtlessness bordering on nonchalance, utterly contrary to the new insights into military tactics gained in recent years, and they have consequently—and quite unnecessarily—suffered huge losses. But their sheer numbers are tipping the scales, all the more so since the aim of the German offensives was to achieve a decisive result *before* the Americans became seriously involved. Since three days ago, the German units have been roughly back where they started.

Arlon lies close to the sector of the front where the latest offensive took place and the Austro-Hungarian units are intended to be reinforcements for the German front line. Today, for the first time, Kelemen sees a small group of American prisoners of war being led past. He finds the sight more than a little demoralising and notes in his journal:

> Their amazingly good physical condition, the excellent quality of their uniforms, the heavy leather in their boots, belts and such, the confident look in their eyes even as prisoners, made me realise what four years of fighting had done to our troops.

On the same day Harvey Cushing writes in his journal:

> After three days in bed with a N.Y.D. [not yet diagnosed] malady which I regarded as the Spanish flu—three days grippe—or what you will. This came on top of two rackety days around Château-Thierry, getting back home supperless, cold and wet, in an open Dodge at 1 a.m. I had suddenly aged and our driver had to help me upstairs—teeth chattering and done in . . .

SATURDAY, 17 AUGUST 1918
Elfriede Kuhr looks at a dead baby in Schneidemühl

A summer's night. Warmth. He is dead now, that little boy of six months who had been Elfriede's favourite. The emaciated child died in her arms yesterday: "He simply laid his head, which seemed much too big for his skeletal body, on my arm and died without as much as a rattle or a sigh." It is now three o'clock in the morning and Elfriede is going to look at his body once more. It is still lying in a bed covered with a net, a bed that has been rolled out into the corridor where it is a little cooler. She has put freshly picked wild flowers around the thin little corpse but the effect is not particularly successful. "Unfortunately, lying there surrounded by the flowers he looked like an ancient dwarf who had been dead for hundreds of years."

As she stands there looking at the body, a faint sound suddenly rises from the bed. It is weak, a dull, muffled buzzing, sometimes louder, sometimes softer, sometimes not there at all. Puzzled by the noise, Elfriede bends forward. Yes, it is coming from the bed. Surely not . . . She looks and listens and realises to her horror that it *is* coming from the dead boy. But there is no way he could have come to life, is there? Yet the sound could be from his little lungs. She bends further forward—yes, it is coming from his half-open mouth. He must be trying to breathe.

She plucks up all her courage, takes hold and forces the boy's jaw open to give him more air.

And she immediately recoils as a large blowfly crawls out of the boy's mouth.

Feeling sick, Elfriede chases it away.

Then she ties the net back round the bed—tight, really tight.

SATURDAY, 24 AUGUST 1918
Harvey Cushing studies frozen hands in Salins-les-Bains

It has been raining almost all day. The journey up the hill is long and hard but is worth the effort. The view is breathtaking, as is the landscape, which is completely untouched by the war. Cushing is part of a small delegation visiting Station Neurologique No. 42, which is housed in the old hill fortress in Salins-les-Bains, south of Besançon.

Cushing is here for purely professional reasons. The army has many neurological hospitals and No. 42 specialises in a particular kind of brain disorder—the sort that results in frozen hands and lame feet. The first of these is of particular interest to Cushing. All the army doctors are familiar with the phenomenon: men whose hands are locked in a kind of permanent cramp, frequently twisted back towards the forearm in impossible-looking positions. A kind of origami of the muscles, yet rarely is there any physical damage to the extremities affected. They have, so to speak, simply frozen solid. Cushing is amazed at the variations and the French doctors have even developed a typology: *main d'accoucheur, main en bénitier, main en coup de poing* and so on.

The affliction often develops after a long period in bandages or in traction, but a different background is also well recognised. The defect frequently affects men who have received a small—indeed, often trivial—wound on the battlefield but who are afraid of being sent back to the front. Their brains, consciously or unconsciously, appear to be overriding the wound's insignificance, worsening its effects.

The treatment consists exclusively of psychotherapy and it is being led by a captain called Boisseau. He is very skilful and Cushing watches in amazement as Boisseau treats a newly arrived "self-deformed" soldier and carefully coaxes the man out of his deformity using words alone. In one room there is a small display of sticks and crutches and corsets and calipers that were used by ex-patients.

The treatment is not guaranteed to succeed. In the village at the bottom of the hill is a barracks to which the patients are sent on discharge. There they are divided into three groups: (a) fully recovered and fit for service at the front, (b) uncertain cases, (c) permanently ill. Cushing and the rest of the delegation watch the first group march past in full battle kit. One of the French neurologists notices one among them who is suffering a relapse and the man is immediately pulled out of the ranks to be sent back to Station Neurologique No. 42, where, after three days in isolation, the therapy will be tried again: "One mind struggling to get control of another that has good reason to resist."

They drive back to Besançon in the pouring rain. Later one of their guides invites them to supper.

SUNDAY, 1 SEPTEMBER 1918
Willy Coppens is confined to bed with a cold

The heat of August is past. It has been an eventful month. Willy Coppens has added to his list of kills by shooting down six more German observation balloons, his speciality. (He has made twenty-seven kills since the start of the year.) He knows the dangers, having returned home several times with holes punched through his aircraft by bullets and shell splinters. The rips are mended with white patches that stand out against the garish light-blue of his Hanriot machine. Just over a week ago he came close to being shot down by a German plane that had sneaked up on him.

Coppens is in a slightly strange frame of mind for all that. On the morning of 10 August he shot down three balloons in the space of an hour and a half, and

> while the flight lasted, all this success, allied with the sense of having escaped from danger, was exhilarating but as soon as I landed and was back in the company of the squadron, the combat which had filled me with such excitement a moment before lost much of its meaning. The joy died away and weariness and tedium took its place.

When they are not flying, their lives are characterised by the restlessness of youth. He and the other pilots are always on the lookout for fun—arranging parties, going to restaurants and to the theatre, playing tennis on the court they have built for themselves at the airfield and devising an endless string of practical jokes. The most recent of these involved telephoning another squadron and tricking the man who answered into believing that King Albert was coming to visit.

Today Coppens is confined to bed with a cold. This is unusual since all the time they spend out in the fresh air and at a high altitude seems to give them a resistance to minor ailments. He is reading a letter from his father, who is still in occupied Brussels. Coppens writes:

> The letter was phrased in the usual highly inventive language we used for this purpose but, reading between the lines, I could tell that he had heard of my latest successes against our hated enemy. But in one sentence, in which he advised me to be careful, I sensed his fear that I would push my luck too far and see it turn against me. Was that a somewhat prophetic apprehension as well as a natural one?

TUESDAY, 10 SEPTEMBER 1918
Elfriede Kuhr is reading a letter from her mother

Autumn has arrived. Most of the street lights are turned off because of the shortage of gas. They have run out of potatoes. Elfriede's grandmother has caught the flu that is going round and spends most of the time lying on the sofa. The brother of one of their neighbours has just had a leg amputated. Elfriede's brother has been given a job as an army clerk. And Elfriede has killed off her pretend alter ego, Lieutenant von Yellenic, because she thinks she is now too big for games of that kind. (She and Gretel gave him a proper funeral. Lieutenant von Yellenic lay in state wearing a cardboard Iron Cross, the ceremony being accompanied by the tones of Chopin's Funeral March and concluded with a final salute from three paper bags that Elfriede blew up and burst. Gretel wept inconsolably.)

Elfriede received a letter from their mother today, addressed to her and her brother:

Children, this autumn is making me depressed. It's raining, it's pouring down and it's cold. And can you believe it—I've lost my ration card for coal. The first thing I have to do tomorrow is to contact the coal merchant. Fortunately, he likes me and won't leave me in the lurch. The soul-destroying work at the office is starting to wear me down and I'm longing for freedom and music. But who's interested in studying music in the current situation? If it wasn't for faithful Fräulein Lap coming for her evening lessons the piano would be utterly silent. I shudder at the sight of the empty music rooms. Everyone in Berlin is calling for peace, but what kind of peace is it going to be? Is it something we can honestly look forward to? We will lose everything if we are defeated. Our brave soldiers! Dear Gil, dear Piete,* keep your fingers crossed for poor Germany! All this blood must not be allowed to have been shed in vain!

MONDAY, 14 OCTOBER 1918
Willy Coppens is wounded over Thourout

If Coppens had known that he was going to take part in a dawn patrol he would have gone to bed earlier. The lights were out and everything

---

* Their mother's pet-names for her children.

was quiet when he arrived back on his motorcycle at about midnight and read the orders for the coming day by the light of a match. He realised he would have to get up much too early.

Now it is five o'clock and he has had no more than four hours' sleep. Coppens knows why they have to rise so early: the Belgian army is going on the offensive this morning in order to increase the pressure on the already hard-pressed Germans. The decisive moment cannot be far away.

The problem is that the weather is misty, overcast and grey. The aircraft have been rolled out of their green tarpaulin hangars but you can hardly see them in the darkness. It is not light enough to fly; not yet, anyway. So they wait.

At 5:30 the artillery away to the east of them opens fire and the flashes of the guns melt into the thin red haze of the rising sun. Coppens has never heard artillery fire of such intensity on this sector of the front. He turns to the man alongside him and says, "Could this be the end of the war?"

One of the staff officers comes up to them at 5:35 with an emergency call from the front lines—they are to destroy the observation balloon at Thourout. The Belgian artillery is being subjected to a very accurate counter-barrage and the German observer directing the fire is almost certainly in the *saucisse* hovering in the air a little behind the enemy lines. Balloons of this kind, anchored by steel cables and equipped with a basket from which one or two observers telephone their observations down to the ground, are used by all the armies. They are a favoured aid for the artillery, but infantrymen hate the sight of them and they provide a welcome if dangerous target for airmen. The "sausages" are protected by clusters of anti-aircraft batteries and it is actually more difficult than people think to set fire to the hydrogen-filled bags. It takes courage and it takes special projectiles, in the form of either incendiary ammunition or rockets.[*] A successful outcome is by no means guaranteed.

At 5:40 Coppens takes off in his patched light-blue Hanriot. He has a new pilot, Etienne Hage, as his wingman. The cloud cover at an

---

[*] The pitting of aircraft against balloons was a case of nineteenth-century technology facing that of the twentieth. Unsurprisingly, modernity prevailed and a balloon of this type had an average lifespan of about fifteen days. The life expectancy of the observers was, however, improved by the fact that, since 1916, balloon crews had been equipped with parachutes (in contrast to pilots; see footnote, 1 May 1917, page 353), although these could not be deployed at altitudes below sixty metres.

altitude of 900 metres is unbroken and both Coppens and Hage fly 100 metres below it. The sun has risen but is only just beginning to penetrate the grey October haze as the two airmen fly towards the front in semi-darkness.

As they approach the lines of trenches Coppens sees that they will have to deal with not one balloon but two. One of them is hanging at about 500 metres over Thourout as expected, but a second is going up over Praet-Bosch—it has already reached an altitude of 600 metres and is still rising.[*] Coppens knows from experience that in a situation like this the lower balloon should always be taken out first because the men on the ground start winching a sausage down as soon as it comes under attack, and now that the Germans are using motorised winches the procedure can be a fairly rapid one. There is also the point that once an observation balloon is at a low altitude it becomes easy for the anti-aircraft batteries to hit an incoming aircraft—in which situation it becomes suicidal to continue with the attack. (British fighter pilots, for instance, will generally never attack a sausage at 300 metres or lower.)

Hage, however, is inexperienced and eager. Coppens is steering towards the Thourout balloon but Hage gets his aircraft in front and thus forces him to attack the higher balloon over Praet-Bosch first. Hage follows suit, leaving the Thourout balloon unmolested for the time being.

At six o'clock Coppens fires his first short burst. He sees the skin of the balloon catch fire and so starts to turn towards balloon number two. Fire spreads slowly in this raw, damp atmosphere, however, and Hage fails to see that the balloon is burning and turns back to attack it again. Coppens is uncertain what to do. He sees that they are already winching down the Thourout balloon and from the corner of his eye he catches sight of some aircraft he is unable to identify. They could be enemy planes. He cannot leave Hage on his own so he goes back and is just in time to see the Praet-Bosch balloon flare up and crumple in flames before spinning down to earth.

Now, at last, both pilots steer towards the Thourout balloon.

The balloon is descending rapidly and by the time they arrive it is already below 300 metres.

Nevertheless, Coppens flies through a storm of exploding anti-aircraft shells and swaying streams of tracer. He is so low that he can

* The maximum altitude for this type of balloon is about 1,500 metres.

hear the "evil barking" of the machine guns, a sound usually drowned out by the noise of the aircraft engine.

Seconds later, at 6:05, he is close enough to open fire. A moment later he feels a violent thump on his left leg and a white wave of pain washes through his body. The shock is so powerful that his right leg shoots out involuntarily, pressing the right rudder pedal to the floor and throwing his aircraft into a downward spiral. Heaven and earth change places again and again. At the same time a spasm of cramp locks his hand on the control stick's trigger and bullets spurt from the spinning, twisting aircraft.

The pain in his leg eases a little and with a great effort Coppens succeeds in pulling out of the spin. His left leg is no longer obeying him—it is hanging lifeless and he can feel the blood pumping out of it. (He learns later that a tracer bullet had penetrated the cockpit floor and struck the lower part of his leg, ripping open the muscles and severing the shinbone and the artery.) He can, however, still use his right foot to control the rudder, since the pedals are linked.

Coppens now has only two thoughts in mind. Firstly, he must reach his own lines—he does *not* want to be taken prisoner; secondly, he must not lose consciousness because if he does he will crash.

Although dizzy with pain and blood loss he rips off his goggles and his leather helmet and stuffs them inside his jacket. He then unwinds the silk scarf that acts as a muffler around his face to protect him from the cold. Cold is what he needs just now. Cold to keep him awake.

And it works.

After crossing back over the Belgian lines he crash lands in a small field by a road. Soldiers rush up to help him and in their eagerness to get him out of the bloodstained cockpit they literally tear the plane to pieces.

Along with two wounded soldiers, Coppens is taken by ambulance to the hospital in De Panne. Weak from blood loss and lashed by pain, he feels as if the bumpy journey in the ambulance is never going to end. He knows the road since he and his friends have travelled it countless times on their way to or from the pleasures of De Panne. As he lies in the windowless ambulance he tries to work out where they are and how much longer the journey is going to take.

At 10:15 the ambulance brakes to a halt outside the Hôpital de l'Océan and he hears the driver shouting that the famous pilot Willy Coppens is dying. He is carried in on a stretcher and while waiting for the doctor he sits up and manages to wriggle out of his leather jacket. That is the last clear memory he has.

After that unconsciousness, fever, ether and chloroform combine to leave only images of a floating, dreamlike kind: operating theatres and white-clad doctors; a tall, slim figure bending over him and pinning a medal on his chest; a man greeting him with a drawn sword and reading aloud from a communiqué. And the thirst, the constant thirst that always accompanies blood loss.

Afterwards he remembers "these dreadful days and never-ending nights" with horror. Even a week later it is still uncertain whether he will survive. His left leg is ruined and has to be amputated.

> My general condition deteriorated and my courage was failing. I no longer had the strength to resist. Being anaesthetised on the operating table every day gradually wore my system down and I became—in spite of all the care I was being given—a nervous wreck.

He sometimes suffers from a depression that is "far too terrifying to be put into words." The nights are the worst.

TUESDAY, 15 OCTOBER 1918
Alfred Pollard collapses outside Péronne

It has been a very unpleasant train journey and he feels cold all the time, even with a blanket to keep him warm. On top of it all, he has a splitting headache and when he does manage to grab a few short and restless snatches of sleep his mind is full of "strange nightmares."

Pollard is on his way to the front. He wants "to feel once more the thrill of 'going over the top.' " That is what he is telling himself. The German army has begun a general retreat and the end seems to be near. But it is not just the excitement of battle that is pulling him, he feels it is a matter of self-respect for him to be there at the deciding moment.

His year has been filled with a variety of tasks behind the front line, most recently selecting active soldiers from the many uniformed non-combatants cluttering the baggage train and the rearward areas. For every man in the trenches there are fifteen or so more involved in various supporting roles, not least in the business of keeping those at the front supplied with rations and ammunition. But the losses the British army has suffered are so great that the shortage of men in the front line has become acute. (France is also having to deal with the same problem and, out of necessity, the French army is now beginning to call up ever younger conscripts—they are filling the ranks with seventeen-year-olds.) The men who have been selected and whom Pollard has to train are anything but willing: they range from people with mild physical handicaps through to convicts who have been freed in order to fight— there are no fewer than eleven convicted murderers among his men. Pollard imposes strict discipline and is a hard taskmaster. The uniform he wears is tailor made.

The news that his unit is on its way to the front again has led Pollard to request leave from his duties in the training camp and he is now on the train to Péronne, where he hopes to be met by someone from the battalion. He is so cold that he is shaking and he is still being plagued by unpleasant fever dreams.

He gets off the train in Péronne a few hours after midnight. It is a cold and starry night. There is no one to meet him at the station so he leaves his batman to guard the luggage. The town is empty, silent, blacked-out and feels almost deserted. It is little more than a month since Australian troops recaptured it. Pollard makes his way out of the town and heads east, steering by the stars. He is bound to reach the front sooner or later and then he will find someone who can tell him where his battalion is positioned.

Pollard's steps become more and more unsteady. He falls over and has trouble getting up. He is ill. He has caught the influenza that is affecting so many people all over Europe, indeed, over the whole world. The disease originated in South Africa but has been called "the Spanish flu" or just "the Spanish."*

---

* The pandemic eventually killed at least 20 million people, more than died in the war itself. (Some estimates say 40 million died, others even claim 100 million.) The first outbreak came during summer 1918 and affected the German army worst. At a critical stage, when it needed all of its troops for the push on Paris, large numbers of men were knocked out by the illness. What made this pandemic so spectacular (apart from the

The road through the night gets narrower and narrower, or is it that his legs are no longer obeying him properly? He is waging what is to be his last battle, a battle between a body that is growing weaker and a spirit that will not accept the fact—the same spirit that has led him to risk his life time after time, in spite of the enormous risks and the unfavourable prospects. Pollard's feverish brain fills with "strange fancies."

He falls down again and when he tries to rise he steps instead "into an abyss." His last memory is of falling and of the fall having no end.

SATURDAY, 26 OCTOBER 1918
Edward Mousley witnesses a bombing raid on Constantinople

Mousley hears the sound of the explosions at about two o'clock in the afternoon. Bombers. He and the others in the large hospital run outside to get a better view. The sky is blue. Seven fast-moving aircraft fly in over Constantinople, followed by a tail of clouds from exploding anti-aircraft fire. The planes drop bombs here and there. Clouds of white smoke rise above the muddle of roofs, pinnacles and towers. Mousley notes with pleasure that the war ministry seems to have been hit.

The aircraft turn in perfect formation (they remind him of a flight of game birds), sweep over the Golden Horn away towards Beyoğlu, drop some bombs on the Galata Bridge and a few at the German embassy. Then they turn again and swoop down towards the main railway station, which lies right by the hospital. A machine gun set up in a neighbouring garden opens fire and its sharp chattering joins in with the distant thump of the anti-aircraft guns. A few more bombs sail down. One of them hits a barracks.

The puffs of smoke from the anti-aircraft guns continue to follow

---

unusually high rate of mortality—in most influenza epidemics the death rate was 0.1 per cent of sufferers, whereas this one claimed 2.5 per cent) was that young adults, usually the most resilient age group, were hit hardest. The reasons for this are still not clear. The symptoms were also unusually severe: those infected suffered a dreadful headache, an extremely high temperature and a painful phlegmy cough. They either died or recovered within three days. Although originating in Africa, Spanish flu was so called because the uncensored Spanish press was the first to report the outbreak upon its arrival in Spain. By then, however, it had already affected several of the warring nations.

the planes as they move around but none of them is hit. Finally, the guns stop their barking and the smoke clouds are dissipated by the wind. An Ottoman plane takes off to attack the raiders. Several Turks standing alongside Mousley point with obvious pride to the solitary plane. Two of the seven raiders break out of the formation and head for the Turkish fighter. Machine guns rattle high in the blue sky and a few seconds later it spins down to earth. The seven raiders then disappear westwards.

Some hours later Mousley is told the results of the raid. In material terms the damage is insignificant. A Turkish colonel is said to have been killed. But the effect on morale is much greater. As well as bombs, the seven aircraft dropped leaflets giving a detailed account of the successes and failures of the various warring parties. Perhaps most importantly, the raid has shattered once and for all the grand sense of invulnerability that has reigned in Constantinople. The city is in a state of shock. Mousley writes in his diary:

> When one realises how slender was the official hold that kept Turkey in the war over many crises, how indifferent provincial Turkey was about entering, and how averse to continuing for the sake of Germany, one can realise how air propaganda and attacks would have brought before them the meaning of this war.

He hears later that the anger stirred up by the raid has not been directed at its perpetrators—the British—but at Germany. Germans have been attacked in Beyoğlu and angry women have been threatening German officers with knives.

WEDNESDAY, 30 OCTOBER 1918
Harvey Cushing hears a young captain telling his story in Priez

Whatever it is that is wrong with Cushing will not go away. Ten days ago he admitted himself to hospital, reluctantly, even though he knew he was in a bad way. Cushing was giddy, had trouble walking, even found it difficult to do up the buttons on his clothes. He is in hospital in Priez and he is now recovering. He is spending his convalescence reading novels, sleeping, chasing flies and making toast at the little open fire.

Even though his body is still failing him his mind is as alert as ever and the professional in him is finding it hard to tolerate the lack of activity. One of the patients in his corridor is a young captain, a fellow American, and Cushing has learned to understand the young man's stammering speech and to recognise the sound of his shambling, jerky footsteps. The young captain is said to be suffering from some kind of shell shock. Cushing's own doctor in Priez knows of his interest in this kind of disorder and he has allowed Cushing to sit in when he is having sessions with this patient.

Today both doctors have carried out a final interview with the stammering young captain and Cushing then summarises the case in his journal.

The patient, referred to as B, is twenty-four years old, a clean-cut, fair-haired young fellow, of medium height and well built. He used to play American football. B does not indulge in alcohol or tobacco and he comes from a good, sound background. He has been in the National Guard since 1911, was stationed on the border during the war with Mexico in 1916, enlisted in 1917, was promoted to ensign eight months later and arrived in France with the 47th Regiment of Infantry in May 1918.

B has been transferred from one of the forward military hospitals to Priez to receive treatment for his serious psychosomatic problems. Apart from a couple of minor wounds (including burns from mustard gas) he was physically uninjured when he left the front line on 1 August, but he was suffering from severe visual and motor disturbance. B himself insisted that all he needed was rest, and a mild degree of force was necessary to bring him to the hospital. When B reached Priez he was blind and could scarcely walk.

As a recent arrival in France, B had been seconded to various units in the front line to observe and gain experience, which meant that he was quickly involved in combat. In May he took part in the British retreat on the Somme; at the beginning of June he was with the Marine Corps when it was given its baptism of fire in Belleau Wood; in the middle of July he was attached to a French unit defending itself against repeated German assaults.

At the end of July he was sent by lorry with his own regiment to the front to the west of Reims, where the French and the Americans were mounting a counter-push. The idea was that the regiment would act as firefighters, to be sent in wherever the attack was getting bogged down. On the night of 26 July they drove through a gas-filled wood and towards morning were dropped off to join an attack that was already under way. Since he was only a lieutenant, B knew nothing about the plan. This was his unit's first real battle and they had scarcely reached open ground before they came under heavy fire. The lieutenant colonel and one of the majors were seriously wounded and the other major and B's captain were killed soon after. This meant that B suddenly found himself the senior officer in the battalion.

In this chaotic situation, a general unknown to B "appeared from somewhere," pointed his finger and said, "You're to cross a river over there and take a town called Sergy." The battalion was already tired after the night's march and shaken by the heavy fire but B formed it up for battle. They advanced through a field of waist-high wheat under heavy German artillery fire, crossed the river (which proved to be hardly wider than a stream) and went on into Sergy. By about ten o'clock in the morning they had cleared the enemy out of the town. Later they came under a very heavy preparatory barrage and the German infantry mounted a counter-attack.

And so it went on. Attack alternated with counter-attack and in the course of five days the little town changed hands nine times. Time after time the battalion was driven out of the town back to the narrow river and the little mill that B had selected as a combined headquarters and dressing station. Time after time they counter-attacked and recaptured Sergy. They had started the battle with 927 men and twenty-three officers and towards the end of the fifth day they were down to eighteen men and one officer—all the rest were dead or wounded.[*] Cushing notes:

> B. admits he was getting rather fed up. He was acting as gas officer, for many of the men were suffering from bad burns and all had been more or less gassed.[†] Then as intelligence officer—in

---

[*] Hardly surprisingly, Sergy (today no more than a large village near the E50 west of Reims) is only about a mile and a half from the second biggest American war cemetery (6,012 dead) of the First World War. The cemetery is set beautifully amid greenery and situated almost exactly where the front line ran in July and August 1918. The "river" is still no more than a brook.

[†] They had been exposed to mustard gas, which can easily penetrate clothing, the soles

other words, as a runner, once or twice by day and two or three times by night, always in the open—a necessity, since lines that he got over to the 168th[*] were soon blown to bits and there was no one at the 168th P.C. who could read flash messages; there was no communication at any time with the rear. Also as medical officer, directing the getting in of the wounded, always under fire, back to the mill; he did two leg amputations himself with a mess-kit knife and an old saw found in the mill. One night they had sent back 83 wounded men on improvised litters.

When sufficiently quiet, the nights had to be spent in searching their own and the enemy's dead for food and ammunition. They once got down as low as twenty rounds of cartridges, and much of the time they used Boche rifles and ammunition—also Boche "potato-masher" hand grenades, which caused at first a good many casualties among the men, for they were timed at three or four seconds instead of four or five like ours. The Boche food was good when they could find it—sausages and bread and Argentine "bully."

The least fatigued men had to be used to get in the wounded, for it was an exhausting process, since they often had to be dragged along a foot or two at a time, as occasion offered. Many men with three or four wounds continued to fight—had to, in fact—and a sound man and a wounded man often fought together, the latter loading an extra gun even when he might not be able to stand. Their only protection was to get in shell holes.

During these days B. saw for the first time a case of shell shock, though he did not know what was the matter with the man—thought he was yellow. Every time a shell would land near,

---

of the shoes and the skin. (Even brushing against an object that has been lying on soil polluted with mustard gas can result in injury, and inhaling the vapour from someone else's gas-infected clothes is enough to cause illness.) Nothing is noticed at first but after about two hours the skin at the affected place begins to go red and after eight to nine hours it starts to swell. After about twenty-four hours masses of small blisters form on the swelling and these blisters then coalesce into a single large zone of injury. The wounds do not heal easily and the worst effects of gas are on the eyes, nose and mouth. In the worst cases the wounds can lead to blood poisoning and death, but as a rule recovery is achieved after six weeks of hospital care.

* The regiment holding the sector to his right.

he would race to shelter, shaking and trembling; but he always came back and got to work. He simply couldn't stand the explosions. They were all pretty shaky from the almost constant artillery fire—high explosive alternating with gas of one kind or another. Many of the men still fighting had mustard burns.

But almost the worst was a "rotten-pear" gas which made them sneeze and often vomit in their masks, so they had to throw them away and take a chance. Everyone was more or less affected, and marksmanship was poor from lachrymation.

On Monday B. was quite badly stunned by a high-explosive fragment which struck his helmet—like getting hit in the temple by a pitched baseball. Men often thought they were wounded—would feel a blow on the leg, perhaps, and see blood and a tear, but on slipping off their trousers would find only a bruise, the blood having come from a neighbor's wound.

The patient tells Cushing and his colleague that they were relieved at sunset on the Wednesday. Even though they had scarcely slept in six days they were forced to march all night and it was not until lunch the next day that they could halt. They were then given hot food and a sympathetic lieutenant colonel forced the men to lie down and sleep.

B himself did not get any rest. He discovered that his code book was missing so he borrowed a motorcycle and rode back to Sergy. He found his code book there in his uniform jacket, which he had folded up and used as a cushion under the head of a wounded man. The man was dead but the code book was still there. Just as B was about to leave the place he found a wounded man who had been forgotten down by the bank of the river. B tried to carry him across the stream but came under fire. The wounded man was shot to pieces and B himself took a violent bang. Dazed, he found the motorcycle and rode away, still under fire.

When he got back people noticed at once that something was wrong. B was shaking and stammering and even found it difficult to sit down. They gave him some whisky to drink and poured ice-cold water over him. Nothing helped. B was feeling extremely ill, was vomiting, suffering from a severe headache, heard whistling in his ears, felt dizzy and began to see a yellowish mist in front of his eyes. He was afraid to go to sleep because he had got it into his head that he would be blind when he woke up. His memories become incoherent after that.

Towards the end of the conversation they ask the patient how he is feeling at the moment:

"The chief trouble now is the dreams—not exactly dreams, either, but right in the middle of an ordinary conversation the face of a Boche that I have bayoneted, with its horrible gurgle and grimace, comes sharply into view, or I see a man whose head one of our boys took off by a blow on the back of the neck with a bolo knife and the blood spurted high in the air before the body fell. And the horrible smells! You know, I can hardly see meat come on the table, and the butcher's shop just under our window here is terribly distressing, but I'm trying every day to get more used to it."

The patient wants to get back to the front to take part in the great final offensive, but he is in no condition to return. Cushing notes the twenty-four-year-old captain's diagnosis: "psychoneurosis in line of duty."

SUNDAY, 3 NOVEMBER 1918
Pál Kelemen hears of the abolition of censorship in Hungary

It is as good a sign as any other. He is sitting eating lunch in the officers' mess in Arlon when an officer in the supply corps comes rushing in with panic in his eyes. It seems that official censorship has been abolished in Budapest and the newspapers can now print *anything and everything*! They get hold of copies of the latest editions that have arrived in the post and see that the front pages are demanding in bold type that Hungarian troops should immediately be brought home. "Put an end to the bleeding in foreign lands for foreign purposes."

The divisional commander immediately issues an order that all mail should be searched and any newspapers confiscated. The news might well have a disastrous effect on fighting spirit—which is already shaky. No sooner said than done. The post is gone through with a toothcomb but no more newspapers are found.

The officers watch tensely for any sign that the news has reached the men but there are only a few "slight incidents" during the afternoon. A few copies of the newspapers turn up during the evening, however—no one knows how or where they come from—and they are passed around the barracks. "Reading aloud to one another laboriously by candlelight, men and non-commissioned officers everywhere discussed only the contents of the papers."

MONDAY, 4 NOVEMBER 1918
Richard Stumpf and five critical moments in Wilhelmshaven

Autumn air. Grey weather. He dresses in parade uniform in honour of the day. Then he and the rest of the crew go off to demonstrate. The attitude of the officers suggests that the sailors might well end up being victorious. The mood has undergone a decisive change. The old Wilhelmine self-confidence has vanished into thin air and those in command are confused, awkward and despondent. After some lame, almost symbolic protests, the crew is permitted to leave the ship. "I can't stop you," the first officer says meekly to Stumpf.

A week ago the whole High Seas Fleet got ready to sail out and give one final heroic war cry, but mutiny broke out on several of the ships.* Richard Stumpf thinks he knows what happened: "Years and years of injustice have been converted into a dangerously explosive force that is now coming to a head." Refusing to obey orders has become an everyday event. Just a week ago Ludendorff, the Supreme Commander, left his command and rumour has it that the Kaiser will soon follow suit and abdicate. A lieutenant on board one of the ships has been killed.

There is a powerful wave of disappointment, rage and frustration sweeping across Germany. It is not just a result of weariness with all the injustice, the war, the high prices and the food shortages, it is also a result of the fact that German propaganda has consistently (and with considerable success) concealed problems and inflated expectations.†

---

* The proposed operation was effectively tantamount to a colossal suicide mission, hatched independently by various naval officers of limited intelligence, keen to save the "honour" of their service at the eleventh hour. Their idiotic plan caused a riot among the sailors, which was the beginning of the German revolution—an irony of history if ever there was one.

† At the start of the year it was still possible to find Germans who expected the war to end

The height from which people's expectations then plummeted was great, much too great. During those beautiful summer weeks of 1914 public opinion allowed itself to be whipped up to such a frenzy that it "transformed all the circumstances of life in such a way that they could only be expressed in terms of heroic tragedy, of a superhuman, even sacred, struggle against the forces of evil."* This meant that for years anything other than total victory became unthinkable. Now, however, in utter disillusion, public opinion has swung to the dark and bitter opposite pole.

Stumpf himself, as ever, feels divided. He thinks it is a pity the war has been lost but, then, perhaps it was impossible to win it right from the start. He welcomes the fact that the day of reckoning has come but finds it disturbing that those who shouted loudest in support of the strong men of the war are now the very people shouting loudest for them to be sacrificed. Perhaps there is an element of bad conscience mixed with his malevolent pleasure. The sense of drama is great and is increasing day by day but he himself feels remarkably unmoved: "I am living through it all without any strong inner emotions."

The mass of uniformed men moves along the quay towards the barracks, which is guarded by armed sailors. What will happen next?

As the demonstrators approach the armed men the latter welcome them with shouts of joy and three cheers. People are pouring in from all sides and the crowd, its numbers growing by the minute, moves on. What is to be done? Now and again someone stops, tries to hold up the procession, tries to give a speech and get a decision made. There is confusion all round. Finally they agree to march to SMS *Baden*, the flagship of the High Seas Fleet, to try to get its crew to join them.

That is where the first of the day's critical moments occurs:

> A verbal duel was fought between the ship's captain and a number of spokesmen for the demonstrators. The prize was the crew of the *Baden*, which was standing lined up on the upper deck. If the captain had been any sort of competent speaker our spokesmen would have had to withdraw without winning over a single

---

with the virtual extinction of Belgium and with large areas of France and Russia being handed over to Germany.

* To quote Frederic Manning.

man. But both the officer, who was deathly pale, and the seamen's council made a rather poor job of it. The result was that about a third of the crew joined our ranks.

The growing host pushes slowly and tentatively on. The march does not have any particular goal, nor is there anyone in particular leading the demonstration. Stumpf and a couple of others fetch their musical instruments and the sounds of the old military marches spur the procession on to move rather more quickly along the quaysides. And the music attracts more people to join them.

The second critical moment occurs on Peterstrasse, where the street is blocked by a platoon of forty armed men under the command of a lieutenant. But the soldiers show no inclination to use their weapons and go and join the demonstrators instead. "It was very funny to see the lieutenant when he suddenly realised he was all on his own." The crowd pushes on, still driven more by collective instinct than by any clear thought.

At a big, locked gate stands a solitary, elderly major. With his pistol drawn he tries to stop the flood of people. This is the third critical moment. But the outcome is more or less inevitable. The gate is lifted off its hinges in an instant and the major is forcibly disarmed. Some men also try to tear off his epaulettes, after which the officer is just swept along in the mass of people. Stumpf cannot help feeling sorry for the old man "who courageously tried to do his duty."

There are now perhaps 10,000 men gathered on the big parade ground, where one speaker after another mounts an improvised platform. The messages vary from exhortations to stay calm and orderly to "the most ridiculous demands"—which are, however, met with storms of applause. Stumpf is convinced that the mood is such that virtually any idea at all would be able to win approval.

Then the great host sets off again, with the people of the town watching guardedly from behind closed windows. Any passing women are greeted with "coarse comments and whistles." A red flag—a coloured bedsheet—flies above the sea of heads and shoulders. They cross the Deichbrücke over the Ems-Jade Canal and arrive at the torpedo boat division. This is the fourth critical moment. The torpedo boat crews applaud them but do not come ashore to join the demonstrators. The explanation follows immediately: "We're having lunch at the moment."

Lunch, indeed, and many of the men begin to talk about food. "We moved on in nervous and aimless haste."

The finale comes outside fleet headquarters. This is the last critical moment. The results of negotiations with Admiral Krosigk, the local commander, are to be announced here.

There is absolute silence as a man climbs up on a large statue in front of the building. Admiral Krosigk has given way on all points: "Our demands have been accepted!" There is applause and rejoicing. It is all about things like improved rations, better conditions for leave, the formation of special committees to supervise military courts, an easing of discipline,* the freeing of the men arrested at the start of the mutiny. Someone shouts: "Down with Kaiser Wilhelm!" The speaker chooses to ignore this. A dockyard worker with what Stumpf describes as "a classic Apache face" steps forward and demands the formation of a "Soviet republic." Applause. The first speaker then exhorts them all to go back to their posts. Laughter.

The demonstration breaks up and they "all head in the direction of the nearest canteen."

WEDNESDAY, 13 NOVEMBER 1918
Pál Kelemen is demobilised and returns to Budapest

Dusk. The *clickety-clack* of the joins between the rails. The train journey continues. It started some days ago when the staff and the last soldiers in the division entrained in Arlon late at night by the light of pocket torches. Since then they have trundled along jerkily and unsteadily, with many inexplicable stops. Through Belgium, through France, through Germany, through Austria. The officers are travelling separately in a special passenger carriage right at the front; the men and the equipment are in ordinary goods wagons.

In Germany they were treated "as if infected with plague." Just as they were during those last days in the west, when the German authorities

---

* For instance, a seaman addressing an officer would now only have to use the officer's title of rank once, at the start of the conversation, instead of at the end of every sentence, as had been the case earlier.

were trying to prevent the rebellious and homesick Hungarian troops from infecting those elements of the German army still in fighting condition. Discipline, which had already been showing signs of crumbling, has completely broken down during the journey. This is largely due to the effects of alcohol: most of the soldiers are very drunk, loud-mouthed, happy and aggressive. Every now and then there is a crackle of shots as soldiers fire their weapons into the air in joy or intoxication.

When they are about to cross into Austria the train is stopped by German officials who demand that they hand over any military equipment, probably to prevent it falling into the hands of the many Austrian revolutionary groups waiting on the other side of the frontier. There could have been some nasty scenes here since the drunken and combative soldiery refused point-blank to give up its weapons. The situation was defused when the Germans satisfied themselves with taking the horses, the kitchen wagons and things of that kind. (When they crossed the frontier and were met by "unshaven, ill-clad, excited civilians with armbands," there was nothing left for them to grab but the divisional typewriters.)

Once they are in Austria the mood becomes more exhilarated and more threatening. At each and every station soldiers hop off, usually filled with relief, at the same time as others hop on, usually filled with alcohol. There has also been more shooting during the last night and day. Theft and threatening behaviour is becoming more and more overt. On his journey to Budapest Kelemen is being accompanied by Feri, his batman; Laci, his groom; and Benke, one of the orderlies. These three help to protect him and have even arranged for his luggage to be hidden in the locomotive's coal tender.

Darkness falls. Lights sweep past outside the windows. Celebratory yells and gunshots can be heard from the goods wagons further back. The train stops and remains at a standstill. The soldiers are becoming more and more impatient and they fire burst after burst through the open doors of the wagons. Some of them are starting to cluster round the officers' carriage, which is now half empty; they shout, wave their fists threateningly and demand money for wine. Shots crash out and the glass in the windows is shattered, the shards and slivers tinkling down onto the floor. Before anything really serious can happen the train jerks into motion and the troublemakers have to hurry to scramble back aboard.

Gradually the housing outside the sooty carriages begins to get denser as they enter the suburbs of Budapest. At about twelve at night the train stops very briefly at a small station in Rákos and Kelemen and his three companions seize the chance to get off. The relief he feels at being back in his home city is short-lived: a railway worker warns him that everything is in a state of chaos and people calling themselves revolutionaries are running round the streets, looting shops and ripping the badges of rank and medals off returning officers, and robbing them of any other possessions they have.

"Deeply depressed" and with his military insignia concealed under his cloak, Kelemen walks out of the little station and searches the dark, silent, empty streets for any kind of transport. He just wants to take his things home with him—his saddle, his firearm, his sword and all the other things he has been carrying round since 1914. After searching for an hour he manages to find a horse-drawn cab which is on its way back to the stable.

With his luggage stowed away under the seat, Kelemen and his companions are driven into the city and reach his parents' house at four o'clock. He rings at the main gate. Nothing happens. He rings again and again. At last the porter appears and approaches cautiously and guardedly across the dark inner courtyard. Kelemen shouts his name, opening his cloak at the same time to show his badges of rank. The porter greets the little group "whispering excitedly" and unlocks the heavy barred gate to let Kelemen and the others slip through.

They take the goods lift up to the kitchen entry. Since he does not want to wake his parents, Kelemen beds down in the clothes closet in the hall.

THE END

So it finally came to an end, for Pál Kelemen and for them all.

Laura de Turczynowicz's war came to an end when she disembarked from the transatlantic liner that had carried her and her three children from Rotterdam to New York. Even though the days at sea had given her time to start adapting to a peacetime existence, she found her meeting with the great city overwhelming. The dense crowds of people filling the busy pavements exhausted her and the high, wide New York buildings filled her with a vague sense of threat—whenever she put her head back to look up she could not avoid the thought that an aircraft might appear and that the aircraft might drop a bomb. But what upset her most was that so few of the people she met were really concerned about what was going on in Europe: "their indifference was almost more than I can bear." She could not know it at the time but she would never return to Poland and she would never see her husband, Stanislaw, again.

Elfriede Kuhr was in the same place as she had been at the start of the war four years earlier—Schneidemühl. At least one scene was exactly as it had been then: there were crowds outside the newspaper office and, just as in 1914, the situation was changing so rapidly that the latest news was announced by means of handwritten billboards, written in blue pencil on newspaper stock. But unlike four years earlier the confusion was

much greater and the unity far less. Elfriede saw a boy weeping inconsolably after someone in the crowd had hit him for making an offensive
remark. There were fewer cheers, too, and many more arguments, and
loud ones. Some soldiers came walking down the street arm in arm and
singing. A lieutenant who started yelling at them had his uniform cap
knocked off and, pale in the face, he had to pick it up from the gutter. Some civilians called the soldiers traitors. Elfriede ran home. Soon
afterwards the doorbell rang: it was Androwski, her brother's friend, and
he threw himself down in a chair, exclaiming, "The war is dead! Long
live the war!" Almost immediately her brother arrived, too. His cap and
belt were missing, the tunic of his uniform was torn, his buttons ripped
off, his shoulder straps likewise and his lapel flashes were hanging loose.
His face expressed shock and confusion. Androwski began to laugh at
the sight of him and, after some hesitation, her brother also started to
smile.

After her death Sarah Macnaughtan was taken from London to Chart
Sutton in Kent. At the end of July 1916, she was buried in the village
churchyard on the hill, in the family grave, in the shade of fruit trees.*
As the coffin was lowered into the ground the mourners could hear the
faint rumble of artillery, borne on a south wind from the battlefield on
the Somme. It was afternoon and the sun was shining.

Richard Stumpf was still in Wilhelmshaven. What had started as madness ended in hysteria. The rumour spread that they had been betrayed
and that troops loyal to the old regime were on their way: "The streets
were like a madhouse. Armed men ran back and forth in all directions—
you could even see women dragging ammunition boxes around. What
madness! Is this how it's going to end? After five years of brutal warfare are we now going to turn our guns on our own countrymen?" He
was sitting writing later when he suddenly heard the sound of cheering,
shouting and running, hooters blowing and shots being fired from small
arms and even from cannon. Signal rockets burst in endless streams of

---

* The epitaph on her gravestone reads: "In the Great War, by Word and Deed, at Home
and Abroad, She served her country even unto Death."

red, green and white up in the evening sky. He thought: "A little more dignity would have done no harm."

Andrei Lobanov-Rostovsky found himself in a training camp in Sables d'Olonne near the Atlantic coast. He and his rebellious company had never been sent to the front and had ended up spending a dull and demoralising time as reserves behind the lines, a period that was then followed by an outbreak of Spanish influenza. He himself lay seriously ill and hallucinating in a fevered state. He recovered, only to be informed that he had been removed from his post as company commander, for which in his heart of hearts he was thoroughly relieved. At the same time he was unlucky in his love for a young Russian woman living in Nice. During this time of general inactivity he continued to devour history books and his studies reinforced his conviction that the Bolsheviks would not be in power for long. Even though he, like many others, sensed that the war was coming to an end, he found it hard to imagine a life without the war and out of uniform. "My own personality had become submerged in the conception of the whole. I think that this was a normal result of war mentality and probably the experience of millions of fighting men." There was talk among his Russian fellow officers about whether they should join the Whites and take part in the civil war that Russia was about to face. Lobanov-Rostovsky was undecided what to do.[*] They were carrying on with grenade-throwing practice as usual when a French officer appeared and announced with great excitement: "Stop all exercises. The armistice is signed." There was "a wild carnival" going on in the town, with people embracing one another and dancing in the streets. The celebrations continued far into the night.

Florence Farmborough's war came to an end the moment the ship carrying her and the other refugees steamed out of the harbour in

---

[*] His keen study of history had convinced him that armed intervention in Russia by a number of the Allied powers would not be a good idea. Great Britain, France, the United States, Japan and the rest of them did not have a real plan. Their original purpose in intervening was not to support the Whites but to keep their great eastern ally in the war. Initially, they were even encouraged to some extent by the Bolsheviks. But Lobanov-Rostovsky now felt that popular support for the Whites was far too weak.

Vladivostock. The ship seemed like a floating palace to her. They went aboard to the sounds of music and when she entered her cabin she suddenly found herself standing in a dream of white sheets, white towels and white curtains at the porthole.* Then she stood on deck and watched this land called Russia, "which I had loved so truly and which I had served so gladly," disappear very slowly until all that was left was a pale, grey shadow on the horizon. And then a thick bluish fog drifted in over the sea and made it impossible for her to see any more. She went down to her cabin and stayed there, making an excuse to the others that she was feeling seasick.

Kresten Andresen's family lived for a long time in the hope that he was a prisoner of war held by the British, interned perhaps in some distant camp, in Africa, for example. They never heard anything more of him and all of their enquiries came to nothing.†

---

* One of the first fellow passengers she met on board was Maria "Yasha" Bachkarova (see footnote, 8 August 1917, page 385), who was now being hunted by the Bolsheviks. The women's units Bachkarova had helped to form had remained loyal to the Kerensky regime right to the end and some of her soldiers had been in the Winter Palace when it was stormed.

† A Christian Andresen, reported missing on 10 August 1916, is buried in the German cemetery at Wervicq-Sud (Plot 4, Grave 140). This may or may not be "our" Kresten. The cemetery is located close to the Belgian border, closer to Ypres than to the Somme, and it is not immediately apparent why Kresten's body would have been moved so far north. There are two possible explanations. His remains may have been moved there during one of the many reburials that took place in France after the war, when the bodies in many small cemeteries were exhumed and transferred to larger cemeteries. (This, for instance, explains why many war cemeteries have mass graves even though the men buried in them are named: whole cemeteries in which the men had been buried in named individual graves were dug up and the bones simply tipped into communal graves. This was a common occurrence.) The second possibility is linked to the first: the body may have been taken to Wervicq-Sud during one of the reburials referred to above, but it may have been brought there from a prisoner of war cemetery on the Allied side of the front. (There were such cemeteries in this neighbourhood.) In that case, what happened to Kresten may have been as follows: he was taken prisoner on 8 August 1916 and transferred north, but died fairly soon afterwards. He may perhaps have been seriously wounded, which would explain why he does not feature in any of the lists of prisoners of war.

· · ·

The end of the war found Michel Corday for once not in Paris but in a small town in the countryside. Like most of the others he had suspected for weeks that the end was close. Right to the finish, attitudes among the people he met varied. Joy at the success was widespread and there were many smiling faces. Some people insisted, however, that they should not be satisfied with the situation, that they should go on, invade Germany and subject the country to the same suffering France had endured. Others hardly even dared hope—they had been disappointed before. There were some who watched guardedly, still holding to the propagandist idea that "peace" was an obscene word. One phrase that could frequently be heard was a rather doubting "Who would have believed this four months ago?" Corday had seen Italian troops on their way home already, full of joy that their war was at an end. And at seven o'clock that morning the local army headquarters received a wireless message that the armistice had been signed. Bells were rung and soldiers danced in the streets with flags and bouquets of flowers in their hands. At lunchtime they heard that Kaiser Wilhelm had fled to Holland.

Alfred Pollard found himself in Montreuil, at the headquarters of the British Expeditionary Force, where his battalion had been sent to do guard duty. At the beginning of November the unit was being shunted round as a mobile reserve without being involved in any fighting, a fact that he regretted for the sake of his soldiers—"I should have hated to miss a stunt of that description"—but was appreciative of it for himself. Pollard had recovered from the bout of Spanish influenza that had caused him to collapse outside Péronne and when the news of the armistice reached them they all went "mad with excitement." The rest of the day was spent cheering, singing, visiting various officers' messes, toasting victory and remembering the fallen. He was probably fairly drunk by the afternoon when someone invited him into the secret rooms at operational command to look at a large map of the location of the divisions of the German army. He noted with pleasure that the clustering of German units was densest where they were faced with the British armies and thinnest where they had to deal with the Belgians and the Americans.

William Henry Dawkins was buried at sunset on the day he died. He was interred at an improvised cemetery immediately south of Anzac Cove, where his body still rests, less than twenty yards from the water's edge.[*]

René Arnaud was back in the front line again, in a shell crater that was temporarily serving as the battalion headquarters. It occurred to him that he had just reached the age of twenty-five but that he had completely overlooked his birthday. A major appeared in the darkness and said that he was there to relieve Arnaud, who was to take up a posting behind the lines. Arnaud "realised at once that the war was over for me, that I had survived, that I was suddenly free of the cruel anxiety that had been weighing on me for three and a half years, that I should no longer be pursued by the ghost of death that had preoccupied me in the same way as it preoccupies old men." He showed his replacement around, without worrying for once about machine-gun fire and exploding shells because "I was gloriously happy and light hearted and it felt as though I were invulnerable."

Rafael de Nogales found himself on a steamship on the way into the Bosphorus. He saw flags everywhere—the flags of the enemy: Italian, French and British. He thought that most of them were flying over houses owned by "Armenians, Greeks and Levantines."[†] In the evening he ended up at a party arranged by some Greek ladies who wanted to celebrate the armistice. Rumours were rife. Some of the leading Young Turks had fled the city in a German motor torpedo boat. A military revolt was being planned in Anatolia "by way of protest against the Allied interference in the internal affairs of Turkey" and, de Nogales adds, this interference will "continue to cause serious armed conflicts as long as the Allies persist in their division of Syria, Palestine, Arabia and Mesopotamia into mandates and protectorates." A week later he went to the war ministry

---

[*] The cemetery is called Beach Cemetery, and lies on the road between Kelia and Suvla. His grave is Plot 1, Row H, Grave 3. It is possible to throw a stone into the Aegean from that point.

[†] De Nogales uses the word as a synonym for Jews.

and for the second time applied for a discharge.* This time his request was granted unconditionally.

Harvey Cushing was still lying in his hospital bed in Priez. On the day of the armistice his batman brought him his shaving mirror and a nail brush and took away his uniform jacket to sew on the new badges: Cushing was being promoted to the rank of colonel. He had been studying newspaper reports of victory for a while, with increasing amazement—how could it have happened so quickly?—and he had been following the advances of the Allied armies on a map with the help of some pins and a length of cotton. At half past four in the afternoon he, with the matron, the hospital padre and a medical colleague, had celebrated the peace in his room. They did so with no great fuss or rejoicing, just sitting in front of the fire, drinking tea and talking about religion and the future.

Angus Buchanan's war ended early, in a field hospital in Narunyu during September 1917. A week or so earlier he and the rest of the 25th Royal Fusiliers had relieved a South African infantry unit. The troops had been completely drained by the appalling heat, and the ranks of both soldiers and bearers were growing thinner by the day. Buchanan himself was one of the weary and sick men. He struggled on for a few days in spite of fever, managing only with great effort to attend the morning parades, but eventually he could no longer walk. Buchanan was carried to the hospital: "I was beaten, hopelessly overcome." They feared for his life. He lay in a hut waiting to be evacuated, first to Lindi and then by boat to Dar es-Salaam. A man in uniform came in. It was O'Grady, the officer commanding this sector, a man Buchanan had worked with earlier. O'Grady said some friendly and encouraging words and expressed his sorrow that things were going so badly. And then, "when he had gone," Buchanan writes, "I hid my face in the gloom of the low grass hut and broke down like a woman."

* See 13 February 1916 for the first, page 218.

Willy Coppens was still in hospital in De Panne. Complications had set in. The wound from the amputation was still open and there was no easing of his depression. (Coppens was now bedecked with medals from virtually every one of the Allied powers, Portugal and Serbia included, but even though he had always been interested in decorations they had been of little help. He knew that he would not be able to wear them in uniform and he also realised that the coming peace would lead to an unparalleled flooding of the medals market.) In the evening he suddenly heard the sounds of tremendous yelling, cheering and laughter bouncing off the walls of the wards, stairwells and corridors. To his ears the rejoicing became contorted to something that almost resembled the last sigh of a dying man, though enormously magnified and distorted. The armistice had just been announced. Coppens himself was confused: "I ought to have felt great joy but it was as if a cold hand took me by the throat. I was beset by anxiety about the future. I realised that a period of my life was over."

Olive King found herself in Salonica, having just returned from England. (The reason for her visit to England was to arrange the necessary official permission for the realisation of her next major project—setting up a chain of canteens to help alleviate the suffering and hardship among returning Serbian refugees and soldiers.) The journey to England had been a confusing experience for her, to put it mildly. She had missed Salonica at first, but this feeling had gradually turned to antipathy and a reluctance to go back there. She did make her return, however, and it proved to be a remarkably happy one. Her unit had moved north long before, following on the heels of the collapsing Bulgarian army. (At the eleventh hour the thousands of soldiers in Salonica had at last been given a proper mission and by September they had forced a hard-pressed Bulgaria to capitulate. The Ottoman Empire soon followed suit and the chain reaction was completed by the capitulation of Austria-Hungary.) Her two vehicles had disappeared along with the advancing forces, her wooden cabin had been moved and was almost empty, but all her possessions had been packed away with great care by her Serbian friends. Before setting off on her journey to Belgrade King went through everything she had collected during the past few years. She thought most of it was just "rubbish" and threw away many of her old clothes, along with heaps of newspapers and news bulletins. All that belonged to the past.

Vincenzo D'Aquila found himself on board a cargo boat just off Bermuda, on his way home to the United States. In all probability it was his American citizenship, combined with the fact that he had never formally been sworn into the army, that saved him. With American public opinion in mind, the Italian authorities had obviously been reluctant to make a martyr of him, so even though he had been kept in Italy and in uniform he had never been sent back to the front. And finally, after all sorts of comings and goings, D'Aquila was given permission to return to the United States. He missed the mailboat to New York but managed to get a berth on the American cargo boat *Carolyn*, sailing from Genoa in September. They took on a load of ore in Gibraltar and then, because of U-boat alarms, the captain opted for the much longer but considerably safer route via Brazil. On their way north from there, one night in November, they saw an unusual sight: a ship steaming through the night fully lit up. At dawn they encountered another vessel and signalled it with flags: "Is the war over?" The answer came, technically correct: "No, it's only an armistice."

Edward Mousley's war came to an end when he stepped aboard the ship that took him from imprisonment in Constantinople to freedom in Smyrna. "Everything is excitement and disorder," he wrote in his journal. "Centuries of captivity are falling from me every second. I am outwardly calm, and too busy to psychologise much on the great end of this awful eternity." A number of other newly freed prisoners of war were on the boat and he shared a cabin with a man who had also been in the artillery at Kut al-Amara and who had pretended to be mad in order to gain his freedom. It was already dark when the boat cast off. The contours of the city faded into the night; first to go were the soft forms of the great mosques and last were the sharp lines of the tall minarets. Mousley went down to his cabin for a while and sat with his companion, smoking and listening to the sound of the waves. When Mousley and his friend went back up on deck the city had disappeared. The only thing to be seen was the gleam of distant lights in the ship's wash. "It was Stamboul: the City of the Eternities, the Beautiful, the Terrible." Neither of them said anything.

Paolo Monelli was at the railway station in Sigmundsherberg in north-eastern Austria. He and the other Italian prisoners of war had been free for several days after overpowering their confused and demoralised guards by a combination of argument and force. Everything had been turned on its head. Some of his fellow countrymen headed down into the town to get drunk and chase women, others began planning a great raid on Vienna. Italian soldiers with Austrian weapons patrolled the railway station and helped to keep order. Troop trains full of Hungarian soldiers steamed past now and again and there was some shooting. The Austrian telephone operators carried on working as usual. Monelli and a small group of other former prisoners listened to an Austrian officer, known to be a friendly fellow, translating the terms of the armistice to them, breathlessly, phrase by phrase. Monelli was enormously relieved to be free and that the war was over, but the feeling was shot through with an element of bitter sorrow. "This is going to be our evil inheritance, or our good inheritance, in any case our irrevocable inheritance—and we are going to be fettered by our memories for ever."

Envoi

On 10 November the priest from the hospital came and made a short speech. Now we learned everything.

I was utterly dismayed during the short speech. The dignified old man was visibly trembling as he informed us that the House of Hohenzollern was no longer to be allowed to wear the German imperial crown, that our Fatherland had become a "republic," that we must pray to the Almighty not to withhold his blessing from this change and not to desert our people in the future. He could not refrain from devoting some words to the royal house, reminding us of its great services in Pomerania, in Prussia, indeed, for the whole of the German Fatherland. Then he began to sob gently to himself and the most profound dejection settled over all the hearts in that little room. I do not think there was a single eye that could hold back its tears. But the old man tried to speak again and began to tell us that we must now end this long war; and since we had lost the war and were now dependent on the mercy of the victors our Fatherland would be exposed to harsh oppression and the fact was that the armistice would result in us having to rely on the nobility of our former enemies—at that point I could take no more. It was impossible for me to remain there. Everything went black before my eyes and I fumbled my way back to the dormitory, threw myself down on my bed and buried my burning face in the covers and pillows [. . .]

The days that followed this were horrible and the nights worse—I knew that everything was lost. One would have had to be a simpleton—or a liar and criminal—to hope for mercy from the enemy. My hatred grew during these nights, my hatred for those responsible for this evil deed. During the days that followed I recognised what my mission was to be [. . .]

I decided to become a politician.

ADOLF HITLER, *Mein Kampf,* 1925

Sources and Literature

Akçam, T., *A Shameful Act: The Armenian Genocide and the Question of Turkish Responsibility*, New York, 2006

Anderson, R., *The Forgotten Front: The East African Campaign 1914–1918*, London, 2004

Andresen, K., *Kresten breve. Udgivne af Hans Moder*, Copenhagen, 1919

Ångström, T., *Kriget i luften. Med skildringar av flygare i fält*, Stockholm, 1915

Anon., *British Trench Warfare 1917–1918: A Reference Manual*, London, n. d.

Anon., *Instruction for the Training of Divisions for Offensive Action*, Washington, 1917

Anon., *Instruction provisoire pour les unités de mitrailleuses d'infanterie*, Nancy, 1920

Anon., *Manual of the Chief of Platoon of Infantry*, n. p., 1918

Anon., *Notes on the Construction and Equipment of Trenches*, Washington, 1917

Arnaud, A., *La Guerre 1914–1918. Tragédie-Bouffe*, Paris, 1964

Barbusse, H., *Le feu. Journale d'une escouade*, Paris, 1916

Bertin, F., *14–18, La grande guerre. Armes, uniformes, matériels*, Rennes, 2006

Bloxham, D., *The Great Game of Genocide: Imperialism, Nationalism and the Destruction of the Ottoman Armenians*, Oxford, 2005

Bouveng, G., *Dagbok från ostfronten*, Stockholm, 1928

Bradley, Carolyn G., *Western World Costume: An Outline History*, New York, 1954

Bruce, A., *The Last Crusade: The Palestine Campaign in the First World War*, London, 2003

Buchanan, A., *Three Years of War in East Africa*, London, 1919

Buffetaut, Y., *Atlas de la Première Guerre mondiale, 1914–1918. La chute des empires européens*, Paris, 2005

——, *The 1917 Spring Offensives. Arras, Vimy, Le Chemin des Dames*, Paris, 1997

——, *Verdun. Guide historique & touristique*, Langres, 2002

Carlswärd, T., *Operationerna på tyska ostfronten med särskild hänsyn till signaltjänsten*, Stockholm, 1931

Christiernsson, N., *Med Mackensen till Przemysl*, Stockholm, 1915

Coppens, W., *Jours envolés. Mémoires*, Paris, 1932

Corday, M., *The Paris Front: An Unpublished Diary 1914–1918*, New York, 1934

Cox, I., "The larks still singing," *Times Literary Supplement*, 13 November 1998

Cron, H., *Geschichte des Deutschen Heeres im Weltkriege 1914–1918*, Berlin, 1937

Curti, P., *Artillerie in der Abwehr. Kriegsgeschichtlich erläutert*, Frauenfeld, 1940

Cushing, H., *From a Surgeon's Journal, 1915–1918*, Toronto, 1936

D'Aquila, V., *Bodyguard Unseen: A True Autobiography*, New York, 1931

Dadrian, V. N., *The History of the Armenian Genocide: Ethnic Conflict from the Balkans to Anatolia to the Caucasus*, New York, 2003

Davenport-Hines, R., *Sex, Death and Punishment: Attitudes to Sex and Sexuality in Britain since the Renaissance*, Glasgow, 1991

———, *The Pursuit of Oblivion: A Social History of Drugs*, London, 2002

Dawkins, W. H., "Letters and diaries," in J. Ingle, *From Duntroon to the Dardanelles*, Canberra, 1995

Defente, D. (ed.), *Le Chemin des Dames 1914–1918*, Paris, 2003

Delaporte, S., *Les Gueules cassées. Les blessés de la face de la Grande Guerre*, Paris, 1996

Erickson, E. J., *Ordered to Die: A History of the Ottoman Army in the First World War*, London, 2001

Farmborough, F., *Nurse at the Russian Front: A Diary 1914–18*, London, 1977

Ferguson, N., *The Pity of War*, London, 1999

Ferro, M., *The Great War 1914–1918*, London, 1973

Fewster, K. (ed.), *Gallipoli Correspondent: The Frontline Diary of C. E. W. Bean*, Sydney, 1983

Figes, O., *A People's Tragedy: The Russian Revolution, 1891–1924*, London, 1997

Fitzsimons, B., *The Big Guns: Artillery 1914–1918*, London, 1973

Flex, W., *Die russische Frühjahrsoffensive 1916* (Der große Krieg in Einzeldarstellungen 31), Oldenburg, 1919

Fox, E. L., *Behind the Scenes in Warring Germany*, New York, 1915

Gately, I., *La Diva Nicotina: The Story of How Tobacco Seduced the World*, New York, 2001

Général de M*** (pseud. Henry Dugard), *The Battle of Verdun*, London, 1916

Generalstabens krigshistoriska avdelning, *Några erfarenheter från fälttåget i Rumänien 1916–1917*, Stockholm, 1924

Generalstabens utbildningsavdelning, *Från fälttåget i Serbien augusti 1914. En strategisk-taktisk studie*, Stockholm, 1935

Gierow, K. R., *1914–1918 in memoriam*, Stockholm, 1939

Gilbert, M., *First World War*, London, 1994

Gleichen, E. (ed.), *Chronology of the Great War, 1914–1918*, London, 1988

Gourko, B., *Minnen och intryck från kriget och revolutionen i Ryssland 1914–1917*, Stockholm, 1919

Griffith, P., *Battle Tactics of the Western Front: The British Army's Art of Attack 1916–18*, London, 1994

Gudmundsson, B. I., *Stormtroop Tactics: Innovation in the German Army 1914–1918*, London, 1995

Guéno, J.-P. and Laplume, Y. (eds.), *Paroles de Poilus. Lettres et carnets du front 1914–1918*, Paris, 1998

Haichen, M. (ed.), *Helden der Kolonien. Der Weltkrieg in unseren Schutzgebieten*, Berlin, 1938

Harries, M. and Harries, S., *Soldiers of the Sun: The Rise and Fall of the Imperial Japanese Army*, New York, 1991

Hedin, S., *Bagdad, Babylon, Ninive*, Stockholm, 1917

——, *Kriget med Ryssland. Minnen från fronten i öster mars–augusti 1915*, Stockholm, 1915

Heyman, H., *Frankrike i krig*, Stockholm, 1916

Hirschfeld, G., Krumreich, G. and Renz, I., *Enzyklopädie Erster Weltkrieg*, Paderborn, 2003

Hirschfeld, M. and Gaspar, A., *Sittengeschichte des Ersten Weltkrieges*, Hanau, 1929

Hitler, A., *Mein kampf. Eine Abrechnung*, Munich, 1925–6

Holmes, R., *Firing Line*, London, 1987

Holmgren, A., *Krigserfarenheter. Särskilt från fyra österrikisk-ungerska fronter*, Stockholm, 1919

Holzer, A., *Das Lächeln der Hänker—Der unbekannte Krieg gegen die Zivilbevölkerung 1914–1918*, Darmstadt, 2008

Horne, J. and Kramer, A., *German Atrocities 1914: A History of Denial*, New Haven, 2001

Johann, E. (ed.), *Innenansicht eines Krieges. Deutsche Dokumente 1914–1918*, Frankfurt-am-Main, 1969

Johansson, K., *K. J. själv*, Stockholm, 1952

Johnston, M. A. B. and Yearsley, K. D., *450 Miles to Freedom: The Adventures of Eight British Officers in Their Escape from the Turks*, London, 1922

Jünger, E., *In Stahlgewittern*, Stuttgart, 1992

Jünger, E. (ed.), *Das Anlitz des Weltkrieges. Fronterlebnisse deutscher Soldaten*, Berlin, 1930

Kearsey, A., *A Summary of the Strategy and Tactics of the Egypt and Palestine Campaign with Details of the 1917–18 Operations Illustrating the Principles of War*, Aldershot, 1931

Keegan, J., *The First World War*, London, 1998

Kelemen, P., *Hussar's Picture Book, From the Diary of a Hungarian Cavalry Officer in World War I*, Bloomington, 1972

King, O., *One Woman at War: Letters of Olive King, 1915–1920*, Melbourne, 1986

Kisch, E. E., *Bland pyramider och generaler*, Stockholm, 1977

Klavora, V., *Schritte im Nebel. Die Isonzofront. Karfreit/Kobarid, Tolmein/Tolmin 1915–17*, Ljubljana, 1995

Koerner, P. (ed.), *Der Erste Weltkrieg in Wort und Bild*, vols I–V, Munich, 1968

Kolata, G., *FLU: The Story of the Great Influenza Pandemic of 1918 and the Search for the Virus That Caused It*, New York, 1999

Laffin, J., *Combat Surgeons*, London, 1970

Lefebvre, J.-H., *Verdun. La plus grande bataille de l'Histoire racontée par les survivants*, Fleury-devant-Douaumont, n. d.

Lettow-Vorbeck, P., von, *Meine Erinnerungen aus Ostafrika*, Leipzig, 1920

Liman von Sanders, O., *Five Years in Turkey*, London, 2005

Liulevicius, V. G., *War Land on the Eastern Front —Culture, National Identity, and German Occupation in World War I*, Cambridge, 2000

Ljunggren, J., *Känslornas krig. Första världskriget och den tyska bildningselitens androgyna manlighet*, Stockholm, 2004

Lobanov-Rostovsky, A., *The Grinding Mill: Reminiscences of War and Revolution in Russia, 1913–1920*, New York, 1935

Ludendorff, E., *Meine Kriegserinnerungen 1914–1918*, Berlin, 1919

Macnaughtan, S., *A Woman's Diary of the War*, London, 1916

———, *My War Experiences in Two Continents*, London, 1919

Malmberg, H., *Infanteriets stridsmedel och krigsorganisation under och efter världskriget*, Stockholm, 1921

Manning, F., *Her Privates We*, London, 1943

Marén, N. G., *Skuggor och dagrar från världskriget. Minnen och stämningar från en studieresa mot ostfronten, Sept. 1915*, Uppsala, 1916

Marlow, J. (ed.), *Women and the Great War*, London, 1998

McDonald, L., *Somme*, London, 1985

———, *The Roses of No Man's Land*, London, 1980

McMoran Wilson, C. (Lord Moran), *The Anatomy of Courage*, London, 1945

Messenger, C., *Trench Fighting 1914–18*, New York, 1972

Meyer, G., *Der Durchbruch am Narew, Juli–August 1915* (Der große Krieg in Einzeldarstellungen 27/28), Oldenburg, 1919

Mihaly, Jo (pseud. Elfriede Kuhr), . . . *da gibt's ein Wiedersehen! Kriegstagebuch eines Mädchens 1914–1918*, Stuttgart, 1982

Miller, H. W., *The Paris Gun*, London, 1930

Moberly, F. J., *The Campaign in Mesopotamia 1914–1918*, vols I–II (Official History of the War), London, 1923

Mollo, A., *Army Uniforms of World War I: European and United States Armies and Aviation Services*, New York, 1978

Monelli, P., *Le scarpe al sole. Cronaca di gaie e tristi avventure di alpini di muli e di vino*, Milan, 2008

Morris, J., *The German Air Raids on Great Britain 1914–1918*, London, 1925

Mousley, E. O., *The Secrets of a Kuttite: An Authentic Story of Kut, Adventures in Captivity and Stamboul Intrigue*, London, 1921

Munson, K., *Fighter, Attack and Training Aircraft 1914–19*, London, 1968

Musil, R., *Diaries 1899–1914*, New York, 1998

Neiberg, M. S., *Fighting the Great War: A Global History*, London, 2005

Neumann, P., *Luftschiffe* (Volksbücher der Technik), Leipzig, n. d.

Nogales, R. de, *Four Years Beneath the Crescent*, London, 2003

Nordensvan, C. O., *Världskriget 1914–1918*, Stockholm, 1922

Ouditt, S., *Fighting Forces, Writing Women: Identity and Ideology in the First World War*, London, 1994

Ousby, I., *The Road to Verdun: France, Nationalism and the First World War*, London, 2002

Pitreich, M. von, *Lemberg 1914*, Stockholm, 1929

Pollard, A. O., *Fire-Eater: The Memoirs of a VC*, London, 1932

Rachamimov, A., *POWs and the Great War: Captivity on the Eastern Front*, Oxford, 2002

Razac, O., *Histoire politique du barbelé. La prairie, la tranchée, le camp*, Paris, 2000

Reichsarchiv, *Der Durchbruch am Isonzo*, part 1: *Die Schlacht von Tolmein und Flitsch* (Schlachten des Weltkrieges vol. 12a), Berlin, 1928

——, *Der Kampf um die Dardanellen 1915* (Schlachten des Weltkrieges vol. 16), Berlin, 1927

——, *Die Tragödie von Verdun 1916*, parts III and IV: *Die Zermürbungsschlacht* (Schlachten des Weltkrieges vol. 15), Berlin, 1929

——, *Flandern 1917* (Schlachten des Weltkrieges vol. 27), Berlin, 1928

——, *Gorlice* (Schlachten des Weltkrieges vol. 30), Berlin, 1930

——, *Herbstschlacht in Macedonien Cernabogen 1916* (Schlachten des Weltkrieges vol. 5), Berlin, 1928

——, *Ildirim. Deutsche Streiter auf heiligem Boden* (Schlachten des Weltkrieges vol. 4), Berlin, 1928

Reiss, R. A., *Report upon the Atrocities Committed by the Austro-Hungarian Army During the First Invasion of Serbia*, London, 1916

Roberts, N., *Whores in History: Prostitution in Western Society*, London, 1992

Rochat, G., "Les soldats fusillés en Italie," *14–18, Le Magazine de la Grande Guerre*, 29 (Dec. 2005–Jan. 2006)

Rommel, E., *Infanteri greift an. Erlebnis und Erfahrung*, Potsdam, 1941

Saunders, A., *Dominating the Enemy: The War in the Trenches 1914–1918*, Phoenix Mill, 2000

Schaumann, G. and Schaumann, W., *Unterwegs zwischen Save und Soca. Auf den Spuren der Isonzofront 1915–1917*, Klagenfurt, 2002

Schaumann, W., *Vom Ortler bis zur Adria. Die Südwest-front 1915–1918 in Bildern*, Vienna, 1993

Schreiner, G. A., *The Iron Ration: Three Years in Warring Central Europe*, New York, 1918

Schwarte, M. (ed.), *Kriegslehren in Beispielen aus dem Weltkrieg*, Berlin, 1925

Sibley, J. R., *Tanganyikan Guerrilla: East Africa Campaign, 1914–18*, London, 1971

Simčić, M., *Die Schlachten am Isonzo. 888 Tage Krieg im Karst*, Graz, 2003

Slowe, P. and Woods, R., *Fields of Death: Battle Scenes of the First World War*, London, 1990

Sonderhaus, L., *Franz Conrad von Hötzendorf, Architekt der Apokalypse*, Vienna, 2003

Stone, N., *The Eastern Front 1914–1917*, London, 1998

——, *World War One, A Short History*, London, 2007

Strachan, H., *The First World War*, vol. I: *To Arms*, Oxford, 2001

Struck, E., *Im Fesselballon*, Berlin, 1918

Stumpf, R., *Warum die Flotte zerbrach. Kriegstagebuch eines christlichen Arbeiters*, Berlin, 1927

Taylor, A. J. P., *The First World War*, London, 1963

Transfeldt, *Dienstunterricht für den Infanteristen des Deutsches Heeres*, Berlin, 1916

Turbergue, J.-P. (ed.), *Les 300 Jours de Verdun*, Paris, 2006

Turczynowicz, Laura de G., *When the Prussians Came to Poland*, New York, 1916

Tylden-Wright, David, *Anatole France*, London, 1967

Wattrang, K., *Det operativa elementet i världskriget*, Stockholm, 1924

Willers, U., *Tysklands sammanbrott 1918*, Stockholm, 1944

Willet, C. and Cunnington, P., *The History of Underclothes*, London, 1951

Williams, J. F., *Corporal Hitler and the Great War, 1914–1918: The List Regiment*, New York, 2005

Wilson, T., *The Myriad Faces of War: Britain and the Great War, 1914–1918*, Oxford, 1988

Winter, D., *Death's Men: Soldiers of the Great War*, London, 1979

Winter, J., Parker, G. and Habeck, M. R. (eds.), *The Great War and the Twentieth Century*, New Haven, 2000

Wirsén, E. af, *Minnen af fred och krig*, Stockholm, 1942

Witkopf, P. (ed.), *Kriegsbriefe gefallener Studenter*, Munich, 1928

List of Illustrations

PORTRAITS

1. Elfriede Kuhr
2. Sarah Macnaughtan, from *My War Experiences in Two Continents* by Sarah Macnaughtan, London, 1919
3. Richard Stumpf, from *War, Mutiny and Revolution in the German Navy—The World War I Diary of Seaman Richard Stumpf*, New Brunswick, 1967
4. Pál Kelemen, used with the permission of Diane Halasz
5. Andrei Lobanov-Rostovsky, used with the permission of Igor Lobanov-Rostovsky
6. Florence Farmborough
7. Kresten Andresen
8. Michel Corday. Engraving bought by the French editor Grégory Martin, credit unknown
9. Alfred Pollard
10. William Henry Dawkins
11. René Arnaud, used with the permission of Laurence Dubrana
12. Rafael de Nogales
13. Harvey Cushing
14. Angus Buchanan, from *Out of the World North of Nigeria* by Angus Buchanan, New York, 1922
15. Olive King
16. Willy Coppens
17. Vincenzo D'Aquila
18. Edward Mousley
19. Paolo Monelli
20. Laura de Turczynowicz, from *When the Prussians Came to Poland: The Experiences of an American Woman during the German Invasion* by Laura de Gozdawa Turczynowicz, New York, 1916

THE WESTERN FRONT

1. SMS *Helgoland,* Richard Stumpf's ship: Bundesarchiv
2. A column of Belgian infantrymen on the beach at De Panne, 17 October 1916: ECPAD (Établissement de Communication et de Production Audiovisuelle de la Défense)
3. Sanctuary Wood, October 1914: IWM (Imperial War Museum)
4. View of Kiel, with the naval base in the background, 1914: Ullstein Bild
5. A street in Lens: Bundesarchiv
6. Fort Douaumont at Verdun under heavy bombardment, 1 April 1916: Ullstein Bild
7. British water carriers at Zonnebeke, August 1917: Ullstein Bild
8. Beach scene in Boulogne-sur-Mer, May 1918: IWM
9. A blown-up bridge at Villers-Cotterêts, September 1914: IWM
10. Péronne, end of March 1918: Ullstein Bild
11. Sailors gathering, ready to demonstrate in Wilhelmshaven, beginning of November 1918: Ullstein Bild

EAST AFRICA

1. The war reaches Africa, 1914: Bundesarchiv
2. German native troops in combat somewhere in East Africa: Bundesarchiv
3. The Pangani River in German East Africa: Bundesarchiv
4. British native troops of the King's African Rifles on parade in Lindi, September 1916: Ullstein Bild
5. The wreck of SMS *Königsberg* in the Rufiji delta, summer 1915: Bundesarchiv
6. A black machine-gun crew under German command somewhere in East Africa: Bundesarchiv

THE EASTERN FRONT

1. The mobilising Russian army gathers horses in St. Petersburg, 31 July 1914: Ullstein Bild
2. Russian prisoners-of-war on the Uszoker Pass in the Carpathians, spring 1915: Ullstein Bild
3. The transport of Russian prisoners captured during the battles of May and June 1915: Ullstein Bild
4. Austrian cavalry crossing the Vistula at Praga in Warsaw, 5 or 6 August 1915: Ullstein Bild
5. German troops in Minsk, 1915: Getty Images
6. View of Elfriede Kuhr's Schneidemühl, 1917: AWM (Australian War Memorial)
7. Red Square, Moscow, October 1917: Ullstein Bild
8. A trainload of homeward-bound Austro-Hungarian troops has stopped in Budapest, November 1918: Ullstein Bild

THE ITALIAN FRONT

1. An Austro-Hungarian supply column near Santa Lucia, October 1917: Bundesarchiv
2. Italian Alpini in their element, 1915: Getty Images

3. Austro-Hungarian mountain troops working their way forward in the Alps, 1915: IWM

4. Cima Undici, 1916: Museo Storico del Trentino

5. Monte Cauriol, 1916: Museo Storico Italiano della Guerra, Rovereto

6. An Austro-Hungarian military hospital on Monte Ortigara, 1915: Museo Storico del Trentino

7. Italian prisoners-of-war and some of the victorious German troops in Udine, October 1917: Museo Storico Italiano della Guerra, Rovereto

THE BALKANS AND DARDANELLES

1. Supplies, the wounded, and swimmers at Anzac Cove, 1915: AWM

2. V Beach on the southern tip of the Gallipoli Peninsula, 1915: Ullstein Bild

3. An Austro-Hungarian supply column in Serbia, October–November 1915: Ullstein Bild

4. Captured Serbian troops on their way to surrender their weapons in Montenegro, February 1916: Ullstein Bild

5. A German aeroplane takes off for combat, watched by members of the local population in Macedonia, 1915: Ullstein Bild

6. A British army camp outside Salonica, April 1916: IWM

7. Salonica immediately after the Great Fire, August 1917: AWM

MIDDLE EAST

1. Fortifications at Erzurum, 1916: Getty Images

2. View over Kut: Ullstein Bild

3. Heavily laden British riverboats on the Tigris, 1916: IW

4. Jerusalem has capitulated and welcomes the victors, 1 December 1917: Getty Images

5. The ruins of Gaza after the fall of the city, November 1917: IWM

6. Under fire on the Palestine front: Getty Images

7. View of Bursa: Ullstein Bild

Index

Abu Hureira, 345–6, 347

Ainsley, Mary, 166, 314, 375

Aisne, France, 267
    1918 German offensive in, 423, 459–62, 464, 465, 486

Albania, 410n

Aleppo, Syria, 141, 218, 219

Alexander Station (Moscow), 116–18

Algeria, 447n

Alpini mountain regiment (Italian army), 173, 196, 249, 402n
    in Battle on Monte Ortigara (1917), 368–72, 377
    see also Monelli, Paolo

Ambulance Américaine (Paris), 97–100

American Red Cross, 171, 434

Amiens, France, 424, 465

Andenne massacre (1914), 106

Andresen, Kresten, xv, 1
    antiwar sentiments of, 29–30, 31, 59, 65–6, 132
    background of, 132
    British Somme offensive and, 286–90
    disappearance of, 290, 500, 500n
    donkey sketched by, 92–3
    at Flensburg training camp, 29, 30–1, 58–9
    French refugees befriended by, 93
    at German front in Billy-Montigny, 223–4, 241–3, 246–7

at German front in Picardy, 63–6, 91–3

injuries and ailments of, 131–3, 241, 247, 273

looting of Lassigny witnessed by, 65–6

monotony and tedium in daily routine of, 224, 241, 246–7, 273

and outbreak of war, 30

in repairing trenches on the Somme, 272–3

shell explosions in Lens experienced by, 182–4

supply kit of, 59–61

Andresen, Thöge, 58

Androwski, Hans, 433

Ankara, Turkey, 326, 390–1

anti-Semitism, 29n, 104, 233, 234, 335

Antwerp, Belgium, 28, 32, 37–8, 39, 51

Anzac Cove (Gaba Tepe), Gallipoli, 121, 502

Argonne, Battle at (1918), 371n, 424

Arlon, Belgium, 472–3, 474, 490, 494

Armenia, 4, 203, 293n

Armenians, 111–15, 227n
    massacres of, 75, 112–13, 114, 140, 219, 227n, 326, 442n

armistice, 424, 499, 501, 502, 503, 504, 505, 506, 507
    German-Russian, 318, 411, 417, 423, 430, 449

Army of the Orient, 188, 433, 434

Arnaud, René, xv
    assault on Mosloy led by, 459–62
    in attempt to receive medical exemption,
        275–6
    in Battle of Verdun (1916), 253–7, 262–7,
        274–5, 276
    in Champagne offensive (1915), 161, 162–4
    dissension in French military observed
        by, 373–4
    and end of war, 502
    and outbreak of war, 86
    in return to regiment at Villers-
        Cotterêts, 459
    and rewritten histiography on the
        Somme, 85–7
Arras, France, 131, 348n
    British offensive at (1917), 317, 348, 353,
        354
Artois, France, French-British offensive in
    (1915), 157, 161, 162
Asiago plateau, 203, 249, 295n, 296n,
    407–8
askaris, 151, 261, 306, 320, 363, 364, 381
Augustów, Poland, 88n, 157–8
Augustów Forest, 5, 158
Australia, 55n, 56, 72, 82, 333
Australia and New Zealand Army Corps
    (ANZAC), 122–3, 236, 483
    Cairo riots and, 109–10
    in convoy from Australia, 54–8, 71
    in Egypt, 71–2, 82–4, 88
    landing on Gallipoli peninsula of, 75,
        115–16, 121
    on Lemnos, 108–9, 110
Australian Expeditionary Force, 57
Austria, 109, 196, 228n, 494
    postwar atmosphere in, 495, 506
Austria-Hungary, 3, 8, 17, 75, 128, 130, 143n,
    196, 204, 415, 424, 449n, 504
    civilian suffering and unrest in, 241–2,
        429, 430, 472, 496
    food shortages in, 241–2, 430, 466n
    railway systems in, 228n, 296n, 343n,
        466n
    Russian retreat from, 118–20, 128, 136n

Austrian air force, 380n, 425–6
Austro-Hungarian army, 4, 20, 65n, 75, 117,
    118, 128, 133, 142, 168, 173, 204, 234, 277,
    290, 292, 296n, 318, 326, 412, 423, 438,
    467, 472, 474
    abolition of censorship and, 490–1
    Asiago plateau offensive of, 203, 249, 250,
        296n, 407–8
    in Battle of Lemberg (1914), 4, 15–16,
        20, 41
    in Battle on Monte Ortigara (1917), 369,
        370, 372
    Caporetto offensive of, 318, 401–3, 414
    in Carpathian mountain passes, 41–3,
        48–50, 75, 96–7, 302
    demobilization of, 494–5, 506
    food and supply shortages in, 96, 216–17,
        343, 416, 438
    guerrilla fighters killed by, 175n–6n
    harsh conditions of, 42–3, 96
    Italian raid on Monte Cauriol and
        (1916), 303
    losses of, 42, 96, 285
    mobilization of, 14–15
    Montenegro occupied by, 213, 216–17, 224
    POWs of, 343, 413, 415–16, 465–7
    Russian Brusilov offensive and, 270, 293,
        296
    Russians driven out of Gorlice by,
        118–20, 128, 156
    Serbia invaded by, 76, 174–5, 180n, 181n,
        213
    in Serbia occupation, 182, 208–9
    STD infections in, 282n
    transport convoys of, 216–17
    uniforms of, 343–4
    see also Kelemen, Pál
Azizi, Mesopotamia, 184, 187

Bachkarova, Maria "Yashka," 385, 385n,
    500n
Baden, SMS, 492–3
Baghdad, 206, 218, 220, 267, 268, 317, 326
    British army's failed advance on, 76,
        184–7, 189, 219–20

Balkans, xi, xii, 10, 62, 131, 180, 336, 352n, 409, 411

Balkan wars (1912–13), 294n

Baltic Sea, 28, 177

barbed wire, 64n, 118, 147, 211, 224, 264

Barbusse, Henri, 289n

Barrès, Maurice, 254n

Base Hospital No. 5, 382, 445
    at Flanders front, 387–90, 396–7, 398–9
    list of day's cases at, 396–7
    in move to Boulogne-sur-Mer, 405, 406
    in sea journey to Europe, 356–7

Basra, Mesopotamia, 4, 184, 186

battlefield communication, 371n, 488

Battle of Verdun, The (Dugard), 266n

Beach Cemetery, 502n

Beersheba, Battle of (1917), 318

Beho Beho, Tanzania, 319–22

Belgian air force, 107, 435, 443, 479
    Coppens's "flying ace" status earned in, 456–7
    Étampes flight training camp of, 190–2, 257–9

Belgian army, 51, 90, 105, 106, 150–1, 238, 365, 405, 406, 465, 473, 479, 501

Belgium, 3, 8, 51, 63, 79, 121, 127n, 153, 154, 161, 324n, 463, 492n
    German invasion of, 3, 32, 37–8, 94–5, 106, 180n
    German occupation of, 39, 51, 106, 176n, 435, 436, 472–3, 477, 494

Belgrade, Serbia, 20, 76, 175, 188, 424

Bell-Irving, Micky, 457, 458

Berlin, Germany, 8, 24, 160, 185, 323n, 328, 395n, 424, 430, 478

Bernard, Tristan, 156–7

Bernhardi, Theodor von, 298

Bethmann-Hollweg, Theobold von, 323, 395n

Beyoğlu, Turkey, 484, 485

Bianchi, Captain, 214, 216

Billy-Montigny, France, 223–4, 241–3, 246–7

black market, 242, 301, 397

Black Sea Fleet, Russian, 177n

Böcker, Captain-Lieutenant, 107

Boelcke, Oswald, 273n

Boer War, 101n, 150n, 238n

Bois de Ville, France, 163, 164

Bolsheviks, 318, 339n, 373n, 404, 406, 416–17, 448, 452, 499, 500n
    German armistice negotiations with, 318, 411, 430n, 449, 449n

Bordeaux, France, 46, 61

Bosna Brod (Bosanki Brod), Bosnia-Herzegovina, 228–9

Bosnia, 209, 228n, 415

Bosniak battalion, 415

Bosphorus, 75, 108n, 502

Boulogne-sur-Mer, France, 405, 406, 431, 445–6, 457

Brazil, 231, 505

bread riots, 317, 334, 336–9

Breendonck, Fort, 39

Bremen (German U-boat), 311n

Brest-Litovsk, Russia, 155, 411, 430

Brest-Litovsk Treaty, 423, 449

Briand, Aristide, 61–2, 81

Bride of Corinth, The (France), 439

British air force, 273, 342, 346, 363, 404, 440
    Constantinople bombing by, 484–5
    severe losses of, 354
    technological advancements in, 352n

British army, 4, 38, 75, 131, 154, 293, 318, 331, 365, 402n, 414, 423, 424, 443, 445, 457, 501
    Army of the Orient of, 188, 279, 433, 434
    Arras offensive of (1917), 317, 348, 353, 354
    barbed wire used by, 64n
    in Battle of Ctesiphon (1915), 76, 186, 187, 220
    in Battle of Neuve Chapelle (1915), 75, 138, 161n
    black battalions used by, 261, 358, 363, 379–80
    Cairo riots and, 109–10
    casualties and losses of, 38, 62, 138, 161n, 165, 186, 260, 308, 321, 330, 345, 446, 483
    criticisms of, 51, 398–9

British army (*continued*)
in East Africa, 150–1, 230–1, 260–2, 274, 293–4, 306–7, 336, 392; *see also* Buchanan, Angus; 25th Royal Fusiliers
Étaples mutiny in, 418*n*
execution of deserters in, 377*n*
in failed advance on Baghdad, 76, 184–7, 189, 219–20
Fifth Army of, 390, 446
55th Division of, 287, 288–9
in fighting at Zillebeke (1915), 165–7
in First Battle of Gaza (1917), 317, 340–3, 345
food and supply shortages in, 130*n*, 161*n*, 205, 222, 223, 243, 246, 260, 268, 274, 309, 345
Force D of, 184–7
German spring offensive of 1918 and, 444, 446, 463
mobilization of, 10–11, 53, 54, 100–2
1915 double-offensive of, 76, 157, 161–4, 165
in Ottoman siege of Kut al-Amara, 76, 189–90, 192–3, 203, 205–7, 218, 219, 220*n*, 222–3, 235–6, 237, 243, 246, 267, 390, 505
in Salonica, 76, 180, 180*n*–1*n*, 188, 279, 433–4
Second Army of, 397, 399
in Second Battle of Gaza (1917), 317, 345–7
Somme offensive of (1916), 203, 272–3, 286–90, 295*n*, 306, 323*n*
in Third Battle of Ypres (1917), 317, 318, 376, 388, 389, 398–400, 406, 416, 436, 446
women barred from the front by, 27, 178, 279
see also Mousley, Edward; Pollard, Alfred
British East Africa, 150*n*, 151
see also East Africa
British Empire, 238*n*, 375, 463
British Expeditionary Force, 127*n*, 310*n*, 418, 501

British navy, 12*n*, 28, 56*n*, 77, 108*n*, 185*n*, 231, 261
in Battle of Jutland (1916), 259–60
blockade of Germany by, 241, 329, 392*n*, 471
in convoy from Australia, 54–8
Mediterranean Fleet of, 447*n*
Q-Ships in, 232*n*
Brusilov, Alexei, 295–7, 384
Brusilov offensive, 203, 270–2, 293, 294, 295–7, 298
Brussels, Belgium, 3, 106, 477
Coppens unauthorized flight over, 435–8
Buchach, Ukraine, 270, 271–2
Buchanan, Angus, xv, 293–4, 306–7, 392
in attack at Ziwani, 363–4
in attack on Beho Beho, 319–22
chickens purchased by, 274, 308, 309
and commanding of pack animals, 248–9
in departure to East Africa, 100–2
and end of war, 503
flora and fauna collected by, 101, 274, 312
in guarding of Uganda railway, 149–50, 151–3, 199–200
hunting by, 260–2, 312, 313
illnesses of, 294, 308, 309, 312, 392, 503
Lindi disembarkment of, 358–9
in march on Moshi, 237–9
and outbreak of war, 100
in storming of Tandamuti ridge, 379–82
Bucharest, Romania, 204, 336
Buckingham Palace, 375–6
Budapest, Hungary, 14, 15, 96, 302, 430, 490, 495, 496
Bulgaria, 76, 95, 112*n*, 180*n*, 424, 449*n*, 504
Bulgarian army, 175, 188, 331, 424, 467, 504
Bursa, Turkey, 447, 467–8

Cairo, Egypt, 72, 109–10
Calais, France, 79, 90, 94
Cameroon, 4, 151, 203, 230–1
Canadian troops, 318, 399, 406
Caporetto offensive, 318, 401–3, 414, 416, 436
Cardiff City Hall, Wales, 154–5

Carpathian Mountains, 84, 117, 118, 290, 295
  Austro-Hungarian army in, 41–3, 48–50, 75, 96–7, 302
Carranza, Venustiano, 417n
carrier pigeons, 371n
Caspian Sea, 247, 449n
Castelgomberto, Italy, 412–13
Castellerio, Italy, 425–6
Catillon, Biéran de, 258
Cattaro (Kotor), Montenegro, 228, 430
Caucasus, 4, 75, 95, 108n, 112n, 134, 225, 226n, 227n, 449n
censorship, 300–1, 322, 324, 388, 446, 454
  Hungary's abolition of, 490–1
Ceylon (Sri Lanka), 58
Chamber of Deputies, 69–70, 365
Champagne, France, 367
  Franco-British 1915 offensive in, 157, 161–4, 373
Château de Chanteloup, 125–6
Château-Thierry, France, 461, 474
chemical weapons, 127, 129, 352, 367, 369, 412, 486, 487, 487n–8n, 489
Cher Ami (carrier pigeon), 371n
cheroots, 207, 278
Chertoviche raid (1916), 210–13
China, 4, 11n
Chlorodyne, 222, 222n–3n
cholera, 43, 59, 134, 155
Chortkov, Austria-Hungary, 233–5
Christians, 113, 172
  massacres of, 112n, 139–41, 192, 219, 326
Churchill, Winston, 108n, 457n
Cima Dodici, 249–50
Cima Undici, 249–52
Clausewitz, Carl von, 298, 299
Clemenceau, Georges, 279n
Coeurs de soldats (Corday), 45
Comédie-Française (Paris), 439–41
Committee on Inventions, 301
communication, battlefield, 371n, 488
Compiègne, France, 70
Constantine I of Greece, 180n

Constantinople, 71n, 95, 112n, 114, 185, 219, 220, 323n, 391, 442
  bombing raid on, 484–5
  POW camp in, 446, 447–8, 505
Coppens, Willy, xv, 105–8, 376–7
  air patrol wounding of, 478–82, 504
  and end of war, 504
  at Étampes flight training camp, 190–2, 257–9
  fatal training accidents listed by, 257–9
  "flying ace" status earned by, 456–7
  German observation balloons shot down by, 456, 476–7, 480
  and German pilot's fatal fall, 443–4
  heroic intervention in dogfight by, 404–5
  leisure time enjoyed by, 413–14, 456–7, 477
  and outbreak of war, 106
  patrol snowstorm experienced by, 426–7
  pilot aspirations of, 105–6, 107, 191
  in unauthorized flight over Brussels, 435–8
  Zeppelin sighting of, 105, 107
Corday, Charlotte, 45n
Corday, Michel, xv, 45–6
  Anatole France visited by, 393–5
  at Bastille Day celebrations, 142–3
  on bias and censorship in wartime press, 299–301, 322, 324–5, 454
  Briand and Sembat's lunch with, 61–3
  in Chamber of Deputies, 69–70, 365
  and end of war, 501
  on France's sex industry, 281–3, 365
  German bombardment of Paris and, 452–6
  Paris air raids and, 439–41
  socialist and antiwar sentiments of, 45, 46, 62, 156, 395
  on train rides through wartime France, 46–8, 156–7, 213–14, 468–9
  waning enthusiasm for war observed by, 142–3, 322–3, 397, 428–9
  on women's wartime fashion, 46, 469–70
Corfu, 208, 279, 434
Coronel, Chile, 56n, 78n

Cossacks, 24, 40, 134, 135–6, 226, 233–4

Cowley, Charles Henry, 246

Ctesiphon, Battle of (1915), 76, 186, 187, 220

Cushing, Harvey, xv, 97–100, 315, 382, 445–6, 452
  as critical of British army's methods, 398–9
  and end of war, 503
  Estaunié's visit with, 464–5
  at Flanders front, 387–90, 396–7, 398–400, 406
  frozen hand phenomenon studied by, 475–6
  head wounds as specialty of, 388, 397
  illness of, 474, 485–6, 503
  injured friend visited by, 457–8
  interesting medical cases observed by, 98–100, 476, 486–90
  list of day's cases made by, 396–7
  Lusitania wreckage seen by, 357
  at McCrae's funeral, 431–2
  POW camp visited by, 445
  sea voyage to Europe of, 356–7
  three-dimensional map studied by, 389
  in train from Paris to Boulogne-sur-Mer, 405–7

Cuy, France, 63–6, 91–3

Dano-German War (1864), 30n, 41

da Pèrgine, Garbari, 252

D'Aquila, Vincenzo, xvi, 168–9, 172
  mental illness of, 214–16, 240, 304–6
  in return to U.S., 505
  at Third Battle of Isonzo, 171–4
  typhus infection of, 194–5, 208, 214–16
  volunteer enlistment of, 145–7

Dardanelles operation (1915), 108–9, 108n–9n

Dar es-Salaam, Tanzania, 308, 503

David, Jacques-Louis, 45n

Dawkins, Arthur, 236

Dawkins, William Henry, xv, 56–7
  Cairo riots and, 109–10
  in convoy from Australia, 54–8, 71
  death of, 123, 502

in Egypt, 71–2, 82–4, 88, 108–10, 120n
  on Gallipoli peninsula, 115–16, 120–3
  in Lemnos harbor, 110
  personal effects of, 236–7

Delcassé, Théophile, 142–3

Delna, Marie, 374

dengue fever, 279, 434

de Nogales Méndez, Rafael Inchauspe, xv, 94, 442–3
  in applying for discharge from Ottoman army, 141, 218–19, 503
  arrival at Third Army Erzurum headquarters of, 93, 95–6
  and end of war, 502–3
  execution of deserter witnessed by, 276–8
  in First Battle of Gaza (1917), 340–3, 345
  Liman von Sanders paid courtesy call by, 441–2
  massacres of civilians witnessed by, 112–13, 114, 139–41, 192, 219
  and outbreak of war, 93–4
  in Second Battle of Gaza (1917), 345–7
  on ship heading down Tigris, 218–22
  Van uprising and, 111–15

De Panne, Belgium, 89–91, 105, 129–31, 456, 481, 504

Diksmuide, Belgium, 436, 437, 456

Dimitriev, Radko, 118

Dinant massacre, 106

diphtheria, 59

Djevded Bey, 114

Dniester River, 270n, 290–3

Douala, Cameroon, 230n

Douaumont, Fort de, 255, 299

Dreadnought, HMS, 12n

Dr. Hector Munro's Flying Ambulance Corps., 50–2

Driscoll, Patrick, 101n

Driscoll's Scouts, 101n

drug abuse, 222n–3n, 365

Dujaila, Battle of (1916), 235–6

Dunkirk, France, 90, 427

dysentery, 155, 222, 308, 309, 312

East Africa, xii, 274, 317, 318, 358–9
  askari soldiers in, 151, 261, 306, 320, 363,
    364, 381
  black battalions used in, 261, 358, 363,
    379–80
  British advance on German colonies
    in, 150–1, 230–1, 237–9, 248, 261, 262,
    293–4, 308–9, 312–13, 319–22, 336, 358,
    363–4, 380
  British army's guarding of railways in,
    149–50, 151–3, 199–200
  British troops departure to, 100–2
  camaraderie among warring whites in,
    381–2
  guerrilla warfare tactics used in, 248,
    308, 320
  harsh climate and terrain in, 150, 152,
    238–9, 260, 261, 294, 308, 320, 321
  horses and mules lost in, 238–9, 249
  hunting by British troops in, 260–2, 312,
    313
  malnourishment and disease in, 260–1,
    306, 308, 309, 312, 358, 392, 503
  see also German East Africa
Eastern Front, xii, 40n, 297, 333, 336, 352n,
    416, 436
  Germany's series of 1915 victories along,
    141–2, 154, 156
  Russian army's 1915 retreat from, 76, 128,
    136n, 142, 144–5, 155, 156, 170, 211
  Western Front trench system vs., 118n
East Prussia, 3, 33n, 44, 67, 160
  Russian invasion of, 3, 4, 17–18, 19–20,
    24, 136n
Egypt, 71–2, 82–4, 88, 112n, 120n, 236
  Cairo riots in, 109–10
Elbe River, 12, 229
England, 129, 223, 359, 429, 504
  German air raids on, 107–8, 440
  German naval attacks on, 78, 78n
English Channel, 28, 89, 105, 106, 107, 446
Enver Pasha, 220
Ernst, Otto, 13–14
Erzurum, Turkey, 93, 95–6
Estaunié, Édouard, 464–5

Étampes training camp, France, 190–2,
    257–9
Étaple mutiny (1917), 418n
Evrard, Lili, 259

Falkland Islands, Battle of the (1914), 78n
Farewell to Arms, A (Hemingway), 402n
Farmborough, Florence, xv, 22, 116–20, 157,
    193, 283, 400
  Bolshevik coup in Russia and, 404
  Chertoviche raid followed by, 210–13
  civilian suffering in Chortkov observed
    by, 233–5
  death first witnessed by, 22–3, 292, 451
  deserted enemy trenches visited by, 267,
    270, 290–1
  in final arduous journey home, 427–8,
    451–2, 499–500
  German breakthrough on the San and,
    133–6
  in march from Minsk, 169–71
  paratyphoid fever of, 307
  in post-revolution Moscow, 427–8
  in return to front at Voloschyna, 366–7
  River Dniester battlefield visited by,
    290–3
  in Romania, 382–5, 403–4
  Russian army's retreat from Gorlice
    witnessed by, 118–20, 133
  winter in Trostyanitse of, 333–5
  wounded in Buchach treated by, 271–2
Ferdinand, Franz, Archduke of Austria, 3,
    10, 82n, 209
Ferguson, Niall, 106n
Feydeau, Georges, 281, 282n
Finland, 174, 430n, 449n
Firefly (British gunboat), 222
First Balkan War (1912–13), 112n
1st Russian Women's Battalion of Death,
    385n
Fiume (Rijeka), Croatia, 228
Flameng, François, 281–2
Flanders, 4, 39, 120n, 131, 162n, 317, 424
  First Battle of Ypres in (1914), 51, 52
  influenza outbreak in, 465

Flanders (*continued*)
  1918 German offensive in, 423, 452, 457
  Third Battle of Ypres in (1917), 317, 318,
    376, 388, 389, 396, 397, 398–400, 406,
    416, 436, 446
Flensburg, Germany, 29, 30–1, 63
Florence, Italy, 305–6
food shortages, 40*n*, 92, 103, 105, 117, 155,
    168, 234, 241–2, 247, 306, 430, 466*n*
  in Austro-Hungarian army, 96, 216–17,
    416
  in British army, 205, 260, 269, 274
  in France, 92, 301, 325, 428
  in Germany, 79–80, 241–2, 301, 329, 392,
    430, 474, 477, 491
  in London, 458
  in Ottoman Empire, 277
  in Russia, 40*n*, 241, 334, 337, 428
  in siege of Kut al-Amara, 222, 223, 243,
    246, 269
Fouccault (French submarine), 380*n*
France, 3, 8, 21*n*, 29*n*, 31, 83*n*, 106, 121, 130,
    180, 211*n*, 231, 254*n*, 279*n*, 287, 293*n*,
    300*n*, 313, 332, 357, 359, 449, 486, 492*n*,
    494, 499*n*, 500*n*, 501
  air raids on, 439–41, 445, 457, 464
  Allied double-offensive in, 157, 161–4, 183
  bias and censorship of wartime press
    coverage in, 299–301, 322, 324–5, 454
  black market in, 301, 397
  Cameroon divided between Britain and,
    203, 231*n*
  civilian unrest in, 373, 428–9, 449
  Corday's train rides through, 46–8,
    156–7, 213–14, 468–9
  destruction in, 63, 65, 81, 92, 445, 455,
    464–5
  food shortages in, 92, 301, 325, 428
  German army's 1917 planned withdrawal
    in, 317, 330–1, 348
  German army's 1918 spring offensive in,
    423, 447, 452–3, 459–62, 464–5, 467,
    468–9, 473–4, 486
  initial wartime patriotism and jubilance
    in, 46–8, 86, 394, 453

looting of villages in, 65–6
propaganda in, 47, 157, 255, 323, 324, 501
prostitution and sexual immorality in,
    70, 281–3, 285, 365, 405–6
refugees in, 46, 65, 93, 94, 283
waning wartime enthusiasm in, 142–3,
    180, 322–3, 394, 397, 428–9, 448
France, Anatole, 46, 393–5, 439, 464
Franco-Prussian War (1870–71), 41, 64*n*,
    162*n*
freebooting, 55, 57–8, 78, 94
"freedom offensive" (Kerensky offensive),
    317, 366, 383–4, 385
French air force, 436, 440
French army, 3, 64, 65*n*, 95, 99, 131, 132, 183,
    217, 311*n*, 331, 354, 414, 415
  attempts to receive service exemptions
    in, 255, 275–6, 283, 307–8
  barbed wire used by, 64*n*
  in Battle at the Somme (1916), 299–300
  in Battle of Verdun (1916), 253–7, 262–7,
    274–5, 276, 295*n*, 299
  carefully worded communiqués of, 87,
    265–6, 287, 454
  casualties and losses of, 62, 161*n*, 164, 254,
    265, 266, 275, 300*n*, 353*n*, 416, 487
  in East Africa, 150–1, 230–1
  in First Battle of the Marne (1914), 81–2
  at front in Billy-Montigny, 224
  general dissension in, 373–4, 410
  late-war confusion and inexperience in,
    459, 460, 461, 483
  Le Chemin des Dames offensive of
    (1917), 317, 353, 373
  mutinies in, 317, 353*n*, 366, 373–4, 416, 436
  1915 double-offensive of, 76, 157, 161–4,
    373
  1918 German spring offensive vs., 423,
    459–62, 463, 486
  Russian battalions in service to, 448,
    449–50
  waning morale in, 275, 353*n*, 373
  see also Arnaud, René
French Revolution, 410
French socialist party, 62

Froidterre, Fort de, 264–5
Fuller, Loie, 61

Gaba Tepe (Anzac Cove), Gallipoli, 121
Galicia (Austria-Hungary province), 15,
    233, 385
    civilian suffering in, 233–5
    Russian invasion of, 3, 15–16, 20, 41, 75,
        142
    Russian retreat from, 117–20, 128, 133, 156
Gallipoli peninsula, 110, 120–3, 441–2
    ANZAC's landing on, 75, 115–16, 121
    evacuation of Allied forces from, 76,
        188n
gas, poisonous, 127, 129, 352, 367, 369, 412,
    486, 487, 487n–8n, 489
Gavrelle, France, 349–52
Gaza, 442
    First Battle of (1917), 317, 340–3, 345
    Second Battle of (1917), 317, 345–7
George V, King of England, 287, 376
Georges-Picot, François, 293n
German air force, 273, 342, 352n, 353, 404,
    413, 433, 443, 456
    air raids by, 18–19, 24, 32, 61, 89, 107–8,
        217, 439–41, 457, 464
    Coppens's first battle with, 354–5
    observation balloons of, 456, 476–7,
        479n, 480
    Willi Kuhr's call-up to, 471–2
    Zeppelins used by, 32, 61, 105, 107–8, 217,
        439, 440
German army, 11, 20, 21n, 40, 44, 53, 75, 76,
    88, 94–5, 99, 137, 138, 144, 148, 149, 155,
    169, 179, 183, 204, 210, 213, 219, 277, 318,
    329, 330, 359, 367, 368n, 383, 394, 401,
    432, 442, 479, 495, 501
    askari soldiers used by, 151, 261, 306, 320,
        363, 364, 381
    atrocities committed by, 98, 106, 176n
    in attack at Gavrelle (1917), 349–52
    in Battle of Opatov (1914), 32–7
    in Battle of Verdun (1916), 203, 242–3,
        253–4, 255–7, 262–4, 265–6, 296n, 299,
        371n

Belgium invasion and occupation by, 3,
    32, 37–8, 39, 51, 94–5, 106, 176n, 180n,
    435, 436, 472–3, 477, 494
    and British attack on Hooge (1915), 138–9
    and British offensive on the Somme
        (1916), 272–3, 286–90
    Caporetto offensive of, 318, 402, 414
    carrier pigeons used by, 371n
    casualties and losses in, 88n, 288
    class system in, 361
    in East Africa, 150, 199, 230, 237–8, 239,
        248, 261, 262, 306–7, 308, 318, 319–22,
        336, 358, 363–4, 380–2
    execution of deserters in, 377n
    in fighting at Zillebeke (1915), 165–7
    in First Battle of Gaza (1917), 341, 342
    in First Battle of the Marne (1914), 46,
        81–2
    food and supply shortages in, 242, 247,
        261, 306
    Franco-British 1915 double-offensive vs.,
        161–2, 163, 164
    French 1917 offensive at Le Chemin des
        Dames vs., 367, 373
    guerrilla fighters killed by, 175n–6n
    guerrilla tactics used by, 248, 308, 320
    influenza epidemic in, 465, 483n
    looting by, 40, 65–6, 103, 106, 381
    mobilization of, 3, 6–10, 12, 30, 66
    1914 march on Paris of, 3, 4, 46, 61, 81
    in 1915 breakthrough at Gorlice, 118–20,
        128, 134n, 156, 254
    in 1915 breakthrough on the San, 133–5
    in 1917 planned withdrawal from France,
        317, 330–1, 348
    1918 Allied counter-offensive vs., 423,
        424, 482, 486–7
    1918 French assault on Mosloy and,
        459–62
    in 1918 push on Paris, 453, 454, 464, 465,
        483n
    1918 spring offensive of, 423, 428, 436,
        444, 446, 447, 452–3, 457, 459–62, 463,
        464–5, 467, 468–9, 473–4, 486
    149th Infantry Regiment of, 6–10

German army (*continued*)
  Ottoman uprisings against, 485
  POWs captured by, 40–1, 104, 124–5, 459, 473, 474
  in rewritten incident on the Somme, 85–7
  Russian Brusilov offensive and, 296, 297
  Russian raid in Chertoviche and (1916), 211, 212
  Serbia invasion by, 76, 174–5, 180*n*, 181*n*, 213
  siege and capture of Antwerp by, 32, 37–8, 39, 51
  STD reduction measures in, 282*n*–3*n*
  at Stokhod front, 294–5, 297–9
  storm-troop tactics of, 402*n*, 414, 444
  Suwalki invasion and occupation by, 25–6, 44, 48, 84–5, 102–5, 124–5, 141–2, 155–6, 159
  waning morale in, 241–2
  see also Andresen, Kresten
German East Africa, 151, 230–1, 261, 262, 293–4, 306–7, 308–9, 312–13, 336, 358
  attack at Ziwani in, 363–4
  attack on Beho Beho in, 319–22
  British troops march on Moshi in, 237–9, 248
  French-British dividing of land in, 203, 231*n*
  storming of Tandamuti ridge in, 379–82
  see also East Africa
Germania (warship), 457
German navy, 11, 12, 177, 230*n*, 359
  in Battle of Jutland (1916), 259–60, 310, 328
  class system in, 360–2
  converted freighters used in, 230–1, 232*n*
  early lack of success for, 77–8, 231
  freebooting in, 55, 57–8, 78
  High Seas Fleet of, *see* High Seas Fleet, German
  Lusitania sunk by, 75, 357
  Pacific Squadron of, 55*n*–6*n*, 78*n*
  POWs captured by, 58*n*
  U-boats of, 75, 77, 181, 232*n*, 245, 311, 317, 323*n*, 328, 356, 357, 380, 505

  waning morale in, 311–12
  see also specific ships and battles
Germany, 3, 4, 22, 29*n*, 30, 55*n*, 78, 88*n*, 94, 98, 106*n*, 130, 131–2, 151*n*, 154, 171, 203, 238, 261, 293, 300*n*, 317, 335, 417*n*, 429, 434, 494, 501
  air raids on, 440, 472
  Andresen's near-evacuation to, 132–3
  animosity toward British of, 11–12, 328, 359
  British blockade of, 241, 329, 392*n*, 471
  chemical weapons used by, 127, 129, 352, 367, 487, 487*n*–8*n*, 489
  civilian suffering and unrest in, 241–2, 360, 430–1, 491–2, 498
  class system in, 360–2
  food shortages in, 79–80, 241–2, 301, 329, 335, 392, 430, 470, 471, 474, 477, 491
  imperialist ambitions of, 11, 104, 143, 226, 238*n*, 324*n*, 359, 395*n*, 449*n*, 463, 492*n*
  influence on Ottoman Empire of, 441*n*, 485
  1918 canon bombardment of Paris by, 446, 453, 454–6, 464
  patriotism and wartime enthusiasm in, 8, 12–13, 39, 284
  peace initiatives of, 204, 323–4, 395
  POWS held in, 40–1
  in prewar naval race, 12*n*
  propaganda in, 13–14, 104, 225*n*, 255, 360, 473, 491
  revolution in, 424, 491, 491*n*, 494, 501, 507–8
  Russian armistice with, 318, 411, 417, 423, 430, 449
  sexual immorality on rise in, 284–6
  unrestricted U-boat warfare waged by, 317, 323*n*, 328, 380
  waning support and enthusiasm for war in, 360, 367, 393, 430, 433, 478, 491–2, 497–8
  war rumors and misinformation in, 7–8, 13, 14, 28, 30
  wave of strikes in, 430–1
Gevgelí, Macedonia, 181, 187–9

Glebovka, 128–9

Goethe, Johann Wolfgang von, 81, 213

Goltz, Colmar von der, 219, 220, 298

Gorizia, Italy, 204, 293n

Gorlice, Austria-Hungary, 117–18, 134n, 254
  Russian army driven out of, 118–20, 128,
    133, 156

Grandcourt, France, 329–31

Great Britain, 3, 8, 11n, 17, 53, 54, 55n, 68,
    71, 106, 154, 211n, 223, 225, 247, 312, 313,
    328, 499n
  German air raids on, 107–8, 440
  Germany's animosity toward, 11–12, 328,
    359
  imperialist ambitions in, 71, 203, 225n,
    231, 238n, 293n
  Macnaughtan's lecture tour of, 130, 153–5,
    179, 225
  risk of economic collapse in, 356, 380
  waning wartime support in, 458
  see also British army

Greece, 112n, 180n, 181, 188, 279

Grenadiers, 2nd Regiment of (Belgian
    army), 106

guerrilla warfare, 106n, 209
  death penalty for fighters of, 176–7
  of forces in East Africa, 248, 308, 320

Guillemont, France, 287, 289

Gumprecht, Ella, 40, 41

Haensch, Dora, 244, 245

Hage, Etienne, 479–80

Haig, Douglas, 287

Halicz, Hungary, 15–16

Halil Pasha, 220, 268n

Hamadan, Persia, 227, 236

Hamburg, Germany, 242, 430

Hamilton, William, 83

Hamisi (African servant), 261, 262

hand grenades, 166, 167, 263, 264, 313, 349,
    350, 351, 488

Hanna, Battle of (1916), 220n

Hansen, Johannes, 288

Hansen, Karl, 288

Harley, Mrs., 126, 127n, 332

Hart prison camp, 466–7

Helgoland, SMS, 11, 12, 12n, 14, 328, 429
  in Battle of Jutland (1916), 259–60, 328
  Jutland anniversary celebration on,
    359–60, 361–2
  in Kiel, 177–8
  lack of action seen by, 28, 77–9, 177–8, 361
  monotonous routine of, 78–9, 310–11, 360

Heligoland Bight, Battle of (1914), 77

Hemingway, Ernest, 402n

Henri Farmans (aeroplanes), 258n

High Seas Fleet, German, 11, 12n, 77, 78, 229,
    231, 310, 359
  in Battle of Jutland (1916), 259–60, 310,
    328
  class system in, 360–2
  mutiny in, 424, 491, 492–4
  SMS Helgoland of, see Helgoland, SMS
  SMS Möwe's triumphant return and,
    230–2

Hindenburg, Paul von, 33n, 88, 103n, 395n

Hindenburg Line, 317, 348, 424

Hitler, Adolf, 371n, 507–8

Holland, 160–1, 171, 436, 463, 501

Hooge, Belgium, 136–9

hospitals, see military hospitals and field
    units

Hotel Astoria, 178, 179, 336, 337, 338–9

Hôtel Terminus, 190–1

Houthulst, Belgium, 353, 456

Hungary, 96, 97, 169, 228n, 295, 344
  abolition of censorship in, 490–1
  civilian unrest in, 430, 496
  see also Austria-Hungary

Ibuki (Japanese cruiser), 56

Immelmann, Max, 273

India, 151, 184, 331, 449n

Infanterie greift an (Infantry Attacks)
    (Rommel), 402n

"In Flanders Fields" (McCrae), 431–2

inflation, 131n, 152, 241, 242, 268, 333, 334,
    491

influenza, 465, 478, 482, 483–4, 499, 501

Intérieurs d'officiers (Corday), 45

Ireland, 203, 231, 357
Isonzo, 75, 76, 407, 472
    Caporetto offensive on, 318, 401–3, 414
    later Italian offensives on, 203, 204, 249,
        293n, 317, 318, 400
    Third Battle of (1915), 76, 168, 171–4
Italian air force, 425–6
Italian army, 75, 142n–3n, 240, 293, 295n,
        331, 433, 501, 506
    Alpini mountain regiment of, see Alpini
        mountain regiment
    in Battle on Monte Ortigara (1917),
        368–72, 377
    casualties and losses of, 173, 303
    collapse at Caporetto of (1917), 318,
        401–2, 414, 416, 436
    D'Aquila's volunteer enlistment into,
        145–7
    execution of deserters in, 377–9
    lack of war updates in, 400–1
    later Isonzo offensives of, 203, 204, 249,
        293n, 317, 318, 400, 401–2
    on Monte Cauriol, 302–4, 309–10
    Monte Panarotta attack by (1915), 195–6,
        197–9
    1917 retreat of, 318, 402, 406, 407, 412
    in retreat from Cima Undici (1916),
        249–52
    River Piave line of defense of, 318, 406,
        407, 414
    in Third Battle of Isonzo (1915), 76, 168,
        171–4
    25th Regiment of, 146, 168–9, 172, 173
Italy, 83n, 143n, 168, 195, 196, 211n, 228, 250,
        336, 352n, 406, 425, 438, 444, 466, 505
    war entry of, 75, 131, 134, 142, 196

Japan, 4, 11, 21n, 94, 95, 499n
    military forces of, 4, 56, 269n
Jerusalem, 277, 318, 345, 442
Jews, 15, 20–1, 85, 113, 277, 293, 384
    anti-Semitism and, 29n, 104, 233, 234, 335
Joffre, Joseph, 162
Jovičić, Milan "Jovi," 332, 333, 434, 463
Julnar, SS, 246, 268

Jutland, Battle of (1916), 203, 259–60, 310,
        328, 359

Känslornas krig (Ljunggren), 284n
Kastamonu prison camp, 326–8, 355, 390,
        391
Kelemen, Pál, xv, 14–16, 169, 343–4
    abolition of censorship and, 490–1
    accident on Caldonazzo mountain road
        witnessed by, 438–9
    at Bosna Brod railway station, 228–9
    in Carpathian mountain passes, 41–3,
        96–7
    demobilization of, 494–5
    dogfight over Castellerio watched by,
        425–6
    in German-occupied Arlon, 472–3, 474,
        490
    Glebovka bread bought by, 128–9
    at hanging of Serbian guerrilla, 176–7
    Isonzo battalion returning from battle
        and, 401–3
    malaria of, 227–8, 301
    Muslim Bosniaks as impressive to, 414–15
    officers' brothel visited by, 182
    at Sátoraljaújhely restaurant, 301–2
    scene of Ferdinand's assassination visited
        by, 209–10
    in Serbia invasion and occupation, 174–5,
        182, 208–9
    transport convoys watched by, 216–17
    wounding of, 48–50, 96
Kemal, Colonel Mustafa (Kemal Atatürk),
        116n
Kerensky, Alexander, 383n, 384, 404, 500n
Kerensky offensive ("freedom offensive"),
        317, 366, 383–4, 385
Kiel, Germany, 12n, 177–8, 424
Kiel Canal, 28, 177
Kiev, Ukraine, 337, 427
Kilimanjaro, 237, 239, 248
King, Mary, 247
King, Olive May, xv, 126
    in evacuation of Gevgelí field hospital,
        187–9

in final departure from Salonica, 504–5
ideological beliefs of, 463
in journey to Gevgelí, 180–1
loss of eyebrows and, 435
medal awarded to, 462–3
procession for shot down German plane
    watched by, 217–18
in raging fires of Salonica, 385–7, 434
romantic affairs of, 332–3, 434, 462
Salonica living conditions of, 278–80, 331,
    333, 433–5
in Serbian military medical service,
    331–3, 385, 434, 435, 462, 463, 504
in set-up of Troyes medical unit, 125–8
King Edward VII, HMS, 231
komidatschi, 175n, 176
Königsberg SMS, 261, 364
Kotur Tepe, 111, 112n, 113
Kressenstein, Friedrich Kress von, 342, 345
Kuhr, Elfriede, xv
    brother's call-up by military and, 432–3,
        471–2
    children's hospital volunteer work of,
        470–1, 474–5
    conflicted feelings of, on war, 245, 367,
        433
    disturbance between warrant officer and
        soldier witnessed by, 244–6
    and end of war, 497–8
    feeding of troops by, 66–7
    food shortages and, 79–80, 335, 470, 471,
        474, 477
    melancholy nocturnal singing heard by,
        143–4
    149th Infantry's Schneidemühl departure
        witnessed by, 6–10
    "peasant's omelette" perfected by, 392
    rise in sexual immorality observed by,
        284–6
    romantic relationship of, 286, 336, 392–3
    Waldecker's coffin procession watched
        by, 408–9
    war cemetery visited by, 158–9
    war stories overheard by, 39–41
Kuhr, Willi, 6, 8, 39, 432–3, 471–2, 478, 498

Kut al-Amara, Mesopotamia, 76, 184,
    189–90, 203, 205–7, 218, 219, 220n,
    222–3, 267, 317, 336, 390, 505
    failed British relief efforts in, 235–6, 237,
        246
    food shortages in, 222, 223, 243, 246, 269

Langemarck, Battle of (1914), 61, 353
Lassigny, France, 63–6, 92
Laval, France, 448–50
Lebanon, 112n, 293n
Le Boulanger (French pilot), 258, 259
Le Chemin des Dames, 459
    French offensive at, 317, 353, 367, 373
Lemberg, Austria-Hungary, 44, 128, 134
    fall of, 141–2, 155
Lemberg, Battle of (1914), 4, 15–16, 20, 41
Lemnos, Greece, 108–9, 110, 122
Lenger, Jørgen, 184, 288
Lens, France, 183–4
Lessing, Doris, 101n
Lettow-Vorbeck, Paul von, 151, 261, 320,
    358, 382
Leverenz, Lieutenant, 392–3
Libeau, Gustave, 413
Libya, 83n
Lille, France, 469
Lindi, Tanzania, 358–9, 363, 364, 503
Liulevicius, Vejas Gabriel, 125n
Ljunggren, Jens, 284n
Lobanov-Rostovsky, Andrei, xv
    in Battle of Opatov (1914), 32–7
    eclipse witnessed by, 21
    illnesses of, 337, 499
    in leading troops across Pisoderi Pass,
        409–12
    at Mokotov camp, 19–21
    and outbreak of war, 20
    oversleeping in Tchapli of, 148–9
    in riot-torn Petrograd, 336–9
    in Russian eastern retreat, 144–5, 147,
        148–9
    Russian Revolution as viewed by, 337,
        410–11, 448, 499
    in snowstorm at Lomza, 88–9

Lobanov-Rostovsky, Andrei (*continued*)
  soldiers' committee election of, 339–40
  on Stokhod front, 294–5, 297–9
  troop rebellion at Laval camp and,
    448–50, 499
Lomza, Poland, 88–9
London, England, 10, 26, 53, 54, 61, 79, 90,
    92, 108, 130, 185, 280, 323n, 345, 376,
    391, 434
  air raids on, 440
  depressing wartime climate in, 457–8
  Macnaughtan's final journey home to,
    247–8
  Waterloo Station in, 100–2
Loos, Battle of (1915), 161, 165
looting, 18, 40, 65–6, 85, 103, 106, 135–6, 175,
    196, 271, 346–7, 381, 387, 496
Loretto Heights, France, 131, 183
Lothringen (Lorraine), 3, 81
Ludendorff, Erich, 33n, 395n, 491
Lusitania, RMS, 75, 357, 471
Luxembourg, 3, 472

Macedonia, 279, 424
machine guns, 296n, 320–1, 343, 418
Macnaughtan, Sarah, xv, 174, 178–80
  antiwar sentiments of, 90, 129–30
  at Antwerp field hospital, 32, 37–8
  death of, 280, 498
  in De Panne, 89–91, 129–31
  fall of Antwerp witnessed by, 37–8, 51
  in final journey home to London, 247–8
  in journey to Antwerp, 26–8
  lecture tour of, 130, 153–5, 179, 225
  on morality of women, 123–4
  nervous breakdown of, 79, 90
  and outbreak of war, 10–11, 27
  in Persia, 224–7, 236, 244
  poor health of, 90–1, 226, 236, 244, 248,
    280
  sense of duty and principles of, 27, 90,
    129, 153, 154
  soup kitchen work of, 68, 79, 89, 90–1,
    129
  at Veurne field hospital, 50–2, 67–9, 89

waning enthusiasm for war effort in,
    129–31, 225, 226, 236
Maktau, East Africa, 149–50, 151–3
malaria, 185, 227–8, 301, 309, 312, 327, 332,
    337, 391, 410, 434
Mann, Thomas, 284n
Marat, Jean-Paul, 45n
Marne, First Battle of the (1914), 4, 46, 62,
    81–2, 406
Marne, Second Battle of the (1918), 423,
    459, 468–9, 473–4, 486
Mashobara (troopship), 110
Maurice Farmans (aeroplanes), 258n, 259
Maxim's (Paris), 281–3
McCrae, John, 431–2
Mediterranean Fleet, British, 447n
Mein Kampf (Hitler), 506–7
mental illness, 214–16, 240, 304–6
  frozen hands and lame feet phenomenon
    and, 475–6
  shell shock and, 116, 123n, 215, 357, 486,
    488–9, 490
Mesopotamia, xii, 4, 192, 219, 221, 293n, 317,
    336, 352n, 423, 424, 502
  British army's failed advance on
    Baghdad in, 76, 184–7, 189, 219–20
  Ottoman siege at Kut al-Amara in, 76,
    189–90, 192–3, 203, 205–7, 218, 219,
    220n, 222–3, 235–6, 237, 243, 246, 390,
    505
  POWs held captive in, 267–70, 326–7,
    390–1, 446–8
Meuse River, 161, 203, 453
Mexico, 417n, 486
Middle East, 71n, 238n, 341, 442
military hospitals and field units, 22–3, 28,
    47, 84, 89, 153, 178, 186, 219, 245, 307,
    313, 381, 400, 405, 431, 457, 503
  Ambulance Américaine (Paris), 97–100
  Andresen treated in, 131–2, 241
  in Antwerp, 32, 37–8
  Base Hospital No. 5, *see* Base Hospital
    No. 5
  Coppens treated in, 481–2, 504
  Cushing treated in, 485–6, 503

D'Aquila treated in, 194–5, 208, 214–16, 240, 304–5
dental surgery in, 100
Dr. Hector Munro's Flying Ambulance Corps., 50–2
in Gorlice, 117–20
interesting medical cases observed at, 98–100, 272, 476, 486–90
Kelemen's malaria treated in, 228
mental illness and neurological disorders treated in, 214–16, 240, 304–6, 357, 475–6, 486, 490
Mobile Field Hospital No. 10, see Mobile Field Hospital No. 10
Mrs. St. Clair Stobart's ambulance unit, 26, 51
in Persia, 225, 227
in Salonica, 278–80, 434
on the San, 134–5, 136
Scottish Women's Hospital, see Scottish Women's Hospital
"souvenir surgeries" performed at, 99
stomach wounds treated in, 271, 272, 403
techniques for treating head wounds in, 388, 397
"trench foot" treated in, 68, 98
Turczynowicz lending hand at, 18–19, 124
in Veurne, 50–2, 67–9, 89
Minsk, Belarus, 169–70
M'Kubwa, Bwana, 313
Mobile Field Hospital No. 10, 84, 117–20, 157, 193, 210
see also Farmborough, Florence
Molodych, 133–5
Monelli, Paolo, xvi, 201, 207–8, 421
Austrian capture of, 412–13
in baptism of fire at Monte Panarotta, 195–6, 197–9
in Battle on Monte Ortigara (1917), 368–72
in communion with dead man, 303–4
in defense of Monte Tondarecar, 407–8
in deterring of nosy military visitors, 325–6
and end of war, 506
execution of deserters witnessed by, 377–9
on Monte Cauriol, 302–4, 309–10
and outbreak of war, 196
in POW camps, 415–16, 465–7
in retreat from Cima Undici, 249–52
in Roncegno bombing, 240–1
troops lack of war updates and, 400–1
Monte Cauriol, Italy, 302–4, 309–10
Monte Cima, 249
Montenegro, 95, 213, 216–17, 224, 228n
Monte Ortigara, Italy, 368–72, 377
Monte Panrotta, Monelli's baptism of fire at, 195–6, 197–9
Monte Santa Lucia, Italy, 168, 171–4
Moscow, 22, 84, 210, 334, 427, 451–2
Alexander Station in, 116–18
post-revolution climate in, 428, 451
Moshi, Tanzania, 238, 239, 248
Mousley, Edward, xvi, 73, 184, 467
British army's failed advance on Baghdad and, 184–7
Constantinople bombing witnessed by, 484–5
failed escape bid of, 446–7, 467
health issues and injuries of, 222, 267–9, 327, 390–1
in Ottoman siege of Kut al-Amara, 189–90, 192–3, 205–7, 222–3, 235–6, 237, 243, 246, 267, 390
as POW, 267–70, 326–8, 355, 390–1, 446, 447–8, 467–8
release from captivity of, 505–6
sonnet written by, 467–8
Möwe, SMS, 230–2
Mrs. St. Clair Stobart's ambulance unit, 26, 51
Munson, Kenneth, 352n
Muslims, 111, 112n, 140, 278
mustard gas, 486, 487, 487n–8n, 489
mutinies, 317, 353n, 366, 373–4, 416, 418, 424, 436, 491, 492–4

Narunyu, 392, 503
nationalism, 13–14, 29, 29n, 39, 60n, 61, 62n, 94, 112n, 220, 254n, 292, 300, 322

Neuralia, HMTS, 102

Neuve Chapelle, Battle of (1915), 75, 138,
    161*n*

Nicholas II, Tsar of Russia, 226*n*, 334, 337

Nicolai Nicolaevich, Grand Duke, 226

North Africa, 83*n*, 331, 448

Northcliffe, Alfred Harmsworth, 1st
    Viscount, xi

Northern Rhodesia, 238

North Sea, 230, 232*n*, 437

Noyon, France, 63, 131

Nureddin Bey, 219–20

oil, 185*n*, 225*n*, 449*n*

Oldenburg, SMS, 12*n*

149th Infantry Regiment (German army),
    6–10

Opatov, Battle of (1914), 32–7

Orvieto, HMAT, 54–8

Østergaard, Peter, 288

Ostfriesland, SMS, 12*n*

Ottoman army, 75, 83, 108, 185, 203, 467
    in Battle of Ctesiphon (1915), 186, 187,
        220
    in Battle of Hanna (1916), 220*n*
    corruption and incompetence in, 219,
        221, 276, 277, 326
    in defense of Gallipoli peninsula, 116*n*,
        121, 122, 188*n*, 441–2
    de Nogales's application for discharge
        from, 141, 218–19, 503
    execution of deserters in, 276–8
    Fifth Army of, 442
    in First Battle of Gaza (1917), 317, 340–3,
        345
    food and supply shortages in, 276, 277
    looting by, 346–7
    losses of, 96, 186, 345
    POW marches and camps of, 267–70,
        326–8, 355, 390–1, 446–8, 467–8
    in Second Battle of Gaza (1917), 317,
        345–7
    siege of Kut al-Amara by, 76, 189–90,
        192–3, 203, 205–7, 218, 219, 220*n*, 222–3,
        235–6, 237, 246, 267, 390, 505

Sixth Army of, 219
    Third Army Erzurum headquarters of,
        95–6
    Van uprising and, 111–15

Ottoman Empire, 4, 71, 108*n*, 111, 112*n*, 134,
    185, 220, 386, 447, 449*n*
    Allied division of, 293*n*, 502
    anti-German uprisings in, 485
    capitulation of, 424, 504
    German influence on, 441*n*, 485
    malnourishment and disease in, 276–7
    massacres of Christians and Armenians
        in, 75, 112–13, 139–41, 192, 219, 326, 442*n*

Pacific Squadron, German, 55*n*–6*n*, 78*n*

Palestine, 29*n*, 277, 318, 341, 342, 343, 424,
    442, 502

Panato, Giovanni, 251

Paris, France, 81, 299, 323*n*, 365, 397, 405,
    449, 452–3, 459, 469
    air raids on, 428, 439–41, 464
    Ambulance Américaine in, 97–100
    Bastille Day celebrations in, 142–3
    Gare de l'Est in, 213–14
    Germany's march on, 3, 4, 46, 61, 81
    Maxim's in, 281–3
    1914 German approach of, 3, 4, 46, 61, 81
    1918 canon bombardment of, 446, 453,
        454–6, 464
    1918 German approach on, 453, 454, 464,
        465, 483*n*
    reopening of Chamber of Deputies in,
        69–70
    soldier beggars in, 366

Pasha Expedition, 277

Passchendaele, Battle of (Third Battle of
    Ypres; 1917), 317, 318, 376, 388, 389, 396,
    397, 398–400, 406, 416, 436, 446

peace initiatives, 204, 323–4, 395
    see also armistice

Peace to End All Peace, A (Fromkin), 293*n*

Persia, 111, 112*n*, 203, 204, 224–7, 236, 244,
    247, 280, 293

Pétain, Philippe, 161

Petrograd, Russia, 174, 247, 323*n*

Bolshevik coup in, 318, 404, 416–17
bread riots in, 317, 334, 336–9
civilian opulence vs. soldier
impoverishment in, 178–80
Piave River, 318, 406, 407, 414, 423, 424
Picardy, France, 63–6, 91–3
Pisoderi Pass, 409, 411, 412
Poincaré, Raymond, 143, 307
Poland, 17, 20, 33n, 88, 104, 155, 179, 297,
449n, 497
wartime destruction in, 33, 43–5, 48,
157–8, 160
Pollard, Alfred, xv
American soldiers disliked by, 416–18
collapse outside of Péronne of, 483–4,
501
digging of trenches by, 52–3, 54
eagerness for combat of, 137, 138, 165, 166,
418, 444, 482
and end of war, 501
German attack at Gavrelle stopped by
(1917), 349–52
Grandcourt patrol led by, 329–31
in Hooge attack (1915), 136–9, 330
influenza of, 482, 483–4, 501
injuries and wounds of, 165–7, 313
in letters to mother, 313–14, 347–9
Mary Ainsley's relationship with, 166,
314, 375
medals awarded to, 313, 375–6
in signing up for British army, 53–4
on the Somme, 306
training of new soldiers by, 482–3
Ponysigne, Jean, 99
Portugal, 203, 238, 294, 504
Portuguese army, 238, 365, 405
Potemkin (Russian battleship), 177n
Priez, France, 485, 486, 503
Princip, Gavrilo, 82n
prisoners of war, 40–1, 58, 90n, 128, 133, 160,
211, 270, 332, 343, 382, 445–7, 473, 474,
500n
boredom and frustration of, 326, 327,
416, 466–7
in Bursa, 447, 467–8

camp living conditions of, 40n, 326–7,
445, 447, 466
in Constantinople camp, 446, 447–8, 505
food shortages and starvation of, 40n,
268, 269, 415
forced marches of, 267–70, 326–7, 415
at Hart camp, 466–7
at Kastamonu camp, 326–8, 355, 390–1
mortality rate of, 327n
release of, 505–6
at Salzburg camp, 415–16, 465–6
treatment of, 40n, 58n, 104, 124–5, 268n,
326, 445, 447
Turczynowicz's encounters with, 18–19,
24, 104, 124
propaganda, 24, 106, 130, 373, 417n, 485
in France, 47, 157, 255, 300–1, 323, 324, 501
in Germany, 13–14, 104, 225n, 255, 360,
473, 491
prostitution, 70, 179, 182, 209, 235, 281–3, 285
Proust, Marcel, 81n, 464
Prussia, 30n, 507
Przemyśl, Austria-Hungary, 42, 75
Punch, 431

Q-Ships, 232n

Rachamimov, Alon, 40n
railways, 7, 21, 40, 181n, 191, 216, 221, 238,
266–7, 297, 300, 308, 341, 363, 471
in Austria-Hungary, 228n, 296n, 343n,
466n
British army's guarding of, in East
Africa, 149–50, 151–3, 199–200
disorganized and slow troop movement
on, 20n, 21n, 88–9, 296n, 459n
Russian demolishing of, 147, 149
strategic use of, 21n, 33n
Ramazani (Selous's African servant), 321–2
Ras al-'Ayn, 269, 270, 326
Rasputin, Grigori, 334
Red Army, 211n
Red Cross, 63, 66, 124, 171, 178, 210, 393, 427,
434
Red Guards, 451

refugees, 15, 16, 24, 34–5, 46, 65, 91, 93, 94, 113, 175, 179, 209, 219, 227n, 271, 277, 283, 332, 410, 451, 499–500, 504
Reims, France, 348n, 465, 486
Reiner, Fritz, 15
Rejitsa, Latvia, 340
Rennenkampf, Paul von, 17, 20
Rhodes, Cecil, 101n
Rhodesia, 151
Richard, Adrien, 258
Riga, Latvia, 177, 318, 402n
Romania, 112n, 243, 294, 300n, 318, 323n, 336, 404
    military hospital in, 382–5, 403–4
    war entry of, 204, 294n, 298
Romanian army, 294n, 299
Rommel, Erwin, 402n
Roncegno, Italy, 240–1
Rufiji River, 313, 320
Russia, 7, 8, 11n, 17, 22, 29n, 106n, 111, 117, 130, 135, 143n, 153, 211n, 225, 226, 247, 294n, 323n, 384, 403, 429, 492n, 500
    anti-Semitism in, 29n, 104, 233, 234
    Bolshevik revolution in, 318, 339n, 373n, 404, 406, 410–11, 416–17, 430n, 433, 436, 448, 452, 499, 500n
    bread riots in, 317, 334, 336–9
    civilian unrest in, 136n, 334, 337, 451
    February revolution in, 317, 334, 337–9, 373
    food shortages in, 40n, 241, 334, 337, 428
    German armistice with, 411, 417, 423, 430, 443
    imminent civil war in, 451, 452, 499
    imperialist ambitions of, 71n, 225n, 293n, 449n
    POW camps in, 40n
    Provisional Government of, 383n
    upgrading of railway network in, 21n
    White, 385n, 430n, 449n, 499
Russian army, 8, 25, 44, 49, 75, 88, 95, 96, 104, 111, 112n, 141, 203, 204, 210, 227n, 268, 293, 331, 339, 365, 405, 406, 441n
    advance into Persia of, 203, 225, 227
    in battles on the San (1915), 133–5

Brusilov offensive of, 203, 270–2, 293, 294, 295–7, 298
    casualties and losses in, 22–3, 36, 88n, 89, 133, 211, 297
    in Chertoviche raid (1916), 211–13
    Chortkov occupation by, 233–5
    East Prussia invasion by, 3, 4, 17–18, 19–20, 24, 136n
    Eighth Army of, 134, 383
    female nurses harassed by troops in, 383
    female soldiers in, 385, 500n
    Galicia invasion by, 3, 15–16, 20, 41, 142
    Gorlice occupation by, 117–18
    Gorlice retreat of, 118–20, 128, 133
    growing dissension and disintegration in, 339–40, 383, 410, 411, 448–50
    improvements made in, 211, 297
    mobilization of, 3, 7, 21, 21n
    1915 large-scale eastern retreat of, 76, 128, 136n, 142, 144–5, 147, 148–9, 156, 170, 211
    1917 failed "freedom offensive" of, 317, 366, 383–4, 385
    Ninth Army of, 270
    POWs from, 40, 104, 124–5, 128, 133, 473
    in Salonica, 331, 409, 410, 448, 449
    scorched-earth policy of, 136n, 147, 149, 170, 233
    supply shortages of, 108n, 118, 135, 147–8, 179, 211, 383
    Third Army of, 118, 133
    see also Lobanov-Rostovsky, Andrei
Russian Red Cross, 178
Russo-Japanese War (1904), 94

Sairt, Turkey, 219
    massacre in, 139–41
Salonica, Greece, 180, 180n–1n, 278–80, 331–3, 386, 409, 448, 449, 504–5
    British troops in, 76, 180n–1, 188, 279, 433–4
    King awarded medal in, 462–3
    procession for shot-down German plane in, 217–18
    raging fires in, 385–7, 410, 434

Salzburg prison camp, 415–16, 465–6
Samsonov, Alexander, 20
San River, 1915 German breakthrough on, 133–6
Sanctuary Wood, 165, 313, 389
Sanders, Otto Liman von, 121n, 441–2
Sandomierz, Poland, 33, 35, 36
San Osvaldo mental hospital, 214–16, 240
Santi Quaranta, 434, 435
Sarajevo, 3, 13, 82n, 182
 Kelemen's visit to, 209–10
Sarıkamış, Turkey, 75, 93
Sarrail, Maurice, 180, 188, 279, 434
Sátoraljaújhely, Hungary, 301–2
Scapa Flow naval base, 231
Schlieffen Plan, 21n
Schneidemühl, Germany, 6–10, 39, 66–7, 143–4, 244–5, 284–6, 408–9, 497–8
 food restrictions and shortages in, 79–80, 335, 392, 470, 471, 474, 477
Schutztruppen, German, 262, 320
scorched-earth policy, 136n, 147, 149, 170, 233
Scottish Women's Hospital
 evacuation of Gevgelí and, 187–9
 in journey to Gevgelí, 180–1
 in setting up of Troyes location, 125–8
Selous, Frederick Courteney, 100–1, 312–13, 321, 322
Sembat, Marcel, 62–3
Serbia, 3, 4, 8, 95, 112n, 143n, 180n, 181, 187, 188, 213, 463, 504
 execution of guerrilla fighters in, 176–7
 German-Austrian invasion of, 76, 174–5, 180n, 181n, 213
 German-Austrian occupation of, 182, 208–9
 refugees from, 175, 209, 504
Serbian army, 279, 331, 385, 424, 434, 462, 465
Sergy, France, Battle in, 486–9
sexual immorality, 284–6, 333, 405–6
 prostitution and, 70, 179, 182, 209, 235, 281–3, 285, 365
sexually transmitted diseases, 282–3, 285

shell shock, 116, 123n, 215, 357, 372, 486, 488–9, 490
shrapnel shells, 65, 115, 116, 134, 163, 183, 184, 189, 206, 251, 255, 256, 288, 289n, 332, 399, 462, 464
 inaccuracy and ineffectiveness of, 34n, 63n, 123n, 264n
smallpox, 234–5
smoking, 207n, 278, 310n–11n, 327
Smuts, Jan, 238n, 320, 358
snipers, 85, 190, 205, 207, 210, 321
Social Democrats, German, 62, 242, 360
socialism, 45, 62, 373, 429
Somme, France, 85–7, 444, 486, 498, 500n
 British-French offensive on (1916), 203, 272–3, 286–90, 295n, 299–300, 306, 323
soup kitchens, 68, 79, 89, 90–1, 129
South Africa, 150n–1n, 151, 238n, 358, 483, 503
Soviet Union, 449n
Spanish-American War (1898), 64n, 94, 417n
"Spanish flu," 465, 478, 482, 483–4, 499, 501
Spee, Maximilian von, 55n–6n
Stanislau, Galicia, 15, 16
Station Neurologique No. 42, 475, 476
Stone, Norman, 42n, 296n
storm-troop tactics, 402n, 414, 444
strikes, labor, 429, 430–1, 449
Stumpf, Richard, xv, 11, 12, 457
 in Battle of Jutland (1916), 259–60, 310
 conflicted feelings about war in, 311–12, 360, 492
 Ernst poem copied by, 13–14
 German workers' strikes and, 429–31
 Germany's class system questioned by, 360–2
 High Seas mutiny and, 491, 492–4, 498
 at Jutland anniversary celebration, 359–60, 361–2
 in Kiel, 177–8
 lack of action seen by, 28, 77–9, 177–8, 231, 232, 361
 monotonous routine of, 78–9, 310–11, 360
 and outbreak of war, 12–13

Stumpf, Richard (*continued*)
  in preparing *Helgoland* for action, 28
  and SMS *Möwe*'s triumphant return,
    229–32
  in Wilhelmshaven, 229–32, 328–9, 429–31,
    491–4, 498–9
Suez Canal, 71, 76, 83, 277, 340, 341
Suwalki, Poland, 5, 6, 17–19, 24–5, 40, 158
  destruction and filth in, 43–5, 48, 104,
    160
  food shortages in, 103, 105, 155
  German invasion of, 25–6, 44
  German occupation of, 84–5, 102–5,
    124–5, 141–2, 155–6, 159
  military hospital in, 18–19
  POWs in, 104, 124–5
  Turczynowicz's final departure from,
    159–60
  Turczynowicz's return to, 43–5, 48
  typhus outbreak in, 84, 102–3, 124
Sykes, Percy, 293
Sykes-Picot Accord, 293*n*

Tamines massacre, 106
Tandamuti ridge, 379–82
Tanganyika, Lake, 151, 238
tanks, 300*n*, 341, 402*n*, 460, 461
Tannenberg, Battle of (1914), 4, 33*n*, 40, 88*n*
Tasim (Albanian batman), 141, 345
Taylor, A. J. P., 180*n*
Tchapli, Ukraine, 147, 148
Teheran, Persia, 227, 244
Tel Armenia, Mesopotamia, 192
Tel el-Sharia, 341, 342
3/4 King's African Rifles, 379
300 Jours de Verdun, Les, 266*n*
Tigris River, 76, 184, 185, 235, 246, 268
  de Nogales's ride down, 218–22
tobacco, 310*n*–11*n*, 345
Togoland (German East African colony;
    Togo), 3, 151
Tours, France, 393, 394
Townshend, Charles, 189, 220, 268*n*, 447*n*
transport convoys, 20*n*, 216–17, 220–2, 246,
    438–9

trenches, trench warfare, 34*n*, 38, 49, 64, 67,
    95, 106, 138, 163, 166, 167, 189, 210, 213,
    251, 252*n*, 256, 257, 294, 296*n*, 298–9,
    311*n*, 329, 330, 348, 362, 374, 385, 398,
    413, 483
  barbed wire and, 64*n*, 118, 224, 264
  in Billy-Montigny, 223–4, 241, 246–7
  conditions in, 53, 118, 122, 273
  D'Aquila's first night in, 168–9, 172
  digging and building of, 52–3, 54, 72, 122,
    147–8, 162, 183, 184, 223, 272, 297
  in Eastern vs. Western Front, 118*n*
  Farmborough's visits to, 267, 270, 290–1
  foot ailment caused by, 68, 98
  gathering of dead in, 263–4
  and German attack at Gavrelle, 349–52
  monotonous and melancholy routine in,
    121–2, 224, 241, 246–7, 273
  shrapnel shells and, 63*n*
  on the Somme, 85–7, 272–3, 286–90
  tacit cease-fire pact among combatants
    in, 182, 224
Trotsky, Leon, 430*n*
Troyes, France, 125–8
Tsingtao (Quingdao), 4, 11, 11*n*, 56
tuberculosis, 82*n*, 283*n*, 307
Turczynowicz, Laura de, xv, 497
  in arduous journey to U.S., 159–61, 171,
    497
  children's illnesses and, 84, 102–3, 155–6
  comfortable prewar existence of, 5–6,
    17, 18
  in flight from German invasion of
    Suwalki, 24–6
  in German-occupied Suwalki, 84–5,
    102–5, 124–5, 141–2, 155–6, 159
  and outbreak of war, 5–6, 17
  POW encounters of, 18–19, 24, 104, 124–5
  in return to Suwalki, 43–5, 48
  volunteer hospital work of, 18–19, 124
Turczynowicz, Stanislaw de, 5, 6, 17, 18, 24,
    44, 85, 104, 142, 171, 497
Turkey, 109, 463, 468*n*, 485, 502
  Van uprising in, 111–15
"turnip winter," 329, 392

25th Royal Fusiliers, 100–1, 199, 308–9,
    312–13, 319, 358, 363, 364, 503
    in departure to East Africa, 100–2
    elite reputation of, 101, 319
    Lindi disembarkment of, 358–9
    losses of, 319, 321
    in march on Moshi, 237–9, 248
    pack animals of, 238–9, 248–9
    in storming of Tandamuti ridge, 379–82
    see also Buchanan, Angus
typhus, 40*n*, 59, 84, 102–3, 124, 134, 220*n*,
    234, 276–7
    D'Aquila treated for, 194–5, 208, 214–16

U-boats, 75, 77, 145, 181, 232*n*, 311, 317, 323*n*,
    328, 356, 357, 380, 449*n*, 505
Udine, Italy, 194, 195, 208, 215, 401
United States, 131, 311*n*, 317, 323*n*, 432, 458,
    499*n*, 505
    Mexican war with (1916), 417*n*, 486
    peace initiatives of, 323, 395
    war entry of, 317, 356, 365, 395*n*
United States army, 416, 423, 436, 458, 465,
    473–4, 486–7, 501
    ban on alcohol in, 406*n*, 418
    in Battle of Argonne (1918), 371*n*, 424
    inexperience of, 417–18, 461, 473
    losses of, 461, 473, 487
    in 1918 Allied counter-offensive, 486–9

VADs (Voluntary Aid Detachments), 27*n*
Van, Turkey, uprising in, 111–15
van Deventer, Louis "Japie," 358
Vaux, Fort de, 266, 371*n*
Verdun, Battle of (1916), 203, 242–3, 253–7,
    262–7, 274–5, 276, 295*n*, 296*n*, 299, 323,
    324, 371*n*
Vergult, François, 258
Verhoustraeten (pilot), 413, 414
Veurne, Belgium, field hospital in, 50–2,
    67–9, 89
Victoria, Lake, 150, 151
Victoria Crosses, 313, 375, 376
Vienna, Austria, 117, 185, 424, 430, 471*n*,
    506

Vie Parisienne, La, 405–6, 407
Villa, Pancho, 417*n*
Viviani, René, 365
Vladivostock, Russia, 451–2, 500
Voie Sacrée, La (Sacred Road), 254*n*
Voloschyna, 366–7

Waldecker, Werner, 392–3, 408–9
war cemeteries, 120*n*, 134, 285, 292–3, 388,
    487*n*, 500*n*, 502
    Kuhr's visit to, 158–9
war credits, 62, 356, 365, 380
Warsaw, Poland, 4, 5, 20, 24, 75, 76, 88, 151
    Russian retreat from, 144–5
Western Front, xii, 55, 108*n*, 118, 121, 162*n*,
    279, 296*n*, 297, 320, 336, 345, 352*n*, 373*n*,
    406, 423, 448, 472
    Eastern Front trench system vs., 118*n*
    Franco-British 1915 double-offensive on,
    76, 157, 161–4, 165, 183, 373
    German 149th Infantry Regiment's
    departure for, 6–10
    German army's planned withdrawal
    from France in, 317, 330–1
    1918 German spring offensive on,
    423, 428, 436, 444, 446, 447, 452–3,
    459–62, 463, 464–5, 467, 468–9, 473–4,
    486
White Russia, 449*n*, 499
Wilhelm II, German Emperor, 12*n*, 90*n*,
    194, 323–4, 360, 424, 433, 491, 494,
    501
Wilhelmshaven, Germany, 232, 328–9,
    498–9
    call for general strike in, 429–31
    High Seas mutiny in, 491, 492–4, 498
Wilson, Woodrow, 323, 395
women
    in ban from front lines, 27, 70
    British army's reluctance to accept
    volunteers of, 27, 178, 279
    German mortality rates among, 471*n*
    Macnaughtan on morality of, 123–4
    prostitution of, 70, 179, 182, 209, 235,
    281–3, 365

women *(continued)*
  as refugees, 93, 94, 175, 179, 219
  rise of sexual immorality in, 284–6,
    405–6
  in Russian army battalions, 385, 500*n*
  and Russian troops harassment of
    nurses, 383
  at Scottish Women's Hospital, *see*
    Scottish Women's Hospital
  symbols of support displayed by, 26, 46,
    47, 63

wartime fashion of, 26, 46, 90, 301,
  469–70
World War II, 40*n*, 269*n*, 328*n*

Ypres, Belgium, 106, 136, 353, 426, 500*n*
Ypres, First Battle of (1914), 51, 52
Ypres, Third Battle of (1917), 317, 318, 376,
  388, 389, 396, 397, 398–400, 406, 416,
  436, 446

Zeppelins, 32, 61, 105, 107–8, 217, 439, 440

Peter Englund is a Swedish historian, who has received numerous prizes in his own country and whose works have been translated into fifteen languages. He has also been working as a war correspondent in the Balkans, Afghanistan, and Iraq. Englund is a member of the Swedish Academy (which awards the Nobel Prize in Literature) and in 2008 was appointed its new permanent secretary, an office he still holds.

A NOTE ON THE TYPE

This book was set in Minion, a typeface produced by the Adobe Corporation specifically for the Macintosh personal computer, and released in 1990. Designed by Robert Slimbach, Minion combines the classic characteristics of old-style faces with the full complement of weights required for modern typesetting.

Composed by North Market Street Graphics
Lancaster, Pennsylvania

Printed and bound by Berryville Graphics
Berryville, Virginia

Designed by Soonyoung Kwon